To Martin C. Hausman,
loyal alumnus of John
Marshall Law School,
with best wishes.

Palmer D Edmunds

LAW AND
CIVILIZATION

By PALMER D. EDMUNDS

A.B., LL.D., KNOX; LL.B., HARVARD
PROFESSOR OF LAW, THE JOHN MARSHALL LAW SCHOOL

Public Affairs Press, Washington, D. C.

FOREWORD

Slowly but surely attention has focused upon the rule of law as the best concept developed by man since the dawn of civilization to bring order and stability into a disordered world.

This gradual centering upon law as a major route to world order and peace makes Professor Edmunds' book most timely and useful. The ever growing realization that civilization is dependent upon law, and that civilization as we know it can best be preserved and advanced by law, should be furthered greatly by his concise historical analysis.

The spotlight of national and world public opinion is now upon law due in part to "Law Day—U.S.A." and the tremendous program to further world peace through law of the American Bar Association. *Law and Civilization* furnishes an essential and useful tool for lawyers and laymen as they move forward on these and other current programs wherein the great principles of law are being explored as a method to govern and guide on-rushing human progress. There is currently a great stretching of many minds to the new horizons of the new legal frontiers and requirements of our day. Events press hard for action in this field. And sound action must be based upon past experience of man in expanding law to the new needs as civilization has unfolded and developed down through past centuries.

While the pages of recorded history are in large part a chronicle of wars and warriors and the weapons they used to kill, destroy and enslave, no one can dispute that the brightest chapters are those which record advances in utilization of law. The Code of Hammurabi, the Ten Commandments and the law of Moses, the Code of Solon, the Twelve Tables of Rome, the Corpus Juris of Justinian, and the Common Law of England are illustrations of such chapters. In every community, city, state or nation, civilization has blossomed and advanced as law has replaced force. Every new high in civilization's progress is accompanied by a new crest in use of the rule of law. History demonstrates that where law has prevailed individual freedom of man has been strong and progress great. Where law is weak or non-existent human slavery, chaos and fear lurk and thrive and human progress is destroyed or retarded.

Taking a broad look at the world community today, it is clear that force remains the controlling factor in most great international decisions. While some governments operate under the rule of law domestically that rule does not prevail internationally. The greatest gap in the growing structure of civilization is indeed the absence of law in the world community. We must translate the immutable principles of law and justice into working legal machinery to regulate relations among nations. There exists no more urgent need than that of developing the legal procedures, methods, principles and institutions which will enable law to replace force in the control of the fate of humanity.

To get the necessary know-how with which to build a "law-ful" world, one can learn much from a review of the way "law-ful" nations came into being. This volume offers an over-all look at this process. The thousands of lawyers and laymen in our country and in many other nations who are now actively engaged in studying ways, means and methods to eliminate lawlessness internationally will profit greatly from this volume's history of law and civilization. That history demonstrates that the use of law has expanded and grown to meet the needs of an advancing civilization down through the ages. But the rapid rush of current events demonstrate that thousands of years are not available to develop the rule of law between nations to the high state it has achieved within nations. We must therefore move quickly to formulate the necessary legal processes for the operation of a new world wherein speedy communications and transportation have shrunk nations to neighborhoods.

The people of our country and other countries do not yet fully appreciate what the rule of law can do for the world by peaceful resolution of disputes which cause tensions and frictions before they fester into conflicts of world-wide import. They do not realize that law in a courthouse offers the best substitute for shooting and bombing on any type of battlefield as a dispute decider between nations. They must be made to fully appreciate their alternatives of decision through law or decision through violence. Experience with violence down through the ages as summarized by Professor Edmunds leaves no doubt as to the choice that will be made provided the people fully understand these alternatives.

While the peoples of the world speak through many different languages and have many diverse forms of government, the rule of law is a universal idea and ideal which all men have in common, even in countries that do not now live under that rule. Elementary principles of right and wrong are common to all legal systems. Justice means the same to people everywhere, even where it is denied by governments which do not adhere to its principles. The motives, techniques and forms used to achieve justice under law in different countries cannot obscure this truth. By placing governments under law nationally we have brought about order and stability within nations. Application of the rule of law would bring a new standard of decency to international relations and create that order, stability and peace which is mankind's greatest desire.

It has been truly said that an idea can be more powerful than an atom, and that nothing can deny an idea whose time has come. Let us hope that the day is not far off when the idea of law replaces terror as the decision mechanism in disputes between nations. Supremacy of law within nations has created freedom of man. Supremacy of law between nations can create freedom for man from the dread scourge of war.

A new world is being born in this century. If it is to be a "lawful" world, thoughtful men must make it so. It will not just happen. Today we can with courage, resolution and devotion write the brightest and noblest chapter in the history of law and civilization. The challenge is here, the opportunity is here, the obligation is here.

We of the twentieth century could make no greater contribution to justify our heritage and to fulfill our destiny, than to have it inscribed large in history that we brought into being a world in which all men live under the rule of law and walk in freedom, in dignity and in peace. Books like that of Professor Edmunds help in bringing this great goal ever closer by presenting the essential information upon which this new world ruled by law must be founded. President Eisenhower is right beyond question in saying that "if civilization is to survive, it (the world) must choose the rule of law."

CHARLES S. RHYNE

President, American Bar Association (1957-58)

INTRODUCTION

Legalistic activity is a striking feature of American culture. The "law man" is the hero of most television westerns. Elaborate codes, frequently revised, characterize our great popular sports. The players' competition depends considerably upon taking imaginative advantage of the rules and much of the excitement for spectators derives from the continuous arbitration. Baseball, football, and basketball each require in addition to team members a surprising number of arbiters, possessed both of professional knowledge and judicial temperament. At what may, perhaps, be called the more serious level of civil affairs, we require, or at least seem to prefer, an astonishing number of legislative bodies. These at national, state, and local levels, and in various geographical varieties, make, unmake, remake, and multiply laws, ordinances, and regulations with a profusion that defies enumeration and confounds classification.

Does all this litigious activity on the part of the American people truly represent great law making any more than finger exercises produce good music or dexterous brush strokes create great art? Organizational ingenuity should not be confused with the understanding and creation of law in its fundamental and urgent sense. Many human institutions, such as chivalry, became most elaborate and most popular just after they had begun their decline.

An able American scholar recently pointed out that in the nineteenth century we were fortunate in being able to confirm our individual liberty outside the sphere of government but that in the complex legal, social and economic circumstances of the twentieth we must learn to sustain our freedom within the processes of government. Here is a problem that vitally concerns every citizen. Palmer Edmunds has for many years been motivated by a desire to show that law and civilization are inextricable. As a lawyer with experience in the workings of our courts and state and federal administrative agencies he has felt and emphasized the responsibility of the legal profession for providing the citizen with materials enabling a better understanding of our American law and its relation to the jurisprudence of the past, as well as to the totalitarian systems of today. The present work exemplifies the scope of his research and effort in this regard. His passion to promote such an understanding of the law has long been a benefaction to the faculty and students at Knox College. Year by year as a teacher of a course on "Law for the Citizen" he persisted in his concern to identify the most important subjects for his lectures and readings and to present these through cases that would best involve and inform his students toward an appropriate appreciation of their legal heritage.

That the American people do not sufficiently appreciate their great legal heritage is due in large degree to neglect of a discipline that once was strongly stressed in the training of the educated gentleman. In most of the universities of the late medieval and early modern period the leading faculty was that of law and this subject was the one "most widely diffused or the most practically influential."

"From a broad political and social point of view" as Hastings Rashdall points out, "one of the most important results of the Universities was the creation, or at least the enormously increased power and importance, of the lawyer-class. Great as are the evils which society still owes to lawyers, the lawyer-class has always been a civilizing agency. Their power represents at least the triumph of reason and education over caprice and bruit force. Lawyers have moderated or regulated despotism even when they have proved its most willing tools: just as in modern democratic communities their prominence must be looked upon as an important conservative check upon democracy."

In our English mother country the learned layman was less likely to pursue seriously that deductive discipline which the canon and Roman law shared with theology in the continental universities. Nevertheless, the English gentleman, destined to serve his monarch in the affairs of his parish and county, was characteristically prepared for his responsibility by some attendance at the Inns of Court where he acquired some familiarity with the workings of that common law which distinguished English jurisprudence from the legal institutions of the Continent.

In the United States the disappearance of the law as part of the generally accepted preparation of liberally educated persons antedated the elimination of theology and the neglect of classical languages. The responsibility for this change, so far as the law is concerned, may probably not be laid to the profession of education so much as to the vocation of the law itself. And it is most appropriate that it is from the latter, the lawyers, that voices should now be heard calling for the restoration of law to curricula which give a nearly universal recognition to the much more novel studies called "social sciences." It is probably not to be regretted that we did not in America perpetuate the eighteenth century tradition of the Etonian who studied casually at Oxford and not very seriously at law in London. If the democratic educational reforms of the nineteenth century are to be fulfilled, however, it is desirable that our legal heritage be understood by the American, if not as a gentleman, then surely as a citizen.

Popular literature and general education are readily available to the citizen who is conscientious about his capacity to discriminate intelligently on issues of foreign policy, voting procedures, and Federal legislation in social and economic areas. School and college courses are, for example, provided so as to make him a good "citizen" in these respects. However, he is least likely to be adequately informed in those more common workaday functions of the courts and the local legislatures which deal with his personal and proprietary prerogatives and responsibilities as father, as husband, as home owner, as shopper and shop keeper. Somehow this part of the layman's education has been neglected, partly because of the tendency of teachers to dismiss these concerns as too homely for academic attention, partly because the lawyers have cultivated the notion that they are too technical for non-professional attention. Similar treatment of the field of medicine would give us a populace ill prepared for modern urban health and sanitation. A similar attitude on the part of engineers would leave us with countrymen poorly equipped for our highly mechanized domestic life. It is all too prevalent a notion, even on the part of those who bother to think about it at all, that somehow our civil rights are taken care of by Supreme Court decisions; the general understanding of the functioning of the Bill of Rights is entirely too static, and an appreciation of an institution such as the jury much too mechanistic. Public opinion is rather recklessly disposed to accept innovations such as loyalty oaths, to tolerate the expanding inquisitorial functions of Congressional committees, or to use "Fifth Amendment" as an insulting phrase. A great chasm separates the layman's notions of our legal heritage from the lawyer's knowledge of our judicial institutions.

A broad historical approach to the legal institutions of the United States, such as is attempted in the present work, provides not only a vivid sense of the rich legacy which we have received from several civilizations but also a sense of stewardship for the precious insights into human freedom which we have recovered from societies which themselves have long since lost their own heritage. We are enlightened by the experience of the Greeks both by observing the fateful poverty of their judicial procedures and by discovering the enduring riches of their philosophy. We learn that the less sophisticated Visigoths gave their women a status which still affects the inheritance of property in parts of the United States. By reflecting on the tyranny of Roman emperors or Japanese Shoguns we justify our intuitive dislike for the secret police of modern totalitarian societies. Some historians may demur over the forthright generalizations made by Dr. Edmunds, but they should note the service which he performs by bridging that gap between the past and the present which historians, despite their promises, are often too timid to cross. It is rewarding to note what Justice Story owed to Cicero, what Justice Brandeis learned from Pericles, or how the ideas of an English philosopher found their way into *Marbury* vs. *Madison*. The living past in American law is exemplified not merely by Alexander Hamilton's remarks about Greek and Roman democracy in a constitutional convention for New York state, but more recently by the analogy between the procedures of Roman praetors and the Illinois Civil Practice Act of 1933. With the preference for the specific instance that is so characteristic of the Anglo-American legal tradition, the author of this work presents not merely living cases from American courts but also sets forth appropriate episodes from a more remote past; for there is something to learn from the misconduct of an unworthy pupil of Socrates or the dialogue of Moses with his father-in-law as well as from the latest litigation of a cosmetics manufacturer.

We may hope that the adaptation of our established legal principles to new technical and human situations may be assisted by the scholarly discoveries of the new social disciplines. But the method of coordinating the older wisdom with novel learning is not self-evident even though the Supreme Court has set a great precedent for pouring the new wine into old bottles. Anthropology, psychology, and sociology have greatly altered our perception of the structure of human behavior but a little anthropology may prove to be a dangerous thing for those who have never drunk at the ancient spring of the law.

HERMANN R. MUELDER

Dean of Knox College, Galesburg, Illinois

PREFACE

World War II brought to the people of the United States a realization that civilization in the high sense that we have come to know it cannot exist under a regime of uninhibited absolutism, contemptuous of law and employing violence and chicanery to attain its ends. How best to turn that realization into the channels of full appreciation of our contrasting American way of life was, during those war years, the subject of much earnest thought.

The purpose of this book is to contribute to a better comprehension of the fundamental part that law plays in undergirding our free institutions. From the author's point of view, any attempt to achieve this end calls for presenting law, not as just a set of rules regulating day-by-day conduct, but as the institution which has made it possible for human beings to live together, develop their varied interests, and attain their present state. It involves renewing acquaintance with the civilizations of the past, taking note of their legal and governmental systems and connecting them with the present. It necessitates an appraisal of the stern juristic positivism forced upon their own peoples and the peoples of the world by the Nazi and Facist regimes, and by the dictators of the Iron Curtain nations who have threatened the peace of the world since World War II came to an end. Calling for ultimate analysis is the nature and content of the system of common law, and its relation to the constitutional system of the United States. The scope of the author's research has been ordered accordingly.

In the process of preparing a work such as this an author becomes deeply conscious of the debt owed to the scholars of the past whose findings of fact and conclusions provide the foundation for those of later eras. The appended references, keyed to the several chapters, evidence the reliance which has been placed upon them, as well as upon the statements of many scholars of the present to whom, also, great obligation is acknowledged. Among those to whom the author is particularly indebted for suggestions and criticisms are Dr. Frank Klingberg, of Southern Illinois University; Dr. Merritt H. Moore, of the University of Tennessee; Dr. Marion J. Bradshaw, of Bangor Theological Seminary; Dr. Stanley K. Norton, of Illinois Normal University; Mr. Kellogg D. McClelland and Mr. Louis Nielson, of Galesburg, Illinois; Mr. Walter F. Dodd, of Chicago; and the author's wife, Margaret B. Edmunds. Special acknowledgment is made of obligation to Mr. M. B. Schnapper, editor of Public Affairs Press, for helpful suggestions as to final arrangement of the manuscript.

To Knox College the author is heavily indebted in a variety of ways. It was in the course of a conversation with Dr. Carter Davidson when the latter was President of Knox in the World War II period that the present book had its origin. From time to time the author has benefited by suggestions from others with whom he has been associated at Knox College as Visiting Professor of Law—particularly Dr. Sharvy G. Umbeck, present President of the College, Dean Hermann R. Muelder, Dr. Alfred W. Newcombe, Dr. Proctor F. Sherwin, and Dr. John A. Houston. To his students at the College the author is unreservedly grateful. Their intense interest and perceptive questions were a real stimulus throughout the continued effort that resulted in the present work.

Whatever may be the shortcomings of this book, it is the hope of the author that the reader will find herein a helpful exposition of law in its relation to the civilizations of the past and present, and at least a hint as to its role in the uncertain future of the atomic age.

PALMER D. EDMUNDS

Chicago, Illinois

CONTENTS

PART I: OVERVIEW

1: The Advent of Law and Government   1

PART II: SYNTHESIS OF LAW AND RELIGION

2: Egypt: Roots of Civilization   20
3: The Influence of the Babylonians   28
4: Heritage From Hinduism   37
5: The Glories of Greece   83

PART III: ROME'S GREAT LEGACY

6: Rome Under the Kings   120
7: The Roman Republic   131
8: The Roman Empire   161
9: The Contributions of Roman Law   173

PART IV: ONE GOD AND THE LAW

10: Judaism and Israel   191
11: Christianity and the Roman Catholic Church   219
12: Islam: Turkey and the Arab States   237

PART V: MAN HIS OWN LAWMAKER

13: From the Hohenzollerns to the Nazis   265
14: Soviet Russia and the Iron Curtain   299
15: The Role of Red China   314

PART VI: CIVILIZATION UNDER THE COMMON LAW

16: Rights of the Individual   324
17: Nature and Sources of the Common Law   343
18: Common Law Liability For Intentional Wrongs   354
19: Common Law Liability For Negligent Wrongs   365
20: Rights and Obligations Arising Out of Contract   375
21: Property Rights and the Common Law   388
22: Crimes and Common Law   390
23: Procedural Aspects of the Common Law   396
24: Equity and the Common Law   403
25: The Common Law's Capacity For Growth   411
26: The Function of Statutes   433
27: Administrative Law   446
28: The Place of Judicial Precedent   465
29: Constitutional Evolution   468

PART VII: EPILOGUE

30: What Does the Future Hold?   474

PART I: OVERVIEW

CHAPTER 1

THE ADVENT OF LAW AND GOVERNMENT

The Progress of a Generation. Millions of citizens of the United States now living have witnessed in their lifetimes developments of science and invention far exceeding the imaginations of their Colonial ancestors. In major degree these wonders have come about within the span of years of persons hardly past middle age.

The student of a middle western college who returned to his home for summer vacation in the sagebrush country of the Pacific Northwest in the year 1909 journeyed for three days and nights by railroad train, followed by a steamboat trip up the rapids of the Columbia River and a stagecoach ride over mountain roads which consumed another day. Vivid within his memory was the afternoon, a few years before, when grade school was dismissed in order that all might for the first time see an automobile which chugged laboriously down the street in a cloud of dust, stopped, and refractorily refused to start.

Electric lights had come into general use, but most students of his generation still studied by gas lamp. His room was heated by a coal furnace, hand-fired by a fellow student who in large part paid his way through college by taking care of a dozen or fifteen furnaces, milking cows and grooming horses which graced the stables of a considerable proportion of the citizenry. If he lived at a distance he came to the campus by streetcar for five cents a ride, or by bicycle. These two-wheeled equipages were common among members of the faculty, although a few of them preferred to travel by horse and carriage.

Our student found occasional relaxation from the rigors of the curriculum by spending a nickel at the "nickelodeon," where the early flickering movies provided entertainment. Occasionally he plunged with a quarter at a legitimate theatre, where a local stock company with weekly changes of bill held the fort with such classics as "East Lynn," "Forbidden Fruit," and "Ten Nights in a Barroom." On state occasions he parted with a dollar at the Opera House, to witness a trav-

1

eling troupe on a one-night stand present an acceptable version of Victor Herbert's "Red Mill," Lehar's "Merry Widow," or some other current Broadway hit which was wandering about the hinterlands.

With the exception of the almost forgotten minor interlude of the short-lived War with Spain in 1898, our country had been at peace since the Civil War. During his campus days our student had been assured in the classroom that wars were a matter of past history, because the world had so developed that they had become an economic impossibility. He was hardly prepared, therefore, to find the world at war within a short time after his graduation. But he did his part. He answered the call for forty thousand young college men to enter officer's training camps, which was issued shortly after the United States declared war on Germany in 1917. Though without previous military training, in ninety days he qualified as a commissioned officer in the armed forces. Assigned to duty, he drilled his men in the musketry and bayonet tactics which he had been taught, and which were based upon the movements of foot and horse soldiers at the Battle of Gettysburg, modified in degree only by the use of machine guns imported from France and England and by field artillery support just beginning to labor in the throes of mechanization. Thus qualified, his outfit went to France. There he had his first sight of airplanes—"flying crates" as they were called—engaging in any kind of operations that carried beyond the barnstorming spectacles which had recently been staged in some large cities, as they made reconnaissance flights in front of the lines and cooperated in the advance of his company in attack by noting and reporting to command headquarters in the rear the white panels which from time to time he displayed on the ground to denote his position. Occasionally, individual planes jousted with those of the enemy, a few hundred or a few thousand feet in the air, like knights of old. As part of his training our young officer had learned visual signaling, with flags. In his rear, soldiers of the Signal Corps strove valiantly to install and maintain telephone lines. He had heard that there was such a thing as radio, making it possible to signal by dots and dashes without wires, but insofar as he was concerned it was yet a mere abstraction.

To make more than bare mention of the contrast between the manner of life of today and that of only a little more than a generation ago would be a work of supererogation. It might be epitomized by saying that now our student might eat his breakfast on his middle western campus and lunch in his Pacific Northwest home. Nickelodeons evolved into the luxurious moving picture palaces of the twenties, later buttressed by sound added to the silent film. But these massive entertainment emporiums bent under the stress of radio broadcasting, which brought music and the spoken word within the walls of every home, and they are now reeling under the impact of television which projects the live screen into the living rooms of the nation. The horse, upon which man depended throughout the centuries for his work and travel, is no more, save to provide diversion for a few riders and the fans of the race track. Streetcars have been pushed aside by tens of millions of motor vehicles, overrunning the city streets, operating on endless ribbons of cement which connect all highways of the nation in an interlacing web. Of the passenger trains upon which the traveler could once reach practically every village of consequence in the nation, but relatively few remain, shoved off the rails as to short trips by the motor car and as to the longer ones by the airplane with its overwhelming advantage of speed.

As to war and its methods, we need only reflect that the atomic bomb, in its way a triumph of the scientific achievement of the ages, brought World War II to an abrupt close by a colossal demonstration of demolition and killing power, and that the H-bomb since perfected carries potentialities of destruction which fairly stagger the imagination. The potentialities of intercontinental missiles, and physical journeys through outer space are beyond present comprehension. Happily, the humane usage of atomic achievements is already apparent in their adaption to medical science and the providing of industrial power, and outer-space travel adds no new element of danger to life on this globe.

What does the future hold? The answer concerns the lives of all of us.

Civilization and Social Order. What have these preceding observations to do with law? For it is law with which we are presently concerned. In today's hurly burly we have little time for reminiscences about the past or superficial discussion about current events within the ken of all.

A moment's thought will reassure us that we have not been proceeding without point. With all good reason we are starting our study with the things that are seen and known, the outward manifestations of a life which seems good to us and which we call civilized. Having them in mind, doubtless there would be unanimous agreement that we are living in a high state of civilization—higher now than it was a generation ago, higher then than it was in the covered-wagon days when pioneers were carrying the Flag across the continent to the west. Because there must be physical life before there can be anything else, because material things play an essential part in promoting the efficiency of the physical side of life there can be nothing wrong about using them as a basis for concluding that we are living in a state of civilization, so far as we know the highest ever attained by man. The greatest pressures of the world today are inexorably toward higher physical standards of living. We look forward to material achievements that will dwarf any yet attained, and say that the cause of civilization will be furthered by their advent.

But some other things demand expression. If only material criteria counted, the Pilgrim Fathers at Plymouth Rock had little, if any, civilization. Lincoln's New Salem was removed from the nomadic life of the Prairie Indians by no more than the thicknesses of a few log-cabin walls. The American citizen is not satisfied with a concept of life which emphasizes only material elements. Physical creations come to flower and pass away; truly, "the things which are not seen are eternal." Civilization embodies something finer, something which overshadows the material—an element of superior moral and intellectual attainment. And so a matter of primary concern to him is the promotion of a high standard of civilization in this more inclusive and truest sense. In short, the citizen wants to retain and improve as to all its elements, seen and unseen, the civilization with which he is blessed today.

We come, then, to our thesis. The good things of life, seen and unseen, come only through civilization. They do not and could not exist apart from it. Civilization comes only through social order. Social order is grounded on law. In stating this thesis we are not overlooking the Marxist philosophy, referred to further hereinafter, that under the so-called ideal society of the proletariat there is no need for law and that it will fade away. That theory has had more than a generation's trial in Soviet Russia. No more bitter fruit has ever matured than that nourished by the blood of murdered thousands, struck down for no other crime than political nonconformity. And the bones of even those who refused to repudiate it when, in the course of this bizarre experiment, the word was given to reverse the course, are bleaching at the end of the liquidation trial.

In spite of its tale of sordid brutalities and moral inconsistencies, Soviet Russia is not without civilization. With the Soviets challenging the United States for supremacy in fields commonly associated with high degrees of human intelligence, to assert that that nation is not civilized would be altogether unwarranted. We will do well to disabuse ourselves at the outset of any idea that civilization is any monopoly of the United States today, or of any nation, or any particular part of the world, or, in fact, of the present day or age in contradistinction to earlier eras. The sound approach lies in the realization that civilization in an acceptable sense of the term has existed throughout at least the period of recorded history. The fact of recorded history is in itself demonstrative of civilization. We will do well to start with the impression that for such a degree of civilization as we today enjoy, we are basically indebted to those peoples of the past who have labored, with only a modicum of the material assets which are ours, to establish a better way of life. Civilization of the future may be the better off by being able to profit by lessons issuing from the experience of the Soviets, as well as from ours.

The Advent of Law. Let us proceed to develop our thesis that without law there cannot be civilization, and that civilization in its manifestations is geared to law. First, what is law?

To imagine a time or situation when there was no law is difficult if not impossible. We think of people as living in relation to each other, and a moment's reflection tells us that such relationship connotes the presence of law. Certainly this must always have been true within the family. If there was a time when there was no law it antedated recorded history, for the presence of some degree of social order is indicated in the accounts of even the earliest times. In fact, absent some sort of social stability, possible only under an orderly regime of law, recordation and preservation of the details of social relationships would have been impossible.

As to what was transpiring prior to the earliest recorded times we do not know. There being no tape recording, microfilming or photographic apparatus, or even the printed word, to preserve for us the account of the human race emerging from its caves and jungles and adapting itself to the wider world, we can only speculate. Starting with the assumption that there must always have been some rules of order within the family, in the nature of things there could hardly have been an extended period when groups of families, however primitive, lived in juxtaposition to each other without some understanding as to their mutual relationships. As long as there were not some understandings and conduct ordered in accordance therewith, there was added to the already fearsome difficulties and dangers imposed by their physical environment the constant threat of molestation and possible annihilation by their fellows, imposing an insecurity that must eventually have become intolerable. Inherent in the very nature of human beings is a yearning for order.

The Desert Island Castaways. Appreciation of the problem will be facilitated by contemplation of the proverbial man cast ashore on a desert island. We should note at the outset—and it is important to do so—that he is at all times subject to the operation of the laws of nature. Unless he is sheltered the rain will wet him, and the sun's rays will burn him. His feet will be cut by contact with sharp stones. Without food, he cannot live. But apart from nature's laws, in this aspect at least, as long as he is alone he is truly monarch of all he surveys. He has full freedom of action. All that he sees and wants is his for the taking and he can use it with impunity. So long as there are sufficient clams and coconuts to satisfy hunger, and leaves with which to improvise a shelter from sun and storm, he can live without physical concern.

Let another castaway appear, however, and the picture is basically altered, especially if clams and coconuts are limited in supply or hard to get. No longer can he in the cool of the morning assemble his dinner in a shady spot by the water's edge and doze off with assurance that it will be awaiting him when he desires it. No longer can he fall asleep at night without fear of molestation by one of his kind who might be motivated to remove him from the scene. The new castaway would, of course, have corresponding fears as to himself.

If these castaways were only animals, when cause for provocation arose they would doubtless "fight it out," and the stronger would from then on dominate, if he did not kill the other. In a crude sense the manifested practice in the animal kingdom that the stronger dominates might itself be thought of as "law." In fact, we sometimes hear references to the "law of the jungle." Certainly any one who has carefully observed a flock of poultry over a period of time is impressed with the accepted routine of all its members under a "picking order," determined originally by physical combat: each fowl accepting and living by a fixed status in relation to the others of the flock. But law in the animal kingdom transcends the realm of force. Any student of ornithology knows that each variety of birds builds its nests in accordance with a distinctive pattern, and that great migrations proceed in ordered routine. There is apparent living order in an ant's nest, although so far as can be observed its aspects are mechanical only.

But we are not here dealing with animals. We are concerned with human beings. The identifying characteristic of human beings is the intangible element that we had in mind when we spoke of civilization as having a higher side than that of the mere physical; the spiritual urge which brought man out of the caves and jungles to commence his arduous trek to civilization in its best sense. It endows him with rationality, with fine sensibilities to understand and appreciate the beautiful, with a conscience that gives him capacity to distinguish what is just and right. With infinite potentialities of development man's spiritual side demands not only that he live physically but that his higher faculties be free to further that development and fulfill the function of lifting him above the level of the animals with which he has physical characteristics in common.

We may reasonably assume that this element, innate in our two castaways, would assert itself in the hypothetical situation which we are considering. After a period of tenseness, perhaps accompanied by unpleasant incidents, there would come mutual realization that in the long run each would be better off to have a companion to make common cause against the difficulties and dangers of the environment than to have to face them alone. It would also be realized that living together would be intolerable without a mutual understanding that each would respect the life and property of the other. And so there would evolve that understanding, perhaps evidenced only indirectly by a period of "help each other" actions, for our two castaways might be of different races or tongues, making interchange of the spoken word impossible. With that understanding, however manifested, came "law" in the sense of a rule of ordered conduct. And with ordered conduct came a state of civilization in the sense of man's emergence from barbarism into a state of living that had some standards as a basis, however crude.

It is not too much to say that law came into being to secure the social interest in general security. Dean Roscoe Pound has pointed out that in its beginnings law was no more than a means toward a peaceful ordering of society, a regulative agency by which men were restrained and the general security was maintained. Law retains this character of a regulative agency and means toward peaceful ordering, although other functions and other ends become manifest as it develops. The Swiss Civil Code expresses the thought by saying in its Introduction that the object of law, or its purpose, is to assure the preservation and the progress of humanity. Its principles, in so far as they are established by the legislator, allow for preventing or settling the conflicts which menace individual liberty and social order.

Law the Framework of Human Freedom. Let it be here noted that in its basic sense law is an indispensable instrument of human freedom. Law is the very framework of human freedom. It is true that without it each of our two castaways appeared to have absolute freedom to do as he wished. But by that very token each was placed in jeopardy by the potential exercise of absolute freedom by the other. Only as each

surrendered his uninhibited freedom under an ordered rule of conduct
was he assured of the physical safety and opportunity to develop his
spiritual side that every human being requires. True within the family, with a greater number of human beings the need for freedom
through law becomes more and more manifest.

At this juncture of history the length of time that the primordial
humans may have gone without "law" is immaterial. It is reasonable,
and sufficient, to say that at some stage the desirability if not absolute
need for order in the group so impressed itself that understandings as
to mutual conduct gradually, perhaps almost imperceptibly, came into
force. At the outset such understandings were doubtless limited, perhaps concerned only with the matter of one human being respecting the
life of another. Whenever such understanding was reached "law" was
born, and with it civilization in the sense of human association on a
basis of recognized standards. That the growth of law through the
ages was a tortuous one goes without saying. We can state with assurance, however, that the development of the law and the state of
order associated with civilization proceeded concurrently.

The foregoing discussion has centered around the individual, the
family and closely knit groups of people. What has been said is as
true in general principle of nations. It has long been realized that it
is to their mutual advantage to live together under recognized rules
of order. History is in large measure a chronicle of their failure to do
so. Whenever a nation has thought it could disregard the broad principles of International Law to its own advantage it has usually not hesitated so to do.

The Advent of Government. We know that human beings have not
yet attained the stage when law is self-executing in the sense of being
universally obeyed. Sanctions by way of vindicating it, invokable in
the courts either by the state itself by way of criminal prosecution, or
by lawsuits instituted by private individuals, depending upon the circumstances involved, are to us a commonplace corollary of the law.
But we are looking back to the time before there were courts, or before
nomadic and illiterate men had even thought of courts. What was to
be done about the individual who did not respect the rule of law?

Obviously, what happened at first was that whoever was aggrieved
took matters into his own hands. It was entirely reasonable that the
self-help thus invoked should seek compensation or revenge in kind.
Thus, if a member of a family had been murdered, surviving members
would themselves seize and kill the person believed to be the murderer.
In all probability there was much of this sort of thing in primitive

times, contributing to the rough system of order that was developing in that era. But self-help had its limitations, which must have been apparent at times when in high-tempered haste vengeance was inflicted upon innocent persons. For what we now know as a deliberate and solemn adjudicative process centering in a formal trial before an impartial tribunal was thus unceremoniously performed by private individuals intensely prejudiced as to the outcome. All members of the group were potential victims of false accusations and punitive action which reintroduced the very insecurities and dangers that the system of order had originally found acceptance to avoid. The advantages of an impartial "ruler" to apply the law could hardly have failed to dawn on the consciousness of at least some of those affected.

The earliest dawn of civilization discloses as the most primitive form of political organization, a wayfaring society grouped about a victorious chief. This powerful personage is supposed to represent the fittest product of the period of barbaric liberty and self-help, which immediately preceded the period of more formal governmental organization. With the accession to power of some one to fill this function—whether or not under the duress of "strong man" tactics—government was "born"; thus came into being a state, in the sense of a people united into one governmental body politic. Hans Kelsen has observed that history presents no social condition in which large communities have been constituted other than by coercive orders. Even the social community of the most primitive of primitives rests on a religious coercive order gradually becoming secularized. It is a legal community. History confirms the saying "wherever there is society, there is law." Professor Paul Vinogradoff has contended that it is impossible to think of law without some political organization to support it; nor is it possible to think of a state without law. The first alternative is absurd, because law requires for its existence and application an organization to put it into force. Although from a wider aspect the function of law may be attributed to all forms of social organization, it cannot last anywhere without leaning directly or indirectly on some kind of political union acting as a safeguard of social order. On the other hand, neither the state nor any other political or quasi-political body, can exist apart from law, in the sense of a set of rules directing its relations and conduct of their members.

There was, moreover, another reason why government came into being. As we have intimated above, recorded history is in overwhelming measure a narrative of wars. Whatever may be his status as a matter of apparent right in the abstract, against organized outside force the individual is helpless. Only through the unifying coordination of government can any group of people defend itself or assert its rights against other groups forcibly challenging them. Wars were as characteristic of primitive times as they have been of the centuries since recorded. Throughout all eras government has provided individuals with protection against external aggression.

In the scholastic concept, according to Joseph M. Snee, man is much more than a social animal, naturally living in community: he is a political being, because his nature demands that he live in political society in order to achieve in a human way the full potentialities of his human personality. Community life is essential, but it cannot be left in a state of anarchy; and mankind knows experientially an essential need to organize politically for the attainment of the common good, unattainable by individual efforts or by private compact. Peace, order, liberty and prosperity are the purpose and the fruit of political society. Out of the raw material of the nation, which is merely a community conscious of its own unity, individuality and will to endure as a distinctive geographical, linguistic and cultural unit, men fashion the body politic, a society rationally organized for the purpose of establishing, maintaining and perfecting the conditions necessary and appropriate for community life to perform its role in the complete development of man. For the most part, these conditions consist in the maintenance of external peace and order, the protection of personal liberty, the regulation of property and commerce in the common interest, and the just settlement of conflicting claims.

The "Strong Man." For our purposes it does not matter whether these things worked out by a sort of common consent, along a somewhat democratic line, or whether some individual of the group possessed of a driving zest for power and taking advantage of outside peril or internal dissension forced recognition of his assumed prerogative to rule. In either case a "strong man" was needed, for under primitive conditions only a strong hand could maintain the order that called for government in the first place. And to insure his unquestionable authority it was essential that he be regarded as of divine lineage, or, at least, as bearing a divine commission. This superstition invested him with a halo of glory and clothed him with sovereign power. The religious sanction guaranteed reverence for his person and obedience to his edicts. He was priest, war chief, judge and legislator.

Though it would place too great a tax on modern credulity to associate divinity with government, there is no difficulty about understanding that government began as an inherently personalized matter.

History has depicted the opportunities which have seemed to keep the way open for it to continue along the same line. When in the seventeenth century Louis XIV of France uttered the expression popularly attributed to him, "The State—it is I," he was only echoing a theme which had its inception when states began, which for centuries was universal, and which with minor variations yet falls upon the ears of hundreds of millions of the peoples of the world.

Taking into account that in its deeper aspects history is in large part the story of injustices perpetrated by government, at first blush it might seem daring to assert that with the advent of government civilization took its most decisive step forward. Nevertheless, there need be no hesitation in so stating. History would adequately document the thesis that even bad governments have been preferable to none at all. Civilization is dependent upon order; order upon law; law upon government. Woodrow Wilson contended that the end of government is the facilitation of the objects of society. This was as true when new-born government of ancient day implemented the maintaining of a degree of primitive order as it is today. We should beware of too much of an ivory tower approach to events of the past. Granting that the first government was a "strong man"—a despot—circumstances made no other government possible. There had to be a beginning, and that was it. Nor did it end there. In various environments and eras since that beginning circumstances have made government by despot inevitable. Through it all, civilization has been maintained, with an upward trend.

International Law and World Government. If we are to be thorough we cannot pass on without referring again to International Law. Thus far the situation between nations has corresponded to the situation between individuals in primitive groups. To remedy breaches of understandings between them, primitive individuals resorted to self-help. Although there have been understandings between nations by way of International Law, self-help has constituted the only remedy for violation. Within the past generation our country has joined in fighting two World Wars to vindicate the rule of law between nations. Whatever may have been the form, in substance it fought for like purpose in Korea.

In all good logic the thought comes that if within groups of people law is an inadequate basis for order unless it has the power of government back of it, by like token law as between nations will not avail without the backing of governmental power. Today's citizen cannot dodge this issue. No apologies need be made for using the term "patriotism" and asserting that as a driving force it has played not only a leading but a highly honorable part in human history. There is no finer emotion than sincere love of country as protecting and promoting a civilized way of life. But the ultimate safety and welfare of one's country may in the future come to depend upon a jural relationship with other nations far more intimate than any known to date. As an ultimate conception it is not in order to deprecate the "one world" or "world government" school of thought, carrying, as it does, far beyond the League of Nations envisioned by Woodrow Wilson but which was too advanced for acceptance by the people of the United States in 1919, and far beyond the United Nations which within the same generation the United States, with vision enlarged by events, sponsored and housed. In the light of this strikingly rapid reversal of national sentiment as to the place of the United States in international relations, manifested within the lifetimes of most of us, one might with some assurance hazard the forecast that the future may bring a general recognition of the necessity of some form of world government if civilization through world order is to be maintained in the atomic age. However insuperable the difficulties may now appear, some kind of workable solution may be forced by the iron hand of circumstances.

A line of thought capable of being buttressed by Soviet authority is calculated to produce some eyebrow-raising. But truth is where we find it. For answers to questions of power in its relation to government there is no better place to go today than to Soviet Russia. The late Andrei Vyshinsky, well-known Soviet jurist, said that the nature of the state is the most important question in the science of public law. The theory of the state is the basis not only of the science of state law but also of law in general, inasmuch as scientific understanding of law is impossible without a correct understanding of the state. Law and state cannot be studied separately and apart from each other. Law draws its force, it obtains its content from, the state.

It is true that Vyshinsky does not use the term "government" but refers to the "state." Thus far we have employed the term "government" rather than "state," with the thought that government is the agency which implements the law. In technical usage the terms are not altogether synonymous. In so far as our general purposes are concerned, however, it is not necessary to encumber the record with an attempt at sharp delineation. Any difference is important only as it bears on the ultimate repository of the power; whether it is the whole people, or a despot. Under our concept the whole people are the state and the government their servant agency, set up and controlled by them to conduct their affairs. Abraham Lincoln expressed it in his immortal Gettysburg Address when he bespoke the resolution "that government of the people, by the people, and for the people, shall not perish from the earth."

With this understanding we can accept Vyshinsky's statement that "law derives its force, it obtains its content from the state," as applicable to us. But although the Soviets make use of the term "people" to the point of endless repetition, it will be obvious from the description of their regime in later pages that their concept of the "state" is not the same as ours. Mr. Vyshinsky made no reference to people. When he spoke of law drawing its force and obtaining its content from the state he was obviously thinking of the repository of power. Implicit in his reference to the state is the concept of Louis XIV in the asseveration attributed to him and to which we have already alluded, "The State—it is I." That dictatorial power reposes in several men rather than in one in no sense alters the principle. Since Vyshinsky has been put forth as an outstanding Soviet jurist it would be the height of presumption on our part to question his statement as applied to Communist Russia. With the understanding that he is talking about a state and government all in one we can accept it freely.

"Who" is the government therefore becomes the all-important consideration, fraught with consequences that extend to the farthest reaches of human life. Under despotism law is one thing. Under democracy it is quite another. There have been, and are today, many different governments, embodying variations of the two extremes. The force and content of the law in each may be determined by close analysis.

Relation Between the Content of Law and Government. As Hans Kelsen has pointed out, the word "law" refers to the specific social technique of a coercive order, which, despite the vast differences between the law of ancient Babylon and that of the United States today, between the law of the Ashantis in West Africa and that of the Swiss in Europe, is yet essentially the same for all these peoples differing so in time, in place, and in culture: the social technique which consists in bringing about the desired social conduct of men through threat of a measure of coercion which is to be applied in case of contrary conduct. The measure of that conduct will be determined by the government which applies the force, and will be strictly geared to governmental ideology.

Starting, then, with the premise that in its practical operation law is integrated with government, the matter of government becomes of vital concern to us in the same degree as the nature and content of the law itself. If law provides the principle, the rule, it is the government which provides the force which implements it. Nor does governmental power stop there. We have inaugurated our study on the premise that there was law before there was government. In the field of international law, as we have indicated, that phenomenon remains manifested today. We are in no sense abandoning that premise when we admit, as we must, the power of government to make law as well as to administer it. For government, once established, is all-powerful, save as it may have been set up democratically and remains under the control of democratic processes. The only restraint upon a despotic government is in the personal inhibitions of its ruler. With or without some limitation, law-making is an inherent prerogative of government.

"Personal" Government: The Despot. The point of view for an understanding approach may be sharpened by glancing at the difference between governments, taking first the despot. Here is personalized power, exercisable without external restraint. We would characterize it, unhesitatingly, as a vicious form of government. We would do so, having fully in mind that there can be benevolent despots as well as evil ones, and that what might fairly pass as good government in many senses has, from time to time in history, come out of despotism. The viciousness flows from the absence of check on despotic power, with its ominous potentialities of arbitrary and oppressive action. In accordance with what we would expect, history has revealed more bad than good despots. Whereas under the administration of a good despot a written code of justice might not add to the procedures of an already beneficent rule, under a bad despot, arbitrarily proceeding according to personal whim, the finest code of law ever produced would be only a scrap of paper. The will of the despot *is* the law; nothing can stop the possessor of despotic power from executing it.

Government "Of the People." Let us consider, on the other hand, a government of the people, using the word "people" not in the bizarre sense in which it is employed by the Soviet politicians of Russia and China in referring to their regimes, but with the Lincolnian meaning of all the people exercising rights as free men under a written constitution sharply limiting the powers of government. Whereas in a despotism the government is, indeed, one of men, we have portrayed here a government not of men but of laws.

The mere description of a true people's government is sufficiently indicative of the basic variation between its laws and the laws of a despotism which, though only the personal unrecorded edicts of a ruler, legally order the lives of the flesh and blood subject to his power. In a despotism there is just one power, the ruler. He makes the law. In a government of the people there is just one power, the people. In so far as there is a ruler, they make him. The people make the law-makers, and, through them, the law. Exercising the rights of free speech and assembly and a free and secret ballot, the people order the course of law and government in accordance with the best interests of all.

The Power of Groups. Before passing on, some further observations appear in order. There would be little disagreement with the broad statement that under our "government of the people" the people order the course of law. But we would be unduly naive if we did not go beneath the surface of the abstraction and note, analytically, what is there. We find the "people," to be sure. But they are not conducting themselves in their various relationships as individuals, or even as families. They are organized into groups, such as labor unions, agricultural federations, trade associations, patriotic and veterans' organizations, and professional societies in great variety, to say nothing of the great business corporations in which millions of citizens are legally united as shareholders. Moreover, a probable majority of Americans are members of religious organizations. These groups exercise what might be said to be the power of private law-making. Few are the citizens who are not affected, if not governed, in important aspects of their lives, by rules which have their source, not in the law laid down by the state, but in rules and regulations promulgated by private groups.

Let us be realistic. In the nature of things, each group is motivated to advance its own particular interest. Under modern ecclesiastical theories of "social action," even religious organizations attempt to join their members in united sociological programs. The political result is that in its actual operation our government is not a government of the people as individuals, but rather a government of groups of people, each attempting to make its own impact decisive upon the formulation of the laws of the land and their administration.

To be strictly accurate we might have to say, then, that we have become a government of groups of people rather than of "the people." Even so, no negation of our democratic principles would be implied. The very fact that organized groups in such number and variety are allowed to live and freely function is in itself the most convincing proof of the existence of democracy. They were not allowed in Hitler's Germany, nor are they tolerated behind the Iron Curtain. As long as the individual citizen is free to join any group of legitimate purpose, and to exercise uninhibited his right of political suffrage, we have, and will continue to have, true government "of the people."

Insulating Government Against Undue Group Pressures. The pressures of groups are by no means confined to the ballot box, but are exerted directly against the several departments of the government. This presents problems, but is no more than a democratic government contemplates. Under the First Amendment to the Constitution of the United States, the right of the people to petition the government for a redress of grievances is guaranteed, as, indeed, in any free government it should be. But like any right, it is not above abuse, as the activities of modern lobbyists from time to time make clear. Senator John F. Kennedy has recently declared that one of the most vexatious problems Congress has faced is represented by the wide variety of efforts by which various groups or individuals attempt to secure the passage or defeat of legislation—the problem of lobbying. Lobbying has attracted the attention of Congress at frequent intervals for more than a century, but, thus far, no effective workable device for coping with the difficulties incident to influencing legislation has been devised. Nevertheless, Senator Kennedy emphasizes that the constitutional right to petition Congress must not be unduly restricted, and he calls attention to the fact that the members of this "third chamber," as he calls them, make a real contribution to the legislative process. The Federal Regulation of Lobbying Act, adopted in 1946, was a forward step in American government, but the time has now come for Congress to adopt an improved law dealing with the activities of pressure groups.

That organized groups may use their financial resources in such a way as to influence, to the national injury, the exercise of the right of the ballot, has long been recognized. Congress has legislated to guard against abuses in this connection. The matter was reviewed historically by the Supreme Court of the United States in the recent case of *United States v. International Union,* in which the Court upheld the validity of an indictment charging the International Union United Automobile Workers with violation of a federal statute forbidding corporations and labor organizations from making a contribution or expenditure in connection with any election for federal office; the indictment alleging that the Union used Union dues to sponsor commercial television broadcasts designed to influence the electorate to select certain candidates for Congress.

Subjecting labor organizations to restrictions in this regard is a recent development. The act before the Court had its genesis in a 1907 enactment forbidding national banks or federal corporations to make money contributions in connection with any election to any political office. Speaking of this 1907 statute, the Court said that as its historical background indicates, its aim was not merely to prevent the subversion of the integrity of the elective process. Its underlying philosophy was to sustain the active, alert responsibility of the individual citizen in a democracy for the wise conduct of government. This act of 1907 was merely the first concrete manifestation for elections "free from the power of money." Subsequent amendments broadened and strengthened the act. In 1939 Congress enacted the Hatch Act, "designed to free the political processes of the abuses deemed to accompany the operation of a vast civil administration." Coming to the 1943 legislation, which brought labor organizations within the purview of restrictions on financial expenditures and contributions, the Court said that the need for unprecedented economic mobilization propelled by World War II enormously stimulated the power of organized labor and soon aroused consciousness of its power outside its ranks. Wartime strikes gave rise to fears of the new concentration of power represented by the gains of trade unionism. And so the belief grew that, just as the great corporations had made huge political contributions to influence governmental action or inaction, whether consciously or unconsciously, the powerful unions were pursuing a similar course, and with the same untoward consequences for the democratic process.

Our Debt to the Past. Though some restraint must be imposed on political action by groups, as we have said they are contemplated by the democratic process. Ours is, indeed, a government of the people, and through our system of law we have the wherewithal to undergird it. Enough has been said to indicate that the course of civilization from the period when there was none to the present has been a tortuous one, however rapidly it may seem to be moving in our generation. For its material progress we are indebted to its whole past. The scientific and commercial achievements which characterize it were not consummated by any present day sleight-of-hand. They are founded upon a process of nature exploration, employing observation and experimentation, making step-by-step advances traceable through remote centuries. Alongside there developed moral standards, arising out of man's experiences as he slowly climbed upward toward higher interpretations of life and living. As we have indicated, the law has made these achievements possible by providing the basis of order without which civilization could not be. And by similar token our legal institutions are indebted to the dimly-lit and awkward processes through which the course of justice has labored since history began. Justice Robert H. Jackson, referring to the superficial belief among laymen that law is all created by "the government," went on to say that a vast proportion of all "law" that is applied today in the courts of our several countries had its real origin long before the government. Some of it is as old as the Scriptures, much of it is traceable in ancient codes, very little is really added by ourselves. Sound law is neither temporary or local. Munroe Smith has summed up the situation by saying that the history of human law, as of all civilization, is largely a history of borrowing.

As we ponder the matter, it does not seem too much to say that our legal debt to the past is greater than is our debt in any other respect. Human relations have presented an ever-present problem, for men have had to live and work together since their creation. Law and government, proceeding largely by fortuitous trial and error, have been constantly operative. Dynasties rose and fell; lawgivers entered and engraved their codes on stone; despots strutted across the stage, sometimes ruthless, sometimes beneficent to the point of evoking deification; democracies and republics flourished and collapsed; empires ruled the world and were crushed to earth; the Church built up within itself a great structure of law and left its cloisters to wield it in the realm of temporal power. Perhaps the narrative of these things seems to be a sordid chronicle of bloody violence and inquisition. Nevertheless, to the student of legal institutions it presents a fascinating story of the development of law and government as the human race struggled through the centuries to attain that liberty of ordered justice which is man's most priceless possession.

Constitutional Forefathers "Not Imbued with Modern Cynicism." Our constitutional forefathers who met in Philadelphia in 1787 to frame the Constitution of the United States knew that story. They did not create, out of hand, the document which provides the basis for our ordered liberties. They were learned men, students of law and government, aware of the enlightenment that history had to offer. They established a pattern for our government calculated to avoid the pitfalls and embody the safeguards which the trials and errors of nations of the past had made manifest. They distinguished themselves through their keen evaluation of these things and their ability to translate into a succinct legal document basic principles of human relationships constituting a unique charter of freedom.   By that document they underwrote our way of life.   With keen discernment Justice Frankfurter has noted that the Founders of this nation were not imbued with the modern cynicism that the only thing that history teaches is that it teaches nothing.   They acted on the conviction that the experience of man sheds a good deal of light on his nature.   It sheds a good deal of light not merely on the need for effective power, if a society is to be at once cohesive and civilized, but also on the need for limitations on the power of government over the governed.

We are living at a time when the way of life established by those Founders is being sharply challenged throughout the world.   The challenge is directly against our legal system and our form of government.   Nothing can better satisfy us that our law as well as our government were good in their conception of immutable principles than to review briefly the background against which our constitutional forefathers worked.   Nor will anything more convincingly remind us that the conception of 1787 remains sound today than to add to this review a few words as to the operation of law and government in those regions responsible for the challenge.

We will proceed, therefore, to turn our glance back to the earliest history of civilization and sketch through the centuries some of the more important events as they cast light on the law and government of the time.   As we proceed, we will be constantly alert to note what the law was, the source from which it came, the manner in which it was administered, and its impact upon the people who were subject to it.

PART II: SYNTHESIS OF LAW AND RELIGION

CHAPTER 2

EGYPT: ROOTS OF CIVILIZATION

Civilization at the Dawn of History. To discover evidences of civilization of a high order at the dawn of history might not seem to be a reasonable expectation. Yet that very phenomenon is provided by ancient Egypt, where, around 4000 B. C., we find people of the Hamite family settled in the Valley of the Nile, and eventually expanding until they occupied Crete, Phoenicia, Syria, Palestine and Cyprus. Several millenia before Greece came to historical notice the Egyptians were demonstrating noteworthy attainment in science and the arts by erecting such monuments as the Great Sphinx and the Pyramids of Gizeh, to say nothing of great engineering and other architectural works.

In the Medical Museum of the Armed Forces Institute of Pathology in Washington, D. C., is a display of "Women and Medicine," which starts with a facsimile of the most ancient known pictorial record of a woman doctor, an Egyptian stele of about 3000 B. C. The legend informs that her small boy patient had poliomyletis and was cured by her intercession with the goddess Isis. Egyptians had worked out a system of writing, the key to which was provided by the famous Rosetta Stone, discovered by the French in the course of the Napoleonic invasion of Egypt in 1798. On the papyrus paper which they invented and manufactured was recorded a literature of great variety, extending from fairy tales for children to treatises on astronomy and medicine. In many ways they demonstrated themselves to have become a people of culture.

What all had transpired before the curtain was lifted on the historical stage at which we have thus glanced has not as yet yielded to discovery, and probably never will. In the tortuous process of establishing the social order that brought about civilization there could not have been any calculated recording of evidence for posterity. Nor, until the social order was in a fair degree of advancement, were there facilities to permit the construction of buildings or monuments that would survive to tell the story circumstantially, or the language that would lend itself to detailed recording that would be intelligible in later ages. Professor Huntington Cairns has aptly said that pre-history, in the investigation of many manifestations of human culture, has accomplished much toward bridging the chasm between anthropology and history, but in the field of social organization this chasm still exists. The origins of customs and institutions are irretrievably lost, even beyond the possibility of discovery by the prehistorian. We may know that the Neolithic man domesticated sheep, cultivated various farinaceous crops, and wore clothing made from the skin of animals, but it is extremely unlikely that we will ever be able to ascertain, except in the most fragmentary fashion—and from the standpoint of theory, valueless—the nature of his social organization.

Religion and Law. Among the indicia of civilization mentioned above, there is no code of law. What, then, as to the law and government which sustained this Egyptian civilization? We can answer, at the outset, that Egyptian law and government were provided by the Egyptian religion.

Thus far in our discussion we have conceived of the evolution of law along rather mechanistic lines. We have thought of the development of law and government as being actuated by some sort of maturing realization that individual safety and welfare could be insured only as there was a system of order, and enforced conformity thereto.

That this in itself would be an adequate explanation would doubtless be conceded. And it would be a momentous explanation, because implicit in it is the operation of human reason, a basic manifestation of man's spiritual attributes. But this is not all. Even more apparent is it that at this dawn of history, men were being guided by their spiritual nature in its higher aspect: the aspect which we commonly think of in terms of religion and the human conscience. Regardless of the reservation that we might hold as to actuation of the primitive man by bare superstition, these were men advanced in civilization. Religion was their law. And even as to superstition, who will say that it is not, in its crude way, a groping of man's spirit toward the light?

It is certainly true, as Lord Macmillan has pointed out, that between the concepts of law and religion, as we now see them, there may well appear to be a wide gulf fixed. Law, we are reminded, is concerned with external behavior, with acts and forbearances and their consequences, or, as it has been put, "with rules of civil conduct enforced by the state." Its sanctions are secular. It does not presume to deal with things of the spirit, but confines itself to mundane matters of contract and delict, property and succession and the maintenance of order by the suppression of crime. As it has been put, criminal law has no mission beyond the preservation of physical quiet. The peace of the soul is not its concern. And civil law is equally indifferent to the spiritual side of life. Anything less reminiscent of the language of inspiration than a modern statute it would be difficult to conceive. Here all is hard and practical.

On the other hand, according to Lord Macmillan, religion concerns itself, not with the things which are seen and temporal, but with the things which are not seen and eternal. Its essence is found in faith and devotion, in an attitude of the soul, though no doubt by works faith may be made perfect. The dictates of religion are not of this world, and its rewards and punishments lie hereafter.

Yet, far apart as would thus seem to be the spheres of religion and law in our day, historically it was not always so. Indeed, these apparent opposites spring from a common origin in the human mind. They both alike share that mysterious word "ought," which is significant of so much that is distinctive of man's higher life and which even reminds us that we owe to a power outside ourselves the obligation to obey the commands of duty, that "stern daughter of the voice of God." Religion, after all, means etymologically only something by which we are bound, which is also the root conception of law. The duties which the law prescribes have by a slow process of evolution separated themselves from those which religion inculcates; but the obligations of religon and law were originally indistinguishable; they derived from a common source, and there are countries where they still remain to a large extent identical, while in all countries they retain traces of their early association.

It is apparent, then, that a religious system is in itself law, and that this is as true today as it ever was. Rules of conduct must, of course, be supplemented by the force of sanctions. Religion can supply them, whether in its own system of ecclesiastical penalties or through the operation of the consciences of its adherents. For the most part, however, religion has operated within the structure of secular government, which has prescribed the laws for all to observe and provided the sanctions calculated to secure their observance. And secular government, throughout history, has drawn heavily, sometimes exclusively, on religious principles and practices for the law which it proclaims and administers. It is hardly too much to say that the most complete observance of laws has been reached through education, based on religious fears and hopes.

The Supreme Role of the Conscience. No one would be so naive as to believe that everything proclaimed in the name of religion has constituted an unimpeachable basis for human conduct. Religion has been conceived and translated into life by human beings, inspired to exercise their highest spiritual capacities. At the heart of religious experience is the human conscience, with its exalted potentialities. To it is entrusted the responsibility for finding and pursuing life's supreme role. But that conscience is, at best, a fallible guide. Getting out of bounds in the persons of men of power, with its functioning invading the precincts of the consciences of others, its operations are capable of unspeakable injustice. Moreover, the noblest principles are susceptible to prostitution by men not measuring up to their spiritual obligations. The spectacle of persecution for failure or refusal to conform to humanly promulgated religious law has stained many pages of history.

But when this has been said, we may conclude from history's brighter pages that the hope of mankind through the better life rests on the working of the human conscience. It must be respected, and have full freedom under law to perform its function. However many or great the injustices that can be traced to its abortive exercise, the emphasis belongs on the demonstrated fact that for thousands of years men have been led by their consciences to search for the eternal verities, and have been inspired to incorporate their findings into rules aimed at promoting the better life, with justice for all. They have always fallen short of the goal. But the law by which we live is the better for their efforts. If it does not seem to have kept pace with the achievements of science, the sufficient reason is that the human soul through which it works is too delicate an instrument to be shaped to formula by the crude hand which split the atom.

Recently it has been said that for all our material abundance, the real strength of America, and the author of its plenty, is the spiritual and moral force of our ideals. In the troubled year 1782 Thomas Jefferson asked the fundamental question: "Can the liberties of a nation be thought secure when we have removed their only firm basis, a conviction in the minds of the people that these liberties are the gift of God?" The power of each man to find his own destiny and to seek his own salvation is the essence of the teachings of the world's great religions, and the well-springs of our political beliefs lie deep in the heart of our spiritual faith. The reawakening of people everywhere to the primacy of things of the spirit reminds us once more of individual responsibility and of the dangers of assuming to judge our fellows. We are reminded, too, that no man is so all-seeing and all-wise that he can create for the rest of us an earthly paradise.

Egyptian Religion As Law. What we find as the curtain goes up on Egyptian civilization amply sustains the thesis which we have been developing. Religious principles and practices, promulgated and implemented by the theocratic Pharaohs who ruled Egypt, constituted the law of the land.

It is admittedly difficult for us to conceive of some of these principles and practices in terms of religion. We cannot imagine divinity in Osiris, the judge of the dead, or in Isis, his wife and sister, or in Horus, their son, or in the other figures of their polytheistic hierarchies. Much less can we accept as a religious concept that which would hold insects and bulls to be emblematic of Osiris and other gods, to be worshipped in that capacity. Perhaps we can presume to judge that our disagreement with such concepts comes about because we are beneficiaries of a process of spiritual development which has brought to us greater enlightenment in matters of the soul. For the purpose of the present principle it does not matter. We would be presuming too much if we judged the early Egyptians as not proceeding in the lights of that ancient day, guided by conscience to follow their religion as they understood it. That they did so is not at all difficult of belief when we take into account that the future life was of paramount importance to them, emphasized by their concern for the embalming and entombment of the dead. Perhaps we should have some reservations about our own spiritual superiority as we ponder the confession which they believed every soul must make before Osiris, some elements of which were: "I have not done evil. I have not blasphemed. I have not slandered any one or made false accusation. I have not cheated. I have not slain any one treacherously. I have not reviled the face of my father. I have not stolen. I have given bread to the hungry and drink to him who was athirst. I have clothed the naked with garments."

The Pharaohs: Priest Rulers. We have spoken of the religious principles and practices of the Egyptians as being promulgated by the theocratic Pharaohs. Implicit in the ancient religions was the concept that the god was the ruler, ordaining some one on earth to represent him in the promulgation and administration of law. This ruler was invested with the attributes of divinity. His judgments had their source in the god and were divinely inspired. The directives of the god were postulated on a dogmatic certainty which booked no qualifying rationalization from any source.

Under such a religious concept, as history has demonstrated, people will accept despotism as their lot. Religious despotism, monarchical despotism, have more than once obtained the sanction, almost the love, of the population which they governed. In religious or monarchical despotism authority is always exercised by virtue of some belief or opinion common to both ruler and subjects; he is the representative, the minister, of another power superior to all human powers. He speaks or acts in the name of divinity, and not in the name of man himself, or man alone. But wherever in a ruler or master the one ruled sees but the individual man—the moment that the authority which presses upon him is not more than an individual, a human will, one like his own, he feels mortified and indignant and struggles against the yoke which he is compelled to bear. By way of anticipation the suggestion might be hazarded here that human liberty had its real advent when people ceased to regard their human rulers with religious or superstitious awe.

But as long as people accepted the divine element in their ruler the word of a theocratic despot was law. Back of it were the double sanctions of religious awe and the king's strong arm. Motivated by strict regard for the tenets of justice, it could be good law. In so far as the Pharaohs lived by the ethical standards implicit in the religion which they administered, their law was good. On an ancient papyrus, on which is inscribed the *Domesday Book of Rameses III*, the king is recorded as saying: "I made the land safe, so that a lone woman could go on her way freely and none would molest her. I rescued the humble from their oppressors. I made every man safe in his home." On the tomb of Rekhmire it is recorded that when King Thutmose appointed him chief judge he commanded him "to do everything which is in accordance with law; to do everything according to the right thereof." The instruction further adjured Rekhmire: "It is an abomination of the god to show partiality. Thou shalt act alike to all, shalt regard him who is known to thee like him who is unknown to thee, and him who is near to thee like him who is far."

But one would legitimately doubt the capacity of priestly rulers to proceed always in a manner worthy of their sacred office. And even though they never departed from the high plane, human fallibility, as always, was capable of working great injustice, the more so as it was coupled with earnest desire to implement the fallible judgment.

As we shall see in later pages, no force is capable of greater wrong than aberrant religious zeal.

Whatever the motive or explanation, every student of the Old Testament is familiar with the side of the Pharaohs and Egyptian law narrated in the Book of Exodus and exemplified in the Pharaoh who said to his people: "Behold, the children of Israel are more and mightier than we. Come on, let us deal wisely with them." We are told how taskmasters were set over the Israelites "to afflict them with their burdens," and, in some detail, how they were made to serve "with rigor." No governmental decree in all history is more harsh than the order to the midwives to kill all male children born to Israelite women. The denouement by way of Pharaoh's daughter saving the life of Moses, encouragingly demonstrative of the humanitarian instinct, only emphasizes the brutality of the current priestly regime.

No "Accommodations Between Conflicting Interests." We cannot but contrast the apparent simplicity of such a legal system, where one man—doubtless with the assistance of other advisers and administrators, but nevertheless himself dominating the scene—declared and administered the law, with the one we know today. Whatever philosophy we may adopt as to its source, our law does not come about through the clear-cut pronouncement of any one man. It is rather a composite of the presently rationalized conduct of all men. In the sense of everyday reality, its source is human, not divine. Clear as to general outline of just principles, its detail, perhaps more often than not, is blurred. For the process of arriving at some sort of a consensus of what is the "rationalized conduct of all men" necessarily involves the intervention of the human mind. Not all minds can agree on what is rational; if they could, there would be disagreement as to how the conclusion should be expressed. In the classic language of the Federalist, the faculties of the mind itself have never yet been distinguished and defined, with satisfactory precision, by all the efforts of the most acute and metaphysical philosophers. Sense, perception, judgment, desire, volition, memory, imagination, are found to be separated by such delicate shades and minute gradations that their boundaries have eluded the most subtle investigations,.and remain a pregnant source of ingenious disquisition and controversy. When we pass from the works of nature, in which all the delineations are perfectly accurate, and appear to be otherwise only from the imperfections of the eye which surveys them, to the institutions of man, in which the obscurity arises as well from the object itself as from the organ by which it is contemplated, we must perceive the necessity of moderating still further our expectations and hopes from the efforts of human sagacity.

Recognizing such limitation the Supreme Court of the United States, dealing recently with "the eternal problem of the law of making accommodations between conflicting interests," declared that there are few areas of the law in black and white. The grays are dominant, and even among them the shades are innumerable." "That is why most legal problems end as questions of degree."

In the light of what has been said about the protestation of Rameses III and the adjuration to Rekhmire, we must conclude that the concept of "conflicting interests" was present in the jurisprudence of ancient Egypt. There have been conflicting interests as long as there has been a human race, and in the nature of things justice finds its main problem in resolving them. But agents actuated by the inspiration of an infallible god are not the ones to distinguish between delicate shades of gray. The experience of the Israelites is enough to indicate that the Pharaohs did not tarry for such a process where their own interests were involved. Perhaps we should assume that they gave more than lip service to principles of justice when there was no issue other than between two humble citizens. As to the king, there was no conflict: he made his own law, in his own supreme interest.

The experience of the Israelites demonstrated, early in history, that the greatest injustice of all can be committed by the government to which one looks for protection, but which rather turns on him and grinds him under a despotic heel. In the relation between man and his government there is, inevitably, a potential clash of interests, calling for accommodation. It will be worth while to keep in mind the possibility that the progress of civilization, in its higher sense, has been rather directly identified with the satisfactory making of accommodations, not only between man and man, but between man and government. Thus far we have not found in religion, on a basis of theocratic absolutism, the way to such justice. We have many centuries to go before we come to the day of Abraham Lincoln, who, even while Civil War was raging in the United States, said: "It is as much the duty of Government to render prompt justice against itself in favor of citizens as it is to administer the same between private individuals."

Chapter 3

THE INFLUENCE OF THE BABYLONIANS

Advancing Civilization. Back around 4000 B. C., we find in the region between the Euphrates and Tigris Rivers, known by the ancient Greeks as Mesopotamia, and sometimes spoken of as the world's oldest highway for the movement of peoples and the transmission of ideas, settlements in the nature of the city states which we will later note in Greece and Italy. Among them were such places as Ur, mentioned in the Book of Genesis, where Abraham received his call to go to Egypt, hereinafter further noted in our consideration of the ancient Hebrews. Each city was ruled by a king and had its patron god. The people were a mixture of non-Semitic Sumerians and Arabian Semitic nomads.

The land was one well fitted to sustain an advancing ancient civilization. Fertile alluvial soil made possible a settled agricultural life rather than the nomadic existence which alone was possible throughout much of the desert and mountainous regions of the Near East. The climate was favorable. Bricks for building purposes could readily be fabricated, and lent themselves to a distinctive architecture which became highly developed. Pottery was made in a multitude of varieties. The ceramic arts flourished. Artisans put copper and other metals to use for both war and domestic purposes.

The Babylonian Empire had its beginning under Sargon, King of the city state of Agade. But it was King Hammurabi of Babylon who, about 2200 B.C., forged all the scattered settlements into an empire which put an end to the harassment long inflicted by the kings of Elam, a country bordering on the east. For some fifteen centuries thereafter Babylon, though subsequently conquered in turn by the Hittites and the Kassites, was the center of empire. In 728 B.C. it was conquered by King Tilgath-Pileser of the Assyrian Empire, which had come to strength in the north. Thereafter, for a period, Babylon was ruled by the Assyrian kings from Nineveh.

Localized Religion. The Babylonians developed cuneiform writing and the art of preserving it on tablets of clay to a degree which laid the foundation for much present enlightenment as to the nature of their civilization, including, especially, their religion. It has already been stated that each city had its patron god. For such god each city provided a temple of large size, dedicated to Baal or Bel, to the moon god, or to whatever god might be the city deity. The temple thus provided was the religious center of the community. But it was much more than that. It housed an extensive library, not only of religious materials, recording such accounts as that of the Creation by the great god Marduk, and of the flood, but also wills, contracts and commercial documents in great variety. Its further content indicated advanced studies by the people of the time into such areas of knowledge as mathematics, geography, and astronomy. Sargon's library at Agane contained works on astronomy and astrology which were copied for the libraries of other cities of the Empire.

In the endowments of these temples we find the precursors of the endowed religious and charitable institutions of today. The temples, moreover, served the purpose of business and legal centers for their communities. Their affairs were administered by a royal priesthood, which was not allowed to get out of kingly control.

As to the content of the Babylonia religion, soothsaying and exorcism played a leading role. The emphasis on astrology led to astro-theological concepts. The heavenly bodies were believed to control life on earth, and the spirits of the stars were identified with the gods of the several planets. Human and animal sacrifices were made to them. To get as near as possible to these gods, temples were placed on the highest possible locations. On the plains, high mounds were first constructed as foundations.

A liturgical element is revealed in the "hymns to the gods" which in their phraseology might be taken to be antecedents of the later Psalms of the Hebrews. Thus, it was declared, "May god, my creator, take mine hands. Guide thou the breath of my mouth, guide thou mine hands. Thou alone art high." However, the emphasis was upon magic rites and incantations to ward off evil spirits. Augury played a determining part, omens being drawn from any and all events. It was not conceived that the dead were judged. All went to the same dark tomb, to drowse through the hereafter in a gloomy underworld, their food the dust of the earth.

Hammurabi's Code. In 1928, twenty-six years after the discovery in 1902 by French excavators at Susa, in ancient Elam, of Hammurabi's Code, Dr. J. H. Hertz read before the Society for Jewish Jurisprudence a paper on the subject "Ancient Semitic Codes and the Mosaic Legislation." The Society was convened in the Inner Temple,

a historic shrine for British and common law lawyers, dating back to
the time of the Crusades. Dr. Hertz brought out how very recent
are the discoveries which have made this vital source material available to us. Said he: "The Babylonian Code has been known for a
quarter of a century, but to my knowledge very little has yet appeared
in this country in regard to either the Assyrian or the Hittite laws.
This is not surprising when we realize that these were discovered a
little more than a decade ago, and have only been edited for the first
time in 1920 and 1921, respectively." Since Botta's unearthing of
Sargon's palace in 1843, and the final deciphering of cuneiform script
in 1857, there has been a continuous archaeological revelation of
ancient civilizations whose very name had for ages vanished from
the lips of men. An unexpected reality has been given to the mythical
and fabulous East, and the kings of Sumeria, Babylonia and Assyria,
of Mittam and the land of the Hittites, seem to have come to life
again. In fact, we know more of the twenty-fifth pre-Christian century in Babylon than of the Fifth Century in Hellas or of the Third
Century in Rome. What would the classical scholar give for the auto-
graph letters of Plato or Pericles; and yet we have the actual originals
of the code of laws, the administrative orders and official letters of a
king who was a contemporary of Abraham and is mentioned in the
early chapters of the Book of Genesis. In all the annals or Oriental
research, no event can compare in importance with the discovery of
this Code of Hammurabi, the oldest document in the development of
human legislation and one of the landmarks in world history.

King Hammurabi: Benevolent Despot. The zenith of Babylonian
civilization was reached under the sixth king of the Arabian dynasty,
best known as Hammurabi, who reigned for 43 years, from 1945 to
1902 B.C. He appears to have been the benevolent despot at his best.
He dealt severely with all bribery and oppression on the part of his
judges and officials. And having the point of view that a written
code accessible to the people is an indispensable condition of justice,
however just the laws themselves may be, he undertook to codify the
Babylonian law and make it accessible to them.

As discovered by J. de Morgan and his French excavators in 1902
at the Acropolis of Susa, the capital of ancient Elam, this code was
inscribed on an enormous block of diorite, measuring 7 feet 4½ inches
in height and 4 feet 11 inches in circumference, covered with 49 col-
umns of writing. Its 8,000 Semitic words, the equivalent of 20,000 in
English, form the longest cuneiform inscription theretofore found. It
consists of 282 paragraphs, and is preceded by a Prologue and closes

with an Epilogue. The Prologue is a fair specimen of the Prunk-schrift, the boasting inscription of Oriental monarchs. Hammurabi boasts of his victories, his greatness, wisdom, love of justice and piety. He is the "shepherd of his people," and declares that the object of his promulgating the Code was "that the strong may not oppress the weak, that the orphan and the widow be protected."

Insight Into Babylonian Life. Nothing can give us such an immediate insight into the cultural and social life of the Babylonias 3900 years ago as this collection of laws. The more so, because it does not lay down general principles, but selects cases which exemplify them. The words of Savigny, the great authority on Roman law, apply here: "Law takes actual life as its starting point." As we read its paragraphs, we catch realistic glimpses of Babylonian life; for the Code deals with the laws of witchcraft, evidence, duties and privileges of royal servants; of tenure, rents and cultivated lands, trade and commerce, deposits and prosecution for debt, of family law, marriage, settlements, divorce, inheritance, adoption, criminal law, slavery, canal-care and tariffs of wages for architects, surgeons and boatmen.

As reflected in the Code, society in the time of the early Babylonians presented certain definite castes: king, court and priests, men of gentle birth (aristocrats and officers), commoners and slaves. The Code contained no laws for the King and very few for the priest. The privileges of the latter were no doubt well known, and the former was a semi-divine person who was above the law, beyond good and evil, so to speak, with perhaps all the gruesome privileges of the early Sumerian absolutism. Among other things these demanded that the king's bodyguard and grooms and gorgeously attired women be deliberately slain around his last resting place. However, the Code recognized appeals to the King and his power of pardon, and had detailed rules concerning some of the King's officers.

It was the gentleman, the commoner and the slave, for whom the Code of Hammurabi legislated. The difference between the social grades could be measured by the various regulations. For example, where bodily injuries were compounded for by money payment, an aristocrat was equal to two commoners, and a commoner to two slaves. Likewise, where capital punishment for theft was commuted by payment, the thief had to pay thirtyfold if the theft was from the royal estate; tenfold if from a gentleman, and fivefold if from a commoner. The commoner was a free man, but subject to corvee, and liable to be sold into slavery for debt or for crime. In case he was enslaved for debt, he regained his freedom after three years.

As D. Oswald Dykes has pointed out, the law of the family occupied a prominent place in the Code. It is noteworthy that it prescribed nothing in the way of a *patria potestas* in the husband. There is no trace of his having, at any time, the extensive powers, extending even to life and death, of the Roman father over his wife and children. The severance of a wife from her own family and her incorporation in that of her husband was never complete and irrevocable, for in certain cases of separation she returned to her father's home. Marriage was monogamous, but with certain provisions for concubinage where there were no children of the marriage. Married women could conduct business, make contracts, and bring suit in their own name.

In many aspects this Code of Hammurabi seems to us a gruesome thing. Note how little value it places on human life. Horrible mutilations abound—of eyes, ears, tongue and hand; and there are 34 crimes for which the death penalty was inflicted; among these, every form of theft. However, there is no denying that harsh and cruel punishments have prevailed through much of history. Even in England pocket-picking was punishable by death until the year 1808, and sheep-stealing until 1832. The Eighth Amendment to the Constitution of the United States, providing that cruel and unusual punishments shall not be inflicted, was a distinct innovation in the field of criminal law.

"Higher Criticism" and the Influence of Mediterranean Law. To the legal scholar, much more interesting than the examination of the detailed regulations of the Code of Hammurabi are the questions connected with what might be called its "higher criticism." Is it the product of one mind, or is it the precipitate of many ages? Again, being the oldest code of laws in the world, what are its influences on younger codes, its traces, in other words, in the history of civilization? In the opinion of Dr. Hertz, the laws incorporated in the Code were not invented by Hammurabi; it would be absurd to look upon the times before him as a period of anarchy. Besides, there is no such thing as starting with a clean slate in law. Every new order must graft itself on the past, must connect itself with the civic institutions that had hitherto shaped the people's life. Writing down the laws, fixing the customary law in legal shape, of course carried some refining with it. This Code was but the amalgamation and adaptation of widely distinct systems of varying antiquity and ethical worth.

Speaking of the Code, Erwin J. Urch has said that it affords a view of Babylonia's administrative ideal and standard of justice. Hammurabi's age was one of strenuous growth, in the course of which the long linguistic and racial conflict was decided in favor of the Semitic. Yet Sumerian culture had left its traces; though having yielded dominance to the newer race, it gave more to the sum-total of Babylonian culture because it had more to give. Hammurabi's Code, in a sense the product of this culture, was not extensively original, though it was far-sightedly adapted to contemporary needs. How much of Sumerian customary law actually passed into the later Semitic law cannot be determined. But the older customs long attached to the land could not have been easily crowded out. The Code and contemporaneous documents present extensive evidence of the social and political structure of Hammurabi's age. An analysis of this structure reveals the age as one of transition.

In the opinion of legal scholars, Hammurabi's Code had a wide influence which spread, through Phoenicia, to Greece and Rome. It would have been quite impossible for the merchants of Phoenicia to have carried on their large trade with Babylonia without adopting the Babylonian system. The Babylonians would treat the Phoenicians either as barbarians—in which case the former would recognize no law as binding, finding right in might—or as commercial equals, when the same principles would govern both parties. The former hypothesis is inconceivable; for the Phoenicians proved themselves capable of holding their own in business transactions with any mercantile nation of antiquity; the latter hypothesis is supported by abundant evidence. Thus the Babylonian law obtained hold in Phoenicia and, as the law of the latter country, became dominant in the countries bordering the Mediterranean. The greater sphere of Phoenician influence was westward. On the isles and shores of that historic body of water which the Romans later called *Mare Nostrum*, but which was once a Phoenician lake, merchants of that race founded trading posts and colonies; and some of the latter, such as Carthage, grew into nations. Wherever he went the Phoenician trader carried a system of business law which, at base, was probably Babylonian. This would account for much of the infiltration of that system into the law of Greece and of Rome. For the latter there was an even more direct source in the neighboring Semitic nation of Carthage, with which Rome at an early period entered into treaty relations.

The "Handwriting on the Wall." As we have noted, the old Babylonian Empire established by Hammurabi was conquered in 728 B.C. by the Assyrian king, Tiglath-Pileser. As he and his successors made conquests they took many of the people into captivity, transplanting them in other regions and placing rulers of their own in command of the provinces. Among the doings of Tiglath-Pileser chronicled in the Old Testament is his defeat of Pekah, King of Israel, "who departed not from the sins of Jeroboam," followed by the carrying away of captives to Assyria. In 722 B.C. King Sargon II overwhelmed the Ten Tribes of Israel, in Samaria, and carried them in captivity to Assyria. "For the children of Israel walked in all the sins of Jeroboam which he did; they departed not from them. So was Israel carried away out of their own land to Assyria until this day." Samaria was made an Assyrian province, and other people were brought in to replace the Israelites.

Under Sennacharib and Asshur-bani-pal, the city of Nineveh became a center of empire, with magnificent palaces and library, described in the Book of Jonah as "an exceeding great city." The conquests of Assyrian armies, which gained a reputation throughout Asia for savagery in their treatment of conquered peoples—verified by sculptured marbles taken from Assyrian palaces showing prisoners having their eyes bored out with spears, and other atrocities—brought the riches of the world flowing into the king's court. Jonah was sent on a mission to bring the city to repentance from its evil ways. The mission was successful. "And God saw their works, that they turned from their evil way; and God repented of the evil, that he had said that he would do unto them; and he did it not."

But Nineveh returned to evil ways. "And it shall come to pass that all that look upon thee shall flee from thee, and say, Nineveh is laid waste: who will bemoan her?" In 606 B.C. Nineveh succumbed to an invasion by the Aryan Medes, with whom the Babylonians joined. The Assyrian Empire fell, and with its fall Babylon returned to the stage to resume once again, but briefly, its role of Empire.

At befitted a powerful ruler of the time, Nebuchadnezzar undertook a program of conquest. With a powerful army he attacked Jerusalem, defeated the army of King Zedekiah of Judah, slew the sons of King Zedekiah and all the nobles, and put out Zedekiah's eyes. After looting the temple of its sacred vessels and burning the city, Nebuchadnezzar took Zedekiah and the remainder of the inhabitants as captives to Babylon. The period that followed is known as the "Babylonian Captivity."

In Baylon itself, vast architectural works were initiated. Shrines were erected for the gods, with walls of gold and silver studded with precious stones. The fame of the Hanging Gardens has lasted throughout subsequent history.

Back of this luxurious magnificence was always the powerful arm of a despotic ruler. The account of Shadrach, Meshach and Abednego as narrated in the Book of Daniel uniquely chronicles the age-old dilemma of a person subject to such a despot. King Nebuchadnezzar set up a golden image and gathered together for its dedication all the subordinate rulers of his provinces. When assembled before the image he commanded that at the sound of the music, all should fall down and worship the image, under penalty of being cast into the fiery furnace. Shadrach, Meshach and Abednego having refused to bow down to the image, Nebuchadnezzar commanded that the furnace be heated "seven times more than it was wont to be heated," and that the trio be cast therein. The flames slew the men who threw them in, but Shadrach, Meshach and Abednego were unscathed: "nor was an hair of their head singed." Thereupon, we are told Nebuchadnezzar reversed himself and made a decree "that every people, nation and language which speak anything against the God of Shadrach, Meshach and Abednego, shall be cut in pieces and their houses shall be made a dunghill."

Subsequent events, however, demonstrated that this apparent reversal of religious affiliation and governmental policy on the part of Nebuchadnezzar was only a passing phenomenon. The Book of Daniel also tells the story of the great feast staged by King Belshazzar, his son, to a thousand of his lords. At Belshazzar's command "they brought the golden vessels that were taken out of the House of God which was at Jerusalem; and the king, and his princes, his wives and his concubines, drank wine in them, praising the "gods of gold, and of silver, of brass, of iron, of wood, and of stone." In the course of the orgy came the handwriting on the wall. Belshazzar, terrified, "cried aloud to bring in the astrologers, the Chaldeans and the soothsayers." They were not able to read the writing. But Daniel, having been brought in at the queen's suggestion, interpreted it forthrightly as foreshadowing the end of the kingdom.

That night was Belshazzar slain, and Darius, the Median, took the kingdom. Some three centuries later the conquering hosts of Alexander brought it under the power of Greece.

In the course of the violent events that we have been sketching the Code of Hammurabi was physically submerged beneath the earth, to lie forgotten and unknown for centuries, coming to light again only within the memories of many now living in a later civilization. Thus we have mute but vivid testimony that civilizations built on foundations of sand fall as well as rise, and that a code of laws for "gentleman, commoner and slave," exempting priests and rulers as above the law, is no more permanent than the despot who promoted it.

CHAPTER 4

HERITAGE FROM HINDUISM

The Pervasiveness of Hinduism. Addressing the American Bar Association in 1930, and referring to the "two hundred millions and more" of Hindus in India, Sir John Simon, Chairman of the Indian Statutory Commission, said: "But what is a Hindu? What is Hinduism? It is an immense pervading system which influences the life of every adherent every waking moment, in all the mere offices of the day, the ablutions of the morning, the consumption of the meal. Every detail of intimate family life is all governed by an ancient traditional code, and Hinduism itself, in spite of its amazing and unifying persisting power, is broken up into something like 2300 castes."

Thus did the speaker emphasize the basic influence upon human life of a religion, for its adherents embodying the supreme law of conduct, professed by the vast majority of one of the world's most populous regions. The word "region" is used advisedly. To speak of India, through all but its most recent history, as a "nation," would hardly be in order, for India as a territorial unit, or a "subcontinent" as it has sometimes been called, never knew absolutely complete political unification.

To the Hindu the events of human life are in themselves without ultimate significance. In its fundamental aspects Hinduism, the individual practice of which is characterized by asceticism, is concerned with the relation of the individual's inner self, the Atman, to the Supreme One, Brahman. But rather than looking to individual eternal life, as does the Christian, the Hindu looks to his absorption in the Supreme One. To achieve this, the individual must go through a process of reincarnations, perhaps in forms other than human, hoping to progress from body to body until the goal of ultimate absorption is attained. Creation itself is conceived of, not in terms of the completed process described in the Book of Genesis of the Jew or Christian, but as eternally continuing in cycles. Thus, Brahma creates, Shiva destroys in preparation for the new cycle, and in the meantime Vishnu aids and comforts. All this finds a home in the atmosphere of resignation and fatalism of the East. We will return to further consideration of these matters when we glance at the Laws of Manu, which lay down a code of conduct for all aspects of life.

The gradations in the timeless Hinduism which come to flower in the concept thus expressed are in scope extreme. To the scholarly adherent it offers continuous challenge to guide the inner self along paths disclosed by processes of metaphysical speculation. To this Brahmanic person the admonitory guidance is adamant: he must ascend to the heights by his own efforts, with no other assistance than that of the sacred teachings; he cannot fall back upon any doctrine of vicarious atonement. On the other hand, Hinduism takes care of the ignorant and superstitious, offering to them the same primitive way of worshipping the gods of nature and cultivating their aid by sacrifice that characterized its earlier manifestations. In modern every-day practice the Hindu's religion touches all phases of his daily life, dictating his role in society, his occupation and his personal habits.

Inscrutable in many of its aspects though it may be, the purpose of the present study would not be served without an earnest effort to understand something of the history and content of Hinduism in relation to the vast influence which it has attained. It is important to note at the outset that Hinduism, in striking contrast to Islam, conceives of a secular government as altogether unrelated to and apart from religion, the latter concerning itself only with man's spiritual attributes and not with temporal power. Nevertheless, as we shall see, in the hands of Mohandas Gandhi it became involved with nationalistic emotions that tempered its traditional peaceful personal asceticism and introduced an element of concern as to secular affairs.

Hinduism's Scriptural Basis: The Vedas, Upanishads and Bhagavad Gita. The scriptural records and teachings of Hinduism, growing out of the lore of the Aryan invaders of India, as hereinafter further described, extend over a period of many centuries. The most ancient were the Vedas, dating back to around 3000 B.C. Believed to have been divinely inspired, they were composed over a period of hundreds of years, as the Aryans established themselves in India, by men and women with aptitude for psalmody. Long existing only in unwritten form, eventually they were transcribed in Sanskrit. There were four Vedas: the Rig-Veda, or lore of ceremonies and rules of conduct, consisting of over a thousand hymns; the Sama-Veda, or lore of music, emphasizing the worship of Indra; the Yajur-Veda, or lore of prayer, with solemn litanies; and the Atharva-Veda, or lore of the Atharvans, consisting of incantations and charms, revealing in its disclosure of popular folklore and superstition.

The Upanishads, or philosophical miscellany, appeared around 800 B.C. The meaning of "upanishad" is "sitting down beside a teacher," with a connotation of being taught something of a confidential nature. The significance of the Upanishads, then, is that they impart secret instruction as to the Vedas. Accordingly, like the Vedas, they were long handed down only verbally, because their secrets were only for the high Brahminic caste. Generally speaking, the theme of the Upanishads is complete renunciation of the world and meditation upon Brahman. Thus, in Tattiriya the exhortation is to meditate upon Brahman as the source of all things. He who meditates upon Brahman as support will be supported. He who meditates upon Brahman as greatness will be great. He who meditates upon Brahman as mind will have great power of mind. He who worships Brahman as Brahman will become Brahman. In Kaivalya, the student who asks his master to teach him the knowledge of Brahman is told to seek to know Brahman by meditating on him unceasingly. A man achieves immortality by devotion to Brahman, not by work, progeny or wealth. Brahman is Brahma, Shiva, Vishnu, and all, One without beginning or end, and the man who knows him conquers death.

About the first century B.C. appeared the Great Epics, including the Bhagavad Gita or Song of God. The Bhagavad Gita was not regarded as divinely revealed scriptural teaching but rather that of prophets and teachers who walked in the way. An epic poem, it sets forth the dialogue between Krishna and Arjuna on a battlefield. Krishna is speaking as God to Arjuna, a warrior. Krishna says that if Arjuna can understand and follow the method of Karma Yoga, or the achievement of union with Brahman, he will be able to free himself from his chains of worldly desire. In this yoga the mind points toward one ideal and does not wander in all directions. Those who are diverted become attached to pleasure and power and cannot attain that concentration which leads the Atman to absorption in Brahman. There is the right to work, but desire for the fruits of work must not be the motive for working. Those who work selfishly for results are unhappy. Wise men reach enlightenment by renouncing the fruit of their actions. Becoming free from the servitude of rebirth they enter a state of blessedness. Throughout the poem the theme of self control is stressed, and Arjuna is admonished to seek thereby aborption into Brahman.

The Beginnings of Hinduism—The Aryan Invasions. The Hinduism manifested in the scriptures which we have just been noting was not a spontaneously revealed religion. It developed with the peoples who followed its way of life and handed down their experiences in song and story from generation to generation. It had its beginnings with the tribes from the Aryan reservoir in Central Asia, which around the year 2000 B.C. commenced making their way through the Himalaya Mountain passes to the river plains of northern India. On these plains the invading Aryans found dark-skinned aboriginal races and Dravidians, the latter also a dark-skinned people who had preceded them into the region. Some of these inhabitants fled into the forests and mountains; others remained to be subjugated.

The religion of the Aryan invaders first found expression in the form of nature worship, in which natural phenomena were held to embody personal attributes, endowed with powers beyond man's control, but amenable to influence by his appeal. Some of the gods in whom centered these attributes were in the heavens, some on the earth, and others in the air between. Receiving a major part of devoted homage was Indra, the god of the rain clouds, and Agni, the god of fire, conceived as a beneficent presence within the household who mediated between the gods and men. Others of the pantheon particularly venerated were Varuna, the all-embracing firmament, Savitar, the sun, and Mitra, the light of day. It was believed that the good offices of these gods could be invoked by sacrificial offerings of food and drink. This strengthened them to fulfill their divine missions, one of which was ministering to mortals.

The father was the priest of his own household. Each tribe selected a chief, who was in charge of the sacrificial rites which constituted the basic expression of the Brahmanical religion. To carry out the details of these rites he designated certain other members of the tribe who were skilled in the priestly rituals.

Origin of the Caste System. In these religious practices, coupled with other events associated with the manner of life of these Aryan peoples as they changed from nomads into settled tillers of the soil, the caste system, a deprecated feature of Indian society, prevailing in effect to this day, had its origin. The highest caste, the priestly, was indigenous in Hinduism.

We have been speaking of a period before the era of writing. The Vedic hymns were handed down, from generation to generation, by certain families who could recite them from memory. Those to whom we have referred as being called upon to conduct the priestly rituals were of those families. These ceremonies became more and more involved, eventually requiring the participation of several priests. The chief priest, who in that capacity was master of all sacred lore, acted as superintendent. He was assisted by a hotar, who interpolated appropriate prayers and liturgical recitations from the Rig-Veda; an udgatar, or chanter, who accompanied the hotar, and who was guided by the Sama-Veda, or lore of chants; and an adhvaryu, who laid the sacrificial fire and made other necessary preparations for the event, and who was guided by the Yajur-Veda, or lore of prayer. Obviously, a considerable degree of learning and professional qualification was involved in the fulfillment of these duties, and the Brahman or priestly class grew in numbers as well as in the esteem of the people whose welfare seemed to be so largely dependent upon them.

Although the Aryan tribes settled themselves in villages to cultivate the soil and live on it, they were not able to do so in peace. From time to time it was necessary for them to defend themselves against forays of the people whom they had driven out, and from the attacks of other invaders. For these purposes a standing military force became necessary. As nations grew out of the informally federated tribes, government administrators and professional soldiers (kshatriyas—meaning "connected with royal power") thus became a segment of the population. Military and civil service became a career of high order. Thus there arose a second distinct group, or caste.

Those who held and tilled the soil (vaisyas—meaning "people"), constituted a third group, whose ranks were gradually swelled by persons who engaged in trade. The vaisyas impressed into service those dark-skinned aborigines who had not escaped them, assigning to them the hard toil and disagreeable tasks. Those thus impressed by the vaisyas constituted a fourth group, known as sudras.

The Vedic hymns depicted the Aryan gods as protecting the Aryan color, and it is obvious how the Sanskrit word for color, "varna," came to mean "caste." A strong motive for avoiding contacts with the lowest group was found in preserving the purity of the faith of the Aryan invaders from pollution by the presumedly inferior religion of the indigenous peoples. Denial of intermarriage between castes was basic to the system.

Development and Working of the Caste System. Much of the early history of Hinduism was marked by a contest for supremacy between the Brahman and military castes. Eventually, some centuries Before Christ, the Brahmans established their right to the highest position. Absolutely hereditary, not even princes could gain admission to its ranks. A learned group, Brahmans were the makers of Sanskrit lit-

erature. The monopoly position which they assumed was maintained
through subsequent history. Addressing the American Bar Association in 1930, Sir John Simon said that the top caste of all, the Brahmans, "one of the most amazing examples of concentrated hereditary
intellectual power," only contains about seven million men. Yet in
large parts of India their monopoly of the priesthood, their tradition
of learning, their past position in former administrations, is such that
they are feared by every other sort of Hindu.

We have already noted the statement of Sir John Simon as to modern Hinduism being broken up into some 2300 castes, indicative of
the ceaseless development of the concept. By way of contrast with
the Brahmans, Sir John further referred to the forty or fifty millions
who had developed, at the lowest end of the scale, as "untouchables,"
included within the Hindu fold largely as the result of Brahman
teaching, and yet denied access to the interior of a Hindu temple; living in a separate little hamlet outside the main village; "in many
parts of India denied the right of using the public water supply; required to take all they need from a different point in the river; in
many cases with children who cannot get access to the ordinary
school; and, what is worst of all, people who do not themselves make
a struggle to get out of their misery; because it is a part of their faith
that their miserable lot is the punishment administered by heaven for
some wrong that they may have done in a previous existence."

Every Hindu belongs to the caste of his parents. No intelligence,
no change of residence, can alter the fact that in that caste into which
he was born he will remain to the day of his death. Under the workings of the caste system, moreover, Hindus cannot eat or drink with
Muslims. And in its operations through the centuries it has attained
such a state of development that as to Hindus themselves a group
of several servants is commonly essential for a household dependent
on hired help: a cook may be disqualified from washing the dishes
or sweeping the floor, and even the dishwasher may be disqualified
from doing other cleaning work.

The Laws of Manu. Establishing their position of preeminence as
givers and administrators of religion, the Brahmans fortified it by
codes of laws. Earliest was the Dharma Sistras, not purporting to be
divinely revealed, or new edicts, but rather a statement of existing
customs, incorporating the caste system. This was superseded by the
Laws of Manu, ascribed to Manu Svayambhuva, a lawgiver sprung
aeons previously from Brahman. It likewise enunciated the caste
system. No other system of laws in all history has exercised a longer-

lasting or more profound influence than the Laws of Manu, interweaving the fabric of Hindu life, and their content merits passing note by way of reference to significant portions of their twelve chapters.

In the first chapter, dealing with the Creation, it is said that God, in order that the human race might be multiplied, caused the Brahman, the Kshatriya, the Vaisya and the Sudra to proceed from his mouth, his arm, his thigh and his foot. He assigned separate duties to them. To the Brahman he assigned the duty of reading and teaching the Veda, and of sacrificing. Since the Brahman sprang from the most excellent part, the mouth, since he was first born and possesses the Veda, he is by right the chief, the highest among men, the incarnation of Dharma, God of Justice. To the Kshatriya he assigned the duty of defending the people, exhorting them to shun the allurements of sensual gratifications. To the Vaisya he assigned the duty of cultivating land, rearing cattle, carrying on trade and lending at interest. To the Sudra was assigned the duty of serving the Brahman, the Kshatriya and the Vaisya. Immemorial custom is stated to be the law, to be diligently observed.

In the second chapter it is stated that a Brahman should shun worldly honor and rather seek disrespect. One should not injure another by thought or deed, nor utter a word calculated to bring uneasiness to a fellow creature. Every man should constantly do what would please his parents and his teacher.

In chapter three the student who has completed his prescribed discipline is directed to take a wife of his same class. But she must not be descended from his ancestors, within the sixth degree. He should not marry a girl with reddish hair, or deformed limb, nor one unduly garrulous or who does not have good health. His wife should possess a good form and walk with grace. Eight forms of ceremony are described. Householders are given a code of conduct, which requires the performance of certain sacraments and adjures that whether a guest comes at an appropriate time or not, he must be properly entertained.

The man who has completed his studies and married is dealt with in the fourth chapter. He is adjured to inflict no injury, or the least possible injury, upon other living things. He may acquire property necessary to his occupation, but he should not desire more than he has, for happiness is based on contentment and discontent brings misery. Though because of his honesty he be poor, he should never contemplate dishonesty, for sinful men are overthrown. He should find satisfaction in truth and justice and in good works, keeping under control his speech, his limbs and his appetite, shunning unlawful wealth and pleasure and even lawful acts which may bring unhappiness to others. He should walk in the good path of his forefathers, not only fulfilling his ceremonial obligations but discharging his moral duties.

The fifth chapter deals with foods, prescribing those which may be eaten and those which are forbidden. Rules for purification are set forth. Many passages deal with women, and express rules in decided derogation of their status. Thus, it is stated that a woman must not seek to be independent. She must not desire to be separated from her father, her husband or her sons. She must maintain cheerfulness in the home, managing it carefully and with frugality. And regardless of the bad qualities of her husband, or his conduct with other women, she must continue to revere him.

The sixth chapter deals with the father of the family who has lived his life according to the law and has attained the status of grandparent. He may then take to the forest for communion with the Supreme Being. Performing the prescribed sacraments, constantly reading the Veda, giving but not receiving gifts and showing consideration for all living things, let him not resort to harsh words, or engage in struggle.

Government and Law. The seventh chapter of the Laws of Manu deals with government, and particularly the king, who is conceived to be of the military class but receiving investiture in accordance with prescriptions of the Veda. God created a king from eternal particles taken from the guardian deities, and therefore he is above all mortals. Having endowed the king with divine origin, however, the code goes on to outline many circumscribing obligations. He is adjured to provide just compensation for the good, and just punishment for the wicked. The king who always speaks the truth, understands the sacred law and carefully hears all cases dispenses proper justice, but just punishment cannot be given by a king who is ignorant and without understanding.

That the king is not to act independently of the Brahmans, however, is indicated by the adjuration that he should heed the Brahmans and abide by their decision. As to matters of administration, the king is adjured to appoint ministers of noble lineage, versed in the sacred books, and brave, and to consult with them consistently on matters of peace and war. Having conquered a country, the king should respect its gods and treat the people with consideration, establishing its laws as declared in their books.

In the eighth chapter it is provided that a king who desires to conduct judicial proceedings must enter the court with composed demeanor, accompanied by Brahmans qualified to give him advice. He may decide cases under the eighteen principal titles of law. The first one of these is debt on loans for consumption; the second, deposits and loans for use; the third, sale without ownership; the fourth, partnership matters; the fifth, subtraction of what has been given; the sixth, non-payment of wages; the seventh, non-performance of agreements; the eighth, rescission of sale and purchase; the ninth, master and servants disputes; the tenth, boundary disputes; the eleventh and twelfth, assault and slander; the thirteenth, larceny; the fourteenth, robbery; the fifteenth, adultery; the sixteenth, family difficulties; the seventeenth, inheritance matters; the eighteenth, gaming.

When the king cannot judge in person, he is adjured to appoint for the purpose a Brahman of high learning, who, accompanied by three assistants, will judge matters brought before the king. Such a group is known as the court of Brahma with four faces. If the judges do not extract the dart which has wounded justice, they will also be wounded by it; when justice is destroyed by evil and truth by falsehood, judges who look on without giving relief will be destroyed also.

The king, or judges, with attentive mind, should begin the trial with due reverence to the deities. The thoughts of witnesses should be discerned by their expressions, countenances and actions. The qualifications of witnesses are prescribed in some detail. They should be sworn, a priest by his veracity; a soldier by his weapons; a merchant by his grain or cattle; and servile man by bespeaking to himself, if he speaks falsely, all possible crimes. A witness who testifies falsely will enter a horrible realm after death.

In a suit for a debt, if the debtor denies it and the evidence establishes the debt, a small fine should be added to the amount of recovery. The rate of interest allowed on loans is dependent on whether or not the loan is secured, and the class of the debtor. Thus, on an unsecured loan the creditor may take 2% a month from a priest, 3% from a soldier, 4% from a merchant, and 5% from a servile man. A surety whose principal does not pay shall pay the debt. Contracts made by intoxicated or insane persons, or by infants or unauthorized agents, are void. A fraudulent pledge or sale should be annulled, as should agreements executed by force or duress. Penalties for defamation are graduated according to the castes involved. Various crimes are dealt with. Blind men, idiots, cripples, men seventy years of age and priests of ancient learning shall not be compelled by the king to pay taxes.

Chapter nine contains provisions relating to inheritance of property and deals with various aspects of the conduct of women. The husband, after conception by his wife, himself takes on the status of an embryo and is born a second time. A wife who drinks spiritous liquor, is incurably diseased, wastes her husband's property, acts improperly, or is barren after the eighth year, may be superseded by another wife. Every father should give his daughter to an excellent youth of the same class even before she has attained the age of eight, but unless the proposed husband possesses excellent qualities it is better that the daughter should never be given in marriage.

Transmigration and Final Beatitude. Chapter ten of the Laws of Manu deals with matters of caste, chapter eleven with sacrifices, and penances for eating prohibited foods. Matters of transmigration and final beatitude are dealt with in chapter twelve. Here it is provided that action, whether mental, verbal or physical, is itself good or evil, and from the actions of men proceed their transmigration. There are ten bad actions: three mental, four verbal, and three physical. Pondering the taking of other men's property, determining to do wrongful deeds, and harboring thoughts of atheism are the three bad acts of mind. Bad language, falsehood, wrongful accusations and idle gossip are the four bad verbal acts. Stealing, hurting sentient creatures without lawful right and adultery are the three bad physical acts. For sinful physical acts a man shall assume after death a vegetable or mineral form; for sinful verbal acts the form of a beast or bird; for sinful mental acts, the lowest human form. Final happiness is found by studying the Veda, observing the requirements of pious austerity, acquiring an understanding of philosophy, controlling the mind and body, refraining from injury to sentient creatures and demonstrating reverence for the divinity. Perceiving at last in his own soul the supreme soul present in all life, he himself shall be absorbed in the highest essence, that of the Almighty.

Observance of the Laws of Manu. The Code of Hammurabi and the Hindu Laws of Manu were simple pronouncements concerning human conduct touching only the very broad and general phases of human interrelation. Most of such ancient "legal" formulations are the decrees of a ruler, seeking ethico-political impositions emanating from the throne and, of necessity, "accepted" by the people. They are not the outgrowth of popular will or need, nor do they have their origins altogether in the developed mores or natural practices of the populace. Nevertheless, the Laws of Manu came into being under religious auspices and prescribed a way of life embodying both religious and secular obligations. As we have noted, the code strengthened its own fibre by incorporating within itself frequent references to the sacred Vedas. Through most of its history there was no government with jurisdiction over all of India. Nor does Hinduism, like Roman Catholicism, possess a corporate ecclesiastical organization capable of administering a system of law, and which might have assumed the prerogatives of government in that regard.

But even though the Laws of Manu had no organized implementing power back of them, no code of laws in history has been more scrupulously obeyed. Their acceptance was brought about, not by direct governmental or ecclesiastical sanctions, but by the simple teachings of continuing generations of Brahmans possessed of the facility of persuasiveness, working, of course, with peoples of noteworthy religious susceptibilities.

References have been noted in the Laws of Manu to custom as the law. Originally applicable only in the area of North India which had been taken over by the Aryan invaders, and apart from the caste system provisions reflecting the particular customs of that region, the element of elasticity incorporated by way of reference to custom as the law enabled the Laws of Manu to be adapted to the varying modes of life and customs of the other peoples of India, living in various stages of social progress, who from time to time were brought under Brahman jurisdiction. Thus, the Laws of Manu provided a workable basis for Hindu law. In the course of time several schools of Hindu law developed, departing in varying detail from the Laws of Manu but retaining its basis provisions.

The Advent of Buddhism. Buddhism began with Guatama, the son of a rich ruler of the Kshatriya caste, who was born about the middle of the sixth century, B.C. Desiring to shield Guatama from knowledge of the hardships and evils of the outside world, his father reared him within the palace walls. Until his young manhood he knew only that cloistered side of life. One day he was taken for a drive. In the course of the journey he saw a doddering old man, obviously afflicted with a loathsome disease, and a corpse. When he expressed concern about these previously unknown aspects of life, his charioteer told him that they were commonplace. On the way back to the palace he saw a man clad in rough monastic garb, but serene of countenance. This person, the charioteer told him, was a man of religion, seeking truth.

Revolting from the life of ease and luxury that he had been leading,

Guatama had the charioteer drive him, in the night, to the edge of a forest. Cutting off his long hair with his sword, he sent it and his royal clothing back to the palace and put on the mendicant's garb which he was to wear the rest of his days. Realizing, as his observation had disclosed, that old age, disease and death are a part of physical life, what he sought was the key to the peace of mind, if not happiness, that would overcome them.

He first studied with several wise men. They did not seem to have the answer. He left them and, for several years, lived as an ascetic in a grove of trees, where he engaged in intensive meditation and made every effort to subdue his bodily appetites. Exercising control over his body by fasting, the resulting physical collapse brought him to the realization that control over body and mind was not the whole answer. Food seemed ordained to sustain the sound body upon which sound meditation is dependent. Thereupon Guatama ate substantially, and sat down under a tree. There he was tempted by Mara, or Satan, to return to his life of ease at the palace. Resisting the blandishments and threats of the Evil One, falling into deepest mental communion under the Bo-tree, or tree of wisdom, he found Enlightenment. It pointed to an eight-fold path, lying between the extremes of a life given to sensuality and a life of ascetic mortification, leading to Sambodhi, or perfect enlightenment, and Nirvana—full peace of mind, marked by the absence of all unhappy cravings and emotions, and the release from all future reincarnations. The eight-fold path called for right views, right intentions, right speech, right conduct, right means of livelihood, right effort, right mindfulness, and right thoughts.

Forthwith Guatama, who had become the Buddha, or Enlightened One, sought out five ascetics whom he had known during his own period of asceticism. He found them in the Deer Park of Isipatana, and disclosed to them his Enlightenment: That by the eight-fold path the suffering that characterizes life from birth to death, and which is brought about by desire and passion, can be made to cease. The five accepted the Enlightenment. Thereupon he ordained them to go out and seek converts, taking from them the following simple pledge: "I take my refuge in the Buddha. I take my refuge in the Dhamma. I take my refuge in the Sangha." As thus used, Dhamma signified the teachings of Buddha, and Sangha the society organized by Guatama, whose members forsook worldly callings and gave their lives to spreading the teachings of Buddhism.

As thus promulgated by Guatama, Buddhism differed from Brahmanic Hinduism in certain noteworthy respects. For one thing, it did not recognize the caste system, which had become adamantly indigenous to Hinduism. One became blessed, not by birth, but by acquiring righteousness through proper conduct, and the key to blessedness was available to all alike. For another thing, Buddhism did not recognize the possibility of union with Brahman, envisioned by the Hindu doctrine. Like Hinduism, however, it recognized the possible place of gods in a polytheistic pantheon. Such a beginning could hardly be called commonplace, though it was obscure. But however its origin might be characterized, the result was one of the great religions of the world. Buddhism eventually spread throughout India into Ceylon, Thailand, Tibet, China, Korea and Japan, reaching a picturesque climax in Burma with its gold-plated pagodas. Today it numbers half a billion human beings among its followers.

In the course of time there developed different schools of Buddhism, with the basic difference turning on the conception of the nature of Gautama. Under the system known as the Mahayana, or "Great Vehicle," followed for the most part in China, Korea and Japan, Guatama, who had not taught prayer to a deity, was himself looked to as a deity. The system known as Hinayana, or "Small Vehicle," followed in Burma, Ceylon and Siam, accepts Guatama simply as a human being, teaching the truths of Enlightenment. The significance of the "vehicle" concept is that it is the vessel which carries men across the stream of re-birth to the shore of Nirvana, and the "Great Vehicle" offers an easier way for all to cross.

In Tibet Buddhism achieved an ecclesiastical hierarchy of hundreds of "living incarnations" of minor spirits of Buddha, headed by the Dalai Lama, exercising absolute temporal and spiritual power as the living incarnation of the Mercy Spirit of Buddha. Tibet Buddhism developed elaborate rituals of prayer and incantation.

The Course of Empire in India. So far as history reveals, the first European impressions of India were gained through the expeditions of Alexander the Great, who led his armies to the Indus River area in 327 B.C. His ambition to push through to the Ganges could not be realized, but he explored the Indus to the head of its delta, where he established a city and named it Alexandria. Thus was discovered a sea route from the great Indus region to the Euphrates. Alexander's Indian Empire did not outlast his death. Seleceus Nictator, who took over the eastern part of Alexander's empire, was unable to maintain his supremacy in India. Eventually he concluded an alliance with Chandra Gupta, who had gained control over a considerable portion of the country.

Chandra's grandson, Asoka, who became emperor in 270 B.C., extended his sway by bloody conquest over all of northern India. His conversion to Buddhism brought his military aggression to an end, and altered his whole manner of personal life and rule. Leaving theological niceties to others who might be concerned with them, he devoted himself to practising the principles of kindness to living things, searching for the higher values of life and the peace which he, as a layman, conceived Buddhism to embody. At the invitation of the king of Ceylon he sent his son, Mahinda, as a missionary to that country, and he also sent missionaries to Burma and other places. As a personal missionary in its behalf, he manifested his own faith by his deeds by way of inaugurating programs of public works calculated to promote the health and comfort of the people and raise their standard of living.

The successors of Asoka were not able to hold together the empire which he had established. There followed centuries of political disunity and confusion, during which the various tribes fought among themselves, and with Tartar, Scythian and Hun invaders from the outside. In such an environment, where survival was dependent on military force, the passive virtues of Buddhism were not at home. The place of the soldier and his use of force was emphasized, by that token solidifying the concept of caste. The more vigorous tenets of Brahmanic Hinduism, with its pantheon of war gods, held a determining appeal. The result was that Buddhism, in its original conception, waned and eventually lost its hold in the land of its birth.

The Gupta Dynasty and the Muslim Invasions. Not until the era of the dynasty established in 320 A.D. by Chandra Gupta II was India united again in any real sense. Under the Gupta dynasty a large part of north India was relatively stabilized for about two hundred years. In favorable environment, and with the encouragement of the rulers, there were noteworthy manifestations of art in its various forms. Sanskrit literature flowered in poetry and drama. Great progress was made in mathematics and chemistry, and in such industries as textile fabrication and metal working. This period ended with the invasions of the Huns from central Asia, who crushed the Gupta dynasty. A century or so later Harshal regained control over much of the Gupta empire, and retained it for more than a generation, but at his death the country became again one of separate states, warring with each other.

Although sporadic Muslim raids and invasions began in the latter part of the seventh century A.D., it was not for five hundred years that they seriously threatened to bring the Indian states under the rule of an invader of a foreign faith. Such was portended, however, and eventually it came about. In 1200 A.D. Mohammed Ghori gained control of northern India. A Muslim kingdom was set up, but it was crushed in 1398 A.D. by the invasion of Amir Timur. In 1524 A.D. the Turk Babur, a descendant of Genghis Khan, invaded the country and defeated the Indian forces. This time the Muslims stayed in power. The Mogul dynasty then established lasted until early in the eighteenth century. It reached its greatest distinction under the rule of Akbar, who came to power in 1556 A.D. Though a Muslim, Akbar pursued a policy of religious tolerance, endeavoring to bring about full cooperation between the adherents of all religions. A tax that had been imposed on non-Muslims was repealed; Hindus as well as Muslims were employed in a government service that set a high mark of efficiency. The Mogul emperors maintained a luxurious court. Under its dispensations art, and architecture in particular, flourished. But even the Mogul emperors never succeeded in conquering all the Indian principalities.

Islam "Takes Hold" in India. Under Akbar's descendants the Mogul Empire went through a process of moral and physical degeneration. The reign of his son, Shah Jahan, was marked by departure from Akbar's policy of religion toleration. Jahan's son, Aurangzeb, who assumed the title of Conqueror of the World the same month that Oliver Cromwell died in England, was the sovereign of a larger territory than had been ruled by any of his predecessors. But he sowed the seeds of his own destruction, and that of his empire. He imposed special taxes on the Hindus, purged them from government employment, and destroyed their temples. He played no favorites, however. His Muslim zeal not being satisfied by these things, he directed his attention to his fellow Muslims, and those not regarded as orthodox in the faith he put to death. A large part of his later reign was spent in attempting to crush rebellions. After his death the Mogul Empire was subjected to increasingly powerful attack by the Mahrattas and the Sikhs from within, and by the Persians from without. Like all the previous regimes of India had done eventually, it fell apart, although it continued in nominal existence until the British government took over the rule of India in 1858.

The degeneration of the Mogul Empire did not carry with it any corresponding degeneration of Islam as a militant religious faith. In spite of the barrier to approach to the Hindus imposed by their caste system, Islam gained in influence as time went on. Hundreds of thousands of natives, particularly in the East Bengal region which, as we shall see, is now East Pakistan, were led by Muslim missionaries to embrace that faith. The widespread establishment of Islam in this melting pot of Hinduism, Buddhism, Jainism and Islam, was said by Professor Stanley Maron to have been due primarily to the efforts of enthusiastic missionaries of the Sufi persuasion who followed the deliberate policy of building shrines to Muslim saints on the sites that had formerly been used for Buddhist and Hindu worship. In this way the people of the area were won over to Islam through their allegiance to Muslim saints venerated for miracles which were in many cases taken over entirely from old Buddhist and Hindu legends.

Because Muslims allowed divorce and Hindus did not; because Muslim women wore the veil and Hindu women did not; because Muslims ate beef and Hindus did not; because Islam practiced animal sacrifice but abhorred idols, and because Hindus abhorred animal sacrifice but worshipped idols, Islam imported alien elements of religious manifestation into Indian life which were always potentially and often actually acutely disturbing. It was true, of course, that adherents of the two faiths found it possible to live together in the villages, where they knew each other as neighbors, and where there was a minimum of aggravating agitation. For centuries they did so. In the cities it was another matter. Tolerance could not survive in the hot fires kindled by nationalistic emotions in the twentieth century, and eventually, as we shall see, when independence came to India it came on the basis of two separate nations, carved out along the boundary lines of these dissimilar faiths.

The English East India Company. In the sixteenth century Portugal developed a commercial empire in the Indian Ocean area, with headquarters at Goa. This power was effectually challenged by the Dutch, who eventually gained control over the archipelago.

But England was not to be left out of the contest for the rich prizes of the trade and commerce of the region. On the last day of the sixteenth century Queen Elizabeth granted a charter to the East India Company. In his History of England, Lord Macaulay said that when this celebrated body began to exist, the Mogul monarchy was at the zenith of its power and glory. Akbar had just been borne to a mausoleum surpassing in magnificence any that Europe could show. He had bequeathed to his posterity an empire containing more than twenty times the population and yielding more than twenty times the revenue of England. It is curious and interesting to consider, Macaulay observed, how little the two countries, destined to be one day so closely connected, were then known to each other. The English had a dim notion of endless bazaars, swarming with buyers and sellers, blazing with cloth of gold, with variegated silks and with precious stones; of treasuries where diamonds were piled in heaps, and sequins in mountains; of palaces compared with which Whitehall and Hampton Court were hovels; of armies ten times as numerous as that which they had seen assembled at Tilbury to repel the Armada. On the other hand, it was probably not known to one of the statesmen in the Durbar of Agra that there was, near the setting sun, a great city of infidels called London, where a woman reigned, and that she had given to an association of Frank merchants the exclusive privilege of freighting ships from her dominions to the Indian seas. That this association would one day rule all India, from the ocean to the everlasting snow, would reduce to profound obedience great provinces which had never submitted to Akbar's authority, would send lieutenant governors to preside in his capital, and would dole out a monthly pension to his heir, would have seemed to the wisest of European or Oriental politicians as impossible as that inhabitants of our globe should found an empire in Venus or Jupiter.

At first only a trading corporation, the East India Company assumed, in effect, the attributes of government itself. Finding the Dutch firmly established in the islands of the region, the Company representatives devoted themselves to the Indian mainland. Overcoming Portuguese opposition, they established friendly relations with the Mogul Emperors. They developed an important textile industry, and trade along many lines. They established the cities of Madras and Calcutta. As Lord Macaulay said, the Company enjoyed, during the greater part of the reign of Charles the Second, a prosperity to which the history of trade of that time hardly furnishes any parallel. Wealth and luxury were rapidly increasing. The taste for the spices, the tissues and the jewels of the East became stronger day by day. Tea, which at the time when Monk brought the army of Scotland to London, had been handed round to be stared at and just touched with the lips, as a great rarity from China, was, eight years later, a regular article of import, and was soon consumed in such quantities that financiers began to consider it as an important source of revenue. The progress which was making in the art of war had created an unprecedented demand for the ingredients of which gunpowder is compounded, and which India provided. Before the Restoration, scarcely one ship from the Thames had ever visited the Delta or the Ganges. But during the twenty-three years which followed the Restoration, the value of the annual imports from that rich and populous district increased from eight thousand to three hundred thousand pounds.

In the latter part of the seventeenth century the East India Company was challenged by the French, who appeared in that area. With the aid of dissident natives they sought to fill the vacuum left by the virtual collapse of the Mogul Empire. The East India Company successfully met this challenge. Taking advantage of England's preoccupation with the American Revolution the princes of Mahratta, Hyberabad and Mysore effectively harassed the Company, but were subdued. However, not until 1849 did British forces conquer the Sikhs, a Hindu sect of the Bengal founded by Nanak, a Hindu leader who preached the abolition of caste. The Sikhs had stood up to the Muslim emperors and had gained a well-merited reputation for military prowess. With their defeat the British came into control of the Punjab. It was the middle of the nineteenth century before the power of the East India Company was extended through most of India.

British Administration in India. It is not surprising that the record of such a powerful, unsupervised organization as the East India Company was not, in its earlier stages, altogether a savory one. But when the situation was brought to light, the English did not hesitate to act. Lord Bryce commented about it frankly. He said that the English went to India as traders. But the men of the sword very soon began to eclipse the men of the quill and account book. The English administration began with extortions and corruption. Officials were often rapacious, sometimes unjust in their dealings with the native princes. But the statesmen and the public opinion of England, even in the latter half of the eighteenth century, had higher standards than those of Rome in the days of Sulla and Cicero, while the machinery which the House of Commons provided for dealing with powerful offenders was more effective than the Roman method of judicial proceedings before tribunals which could be, and frequently were, bribed.

The first outbreak of greed and corruption in Bengal was dealt with by the strong hand of Clive in 1765. It made so great an impression at home as to give rise to a provision in a statute of 1773 making offenses against the provisions of that act, or against the natives of India, punishable by the Court of King's Bench in England. By Pitt's Act of 1784, a Special Court, consisting of three judges, four Peers and six members of the House of Commons, was created for the trial in England of offenses committed in India. Lord Bryce went on to say that soon after this came the famous trial which is more familiar to Englishmen than any other event in the earlier relations of England and India. The impeachment of Warren Hastings has often been compared with the trial of Verres. Hastings, like Verres, was not punished. But the proceedings against him so fixed the attention of the nation upon the administration of India as to secure for wholesome principles of conduct a recognition which was never thereafter forgotten.

Addressing the American Bar Association in 1930, Sir John Simon, chairman of the Indian Statutory Commission, said that in the history of the Indian Civil Service "I know of no case, in spite of the abuse and contumely poured upon the British administration, where any man or any newspaper has said there is in the British-Indian Civil Service a man who has accepted a secret bribe."

Nevertheless, as a practical matter, hardships and abuses were almost inevitable because of the sheer difficulties involved in administering so vast a realm. Thus, to solve the problems inherent in collecting taxes in the areas under their government control, the British introduced a system which was maintained throughout their rule, and was inherited by the Indian government when it became independent. Under the workings of the system the duty of collection was turned over to persons appointed for that purpose, known as zamindars. In effect, they became landlords, in control of the land. The amount which they were required to turn over to the government was stipulated, but they were not restricted as to what they could collect in the first instance. This system came to cover a large portion of the agricultural land of India. Needless to say, the abuses perpetrated under it made a continuous contribution to the hardships of the masses of Indian people.

Looking to the future, some of the governors-general of the nineteenth century sponsored enlightened programs. Thus, Lord William Bentinck, who was governor-general from 1828 to 1835, did many things to improve the lot of the people. He lessened the tax burden and opened the way for educated natives to enter the service of the East India Company. He abolished suttee, or widow-burning, a rite which, although it was not authorized by early Hinduism, had become established by long tradition to the extent that hundreds of widows were burned to death annually, by making all who aided or abetted it guilty of criminal homicide. He also suppressed the Thugs, a Hindu sect built around worship of the goddess Kali, to whom were sacrificed human victims who had been murdered by strangulation, and took steps to stop the practice of killing female babies, who were often regarded as unbearable economic handicaps. His accomplishments were epitomized by the inscription by Lord Macaulay on his statue at Calcutta: "He abolished cruel rites; he effaced humiliating distinctions; he gave liberty to the expression of public opinion; his constant study it was to elevate the intellectual and moral character of the natives committed to his charge."

Lord Bentinck's program was earnestly renewed by Lord Dalhousie, who was governor-general from 1848 to 1856. He initiated a comprehensive program of public works, introduced a postal and telegraph service at reasonable rates, and promoted a national plan of education. In his zeal to bring the benefits of British rule to the people he stopped the practice of the East India Company, which had theretofore been in force, which had enabled the Indian princes to adopt successors if they had no heirs, and thus perhaps perpetuate a corrupt rule over their subjects. It has been indicated that the British did not control the whole of India. We will refer to this again hereinafter. Suffice it to say here that the princely rulers of many Indian states had been allowed to maintain their dynasties, and rule locally in their own way, and the right of their bodily heirs to succession had been recognized. It was the practice of these princes to adopt an heir, if there was not one of the body, and the previous British practice had been to recognize such adoption. Lord Dalhousie refused to recognize the Hindu law by which this was accomplished, and when succession depended upon adoption the state was brought under British rule. In this manner several Indian principalities which had been under notoriously bad native rule were made subject to British administration and law.

The spirit of British administration of those days was aptly expressed by Henry Lawrence: "We cannot expect to hold India forever. Let us so conduct ourselves that when the connexion ceases, it may do so not with convulsions but with mutual esteem and affection, and that England may then have in India a noble ally, enlightened and brought into the scale of nations under her guidance and fostering care."

The Law Applied by the British. Other than the purely religious law the English administrators in the days of Clive and Hastings found two great systems of customary law—the Muslim and the Hindu. It embodied four elements.

First, it contained a large and elaborate system of inheritance and family law, the Muslim pretty uniform throughout India, though in some regions modified by Hindu custom; the Hindu less uniform. Each was utterly unlike English law and incapable of being fused with it. Each was closely bound up with the religion and social habits of the people. Each was contained in treatises of more or less antiquity and authority, some of the Hindu treatises being very ancient and credited with almost divine sanction; the Muslim treatises of course posterior to the Koran and consisting of commentaries upon the book and upon the traditions that had grown up around it.

Second, the body of law found contained a large mass of customs relating to the use and occupation of land and of various rights connected with tillage and pasturage, including water rights, rights of soil accretion on the banks of rivers, and forest rights. The agricultural system and the revenue system of the country rested upon these land customs, which were of course mostly unwritten, and which varied widely in different districts.

The third element was a body of customs, according to the English idea scanty and undeveloped, but still important, relating to the transfer and pledging of property, and to contracts, especially commercial contracts. Fourth, and last, were certain penal rules drawn from the Muslim law, and more or less enforced by Muslim princes.

Obviously, these elements did not cover all fields of law. There was hardly any law of civil and criminal procedure, because the methods of justice were primitive. There was little or no law of torts or civil wrongs. In the law of property, of contracts and of crimes, some departments were wanting, or in a rudimentary condition. Of a law relating to civil and constitutional rights there could of course be no question, since no such rights existed.

In this state of facts the British officials took the line which practical men, having their hands full of work would naturally take, viz., the line of least resistance. They accepted and carried on what they found. Where there was a native law, they applied it, Muslim law to Muslims, Hindu law to Hindus, and in the few places where they were to be found, Parsi law to Parsis and Jain law to Jains. Thus, men of every creed—for it was creed, not race or allegiance by which men were divided and classified in India—lived each according to his own law, as Burgundians and Franks and Romanized Gaul had done in the sixth century in Europe. The social fabric was not disturbed by the land customs and the rules of inheritance were respected, and of course the minor officers with whom the peasantry came in contact continued to be natives. At the outset the villager scarcely felt that he was passing under the dominion of an alien power. His life flowed on in the same equable course beside the little white mosque or at the edge of the sacred grove. A transfer of power from a Hindu or Muslim sovereign would have made no more difference to him than did the establishment of British rule, and life was more placid than it would have been under either a rajah or a sultan, for the marauding bands which had been the peasants' terror were soon checked by British officers.

As Lord Bryce emphasized, not only did things so continue for a generation, but they have so continued to recent times as respects those parts of law which are interwoven with religion, such as marriage, adoption (among Hindus) and other family relations, and with the succession to property. In all such matters native law continued to be administered by the courts set up by the English. When cases were appealed from the highest of these courts to the Privy Council in England, that body determined the true construction to be put on the Koran and the Islamic Traditions, or on a passage from the mythical Manu, in the same business-like way as it would the meaning of an Australian statute. Except in some few points the Sacred Law of Islam and that of Brahmanism remained unpolluted by European ideas. The significance of this was, of course, that elementary principles of right and wrong are common to all legal systems. This was well brought out by Lord McMillan, Chairman of the Executive Committee of the English Society of Comparative Legislation. In responding to a toast to the Society, he stated the Society might justly "blow its own trumpet." People sometimes asked him "How on earth do you manage in the Judicial Committee of the Privy Council to administer Hindu Law one day, Mohammedan Law the next day, French Law the following day, Roman-Dutch Law the next day, and so on through the whole gamut of jurisprudence?" After a good many years, Lord McMillan went on, the great truth has been borne in upon the Privy Council that throughout the world justice is one thing, and that the motives, techniques and forms which it assumes in different countries are only its trappings. One found in all three different systems that the same simple object was in view of doing what is right and just and that the mere forms in which justice clothes itself in different lands are important, no doubt, but they are not the essence.

Conspicuous among the portions of Hindu law that have continued in operation even after Lord Bryce's generation is that pertaining to marriage. Most such marriages are still negotiated by parents of the parties, the parents of the girl looking for a husband with a lucrative position and of a wealthy family, whereas the size of the girl's dowry is the convincing point for parents of a prospective bridegroom. Parents unable to make a suitable match directly insert an advertisement in the classified section of a newspaper, where the matrimonial column is a most popular feature. The field being limited by the caste system, the matrimonial advertisements usually specify the caste. Sometimes wealthy parents buy their daughter into a higher caste; if they are hard-pressed for cash, parents of a man are likely to accept a tempting offer and let their son marry a lower-caste girl.

The Indian Mutiny—Direct Rule by the British Crown. The beneficent British rule which Lord Bentinck and Lord Dalhousie exemplified with the motive of raising the standard of living of the Indian people and qualifying them for eventual self-government was brought to a sudden end by the Mutiny of 1857. Whatever the deeper grievances, the explanation commonly given for the starting of the mutiny by Sepoys of the Bengal army is that they were issued cartridges greased with animal fat, unclean to Muslims as well as Hindus. Whatever feelings of friendship had grown up between the native peoples and the English were blasted away. English officers and Europeans who could be reached were killed. The revolt spread quickly and widely. More than a year of fighting was required before order and control were again restored.

With the Indian Mutiny of 1857 the career of the East India Company came to a close. By the act of 1858, the British Parliament transferred the administration of affairs in India from the Company to the Crown. The act provided that India should be governed by the sovereign of England through a secretary of state for India, assisted by a council of fifteen members. The British administrator in India, the governor-general, was given the title of Viceroy. He headed an executive council upon which Indians had minority representation, and which had limited law-making powers. Each of the eleven provinces which were under full British control had an executive council similarly constituted.

It is essential to keep in mind that the British did not have full control over all of India. A unique situation was presented by the princely states to which we have already referred in relation to Lord Dalhousie's program. The dynasties of many of them were of long standing, some rulers claiming descent from the planets or other heavenly bodies. They varied in size from a few square miles to Hyderabad, with about sixteen million inhabitants and with a territory corresponding in size to that of Korea. Kashmir, another large princely state, was destined to make for particular trouble when Great

Britain withdrew from India. By treaty with each, these states were left nominally independent, but their foreign relations were committed to British hands.

Referring to the problem added by the princely states, Sir John Simon said that it meant that one-third of Indian soil was not British at all. They were often governed on feudal principles, with a great potentate, entitled to say, "I have got my treaty with you, and I call upon the British raj (rule) to honor its bond"—a difficulty all the greater because these Indian states were areas not naturally cut off by frontiers and scientific barriers from the rest of India. India was thus a patchwork, and the complications for statesmen were immensely increased thereby.

A further great problem of security from outside attack, as well as internal contrasts, which had always faced the statesmen having responsibility for India, was stated by Sir John as without parallel in any other part of the world—an immense frontier problem, the problem of the northwest frontier of India, that great stretch of mixed mountain country cut through here and there by a pass like the Khyber Pass leading down to Peshawar. "Why, gentlemen, the contrast between that part of India and the India of the plains has got to be seen to be believed," said Sir John. "There you see some hardy, fanatical tribesman in his white robes, spending much of his time on a tower with a rifle in his hand looking around—I will not say whether for his neighbor or his enemy—with his women folk and his cattle and his chickens inside a fortified farmstead, cultivating a bit of stony ground, seeing the caravans of camels pass along, as they have done for hundreds and perhaps thousands of years, by the road by which Alexander marched into India, by which so many invaders have marched into India since. And this hardy tribesman regards looting and fighting and struggling as one of the natural occupations of existence."

Thus, in the 1920's, when the British constructed a railroad line to the Afghan frontier, it was said that the job required almost as much diplomatic skill as it did engineering. The tribesmen did not like the idea. Finally, an engineer put over the plan by pointing out to the tribesmen the looting opportunities that would be offered by a richly laden train running up to the frontier on a regular schedule.

British sovereignty over the vast, heterogeneous area, problems and all, was formally exemplified in 1877 by a magnificent ceremony at Delhi, in the course of which Queen Victoria was crowned Empress of India.

Nationalistic Ferment. For the first time in its history all of India came under a semblance of unified rule after the legislation of 1858. Following the reaction inevitably caused by the Mutiny and its aftermath, the British desire to ameliorate the conditions of the people and to promote their qualification to participate in a democratic system was again evidenced. To cope with the periodic famines that afflicted the country as a result of drought, a far-reaching governmental program was initiated and carried through, including irrigation projects, improved roads, and extension of the railway systems to facilitate distribution of foodstuffs. The keeping of slaves was made a criminal offense. Under Lord Ripon, the provinces and their local units were given increased powers, and the local governments were increasingly entrusted to the native people. Further legislation by the English Parliament looked to increasing participation by the Indian people in their central government. Again and again it was asserted by Lord Cromer, who knew, as few men know, that region where colonial government abuts on foreign policy, that the reason why the British Empire proved so little irksome to the other nations of the world, and provoked so little practical obstruction, lay, and lay only, in the fact that, despite its obvious shortcomings, the verdict of history did in fact acknowledge that it approached colonial questions in the spirit of men administering a trust.

Nevertheless it was inevitable that the changed conditions brought by British rule should lead to unrest, and, eventually, to nationalistic ferment. We have already noted that in so far as law was concerned, the British rule brought no innovation, for British administrators and courts applied the law of Hindus and Muslims as they found it. But other factors were involved. The center of Indian life was the village, with its simple community government, where life had gone on unchanged for almost countless generations. Its people subsisted upon the fruits of the soil tributary to the village, generally held in common, and all their other needs were taken care of by the products of the local handicrafts. As we have seen, under British rule a system of landlordism was instituted in connection with the collection of taxes. Out of this arose an oppressive debt structure. Textile fabricating and other industries had attained sizable proportions. But England looked to India as a market for her own industrial products. Wanting only raw materials from India, she was in a position by tariff regulation to differentiate in her own favor. Under the policies which were introduced Indian industry declined. With the improvement of transportation the long-existing isolation of the Indian villages was brought to an end. English products reached remote areas, emphasizing that there was an "outside world." Great numbers of people left their primitive huts, made of mud, straw and cattle dung, seeking employment in the growing cities. There they lived in even more trying slum conditions, sleeping packed together in small rooms, or, on warm nights, in the streets. Then, as always in recent history, India was an overpopulated land, characterized by poverty, unsavory surroundings and disease.

The impact of these economic changes which attended British rule was intensified in the nineteenth century by the increased printing of books and newspapers. The fruit of the educational program initiated by Lord Dalhousie was ripening in the form of hundreds of thousands coming out of the secondary schools, and thousands in the colleges and universities. Only a small minority enjoyed these opportunities. Nevertheless, according to Sir John Simon, the Indian educated minority presents one of the most amazing spectacles on earth: "There you see a man, speaking and even thinking in the foreign language of English, competing in examination with the best British brains, arguing, as My Lord Dunedin would agree, his case before the Privy Council with great subtlety, knowledge and distinction, and he has acquired his great intellectual grasp and range because he has learned to adopt western education, western philosophy, western outlook, while he is really the recipient and transmitter of the ancient traditions of the East."

British impact on the thought and education of India, was considerable. This impact, while intimate, was a forced one, and inevitably aroused hostility and defiance; but it also created a kind of "Hindu-British (or European) synthesis," which Percival Spear calls "the working creed of modern India." British influence is still strong in independent India, as even the most casual visitor can attest. For every Indian political thinker who derives his inspiration from the thought of ancient India, there are probably a dozen who know more about Western than Indian thought and who are more at home discussing the ideas of Harold J. Laski than when interpreting the *Santiparvan* or the *Manusamhita*. Since Lord Macaulay's famous Minute of 1835, the English pattern of education has been the prevalent system in India. "It is possible," argued Macaulay, "to make natives of this country thoroughly good English scholars and to this end our efforts might be directed." Seldom have efforts been more successful. Most of the leaders of Indian thought and politics in the past century or more, including those who have been most anti-British and those who have preached the necessity of going back to the Vedas and of following Vedanta, have been under strong Western influence, and many have studied abroad.

It is understandable then, as Sir John Simon has pointed out, that in Indian towns of size there came to be found a cultivated and educated minority. Not only were there a growing number of people able to read with understanding the thoughts of the western world, along with chronicles of their local grievances, but large numbers who were not yet literate were within the sphere of influence of those who could read and who were becoming imbued with western concepts of human liberty. And, from a different but very important point of view, emphasis must be placed upon an event around the turn of the twentieth century which in Asia possessed a significance not appreciated in the West—the Japanese victory over Russia in 1905. No longer did the West appear as an invulnerable power, resistance against which was doomed to failure.

In this environment of growing self-consciousness of a life that was economically harsh and politically subordinated, the British government compounded difficulties for itself by failing to continue the beneficent course which it had initiated before the Indian Mutiny of 1857, even after the reaction to that event had presumably run its course. Steps were taken which looked rather to the other direction. A measure sponsored by Lord Ripon, looking to elimination of the special privilege of Englishmen to be tried only by English judges, was not adopted. Service in governmental positions for which at an earlier period Indians had been encouraged to qualify was progressively narrowed for them. The press was made to feel that it was not altogether free. Such legislative measures as did have a bearing on the scope of Indian autonomy fell disappointingly short of providing it.

It was not at all surprising, then, that signs of ferment appeared among the educated Hindus, and that at the lower levels, from the late nineteenth century on, sporadic incidents of revolutionary violence occurred. In their earlier stages, however, these things did not portend a complete breaking of relationship with Great Britain. This was strikingly confirmed at the time of World War I. The German Hohenzollerns, with ample reason to believe that Indian soil would be fertile ground for the seeds of revolt against Great Britain, broadcast them with confidence. They did not germinate. The Indian people had developed feelings of grievance against Great Britain, but inherently, though they did not relish being pressed to admit it, they respected Great Britain as the force which had brought them a sense of peace and security that they had never known before. Rather than revolting, India rallied to the support of the Allied Powers with substantial contributions of man power and material.

Indian Government Following World War I. Following World War I, in 1919 the British Parliament enacted the Government of India Act, which broadened the basis for suffrage, provided for provincial legislatures, and established a foundation for a federal union of the provinces and princely states. The provincial legislatures were constituted on a primarily religious basis—Muslims elected by Muslims, Hindus by Hindus, Sikhs by Sikhs, Indian Christians by Indian Christians, Europeans by Europeans. It was within the power of those legislatures to give women the right to vote and to serve as legislators. In each province there was a system by which certain Indians filled certain places on the Executive Council, such as Education, Public Health, Roads, and Local Government. Viewed in perspective, the Government of India Act embodied significant concessions to Indian autonomy, along with recognition of the internal divisions which militated against political unity.

Speaking of his experience in administering this Act as Viceroy, Lord Reading pointed out that on his arrival in India he found that the leading positions in political life were occupied by Indian lawyers, many of them trained in England, all of them practicing in courts of justice established under the English legal system and adjusted to the requirements of India, and pleading in English. Lord Reading placed in the forefront of English achievements in India the reign of peace practically from the time of English rule, the introduction of justice under the system of common law, of integrity pure and undefiled in administration. English education had proceeded far since the days of the Macaulay Minute in 1835. As it spread, educated men in India learned to speak English remarkably well, the flood gates were opened of English political history, of individual freedom, of integrity in public service, of English literature, with the result that the Indian demands were for constitutional government in main respects similar to that of England. Following 1921 there were provincial legislatures and the central legislature. "The debates take place in English, rarely is a speech made in another tongue, especially in the Central Legislature, where otherwise a member from Madras would not understand a member from the Punjab, a member from Bengal would not understand a member from Burma. It is the lingua franca," Lord Reading reported.

Reference has already been made to the problems imported by the princely states, and to the contrasts between the peoples as affecting the unity of India. In these remarks of Lord Reading may be found the key to the aspirations of the leaders of India on the one hand, and to the almost insuperable limitations on their realization, on the other. The educated classes, grasping the ideals of freedom, were motivated to pursue them. But not only were the masses without capacity to do their part, but the situation was almost hopelessly complicated by lack of anything like a common language. The census of India records some 220 dialects. Leaving that aside, there are a score of prominent languages, with no single Indian tongue prevailing over the whole Indian continent. There is nobody who can communicate with the whole Indian people by using any given form of Oriental speech; and there are vast areas in India where the language is not only different from elsewhere, but it comes from an utterly different family of speech—not like the contrast between English and French, not like the contrast between the languages of Europe, but tongues so utterly different that there is not the remotest prospect of getting that available bond which is presented by the bond of the American language. English is the uniting tongue of India. Out of the 320,000,000 inhabitants of India, there is a minority of two and one-half million, most of them highly cultivated and most intelligent people—lawyers, journalists, politicians and statesmen —people to whom English, the language which Britain brought, is the inevitable medium of communication between one part of India and another. But to the mass of the Indian people, English is of course entirely incomprehensible.

Pointing out the further difficulties involved, Sir John went on to point out that in India "you have stage upon stage, unit upon unit, vast complexes of people and races and nations which differ from one another in almost every conceivable respect, but have this in common that not one of them can claim as his natural Oriental inheritance the principle of government by means of representative institutions as you and I understand them." Moreover, although great efforts were made under the constitution which was established in 1919 to make the franchise wide, when the Commission went to India and examined the figures of electors it found that less than three per cent of the whole population was exercising a political vote, and that, even so, the greater part of those who were casting their vote were illiterate, not only in English but in any language whatever. The Commission made great efforts to find ways by which this franchise can be extended, "but all idea under the circumstances of India today that you can by a sweep of the hand establish universal suffrage even for men, much less for women, is only possible as people utterly misunderstand the real character of Indian difficulties."

Gandhi and Nehru. Viewed in impartial perspective, and taking into account the complex problems involved, the Government of India Act of 1919, which went into effect in 1921, embodied significant concessions to Indian autonomy, along with recognition of the divisions which militated against political unity. Nevertheless, it did not satisfy the nationalistic aspirations of the Indian National Congress as they had matured. We must glance briefly at that body and its history.

Whatever may have been the original causes, in recent times ferment among peoples who have been under outside rule has found consummation in terms of nationalistic activity. The history of the development of such activity in India, stemming from the ferment of discontent of which we have spoken hereinabove, has been inseparably connected with the Indian National Congress, which was established in 1885. That year there convened at Poona a group of men, some of them Muslims but for the most part Hindus, who, without initial motive of separation from British rule, nevertheless embarked upon a course of collaboration that developed inexorably toward that end. Within a generation it had become a powerful agency, working for Indian independence, but contemplating its attainment by none other than peaceful means.

Not until after World War I did the National Congress adopt what could be called a policy of extreme nationalism. At that juncture it came under the domination of Mohandas K. Gandhi, born of the Vaisya caste, who carried it to the people and promoted its expansion on a mass basis. A devout Hindu, he combined great political astuteness with an appealing asceticism that translated him, in the estimation of millions of his countrymen—to say nothing of many people of other lands—to a status closely approaching divinity. Destined to meet his end in 1948 at the hand of a Hindu fanatic after he had attained his goal of Indian independence, he did not believe in violence or the use of force. His tactics were rather those of hunger strikes and other manifestations of passive resistance.

The philosophy of Gandhi, as Albert Schweitzer has observed, "is a world in itself." Gandhi never tried to evolve a consistent political philosophy; his writings, statements and actions are full of contradictions and inconsistencies. It is difficult to trace the origins of his teachings; he took his ideas from many sources, and adapted them in the light of his own experiences and observations to the needs of his country as he envisioned these needs. His political ideas were "an organic part of his philosophy of life," which was essentially religious in character. To him "there are no politics devoid of religion." "Better than anybody else" he "appreciated the supreme role of moral persuasion in social and political changes." He preached the "superiority of one's conscience over any mighty power in the world." His analysis of the relations between ends and means and his philosophical justification and explanation of *ahimsa* and *satyagraha* deserve the careful attention of students of political thought.

Gandhi's first conspicuous activity was by way of opposition to the Rowlatt Act, enacted after World War I to be in force for a three-year period, with the purpose of aiding in curbing terroristic violence by extremists who had been imprisoned during the war, but who were released thereafter. By way of protest Gandhi proclaimed a hartal, or day of prayer, with all work to cease. Not all of his followers observed his adjuration to conduct themselves peacefully. Riots broke out at Delhi, bringing death to many, and violence spread to other places. English soldiers and civilians were killed. At Amritsar General Dyer, in command of a small force of British soldiers, proclaimed a local state of martial law. When a large crowd assembled in violation of orders, he gave the word to shoot, and several hundred Indians were killed. This incident resulted in Gandhi's suspending for the time being his passive resistance program, but it provided powerful fuel for the growing fire of Indian nationalism. Although he had previously indicated that the National Congress would support the Act of 1919, when the show-down came he turned against it, basing his change of position on the ground that the British government had not adequately repudiated the action of General Dyer at Amritsar, and on the further ground that Indian Muslims were being wronged by the proposed Treaty of Sevres, by which Turkey was to be virtually emasculated, with attendant general threat to the interests of Muslims everywhere. By thus making himself the champion of the Indian Muslims, he obviously greatly strengthened his tactical position as the leader of all India.

When the Act of 1919 went into effect Gandhi confidently ordered a program of general passive resistance. At first the Muslim League, at which we will presently glance, joined. But the honeymoon between Hindus and Muslims in this connection was short-lived. Adherents of both faiths got out of hand and assaulted each other, with bloody results. Gandhi's own followers engaged in violent attacks upon government officials. Gandhi, imprisoned, called off the passive resistance campaign, but the passions aroused continued on.

At this juncture mention must be made of the Nehru family, which had its antecedents in the Kashmir Brahmans. The father, Motilal, was brought to active interest in the National Congress by his son, Jawaharial, a lawyer, educated at Harrow and Cambridge. Jawaharial married a girl of his own high Brahman caste, and when he returned from his schooling in England he settled down to the life of a wealthy Indian. But he was highly active intellectually, and an eager reader. He found attraction in Marxism and the Gandhi leadership of the National Congress, and formulated for himself a philosophy which in a sense combined the two. He was not a Communist. His disagreements with Gandhi were many and deep. Inclined to agnosticism, he thought that the mysticism emphasized by Gandhi was not what India needed. But in this as well as in other things he deferred to Gandhi, who sensed in him a powerful young ally. At the time he visited the United States in 1949 it was said that he was a relentless self-driver, working a nineteen-hour day, beginning with Yoga exercises that included standing on his head.

Of one thing Jawaharial Nehru was certain, and that was that the whole system known as colonialism had to go. Not clear, perhaps, as to the form of political and economic structure that would supplant colonialism, from the outset of his activity in the National Congress he was an uncompromising advocate of Indian independence.

Independence Movement. In 1928 Lord Birkenhead, Indian Secretary of State, having suggested that the Indian parties submit their draft of a proposed plan for Indian government, Motilal Nehru was named chairman of the several Indian groups, including the Muslim League. It was then that the difficulty of arriving at a plan satisfactory to both Hindus and Muslims became unmistakably apparent. In spite of disagreements between the National Congress and the Muslim League, however, a plan was worked out, and by resolution the Congress called upon Great Britain to accept it within one year, under threat of a program of passive non-resistance against the government. The British government did not accept the plan, but made proposals for a conference in the matter.

The Muslim League was favorable to acceptance of the conference proposal. Gandhi announced that the National Congress would participate only with the conclusive understanding that a plan of full dominion status for India would be adopted at such a conference, to come into immediate effect. Thereafter the National Congress convened. It passed resolutions ordering its constituents to take a pledge of complete independence from Great Britain on a day fixed, and to resign from provincial legislatures of which they were members. Preparations were announced for withdrawing all voluntary association from the British government, and for civil disobedience, including nonpayment of taxes. Subsequently, under Gandhi's direction, in March of 1930, this program of civil disobedience got under way. In accordance with what the previous history of such a program indicated, the campaign made a quick transition from non-violence to rioting and bloodshed. The Muslims did not cooperate. As before, Gandhi was imprisoned, and the situation was brought under control.

Late in 1930 a round-table conference was called in London, and was attended by representatives of the Muslim League and other Indian groups, with the exception of the National Congress. In the absence of representatives of the latter body, a plan was drafted. To insure the participation of the National Congress, Gandhi was offered amnesty. He appeared at a second conference in 1931, objected to much that had been done at the first conference in his absence, and claimed for the National Congress the prerogative of representing all parties of India. No definitive result was reached. When he returned to India, having ordered a renewal of civil disobedience, he was again imprisoned.

A third round-table conference, without representation by the National Congress, was held in London in 1932. Agreement was reached on a framework for an Indian constitution, and, embodying such a proposed constitution, there issued the White Paper of 1933. Study by a Parliamentary committee followed, and in 1935 Parliament adopted the India Bill which notably enlarged the scope of Indian self-rule. Gandhi's further attempts to oppose the working of the measure by civil disobedience campaigns having failed, he retired from active leadership of the National Congress and Jawaharial Nehru took over.

Though Nehru vigorously opposed the new measure at the outset, when the new governmental organization became effective in 1937 the National Congress was brought to cooperate, and it proceeded to acquire control over most of the provincial governments. Muslims were kept out of office. But things were not running smoothly in the National Congress. A schism manifested itself, with the development of a strong group displaying leftist tendencies that carried far beyond the orthodox socialistic policies of Nehru. Led by Subhas

Chandra Bose, this group succeeded in carrying the Congress election in 1938 and electing Bose president. Under pressure from Gandhi, the Congress forced Bose to resign his office, which he did. He then operated in a manner which, with the coming of World War II almost at hand, soon became altogether subversive.

The Muslim League. A number of references have already been made to the Muslim League. We have noted the statements of Sir John Simon, chairman of the Indian Statutory Commission, calling attention to the handicaps of illiteracy and lack of a common language attached to the effort to promote independent democratic government in India. Sir John went on to direct attention to another difficulty which he characterized as much more fundamental: "Self-government does not really mean that everybody governs himself. It means that every citizen is willing to be governed by the votes and judgment of others in return for their franchise."

India did not provide this kind of a setting. Sir John referred to the seventy million Muslims—monotheistic, iconoclastic, hating and despising the idols in the Hindu temples, remembering the traditions of a conquering martial race, proud of the magnificent monuments which their Mongol ancestors erected, never forgetting that in the long ago they came through the passes of the Hindu Kush, ran over the plains, and made themselves masters of the land, and asked, "What is their position in this three hundred millions of accumulated humanity that you so simply call India?" By way of reply to the question, he said that nothing would induce those seventy million Mohammedans to vote on the same register as citizens living in the same street that were also Indians, but also Hindus. They insist that they should have their own list of voters, that they should elect their members, that they should be secure in their own local government, and if they had their way they would like to secure in every branch of the public service, administrative, judicial service and everything else, that the Mohammedans have there what they would call their fair proportion.

Such a setting explains the Muslim League, which was organized at Decca by a group of Muslim leaders in 1906. The growth of the National Congress, which was throughout a predominantly Hindu group—and could hardly have been otherwise in a country where the Hindus were in such great majority—was viewed with misgiving by Indian Muslims. Hinduism as a religion was separated from the state, but as events developed the Muslims came to fear that the leaders of the National Congress were looking to the consolidation of Hinduism within the Indian government, to the exclusion of other religions. With reason, they feared for their own Muslim faith.

In the background, moreover, there were other perhaps less direct but withal potent reasons for fear as to the future of Indian Muslims. By virtue of their faith, Muslims regarded all men as equal, yet under the caste concepts of the Hindus, as we have seen, they were made to sense their own assumed inferiority by such things as having to use separate public drinking fountains. On the whole, the Muslims were on a lower economic and educational level. They were handicapped in trading and amassing wealth by religious injunctions against receiving interest profits. Instinctively, they sensed the greater power of the Hindus, who with their superior qualifications were in position, not only to exercise an outstanding influence in both private life and government service, but to prevent the Muslims from progressing to a position of individual equality. And, of course, the Muslims had not forgotten that until the British took over *de jure* as well as *de facto* control of India in 1858, Muslim emperors had been the rulers of India for many centuries.

For many years after it was organized the Muslim League did not play a very distinctive part in Indian affairs. It did not openly promote division along religious lines. Through the period of World War I it cooperated with the National Congress to promote the general interests of Indian independence. Interestingly enough, the League's leadership at the critical juncture of which we have been speaking in a way paralleled that of the National Congress. What Nehru was to the latter body, Mohammed Ali Jinnah was to the Muslim League.

The son of Jinnah Poonja, a wealthy merchant of Karachi, he developed into a lanky youth, over six feet tall. When he was sixteen years old his father sent him to England to receive his higher education. Studying at Lincoln's Inn, where his fellow students knew him as the "tall thin boy with the funny long yellow coat," he made good use of his time and talents. Returning to India, he married a Parsi girl, who as a member of that sect had grown up as an adherent of Zoroastrian doctrines, but who at marriage espoused the Muslim faith.

Jinnah set up a law office in Bombay, and practiced successfully. Believing in cooperation between Muslims and Hindus, he first identified himself with the National Congress, and rose to a position of leadership in its ranks. But he also identified himself with the Muslim League. He did not agree with Gandhi's non-resistance policies, and in 1921 withdrew from the National Congress. Thereafter for several years he spent much of his time practicing law in England, where, as subsequent events proved, he made many important contacts with high British officialdom.

Such events as a militant Hindu movement to proselyte among the Muslims, and the short shrift given to Muslim proposals at the 1928 conference of which we have spoken, galvanized the League into activity. Jinnah returned to India and assumed leadership, with such effectiveness that he came to be known to his followers as the Quaid-i-Azam, or "great leader." Originally he supported the India Act of 1935. But having been disillusioned by its operation he became convinced that the only solution of India's problems lay in setting up two independent states: a Muslim state of Pakistan, as well as an Indian state; the former to be carved out of existing British India. Voicing the differences between Hindus and Muslims, he emphasized what we have already noted: that they belong to two different religions, philosophies, social customs and literatures. They neither intermarry nor interdine. They belong to two different civilizations, based on conflicting ideas and conceptions. To yoke together two such nations, one as a numerical majority and the other a minority, would lead to growing discontent and the final destruction of any fabric that might be built up for the government of such a state. To promote the end of two separate nations, by constitutional means, he struck out to make the Muslim League a vigorous force.

At the League meeting in Lahore in 1940 a resolution was passed calling for the creation of sovereign Muslim states where the Muslims were numerically in the majority, as in northwestern and part of eastern India. With the advent of World War II the League asserted political domination in these areas, and in 1942 Jinnah proposed that they constitute the independent state of Pakistan.

Developments of the World War II Period. When World War II broke out, the Viceroy summarily declared India to be included among the powers fighting Germany. He did this without referring the matter to Indian opinion. To show their resentment, all the provincial ministries resigned in 1939, not to resume popular government until 1945. The political climate of the country was further reflected by the National Congress, which took a position of absolute non-resistance, and refusal to aid the war effort of Great Britain. Gandhi went so far as to urge Englishmen not to resist Hitler and Mussolini.

The fires of political dissatisfaction were fed by the economic concomitants of the war, which brought disruption into Indian life and intensified the chronic shortages of food and other necessities.

In 1942, when the Japanese forces were approaching India, Sir Stafford Cripps was sent from Great Britain with an offer of Indian dominionship through a constituent assembly at the war's end. The offer was not accepted. The National Congress was not satisfied, because independence was not granted at once, and because the Muslims and princely states would not be obliged to enter the union. The Muslims rejected it because, as we have seen, they had decided that they should have an independent state of their own. When it became evident that the Cripps proposals were unacceptable, the National Congress followed with a resolution announcing a campaign of civil disobedience unless Great Britain quit India at once. Gandhi and Nehru were arrested and imprisoned. Sabotage and rioting followed. Hundreds were killed and injured throughout India. But in spite of these occurrences, India rendered effective aid to the military effort of the United Nations.

In June, 1945, Lord Wavell invited representatives of the various Indian groups to a conference at Simla, at which he proposed a new constitution for India, to be drawn up by the Indian people. As an immediate step toward independent rule he proposed an all-Indian executive council, to be selected in proportions which would give a balanced representation of the main communities, including equal proportions of Muslims and Caste Hindus. Contending for the principle of an independent Pakistan, Jinnah, on behalf of the Muslim League, refused to accept the proposition, and the conference broke up without direct result.

Shortly thereafter the Labor Party, with a long-standing policy of self-government for India, won the election in Great Britain. At the opening of the new Parliament the early realization of full self-government was promised in the King's speech. Preparations were begun looking to working out what it was anticipated would be the orderly consummation of such a program in due course. However, India was in no mood for temporizing. The end of the war brought renewed outbursts of nationalistic ultimatums. The temper of the country was demonstrated when Subhas Chandra Bose partisans were put on trial for treason. As we have seen, Bose had been forced out of the National Congress presidency. After the war began, he visited Hitler and the Japanese authorities, and organized a "Free India" government and army, under Japanese protection. With the turning back of the Japanese forces his efforts came to naught. He himself was killed in an accident, but after the war a number of his officers were brought to trial at Delhi. The adverse reaction of all parties, including the Muslim League, was quick and violent. Riots broke out in various places. Sailors of the Indian navy mutinied, and in a number of cities the police refused to enforce order.

On March 15, 1946, Prime Minister Atlee declared in the House of Commons: "I am quite certain that at the present time the tide of nationalism is running very fast in India, and, indeed, all over Asia." The Prime Minister emphasized that the idea of nationalism had spread through all groups, religious and political as well as through the army and civil service. A Cabinet Mission was about to leave for India to discuss the matter. As to this, the Prime Minister said: "My colleagues are going to India with the intention of using their utmost endeavors to help her attain her freedom as speedily and fully as possible. What form of government is to replace the present regime is for India to decide. I hope that the Indian people may choose to remain within the British Commonwealth. But if she does so elect, it must be by her own free will. If, on the other hand, she elects for independence, in our view she has a right to do so."

The Cabinet Mission thus delegated met with Gandhi, Nehru, Jinnah and others at Simla. The British emissaries made it plain that it was for India itself to say what it wanted. Jinnah in behalf of the Muslim League was adamant that that party would join in constituting a provisional government only if the plan for Indian independence was postulated upon complete Muslim separation and the setting up of an independent state of Pakistan. Gandhi and Nehru were equally adamant that the National Congress would not proceed if a disunited India would be the result. The conference ended without direct result.

On May 16, 1946, the British government announced plans for an independent federal regime in India, rejecting the Muslim demands for the separate state of Pakistan. The Viceroy, Lord Wavell, asked Nehru, president of the National Congress, to form an interim government. The Muslim League announced that it would not participate. Adopting the tactics previously employed by Gandhi and Nehru, Jinnah called for a hartal, or work stoppage, to protest rejection of the Muslim plan for Pakistan. Communal riots resulted. What was characterized as the largest communal riot in the history of India broke out in full fury at Calcutta, where in a few days over four thousand people were killed in an outburst of religious warfare. The violence spread to East Bengal, where Muslims were in majority, and to Bihar, where Hindus were in majority, and to Bombay and the Punjab.

In September, officials selected by the National Congress took office and for the first time since British rule of India, native Indians were in positions of authority in the central government. But it was not a regime that could effectively rule. To deal with the tangled situation Lord Mountbatten was sent to replace Lord Wavell as Viceroy. Accepting the fact that an India uniting Hindus and Muslims in one nation was a political impossibility, he entered into conferences with the Indian leaders looking to the withdrawal of Great Britain on a basis of turning over the existing British rule to two separate nations, India and Pakistan. The princely states were given the alternative of independence, or identifying themselves with either India or Pakistan through accession. The maharajas of these states, foreseeing the demise of their personal power—which was ultimately actually symbolized by the sale of their ceremonial elephants after Indian independence for as little as $60 a head—protested strongly but ineffectively. With the exception of Hyderabad and Kashmir they later accepted the program of independence, which granted all princes a privy purse for living expenses, by acceding to either India or Pakistan. With the acquiescence of the National Congress in such a solution, the goal of Indian independence was close at hand.

India and Pakistan Become Independent Nations. The regime of the "pukka sahib," or British governmental administrator, came to an end with the Indian Independence Act of 1947, effective in August of that year. Britain pulled out of India. By the terms of this Act, both India and Pakistan remained members of the British Commonwealth for one year, at the end of which period they were free to withdraw. Neither withdrew from the Commonwealth. Some difficulty was presented as to the continued membership of India, as a republic, because the Statute of Westminster of 1931 declared that members of the Commonwealth must express their unity by a "common allegiance to the Crown." India did not propose to do this. At a conference of the foreign ministers of the eight countries making up the Commonwealth in 1949—the United Kingdom, Canada, Australia, New Zealand, South Africa, India, Pakistan and Ceylon—it was agreed that India could remain a full member of the Commonwealth by acknowledging the King "as a symbol of the free association of its independent member nations, and, as such, the Head of the Commonwealth." With only two dissenting votes the Indian Constituent Assembly approved this settlement. Nehru realistically said: "We join the Commonwealth obviously because we think it is beneficial to us and to other causes in the world that we wish to advance. It is good to keep a cooperative association going which might do good in this world." The change of Great Britain's status as a world power thus brought about was indicated by the phraseology of a state paper in 1949, which referred to the British king, not as the "Emperor of India" of more resplendent days, but as, simply, "the Head of the Commonwealth."

Never before had the world beheld the spectacle of two great nations coming into independent existence by absolutely peaceful means, and proceeding without previous experience on the course of free, democratic government.

The Republic of India, with a population of some 350,000,000 people, strongly protesting the partition and beaming to the United States the slogan, "you did not allow the South to secede in 1861," nevertheless commenced with enthusiasm its career of nationhood. From the standpoint of language diversification, general illiteracy and poverty of the people, it was handicapped in the same manner as Pakistan. Some 40,000,000 of the people within its boundaries were Muslims. But it had the advantage of possessing most of the administrative machinery of government, with a personnel somewhat experienced in many of its details, and its territory was geographically intact.

On the other hand Pakistan, with a population of some 80,000,000 people, did not inaugurate its history as the world's fifth most populous nation under outwardly auspicious circumstances. It had to set up a new capital at Karachi. It was divided into two parts, one on the east and one on the west of India, separated by a thousand miles of distance geographically and by basic economic differences. From the outset it was confronted with the problem of caring for the millions of the refugees of which we will presently speak. Probably 90% of its people were illiterate. The official language, Urdu, was not spoken by a majority of the Pakistan population. Agriculture was what practically all of its people were dependent upon. Including no major industrial area, and with practically no basic raw materials in the form of coal and iron, it was under the necessity of importing most manufactured goods. It was lacking in people trained in business, in the professions, and in public administration. It was faced with large claims for compensation for property left in Pakistan by Hindus and Sikhs who fled the country, whose holdings were not balanced by what was left in India by the less affluent Muslims who had fled that country.

Mohammed Ali Jinnah, who was in large measure responsible for Pakistan's existence and who would have been a continuing tower of strength in its establishment as a sound and strong nation, died in 1948. His able successor, Liaquat Ali Khan, was assassinated in 1951. Pakistan's difficulties were further compounded by developments in the neighboring princely state of Kashmir, whose maharajah at the outset did not accede to either India or Pakistan. Kashmir had a population of about four million people, of whom three million were Muslims, but the maharajah was a Hindu. With his own troops he savagely suppressed a Muslim revolt. Thereupon fanatical Muslim tribes of the Northwest Frontier Province went to the aid of their co-religionists. On October 26, 1947, the maharajah acceded to India, which sent Indian troops to repel the tribesmen. Pakistan followed with moral, material and military support for the Kashmir Muslims, with the result of an undeclared war on Kashmir soil. A cease-fire was arranged by the United Nations, and a decision was reached to settle by plebiscite Kashmir's affiliation, but to date the plebiscite has not been held. Some half-million Muslims fled to Pakistan, thus greatly adding to the rehabilitation problem which confronted that country from the outset of its existence.

On the brighter side, Pakistan commenced with some sources of economic strength. It produced a surplus of such basic products as cotton, wheat and jute. Within a few years, with the aid of outside agencies, it had under way new flood control, reclamation and irrigation projects, and industrial facilities. In a sense not altogether happy, a spirit of internal unity was promoted by the resentment toward India, fed by the events which preceded the withdrawal of the British. From the spiritual point of view Pakistan commenced with the strength inherent in a common, militant religion. The leaders of that country commenced by laying great stress on the Shariat, or teachings of the Koran and the Traditions of Islam. Nor was, or is, the point of view of the Islam of Pakistan one of blind adherence to ancient precepts, not in keeping with modern human needs. Prime Minister Liaquat Ali Khan stated before his assassination that for the government there was only one "ism"—Islamic socialism, which means that every person in the land has equal rights to be provided with food, shelter, clothing, education and medical facilities. If this would not seem to be in keeping with Islamic orthodoxy, it would indicate that Islam is amenable to the needs of social change.

Aftermath of Travail. The theory of the final settlement out of which came the nations of India and Pakistan was that the Muslims had their independent state of Pakistan and the Hindus their independent state of India. But the lines were man-made, not at all related to geography or previous history. The theory was one thing, its application another. Not all Muslims lived in the territory allocated to Pakistan; not all Hindus lived in India. In fact, millions of Muslims lived in the India area, millions of Hindus in Pakistan.

The advent of partition brought scenes of hardship and death hardly matched by any other event in history. Rioting began in various places, particularly in the vicinity of the boundary line between India and Pakistan which had been drawn through the Punjab. Hindus and Muslims attacked each other with increasing ferocity, putting villages to the torch and killing their inhabitants. As the terror spread, hundreds of thousands of Muslims abandoned their homes and sought to make their way out of India to Pakistan, and hundreds of thousands of Hindus left their homes in Pakistan for India. Photographs taken at the time portrayed scenes beggaring word description. The roads were clogged for miles on end with caravans, made up of bullock carts piled high with personal possessions, babies and the infirm riding on top of the loads, those able to walk trudging alongside carrying all that their backs would bear. Railroad trains made up of cars of every description were jammed with fleeing humanity. Every foot of the top of passenger cars was occupied by men and women, clinging desperately to this means of escape.

Faced with this initial crisis, the new governments of both nations collaborated in hastily improvised but effective programs of evacuation under military auspices. Within a few months there had been a transmigration of several million people. Before the movement was substantially completed over six million Muslims had entered Pakistan from India, and over five million Hindus had come to India from Pakistan. Hundreds of thousands of Hindus and Muslims had been killed.

With the subsidence of violence and terrorism, the problems of rehabilitation of these millions became at once acute, and continued on. For a time physical housing could be accomplished by the expedient of tent cities, stretching across the landscape as far as the eye could reach, some of which sheltered several hundred thousand people. But resettlement as a permanent solution provided baffling problems to the new nations which have not yet been altogether solved.

Constitutional Government in India. The preparation of constitutions for India and Pakistan was obviously not a simple matter, but in India intensive application was given to the matter. Interestingly enough, the chairman of the drafting committee, B. R. Ambedkar, had been born an untouchable. Throughout his early life he had known the humiliation and indignities that such a status involved. But he had had the good fortune, through the encouragement of his family and the financial assistance of the Maharajah of Baroda, to attend institutions of higher learning in India, and Columbia University in the United States. At the latter institution he gained the Ph.D. degree. In 1950 the constitution for the Republic of India was ready, setting up a federation of seventeen states, based largely on language differences.

The Constituent Assembly which framed the document relied on a number of patterns: English constitutional law was the guiding factor for the parliamentary system of government, American constitutional law for conceiving a bill of rights, and Canadian and Australian constitutional law for reconciling federalism with the system of government adopted. Among other things, it set forth as a function of the state "to promote the welfare of the people by securing and protecting as effectively as it may a social order in which justice, social, economic and political, shall inform all of the institutions of the national life." It featured abolition of untouchability, free elections, freedom of speech and democratic courts. Not the least important provision was that granting self-rule to the villages. Hindi was made the official language, but English was retained for use until 1965.

Similarity to Constitutional Government of the U. S. Summarizing as to the constitutional system of India, Justice Douglas pointed out the constitutional systems of the United States and India are founded on the concept of popular sovereignty and universal suffrage. Each adheres to the federal form of government, despite differences in emphasis and detail, and each recognizes an area of free trade. India, like America, has respect for the system of checks and balances. Each relies on an independent judiciary as a guardian of constitutional rights. The Indian Constitution, like our own, recognizes the basic rights of free expression, free religion, and separation of Church and State. Each Constitution contains guarantees designed to insure fair treatment to the defendant in a criminal prosecution, such as provisions against self-incrimination, a right to be informed of the charges against him, and the right to counsel. Each honors the Great Writ—habeas corpus—as an instrument of freedom. Both India and America afford protection to property rights from arbitrary governmental action. Though India has no Due Process clause, it has other protective provisions that serve essentially the same function in the field of social legislation. Each recognizes that modern conditions frequently require delegation of authority to administrative agencies, but each also recognizes that judicial control is needed to keep the agency within the authority delegated and to insure that the authority will be exercised fairly. Above all, the Indian Constitution, like our own, guarantees equal protection to all, regardless of race, creed or color. However, certain of our basic guarantees, such as the right of privacy and guarantee of jury trial, find no counterparts in the Indian Constitution, while the latter contains provisions on social and economic rights not dealt with in the American Constitution.

Under the Indian Constitution, the first national general elections were held in 1951. To meet the difficulty presented by illiteracy a distinctive symbol was given to each political party. Ballot boxes marked with this symbol were provided, and the voter registered his preference by dropping his ballot into the box bearing the symbol of his choice. The National Congress Party headed by Nehru led the field. Women ran strong, many being elected to parliament. The important part thereafter played by women in Indian affairs was exemplified by Mrs. Vijaya Lakshmi Pandit, a sister of Nehru. She had been the first woman elected member of an Indian provincial government, and had served as Minister for Municipal Affairs and Public Health in the Government of the United Provinces. She became chief of the Indian delegation to the United Nations, where she had a leading part in a number of the dramatic episodes which marked the earlier years of that body.

The Constitution of Pakistan. Pakistan was hampered in framing a constitution because of differences between its religious and political leaders over the nature of the state that should be set up. The orthodox Muslim leaders stood fast for an Islamic religious state. More practical men, and political scientists having in mind the minority of Hindus and adherents of other religious faiths in East Pakistan, disagreed. Unfortunately, the matter was allowed to lag. The more populous but physically smaller East Pakistan came to feel that its interests were being neglected in favor of the more affluent western part of the nation. At a general election in East Pakistan in 1954, a coalition voted down the Muslim League candidates on an economic program of agrarian reform. A month later the central government at Karachi ousted the new regime and took over direct control. Local control was later restored, but not before the idea of an East Pakistan independent of West Pakistan had opportunity to crystallize. In October of 1954 the Governor-General dissolved the central assembly and directed Mohammed Ali, Pakistan ambassador to the United States, to form a new government. National elections were called for in 1955. Work on the constitution was speeded up, and it was completed and adopted in 1956. Its preamble states that the Muslims of Pakistan should be enabled to order their lives in accordance with the teachings and requirements of Islam, as set out in the Holy Koran and Sunna, but it also states that adequate provision should be made for the minorities freely to profess and practice their religion and develop their cultures. The fundamental Islamic nature of the document is indicated by the provision that no law shall be enacted which is repugnant to the injunctions of Islam, and that non-Muslims are not eligible for the presidency. The promotion of the social and economic well being of the people is recognized as a purpose of government. The constitution creates a unicameral legislature, with membership equally divided between East and West Pakistan, provides for an independent judiciary, and includes a bill of rights granting freedom of speech and religion, and abolishing untouchability. Thus commenced the career of two of the most populous countries of the earth as sovereign nations.

Persisting Problems of Caste and Minorities. Ten years have elapsed since India and Pakistan became independent nations. However much has been accomplished, deep-lying problems, having their source in the religious differences between Hindu and Muslim, remain to be solved. Recently writing from India, A. M. Rosenthal, discussing the short-lived attempt of Prime Minister Nehru to lead the country from a position above political office, said that one of the motives behind the attempt was the fear that the country was sliding back into antagonisms between the two religions—"communalism" is the word the Indians use—and that the phenomenon of caste within the Hindu community was growing stronger. Nehru did not leave office, but at a series of political meetings he urged the Congress Party to take action by way of ameliorating the situation. At his insistence resolutions were prepared saying that the minority should be given full opportunity to enter the public service of India; that all children whose mother tongue was said by their parents to be Urdu, the language of Muslims, should receive instructions in that language; that documents in Urdu should be accepted by all courts, and that government offices and training for teachers of Urdu should be established.

These efforts of Nehru brought him under strong attack from Right-Wing Hindu orthodox parties. One party publication went so far as to say that he was playing with fire, without knowing what he was doing, and that he would make a better Prime Minister of Pakistan than of Hindustan.

Certain portions of the Hindu law, dealing with marriage, succession to property, guardianship and adoption, were codified by the Indian Parliament in 1955 and 1956. Presumably they are furthering the abolition of caste.

CHAPTER 5

THE GLORIES OF GREECE

Gods and Kings. Early Greek history is largely built around gods and kings. The legends depict a race of heroes of divine lineage from whom the Greeks claimed descent. During this period, as narrated by Homer in the Illiad and the Odyssey, rule was by kings who were given the scepter by Zeus. When they ceased to exercise the essential qualities of courage and wisdom the scepter departed from them. These kings were at once priests, generals and judges. However, their power was limited by custom, and there was an advisory council of nobles, and an assembly of freemen without definite power but foreshadowing the popular assembly of later eras. In the trial scene on the shield of Achilles, the council and people standing by are obviously participating.

As we shall presently emphasize, Greece was never a truly united nation politically. Only in its religion was there an overall influence that made for unity. But by its nature the Greek religion did not exert the centralizing cohesive force that later made the Christian religion a powerful unifying agency through the centuries that followed the fall of the Rome or that made Islam the foundation of an Islamic state that for several hundred years constituted the world's most powerful empire.

At the summit of the Greek hierarchy was a council of twelve gods and goddesses, headed by Zeus, the father of gods and men. Among others were Apollo, the god of light, music and prophecy; Athena, the goddess of wisdom, and Aphrodite, the goddess of love and beauty. The gods and goddesses were presumed to reside on Mount Olympus and in the stratosphere above. They were conceived in attractive form. It has been said that under the magic spell of art the baleful and terrifying shapes of barbarous religion retreated and the world of imagination was peopled with gracious and attractive figures. The Greek pantheon is, for all its defects, a world of dignified and beautiful humanity. On the whole, the gods which are its citizens are humanized and humane, the friends and allies of men who therefore feel themselves not abased or helpless in their relations with them.

It was believed, moreover, that the gods did not hold themselves aloof from men, but rather revealed themselves to humans. In this connection Marion J. Bradshaw has called attention to the narrative of Paul healing the cripple and what happened thereafter. The aftermath is related in the Book of Acts as follows:

> And when the people saw what Paul had done, they lifted up their voices, saying in the speech of Lycaonia, The gods are come down to us in the likeness of men.
> And they called Barnabas, Jupiter; and Paul, Mercurius, because he was the chief speaker.

Nevertheless Greek religion was a thing of mystery, and godly desires were expressed only through signs and portents that required priestly interpretation.

Delphi and Olympia. Symbolic of the system was the oracle of Apollo, at Delphi. In a temple which was erected over a fissure in the rocks from which rose vapors, considered to be the breath of Apollo, a priestess known as the Pythia, after a period of coma or convulsion, purported to give Apollo's answer to questions. These answers were translated by attendant priests. The Delphi oracle was known throughout the world of that time, and was consulted not only by the Greeks but also by the Romans and other peoples. The importance attached to its utterances is manifest in the belief that no new colony could succeed without its approval.

In his life of Alexander, Plutarch tells of Alexander going to consult the Delphi oracle about the oncoming war with the Persians. He happened to arrive there on one of the days called inauspicious, on which the law permitted no man to put his question. At first he sent to the prophetess to entreat her to do her office, but finding she refused to comply and blaming the law as her excuse, he went himself and drew her by force into the temple. Then, as if conquered by his violence, she said: "My son, thou art invincible." Alexander, hearing this, said he wanted no other answer for he had the very oracle he desired. Further emphasizing the seriousness with which Alexander, as a representative Greek ruler took his religion, Plutarch relates that as soon as he had risen each day he sacrificed to the gods.

Another aspect of the religious system, honoring Zeus as supreme god, centered in the games at Olympia. Originally a form of ceremonial sacrifices, they consisted of various kinds of athletic contests. Participation was limited to Greeks free from sin against the gods. Consistent with the acceptance of Christianity as the Roman state religion when that juncture arrived centuries later, and with Greece

then a part of the Roman Empire, Emperor Theodosius put an end
to the Olympics.

In so far as the future life was concerned, Greek religion held that
the delightful Elysian Fields were reserved as the eternal haunt of
only the favored few heroes of the race. The masses were fore-
ordained to take up abode in the joyless caverns of Hades.

The City States. The emergence of the individual point of view
as opposed to that of the tribal custom formed the foundation upon
which human society could build its betterment. All history as studied
today in schools, be it Greek, Roman, foreign, or English, shows only
the combination of separate individual personalities into a pattern or
community that differed in different ages and was called by different
names according to the shape it took. The most studied period of
classical history describes an intensified form of such corporate organization, the city state.

As we have said, Greece was never a truly united national politically. It was rather an aggregation of some one hundred independent
city states, situated not only on the Grecian peninsula but also, in
later periods, as a result of a process of colonization, scattered throughout the Mediterranean World from Asia Minor to as far west as southern Gaul and Spain. Geographical considerations had much to do
with this condition of separation, but it was further promoted by the
fact that each one of these city states had its own religious deities
to command the veneration of its populace.

The loyalty of the Greek was to his own state community. He did
not live in an atmosphere of dominance by a central authority. As
events demonstrated, there was lacking the sort of central government
essential to putting up a strong front against external aggression.
It is true that the Greek states joined in the Amphictyonic Council,
which was set up with the primary object of protecting the Delphic
Oracle and other shrines. As described in *The Federalist*, all its members retained the character of independent and sovereign states, and
had equal votes. This Council had a general authority to propose
and resolve whatever it judged necessary for the common welfare of
Greece; to declare and carry on war; to decide, in the last resort, all
controversies between the members; to fine the aggressing party; to
employ the whole force of the confederacy against the disobedient;
and to admit new members. The Amphictyons were the guardians of
religion, and of the immense riches belonging to the Temple of Del-
phos, where they had the right of jurisdiction in controversies between the inhabitants and those who came to consult the oracle. As

a further provision for the efficacy of the federal powers, they took an oath mutually to defend and protect the united cities, to punish the violators of this oath, and to inflict vengeance on sacrilegious despoilers of the Temple.

In theory, and upon paper, this apparatus of powers seemed amply sufficient for all general purposes. In several material instances they exceeded the powers enumerated in the Philadelphia Articles of Confederation of 1778. The Amphictyons had in their hands the superstition of the times, one of the principal engines by which government was then maintained; they had a declared authority to use coercion against refractory cities, and were bound by oath to exert this authority on the necessary occasions. Very different, nevertheless, was the experiment from the theory. The powers were administered by deputies appointed wholly by the cities in their political capacities; and exercised over them in the same capacities. Hence the weakness, the disorders and finally the destruction of the confederacy. The more powerful members, instead of being kept in awe and subordination, tyrannized successively over all the rest. It happened but too often, according to Plutarch, that the deputies of the strongest cities awed and corrupted those of the weaker; and that judgments went in favor of the most powerful party. Even in the midst of defensive and dangerous wars with Persia and Macedon, the members never acted in concert, and were, more or fewer of them, eternally the dupes or the hirelings of the common enemies.

Had the Greeks been as wise as they were courageous, as, the Abbe Milot pointed out, they would have been admonished by experience of the necessity of a closer union, and would have availed themselves of the peace which followed their success against the Persian arms, to establish such a reformation. Instead of this obvious policy, Athens and Sparta, inflated with the victories and the glory they had acquired, became first rivals and then enemies; and did each other infinitely more mischief than they had suffered from Xerxes. Their mutual jealousies, fears, hatreds and injuries ended in the celebrated Peloponnesian War; which itself ended in the ruin and slavery of the Athenians who had begun it.

Sparta. With this background, let us look more closely at the nature of the Greek city states as exemplified by Sparta and Athens, considering first Sparta, which arose out of the Dorian invasions in the eighth century B.C. According to tradition Lycurgus, who had acquired divine wisdom through priestly contacts, prepared a constitution for Sparta, presented it to his people, exacted from them an oath to obey it, and then went into exile. To achieve his assigned purpose he was under the necessity of mixing a portion of violence with the authority of superstition, and of securing his final success by a voluntary renunciation, first of his country, and then of his life. The Lacadaemonians believed that their legislator was not Lycurgus, but Apollo. The veritable legislator among the ancients was not a man, but a religious belief which men entertained.

Under the constitution of Lycurgus there was a sharp division of classes. A group of noble families of allegedly heroic descent constituted an oligarchy which was the state, with all powers of government. This group was in a minority. The majority were people who had been subjugated, an inferior class, allowed to hold their land but heavily taxed and subject to military service. Below them were the helots, or slaves, regarded as the property of the state and farmed out for labor upon the estates of the Spartan lords.

At the beginning of the historic period the government was composed of two kings, the Senate of Elders, the Ephors, and the General Assembly. The two kings embodied the functions of high priest and military commander. They also exercised certain judicial powers. They presided over the Council and had absolute military authority. The Senate of Elders was composed of twenty-eight members, chosen by the General Assembly. Required to be at least sixty years of age, they held office for life. They exercised judicial duties, and prepared measures for presentation to the General Assembly. The Ephors were a body of five, elected by the General Assembly. Originally designed to be a check on the kings and Senate, they eventually assumed the main administrative activities of the state. The General Assembly was composed of the citizens not less than thirty years of age. It elected priests and magistrates. Though presumably having the power to pass laws, it acted only to accept or reject the measures presented to it by the Senate.

On the face of it, a government so constituted was not altogether inconsistent with a measure of democracy. But Sparta affords a demonstration that even a democratic government may lend itself to oppressive use if the policy back of it is directed to oppressive ends. In the day of our constitutional forefathers it was said that though nominally a republic, Sparta was little better than an armed camp. In an era when sword and spear were the basic weapons of war, and military defense or conquest depended entirely upon the physical strength of individual men, the policy of Sparta as an avowed military state is understandable. And history affords no better example of governmental policy geared to the attainment of a particular end. Scant respect was paid to the institution of marriage, which was customarily consummated by the forcible abduction of the bride. For a wife of a feeble husband to have children by another man was an approved practice. Meals were eaten at public tables, to the content of which every citizen was compelled to contribute. Children were regarded as state property; every male infant was brought before the Senate of Elders and condemned to exposure in the mountains if it did not appear sound. At the age of seven, boys were taken over by trainers who schooled them in exercises calculated to promote bodily strength. As a religious rite, and to accustom them to pain, they were subjected to beatings. To promote self-reliance, they were sometimes compelled to forage for their food, and if detected in the process of acquiring it through means regarded as improper they were severely punished.

Above the stern code of discipline which thus governed Spartan life there was a supreme rule of conduct to which every true Spartan adhered. It was expressed by Damaratus, an exiled Greek, in what he told Xerxes when the latter was leading his great Persian army to the invasion of Greece in 480 B.C. According to Herodotus, Damaratus told Xerxes that the Spartan soldiers were free—but not entirely free. For they had a master, and that master was law, which they feared much more than the subjects of Xerxes feared him. Whatever that master commands, they do, and his command never varies: it is never to retreat in battle, however great the odds, but always to stand firm, and to conquer or die.

We may take it that this "law" was not written in statute books, or even promulgated by magisterial decree. It was rather embodied in an inflexible customary mode of conduct, illustrating early in history how custom may become the basic component of the law by which mankind lives—or, perchance, dies.

So trained and so indoctrinated, Spartan soldiers fought and died like supermen at Thermopylae. But there was another side. In its war making Sparta wasted little time on what might be thought of as military chivalry. Thus, when Sparta conquered Messenia and attacked Argos, after defeating the Argives it annihilated their army by setting fire to the sacred grove in which it had sought sanctuary. In the later Pelopennesian War with Athens, the Spartans captured the city of Plataea, killed all the men, sold the women as slaves, destroyed the city, and made a pasture where it had been. More might have been expected from the Athenians, but, as we shall presently see, it was not forthcoming.

Early Athens. In the prehistoric period Athens, like the other city-states, was governed by kings of presumed divine lineage. The historic period found Athens changed from the monarchy of Homeric tradition to an oligarchy of nine Archons, chosen by the nobles from among themselves. Ultimate authority rested in the Council of the Aeropagus, composed exclusively of ex-Archons, whose members held office for life. This body had both judicial and political functions. There was an Ecclesia, or General Assembly, based on military qualification, but without real power. There were no written laws, leaving the way open to the exercise of arbitrary discretion by the officials of the state. Along with the ultimate political authority, the desirable land was held by the nobles. Most of the people were either tenants, subject to be seized into slavery for non-payment of rent, or small land-holders who were chronically in debt and therefore in jeopardy of a like fate. The list of crimes was large. Even such lesser ones as would be classified today under the head of disorderly conduct were punishable by death.

The Codes of Draco and Solon. Apparently as a concession to the unrest that grew out of such conditions Draco, one of the Archons, was commissioned to prepare a written code of laws. The Draconian Code, promulgated in 621 B.C., met the test of being formal written law, but it merely declared the existing harsh customs and practices that put the lower classes at such a disadvantage in their relation to the nobility. It was said that Draco wrote his laws not with ink but with blood.

To further allay the continuing unrest, a commission to draft a further code was given to Solon. One of the functions of law is to balance the interests of the classes of the society in which it operates. Solon's Code provides a historic example of this, accomplishing, as it did in effect, a considerable measure of non-revolutionary emancipation of the lower classes of Athenian society. At the same time, it did not so change the existing order as to upset a stable balance. Plutarch said that Solon did not make any concessions in behalf of the powerful, nor in the framing of his laws did he indulge the humor of his constituents. Where the former establishment was tolerable, he neither applied remedies nor used the scalpel, lest he should put the whole in disorder and not have power to settle or compose it afterwards in the temperature he would wish. He only made such changes as might bring the people to acquiesce in by persuasion, or compel them to by authority, making, as he said, "force and right conspire." Hence it was that having the question afterwards put to him whether he had provided the best of laws for the Athenians, he answered: "The best they were capable of receiving."

Among other things, Solon's Code broadened the right of suffrage. All were admitted to the Ecclesia. The load of the debtor class was lightened by depreciation of the currency, cancellation of debts to the state and outlawing the practice of selling debtors into slavery for nonpayment of debts. The power of the nobles, diluted through the extension of suffrage, was nevertheless retained in their sole right to be members of the Council of the Aeropagus.

Solon was reported by Plutarch to have said that it seemed that a ruler, whether king or tyrant, is held in more esteem by the citizens when he combines democracy with monarchy. Accordingly, the Ecclesia was given power to pass laws, call magistrates to account, and elect Archons. A Council of Four Hundred was established, to be elected annually by the people and through which all business was to be introduced to the Ecclesia. It is noteworthy that all citizens were required to take part in all political contentions, under penalty of forfeiture of citizenship.

The status of women was not advanced by Solon's Code. In this day, when women participate fully in the political affairs of the United States, and of such nations as India, it should be emphasized that in Greece women had no political rights, and even held a lowly place in the home. Their status in the political and economic sense was lower than that of their earlier Babylonian sisters. Only in Plato's ideal state, of which we shall later speak, were they admitted to their own. However, the Code provided that no marriage dowries be given; the bride was to bring with her only three suits of clothes and some household goods of small value. The marriages were not to be made with mercenary or venal view, but should be cemented by the endearment of children and overt instances of love and friendship.

Testamentary Disposition of Property. One notable innovation in Solon's Code provided for the testamentary disposition of property. In the primitive eras, wills were unknown. We have taken note of the Code of Hammurabi as containing provisions for inheritance of property, but with no mention of testamentary instruments. Before the days of Solon, no provision for testamentary disposition was made in Greece. As Chancellor Kent said, family convenience and a sense of the absolute right of property introduced the use of testaments in the more advanced progress of nations. The Attic laws of Solon allowed the Athenians to devise their estates, provided they had no legitimate children and were competent in mind, and not laboring under any personal disability. If they had children, the power to devise was qualified, allowing the parent to devise if the sons died under sixteen; or, in the case of daughters, with the condition that the devisees should take them in marriage.

Separation of Governmental Powers. Reference to Solon's Code cannot be concluded without emphasizing its import as making for a separation of governmental powers, a basic feature of the government of the United States. Thereby the possibility of one person or group asserting complete authority over all was greatly reduced. In past history the asserting power had been the king. Under a democracy, it could be the demos. By Solon's Code, the Aeropagus was made the supreme interpreter and guardian of the laws, with power to set aside certain resolutions of the Ecclesia and Four Hundred. Thus, the Aeropagus occupied a place somewhat like that of the Supreme Court of the United States. The value of these safeguards was tested and approved in the stormy years extending from the expulsion of the Pisistradae to the end of the Persian Wars. To them was due in no small measure that union of prudence and energy which enabled Athens to overcome seemingly insuperable odds. In consequence, the Aeropagus stood higher in public confidence and respect than it did during the two decades following the retreat of Xerxes.

The Constitution of Clisthenes. It is no disparagement of Solon's Code to say that it was in trouble from the beginning. Capitalizing on the resentments that followed its initiation, Pisistratus, Solon's nephew, who in today's vernacular would be classified as a demogogue, and who pioneered in that capacity in Athens, plotted to seize the government. Having wounded himself on purpose, he drove into the market place and endeavored to inflame the minds of the people by telling them that his enemies had laid in wait and assaulted him on the ground of his patriotism. By this subterfuge he succeeded in having a small guard of soldiers voted to him to protect him from the allegedly disgruntled nobles. With this nucleus he was able to seize control and set himself up as a tyrant. Solon, who had opposed the grant of the bodyguard, told the public it would have been easier for them to repress the advances of tyranny and prevent its establishment, but now that it was established it would be more glorious to demolish it. His advice went unheeded. Although the rule of Pisistratus was mild, and Athens prospered, his sons were lacking in the necessary qualifications. Their role was cut short by the assassination of one and exile of the other.

With the support of the lower classes Clisthenes then came to power. By his action all free inhabitants, including emancipated slaves and resident aliens, were granted citizenship. The number of the Council of the Aeropagus was raised to five hundred, fifty of them acting in rotated terms to constitute an interim committee of the Council. The chairman of this committee presided over the Council. There was instituted the practice of ostracism, by which any person who had excited the suspicion of the people could, by a vote of six thousand at a meeting of the Ecclesia, be banished from Athens for ten years. Clisthenes strengthened the position of the city by entering into treaties with Sparta and other Greek city states.

Athens Destroyed. Commencing in the sixth century B.C., the Greek cities were the object of invasion by the kings of the Persian Empire. In 490 B.C. the Athenians, under Miltiades, turned back the hosts of Darius at the Battle of Marathon, which is sometimes said to have marked the beginning of European history. To avenge this defeat Xerxes ten years later brought a tremendous Persian host across the Hellespont. The lack of unified counsel and action that only a strong central government could have provided proved almost fatal to the Greeks. But under the leadership of Themistocles a number of Greek cities, including Sparta, had combined their resources under Spartan command.

Had it not been for the treachery of a renegade Greek, the Persian invasion might have been repulsed. But as a result of this treachery the army of Xerxes was led around the Thermopylae Pass, valiantly held by Leonidas and his handful of Spartans. Athens was abandoned to the invaders, who seized and burned it. In the light of subsequent events this was not decisive, for the Persian fleet was defeated at Salamis, the Greeks won victories at Plataea and Mycale, and the Persian forces were driven back into Asia. As later history confirms, it was thus determined that the East was not to rule the West.

Athens Rebuilt. In leading the successful resistance to the Persian invasions Athens had risen to great heights of military power and influence. The city was, of course, in ruins. But Themistocles led in its rebuilding, and the fortification of the naval port of Piraeus. The future held many sordid events in store. Nevertheless, it was the beginning of an Athenian Golden Age, the fruits of which were destined to survive material decline and to provide the nourishment for future civilization.

In 477 B.C. representatives of the maritime cities met at the temple of Apollo in Delos for the purpose of uniting to build a naval force for mutual protection. The delegates formed the Confederacy of Delos. Government of this free association was to be in the hands of a conference of representative delegates, convened yearly on the sacred island of Delos. There, in the temple of Apollo, was to be the treasury. Aristides was chosen president.

Unfortunately, under the workings of the Athenian "democracy" of which we shall speak in greater detail presently, Themistocles fell from favor and was ostracized. Cimon, the son of Miltiades, who had gained popularity for his part in defeating the Persians, came into leadership. Following the apparently logical course of maintaining close relations with Sparta, he undertook to assist the Spartans in crushing a revolt of the helots. The difficulties in which modern democratic states find themselves when they support their allies in policies restrictive of colonial independence are reminiscent of the trouble which thus came to Cimon. He was undone by it, and in 461 Pericles, with whose name is commonly associated the "Golden Age of Athens," of which we shall presently further speak, came into power.

An Empire by Chicanery. The historian Polybius held the morality of Greek statesmen in low esteem, saying that a Greek statesman, if entrusted with a single talent, though protected by ten checking clerks, as many seals and twice as many witnesses, yet could not be induced to keep faith. Whether or not this was a just appraisal, it is clear in the light of events that the standard of Athenian official conduct was not uniformly immaculate.

From the outset, Athens had assumed control of the Confederacy of Delos. In accordance with the arrangement agreed to, the various cities were assessed ships for a confederacy navy. Some of the cities preferred to send money rather than ships. This money was to be used for building ships. The ships so built were, however, added to Athens' own navy. The treasury was moved from Delos to Athens, moreover, and its contents subjected to diversion to finance the undertakings of Athens, civil as well as military. When this state of affairs became known and Naxos sought to withdraw from the Confederacy, the Athenian navy was used to compel Naxos to remain. It was also used to enforce the exactions which other cities were finding to be increasingly onerous. In such manner, by breach of trust and in disregard of solemn agreements with her sister states, Athens made herself physically strong and created for the time being an empire which she ruled by force.

Whether, in view of the potential menace of further invasion from the East that could be met only by united Hellenic effort, this imperialistic policy was justifiable in the common interest, is a question not readily susceptible of confident dogmatic resolution. Citizens of the United States may sense some parallel in the resolution by Civil War of the problem of the right of the several states to secede from the Union.

In the meantime, in 445 B.C., the matter of the growing rivalry of Sparta was temporarily solved by the Thirty Years Truce. At this time, also, encouraging the developments of the Golden Age, there was peace at Rome and Carthage in the western Mediterranean.

The Rule of the Masses. Having noted the measures adopted by Pericles to strengthen Greece against external aggression, it is essential to note the internal situation. Pericles brought about governmental changes which stripped the Aeropagus of its powers. Thenceforth the General Assembly assumed, in effect, the whole power of government. The theory of absolute political equality was vigorously carried out. In his celebrated funeral oration, honoring Athenians who had died in battle, Pericles referred to it as "Democracy, or the Rule of the Masses." The lower classes were made eligible to be Archons. The degree to which all citizens were conceived to be equal was demonstrated by the practice of filling public offices by lot rather than by election. Under the policy of universal participation in the affairs of government, practically every citizen was carried upon the state payroll in some connection. Implementing the equality theory even as to luxuries, provision was made for free tickets to the theatre and ceremonial banquets.

We shall have more to say presently about the excesses of Athenian democracy. Suffice it to refer here to Plutarch's quotation from the life of Pericles: "So the comic writers speak of the people of Athens as of a horse wild and unmanageable—which listens to the reins no more, but in his headlong course bears down the very friends that feed him." Plutarch's thought is reflected to a degree in the conclusion of C. H. McIlwain that the Greek notion was that the state made the laws, while, by contrast, constitutionalism as we live under it presumes that the law makes the state.

"Inner Circle" Citizens; Slavery. However, the Athenians of the time of which we are speaking saw to it that these aforementioned emoluments did not become too widely diffused. A law was enacted

circumscribing Athenian citizenship for the future by limiting it to persons born of an Athenian father and an Athenian mother. Perhaps no governmental regime ever hewed more consistently to the line of promoting equal privileges for all citizens—or, incidentally, took better precaution to insure that the future base for such privilege would not be too greatly broadened.

There is a further consideration, too, to be noted. "Equal privileges for all citizens," we have been saying. "Citizens" did not include slaves, of whom there were many, indeed, in Athens. Slavery was an accepted social institution in Greece. De Toqueville said that the most profound and capacious minds of Rome and Greece were never able to reach the idea, at once so general and so simple, of the common likeness of men, and of the common birthright of each to freedom. They strove rather to prove that slavery was the order of nature, and that it would always exist. We find some assurance, however, that the slaves of Greece were treated with a degree of humane consideration for their personal comfort that transcended that accorded to their unfortunate counterparts in Egypt, Babylonia and Rome.

The "Golden Age." One receives a false impression of a "Golden Age" unless it be considered in the light of its background. Before speaking more in detail of the "Golden Age of Athens" in the rule of Pericles, we have therefore said something as to that background. This Golden Age got under way with the rebuilding of the city after its destruction by the Persians. "We are lovers of beauty," said Pericles in his funeral oration, "and with us it is within the reach of all." And, referring to the Athenian respect for law and anticipating those Stoic principles of natural law which were later woven into the fabric of the Roman law, he said that "least of all do we ignore those rules which derive their unwritten sanction from the individual's sense of honor."

With reservations, perhaps, as to whether in matters of "honor" the Greeks of the time fully met Pericles' expressed ideal, in the realm of beauty, at least, it is not out of order to refer to the age as a golden one. The period was one of achievement in architecture, art and drama, as exemplified by the Parthenon, sanctuary of the virgin goddess Athena; the art of Phidias, and the works of Aeschylus, Sophocles and Euripides. It was an age, also, in which the Greeks broadened the horizons of science. The rudiments of Greek science were doubtless traceable to the ancient civilizations of Egypt and Babylonia. But in the larger sense the Greeks were not only supreme artists, but also the pioneers of thought. They first took the measure of the universe in which they lived, asserting the mind of man to be its measure, and it amenable and subject to reason. The world they lived in was not only beautiful to the imagination, it was also reasonable, penetrable, and governed by the intellect.

Insofar as individual Greeks were concerned, without question high-minded Greek citizens of the time lived by a code of noble ideals. Justice Brandeis was fond of quoting from Pericles' funeral oration: "An Athenian spends himself in the service of the city as if his body were not his own, and counts his mind most his own when he is employed in her business."

Perhaps it should be said in passing that there are those who would emphasize another side of the Greek people, not altogether inconsistent with life in a golden age and to many not apparent through the veneer of artistic and intellectual glitter. They would call attention to and perhaps moralize upon the fact that erotic songs and poems were popular in ancient Greece, and were an accepted part of the nation's culture. Greek drama, which was closely connected with religion, was frequently obscene.

Having in mind the background of the "Golden Age of Athens" will enable one to better understand that it was short-lived. Plutarch tells us that after the death of Pericles in the plague of 429 B.C., "much corruption and a rage of wickedness" broke out upon the commonwealth, which he by proper restraints had palliated and kept from dangerous and destructive extremities.

Democracy and Tyranny. "Golden Ages" come and go. They are not inherently dependent on any particular form of government. The one in ancient Greece did not last, any more than did such ages under the emperors of Rome, or under the Muslim dynasties of medieval India. The democracy of Greece is of interest, not because of any close relationship between it and the artistic achievements of which we have been speaking, but rather because of its workings in the general affairs of men.

Greek democracy demonstrated that democratic institutions can be not only dangerously inefficient but that in their pure form they afford great opportunity for the unscrupulous manipulations of dangerous men. Writing over two thousand years ago the historian Polybius pointed this out. He said that the Athenian demos was always in the position of a ship without a commander. In such a ship, if fear of the enemy, or the occurrence of a storm, induces the crew to be of one mind and to obey the helmsman, everything goes well;

but if they recover from this fear and begin to treat their officers with contempt, and to quarrel with each other because they are no longer all of one mind—one party wishing to continue the voyage and the other urging the helmsman to bring the ship to anchor; some letting out the sheets and others hauling them in and ordering the sails to be furled—their discord and quarrels make a sorry show to lookers-on; and the position of affairs is full of risk to those on board engaged in the same voyage. The result has been that, after escaping the dangers of the widest seas, and the most violent storms, they wreck their ship in harbor and close to shore. "Therefore I say no more about it, or the Theban constitution, in both of which a mob manages everything on its own unfettered impulse," said Polybius, "a mob in the one city distinguished for its headlong outbursts of fiery temper, in the other trained for long habits of violence and ferocity."

Writing in modern times, Edward Van Dyke Robinson observed that in the case of Greece, the powers exercised by the Athenian Assembly and the Spartan Ephors needed but to come into the hands of one man, and behold a tyrant, master of the life and fortune of every citizen. The tyrant could be killed, but the tyranny remained. Whatever its form, the government was equally and necessarily a despotism; for its power over the individual was legally and morally unlimited. And when religion had lost its hold, when law no longer counted as a gift of the gods, but as an arbitrary command of a chance majority, when men came to contend not for principle but for plunder, and in the contest employed the power of the state as their chief and most effective weapon, then the full consequences of the omnipotence and centralization of government were brought to view. It is doubtful if history contains any page more sickening than that recording the events in Greece between the beginning of the Peloponnesian War and the Sack of Corinth.

So it was that the democratic institutions of Greece, which had come to vest all power in the popular assembly, provided an invitation and a training school for political maneuver and manipulation, the workings of which belied "golden age" refinement and higher beauty, and led to gross evils. Speaking of Greek and Roman democracy on the floor of the New York convention in June 1788, Alexander Hamilton pointed out it had been observed that a pure democracy, if it were practicable, would be the most perfect government. Experience had proved that no position in politics is more false than this. The very character of ancient democracies in which the people themselves deliberated, was tyranny. When they assembled, the field of debate presented an ungovernable mob, not only incapable of deliberation, but prepared for every enormity. In these assemblies, the enemies of the people brought forward their plans of ambition systematically. They were opposed by their enemies of another party, and the people subjected themselves to be led blindly by one tyrant or by another. Athens, when she had sunk so low that the lot decided the appointment to all important offices, would at that period have been freest, while in fact her government had become a plain democratic absolutism, one of the very worst of governments.

The working of such processes in Athens was exemplified by the action of the Assembly in voting the death penalty for the officers commanding the Athenian fleet at the Battle of Arginusae against the Spartans. The Athenian fleet won the victory. Orders were given to rescue the Athenians on the Athenian ships which were wrecked in the battle. Because of a severe storm it was impossible to carry out these orders. Nevertheless, over the vigorous protest of Socrates, who was presiding over the Assembly, that body persisted in carrying through the trial and imposing the death sentence for disobedience.

In short, Athenian democracy gave a demonstration for all time that there is such a thing as democratic tyranny. The Greek sentiment of local patriotism, of which we spoke at the outset, expressing itself in many city states, each with its own gods and sovereign in its own right, was not at home in the empire which Athens had achieved by sharp practice and force of arms. The individual of high ideals, immortalized by Pericles in his funeral oration, stood in constant peril of the demagogue, as we shall see dramatically demonstrated in the case of Socrates himself. As was stated in the Federalist, had every Athenian citizen been a Socrates, every Athenian assembly would still have been a mob.

Savagery and Treachery. The excesses of Athenian democracy were strikingly demonstrated, not only at home but also in the relations of Athens with her sister states. Thus, when a rebellion was suppressed in Mytilene, the Assembly, under the urging of Cleon, decreed that all the men of Mytilene should be killed and the women and children sold as slaves. In 416 B.C. the island of Mekos was wantonly invaded, and commanded to acknowledge subserviency to Athens. The Melians, who had been an independent city state for many centuries, refused. After a seige of several months the Athenian forces gained possession. All the men were put to death, the women and children were sold into slavery, and the island was repopulated by Athenian settlers.

The length to which treachery as well as savagery could go under such a regime was well exemplified by Alcibiades, an unworthy pupil of Socrates, whose bizarre career is identified with many pages of history. Exhorting the Assembly, and against the counsel of more discerning men, he induced almost unanimous approval of a great expedition to conquer Sicily, and was made one of the generals in command. Under a reversal of confidence, which developed while the expedition was enroute, he was summoned to return. Fearing to do so, he played the part of traitor and went over to Sparta. Through his machinations the Greeks were conclusively repulsed in Sicily. Although they might have escaped by sea had they moved promptly, as military tactics dictated, the religious fears of their leaders, brought about by an eclipse of the moon, led them to delay until they were set upon and practically annihilated. In the course of the repercussions in Athens the nobles attempted to overthrow the government and resume their former control. The Greek military refused to acquiesce. In the meantime, finding himself in trouble with the Spartans, Alcibiades had gone over to the Persians. But so strong was the feeling that he was the "indispensable man" that he was recalled to Athens to take military command. His history did not end at that point. After subsequent military defeats he was deposed, and eventually had to flee for his life.

Thus, over and over, was enacted the drama of bloodshed and treachery which comes perilously close to epitomizing the political life of Greece in the period of its fullest democracy.

The Judicial System. Democracy found other applications in its working in the Athenian judicial system. The volume of litigation was large. In the period of Athenian supremacy not only all cases arising in Athens itself but also, disregarding concepts of venue that are indigenous in America's legal system, all important cases arising throughout the whole empire were brought to Athens for trial in the Athenian courts. All civil jurisdiction was vested in a tribunal which was composed of six thousand jurymen, chosen annually by lot from the citizenry and divided into panels of five hundred each known as dicasteries.

Each case was assigned by lot to one of these dicasteries; the assignment by lot being on the theory of foreclosing bribery. Sometimes more than one dicastery participated in a hearing. Each citizen was expected to plead his own case. Handbooks, called rhetorics, and telling citizens how to conduct their cases, were written by professionals. One of these was prepared by Aristotle. In the course of time there developed "speech writers" whose activities eventually led them to fulfill the various forensic functions of lawyers. There were no instructions as to the law, the jurors being in effect judges as well as triers of the fact. Their oath was to judge according to their best judgment or conscience. There was no appeal from a dicastery decision; no higher tribunals were provided for appellate review.

Civilization reached a truly high peak in Greece, particularly in Athens. Writing was in general use. Public archives were established for the reception of documents. Trade and commerce were extensive. Here art found its masters. Here lived the father and founder of the science of medicine. The universe was explored, the sun known to be the center of the planetary system, the earth discovered to be round, and that the moon shines upon us with a reflected light of the sun. Geometry and astronomy were known sciences, improved upon since that time only to a limited extent. The eloquence of Demosthenes continues to reverberate in our ears, and the philosophy of Plato and Aristotle still, to a large extent, sways and molds the modern mind.

Here, in any event, we should expect to find a system of laws comparable to our own, a system devoid of superstition, perfect in procedure, and placing human rights on the high level to which they belong. But we are disappointed, and are led to suspect that general education and general intelligence were not on as high a level as the content of Greek literature would seem to indicate. No code of laws worthy of the name has come down to us. Even in Athens we find courts proceeding to condemn animals and inanimate objects which caused the death of a human being. While there was, apparently, a sufficient number of courts, and while certain cases for the repayment of debts—in order that property rights might be fully protected— were triable within thirty days after they were commenced, there were no judges, learned in the law, to direct the triers of facts, or to insure the decision of cases according to the law of the land. No written pleadings were required to define the issues. In fact, we find no evidence of a profession of lawyers, a profession absolutely necessary for a well-organized and stable system of law.

Jurors Make the Law. The reason, then, why the jurors who heard the cases received no instructions as to the law was simple: There was no general body of formal law and there were no judges, learned in the law. In practice Solon's Code had become largely disregarded, or abrogated, except as dicasteries chose to follow it. The Greeks did not develop, and adhere to, a systematic body of jurisprudence such as that which matured in Rome, and in England and the United States under the common law system.   Except to the small extent that statutory regulation and rules established by custom required—and these stood to be overruled by popular action if the dicasteries felt so moved—the common notions of justice which gained acceptance at the time by the dicastery hearing the case governed the decision.

These notions of justice were not allowed to materialize as the innermost solid concepts of right and wrong of those men charged with making the decision.   They were swayed by all the wiles of persuasion that forensic artisans could invoke.   In his Rhetoric, Aristotle defined rhetoric as the art of persuasion, to be effected either by working on the emotions of the jurors themselves, or by giving them the right impression of the speaker's character, "or by proving the truth of the statements made."   With all deference to Aristotle's great attainment, the content of the work is not reassuring in its relation to the processes for getting at the truth as practiced before the dicasteries.

With all its nobility and elasticity the Greek intellect was quite unable to confine itself within the strict waistcoat of a legal formula, and, if we may judge them from the peoples' courts of Athens, the Greek tribunals exhibited a strong tendency to confound law and fact. The arguments of the orators and the forensic commonplaces preserved by Aristotle in his treatise on Rhetoric, show that questions of pure law were constantly argued on every consideration which could possibly influence the minds of the jury.   No durable system of jurisprudence could be produced in this way.   A community which never hesitated to relax rules of written law when they stood in the way of an ideally perfect decision on the facts of the particular case would only, if it bequeathed any body of jurisprudence to posterity, bequeath one consisting of the ideas of right and wrong which happened to be prevalent at the time.   Such jurisprudence would contain no framework to which the more advanced conceptions of subsequent ages could be fitted.   It would amount at best to a philosophy marked with the imperfections of the civilization under which it evolved.

Accordingly, Greece never developed a complete system of private law—that portion of the law of the state which deals with the mutual relations and transactions of private individuals between themselves. This was something that remained for the more stable Romans to achieve.

Later Greek History.   Our primary purpose to note the development of the law and government of Greece would not be materially furthered by attempting more than a brief summary of the later events of Greek history. By the victory of Sparta in the Peloponnesian War, Athens was brought to a state of humiliating ruin from which she never fully recovered. For the time being the Athenian democracy was overthrown, and rule by the Thirty Tyrants was supported by Spartan soldiers. Spartan rule by force and treachery was ended with defeat by the Thebans under Epaminondas at Leuctra in 371 B.C. This brought Thebes into ascendancy. Messenia was liberated from Spartan control, and the freed Spartan helots built a new city, Messene.

Philip and Alexander the Great. But Thebes, like all other Greek cities, was weak from the ravages of war. The way was clear for the rising power of Macedonia to assert itself through Philip of Macedon. In his famous Philippics Demosthenes urged Athens to rally to save itself and its sister Greek cities. The Athenians were lethargic until Philip, acting under a commission to punish the Phocians for sacrilege in making secular use of lands consecrated to the Delphian Apollo, invaded central Greece. The hastily recruited Athenian and Theban forces were defeated at Chaerones in 338 B.C. by the Macedonian forces of Philip under the command of his son, Alexander, a pupil of Aristotle, who, as later events were to prove, had outstanding talents, military and cultural.

Greece thus came under Macedonian rule. At Corinth, under the dictate of Philip, a union of the Greek cities was accomplished, with the provision that each city was to furnish a contingent for a powerful military force to invade Persia. Following Philip's assassination, the Thebans revolted but Alexander, who had taken over, defeated them, razed Thebes to the ground and sold most of them as slaves.

In 334 B.C. Alexander led his forces across the Hellespont, and his invasion of Asia was on. After defeating the Persians at Issus he laid siege to and conquered Tyre, selling thousands of its inhabitants into slavery. The Jewish priests at Jerusalem, taking note of what he had done to Tyre, gave Alexander their allegiance. Egypt was the next conquest. Here he was crowned Pharaoh and established the city of Alexandria. At the temple of Zeus Ammon in the Libyan desert the priests announced that the oracle had designated Alexander as the son of Zeus, who was destined to rule the world. Thenceforth a world united by Greek learning and under Greek institutions was his goal.

Having routed the hosts of Darius at the Battle of Arbela, he conquered Babylon and Susa, taking vast quantities of loot. Conquering

Persepolis, he took still more loot, and also destroyed the palaces of the Persian kings and sold large numbers of the inhabitants into slavery.

At this stage Alexander laid claim to be ruler of Asia as well as of Greece, and assumed the role of an Oriental monarch. Leading his forces to the East, he carried his conquests to the Indus River in India, as we have seen. The greater his conquest, the greater his determination to Hellenize the world, with Greek the universal language. Ancient Babylon was to be the capital. Looking to this "one world," he encouraged intermarriages. He himself married a daughter of Darius III; many of his soldiers married Asiatic wives. Threatened by mutinous plots against his command, he put them down, but before he was able to consolidate his victories he was attacked by a fever and died in 323 B.C.

The great empire that Alexander had envisioned did not materialize. But through his conquests the language and culture of Greece were spread over a vast expanse of Asia. In turn, the Oriental influence, in general demoralizing rather than otherwise, was afforded entree into the West. Perhaps the most important aspect of Alexander's conquests was the foundation thereby laid for the later transmission and reception of Christianity.

After his death his empire fell into four parts—Macedonia and Greece, Thrace and western Asia Minor, Syria and the territory to the east, and Egypt. Eventually all fell to Rome. Macedonia and Greece were conquered by the Romans in 146 B.C., at which time Corinth was destroyed, its men killed, and its women and children sold into slavery. Syria became a part of the Roman Republic in 63 B.C. A succession of Ptolemies ruled Egypt until the death of Cleopatra in 30 B.C., when Egypt became a Roman province. Under the first Ptolemy, Alexandria in Egypt became the world's intellectual center.

The Legacy of Greek Philosophy. It would seem that, in so far as law goes, we have no jurisprudential heritage of consequence from Greece. In our sketch of Greek democracy we have noted a pragmatic dispensation of day-by-day justice, affording no legal content of more than passing interest to the citizen of today. Nevertheless, as Roscoe Pound has aptly said, in the realm of law and lawyers, as in nearly every other connection in the social sciences, the germs of our institutions are to be found in Greece.

The Greeks recognized the dignity of the human mind, and the importance of cultivating within it that freedom from passion and prejudice which enables reason to work its way through the labyrinth of searching thought, to truth. If this recognition was not given its proper due in the forensic jousting which characterized the working of the legal processes of Athens—and from all appearances it was not —it was nevertheless the starting point for the great minds of Athens whose contributions have enriched the world in the larger, permanent sense. And whatever may have been the dangers and abuses of Athenian democracy, it gave encouragement to the processes of thinking and provided an impetus for learning. Development of the mental powers by intellectual discipline was recognized as in itself a sufficient end. There was an awareness of the need for education as a preparation for citizenship. About the middle of the fifth century B.C. the Sophists appeared. They raised questions about everything, including the gods of the national religion. Although there was no constructive element in their approach to thought, in their wandering over Greece they stimulated the minds of the people and prepared them to assimilate the mental pabulum to come.

Before we draw the curtain on Greece we will do well to take brief note of the contribution made by the great minds of that country to the content of the world's philosophy, law and other fields of learning.

Anaxagoras. Our present purpose will be served by making mention of a few of the Greeks whose names are associated with higher learning in an outstanding way. Among these was Anaxagoras. Based on his observation of the celestial bodies and other manifestations of nature, Anaxagoras, the teacher of Pericles, introduced the conception that the world was not a product of chance but was rather the product of reason, which rules in all forms of life. His deduction was that everything in the universe was originally present in a state of infinitesimal fragments, inextricably admixed with the fragments of other things in a confused state. Through the operation of reason the like elements were brought together into their complete entities, these entities were coordinated in their relationship with each other, and the universe made to proceed along its ordered course. With the universe assembled these processes remain in continuous operation, manifested, for example, by what occurs to the body when it goes through a state of dissolution after death, its elements proceeding into new aggregations.

Such theories as these were not safe for the teacher in ancient Athens. The doctrine that unified reason was the creator and guide of the universe was manifestly at odds with Greek polytheism. Like Galileo of a later century, Anaxagoras found himself in conflict with the law. He was prosecuted under a decree that those who disputed the existence of the gods, or introduced new opinions about celestial appearances, should be tried before an assembly of the people. He escaped penalty because Pericles, not expecting any indulgence for him, caused him to quit the city.

Socrates. Few names in history are better known than the name of Socrates. His trial is one of the classics of ancient annals. The charge brought against him, corresponding to a present-day criminal indictment, was: "Socrates is guilty of crime, first, for not worshipping the gods whom the city worships, but in introducing new divinities of his own; next, for corrupting the youth. The penalty is death."

A modern criminal lawyer would probably move to quash such an indictment for indefiniteness, or demand a bill of particulars regarding "corrupting the youth" and "new divinities." The procedure of Athens knew no such refinements, and Socrates went to trial. He had not always been circumspect in his references to the accepted divinities. What was probably much more to the point, he had been critical of some aspects of Athenian democracy. That it was fairly open to criticism is obvious from what has heretofore been said. Today, such criticism would be regarded as an element inherent in the democratic process, essential to its successful working. Socrates had been guilty of nothing more than assuming and exercising the right of free speech.

The trial was before a dicastery of five hundred jurors. A majority of them were not impressed by his words, "If you propose to acquit me on condition that I abandon my search for truth, I will say: I thank you, O Athenians, but I will obey God, who, as I believe, set me this task rather than you, and as long as I have breath or strength I will never cease from my occupation with Philosophy." The sentence was death. The story of how he drank the hemlock has since been familiar to every generation which has had access to the fountain of Greek history.

The Offended Politicians. What were the beliefs and teachings of this man which made him so dangerous that he had to be killed? By reference to Plato's Apology, Crito and Phaedo we find significant enlightenment in the matter. In retrospect it would seem that his downfall was brought about not so much on account of his abstract ideas and teachings as because he offended the politicians who essayed to control the Athenian democracy. At his trial he disdained the apologetic tactics which might have gained acquittal or mitigated his punishment.

The shallowness of motivation of the charges is apparent from his statement of defense, as transcribed in the Apology. Explaining how he happened to start his career as an instigator of philosophical dialogues on the streets of Athens, he said his friend, Chaerephon, visited the oracle at Delphi and asked the oracle to tell him whether any one was wiser than Socrates. The Pythian prophetess answered that there was no man wiser. When Socrates heard this from his friend he said to himself: What can the god mean, and what is the interpretation of this riddle? For I know that I have no wisdom, small or great. What then can he mean when he says I am the wisest of men? And yet he is a god and cannot lie; that would be against his nature. After long consideration, continued Socrates, I thought of a method of trying the question. I reflected that if I could find a man wiser than myself, then I might go up to the god with a refutation in my hand. I should say to him, "Here is a man who is wiser than I am, but you say I am the wisest." Accordingly, I went to one who had the reputation of wisdom, and observed him—his name I need not mention; he was a politician whom I selected for the examination— and the result was as follows: When I began to talk with him, I could not help thinking that he was not really wise, although he was thought wise by many, and still wiser by himself; and thereupon I tried to explain to him that he thought himself wise, but was not really wise; and the consequence was he hated me, and his enmity was shared by several who were present and heard me. So I left him, saying to myself, as I went away: Well, although I do not suppose that either of us knows anything really beautiful and good, I am better off than he is—for he knows nothing, and thinks that he knows; I neither know nor think that I know. In this latter particular, then, I seem to have slightly the advantage of him. Then I went to another who had still higher pretention to wisdom, and my conclusion was exactly the same. Whereupon I made another enemy of him, and of many others besides him.

"I Would Run the Risk, Having Law and Justice With Me." Coming to the matter of his own principles, Socrates said that a man ought not to calculate the chance of living or dying; he ought only to consider whether in doing anything he is doing right or wrong—acting the part of a good man or of a bad. "I do nothing," said he, "but go about persuading you all, old and young alike, not to take thought for your persons or your properties, but first and chiefly to care about the improvement of the soul. I tell you that virtue is not given by money, but that from virtue comes money and every other good of

man, public as well as private. This is my teaching, and if this is the doctrine which corrupts the youth, I am a mischievous person. Strange, indeed, would be my conduct, O men of Athens, if I, who, when I was ordered by the generals whom you chose to command me at Potidaea and Amphipolis and Delius, remained where they placed me, like any other man, facing death—if now, when, as I conceive and imagine, God orders me to fulfill the philosopher's mission of searching into myself and other men, I were to desert my post through fear of death or any other fear; that would indeed be strange."

We have already referred to the death sentence imposed by the Assembly upon the Athenian generals who did not effect a rescue of the Athenian naval personnel whose ships were wrecked in the Battle of Arginusae, and against which Socrates protested. Alluding to this, Socrates told the jurors: "I gave my vote against you, and when the orators threatened to impeach and arrest me, and you called and shouted, I made up my mind that I would run the risk, having law and justice with me, rather than take part in your injustice because I feared imprisonment and death."

In Plato's Crito, recording the conversation between Crito and Socrates in his prison cell, Socrates is said to have replied to Crito's question as to doing evil in return for evil, "which is the morality of the many," that "we ought not to retaliate or render evil for evil to any one, whatever evil we have suffered from him." The Bible student will find this reminiscent of the injunction of Solomon, "If thine enemy be hungry, give him bread to eat, and if he be thirsty, give him water to drink" and anticipatory of Paul's teaching "being reviled, we bless, being persecuted, we suffer it."

We have emphasized the intellectual atmosphere which developed in Athens, and the respect accorded to the operation of the mind. Without question there had been much latitude of expression in the Athenian democracy. At times it probably went to extremes. But when it did, it was popularly slanted, and met with toleration because it tallied with mass approval. There was no fundamental law which guaranteed the right of free speech. In the absence of such, the advocate of the minority point of view spoke at his peril, and he who made unpopular utterances in his own individual behalf was in extreme jeopardy. The trial of Socrates demonstrated for all posterity that only by constitutional guaranty can the right to raise a minority voice be freely assured.

In his Phaedo, after discoursing on the nature of the other world to which the soul goes after death, Plato quotes Socrates as saying that as a man of sense he is not confident of the exact truth of the description. "But I do say," said he, "that inasmuch as the soul is shown to be immortal, he may venture to think, not improperly or unworthily, that something of the kind is true. The venture is a glorious one, and he ought to comfort himself with words like these. Wherefore I say, let a man be of good cheer about his soul, who having cast away the pleasures and ornaments of the body as alien to him and working harm rather than good, has sought after the pleasures of knowledge, and has arrayed the soul, not in some foreign attire, but in her own proper jewels, temperance and justice, and courage, and nobility, and truth—in these adorned, she is ready to go on her journey to the world below, when her hour comes."

Plato's Republic. It has been said that Plato found philosophy a city of brick and left it a city of gold. It is hardly necessary to attempt an amplification of such an encomium. Plato believed the human mind to be capable of ascertaining absolute truth, and that reason enabled such truth to be used as the guide for life. He was a student of Socrates, and in his writings imitated the method of Socrates in conversation. Socrates himself was depicted as a participant in many of the dialogues. It is not always possible to know whether the thought expressed originated directly with Socrates, or was that of Plato himself. For all practical purposes it does not matter.

Of classic interest is the Republic, in which Plato dealt with the makeup and organization of the ideal state. In attempting to arrive at this consummation he went at length into a consideration of "justice." A proper understanding of his thought is conditioned upon the realization that "justice" was considered by him not in the popular limited sense as what is right as between conflicting interests, but rather is the broader aspect of what is virtuous and good—that which promotes and makes possible the best in man.

Plato introduced his consideration of justice by pointing out that it is sometimes spoken of as the virtue of an individual, sometimes as the virtue of the state. Because it may be more readily discernible in the larger framework of the state, its analysis may profitably start there. A state arises out of the needs of mankind. No one is self-sufficing, but all of us have many wants. Many persons are needed to supply those wants. One takes a partner for one purpose and another for another; and when these partners and helpers are gathered together in one habitation the body of inhabitants is termed a state. The aim in founding a state is not the disproportionate happiness of any one class but the greatest happiness of the whole.

Each Citizen to His Own Talent. In the interest of justice, each person in the state belongs in the niche for which his natural qualifications have endowed him. "There are diversities of natures among us which are adapted to different occupations." The shoemaker was not allowed to be a husbandman, or a weaver, or a builder, "but to him and to every other worker was assigned one work for which he was by nature fitted, and at which he was to continue working all his life long and at no other. Justice is this principle or a part of it."

But the state involves more than an aggregation of people working in a routine society. These constitute one element—the masses. There are two others: the "guardians," or rulers, and the warriors. Here, too, the principle of fitness for the job is applicable. Those would be guardians who are physically brave and strong and have the mental quality of the love of wisdom, which is philosophy. The good and noble guardian of the state will unite in himself philosophy and spirit and swiftness and strength.

Rulers Must Obey the Laws. Plato's high concept of justice as we would use the term in its relation to clash of interest between man and man is indicated by the statement that the rulers should be those to whom would be entrusted the office of determining suits at law. And a basic principle—one which we will later on note in the Ten Commandments, ultimately embodied in the Roman law and the common law of England and America—is the admonition that suits are not decided on any other ground but that a man may neither take what is another's, nor be deprived of what is his own.

Long anticipating the pronouncement of Lord Coke of England that the law is above the King, Plato said that the guardians themselves must obey the laws, and they must also imitate the spirit of them in any details that are entrusted to their care. Judge Wilkin has said that twenty-five hundred years ago Plato, in his philosophy of morals, law and government, which has been referred to as the most brilliant achievement in the entire history of human thought, stated that the ideal government would be a government of law; strong enough to maintain law and order and itself subject to law.

"Men of Gold, Silver, Brass and Iron." In postulating his ideal state upon each person performing his own separate function, Plato recognized the human being as a person with a part to play in his group. It would hardly have been consistent had Plato advocated a class society which denied the individual a right of opportunity to achieve the place for which he was best adapted. He did not do this. He went far, also, in according equal rights and duties to women in

accordance with their individual capacities, concluding, "let our women strip, and let virtue be their robe." It was his position that each should find his role according to his qualifications.

"Citizens, we shall say to them in our tale," he declared, "you are brothers, yet God has framed you differently. Some of you have the power of command, and in the composition of these he has mingled gold, wherefore also they have the greatest honor. Others he has made of silver, to be auxiliaries; others again who are to be husbandmen and craftsmen he has composed of brass and iron; and the species will generally be preserved in the children." But as all are of the same original stock, a golden parent will sometimes have a silver son, or a silver parent a golden son. And God proclaims as a first principle to the rulers, and above all else, that there is nothing which they should so anxiously guard, or of which they are to be such good guardians, as of the purity of the race. They should observe what elements mingle in their offspring; for if the son of a golden or silver parent has an admixture of brass and iron, then nature orders a transposition of ranks, and the eye of the ruler must not be pitiful towards the child because he has to descend in the scale and become a husbandman or artisan, just as there may be sons of artisans who having an admixture of gold or silver in them are raised to honor, and become guardians or auxiliaries. "For an oracle says that when a man of brass or iron guards the state, it will be destroyed."

History has demonstrated only too emphatically the truth of this oracular assertion about men of "brass or iron" controlling the destiny of states. Millions now living have witnessed its exemplification.

Community of Wives. In his zeal to promote "golden" sons, however, Plato espoused practices that carry beyond the pale of the moral concepts of civilization. He proposed that women would be selected and given to the guardians of the state, to live in common houses and meet at common meals. "None of them will have anything especially his or her own," he proposed. "They will be together, and will be brought up together. The best of either sex should be united with the best as often, and the inferior with the inferior as seldom, as possible." The braver and the better youth ought to have as many sons as possible. The proper officials will take the children of the good parents to the fold, and there will place them with certain nurses who dwell in a separate quarter. The offspring of the inferior, or of the better if they are deformed, will be taken to some mysterious and unknown place."

Education for All. Education for all was stressed by Plato. "If our citizens are well educated, and grow into sensible men, they will easily see their way through all these, as well as other matters which I omit," said he. The state, if once started well, moves with accumulating force like a wheel. For good nurture and education implant good constitutions, and these good constitutions taking root in a good education improve more and more. "This is the point to which, above all, the attention of our rulers should be directed—that music and gymnastic be preserved in their original form, and no innovation made. They must do their utmost to maintain them intact. And when any one says that mankind must regard the newest song which the singers have they will be afraid that he may be praising, not new songs, but a new kind of song; and this ought not to be praised, or conceived to be the meaning of the poet; for any musical innovation is full of danger to the whole state and ought to be prohibited. So Damon tells me, and I can well believe him—he says that when the modes of music change, the basic laws of the state always change with them."

As to the warrior class, they must be given such education as will have the greatest tendency to civilize and humanize them in their relations to one another, and to those who are under their protection. None of them should have property of their own beyond what is absolutely necessary. "We will tell them they have gold and silver from God. The diviner metal is within them, and they have therefore no need of the dross which is current among men."

How War Comes. The need for warriors Plato indicated in terms only too often identifiable with history. Ultimately, said he, the country which was enough to support the original inhabitants will be too small, and not enough. The ranks of the agriculturists, artisans and tradesmen who supply the necessities of food, clothing and shelter will be augmented by others who provide the "relish" for the food, and other luxuries. The country which was enough to support the original inhabitants becomes too small. "Then a slice of our neighbor's land will be desired by us for pasture and tillage, and they will desire a slice of ours, if, like us, they exceed the limit of necessity. And so we will go to war. Then, without deciding as yet whether war makes for good or evil, this much we can say, that now we have discovered war to be derived from causes which are also the cause of most of the evils in states, private as well as public."

The Just Man. Of necessity, of course, Plato finally granted that the ideal state of which his characters had been speaking was unattainable. His conclusion was that until philosophers are kings, or the kings and princes of this world have the spirit and power of philosophy, and political greatness and wisdom meet, and those commoner natures who pursue either to the exclusion of the other are compelled to stand aside, cities will never have surcease from their evils, nor will the human race. Plato was thus thinking of greatness of qualification in terms of rulers. With a government of the people, the same thought would have to be carried to the people themselves: "political greatness and wisdom" must meet in the people who are the government.

But whatever might be said as to the perfect state, Plato insisted that the principles brought out in the analysis looking to such a state have application to the ascertainment of who is the just man. The justice of the state consists in each citizen doing well with his own work. The individual in whom the several qualities of his nature do well their own work will be a just individual. Anticipatory of Paul's reminder that "for as we have many members in one body, and all members have not the same office" Plato said the just man does not permit the several elements within him to interfere with one another, or any of them to do the work of others—he sets in order his own inner life, and is his own master and his own law, and at peace within himself. When he has bound together the three principles within him, which may be compared to the higher, lower and middle notes on the scale, and the intermediate intervals—when he has bound all these together, and is no longer many but has become one entirely temperate and perfectly adjusted being, then he proceeds to act, if act he must, whether in a matter of property, or in the treatment of the body, or in his business; always thinking and calling that which preserves and cooperates with this harmonious condition just action, and the knowledge which directs it, wisdom. That which at any time impairs this condition he will call unjust action, and the opinion which directs it, ignorance.

Nothing is more closely related to wisdom than truth, Plato insisted. The same person cannot be a lover of wisdom and a lover of falsehood. He whose desires are for knowledge in every form will be absorbed in the pleasures of the spirit, and will hardly sense bodily pleasure. He will never entrust his bodily functions to the irrational pleasures of the beast within him. He will not be dazzled by the popular idea that wealth means happiness.

Accordingly, such a man would never be guilty of sacrilege or theft, or treachery either to his friends or to his country, neither will he ever break his covenant where there have been oaths or agreements. He will be more unlikely to commit adultery, or to dishonor his father and mother, or to be remiss in his religious obligations. Expressing the thought later enunciated by Christ that "for what is a man profited if he shall gain the whole world and lose his own soul" Plato said that a man would not profit if he received gold and silver on the condition that he was to enslave the noblest part of him to the worst.

Short Shrift for Individual Freedom. As exemplified by the fate of Socrates, we have seen that Greece accorded short shrift to individual freedom in the sense in which it is conceived by the citizens of the United States—the right to differ in opinion from the majority, to voice such difference, and, within limits set only by recognition of similar individual rights of others and the police power of the state, to act accordingly. Man appeared to the ancients in his highest and noblest character when they considered him as a member of the state or as a political being. Men could rise no higher in their view. Citizenship was in their eyes the highest phase of humanity. To Plato, it was a mistake to think that laws can be given for the public conduct of states, but that the private life of citizens may be left wholly to the care of itself. The modern notion of individual freedom would have seemed monstrous to Plato.

With all respect to Plato and his profound philosophical compatriots, it may be said that they did not have a monopoly on Greek thought. We must digress to say that happily, other Greeks bequeathed signs of greater discernment in this regard, showing consciousness of the concept of the conscience in the role of guide for human action and awareness of the tragic consequences which ensue when freedom to stand on it is denied.

Such was the theme of Sophocles in his Theban play, Antigone. To make an example of Polynices, who had presumed to invade the city, King Creon ordered that his dead body should be disgraced by being left, unburied, where it lay, to provide a feast for carrion birds. To Antigone, his sister, this was unthinkable. After she was caught in the act of pouring a layer of earth over the body from a bronze urn, she was brought before Creon, who asked her if she knew the order forbidding the act, and had dared to contravene it. Her reply was an inspiring classic of defense, but her words were unavailing and, in the due course of dramatic progression, she was led to her fate.

Aristotle. Aristotle was a fit successor to his master, Plato. His studies and writings were exhaustive, carrying him into the whole world of knowledge. Thus, he raised the question as to what is the chief good of man. He answered it by saying that it consists in the evocation of man's highest faculty, reason. The greatest happiness is to be found in the contemplation and speculative thought by which reason is exercised and developed. Agreeing with Plato, he tied the individual in with the state. Neither virtue nor happiness can be attained by the individual separately. Moral development and the realization of personal powers require as external conditions a settled community, social habits, the restraint and protection of law, and a wisely regulated system of public education. The state is a primary necessity to man. Its mission is to train men for noble lives.

As to free citizens, Aristotle recognized a personal dignity that would afford them latitude to develop their internal control over prejudice and passion and thereby bring them freedom as the Greeks conceived it. But he looked upon women as stunted men, inferior by nature, and therefore not deserving of the emancipation suggested by Plato. Likewise, he held slavery to be in accordance with nature, and regarded it as justifiable to make war on and reduce to slavery those races which were presumably inferior and therefore destined by nature for such a lot. Inferior peoples found their highest expression in serving the Greek "master race."

"A Government of Laws." Consistent with his general philosophy, Aristotle identified law with reason. The rule of law, he said, is preferable to that of any individual, and he who bids the law to rule may be deemed to bid God and Reason alone rule, but he who bids man rule adds an element of the beast; for desire is a wild beast, and passion perverts the minds of rulers, even when they are the best of men, whereas the law is reason unaffected by desire. As Judge Jerome Frank has pointed out, it is from Aristotle that we derive the concept of "a government of laws and not of men."

Speaking on the same theme, Edwin S. Corwin observed that nearly two thousand years after Aristotle, the sense of his conclusion, condensed into Harrington's famous phrase "a government of laws and not of men," was to find its way successfully into the Massachusetts Constitution of 1780, and into Chief Justice Marshall's opinion in *Marbury v. Madison.* The opposition which it discovers between the desire of the human governor and the reason of the law lies, indeed, at the foundation of the American interpretation of the doctrine of the separation of powers and so of the entire American system of constitutional law.

The Separation of Powers. The principle of the separation of powers as we know it in our government, and as we will deal with it in due course, arises from the same concept as "a government of laws and not of men." We have already noted its recognition by Solon in his Code. Aristotle himself developed the doctrine in some detail. In his Politics he said that there are three elements in every government, which the good lawgiver must consider separately as to their utility. If these are found, the government will be sound; and governments differ from each other in so far as any one of these elements is different. One of these three is that which deliberates concerning the common welfare; the second has to do with administration; and the third with judicial action.

Commenting on this, Edward Van Dyke Robinson observed that we have here the familiar division into legislative, executive and judiciary. This distinction was made, the way was open for further advance. Aristotle had distinguished the three parts of a mixed government, he had also distinguished the three functions of government. Why did he not combine the two ideas and assign each function to a separate organ? Had he done so, he would have anticipated Locke and Montesquieu.

But this combination, obvious as it seems today, was not then possible. It presupposes what it took two thousand stormy and eventful years to create—the national representative system. For the division of power in this its modern form rests upon one fact alone—that the sovereign does not act directly except when ordaining and amending the constitution; whence it follows that the several organs of government created by the constitution stand upon an equal footing as regards each other, each being supreme in its own sphere. But so long as the sovereign, whether the one, or the few, or the many—especially if the many—is in his own person a part of the government, the other parts must necessarily be subordinate appendages. Such a sovereign was the Greek Assembly, and for this reason the modern division of power was, in ancient times, not only impossible, but even inconceivable.

Natural Law. The concept of natural law, which as we shall see further in our consideration of Roman law has played such an important part in the development of law, was embodied in Aristotle's thinking. He recognized the existence of a natural as well as of a legal justice, mentioning as an ordinary device of rhetoric the distinction which may be drawn between the written law and the common law which is in accordance with nature and immutable. Particular law, Aristotle said, is that which each community lays down and applies to its own members; this is partly written and partly unwritten. Universal law is the law of nature. For there really is, as every one to some extent divines, a natural justice and injustice that is binding on all men, even on those who have no association or covenant with each other. It is this that Sophocles' Antigone clearly means when she says that the burial of Polynices was a just act in spite of the prohibition of Cleon; she means that it was just by nature's inherent principles: "Not of yesterday or today, but everlasting."

Equity. Aristotle was the first philosopher to clarify the conception of human rights. As Professor Barna Horvath has said, Aristotelian justice, symbolized by the emblem of the balance, requires an exact accounting of what is due each one, whether in distributing rewards according to merits, or in redressing wrongs to property, wrongs in contracts, as well as torts and crimes.

In this connection it is particularly interesting to take note of what Aristotle had to say about that segment of every system of jurisprudence which in legal terminology is known as equity. It is sometimes said that equity is as old as Aristotle. This is confirmed by his analysis. In his Nichomachean Ethics he raised the question as to the relation of equity to justice. He said that equity, though just, is not the justice of the law courts, but a method of restoring the balance of justice when it has been tilted by the law. By way of elucidation he went on to say that the need for such a rectification arises from the circumstance that law can do no more than generalize, and there are cases which cannot be settled by a general statement. So in matters where it is necessary to make a general statement, and yet that statement cannot exclude the possibility of error, the law takes no account of particular cases, though well aware that this is not a strictly correct proceeding.

Yet this does not make it a bad law, the error lying not in the law or the lawgiver but in the nature of the case; the data of human behavior simply will not be reduced to uniformity. So when a case arises where the law states a general rule, but there is an exception to the rule, it is then right when the lawgiver owing to the generality of the language left a loophole for the error to creep in, to fill the gap by such a modified statement as the lawgiver himself would make, if he was present at the time, and such an enactment as he would have made, if he had known the special circumstances.

So although it is true that equity is just and in some circumstances is better than justice, it is not better than absolute justice. The most we can say is that it is better than the error which arises from the unqualified language in which absolute justice must be stated. Equity essentially is just this rectification of the law, where the law has to be amplified because of the general terms in which it has to be stated.

This in fact is the reason why everything is not regulated by law; it is because there are cases which no law can be framed to cover, and which can be dealt with only by a special rule. It is useless to apply a definite measure to something indefinite; we must be like the Lesbian architects and use a leaden rule. Just as that rule is flexible and can be bent to take the shape of the stone, so a special decree or rule can be made to fit the peculiar condition.

Aristotle then proceeded to pay his respects to the equitable man, saying that he is one who by deliberate choice has taught himself the habit of doing equitable things, who is not a stickler for his rights to the disadvantage of others, but refrains from pressing his claims even when he has the law on his side.

Demosthenes. Demosthenes is ordinarily thought of as a distinguished orator rather than a philosopher. Some of his utterances, however, embodied a noteworthy philosophic content. Of particular present interest, because it is expressive of the concept of natural law which we have previously noted as embodied in the thinking of Aristotle, was his statement in his famous oration on the Crown, in 330 B.C.: "Among all other peoples I find these principles in a manner defined and settled: Does a man wilfully offend? He is the object of wrath and punishment. Has a man erred unintentionally? There is a pardon instead of punishment for him. Has a man devoted himself to what seemed for the general good, and without any fault or misconduct been, in common with all, disappointed of success? Such a one deserves not obloquy or reproach, but sympathy. These principles will not be found in our statutes only. Nature herself has defined them by her unwritten laws and the feelings of humanity."

Here, in short, is a law higher than the formal legal enactments of man. From the brief context of Demosthenes' statement, its general purport is clear. It expresses justice in moral terms that all can understand, and that all thinking men can approve. The one who inflicts intentional injury is blameworthy; the one who does not mean to harm is not. And although this higher law is unwritten, it is revealed to men through their "feelings" as human beings—in other words, their consciences.

The Stoics and Epicureans. The waning political power of Hellas was not accompanied by a concurrent decline in philosophical thought. Following Aristotle came the Stoic school, founded by Zeno, a Phoenician merchant, about 310 B.C. It derived its name from the Stoa, or porch, at Athens, where the disciples of the school assembled.

Modern Christians too often fail to take into account the fact that

the thinkers who formulated and defended orthodox doctrines were
under the influence of philosophical pattern of the Graeco-Roman
world.   Most of us on reading "I and the Father are one" rightly
enough take it and treasure it as a unique and dependable declaration of the status that Christ alone had.   We little realize that such a
relationship to God is implicit in Stoic philosophy, then the dominant
thought of educated men.

The Stoics believed in the equality of all men, under a universal
Reason, to which all men ought to conform.   Man's duty was to live
and develop himself in conformity with that Reason.   A virtuous
life was the end in itself.   That desideratum was attained by rigid
adherence to the dictates of duty, which embodied the obligation to
help other men as members of the same human family.

As Edward S. Corwin has said, while Aristotle's natural justice was
conceived primarily as a norm and guide for law makers, the *jus
naturale* of the Stoic was the way of happiness for all men.   The
supreme legislator was nature herself; nor was the natural order the
merely material one which modern science exploits.   The concept
which Stoicism stressed was that of a moral order, wherein man,
through his divinely given capacity of reason, was directly participant with the gods themselves.   Nature, human nature and reason
were one.   The conception was manifestly an ethical, rather than a
political or legal one, and for good cause.   Stoicism arose on the ruins
of the Greek city state.   Plato's and Aristotle's belief that human
felicity was to be achieved mainly by political means had proven illusory; thrown back on his own resources, the Greek developed a new
outlook, at once individualistic and cosmopolitan.

On the other hand, Epicurus, a contemporary of Zeno, headed a
school of thought which held that the world was not a creation of
divine power, ordered by reason, but an accident.   It was not believed that there was such a thing as settled principles of right and
wrong.   It was for each individual to determine his conduct by his
own apparent self interest.   Pleasure was held to be the highest good.
Virtue was not decried, but it was regarded as only a means to the
end of achieving pleasurable satisfaction.   As conceived by Epicurus,
a good life probably extended to no more harmful pursuits than reading good literature and conversing with stimulating friends, as intellectual activity would presumably bring the greatest happiness.
But such a philosophy, as it reached the masses, became, almost inevitably, one of "eat, drink and be merry, for tomorrow we die."

The Continuity of Greek Culture.   We may well leave it to Lord

Bryce to pronounce the Epilogue. He said that the Greek type of civilization, and to some extent the Greek population also, spread out over the regions around the eastern Mediterranean and the Euxine. Presently the conquests of Rome brought all those regions, as well as the western countries as far as Caledonia, under one government. This produced a uniform type of civilization which was Greek on the side of thought and literature and of art, Roman on the side of law and institutions. Then came Christianity, which in giving to all these countries one religion and one standard of morality, created a still deeper sense of unity among them. Thus the ancient world, omitting the barbarous north and the semi-civilized heathen who dwelt beyond the Euphrates, became unified, the backward races having been raised, at least in the upper strata of their population, to the level of the more advanced. One government, one faith, and two languages were making out of the mass of races and kingdoms that had existed before the Macedonian conquest a single people, who were at once a nation and a world nation.

The process was not quite complete when it was interrupted by the political dissolution of the Roman dominion, first through the immigration of the Teutonic peoples from the north, then by the terrible strokes dealt at the already weakened empire by the Arab conquerors from the southeast. The results that had been attained were not wholly lost, for Europe clung to the Greco-Roman-Christian civilization, though in a lowered form and with a diminished sense of intellectual as well as political unity. Several centuries passed. Then, at first faintly from the twelfth century onwards, afterwards more swiftly from the middle of the fifteenth century, when the intellectual impulse given by the Renaissance began to be followed by the rapid march of geographical discovery along the coasts of Africa, in America, and in the further East, the process was resumed.

And so we draw the curtain on Greece, politically defunct, but leaving a cultural heritage destined to permanently enrich the spiritual life of mankind. Modern Greece, an honorable nation without the emoluments of physical power, points with dignity to the leading role it played in the earlier acts of the world's great historical drama.

PART III: ROME'S GREAT LEGACY

CHAPTER 6

ROME UNDER THE KINGS

The Beginnings of Rome. In spite of Rome's great part in history and its great legacy of law and legal institutions, it is not possible to give an accurate account of its beginnings. Legend has it that it was established about the middle of the eighth century B.C. by the Etruscans. Suffice it to say that settlements on the seven hills were eventually combined together to constitute the city state of Rome, and a government came into being.

As we first know them, its peoples manifested a culture indicative of a fairly advanced civilization. Rome was governed by a rex, or king, who exercised power of a patriarchal nature. He was the supreme judge in all private and public matters, the commander-in-chief in time of war, and the source of all magisterial power. All inferior officers were subject to his power and removal. The Roman kings, or Tarquins, were Etruscans, and it has been said that they were not of the Italian race.

The Basic Importance of Religion. It is well to emphasize at the outset the basic importance of religion in Roman life. From the earliest period many centuries before the birth of Christ through the era following the decree of the Emperor Constantine integrating Christianity with the state, religion provided a decisive influence on both public and private life. As with the ancient Egyptians, Babylonians, Hebrews and Greeks, law was a part of religion. Polybius said that a "scrupulous fear of the gods" was the "very thing" that kept the Roman commonwealth together. Not the least important of the functions of the early kings was that of high priest of the national religion.

Many Roman gods and goddesses were identified with those of Greece. Greece had its Zeus: Jupiter held the corresponding place at the top of the Roman pantheon. Other Roman divinities personified the various aspects and activities of life. Mars was the god of war, Vulcan the god of fire, Neptune the god of the sea, Mercury the god of trade, Apollo the god of healing, Venus the god of love, Juno the goddess of married life, Minerva the goddess of learning, Diana the moon goddess, and Ceres the goddess of growing things. Vesta was the goddess of fires on the household hearths, and in the temple of Vesta sacred fires were kept burning continuously by Roman virgins. In the sense of personal freedom these vestal virgins were privileged above all other Roman women. They could not marry, but were freed from the absolute control of their fathers of which we shall presently speak. The sacred repute of their office was exemplified by the fact that a criminal on the way to execution who chanced to meet a vestal virgin was forthwith freed. In addition to the national gods of Rome, each locality had its patron god.

All activities of life were ordered to rendering the gods their due. Not to conform to their exactions was to insult them; to insult them was to break the law. But a reciprocal arrangement was presupposed: the gods rewarded the reverence paid them by providing the appropriate bounty. When public calamities or crop failures occurred the fault was deemed to lie in the failure of men to do right by the gods, and efforts to appease the gods were redoubled. So strong was the feeling of obligation to the gods that when it came to be admitted that the will of a man or vote of the people might make law, it was thought to be still necessary that religion should be consulted, and that there should be some attestation of the augurs that the gods approved.

As did the Greeks, the Romans conceived of the gods coming down from heaven. Amazing testimony to the genuineness of this religious belief is found in the detailed and shocking report, by Josephus, of a discreditable incident connected with the Temple of Isis in Rome, in 33 A.D. Because of the immoral use to which this belief lent itself in this unworthy case, the Emperor Tiberius ordered the crucifixion of the priests of Isis, had their temple demolished, and gave orders that the statue of Isis be thrown in the river Tiber.

The Roman religion before Christianity offered no guide or inspiration to conduct on the basis of ethical principles. Nor in it was reason a factor. Rather, the governing motive was what Professor Brendan F. Brown has characterized as a non-philosophic paganism, deifying the emotions and indorsing irrational excesses, such as those included in the worship of Bacchus.

As time went on, religion evolved into an effective implement of Roman imperialism. To bring conquered lands into immediate religious unity with Rome, centers were established therein for worship of the Roman emperor. For this purpose temples were erected, manned by an appropriate priesthood, and elaborate observances and festivals were promoted. Needless to say, the cost was met by local exactions.

Patricians, Clients, Plebeians and Slaves. There were four sharply defined classes of people in Rome: the populus Romanus, or patricians; the clients; the plebeians, and the slaves. The patricians were those who traced descent from the old Etruscan families. The clients would be referred to today, colloquially, as "hangers-on" of the patricians. In the main they were freed slaves, and their descendants and conquered people who had not been made slaves. Slaves were what the term implies, being for the most part captives taken in the numerous conquests engaged in by Rome. All others—and they were very numerous—were plebeians. Most of them were persons who had come to Rome from elsewhere and taken up abode there, attracted by the apparent prosperity of the Romans, and finding it agreeable to work for them.

All but the slaves were free persons. However, only the patricians enjoyed all the rights of Roman citizenship, which included the right to hold and bequeath property, to contract a religious marriage, to vote, to hold office and to appeal to the popular assembly from a magistrate's decision in a criminal case. Patricians were not subject to torture as witnesses, except when accused of treason. They claimed for themselves the exclusive right to occupy the public lands. The main concern of clients was not in individual rights, but rather to retain their "hanger-on" status, which was rewarded by support in some financial form from their patrician patrons. The plebeians belonged to no gens and were not within the operative pale of the Roman religion. They were held liable for taxes and for military service, in return for which they were regarded as citizens and granted the right to engage in trade and, within limits, to hold property and slaves, but they were denied other rights accorded to Roman citizens, including the right to marry patricians, to marry religiously, or to hold important offices of state. They were not exempt from torture when called as witnesses.

Those who were brought to Rome as slaves were committed to a status from which there was no escape, save as an enlightened owner might confer the boon of freedom. The status was hereditary. Having power of life or death over his slaves, the master could compel them to be gladiators or prostitutes. Such marriage relations as were allowed between them were dissolvable at the owner's whim. Slaves were subject to torture to compel them to give evidence.

Slavery itself was an accepted ancient institution, but it would be disappointing if history recorded no objection to this matter of slave torture. It is reassuring to note that it does. As Justice Joseph Story pointed out, Cicero, though he lived in a state wherein it was usual to put slaves to the torture to furnish evidence, denounced the absurdity and wickedness of the measure in terms of glowing eloquence, as striking as they are brief. They were conceived in the spirit of Tacitus, and breathe all his pregnant and indignant sarcasm. Ulpian, also, at a still later period in Roman jurisprudence, stamped the practice with severe reproof.

Unfortunately for later generations of human beings, the practice of torturing persons for the purpose of extorting admissions of wrong-doing which started with the slaves of Rome did not stop with them, but extended and spread itself throughout western Europe. The ecclesiastical courts, to which we shall later refer in dealing with the Church, took it up. The practice of interrogation on mere suspicion because of rumor became the usual procedure in ecclesiastical courts throughout Christendom, including England. Heresy was more likely to be committed in the mind than it was by deed or by word. Witnesses to a man's non-conformist thoughts, or even to his repute, sometimes were difficult if not impossible to procure. Such interrogation was initiated by the judge himself, acting not on formal accusation, but by simple virtue of his office, i.e., *ex-offico*. The oath which those suspected of heresy were compelled to take, in the hope that a confession sufficient to establish guilt could be wrung from their reluctant lips, became known as the oath *ex-officio*. Up to the middle of the seventeenth century torture was used to extort confessions, and there was no serious contention that such extorted confessions were inadmissible against the victim. The practice was finally disapproved by the common law, and in the United States was outlawed by the Fifth Amendment. But compulsory self-incrimination is today part of the established procedure in the law of continental Europe.

The Roman Family. In the present study we are not stopping to quibble about technical definitions of "law." We are concerned in a broad way with the conduct of human beings in organized society, and it is obvious to any observer that their external motivation is not traceable to any one source, to the exclusion of others.

To be sure, we ordinarily think of "law" as the law of the state, by which, of course, all must live. But as we have already noted, we do not live altogether as individuals, but rather as members of groups. At the basis is the family association. Outside and beyond that are the churches, labor unions, trade associations, social and professional organizations to which one or another nearly every individual belongs. Even the modern American family lives under some customary rules of conduct. These external associations are constituted and conducted under definite ordered systems of their own, in conformity, of course, to the basic law of the state.

In the large sense we have, then, what are in effect two systems of "law," one public and the other private. In the light of what was said at the beginning of this study, we might well conclude that there was private law before there was public law, because public law contemplates a degree of governmental organization that came only with the advance of civilization beyond its primitive stage. The natural tendency of public law, once in operation, is to encroach on private law and to tend to occupy the entire field of regulating conduct. To the extent that it does not occupy that entire field is latitude reserved for action not under the sanction of the state. As we would see it, this is in the interest of freedom.

The Roman state originally stayed out of the realm of the family. This is something of no small significance. The oldest period in Rome was distinguished by a thorough separation of private life from the public power of the kings and their successors, and by joining such an independence of citizens with the strongest force of public authority; whereas with other peoples either the individual liberty or the concentration of authority was wanting, or did not fully develop. The old Roman idea of protecting private life without interference in the exercise of ownership became the foundation of law for all European people.

Under the religious concept that the soul lived on and assumed divine attributes—to bless and protect its posterity if its needs were met after death of the body, to bring ill fortune if they were not— the family was the basic unit of Roman life. History affords no better example of a comprehensive system of private law than that demonstrated by the early Roman family. In the last analysis, the Roman king and his consular and emperor successors ruled not individuals, but an aggregation of families.

The Paterfamilias as High Priest. On the family hearth burned a perpetual sacred flame, into which blended the family Lares and Penates. There being no over-all ecclesiastical organization, no churches, no religious assemblies and no holy writings in the nature of scriptures, each family constituted its own center of religion, without external surveillance. In the exercise of its autonomy, each family maintained its own secret forms of worship. But whatever the form, cultivating the good graces of the household divinities was the direct concern of each member, drawing all together in close unity.

The place of the family as a unit in Roman society is indicated by the fact that the family, not individuals, owned the land occupied by its members. The lawgiver was the father, or paterfamilias. In his dual capacity of high priest and family head he exercised dictatorial powers. He could do as he willed with its members, including the slaves attached to it, even to the extent of having them put to death. In fact, sons and slaves were, for family purposes, on much the same basis. As the Apostle Paul said in his Epistle to the Galatians, "the heir, as long as he is a child, differeth nothing from a servant, though he be lord of all." Although his sons could hold government offices, within the scope of operation of family law they remained subject to their father. By virtue of such power Fulvius, an associate of Catiline, was put to death by his own father. During his lifetime the father could by formal ceremony emancipate his sons. Otherwise, only with the father's death were they released from paternal domination. At that juncture each became a paterfamilias in his own right.

The Position of the Roman Woman. If even the sons were thus subject to the absolute power of the paterfamilias, it would go without saying that the same would be true as to the feminine members of the family. Originally, they had no rights under Roman public law, and within the family only such as their father or husband vouchsafed. A daughter could not be emancipated, as could a son, and, if she did not marry, after her father's death was under the control of a guardian.

Feminine subordination was particularly emphasized in relation to marriage. When a daughter reached the age of seven years she could be betrothed by her father to the man of his choice. With its inherent logic the Roman law regarded the marital relation for what it was—a consensual one—but with its genius of pragmatic improvisation it imported the fiction that the choice was adopted by the girl. Even in the later Empire the power of the paterfamilias in this regard was confirmed. By the Theodosian Code it was provided: "If a father should enter into a pact concerning the marriage of his daughter and he should not be able to reach the time of the marriage because he perished by human lot, the decision which is proved to have been made by the father shall remain valid and binding between the betrothed, and a compromise shall not be permitted to have any weight if it is proved to have been made by the guardian to whose administration the interests of the minor pertain." The provision goes on that such "compromise" should not be admitted as against the father's wish, because the tutor or curator might be bribed, and "frequently even the determination of the woman herself is found to work against her own interests."

When a woman was married, her father's power over her ceased, but she came under the power, or *manus,* of her husband. An unmarried daughter could inherit property from her father, but it was controlled by her guardian; when she married it became vested in her husband. Upon the death of her husband a wife took a share of his estate, but she could not personally possess it: control over it was vested in a guardian who was one of her husband's male relatives. At no stage and in no way could she dispose of her property by will. In another sense, however, the Roman matron did not fare so badly. She was the mistress of the household, without menial duties if there were slaves to do the work. In that realm she was highly honored. Unlike her Greek sisters she was not restricted from outside contacts. She freely attended the theatre and other spectacles, and took part in social events along with her husband and other men.

Later Relaxation of Paterfamilias Controls. The Roman family as thus conceived and functioning provided a closely knit disciplinary basis for Roman life. In it were implicit the qualities of obedience and loyalty. Developed around the family hearth, these qualities carried through to the higher levels of the state. Roman history might not have been as it is had not these qualities of obedience to law and loyalty to Roman institutions been demonstrated by the Roman citizenry through the vicissitudes of centuries.

But basic as was and is the family in the scheme of things, and with due deference to the contribution to freedom in the sense that the conduct of family life was not interfered with by the early Roman state, it is obvious that the paterfamilias concepts that we have been considering are not compatible with true individual dignity. Nor did they indefinitely continue in their initial extremity. The enlightenment of later centuries, finding expression in the *jus gentium* which will be considered hereinafter, and the influence of the Christian religion introduced concepts which were calculated to weaken if not to shatter the idea of the family as a pagan religious unit, thus paving the way to modification or abrogation of the powers exercised by the paterfamilias, as well as improving the status of women.

Such was, indeed, the consummation. The Justinian Pandects disclose, for example, that Emperor Trajan ordered a son released from paternal authority on account of cruel treatment. The power of selling a child, at first unlimited, was restricted and finally abolished. Important matters became subject to consideration by a family council. The original idea that the wife should be under the *manus* of her husband finally gave way to the concept of free marriage in which the spouses were legally independent of each other, with independent property rights during the marriage and with the wife having full power of testamentary disposition.

The Senate and Comitia Curiata. In the early period, as we have seen, Rome was governed by a king, whose power, in the last analysis, was supreme. But history reveals the presence of other governmental institutions, in the form of the senate and *comitia curiata.*

The Senate, consisting of the heads of the ancient clans, nominated the king for election by the *comitia curiata* and, in theory, gave counsel to him. It initiated the important measures submitted to the *comitia curiata.* As time went on it asserted the power to make laws pertaining to matters of religion and took upon itself other prerogatives, which, as Roman conquests extended Roman power, came to include the government of conquered provinces. Eventually, under the Empire, the senate usurped practically all legislative power; this was not particularly significant, because at that stage the emperor was a virtual dictator.

The *comitia curiata*, Rome's original popular assembly, which met in the comitium at the end of the forum, was made up of patricians. The patrician order was originally divided into three tribes, each composed of ten *curiae.* Each *curia* was in turn divided into ten *gentes.* A *gens* was made up of families, not necessarily immediately related by blood, but each of which had a pedigree tracing to some ancient ancestor of nobility and united for common religious rites.

It is important to note that voting in the *comitia curiata* was by *curiae*, the vote of each *curia* being determined by a majority thereof. The vote of the individual Roman counted only in this way. The Roman citizen did not exercise his right of suffrage in the direct manner to which the people of the United States have always been accustomed. Much less did the Roman vote as a member of a political party, for there were no political parties as such in Rome.

The *comitia curiata* had no power to initiate legislation or to debate legislation proposed by the king. It met only on the king's call, and could only assent to or disapprove such measures as he proposed. But without its ratification the penalty of death could not be inflicted. It

exercised some powers which we would think of as judicial, by way of
validating wills and approving adoptions. These latter powers it
continued to exercise after other popular assemblies, the advent of
which we will hereinafter note, had superseded it in the exercise of
legislative functions.

Symbolism of Early Law. An appreciative understanding of the
development of Roman law to its culmination as a body of jurisprudence that even today exercises world wide influence will be facilitated
by emphasizing that in its early state its concepts were narrow, indeed, and characterized by the manifestations of symbolism which
are commonly associated with primitive societies. In its earlier days,
this symbolism was essential to its successful application. As the
priest chanted his ritual, imploring the gods by a fixed and unalterable formula, the least departure from which would make the prayer
wholly inefficacious, so, too, the early contracts required a fixed and
unalterable symbolism and ritual.

Thus, the early Roman law did not recognize as legally enforceable
the simple contract of sale or hire, or of pledge, which is so common a
feature of modern life. The only contracts which were legally enforceable were sale—*mancipatio*—and loan—*nexum*—as constituted
per aes et libran, i.e., by the old ceremony of having the price to be
paid or the loan to be advanced weighed out by a *librepens* or weigher
—a functionary—in the presence of five witnesses, accompanied by
appropriately formal solemn words of sale or loan. The *librepens*
was a survivor of the days when, the medium of exchange being copper, a sale involved a weighing out of the required quantity. There
was no recognition by the law in any true sense of a contract of agency
whereby one acting for another might render the latter liable to a
third party without being liable himself, a contract upon which so
much of the business of modern life depends.

As we have noted, a will could be validated by application to the
comitia curiata, resulting in something analogous to what we would
call a private legislative act. Otherwise a testamentary disposition
had to take the form of a sale by the intending testator, with the
copper and scales, and with five witnesses, to a friend. On the
testator's decease this friend would be required to recognize the appointed heir or heirs, against whom legatees and creditors would make
their claims. But no recognition of testamentary trusts was given,
nor was recognition accorded to trusts *inter vivos,* which have so important a place in today's social and legal arrangements.

Again, if a citizen made no will and died intestate, the claims of

affection and blood relationship were ruthlessly set aside as against
all who did not come within the agnatic circle, from which were excluded all descendants of the female line, as well as any son or grandson who had been emancipated from his paternal authority and any
daughters who had contracted marriage.

A Roman citizen who desired to emancipate his son from parental
control or free his slave had to appear before a magistrate. A friend
of the person to be emancipated, or freed, or an official representing
himself to be a friend, touched such person on the head with a wand
and claimed him as a free man. When the *assertor liberatis* had thus
fulfilled his office, the paterfamilias turned the new freeman around,
in token that he might go where he liked, and gave him a gentle blow
on the cheek, whereupon the magistrate pronounced the emancipation
or liberation complete.

The Servian Reforms. A basically important aspect of Roman history throughout the period of the kings and the Republic was the
constant pressure of the plebeians for full participation in the rights
enjoyed by other citizens. Because, as we have noted, the plebeians
enjoyed certain property rights, this was not a class struggle in the
full sense of the term. In this effort, made under the handicap that
political activities by plebeians were regarded as sacrilegious, but
meeting with growing success as they advanced from one foothold to
another, will be found much to explain the development of Roman
government and law.

The second Etruscan king, Servius Tullius, gave an early impetus
to this advance of the plebeians by what are known as the Servian Reforms. Originally the Roman army had been made up of patricians,
but there were not enough of them to fight Rome's expanding battles.
By decree of Servius Tullius, all landowners between seventeen and
sixty years of age were ordered into the ranks for periods of service.
In place of the three original patrician tribes within the city, four
new tribes were created, and a number of new tribes were created outside the city, constituted on a territorial basis of residence. Because
plebeians were qualified land-owners, for military purposes this broke
down the distinction between them and the patricians and brought
them together into the Roman armed forces. Even though plebeian
rights were not at this juncture directly enlarged, the move greatly
strengthened the plebeian position.

Apparently proceeding on the theory that it would be wise to
mollify the plebeian urge by granting to the plebeians a semblance
of further recognition, Servius Tullius approved the institution of new

assemblies, which, in the course of time, superseded the *comitia curiata*. One was the *comitia centuriata*, which was drawn from the soldiery under the new dispensation, and which included plebeians as well as patricians. Like the *comitia curiata*, it had no power to initiate legislation, and at the outset all measures which required a religious sanction had to go to the *comitia curiata* for confirmation. But to it a Roman citizen could appeal against sentence of death. Ultimately it succeeded the *comitia curiata* in political power, and by it was enacted Rome's first code of law, the Law of the Twelve Tables, which will be further considered hereinafter.

Other assemblies which came out of the Servian Reforms were the *comitia tributa*, constituted according to geographical districts, and which therefore included both plebeians and patricians, and the *concilium plebis*, consisting entirely of plebeians. The *plebiscita* of these bodies were not law, but were significant as indicating plebeian desires.

No Formal Constitution. One who does not understand the manner in which the word "constitution" is used in Roman affairs may gain the erroneous impression that the Roman government operated under a formal constitution, in the same sense as does the government of the United States. Neither at the outset, nor ever, did Rome have a formal written constitution in the sense in which we would employ the term. As reported by Cicero, Cato held it to be Rome's chief virtue that it was the product, not of one genius but of many, established not during the lifetime of one man but by various men in various generations.

The term "constitution" as used with regard to Roman law and government is applied to pronouncements by the Emperors during the Empire. As will be apparent, the Emperors assumed all powers of government, and their "constitutions" were in effect legislative enactments, judicial judgments or executive orders, as the case might be. Some of them were really general legislative enactments; some were judicial decrees adjudicating lawsuits; some were declaratory statements as to the law; some were mandates to subordinate government officials. One form of "constitution" was the oration, or address, by the Emperor to the senate, recommending legislation. Because the recommendation was always adopted it became law as a matter of course. Under a similar regime in the United States, all of the President's messages to Congress would become, *ipso facto*, the law of the land.

CHAPTER 7

THE ROMAN REPUBLIC

The Kings Depart; Wars and Conquests Begin. In spite of concessions granted, the rule of the Tarquin kings was on the despotic order. The impact of the rising power of the citizenry brought about the expulsion of the last of these in 510 B.C., at which time the Roman Republic may be said to have begun. It did not start under auspicious circumstances.

In the nature of things there was grave internal disorder. Resentment occasioned by the expulsion of the kings was manifested by threats of Etruscan invasion. But the new Republic survived the crisis, and started on its way to virile expansion. First successfully resisting invasion, Roman armies gradually pressed out in almost continuous military conquest, until by around 300 B.C. they had occupied most of the Italian Peninsula. People like the Samnites, who would not stay conquered, had to be reconquered, and again reconquered.

In 264 B.C. the Roman armies started their subjection of Mediterranean lands by invading Sicily, held by the Carthaginians. Carthage was eventually destroyed in the great Punic Wars, which came to an end in 146 B.C., but not until Rome's resources of men and material had been drained to the point of exhaustion. Rome's control over North Africa was confirmed by the defeat of Jugurtha in 106 B.C.

In the East, Philip of Macedon was defeated in 197 B.C., thus opening the way to complete Romanization of the Balkan Peninsula. On the far West, the Spanish Numantians were conquered in 133 B.C., and the Marians in 72 B.C. Pompey conquered Syria in 64 B.C., and, as it has been said, by taking advantage of the religious scruples of the Jews against fighting on their Sabbath, captured Jerusalem in 63 B.C.

As James Bryce observed, the Romans, though they did not start out with the notion of conquering Italy, much less the Mediterranean world, came to enjoy fighting for its own sake, and were content with slight pretext for it. For centuries they were always more or less on the go somewhere. Rome did not march so swiftly as England did later from conquest to conquest. Not to speak of the two centuries during which she was making herself supreme in Italy, she began to conquer outside its limits from the opening of the First Punic War in 264 B.C., and did not acquire Egypt until 30 B.C., and South Britain until 43-85 A.D. Her Eastern conquests were all the easier because Alexander the Great's victories and the wars waged by his successors had broken up and denationalized the East, much as the Mogul Emperors afterwards paved the way for the English in India.

Law and Military Force. It seems somewhat anomalous to accord to war and military conquest so prominent a reference in a discussion presumedly devoted to the law. In their substance and application the processes of the sword are commonly regarded as the antithesis of the civil law. But if there is any anomaly, it is inherent in history itself, for historical annals are in large measure a chronicle of the relationship between military force and the legal institutions through which law finds life and application.

Sometimes such force has been employed in derogation of justice. Sometimes it has been employed to promote it. Thus, as every schoolboy knows, the constitutional system of the United States traces directly to the freedom from British rule achieved by the Revolutionary War. The citizen of today who has memories of the two World Wars in which the United States has recently participated is aware that they were fought for the basic purpose of upholding the rule of law as opposed to unbridled autocratic power, contemptuous of human rights.

It is probably best to leave it to each reader to develop his own rationalization as to the right or wrong of Roman conquest. Certainly, Roman law and institutions were not established throughout the world at the invitation of the peoples concerned. But on the theory that they steadily expanded the boundaries within which law and order of at least a relatively enlightened nature supplanted a more primitive relationship, a persuasive case can be made for them. The consideration that is of major interest to us is that with the effective use of the sword, the Romans combined a noteworthy facility for supplementing force with law—and making that law "work."

Whatever may be the conclusion as to the right or wrong of Roman conquest, we must respect Roman law and institutions for having provided the basis of order that made such stupendous military accomplishments possible. Perhaps for the simple reason that she was self-centered and did not undertake such an aggressive program of conquest, Greece did not develop the centralized stable institutions that

THE ROMAN REPUBLIC   **133**

would have supported such a program. In the light of the great military pressures under which the Roman Republic constantly strained, perhaps the wonder is not that greater solicitude was not shown for individual rights, but rather that the way of the Roman was not harder than it was. Under such circumstances it is perhaps to be marveled at that a governmental system which had such substantive as well as formal regard for principles of justice and out of which developed in the later days of the Republic men of ideals whose scholarly productions constituted the basis for the great codes of Roman law, could be sustained as long as it was.

What appears to be clear from Roman history is that free governmental institutions, however democratically conceived, and however strongly supported by the citizenry, cannot indefinitely sustain a program of all-out militarism. Autocracy, constantly approaching closer and closer, will finally enter and take over. The cycle of "strong man" to democracy, and back again, has been completed.

Treatment of Conquered Peoples. As we have noted, the first conquests of Rome were made in Italy. They did not, however, involve any legal changes, for conquest meant merely the reduction of what had been an independent city or group of cities or tribes to vassalage, with the obligation of sending troops to serve in the Roman armies. Local autonomy was not, as a rule, interfered with, and such autonomy included civil jurisdiction. So the Italic and Greco-Italic cities continued to be governed by their own laws. With the annexation of Sicily the first provincial government was set up, and the legal and administrative problems with which Rome had to deal began to show themselves.

It seems in order to say, then, that at the outset Rome built up her power in an enlightened manner. The conquest of Italian communities was supplemented by treaties which manifested a high degree of workable statesmanship. The conquered peoples yielded sovereignty to Rome, but were allowed to retain varying degrees of their own law and established institutions. They were commonly permitted to elect their local magistrates and mobilize their own troops to fill quotas for the Roman army. There was present all the time in the Roman provinces a people's law to be administered in the local tribunals of the particular province, municipality, or other political subdivision. We have the most abundant evidence on this head in relation to the Jews, after they had submitted to the Roman yoke, and who were still permitted to follow their own laws in the time of our Saviour, and down to the destruction of Jerusalem.

Moreover, they were granted the rights of *connubium, commercium* and *recuperatio*. *Connubium* was the right of intermarriage, *commercium* the right to carry on trade, and *recuperatio* the right to have questions between citizens and those aliens who enjoyed the privilege, or between aliens *inter se*, referred for trial to sworn *recuperatores*, a court probably composed of an equal number of arbiters from both nations and an umpire or overman. Such court sat at the place where the contract was made, and applied the law of that place. Treaties containing such provisions appear to have been made with most of the Italian communities, including the Greek colonies in South Italy and Sicily. By treaty in 493 B.C. between Rome and a Latin confederacy of some thirty cities it was provided that disputes arising out of private contracts between their respective citizens should be determined within ten days by the tribunal of the city where the contract was entered into.

In the process the Roman law, although not everywhere in effect as such, inevitably broadened in scope and content. Broadly comparing the law of Rome with that of Greece, Paul Vinogradoff decided that the older *Jus Civile* of Rome as well as the law of the Greek city states presents combinations of legal rules which depend upon one dominant fact—the nature of the city commonwealth. But the law of the Greek states can be more clearly imagined as existing on one plane, namely in the stage of the city commonwealth, while the law of Rome gradually became the law of an empire and lost its municipal complexion.

Outlying Provinces. Beyond the immediate vicinity of Rome itself, as Bryce pointed out, the territories conquered by the Romans were of three kinds. Some, such as Egypt and Macedonia, had been under their own princes, monarchies practically despotic. In these, of course, there could be no question of what we call popular government. Some had been tribal principalities, monarchic or oligarchic, such as those among the Iceni and Brigantes in Britain, the Arverni in Gaul, the Cantabrian mountaineers in Spain. Here again, free institutions had not existed before and could hardly have been created by the conqueror. The third kind consisted of small commonwealths like the Greek cities. These were fitted for self-government, which, indeed, they had enjoyed before they had been subjected to Rome. Very wisely, municipal self-government was to a large extent left to them by the rulers down till the time of Dicoletian. But they were all placed under the governor of the province; most of them paid taxes, and in most both the criminal and the higher civil jurisdiction were in the hands of imperial officials.

How the Romans adapted their methods to circumstances is illustrated by the manner in which they dealt with the Toulouse region of southern Gaul. After the attack of Hannibal through Spain and southern Gaul had been crushed, the Romans sought to make secure their route from Italy to Spain. The Roman senate founded at the mouth of the Aude the city of Narbonne and sent there a colony of Roman citizens to establish Roman civilization and learning. Toulouse was then a capital of a people designated by Roman historians as Tolosates. It soon became a dependency of Narbonne. The consul Fabius, in occupying the country inhabited by the Tolosates, did not wish to impose an onerous yoke on the natives. He demanded only the taxes already paid by them for public purposes. Some years after the founding of Narbonne the Roman civilization radiated from this center into the whole country, and the use of the Latin language became common. The Romans of Narbonne entered into a treaty with the Tolosates and placed a garrison in the city of Toulouse, leaving its people altogether free. The purpose was to cover and protect the route to Spain, and to make the Tolosates allies.

When the Cimbri approached through Gaul to invade Rome, about 113 B.C., some of the people of Toulouse, regarding them as conquerors, pronounced in their favor. The soldiers of the Roman garrison were held as prisoners. Members of the faction wishing to continue under Roman rule sent secret emissaries to Cepio, the Roman consul, to advise him of the conspiracy. Forthwith he marched with his soldiers into Toulouse "which he freed from the traitors during the night." Then to punish the rebellion he authorized wholesale looting. There were numerous temples in Toulouse, rich in gold and precious objects brought, it is said, from the Delphi temple. These riches were seized, and Cepio started them under convoy to Rome. Near Marseilles the convoy was overcome in an ambush which Cepio was alleged to have himself arranged. He did not profit, however. To prevent the Cimbri from penetrating Italy he was forced to leave Toulouse and march his army rapidly to the banks of the Rhone. His forces were annihilated. When news of the disaster reached Rome the senate condemned his memory to public contempt and seized his property. The people of Toulouse attributed these misfortunes to the sacrilegious pillage of the temples of their gods. Since then, when one wishes to describe some one whose affairs have not gone well he says, "He has the gold of Toulouse." Marius, having conquered the

Cimbri, treated the people of Toulouse as conquered people. They lost their independence and fell into the hands of proconsuls who crushed them with taxes. Nevertheless, under the civilizing influence of the Romans, trade and culture developed and flourished. The customs, the laws and above all the language of the Romans soon came into use.

Of the introduction of any free institutions for the Roman nation at large, or even for any province as a whole, there seems never to have been any question. Among the many constitutional inventions we owe to the ancient world, representative government finds no place. A generation before the fall of the Republic Rome had missed her opportunity when the creation of such a system was most needed and might have been most useful. After her struggle against the league of her Italian allies she consented to admit them to vote in her own city tribes, instead of taking what seems to us moderns the obvious expedient of allowing them to send delegates to an assembly which should meet in Rome.

Subject to the general principle that the power of the emperor was everywhere supreme and absolute, the Romans recognized, at least in the earlier days of the Empire, considerable differences between the methods of administering various provinces. A distinction was drawn between the provinces of the Roman people, to which proconsuls or propraetors were sent, and the provinces of Caesar, placed under the more direct control of the emperor, and administered in his name by an official called the *praeses* or *legatus Caesaris,* or sometimes, as was the case in Judaea, at the time when it was ruled by Pontius Pilate, by a procurator, an officer primarily financial, but often entrusted with the power of a *praeses.* Egypt received special treatment because the population was turbulent and liable to outbursts of religious passion, and because it was important to keep a great cornfield of the Empire in good humor. The distinctions between one province and another tended to vanish as the administrative system of the Empire grew better settled and the old republican forms were forgotten.

The Denouement: Slavery and Booty. Roman history would present a more attractive chronicle if the high order of relationship which we have depicted as originally applying to the Italian communities, and the governmental methods employed as to the distant provinces, told the whole story of Roman control and administration. Unfortunately, there are other chapters. After the earlier period of conquest, and especially after conquest carried beyond the boundaries of the Italian Peninsula, there were sordid manifestations which cannot be passed unnoticed.

We have already spoken of one aspect of these manifestations—the seizure of conquered peoples and taking them to Rome for impressment into slavery. Scores of thousands of slaves were thus often impressed at one time. Nearly a hundred thousand Jews were made slave captives by Titus when he destroyed Jerusalem in 70 A.D. Slave labor made possible the great system of Roman highways and other public works. From another point of view, Rome profited by the fact that many slaves were highly educated people, and could be put to use in higher capacities. As an institution slavery, of course, existed everywhere in antiquity. It was a part of Hebrew culture from early times. Joseph was sold by his brethren to the Ishmaelites for twenty pieces of silver. But immediately after the giving of the law on Mt. Sinai the Lord proclaimed that if a man be found stealing any of his brethren of the children of Israel, and maketh merchandise of him, or selleth him, then that thief shall die. It is true that Paul appears to have counseled slaves to obey their masters. "Let as many servants as our under the yoke count their own masters worthy of all honour." But warrant cannot be found for saying that slavery was approved by Christ or his apostles as an institution. And by the time of Justinian there was recognition of the incompatibility of slavery with the natural law.

Another repulsive aspect was looting the treasures and resources of conquered peoples, and imposing oppressive indemnities and taxes. The soldiers of the early Roman Republic idealistically served their country at their own expense. As time went on, they came to be paid. Their emoluments were increased. Finally, they came to look for lush reward in the booty acquired by conquest. Unfortunately for the men in the ranks, this did not always work out to their best advantage: the commanders of the Roman forces pocketed the money appropriated for their pay and upkeep, retained the best part of the booty, and quartered them on the occupied people for food and housing. Rome itself came to look to the conquered provinces for the indemnities and revenue which would enable the people at home to enjoy the increasing bounties of the Roman state without cost to them.

Thus, policies of downright brutality and injustice superseded the statesmanlike practices which initially took much of the sting out of the process of conquest. It was a change which worked for the ultimate downfall of the Republic.

Limitations on Roman Citizenship. In the light of the principles of territoriality, implicit in the law of the United States, the Roman law was narrow, indeed, in withholding its applicability from those who, though free residents in Rome or Roman provinces, were not Roman citizens. Thus, the protection accorded by the Bill of Rights of the Constitution of the United States is not couched in terms of citizenship, but of "people" and "persons," with the result that even aliens may be entitled to invoke its provisions.

Rome departed from the usual practice of the city republics of the ancient world. No man enjoyed any rights at all, public or private, except a citizen of the Republic. A stranger coming to reside in the city did not, no matter how long he lived there, nor did his son or grandson, obtain any rights, unless he was especially admitted to become a citizen.

From this principle Rome as she grew presently found herself obliged to deviate. She admitted one set of neighbors after another, sometimes as allies, sometimes in later days as conquered and incorporated communities, to a citizenship which was sometimes incomplete, including only private civil rights, sometimes complete, including the right of voting in the assembly and the right of being chosen to a public office. Before the dictatorship of Julius Caesar practically all the Italians, except the people of Cisalpine Gaul, which remained a province until 43 B.C., had been admitted to civic rights. Citizenship, complete and partial (i.e., including or not including public rights) had also begun to be conferred on a certain number of cities or individuals outside Italy. Tarsus, in Cilicia, of which St. Paul was a native, enjoyed it, so he was born a Roman citizen. The process of enlarging citizenship went on with accelerated speed, in and after the days of the Flavian Emperors. Early in the third century A.D. every Roman subject was by imperial edict, made a citizen for all purposes whatsoever.

Paul: "I Was Free Born." For those who were Roman citizens, Roman citizenship had its majestic aspect in the concept that the rights of Roman citizens accompanied them to the farthest reaches of the Roman state. The governors of conquered provinces were empowered to administer it in their behalf.

How the Roman law worked for the Roman citizen abroad is illustrated by its application to the Apostle Paul. Few scenes of recorded history are more dramatic in their implications than that of St. Paul, a Roman citizen, denounced by the Jerusalem mob and sentenced to be scourged. In the later period of the Republic any Roman citizen who was convicted in a province on a criminal charge had the right of appeal to Rome. Provincial subjects had no such right. When Paul said, "I was free born," his captors unbound and "departed from him."

The Government of the Republic. We may well preface a brief look at the government through which Rome built up her strength at home and expanded her power abroad by reference to the conclusions expressed by Polybius, writing after the popular assembly, augmented by the power of the tribunes, asserted unmistakable power on the part of the people. Polybius found in the government of the Roman Republic the separation of powers which has already been spoken of in relation to Greece, and which characterizes the government of the United States. He referred to the Roman Republic as having three elements, each of which possessed sovereign power, and said that their respective share of power in the whole state had been regulated with such a scrupulous regard to equality and equilibrium that no one could say for certain whether the constitution as a whole were an aristocracy, or democracy, or despotism. And no wonder, said he, for if we confine our observation to the power of the consuls we should be inclined to regard it as despotic; if to that of the senate, as aristocratic; and if one looks at the power possessed by the people it would seem a clear case of democracy.

Taking note, first, of the consuls, it is understandable that the citizens of the Republic, having expelled the last of the Tarquins in a revolt against kingly despotism, were desirous of providing an arrangement calculated to avoid future oppression. To avoid the concentration of power in one man they vested it in two successors to the king, known as consuls. Nominated by the senate from the ranks of the patricians, these men were elected for one year by the *comitia centuriata*. Being the successors to the king, their power was comprehensive. It included command of the military, the convening of the senate, and the administration of justice in all its aspects, civil and criminal. But from an early date a citizen had the right of appeal to the *comitia centuriata* from consular sentences of death or scourging, and from some other crimes as well. While in office consuls could not be thwarted by any legal process, or impeached. After expiration of their terms, however, they were subject to prosecution for misconduct.

The anomaly of having two chief executives with concurrent powers is at once apparent. Each consul could veto the acts of the other. Obviously, this might weaken the government fatally at a critical juncture. To obviate such a dire possibility, provision was made for an official, called a dictator, to be named for a period of six months in time of danger, and who as such would exercise supreme power.

It was stated in *The Federalist* that history records many instances of mischiefs to the Republic from the dissensions between the consuls, and between the military tribunes, who were at times substituted for the consuls. But it gives no specimens of any peculiar advantages derived to the state from the circumstance of the plurality of these magistrates. That the dissensions between them were not more frequent or more fatal, is matter of astonishment, until we advert to the singular position in which the Republic was almost continually placed, and to the prudent policy pointed out by the circumstances of the state, and particularly by the consuls, of making a division of the government between them. The patricians engaged in a perpetual struggle with the plebeians for the preservation of their ancient authorities and dignities; the consuls, who were generally chosen out of the former body, were commonly united by the personal interest they had in the defense of the privileges of their order. In addition to this motive of union, after the arms of the Republic had considerably expanded the bounds of its empire, it became an established custom with the consuls to divide the administration between themselves by lot—one of them remaining at Rome to govern the city and its environs, the other taking command in the more distant provinces. This expedient must, no doubt, have had great influence in preventing those collisions and rivalships which might otherwise have embroiled the peace of the Republic.

As time went on a force of assistants to handle the growing business of state became necessary. But the choice of the necessary subordinate magistrates, who corresponded to modern civil servants, was not delegated to the consuls. The quaestors who collected taxes and handled the public finances, and the censors, who took a census of the people and their property, assigned them to their positions in the different classes, and were charged with the promotion of morality, were elected in the same manner as consuls. Like the consuls, originally they were patricians. Cato the Censor, who sternly insisted in the era when the Roman Republic had begun to decline that there be a return to the hardy virtues of the past, made for the censor's office a place in history.

The senate, fortified by tradition, was an advisory and administrative rather than a legislative body. In that capacity it was actively identified with the routine of government, and continuously exercised great influence over its affairs. Polybius explained how it could add to or detract from the success of generals by granting or withholding the appropriations for "triumphs" which celebrated their victorious campaigns. Until the later years of the Republic it was supreme over the military power. Its members were never popularly elected and it came to be largely constituted of those who had served as consuls and senior magistrates.

The Plebeian "Sit-Down"—The Tribunes. In the choice of consuls and other magistrates the plebeians, through their inclusion in the *comitia centuriata*, had a voice, though because they were in a minority it was not a determining one. Long a debtor class, with little hope of bettering themselves economically, their position was measurably weakened by the disorder attending the expulsion of the kings and the setting up of the new government. Under the existing procedures, as in ancient Greece, debtors who did not pay their debts could be sold as slaves. Revulsion against such conditions led the plebeians of the army, in 494 B.C., to ignore orders to take the field for a campaign. Instead, they entrenched themselves on the Mons Sacer, near Rome, and demanded an end to the measures which oppressed them.

This maneuver, of which the "sit-down" strikes of the modern era are reminiscent, demonstrated the revolutionary strength of a group of citizenry acting cohesively in a manner not in itself violent. Because those who engaged in it were members of the armed forces it was, in effect, a form of mutiny. It anticipated the "passive resistance" tactics introduced, in modern times, by Mohandas Gandhi in India and of which we have spoken in this connection. At any rate, it achieved results. In what was in effect a contract between two classes of citizens—and therefore a unique form of law—it was provided that thereafter the plebeians should have certain magistrates elected from their own ranks by the *concilium plebis*, to be known as tribunes, with authority to protect them from the senate, consuls and patrician magistrates. If the tribunes interposed their veto, the senate could not make decrees, or meet. Furthermore, debts were cancelled, and debtors who had been sold into slavery were set free. The authority of the tribunes was exercised, interestingly enough, by calling down a curse upon whoever would impede them in the performance of their duty to protect the plebeians from oppression. As assistants to the tribunes there were elected *aediles*, plebeians whose duty it was to supervise the streets and public places and manage the public observances.

It was a rather strange method of protection, but it fairly achieved its immediate purpose. Moreover, the power of the tribunes, who were abolished during the interlude of the Decimvirs but were restored thereafter, grew until in the last century B.C. they exercised a determining influence over the affairs of state. No modern government has an officer with similar function.

Religion Under the Republic. We have already noted the basic part religion played in general, and in constituting the foundation for the life of the Roman family. Under the Republic its public influence was, if anything, expanded. With the passing of the kings, their priestly powers came to be exercised by four sacred colleges, known as the Keepers of the Sibylline Books, the College of Augurs, the College of Heralds, and the College of Pontiffs. The destiny of the state was in large measure in the hands of these religious functionaries.

The Sibylline Books were reputedly the recorded utterances of Greek Sybils, or oracles, which related to the destiny of Rome. They were guarded with great care, and interpreting them at critical junctures by their keepers was regarded as a supreme responsibility.

The duty of the College of Augurs was to interpret natural manifestations, such as the flight of birds, through which Jupiter was presumed to make known his directions as to the conduct of public affairs. Public acts were from time to time suspended on the ground that the omens had been found to be unfavorable. For reasons that the modern reader can perhaps understand better than the Roman citizenry of that time, this gave the rulers an effective veto over popularly approved legislation and action that they did not like. In the course of his career, Cicero was a member of the College of Augurs.

The College of Heralds was charged with foreign relations. One of its most important functions related to the making of war. When it was decided to go to war with another country, a member of the College hurled across the boundary a spear dipped in blood, by way of a declaration. The cynic might be moved to remark that this manifested a high state of international chivalry, in relation to which the Japanese attack at Pearl Harbor some two thousand years later stood out in sad degenerative contrast.

The College of Pontiffs: A Legal Monopoly. The College of Pontiffs constituted the supreme religious body of Rome, regarded as having full insight into supernatural matters. Its head was the *Pontifex Maximus,* who appointed the other members. In so far as religion went, it was deemed necessary to invoke the advice of these priests as to questions of religious observances and relationships which did not center in the family itself.

But the prerogatives of the College of Pontiffs carried beyond the realm of religion into that of law, and in a manner which vested them with what amounted to a legal monopoly. Inasmuch, as we have stated, the popular assemblies were without legislative power in the sense that we think of it, in the early history of Rome there was no body of statutory law. In fact, there was no clear-cut body of law of any sort which citizens could understand, and by which they could live. Among the Romans, however, as among all primitive peoples, there existed a body of customs which governed them in their relations with each other, as well as to the gods. As we would expect of a people who had attained such a stage of civilization, in this body of customs there were rules regarding such matters as contracts, and holding and transferring private property, including disposition of it by will.

In accordance with the acknowledged relationship of people and state to the gods, these customary rules of conduct were of divine significance. The law participated in the mysterious character of religion, and the legal formulas, like those of religion, were kept secret. Logically enough, then, they were deemed to be fully known and understood only by the College of Pontiffs. Such legal writings and opinions as had developed were locked securely in the archives of this sacred College. The priesthood influence extended throughout the whole area of the law. The magistrates themselves called upon the priests for advice as to the formalities to be employed in the transaction of legal affairs in general (*cavere*) or the prosecution of actions (*agere*). Moreover, the priests exercised the function known as *respondre*, meaning the answering of questions about the law as it applied to particular cases.

All this meant that the law was beyond the ken of the ordinary citizen; in fact, that the law had its existence in the realm of the occult. Today we regard it as axiomatic that only laws which it is possible for every citizen to know, and the content of which can be freely ascertained, are at all consonant with that minimum of protection which we think of as due process of law. Romans of the early periods were without a semblance of such protection, and without guarantees of any kind against oppression in application of the customary law as interpreted under such secret priestly auspices.

Although the College of Pontiffs eventually lost its legal monopoly, as we shall hereinafter see, it continued to remain of high importance in the religious life of Rome. However, taking into account that such men as Julius Caesar served in his time as Pontifex Maximus, one might be pardoned for not being highly impressed with its spirituality.

The Law of the Twelve Tables. Just as their counterparts of ancient Greece had felt the need for and forcefully demanded laws in a definite form, available to all citizens and setting forth in some definite manner such rights as they possessed, as well as their obligations, the Roman plebeians, ever conscious that their welfare was subject to the caprice of a priesthood over whose personnel and tenure they had no say, pressed for such laws.

There is perhaps some significance in the fact that plebeian agitation took the form of this demand for written laws, rather than for reform of the official hierarchy. Their efforts were successfully consummated in 451 B.C. when the *comitia centuriata* enacted the Law of the Twelve Tables. Its text was framed by a commission of Decimvirs after careful deliberation, including a period of research in Greece. It was written on twelve bronze tablets, fastened to the rostra of the Forum, where all could read.

The Law of the Twelve Tables was not a code in the modern sense, but rather a compilation of the customary law of which we have spoken above, in a form available to the public. Apart from its practical importance, it is noteworthy as marking recognition of the right of the individual to be recognized, as such, by the law, and of the right to be dealt with accordingly.

Unfortunately for the purpose of today's direct enlightenment, the Twelve Tables did not survive, but at some stage were lost or destroyed. From the hundred or so fragments which were later found it was possible to determine their general content. The First Table related to the procedure in a civil lawsuit. For example, a person summoned before a magistrate was bound to go, but if he were aged or sick an ox team must be provided for him. The Second Table provided for bail and the summoning of witnesses. The Third Table gave debtors thirty days before steps could be taken against them, but unless they paid they might be put in irons for sixty days, during which time they could be ransomed. After that the creditor could sell the debtor as a slave, or kill him. The Fourth Table dealt with family matters, establishing the life and death right of the paterfamilias of which we have spoken, and who was ordered to destroy deformed children.

The Fifth Table related to inheritances and wills. The testamentary power was unlimited. Wills were executed with great ceremony, before five citizens representing the people. The transaction was in the form of a purchase of the inheritance. The Sixth Table dealt with ownership and conveyance of property and the Seventh with the rights of adjoining property holders with regard to such things as boundaries, rights of way and overhanging trees. The Eighth dealt with tortious wrongs, providing for penalties and compensation ranging from death at the hands of the injured person who was robbed, for example, to forfeiture of a four-footed beast which had committed depredations. The Ninth Table related to public law, providing that a judge or arbiter taking a bribe was subject to capital punishment, that death should be the punishment for treason, and that only the *comitia centuriata* could pronounce a capital sentence. The Tenth Table, relating to funerals and burials, brought religion and law together in that regard. The Eleventh Table reiterated the prohibition of marriages between patricians and plebeians, and the Twelfth dealt with a number of miscellaneous matters.

Much of the content of the Law of the Twelve Tables was obviously procedural, looking to guaranteeing certain practices and standards on the order of what we think of as due process of law. This is not without significance, as it indicates early recognition of the extent to which procedural methods strike to the heart of human rights. Doing justice may well turn on whether a party receives fair notice before he is charged with offense or liability. It may well turn on his right to bail, the qualifications of those who judge him, or the rules relating to testimony. Though the Law of the Twelve Tables was limited in substantive content, it must be remembered that the society of 451 B.C. was a relatively simple one, not industrialized, and without the complexities of social and business relationships of later eras that called forth a correspondingly greater body of legal rules and regulations to deal with them.

It has been noted that before the Law of the Twelve Tables there was a right to appeal to the *comitia centuriata* in criminal cases, and that only the *comitia centuriata* could confirm the death sentence. As a matter of expediency the handling of these matters came to be delegated by the *comitia centuriata* to *questiones,* or commissions, which eventually became permanent criminal tribunals.

Further Plebeian Progress—Valerio-Horatian Laws. As part of the procedure to secure the Law of the Twelve Tables the Decimvirs who were commissioned to frame them had been vested with the power of the state, in place of the consuls and tribunes. Appius Claudius, chairman of the board after the Law was promulgated, instituted a tyrannical regime. Desiring Virginia, the daughter of a plebeian, in his official capacity he decreed her to be a slave. Rather than to have her taken by Claudius her father killed her, then took the story to the army. Reflecting, as we may reasonably believe, the respect felt for Roman womanhood, the soldiers entrenched themselves on Mons Sacer, as they had done before upon the occasion already mentioned, and held out for resignation of the Decimvirs and restoration of the consuls and tribunes. Their effort was successful.

Further laws were then enacted under the sponsorship of the newly-chosen consuls, Valerius and Horatius, which provided that *plebiscita* passed by the *concilium plebis* should have the same force as enactments of the *comitia centuriata,* and that the tribunes be permitted to sit at the door of the senate. From this foothold the tribunes eventually gained great power, including that of convening and presiding over the senate. The extent of tribune power and influence at the late stage of the Republic is indicated by Plutarch's narration in his Life of Cicero. Clodius, after his acquittal from a criminal charge arising out of his attempt at a rendezvous with Pompeia, wife of Caesar, was elected a tribune of the people. He immediately attacked Cicero and left neither circumstances nor person untried to ruin him. He won the people with popular laws and the consuls by decreeing them large and wealthy provinces. He registered many indigent persons as citizens and armed a body of slaves for his constant attendants. After Cicero fled Rome, Clodius procured a decree of banishment against Cicero which prohibited him fire and water and admission into any house within five hundred miles of Italy.

So important were these Valerio-Horatian Laws that they have sometimes been referred to as Rome's Magna Charta. Shortly thereafter, in 445 B.C., a tribune, Gaius Canuleius, secured the passage of a law referred to as the Canuleian Law, legalizing marriages between plebeians and patricians. Under the Licinian Laws of 367 B.C. the plebeians gained rights in the public lands theretofore restricted to patricians; the right to hold one of the two consulships, and the right to five of the ten keepers of the sacred Sibylline Books in the Capitoline Temple.

It having developed that the *concilium plebis* could not enact *plebiscita* without the consent of the senate, through the "sit-down" tactics which had brought results in earlier periods the plebeians brought matters to a head in 267 B.C. and gained the agreement that thenceforth *plebiscita* of the *comitia tributa* were to have the force of law without senatorial consent. The *comitia tributa,* or assembly of tribes, thus became, in theory at least, the most powerful legislative body.

Speaking of the Roman legislative system, the Federalist said it was well known that in the Roman Republic the legislative authority, in the last resort, resided in two different political bodies—not as branches of the same legislature, but as distinct and independent legislatures, in each of which an opposite interest prevailed: in one, the patrician; in the other, the plebeian. The *comitia centuriata*, in which the people voted by centuries, was so arranged as to give a superiority to the patrician interests; in the *comitia tributa*, in which numbers prevailed, the plebeian interest had an entire predominancy. Many arguments might have been adduced to prove the unfitness of two such seemingly contradictory authorities, each having power to annul or repeal the acts of the other. But a man would have been regarded as frantic who should have attempted at Rome to disprove their existence.

A possible explanation of the acceptable functioning of such a system lay in its inherent weakness in actual operation. Because under the operation of the system all citizens had to come to Rome itself to vote in their tribes, the right of suffrage to all living outside Rome was an empty one. In no real sense could the government be called representative. As events finally demonstrated, in the last analysis it was not under the people's democratic control. Nevertheless, the gains which these measures brought were noteworthy.

Interpreting the Law of the Twelve Tables. For several hundred years the Law of the Twelve Tables constituted the basic law of Rome. Of such importance was it thought to be, and in such high esteem was it held, that preceding the time of Cicero it was customary for schoolboys to commit it to memory. But no formal statement of the law can be made that will literally fit every situation, even as of the immediate era of enactment. As we have seen, this had been realized by Aristotle. Much less can a formal statement anticipate the demands of decades in the future. Justice Cardozo put it well when he said that no doubt the ideal system, if it were attainable, would be a code at once so flexible and so minute, as to supply in advance for every conceivable situation the just and fitting rule. But life is too complex to bring the attainment of this ideal within the compass of human powers.

In other words, anything in the nature of a formal code, rigidly interpreted, cannot fully meet the needs of present justice, and without elasticity of application it cannot afford adequate guidance for the future. Here, of course, is demonstrated by way of contrast the great vitality of the English common law, which does not rest on formal codification and which has full latitude to conform itself to the changing conditions of human society, overruling or otherwise superseding by judicial opinion those principles which should be changed.

The Romans proceeded realistically in the light of the realization that if the Law of the Twelve Tables was to afford the necessary guide for conduct, it must be held open to processes of interpretation that would give it adequate application for present and future purposes. The necessity of supplementing it with an interpretative process enabled the College of Pontiffs, as the "experts" in the law, to continue the legal monopoly that they had previously asserted and maintained. So it was that the enactment of the Law of the Twelve Tables did not dislodge the College of Pontiffs from its hold over the law. Retaining the prerogative of interpretation, they had it within their power not only to "interpret" but also to make substantive additions under the guise of interpretation. By the last century of the Republic the Law of the Twelve Tables had been encrusted by a growing mass of "interpretation" which had so modified and supplemented its primitive and scanty provisions that for all practical purposes the interpretation and not the text was the law.

The Roman Praetor. Roman citizens were the gainers by having, in the first place, written laws in the form of the Law of the Twelve Tables. They were the gainers, in the second place, by having an interpretative process at work to adapt that law to situations not within its literal purview, even though the interpretation was in the hands of a priesthood over which they had no direct control. A further gain of another sort was imported, under the Licinian Laws of 367 B.C., by the creation of a judicial magistrate known as a *praetor.* Later, by way of distinction from the *praetor peregrinus,* whose office was created over a century thereafter, the *praetor* created by the Licinian Laws came to be known as the *praetor urbanus.*

Originally, the two consuls had administered justice, along with their other duties. Under the new law this function was vested in the *praetor,* whose office was regarded as of concurrent dignity. A judge in the modern sense, he sat in the city of Rome. In theory, like the two consuls, he inherited the kingly power of command, with jurisdiction to issue orders and enforce them by fine or imprisonment. With impressive formality he was ensconced on an ivory chair, wearing a white robe ornamented with purple.

In the early form of praetorian procedure the plaintiff summoned the defendant before the *praetor* by touching him on the ear in the presence of witnesses. Each party had to give security for his further appearance. When the *praetor* was ready to hear the case, each party stated his position. The plaintiff then took hold of the thing claimed, or a symbol of it, or moved as if to attack the defendant. The *praetor* interrupted, and called upon each party to justify his claim. Each then wagered a sum that his position was just. The loser stood to forfeit this to the public treasury for the expense of sacrifices to the gods. It has been said that this procedure grew out of the primitive practice where each adversary swore on oath by the gods that his position was right, and the magistrate, acting under the logical assumption that one or the other had sworn falsely, hastened to adjudicate a settlement so that one of the outraged gods might not inflict his wrath upon the people as a whole. Such a concept was manifestly in line with the modern theory of the law as an instrument to keep the peace. But in its modern application, of course, the concept is hardly concerned with the possibility of breach of the peace from the direction of the starry firmament.

Whether taking the form of a wager, or a later form more consonant with modern procedural methods of arriving at an issue to be tried, the case thus initiated was assigned by the *praetor* to a *judex*, or juryman, or sometimes to several *judices*, for hearing and decision. The *praetor* issued to the judex an appropriate formula in the way of instructions as to the judgment appropriate to the facts as they might be found. One will at once sense the profound difference between such procedure as this, and that of Athens, where a mass of five hundred people, subjected to demogogic persuasion, in effect made their own law of decision.

Originally, the *judices* were patricians of high standing, such as senators. For the most part they were not learned in the law. As would be expected, and as we have already indicated, they frequently consulted the priests of the College of Pontiffs, and their decisions reflected the priestly opinions. The decision of the *judex* in the case was not regarded as constituting a binding precedent for succeeding cases. Nevertheless, a body of precedents tended to develop.

Being vested with inherently the same military authority as consuls, *praetors* could be appointed for the provinces. In the course of time *praetors* were accordingly sent to such places as Sicily, Sardinia and Spain. By the time of the Emperor Augustus there were sixteen of them.

The Praetorian Edict—Jus Honorarium. At the outset the Roman *praetor* was not regarded as having legislative powers. He was a judicial officer, and his duty was to administer the legislative law in the form of the Law of the Twelve Tables—the *"jus civile"* as it came to be called in its application to Roman citizens. But though, as we have emphasized, the Law of the Twelve Tables was a great step forward, it was a rigid thing and its procedures, even though liberally interpreted along the lines we have indicated, were too inelastic to make possible the redress of many patent wrongs. Because the *praetor* had inherited kingly attributes he was deemed to have the power to prescribe the rules and methods in accordance with which he would perform his function. These could extend to supplement the prescriptions of the Law of the Twelve Tables.

By the exercise of this power the basic inelasticity of the Law of the Twelve Tables was effectively redressed. As each *praetor* assumed office, he promulgated what was known as an edict, in which were set out the rules and methods that he proposed to follow during his term of office. In his edict he enunciated available remedies and indicated under what circumstances they could be invoked. This edictal Roman law was known as *jus honorarium.*

The praetorial edict was not altogether a personal document. It tended to embody much that had been included in the edicts of his predecessors. Moreover, he generally consulted his jurist friends, and incorporated principles currently held by them. American lawyers of today will recognize in the latter practice a precedent for such modern law-making methods as that of the Supreme Court of the United States in appointing, in 1935, a committee of distinguished jurists to draft the Federal Rules of Civil Procedure. Similarly, the Illinois Civil Practice Act, enacted by the Illinois General Assembly in 1933, was drafted by committees of the organized Bar and submitted for wide professional suggestion and criticism before it was presented to the legislature in final form.

Obviously, the praetorian edicts—the *jus honorarium*—became in themselves important repositories of law. The breadth of their eventual scope is indicated by the fact that they came to embody commercial customs of the Mediterranean area which harked back to the days of the Babylonian Empire.

In a real sense this was legislation. The legislative aspects were emphasized by the fact that no *praetor* was bound by the rules promulgated by his predecessor, but was free to make his own. For reasons that we have already noted, the tendency to expand the scope of his edicts was almost irresistible, and the advice that came to him from his jurist friends provided the wherewithal for added content. The result was that Roman law of the particular era was, through this process, supplementing that of interpretation of the basic law, kept reasonably abreast of the times. As Austin said, the obvious truth is that in Rome, as in most other communities, such has been the incapacity, or such the negligence, of the sovereign legislature, that unless the work of legislation had been performed mainly by subordinate judges, it would not have been performed at all, or would have been performed most ineffectually.

The Equivalent of English and American Equity. In the praetorian edict we find something equivalent to the English and American equity—a system in which an officer, not historically judicial, exercised discretionary power to develop and apply remedies carrying beyond the previously existing law.

But although the Roman *praetor* and the English chancellor—of whom we will have more to say in the appropriate connection later—exercised the same prerogative of discretionary dealing with a case, the process of approach was manifestly different. The *praetor* announced by his edict beforehand under what circumstances he would award certain remedies. In a given case his problem was only to determine if the facts brought it within the purview of his previous edict. The English chancellor, on the other hand, issued nothing in the nature of a praetorian edict. He waited until a case was brought before him and all the facts were in. After he had made his findings of fact he determined whether or not the relief prayed should be granted. Whereas the Roman *praetor* determined and promulgated all his principles beforehand, the English chancellor left such determination to a piecemeal consideration as cases presented themselves. In time, of course, this distinction became minimized. The English chancellors developed a body of precedents altogether as comprehensive as the praetorian edicts. Equity became a segment of English jurisprudence, with its well-understood boundaries and general content.

Comparing the Roman and the common law systems of law, Hessel E. Yntema noted that in each system the scheme of rights had become rigidly formalized and had to be supplemented, corrected and eventually superseded by a parallel system of equitable remedies, introduced by the authority of a magistrate—the *praetor* in Rome, the chancellor in London.

The Praetor Peregrinus. As a natural concomitant of Roman expansion, commerce with the rest of the world grew apace. Outsiders came to Rome to do business. Romans went to other parts of the world to develop trade. There were special forms of transactions from which aliens were originally excluded; as to others, aliens could be parties, but without the rights of citizens. Legal problems came to a head for which the *jus civile* of Rome did not provide an adequate solution, or perhaps was regarded as having no application at all.

For example, we have noted the formality of *mancipatio* which the Roman law provided for a sale of goods. In some countries a sales transaction was legal and binding without any such formality as the Roman law prescribed. The *jus civile* of Rome could not recognize the validity of a contract of sale, even though made in such other country where it was valid. The Roman mind, holding to narrow logic, was without the elasticity to solve the problem by simply recognizing and adopting the principle, elementary in our common law of Conflict of Laws, that a contract valid where made can be properly accepted as valid everywhere. Moreover, as we have seen, the Roman law was held applicable only to Roman citizens.

Roman logic not providing a solution to such problems, the Roman genius for legal improvisation found the way out of the difficulty by creating, in 242 B.C., the office of *praetor peregrinus*, or foreign praetor, and vesting him with jurisdiction to adjudicate disputes between foreigners, or between a foreigner and a Roman citizen. In effect, he was empowered, in such adjudication, to "make" or "use" whatever law would accomplish the purpose of a just and expedient solution.

The Jus Gentium. The *praetor peregrinus*, thus commissioned, proceeded accordingly. The way was open for him to hold, for example, that a contract made in another country under the law of which it was valid should be upheld in Rome, even though it did not meet the requirements of Roman law. By the sequence of such holdings in the variety of cases that came before the *praetor peregrinus* there developed a body of legal principles, drawn in large part from the law of the surrounding communities with which the Romans had contacts, known as the *jus gentium*. It became, in part at least, what is now referred to as the law merchant—that part of the law of nations, grounded upon principles of natural equity, regulating the transactions of men who reside in different countries and carry on the intercourse of nations independently of the local customs and municipal law of particular states.

Through this process the early Roman contract law was greatly broadened. As we have seen, the Roman law did not uphold agreements which represented mere mutual consent of the parties. There had to be a formal ceremony, accompanied by symbolism, before a contractual undertaking was legally validated. Contrary to all these traditions of the Roman law, during the period of the *praetor peregrinus* contracts upon the mere consent of the parties came to be upheld. This principle was extended to contracts of sale, letting and hire, partnership, and agency or mandate. Commercial expediency demanded such a result. The same was true of the four contracts that under old Roman law involved the delivery, or token delivery, of something: namely, the *mutuum,* or simple loan of money without any ceremony of the copper and the scales, the *commodatum,* or contract of gratuitous loan for use, the *depositum,* or contract of gratuitous deposit, and the contract of simple pledge by delivery over of property with that object.

Another important element of law that gained adoption in the *jus gentium* was the conception that good faith must be an ingredient of enforceable contracts. It became a defense that the party seeking to enforce a contract had taken a fraudulent advantage in its procurement, or had otherwise not shown good faith. By like token, such a contract might be rescinded on application of the injured party. No one should be thus enriched at the cost of injury to another. The guiding principle of modern equity that "clean hands" are essential to the awarding of relief is the modern counterpart of the *praetor's* good faith doctrine.

Fusion of the Jus Civile and the Jus Gentium. It is obvious that the *jus civile* and the *jus gentium* were in their inception two separate bodies of law, administered by different tribunals. It was perhaps inevitable that in the course of time they should become fused, even if that result were not attained by direct methods. The student of jurisprudence is familiar with the course of events in the United States, where separate courts of law and equity were set up, and law and equity were long applied under different procedural systems. In time, the same courts were empowered to apply both, and the last vestiges of procedural differences have largely disappeared. In Rome, however, the fusion of *jus civile* and *jus gentium,* was more directly accomplished, when under Emperor Hadrian the *jurisconsult* Julian revised the edicts of all the *praetors* and consolidated them. His work was ratified by the senate, and changes thereafter were forbidden. This prohibition of change was altogether in keeping with the point of view of an emperor who could not tolerate the alteration of the law by any group or agency other than himself. Later emperors, by like token, did not regard themselves as precluded from making changes in Julian's work when they so desired.

The Advent of the Legal Profession. What had been, as we have seen, a legal monopoly of the College of Pontiffs for many centuries, was broken in 254 B.C. when Tiberius Coruncanius, the first plebeian Pontifex Maximus, proclaimed his readiness to lift the veil of priestly secrecy which had previously shrouded the general body of law, and give public information on legal matters. The way was thus opened for secular citizens to become experts in the law, capable of giving legal advice to citizens who sought it. Here was the beginning of the legal profession. *Jurisconsults,* as they were called, who achieved a high degree of scholarship, gave opinions called *responsa prudentium,* not only to the persons who consulted them but also to the *praetors* and *judices* to whom the actual trial of cases had been assigned. These *responsa* exercised great influence over the formulation and growth of the law.

Such scholars as Mucius Scaevola, who wrote a treatise on the *jus civile* and was the teacher of Cicero, and Manilius and Cato Younger of this era left in this manner an outstanding heritage. Other great Roman *jurisconsults* were Gaius, Papinian, Paulus, Ulpian, Modestinus, Sabinus, Julianus and Marcellus. There was also, of course, a role for lawyers to play as forensic advocates, and those who had oratorical talent and devoted themselves to this aspect of the profession found opportunity to bring themselves before the people in a conspicuous manner. Just as it does in modern times in democratic nations, a legal career often led the way to political achievement in the Roman Republic. Cicero, perhaps the most famous lawyer of all time, was a master of forensics and was a leading figure in the Republic's last turbulent days.

Influence of Greek Philosophy. A classic statement of the professional qualifications of a lawyer was made by Cicero, who said that a lawyer must be skilled in the laws and usages among private citizens, in giving opinions, in bringing actions, and in guiding his clients aright. More pertinent for present purposes, perhaps, is the opinion of Cicero as to how these qualifications should be gained. He contemplated the training of the lawyer as going beyond gaining a bare and literal knowledge of the Law of the Twelve Tables and the praetorian edicts. Its ultimate basis was an understanding of philosophy.

Fortunately, circumstances had so developed as to open the way for such philosophical interest and insight. During the second century B.C. Greece was incorporated in the Roman Republic. At that time

Greece had, of course, reached a stage of political decadence. Her great philosophers had had their day, and her culture was in decline. But the Greeks had been inspired by the higher impulses of life. The tides of Hellenic thought still ran strong. Greeks who were brought to Rome following the Roman conquest of that country tutored the Roman youth. Athens became an educational mecca for the sons of Roman patricians. Greek philosophy gained ascendancy in Rome.

The Natural Law. It would go without saying that Plato and Aristotle and the Stoics had much to offer by way of stimulus to legal thinking. Roman ears were receptive to their teachings. The extent to which they influenced Roman legal thought is epitomized by Cicero's statement: "There is a true law, a right reason conformable to justice, diffused through all hearts, unchangeable, eternal, which by its commands summons to duty, by its prohibitions deters from evil. Attempts to amend this law are impious, to modify it is wrong, to repeal it is impossible."

Cicero identified true law and right reason with those qualities of human nature whereby man is associated with the gods. In the natural endowment of man is to be found the true source of laws and rights. We are born for justice, he said, and right is not the mere arbitrary construction of opinion but an institution of nature. To command the approval of the human conscience the positive law of the state must meet the test of conformity to this higher law. As Roscoe Pound said, one of the chief characteristics of the natural law jurisprudence is its identification of law and morals; of what ought to be the law, as the particular jurist sees it, with what it is. This mode of thought was of the highest service in Roman legal history. As the influence of the Greek philosophers worked in Rome, the Roman *jurisconsults* gradually became more and more emancipated from the narrow rigidity of the traditional national jurisprudence. Their views were widely impressed on Roman society. Almost all of them were men of wealth and rank. They were in the habit of giving advice without fee in matters of business as well as law, and were consulted, as Cicero said, "about all things, human and divine." The houses of those of them who attained a high reputation were thronged with citizens. Along with this manifestation there was a rise of legal authorship, promoting the development of a scientific body of legal principles, impregnated with natural law concepts.

That these "natural law concepts" made a contribution of the highest importance to Roman law goes without saying. We will take further note of them when we come to appraise Rome's legacy to the world's jurisprudence.

Demise of the Republic. Thus far in our consideration of the Roman Republic we have traced a course of history which would seem to have been marked by a rather consistent development of democratic institutions, functioning to bring about ameliorative legislation and administration, and providing salutary legal processes for the growth of a progressive jurisprudence. We have seen the Roman plebeians forge steadily ahead in gaining political rights, and have witnessed enlightening developments in the body of Roman law and the manner of its administration. We have seen Roman government and law extended over much of the world of that day, bringing stability to regions that had hardly before known what it was to be free from disorder.

That these things represent progress of the highest order is hardly open to question. We would reasonably expect that with their attainment the Roman Republic would be set for a long period of prosperity under a reign of justice. We are hardly prepared to realize that the era which saw these developments come to a sort of fruition in acceptance of the nobler elements of Greek thought as the embodiment of the higher thought of Rome marked the beginning of the end of the Roman Republic. But we have come to the dispute between Marius and Sulla, which ended only with the crushing of the Republic's governmental institutions and the initiation of a reign of terror.

Bitter Fruits of Oppression. We will speculate further hereinafter about the factors that brought disaster to the Roman Republic. Certainly one cause is to be found in those oppressive policies of Rome with regard to conquered peoples which we have already mentioned, including the seizure of great numbers of them and bringing them to Rome as slaves. Only fear of force would prevent reprisals on the part of such peoples, and when opportunity presented itself, such reprisals were almost sure to come. Thus it was that the natives of the Roman province of Asia Minor, to which far-off region Roman power had been extended, connived with Mithridates the Great to put to death all Romans in that region. Roman sentiment for revenge burned fiercely. In the dispute between Marius, under whose consulship Jugurtha of Numidia had been subdued, and Sulla, as to who should command the avenging forces to be sent to Asia Minor, Sulla marched his legions into Rome, forced legislation effectively depriving the popular assemblies of power, and had Marius and ten companions proscribed. After Sulla's departure, Marius retaliated by inaugurating a period of bloody violence, in the course of which the leaders of the senate were executed and the consul Octavius was assassinated and his head put on public display.

Returning from the Mithridatic War, Sulla, himself and his army richly rewarded with tremendous loot seized from Greek temples and the proceeds of crushing indemnities, assumed dictatorial powers and proscribed thousands of the leaders of Rome. Murder and confiscation were made the order of the day. The senate confirmed Sulla as dictator, and vested in him full power to make laws. He proceeded to restore to the senate powers which it had not exercised for centuries, and to curtail the power of the tribunes.

The changes thus effected were short-lived. In 71 B.C. Pompey led the Roman forces that finally put down a slave revolt led by Spartacus, a slave gladiator, and by way of reward was named consul. Forthwith, he abolished the decrees of Sulla. But from then on the government of Rome was with little regard for the previously established, hard-won, republican institutions.

Final Days Under Antony and Cleopatra. A state of low morals in high places accompanied the violence that ushered in the Republic's final days. Illustrative was the looting of Sicily by Verres, the Roman governor. Not only did he impose the most onerous burdens on the people. He took bribes in his judicial capacity, sold the subordinate offices, and confiscated for himself whatever property he desired. It will be recalled that Cicero came into prominence by prosecuting him when he was subsequently impeached. Cicero perpetuated his own name by his philippic before the senate in 62 B.C., exposing the conspiracy of Catiline and others to murder the consuls, plunder the city and renew the proscriptions of Sulla.

The last years of the Republic witnessed a succession of dramatic events. Pompey, invested with dictatorial powers, cleared the Mediterranean of the scourge of pirates who had taken virtual possession of it, conquered Syria and Phoenicia, and captured Jerusalem. Following the exposure of the Catilinian conspiracy came the First Triumverate, by which Pompey, Crassus and Caesar ruled Rome and its provinces. Caesar's conquest and Romanization of Gaul made him a hero and aroused to a high pitch the jealousy of Pompey, who remained in Rome. Pompey initiated in the senate a decree ordering Caesar to disband his army and resign. Instead, Caesar at the head of his troops crossed the Rubicon, which amounted to a declaration of war, and marched through Italy toward Rome. Pompey and the senate fled. Pompey died by assassination. Caesar was supreme.

The senate named him perpetual dictator and gave him the title of Pontifex Maximus and Imperator.

Caesar played to the masses. In the few years that remained to him before his assassination in the senate by Brutus he put into effect many public decrees abolishing class distinctions and broadening the scope of Roman citizenship. With his death the tempo of events was accelerated. After Mark Antony's dramatic funeral oration, Brutus and the other conspirators fled. Antony usurped power. Following internal war between the forces of Antony and Octavius, adopted son of Caesar, the Second Triumverate was formed. As Plutarch said in his life of Cicero, they divided the empire among themselves as if it had been a private estate. By the terms of the agreement Octavius was to have the government of the West, Antony of the East, and Lepidus of Africa. Each was to turn over such friends as were *persona non grata* to the others of the Triumverate. Two hundred persons were proscribed.

In accordance with this sordid deal Cicero was given up for slaughter by Octavius. His head was set up in front of the rostra from which he had in life so eloquently spoken. Thus, as Plutarch put it, "they showed that no beast is more savage than man when he is possessed of power equal to his passion."

Brutus and Cassius having committed suicide after defeat of the forces which they had rallied to restore the Republic, Antony went to Egypt to insure that that country would cease its assistance to his enemies. The story of how the conqueror was "conquered" by the pulchritude of Cleopatra, how he determined to make Alexandria the Roman capital, how he joined his ships with those of Egypt to resist the attack by Octavius as the champion of Rome, and fled with Cleopatra in defeat, how he later committed suicide when she falsely sent word that she was dead, and, finally, how she put the asp to her breast when Octavius proved immune to her feminine wiles, stands high among the dramatic tales of history.

Thus, in 31 B.C., ended the dynasty of the Ptolemies of Egypt. Egypt was thereafter a Roman province. And though Rome remained a nation, destined to attain still greater heights of material power, with the death of Antony the curtain fell on the Roman Republic.

Why Did the Roman Republic Fall? For one highly important thing, it might be said that it was not a Republic, in so far as that term connotes a government in which the people exercise full representative control. Its suffrage procedures, in which the people voted by groups rather than as individuals, was only awkwardly adapted to registering the undiluted voice of a citizen constituency. Without political parties there were no agencies for the development of political thought in an organized manner. In the last analysis the broad powers held by public officials to administer justice, convene the popular assemblies and command the army were not subject to constitutional limitation, and were beyond the pale of any workable popular control.

But however much the political institutions of the Roman Republic failed the people, questions of honesty and integrity aside, there is certainly a serious question as to whether any government which makes war and conquest a primary business can tolerate individual personal rights in any degree and democratically survive. But questions of honesty and integrity cannot be put aside. Some two centuries before the demise Polybius had written with pride of the high fidelity of Roman officials, saying that it was a rare thing to detect a man who had his hands in the public purse. This high standard did not continue. As we have seen, Rome's far-flung conquests lent themselves to growing graft and corruption which befouled the whole body politic.

It can hardly be expected that the rulers will rise above the ruled. More could hardly have been expected of the rulers of Rome when the morality of the masses had declined. Under the conditions that we have noted, such decline was almost inevitable. At the beginning, Romans as simple agriculturists had little wealth. They were later degraded by the proceeds of lush conquests which invited indulgence in luxury and idleness. Small land holders had lost their holdings because of enforced absence as soldiers in the never-ending wars. There was nothing in the mechanistic Roman religion to promote a high standard of personal conduct. Even such elevating qualities as might have been discernible in it upon close inspection had been nullified by positively debasing aspects of the religious practices which found their way back to Rome from conquered lands.

Moreover, the finer sensibilities of the masses of Romans were dulled by the oppressive policies visited on other human beings all over the world. The presence in Rome of hundreds of thousands of slaves, in large part of alien stock, not only testified to the degradation of such sensibilities but also made for an intense degree of economic demoralization that contributed measurably to the debacle. The freemen of small means could not compete against slave labor.

One generalizes here at his peril, but if a generalized conclusion were attempted, it would be along the line that the liquidation of the Roman

Republic was brought about, not so much by the failure of Roman institutions and law as by the moral inadequacies of rulers and people alike which brought about their perversion.

CHAPTER 8

THE ROMAN EMPIRE

Dawn of Power. The Empire began in 27 B.C. when Octavius was invested with imperial power, adopting the title of Imperator, and receiving from the senate the honorary name of Augustus. When, according to the historian Tacitus, after the destruction of Brutus and Cassius there was no longer any army of the commonwealth, when Pompeius was crushed in Sicily, and when, with Lepidus pushed aside and Antony slain, even the Julian faction had only Caesar left to lead it, then dropping the title of triumvir, and giving out that he was a consul, and was satisfied with a tribune's authority for the protection of the people, Augustus won over the soldiers with gifts, the populace with cheap grain, and all men with the sweets of repose, and so grew greater by degrees while he concentrated to himself the functions of the senate, the magistrates and the laws.

Such was indeed the fact. Allowing the vestiges of the Republic to remain, Augustus proceeded with calculated thoroughness to assume the powers of an emperor. The consuls were continued, but were virtually stripped of power. With the acquiescence of the senate he nominated the magistrates for election by the popular assemblies and, after they were elected, controlled their subsequent actions. He vetoed the "veto" of the tribunes. He altered the composition of the senate itself by reducing the number of senators from one thousand to six hundred, in the process eliminating those regarded as unfriendly, and adding others upon whom he could personally depend. He organized the praetorian guard, an emperor's bodyguard which from time to time played an important part in Roman affairs until it was disbanded by Septimus Severus some two centuries later. To command it he named a praetorian prefect. At first military, this office evolved into the highest judicial office of the Empire, without military jurisdiction. In subsequent times it was filled—to its credit it must be said—by such distinguished jurists as Ulpian, Paulus and Papinian.

With sagacious insight, Augustus accorded deference to the important place that the law had gained in Roman life. He enacted that the *responsa* of designated jurists be solicited in appropriate connections and announced with the emperor's sanction in formal manner.

The working of the regime of Augustus in southern Gaul has been described by saying that having completely subdued the Gauls, he imposed on each province a Roman administration. Each one had its proconsuls, its censors, its praetors, its consuls; each city had its council to deal with important matters. Toulouse had its senate of decurions, which in the provinces was like a feeble image of the Roman senate. The grateful people dedicated their altars to Augustus as to a god. It was not the same for his successors who, riddling with taxes the provinces subject to their domination, made themselves hated by their exactions and perished miserably by poison or the sword.

Wine and Circuses. Under other circumstances the citizens of Rome might have taken notice that their new ruler was in effect ignoring the republican institutions under which Rome had risen to greatness during the preceding centuries, and, inspired by determination to preserve those institutions, they might have been able to check his autocratic usurpation. But circumstances were not of the sort that prompted such serious thought or effort. They found themselves in a period of relaxation and apparently growing prosperity. As Tacitus said, there were doles of corn, wine and oil for hundreds of thousands of the multitude, the wherewithal being exacted from the conquered provinces. The hard work was done by slaves, recruited, as we have seen, by war and kidnapping, and often brutally treated. There was ample time for "play." The theatre lacked the appeal that it had in Greece, but one may hasten to say that this was not because its presentations were dull or unduly moral. Both Plautus and Terence wrote obscene plays, with characters such as libertines and prostitutes, while adultery and seduction were among the subjects bawdily treated.

Public taste ran strongly to spectacles of actual violence and death. Animal baiting had become too tame. Gladiatorial combats of every conceivable variety were staged by social-climbing families and emperor alike, with differences only in scale. To meet the call for gladiatorial talent, seminaries for such training were established throughout Italy. Great audiences were thrilled to decide by thumb-motion whether a wounded gladiator should be spared or should die by the hand of his conqueror. The dead were dragged from the arena with hooks; the pools of blood were coated with dry sand; the show continued; other men entered to fight and die.

Thus, freed from the time being from the rigors of war as such, their physical needs comfortably met, and with dull moments only as they failed to take advantage of the diversions so bountifully provided, the citizens of Rome found their new empire duly satisfying. But no American fails to note the implications inherent in the conclusion of the historian Gibbon, after he had pointed out that the frequent and regular distribution of wine and oil, corn and bread, of money and of provisions, had almost exempted the poorest citizens of Rome from the necessity of labor, that it was artfully contrived by Augustus that, in the enjoyment of plenty, the Romans should lose the memory of freedom.

Revival of Religion and Art. Taking into account the background just sketched, it seems somewhat anomalous that Augustus should have been, as historians have said, gravely concerned about the decay of the religious faith and practices of the people, and that he should have attempted to counteract it by restoring old shrines, erecting temples, and urging renewed veneration for Rome's ancient gods. Perhaps in all this he may be credited for sensing that his people were not living up to the religious traditions of Rome, and with the worthy motive of encouraging higher standards of conduct through renewed attachments to the symbols of deity. But we have in mind that there was little or no connection between the Roman religion and moral ideals. The reasonable belief is that the main concern of Augustus was to make religion a personal ally through identifying it, with renewed emphasis, with the state which he ruled, and by promoting its tranquilizing influences to divert the public mind from projects that might not bode well for the peace of his realm.

By the time of the later period of the Republic there had developed an intellectual class of note. The materialistically sordid era of Augustus would hardly have seemed the time for a flowering of the arts and letters. Nevertheless the roots had not died, and were yet capable of nourishing the superstructure of the plant. Many public architectural masterpieces were erected. Even more impressive were the achievements in literature. Those historians who theorize that Augustus encouraged the activities so well exemplified by Virgil, Horace, Livy and Ovid in order to divert the talents of men of intellectual attainment from political machinations that might have threatened his regime are on reasonably sound ground. However this may be, the era of Augustus witnessed outstanding contributions of men of culture, which were not without effect in adding finer concepts of human relationships. These, directly and indirectly, exerted a measurable impact for the better on Roman life and law.

All seemed serene in Rome. But an ominous cloud was rising in the north, in the form of growing strength of the threatening Germanic tribes. Thinking to bring them under control, Augustus dispatched an expedition to the region beyond the Rhine, under Quintilius Varus. The disaster which came to this expedition unmistakably indicated the force which was to threaten the Empire thereafter, and which would eventually topple it from its foundations. One of its great weaknesses was that its frontiers were not easily defensible against attack from the Teutonic tribes in the West, and from the Persians and Parthians in the East.

But the Rhine seemed a great distance in those days, and, in fact, more than two centuries of relative security stretched immediately ahead.

Tiberius, Caligula and Claudius. The manipulations of Augustus left the government without any stabilized plan of successorship upon his death. Presumably the senate had the power to choose the Emperor, but, as we have seen, the senate had been reduced to a condition of impotence. In the choice the way was left open for intrigue and force to dominate.

Following Augustus came a line of emperors, the names of most of whom have since been synonymous with tyranny. During the reign of Tiberius, adopted stepson of Augustus, Jesus Christ was tried before Pontius Pilate, governor of Judaea, under the patronage system of the Roman Empire, and crucified. Tiberius resurrected the law of *majestas*, making it a capital offense to speak disrespectfully of the emperor. In consequence, many leading citizens met death and their property was confiscated; informers provided the leads. Only those prominent persons who curried favor with Tiberius survived, and trapping others into appearance of disloyalty was a common method of currying favor. In his Annals Tacitus tells how, while three senators hid in a ceiling above a room, others drew Sabinus, a loyal citizen, into conversation, and induced him to make statements which were employed as evidence to condemn him to death. Fittingly enough, Tiberius himself came to a violent end by being smothered to death.

Caligula set an example of dissipation. The normal excitement of the arena so paled for him that at times he ordered spectators to be thrown to the lions. Claudius, who succeeded him, having subjugated southern England, had a naval battle staged upon a large lake with ships containing thousands of gladiators. His career was terminated by his fourth wife, Agrippina, who poisoned him to insure the succession of her son, Nero.

The Era of Christian Persecution. From the standpoint of broad perspective it seems in order to view the period of some two and one-half centuries, commencing with the reign of the Emperor Nero in 54 A.D., as the era of Christian persecution. Living in an age of enlightened American justice, as we are, we can hardly grasp, in its stark reality, much if not most of what went on in those remote times. Accustomed, as we Americans are, to look to the state for protection, it is difficult to realize that the state as then conceived not only did not accord protection against persecution, but was itself the persecutor.

At first thought, too, it would seem that the doctrines of Christianity were in general harmony with the concept of the Roman state as embracing all mankind, and therefore would have been favorably received. For as Paul said to the men of Athens, God that made the world and all things therein "hath made of one blood all nations of men for to dwell on all the face of the earth." But this was not the case. To the Roman emperors the Christians were a subversive group who, because they refused allegiance to the pagan religion and would not make obeisance to the emperor as its godhead, were guilty of treason. It was as simple as that. Having this in mind contributes materially to a better understanding of what went on rather consistently during the early centuries of the Roman Empire, although we are so accustomed to the nomenclature of "persecution" that there is no occasion to employ other characterization.

The Christian persecutions commenced with Nero, who accused the Christians of starting the conflagration that burned Rome, in order to discredit the story that he, himself, was responsible. Christians were thrown to the lions of the arena and put to death by torture. Among other acts of perfidy, Nero charged his old tutor, Seneca, with treason, ordered him to commit suicide, and confiscated his estate.

Under the later Emperor Vespasian Jerusalem was taken, the Temple sacked, and the Jewish nation scattered. The Emperor Domitian, who came to power in 81 A.D., feuded with the senate and proceeded ruthlessly against the Christians because they refused to offer obeisance to statues of himself. At his death, by assassination in his own household, the senate ordered his name to be blotted from the records of the government.

Trajan and Anonymous Informations. Trajan, who was born in Spain, came to power as the first emperor from the provinces, thus reflecting the expanded scope of the Empire. In the course of his rule he vigorously prosecuted the Christians, but, strangely enough, apparently with some recognition of principles of enlightened legal procedures. Of particular interest is some of the correspondence between him and Pliny the Younger. Pliny wrote to Trajan with regard to what should be done with the Christians, asking whether "repentance" should earn a pardon, or if "when a man had once been a Christian he gains nothing by leaving the sect." There was no written or stated law which dealt with the situation. Trajan replied that when "these people" were summoned and convicted they must be punished; "but when the accused denies that he is a Christian, and gives proof by adoring our gods, whatever suspicion he may have previously incurred, he should earn pardon for repentance."

Pliny further wrote to Trajan as to the best method of handling the prosecution of Christians, referring to "an anonymous information" containing a charge against several persons, who, upon examination, denied that they were Christians, or had ever been Christians. Trajan replied: "You have adopted the right course, my dearest Secundus, in investigating the charges against the Christians who were brought before you. Anonymous informations ought not to be received in any sort of prosecution. It is introducing a very dangerous precedent, and is quite foreign to the spirit of our age."

Hadrian and Usurpation. In the year 117 A.D. Trajan was succeeded by Hadrian. From the time of his accession, and perhaps from an earlier period, the supreme legislative power originally covertly exercised by the emperors, was openly assumed. Instead of emitting their decrees through the popular assemblies or the senate, they legislated avowedly as monarchs and autocrats, and promulgated their commands in Imperial constitutions.

These Imperial constitutions were of two kinds—general and special. By a general constitution (*edictum*) the emperor, acting in his legislative capacity, established a law of a universal or general character, and not regarding specifically a single case or person. Special constitutions were of various kinds, but agreed in this: that they referred to specific single cases or persons. One kind was called an extraordinary mandate, and was an order addressed to a civil or military officer, for the regulation of his conduct in the execution of his office. The most important of these special constitutions were *decretes* and rescripts which were made by the emperors in their capacity as sovereign judges; a *decrete* being an order made on a regular appeal from the judgment of a lower tribunal, and the rescript being an order preceding the judgment of the lower tribunal, and instructing the lower tribunal how to decide the case.

Thus was illustrated how in a nation with Rome's enlightened back-

ity by his successors, the municipal governments were stripped of all vestiges of autonomy and converted into mere tax-collecting agencies for the emperor. Upon them was thrust the responsibility for collecting and transmitting to the royal seat the levies which, in ever-increasing amount, the emperors found necessary to maintain an empire which, in spite of its imposing facade of absolutism, was fast heading into decadency. The local welfare was dealt a fatal blow.

The decurionate had formerly been an office sought by members of the middle class for the honor implicit in it. Now it could not be avoided by those eligible. If they did not come forward and volunteer, they were viciously searched out and compelled to serve, at their own expense. They were forbidden to leave their municipalities. Their property was in effect bonded for such service, and and could not be sold. Each decurion, moreover, was jointly liable with the others. If one became bankrupt, or otherwise defaulted, those remaining had to bear the loss, and they had the further obligation, under penalty, to find and return the defaulter if he had become a fugitive.

The augurs of Rome might well have found such a state of affairs direly portentous.

The Era of Church Supremacy. The system of succession set up by Diocletian was violated by Constantine, who assumed power in 306 A.D. and fought for many years to overcome challengers to his rule. At the Battle of the Milvian Bridge Constantine's army fought under the standard of a Christian cross, adopted by him as the result of an alleged revelation as he prayed to a pagan divinity. Having won the battle, he accepted to the full the implications which he felt were involved, and dramatically reversed the policies of his predecessors with regard to Christians. In 313 A.D. he issued a decree granting Christians and all others full liberty of following that religion which each might choose. Subsequently, he made Christianity the religion of the Roman state.

Thus, by a strange turn of events, we enter a long era which not inaccurately might be characterized as the era of church supremacy. Official intolerance reversed its former course and proceeded to vent itself against non-professors of Christianity. The full power of autocratic government was dedicated to the extermination of heretics who did not accede to the dogmas of the Council of Nicea. Differences over the nature of the Divine Trinity and whether the Father and the Son were of the same or only similar substances became issues of loyalty, not merely to the church but also to the state, and, indeed, to a total way of life, to civilization itself. The "unity" of the church to the end that its power might be unimpaired was the desideratum. How far the effort to insure it went is pointed out by Marion J. Bradshaw, who noted that for the Council of Nicaea the unity of the church would be broken if some congregations knelt in prayer and some stood; so Nicene canon law ordered all to stand.

Division of the Empire. Along with the promotion of Christianity, Constantine was concerned to establish the Roman Empire even more firmly upon the basis of despotism exemplified by the monarchies of the East. To that end he moved the capital to Byzantium, on the Bosphorus, building a magnificent new city and naming it Constantinople. With the death, in 395 A.D., of the Emperor Theodosius the Great, who in his reign outlawed all religions but Christianity, the Roman Empire became in effect divided into two parts, the East and the West. Thenceforward, as Bryce pointed out, there were two legislative authorities. For the sake of keeping the law as uniform as possible, arrangements were made for the transmission by each emperor to the other of such ordinances as he might issue, in order that these might be, if approved, issued for the other half of the Empire. These arrangements were not, however, fully carried out, and before long the Western Empire drifted into so rough a sea that legislation practically stopped. The Great Codex of Theodosius II was promulgated in the Western as well as the Eastern part of the Empire, whereas the later Codex and Digest of Justinian, published nearly a century later, was enacted only for the East, though presently extended by reconquest to Italy, Sicily and Africa. Parts of the Theodosian Code were embodied in the manuals of law made for the use of the Roman subjects by some of the barbarian kings. It continued to be recognized in the Western provinces after the extinction of the imperial line in the West in 476 A.D. It was indeed, along with the manuals aforesaid, the principal source whence during a long period the Roman population drew their law in the provinces out of which the kingdoms of the Franks, Burgundians and Visigoths were formed.

The Eastern Empire continued until 1453 A.D., when, as we shall further see in our consideration of Islam, Constantinople was captured by the Turks. But the Roman heritage waned. Greek replaced Latin, even the Roman law being written and employed in Greek. Greek refugees fleeing from the Muslim ravagers brought to Western Europe many precious manuscripts of the great literature of ancient Greece. By happy coincidence, John Gutenberg had invented printing with movable type in the era that these manuscripts thus became available, affording a medium for their publication and wide dissemination.

From the time of the division the Western Empire was under attack by successive waves of invaders—Goths, Vandals, Burgundians and Huns. Rome fell to the Vandals from Africa, who in 455 A.D. sacked it and impressed thousands of its citizens into slavery. In 476 A.D. the child-emperor named as such by the interloper Orestes was dethroned by Odoacer, chief of a force of German invaders, and the Empire of the West came to an end. Justinian, the Eastern Emperor at the time, reconquered Italy in 553 A.D. and purported to restore the Western Empire, but a few years later it was taken over by the Lombards.

An abortive attempt to restore the Western Empire was made in 800 A.D. when Charlemagne knelt on Christmas Day in St. Peter's Cathedral in Rome, and the Pope pressed upon his brow the diadem of the Roman emperors. By that act there was added another seven hundred years of an uneasy marriage of Church and State. Lord Bryce said that from the fifth to the sixteenth centuries, whoever asked what was the source of legal sovereignty, and what the moral claim of the sovereign to the obedience of subjects, would have been answered that God had appointed certain powers to govern the world, and that it would be a sin to resist his ordinance. From the eleventh century onwards, it was admitted in Western Christendom, though less cordially in France, Spain or England than in Italy and Germany, that there were two legal sovereigns, and according to the view more generally held, each was *de jure* absolute, the Pope in spiritual, the Emperor in temporal matters. Both Pope and Emperor were above all positive secular law, but subject to the law of nature and the law of God, these being virtually the same.

Those who are curious may learn from the financial and economic histories of the Middle Ages that this was a period of administrative absolutism when the common man was a slave or a serf; when men had to attach themselves to some armed knight or baron or duke or similar powerful individual for physical protection; and when each strata of the people was cabined and confined within a legal system which was an unyielding as those of antiquity, and largely for the same reasons. Protection of life, liberty and property was solely by might. With such theories of the law being currently accepted by those in authority, and the people confronted with all the horrors of excommunication and eternal damnation if they contested the exercise of unjust and oppressive administration of the laws, it is no wonder that this period in the world has become known as the Dark Ages.

We may appropriately draw the curtain on Rome by saying that once again, in modern times, a would-be Caesar strutted upon the stage, proclaiming his destiny to restore Rome to its ancient grandeur when the Mediterranean was a "Roman lake." The role fizzled. History does not record that any of his assassinated predecessors were put on display, strung up by the heels, as was Mussolini. That the world was shocked by this desecration of a human body, however great its aberrations when it was morally activated, afforded evidence of some elevation of the spiritual standards of the human race. Since then a democratic nation, Italy, like Greece, points with dignity to the heritage bequeathed by Rome to the civilized world.

CHAPTER 9

THE CONTRIBUTIONS OF ROMAN LAW

Law From Violence, Conquest and Corruption. The impression that would reasonably be gained from the foregoing sketch of the power that conquered the ancient West and much of the East by force of arms, and ruled it by a combination of force and imposed law for over a thousand years is not one of a society consciously concerned with ordered progress promoted by a program of internal and external justice. For the most part, the portrayal is rather one of a series of despotic governments, much of the time imposing their will upon the less fortunate classes of the inhabitants of Roman territory, almost constantly engaged in strife, and promoting an agenda of conquest.

Even during the more stable periods of the Republic these things went on. Through long periods we have noted the promotion of a licentious way of life, with its concomitant of corruption from the lowest ranks to the highest levels of the government itself. At some times more conspicuously than others, the record depicts unmistakable cruelty, accompanied by the use of unmitigated force, internally as well as externally. In no connection, as we shall further see, was this more marked than in the attempt to impose observance of dictated formulae of the Christian religion.

One would hardly look to the sources of such a chronicle for the elements of a worthy system of justice, or for the first complete system of law dealing with the mutual relations and transactions of private individuals with each other disclosed by history. And yet, it is precisely there that we find these very things.

In our observations dealing with the development of the *jus honorarium*, the *jus gentium*, and the impact of Greek philosophical thought we have anticipated much of the explanation. The institutions of the Republic made such a development possible, and in general promoted it. After all, the violence, conquest and corruption which stand out so blatantly were the manifestations of that human depravity which exists apart from and in spite of governmental institutions and laws, however salutary. Unfortunately, such manifestations are not unknown to us today. Beneath the repulsive surface, the better side of man was evolving a growing sense of justice that found general expression in the public assemblies, and which achieved specific translation in the works of the *praetors,* the *jurisconsults* and the great legal scholars who throughout the period of the Republic and early Empire laid the foundations for the Theodosian Code and the subsequent great classic of jurisprudence, the Corpus Juris Civilis of Justinian.

True, the emperors who followed Augustus with a profusion of personal "constitutions" appeared to be ruthlessly dictatorial in their manner of laying down the law. But upon a closer look it would seem that although they held no concern for the right of the people to have a voice in making the law by which they were governed, they had real respect for its substance as affecting the private lives of Romans, and for the manner of its administration. The emperor reserved for himself the right to hear all appeals, and to give opinions. But by way of aid, not only for governmental purposes in general but in all judicial matters, he surrounded himself with a group of advisers which came to be known as the Imperial Consistory. In this group were generally found the leading jurisconsults of the time. To be sure, force of circumstances permitted them to be hardly other than obsequious. Nevertheless, the head of the state thus created a favorable formal setting for respect for law and its purpose, with opportunity to promote its influence for justice in Roman life.

Emphasizing what might be said to be two of the concrete contributions which Rome made to the world, Guizot points out that the two elements of Roman civilization which passed from the Roman civilization into ours were, first, the system of municipal corporations, its regulations, its habits, its principle of liberty—a general civil legislation, common to all; secondly, the idea of absolute power—the principle of order and the principle of servitude. Order, of course, is the basis of civilization. Rome's contribution in that regard was distinctive. It remained for the common law in particular to modify the rigidities of "absolute power" to bring the power concept into working conformity with ideals of human freedom as we know them.

The Theodosian Code. The earnestnesses with which the better emperors, at least, took their responsibilities in the matter of the law, finds demonstration in the project initiated by Theodosius II, which resulted in the first official codification of Roman law after the Law of the Twelve Tables. In 438 A.D., nearly a century before the Corpus Juris Civilis of Justinian, Theodosius II, in collaboration with Emperor Valentinian III of the West, promulgated the Theodosian

Code, covering both public and private law, including criminal, civil, administrative, military and ecclesiastical provisions.

Some of the circumstances surrounding the preparation of this Code are disclosed by the minutes of the Roman senate of December 25, 438 A.D., which had assembled on that day to hear about it. In keeping with the low estate to which the senate had descended, in so far as its governmental prerogatives were concerned, the minutes manifest an understandable obsequiousness on the part of that body in relation to the emperor. But beneath this somewhat disgusting, but superficial manifestation, is apparent the hard core of real legal achievement. At the outset of the proceedings, Praetorian Prefect Glabrio Faustus, who presided, declared grandiloquently: "The felicity that emanates from our immortal Emperors proceeds in its increase to the point that it arrays with the ornaments of peace those whom it defends in the fortunes of war." Alluding to his previous attendance at the wedding between the daughter of Theodosius, and Emperor Valentinian III, which took place in Constantinople, Prefect Faustus continued: "After the nuptials had been felicitously solemnized, the most sacred Emperor, our Lord Theodosius, desired to add the following high honor also to this world, namely that he should order to be established the regulations that must be observed throughout the world, in accordance with the precepts of the law which had been gathered together in a compendium of sixteen books, and those books he had desired to be consecrated by His most sacred name. The immortal Emperor, Our Lord Valentinian, with the loyalty of a colleague and the affection of a son, approved the undertaking." Thereupon, as indicated by the minutes, the assembly shouted: "Thou are newly eloquent! Truly eloquent!"

Continuing, Prefect Faustus announced that "the most Sacred Emperor" ordered copies to be delivered "from his own divine hand" to Prefect Faustus and the Prefect of the Orient, "one to each of us, in order that they might be dispatched throughout the world with all due reverence." He then said: "If it please your Magnificences, let your Magnificences order that these very laws be read to you by which they ordered that this undertaking should be performed in order that we may obey with proper devotion the most carefully considered precepts of the immortal Emperor." Whereupon the assembly shouted: "It is right, it is right! So be it!"

From the statements of Prefect Faustus it appears that when Emperor Theodosius ordered the Code prepared he prescribed as a model the works of Gregorius and Hermogenes, both distinguished law professors whose writings had attained wide usage and general acceptance. He ordered that "after the pattern of the Gregorian and Hermogenian Codes, a collection shall be made of all the constitutions that were issued by the renowned Constantine, by the sainted Emperors after him, and by Us, and which rest upon the force of edicts or sacred imperial law of general force." Nine eminent legal scholars, most of whom were Greeks, had been named for the task. "We are confident that these men who have been selected by our Eternity will employ every exceptionally learned man, in order that by their common study a reasonable plan of life may be apprehended and fallacious laws may be excluded."

After Prefect Faustus had completed his reading there was a chorus of approving shouts. Forty-three in number were recorded, most of them shown as having been repeated a number of times. Among them were: "Augustus of Augustuses," "God gave you to us, God save you for us," "a third term for you in the consulship," and "our hope is in you, you are our salvation."

The Corpus Juris Civilis of Justinian. The Emperor Justinian, probably of Slavic ancestry, who came to power at Constantinople in 527 A.D., left two great monuments of his forty-year reign. One was the Church of Sancta Sophia, which survived the Roman Empire to become a Muslim mosque when Constantinople fell to the Turks in 1493, and which became a museum in the regime of modern Turkey. Of far greater importance was the Corpus Juris Civilis, the culminating compilation of Roman law and a priceless contribution to justice and civilization. Although Justinian's name has ever since been attached to this body of law, it was not his personal work but that of commissioners appointed by him. It included the following elements:

These commissioners first compiled a code embracing the imperial constitutions. Next, in the field of jurisprudential law, they assembled the Digest or Pandects, divided into fifty books, arranged on the model of the perpetual edict, and embodying selections from writings of the great jurists covering the various areas of the law. For example, Justinian's Digest contains some six hundred extracts from the works of Papinian, who, as we have seen, lost his life because he refused to approve as legal the murder of Gata by his brother, Caracella. This was an encyclopedic production, and Justinian ordered a work of an abbreviated nature, suitable for a legal study text. The Institutes of Gaius, who died around 180 A.D., served as a basis for Justinian's Institutes, an abbreviated repository for basic principles of law arising out of Roman life and trade and contact with the world.

Subsequently there came a second code, and Novellae, which incorporated changes in the legislative law.

The vital source of the decisive influence of Roman law in western culture is the fact that it was, once for all, embodied by the Emperor Justinian in this Corpus Juris, the authoritative form in which, like the Bible in things spiritual and the works of Aristotle for philosophy, it was received as the epitome of justice in later times. Well did the Supreme Court of the United States say that due process of law, in spite of the absolutism of continental governments, is not alien to that code which survived the Roman Empire as the foundation of modern civilization in Europe, and which has given us that fundamental maxim of distributive justice, *suum cuique tribuere* (to render to every man that which belongs to him). For the first provision of Justinian's Institutes is: "Justice is the constant and perpetual wish to render every one his due." The second is: "Jurisprudence is the knowledge of things divine and human; the science of the just and the unjust." The third is: "The precepts of the law are, to live honestly, to hurt no one, to give every man his due."

Virility of Principle and Content. In the light of the considerations of which we have spoken, it is understandable why the Theodosian Code and the Corpus Juris Civilis of Justinian did not suffer the same fate of oblivion as did Hammurabi's Code. In the Roman law was a virility of principle and content that sustained it through long periods of tribulation during which it was relatively impotent, and which ultimately brought it back to bloom in full vigor.

Commenting upon developments in France at this juncture, William Wirt Howe said the barbarian conquerors could overrun the country but they could not divest themselves of the reverence which they had for the institutions of the empire, and especially for the system of law which, in the scientific development of the early jurists, appealed to them in the same way that Greek sculpture appeals to an American artist. So we find them framing codes for their conquered subjects based on Roman law, no doubt preparing such compilations with the help of such jurists as they could employ. Thus, we have the Edict of Theodoric, the Ostrogoth, who for a time reigned over a part of South Gaul, a work probably prepared by Cassiadorus, a Roman jurist and philosopher who was attached to the court of Theodoric. This code was promulgated about the beginning of the sixth century.

We find, also, the underlying part of the French law, the Breviary of Alaric II, sometimes called the Roman law of the Visigoths, or

West Goths, which had its domain in Southern Gaul because South Gaul as well as Spain was part of the Visigothic kingdom. Alaric II, son of Euric, was proclaimed king and honored at Toulouse by delegates of the principal cities under his rule. He did not seek at first to make new conquests, but rather to conserve those of his father. He governed well. Just as his predecessor had given a code to the Visigoths, he desired to give to the people subject to him and therefore accustomed to Roman manners and customs a commentary on the Theodosian Code, which would govern them for the future. This commentary, prepared by Gouarich and the jurisconsult Ancan, was approved in a general assembly and promulgated at Toulouse, under the name of the Breviary d'Alaric. By virtue of this important document the Roman law was preserved during the centuries in the South of France. From that date the subjects of Alaric followed the Roman law if they were Gauls, the ordinances of Euric if they were Goths, or special regulations if one was a Gaul and the other a Goth. This new law prohibited, under pain of death, marriage between provincials and barbarians.

The Breviary of Alaric II in fact antedated by some years the works of Justinian. It contained sixteen books of the Theodosian Code, a collection of imperial constitutions of more recent date; the Institutes of Gaius compressed into two books and sometimes referred to as the Gothic Epitome of Gaius; some *sententiae* or opinions of Paul; some portions of the Gregorian and Hermogenian Codes, and, finally, a passage from the writings of Papinian. In this way, amid the many changes of this turbulent epoch many of the best portions of the classical law were not only preserved but put to use in the interest of a new governmental order. The Breviary of Alaric II became law for Western Europe, at least until the revival of legal studies in the twelfth century. It was one of the sources of Portuguese and Brazilian law.

Revival of the Twelfth and Thirteenth Centuries; Las Siete Partidas. The study of Roman law was revived in the twelfth and thirteenth centuries at the University of Bologna, and was pursued with vigor there and at other centers of learning, such as the Universities of Toulouse, Montpellier and Paris. Justinian's Corpus Juris Civilis constituted the basis for instruction.

It is probable that the jurisconsults of Spain is this era began to take part in this revival of study of Justinian's works, which spread throughout Italy, France and England. In the year 1255, Alfonso the Learned, the king of Castile, promulgated the Fuero Real. This work was preliminary to the framing and promulgation of Las Siete Partidas, one of the most important and interesting codes that has ever been published in the course of legal development. It was finally promulgated in the year 1348. It is divided into seven parts, as its name implies, this division possibly being an imitation of the seven parts of Justinian's Digest, and having perhaps some reference to the supposedly sacred character of that number.

By a royal decree of 1530 the Partidas were extended to the Spanish colonies. It is said that such extension gave the Partidas the widest territorial force ever enjoyed by any law book. They are still authoritative as fundamental law in many Civil Law countries that were formerly part of the Spanish Empire. When the French colony known as Louisiana was ceded to Spain in 1760, the code known as Partidas was introduced, and became a really large part of the fundamental law of that vast domain. Portions of it were translated into French for the benefit of the inhabitants. Some of its provisions remained as part of the law of the State of Louisiana, and are referred to in the earlier decisions of the Louisiana Supreme Court. The Spanish law remained in force in Texas until 1840 and the Partidas are frequently cited in the early supreme court reports of that state. In California the Spanish law continued for a decade longer and there, too, the Partidas were often invoked by the early judges.

The Law of Northern France. We have noted the incorporation of Roman law in the law of southern France. But French law was not destined to be entirely Roman in its character. As William Wirt Howe has emphasized, another important influence was added in the form of what are commonly referred to as the barbarian laws, such as those of the Salian Franks, the Riparian Franks and the like. These were Teutonic customary laws, and were in nature what might be expected from such peoples at such a period of their development: systems in which the primitive ideas of family, clan, status, torts and penalties play a large part. Their customary laws derived from local grants and charters, and from the feudal system as differently applied in different provinces. There were many of these different jurisdictions, each with its customs, receiving its name from the province in which it prevailed, such as the Custom of Orleans, the Custom of Normandy, the Custom of Brittany, and the like. Naturally, one of the most important among them was what was called the Custom of Paris. That city had become more and more the center of civilization and learning, and was distinguished for its revival of the study of Roman law. When, therefore, in the seventeenth century France began to take up seriously the project of colonization in America, and to provide some kind of law for her possessions in the Western World, it was prescribed that the laws, edicts and ordinances of the realm of a general character, and the Custom of Paris, should be extended to those colonies.

To the coverage of these customary laws there was to be added, as indicated, the general law of the realm, which was constantly being changed or modified by the "capitularies" and ordinances of the kings. The power of the monarch came to be more and more displayed in these edicts, which resembled the constitutions of the Roman emperors.

Obviously, there was present a great diversity of law between the various regions and kingdoms of Western Europe during this era. It was said that in traveling through France by the common mode of travel of those times, one changed law oftener than he changed horses.

The Code Napoleon. The most influential of all Civil Law Codes in the modern world is the Code Napoleon, promulgated by the Emperor Napoleon. Its Roman law foundation may be traced to French universities at Toulouse, Paris and Montpellier, whose establishment was inspired by the law studies at Bologna, and at which Justinian's Corpus Juris Civilis constituted the basis for instruction. In the eighteenth century the French jurist, Pothier, produced his *Pandectae Iustiinianae in Novum Ordinem Digestas.* The Custom of Paris had been increasingly influenced by Justinian. In 1800 Napoleon, as First Consul, ordered a civil code prepared. In essence, it was a compendium of the rules of Roman law then recognized as in force in France, as interpreted by Pothier and other French jurists. In 1804 it was promulgated. That same year it became the model for the Civil Code of Belgium, and in 1808 for the Civil Code of Louisiana. In the further course of the nineteenth century it became the model for civil codes in Austria, Greece, Holland, Hayti, Bolivia, Peru, Chili, Italy, Quebec, Portugal, Argentina, Uruguay, Mexico, Nicaragua, Guatamala, Honduras, Spain and Salvador.

Speaking of the Napoleonic codes, and particularly of the Code Civil, Roger Houin recently stated that due to the lucidity and precision of the style employed by their authors, the unification of law that they effected in the interior of France, the introduction that they brought about in private law of the great revolutionary principles of liberty and equality of individuals, these monuments of law continue to form the basis of French legislation, and, regarded as "written reason," they have exercised a significant influence in the entire world.

Although the conquest of the world by the Roman Empire came to an abrupt end, the conquest of the world by Roman law continues and there is no sign that it will pass away as long as mankind endures. Today it rules a wider empire than the Caesars ever knew and its empire is ever widening.

The basic difference of concept between the common law and the civil law is brought out in the Code Napoleon. As we shall see further, common law is essentially judicial law. At the beginning of his Civil Code Napoleon put in a provision forbidding judges from laying down any general rule of law. And such is the spirit and the general practice today in all Civil Law countries. It is not considered to be the business of judges to make law; their task is to apply it to the specific cases brought before them. It follows that they should not formulate rules of law in their own words. That has been authoritatively done, once for all, by the codes. Neither should they be influenced in their decisions by what other judges have held upon similar facts, for the others may have been wrong, and it is not desirable that errors should be repeated. The result is that the application of law does not give rise itself to new rules of law.

The Leaven of Roman Jurisprudence—Natural Law. The study of Roman governmental institutions and Roman law has been a fascinating one for historians, political scientists and lawyers of all succeeding generations. The origins of Roman law and the part it has played have provided material for many commentaries. As we approach the close of this brief sketch it is in order to emphasize more than has been attempted heretofore two elements which seem particularly noteworthy as leavening the content and administration of Roman jurisprudence, and which contributed to the virility of principle which brought it through great vicissitudes and commanded for it such universal acceptance—the concept of natural law, and Christianity.

Like all earnest men, the Romans were moved by schools of thought which embodied truth as the desideratum. In the Roman sense, Greece was a failure as a nation. Yet as we have seen, the Romans held Greek thinking and Greek philosophers in high esteem. The philosophy of natural law, with the key to its ascertainment of what is right and good provided by the human conscience, greatly influenced the Roman jurists and *praetors*. From the end of the Republic, Roman jurisprudence identified law and morals, subordinating law and the makers of law, whether judges or legislators, to the overriding veto power of the ethics of natural law.

Natural law concepts proceed with the thought of law as a body of jurisprudence extending through a commonwealth of all mankind, ordained to govern the social relationships between all men in like manner as the laws of gravity and other manifestations of the physical world govern life's material aspects. Natural law philosophy as to the content of at least part of this body of jurisprudence has played so important a part in legal thinking that it merits exposition extending beyond the mere generalization that it is grounded on unwritten principles of universal justice, translating themselves into rules of moral conduct susceptible of revelation through the conscience with which each man is equipped.

As to its source and ultimate development, Sir Frederick Pollock said that natural law as conceived by mediaeval scholars was derived partly from the Aristotelian distinction of natural and conventional justice, partly from the Latin exposition, led by Cicero, of the same idea in its later Greek forms, and partly from the still later special adaptation of it by the classical Roman jurists.

Blackstone's Exposition of Natural Law. Because our Revolutionary forefathers and the framers of the Constitution of the United States were under the strong influence of natural law philosophy, it is appropriate that we should turn for a somewhat more detailed exposition of it to Sir William Blackstone, whose commentaries on the laws of England, widely read and influential in the American colonies, evaluated it in the light of historical perspective.

Speaking first of all of law in its broad sense, he said that law in its most general and comprehensive sense signifies a rule of action, and is applied indiscriminately to all kinds of action, whether animate or inanimate, rational or irrational. Thus we say, the laws of motion, of gravitation, of optics, or mechanics, as well as the laws of nature and of nations. And it is that rule of action which is prescribed by some superior, and which the inferior is bound to obey. Thus, when the Supreme Being formed the universe, and created matter out of nothing, he impressed certain principles upon the matter from which it can never depart, and without which it would cease to be. If we further advance from mere inactive matter to vegetable and animal life, we shall find them still governed by laws; more numerous, indeed, but equally fixed and invisible. The whole process of plants, from the seed to the root, and from thence to the seed again; the method of animal nutrition, digestion, secretion, and all the other branches of vital economy—are not left to chance, or the will of the creature itself, but are performed in a wondrous involuntary manner and guided by unerring rules laid down by the great Creator.

This, then, said Blackstone, is the general significance of law, a rule of action dictated by some superior being; and in those creatures which have neither the power to think nor to will, such laws must be invariably obeyed, so long as the creature itself subsists, for its existence depends on that obedience. But laws, in their more confined sense, and in that which it is our present business to consider them, denote the rules, not of action in general, but of *human* action or conduct: that is, the precepts by which man, the noblest of all sublunary beings, a creature endowed with both reason and free-will, is commanded to make use of those faculties in the general regulation of his behavior. Blackstone went on to say—and he might well have emphasized it more than he did—that man, considered as a creature, must necessarily be subject to the laws of his Creator, for he is entirely a dependent being. Any human law must be in conformity with this basic law of nature, or it will not work. And, consequently, as man depends absolutely on his Maker for everything, it is necessary that he should in all points conform to his Maker's will.

Digressing momentarily from Blackstone, it might well be said that these principles are of even greater pertinence today, when man must relate his conduct to the released manifestations of atomic fission and outer-space phenomena, than they were conceived to possess by the Greeks and Romans, and even by the philosophers of eighteenth-century England. If men are to stay alive and live together, their law must indeed be geared with nature's physical fabric. Blackstone went on to say that man can accomplish this as part of the very law of nature itself. For as God, when he created matter and endued it with a principle of mobility, established certain rules for the perpetual direction of that motion; so, when he created man and endowed him with free-will to conduct himself in all parts of life, he laid down certain immutable laws of human nature, whereby that free-will is in some degree regulated and restrained, and gave him also the faculty of reason to discover the purport of those laws.

Considering the Creator only as a being of infinite power, He was able unquestionably to have prescribed whatever laws he pleased to his creature, man, however unjust or severe. But as He is also a being of infinite wisdom, He has laid down only such laws as were founded in those relations of justice that existed in the nature of things antecedent to any positive precept. These are the eternal, immutable laws of good and evil, to which the Creator in all his dispensations conforms; and which he has enabled human reason to discover, so far as they are necessary for the conduct of human actions.

Such, among others, are these principles: that we should live honestly, should hurt nobody, and should render to every one his due; to which three general precepts Justinian has reduced the whole doctrine of law.

But, continued Blackstone, if the discovery of these first principles of the law of nature depended only upon the due exertion of right reason, and could not otherwise be obtained than by a chain of metaphysical disquisitions, mankind would have wanted some inducement to have quickened their inquiries, and the greater part of the world would have rested content in mental indolence and ignorance, its inseparable companion. As therefore the Creator is a being not only of infinite power and wisdom, but also of infinite goodness, he has been pleased to so contrive the constitution and frame of humanity that we should want no other prompter to inquire after and pursue the rule of right, but our own self-love, that universal principle of action. For he has so intimately connected, so inseparably interwoven the laws of eternal justice with the happiness of each individual, that the latter cannot be attained but by observing the former; and if the former be punctually obeyed, it cannot but induce the latter.

In consequence of which mutual connection of justice and human felicity, the Creator has not perplexed the law of nature with a multitude of abstracted rules and precepts, referring merely to the fitness or unfitness of things, as some have vainly surmised; but has graciously reduced the rule of obedience to this one paternal precept "that man should pursue his own true and substantial happiness." This is the foundation of what we call ethics or natural law. For the several articles into which it is branched in our systems amount to no more than demonstrating that this or that action tends to man's real happiness, and therefore very justly concluding that the performance of it is a part of the law of nature; or, on the other hand, that this or that action is destructive of man's real happiness, and therefore that the law of nature forbids it.

This law of nature, being coeval with mankind, and dictated by God himself, is of course superior in obligation to any other. It is binding over all the globe, in all countries, and at all times; no human laws are of any validity if contrary to this; and such of them as are valid derive all their force and all their authority, mediately or immediately, from this original.

Reason and Revelation. In order to apply this to the particular exigencies of each individual, Blackstone went on, it is still necessary to have recourse to reason; whose office it is to discover, as before observed, what the law of nature directs in every circumstance of life, by considering what method will tend the most effectually to our own substantial happiness. And if our reason were always, as in our first ancestor before his transgression, clear and perfect, unruffled by passions, unclouded by prejudice, unimpaired by disease or intemperance, the task would be pleasant and easy; we should need no other guide but this. But every man now finds the contrary in his own experience; that his reason is corrupt, and his understanding full of ignorance and error.

This has given manifold occasion for the benign interposition of Divine Providence; which in comparison to the frailty, the imperfection, and the blindness of human reason has been pleased at sundry times and in diverse manners, to discover and enforce its laws by an immediate and direct revelation. The doctrines thus delivered we call the revealed or divine law, and they are to be found only in the Holy Scriptures. These precepts, when revealed, are found upon comparison, to be really a part of the original law of nature, as they tend in all their consequences to man's felicity. But we are not from thence to conclude that the knowledge of these truths was attainable by reason, in its present corrupted state; since we find that until they were revealed, they were hid from the wisdom of ages. As then the moral precepts of this law are indeed of the same original with those of the law of nature, so their intrinsic obligation is of equal strength and perpetuity. Yet undoubtedly the revealed law is of infinitely more authenticity than that moral system which is framed by ethical writers and denominated the natural law. Because one is the law of nature expressly declared so to be by God himself; the other is only what by the assistance of human reason we imagine to be that law. If we could be as certain of the latter as we are of the former, both would have an equal authority; but till then they can never be put in competition together.

Blackstone continued that upon these two foundations, the law of nature and the law of revelation, depend all human laws; that is to say, no human laws should be suffered to contradict them. There are, it is true, a great number of indifferent points, in which both the divine law and the natural law leave a man at his own liberty; but which are found necessary for the benefit of society to be restrained within certain limits. And herein it is that human laws have their greatest force and efficiency; for with regard to such points as are not indifferent, human laws are only declaratory of and act in subordination to the former. To instance in the case of murder: this is expressly forbidden by the divine, and demonstrably by the natural law, and from these prohibitions there arises the true unlawfulness of this crime.

Those human laws that annex a punishment to it do not at all increase its moral guilt, or superadd any fresh obligation *in foro conscientia* to abstain from its perpetration. Nay, if any human law should allow or enjoin us to commit it, we are bound to transgress that human law, or else we must offend both the natural and the divine. But with regard to matters that are in themselves indifferent, and are not commanded or forbidden by those superior laws; such for instance, as exporting of wood into foreign countries; here the inferior legislature has scope and opportunity to incorporate and to make that action unlawful which before was not so.

Speaking in this same connection, Sir Frederick Pollock has said that justice as a necessary element of the state is divided into natural and conventional. Rules of natural justice are those which are universally recognized among civilized men. Rules of conventional justice deal with matters which are indifferent or indeterminate until a definite rule is laid down by some specific authority. Such are all rules fixing the amount of fines or other money payments. The rule of the road may furnish as good a modern example as any. Reason suffices to tell us that some rule is desirable on frequented roads, but whether we shall take the right or the left can be settled only by custom or legislation; and in fact the rule differs in different countries.

The Law of Nations. If any man were to live in a state of nature, unconnected with other individuals, observed Blackstone, there would be no occasion for any other than the law of nature and the law of God. Neither could any other law possibly exist, for a law always supposes some superior who is to make it, and in a state of nature all are equal without any other superior but Him who is the author of our being. But man was formed for society; and as is demonstrated by the writers on that subject is neither capable of living alone, nor has the courage to do it. However, as it is impossible for the whole race of mankind to be united in one great society, they must necessarily divide into many; and form separate states, commonwealths and nations, entirely independent of each other. Hence arises a third kind of law, to regulate this mutual intercourse, called the "law of nations" which, as none of these states will acknowledge a superiority to the other, cannot be dictated by any; but depends entirely upon the rules of natural law, or upon mutual compacts, treaties, leagues and agreements between these several communities; in the construction also of which compacts we have no other rule to resort to but the law of nature; being the only one to which all the communities are equally subject;

and therefore the civil law very justly observes that *quod naturalis ratio inter omnes homines constituit, vocatur jus gentium.*

Any mention of the law of nations, and particularly in relation to natural law, would be incomplete without reference to Grotius.

Hugo Grotius, Holland's famed jurist and humanist, was appalled by savagery in the Thirty Years War, which ended with the Peace of Westphalia in 1648, and which was perhaps more brutally waged and more destructive of life than any war prior to World War I. He set himself to think out the principles upon which laws might be based for mitigating the horrors of hostilities. The application of these principles is given in his book *De Jure Pacis ac Belli,* which was published in 1625. As a model for his work there existed certain codes of maritime law which had governed the practice of sailors and merchants in ancient or contemporary traffic in the Mediterannean or other seas. On other than maritime questions the practice of permanently accrediting ambassadors, the rule since the end of the fifteenth century, was beginning to provide in embryo a crystallization of diplomatic practice. It was not, however, a mere codification (with additions) of existing law, which Grotius gave the world. As the Roman *praetor peregrinus,* in working out to meet the needs of the ancient world a practical system of law, invoked a system of ideal principles of right and wrong, familiar to the Stoics, to improve and perfect the code of laws which he administered, so this same ideal eternal justice, the *ius naturale,* was invoked by Grotius to shape and regulate the code of international practice which was once more to "make men free" from the worst features of institutional rivalry in the new order of the world. Then he worked out a judicial expression for world organization, which other prophets like Cruce and Sully had but dreamed. In tracing the progressive steps towards some system of world organization we can see that the debt owed to both is great, to the more statesmanlike vision as well as to the more poetic.

America's Debt to Natural Law. American law is indebted to natural law concepts for much of its trend and content. The extent of the obligation might be gauged with some exactness by a process of historical analysis. For our purposes this is unnecessary. It is sufficient to realize that there is a debt.

It is unnecessary to go far for symbolic exemplification. In the third century A.D. the Roman jurist Ulpian wrote the strangely familiar sentiment, "by natural law, all men are equal, are created equal." What American has not been thrilled to read the immortal paragraph introducing the Declaration of Independence: "When in the course of human events it becomes necessary for one people to dissolve the political bands which have connected them with another, and to assume among the powers of the earth the separate and equal station to which the Laws of Nature and of Nature's God entitle them, a decent respect to the opinions of mankind requires that they should declare the causes which impel them to the separation. We hold these truths to be self-evident, that all men are created equal, that they are endowed by their Creater with certain unalienable rights, that among these are life, liberty, and the pursuit of happiness."

However intangible such an idealistic concept, it sparked the American Revolution. Americans today are its living beneficiaries. It should not be at all difficult for us to understand that in the era of its recognition by Roman jurists it worked to lift the Roman judicial processes to a higher plane. Through their working it, in turn, was elevated and strengthened for transmission to posterity.

A very recent expression of natural law philosophy in its relation to present-day law and political institutions was made at the observance of the Bicentennial of John Marshall at the Harvard Law School by Joseph M. Snee, who stated that natural-law philosophy conceives the function of political authority to be far more basic than the mere preservation of external order by imposing an armed truce upon Hobbes' "warre of every man against every man." The purpose and duty of the body politic is to provide the means necessary or conducive to the full human life, or, as Aquinas would express it, to promote the common good, to provide an order of justice and liberty. Its sphere of authority extends to every external human activity which affects the common good, which strengthens or debilitates the capacity of the community and its members to play their role in the development of the truly good life. The world of commerce and property is by no means excluded; the laissez-faire concept of an untouchable and sacrosanct liberty of contract or the idea of an absolute right of private property is completely alien to the natural-law thought of St. Thomas and the scholastic tradition. Despite its necessity and pervasive character, the authority of political society is not, however, without its limitations. It is limited by the very necessity which calls it into being—the nature of man. It must constantly be kept in mind that the body politic is nothing but the rational self-organization of a human community for the specific purpose of promoting the common good by the establishing of optimum conditions for the perfect development of the human personality of its members.

The Influence of Christianity. We shall deal further with Christianity hereinafter. Suffice it to say here, in passing, that in the recognition of Christianity by Constantine, the philosophy of Stoicism was superseded by that of the Christian Gospel. Thereafter, as Professor Brown has said, Roman law responded to the influence of a new concept of natural law, more authoritative and more discriminating than the Stoical, as to the difference between reason and instinct. A personal God was now postulated instead of a materialistic pantheism. The result was that the law of Rome became even more sensitive in the necessity of discriminating between good and bad faith, between the deliberate and the accidental injury, and between the letter and the spirit of the law, than ever before.

The "Invisible Commonwealth of Civilized Nations." We have already commented upon the debt of our law to the natural law, as the concept was recognized and amplified by the Roman jurists. To some extent the debt extends to the more mechanistic content of the Roman law. Speaking as a German scholar as well as a student of the common law, Professor Rudolf Leonhard said that formerly the opinion prevailed in Germany that the English law was wholly free from Roman ideas. Every one knows from the excellent works of Sir Frederick Pollock and Professor Maitland that this opinion was long ago refuted. In reality Roman law was received by Germany and also England and America. But in England and America, this reception was more a reception of ideas, in Germany more a reception of a code. In England and America there was a reception only of doctrines or terminologies, on the Continent there was a reception of the totality of the Roman texts.

As Rudolf Leonhard summed it up, Roman ideas of law invade the whole wide territory for which the Christian Church created a common civilization. From Rome came the universal empire of antiquity. From that empire arose the universal church of the Middle Ages. From that Church arose the invisible commonwealth of civilized nations. This community is not one of law alone, for the law never remains uninfluenced by other branches of culture. But the members of this family of nations are related in the first degree with respect to ideas of law, because, first through the influence of the Universal Church, and later through the international science of Bologna, Roman and Canon law came to be a common fundamental basis of law for the community of civilized peoples. In later times nations have become more and more separated, but the remembrance of the common source of their thinking has kept them from absolute division. In this way certain Roman ideas have been preserved as a common treasure of law which can be easily recognized by the terminology of juridical science.

PART IV: ONE GOD AND THE LAW

Chapter 10

JUDAISM AND ISRAEL

Beginnings of Hebrew History. The history of the Hebrews begins around the year 2000 B.C. when God appeared to Abraham, when he was in Ur of the Chaldees, near the River Euphrates, "and said unto him, Get thee out of thy country, and from thy kindred, and come into the land which I will shew thee." Thereupon Abraham left Mesopotamia and dwelt in Charran until his father died, after which he went on to Canaan.

After various experiences, including a journey into Egypt, Abraham and his nomadic tribe were sojourning in a fertile area in Canaan. Following a successful attack by a combined force of Hebrews and Canaanites, which Abraham led, and which gained the favor of King Melchizedek and other Canaanite rulers of the area, the Lord promised him that his seed would be as the unnumbered stars; that they would be afflicted in a strange land for four hundred years, but that thereafter they would return to Canaan. "In the same day the Lord made a covenant with Abraham, saying, Unto thy seed I have given this land, from the river of Egypt unto the great river, the river Euphrates."

Thus we are introduced to the covenant upon which Hebrew history is grounded. The concept of a covenant, a relation of mutual understanding between man and man, was basic in every-day Hebrew life. To the extent that it defined agreed mutual rights and obligations it embodied a law of conduct that was accorded high respect. It promoted the harmonious human relationships that made for happiness. Of equal importance with the covenant was the symbolism under which it arose or by which it was manifested. Covenants in those ancient days were not always lived up to, any more than they are now. The flesh was, and remains, weak. But they created a norm for conduct.

In the present connection we shall be dealing with covenant in the exalted realm where Yaweh, or Jehovah, is one of the parties. A covenant by Jehovah must needs be an eternal verity. With these considerations in mind we can understand the implicit faith of the leaders of the Hebrew people that Jehovah would sustain them through their vicissitudes. We can understand, too, that Jehovah was not unmindful that His people had covenanted to obey His law, and that when they failed to do so they did not merit the protection of Jehovah. All in all, we shall be in position to better appreciate the significance of the events of history at which we are about to glance.

Moses and the Exodus. Abraham's descendants did, indeed, multiply and, in due course, made their way into the "strange land" of Egypt, where they and their successive generations carried on their nomadic lives. Moreover, Jehovah's prediction that the Israelites would be afflicted in the "strange land" for four hundred years was borne out. We have already noted the law of the Pharaoh who said, "Behold, the people of the children of Israel are more and mightier than we are: Come on, let us deal wisely with them." Thereupon taskmasters were set over the Israelites to afflict them with their burdens. The Egyptians made the children of Israel to serve with rigor. And they made their lives bitter with hard bondage, in mortar and in brick, and in all manner of service in the field. The Egyptian king ordered the Hebrew midwives to kill the male sons of Hebrew women, but Moses was saved by Pharaoh's daughter.

In due time, when Moses was grown, he went out and looked on these burdens. Seeing an Egyptian smiting a Hebrew, he slew the Egyptian and hid his body in the sand. When the next day he took to task a Hebrew for smiting another Hebrew, the former betrayed Moses to the King. Moses had to flee for his life to the land of Midian. There he drove away shepherds who were preventing the seven daughters of the priest of Midian from watering their father's flocks, was invited to live in the priest's household, and eventually married Zipporah, one of these daughters.

Forty years went by. The Hebrew people cried to Jehovah. Jehovah heard their cry and remembered his covenant with Abraham. He appeared, in a burning bush, to Moses, tending the flocks of his father-in-law, and said, "I am the God of thy father, the God of Abraham, the God of Isaac and the God of Jacob. I have surely seen the afflictions of my people which are in Egypt. And I am come down to deliver them out of the hands of the Egyptians. Come now therefore, and I will send thee unto Pharaoh, that thou mayest bring forth my people, the children of Israel, out of Egypt. Go and gather the elders of Israel together, and say unto them, The Lord God of your fathers, the God of Abraham, of Isaac and of Jacob appeared unto me, saying, I have surely visited you and seen that which is come to you in Egypt. And I have said, I will bring you up out of the affliction of Egypt."

After demurring—quite understandably—Moses undertook the assignment to return and "gather the elders together" and to confront Pharaoh with the demand that the Israelites be freed. Pharaoh refused. In spite of a series of manifestations, including the turning of Aaron's rod into a serpent, plagues of frogs, flies and locusts, and physical afflictions in the way of boils, Pharaoh refused to obey the divine decree to let them go until all the Egyptian first-born died in a night. Thereupon Pharaoh called for Moses and said, "Rise up and get you forth from among my people."

Guided by a cloud by day and a pillar of fire by night the Israelites proceeded on their way. The pursuing Egyptian hosts were overwhelmed in the Red Sea. "And Israel saw that great work which the Lord did upon the Egyptians: and the people feared the Lord, and believed the Lord and his servant Moses." In token of deliverance they sang the eloquent "Song of Moses," with its theme, "The Lord shall reign for ever and ever."

These events in the history of the ancient Hebrews were much in the minds of our Revolutionary forefathers as they deliberated in Philadelphia. A committee appointed the same day the Declaration of Independence was adopted, consisting of Jefferson, Franklin and Adams, to prepare a device for a seal of the United States, proposed as such device Pharaoh sitting in an open chariot, a crown on his head and a sword in his hand, passing through the dividing waters of the Red Sea, in pursuit of the Israelites, with rays from a pillar of fire beaming on Moses, who is represented as standing on the shore extending his hand over the sea, causing it to overwhelm Pharaoh, and, underneath, the motto, "Rebellion to tyrants is obedience to God." The chief textbook of the Constitutional forefathers was Algernon Sidney's *Discourses Concerning Government*; Sidney's works were to be found in the libraries of Franklin, Adams, Jefferson and many others of the scholars, statesmen and divines of the time. Sidney was a student of the Hebrew Commonwealth and analyzed its government discriminatingly.

The human quality of the Israelites was demonstrated only three days after their deliverance from the Red Sea, when, after journeying in the wilderness without water, they came to the waters of Marah and found them bitter. "And the people murmured against Moses, saying, What shall we drink?" This was only the first of several such incidents. On the fifteenth day of the second month after their departure the whole congregation of the children of Israel murmured against Moses and Aaron in the wilderness. "And the children of Israel said unto them, Would to God we had died by the hand of the Lord in the land of Egypt, when we sat by the flesh pots, and when we did eat bread to the full: for ye have brought us forth into this wilderness, to kill this whole assembly with hunger." At Rephidim the people murmured so strongly for lack of water that Moses cried unto the Lord, saying, "What shall I do unto this people? They be almost ready to stone me." In all these instances, of course, it is evident that Jehovah was testing the people. Their needs were eventually met.

The Hebrew Commonwealth. What Oscar S. Straus has characterized as the Hebrew Commonwealth embraces that period of the history of the children of Israel, from the Exodus to the selection of Saul as king, that is, during the administration of Moses, Joshua and the judges, about 550 years, according to the generally approved chronology from about 1650 B.C. to 1099 B.C. That the Israelites while in Egypt were under some definite discipline and regulations of their own is to be inferred not only from the fact that when they left Egypt they did not go forth like a tumultuous rabble, but marched as an organized army under regular leaders, but also from the circumstance that when Moses was first sent to deliver God's message to the children of Israel he was directed, as we have seen, to "gather the elders of Israel together," and he literally followed the express direction. Straus emphasizes that the Hebrew Commonwealth, unlike the other republics, both ancient and modern, was an original government. It was not constituted from the remnants of a shattered monarchy, nor did it belong to that class of governments which were originally formed from the seeds of their own dissolution. The governing power was exercised by the people, and not arrogated by the few, or retained by aristocratic families who might thereby have the means of constituting themselves an hereditary senate. The children of Israel, when they escaped from the thraldom of Pharaoh, like the people of America when they severed their allegiance from the king, were peculiarly fortunate in having no titled classes with exclusive privileges to contend against, no institutions among them which had outlived their usefulness, no old ruins to rebuild. They were peculiarly fortunate in having the power of organizing for themselves such form of government as they in their most deliberate judgment, guided by the experiences of all nations, might elect.

It it possible to discern a division of powers as established by Moses in such government as was possible under the nomadic circumstances of the Israelites during the progress of the exodus. Military command was assigned to Joshua, as indicated by the order to Joshua, when Amalek and his forces threatened, to "choose us out men" and to go out to fight with Amalek. Priestly duties were in Aaron's province, his priesthood being confirmed by the Lord on Mount Sinai and the blossoming of his almond rod.

Moses himself assumed the responsibility for conduct of the civil government. The verses from the Book of Exodus which narrate the colloquy between him and his father-in-law, Jethrow, is not only enlightening in this regard but also evidences the beginning of a true legal system.

And it came to pass on the morrow, that Moses sat to judge the people: and the people stood by Moses from the morning unto the evening.

And when Moses' father-in-law saw all that he did to the people, he said, What is this thing that thou doest to the people? Why sittest thou thyself alone, and all the people stand by thee from morning unto even?

And Moses said unto his father-in-law, Because the people come unto me to enquire of God:

When they have a matter, they come unto me: and I judge between one and another, and I do make them know the statutes of God and his laws.

And Moses' father-in-law said unto him, The thing that thou doest is not good.

Thou wilt surely wear away, both thou, and this people that is with thee: for this thing is too heavy for thee: thou art not able to perform it thyself alone.

Harken now unto my voice, I will give thee counsel, and God shall be with thee: Be thou for the people to God-ward, that thou mayest bring the causes unto God:

And thou shalt teach them ordinances and laws, and thou shalt shew them the way wherein they must walk, and the work that they must do.

Moreover, thou shalt provide out of all the people able men, such as fear God, men of truth, hating covetousness; and place such over them, to be rulers of thousands, and rulers of hundreds, rulers of fifties, and rulers of tens:

And let them judge the people at all seasons: and it shall be, that every great matter they shall bring unto thee, but every small matter they shall judge: so shall it be easier for thyself, and they shall bear the burden with thee.

If thou shalt do this thing, and God command thee so, then thou shalt be able to endure, and all this people shall also go to their place in peace.

So Moses harkened to the voice of his father-in-law, and did all that he had said.

And Moses chose able men out of all Israel, and made them rulers of thousands, rulers of hundreds, rulers of fifties, and rulers of tens.

And they judged the people at all seasons: the hard cases they brought unto Moses, but every small matter they judged themselves.

This Biblical episode may well account etiologically for the institution of various kinds of courts and the general idea of an appellate court.

Mount Sinai and the Ten Commandments. Of paramount interest is the event on Mount Sinai, where, after 40 years of wandering, and in a symbolic atmosphere of lightning and thunder, Moses received from Yaweh, or Jehovah, the Two Tables containing the Ten Commandments. After the Israelites came into the wilderness of Sinai the Lord called to Moses out of the mountain, commanding him to tell the children of Israel that "if ye will obey my voice indeed, and keep my covenant, then ye shall be a peculiar treasure unto me above all people: for all the earth is mine." Having been so informed, "all the people answered together and said, All that the Lord hath spoken we will do." God spoke all these words:

Thou shalt have no other gods before me.

Thou shalt not make unto thee any graven image, or any likeness of anything that is in heaven above or that is in the earth beneath; or that is in the water under the earth; Thou shalt not bow down thyself to them, nor serve them: for I the Lord thy God am a jealous God, visiting the iniquity of the fathers upon the children unto the third and fourth generation of them that hate me; and shewing mercy unto thousands of them that love me and keep my commandments.

Thou shalt not take the name of the Lord thy God in vain: for the Lord will not hold him guiltless that taketh his name in vain.

Remember the Sabbath day to keep it holy. Six days shalt thou labor and do all thy work. But the seventh day is the Sabbath of the Lord thy God: in it thou shalt not do any work, thou, nor thy son, nor thy daughter, thy manservant, nor thy maidservant, nor thy cattle, nor thy stranger that is within thy gates. For in six days the Lord made heaven and earth, the sea, and all that in them is, and rested the seventh day: wherefore the Lord blessed the Sabbath day and hallowed it.

Honor thy father and thy mother: that thy days may be long upon the land which the Lord thy God giveth thee.

Thou shalt not kill.

Thou shalt not commit adultery.

Thou shalt not steal.

Thou shalt not bear false witness against thy neighbor.

Thou shalt not covet thy neighbor's house, thou shalt not covet thy neighbor's wife, nor his manservant, nor his maidservant, nor his ox, nor his ass, nor anything that is thy neighbor's.

When, after an absence on the mountain for forty days Moses came down with the two tables of stone, he found the people offering sacrifices to a golden calf. Enraged, he cast the tables out of his hands and broke them and destroyed the calf. Subsequently, he interceded with Jehovah to forgive the Israelites, and "The Lord God, merciful and gracious, longsuffering, and abundant in goodness and truth, keeping mercy for thousands, forgiving iniquity and transgression and sin," wrote on and handed to Moses two new tables. When Moses came down from the mountain his face so shone that the people were afraid to come near him.

The Promised Land. Moses was not to set foot on the promised land. When the children of Israel arrived in sight of it Moses "spake in the ears of all the congregation of Israel" a final "Song of Moses." He recounted to them their hardships, their toils, their sufferings and their triumphs. He admonished them to obey the law and assured them that "The eternal God is thy refuge, and underneath are the everlasting arms." From the top of Mount Pisgah he viewed the promised land from afar, and died.

The Period of the Judges. The Hebrew conquest of Canaan was never completed in the sense that the Israelites became free from the danger of attack. The Hebrew Commonwealth was an amphictyony —tribes held together to a religious compact. The existing environment did not lend itself to the development of an organized and stabilized government and although their covenant with Jehovah was a unifying force, it was constantly subjected to what we would think of today as the "subversive" influences of the peoples around them who worshipped pagan gods.

Under such circumstances, it is not surprising that for a period of some two centuries of their earlier sojourn in Canaan there is revealed a recurring pattern of the Israelites departing from this covenant with Jehovah; Jehovah thereupon ceasing to protect them; the Israelites, after being oppressed, repenting and Jehovah, thereupon, forgiving the aberration and renewing his protection under the covenant. The method by which the Israelites were delivered from one fall from grace after another was not standardized.

During this period the government was conducted by "judges," who, however, were rulers in the full governmental sense rather than judicial officers alone. They adjudicated not only individual but also intertribal difficulties. One of these judges, Deborah, was a woman, who dwelt under the palm tree of Deborah in Mount Ephraim, "and the children of Israel came up to her for judgment." In some instances they were divinely commissioned to lead. Thus, after the Israelites were oppressed by Midian, an angel of the Lord appeared to Gideon and said to him, "The Lord is with thee, thou mighty man of valor. Go in this night, and thou shalt save Israel from the hand of the Midianites: have I not sent thee?" Gideon asked for a sign to confirm the commission. After it had been provided through a fire consuming a sacrifice of flesh and cakes placed upon a rock Gideon undertook and successfully carried out the mission, "and the country was in quietness forty years in the days of Gideon."

That in other instances these judges were commissioned by the people is indicated by the account of Jephtah in the Book of Judges. Israel having fallen from grace was menaced by the Ammonites. Because Jephtah was the son of a harlot, his brothers who were legitimate forced him into exile, where he gained prowess as a military man. The elders of Gilead went to induce him to return and lead the forces of Israel against the Ammonites. Jephtah asked, "If ye bring me home again to fight against the children of Ammon, and the Lord deliver them before me, shall I be your head?" Whereupon the elders replied, "The Lord be witness between us, if we do not so do according to thy words." Then Jephtah went with the elders of Gilead, and the people made him head and captain over them. Jephtah judged Israel six years.

Among the best known of the judges was Sampson, son of Manoah of the tribe of Dan. The angel of the Lord appeared unto his wife, who is not named, and told her she would bear a son. "The child shall be a Nazarite unto God from the womb: and he shall begin to deliver Israel out of the hand of the Philistines." His career as a deliverer by sheer personal prowess was interwoven with Philistine women, one of whom he married and who was later "given to his companion, whom he had used as his friend." His later relations with Delilah, who by her feminine wiles drew from him the secret that his strength lay in his unshaven head, had his head shaved while he slept, caused his eyes to be put out when he could not break the bonds with which he had been secured, and at the end perished along with three thousand Philistines when Sampson, whose strength had returned as his hair grew out again, pulled down the pillars of the temple in which they had assembled to celebrate the triumph of their god Dagon over Jehovah, provided the elements of one of the most famous episodes of history.

The Hebrew Kingdom—Saul and David. Through the times that we have been considering the moral fiber of the Hebrews was being constantly weakened by the temptation to forsake Jehovah's law and embrace that of the divinities of the Canaanites. Though the Israelites were again and again restored to power, the Philistines made increasing inroads upon them and eventually inflicted upon them a disastrous defeat and captured the Ark of the Covenant. At this juncture "all Israel knew that Samuel was established to be a prophet of the Lord." Under his leadership the Philistines were subdued, "and they came no more into the coast of Israel: and the hand of the Lord was against the Philistines all the days of Samuel."

When Samuel was old he made his sons judges over Israel. But his sons walked not in his ways, but turned aside after lucre, and took bribes, and perverted judgments. Then all the elders of Israel gathered themselves together and said unto Samuel, "Behold, thou art old, and thy sons walk not in thy ways: now make us a king to judge us like all the nations." Samuel protested and the Lord supported his protest, telling Samuel to explain to the people the hard lot that would be theirs under a king. "And ye shall cry out in that day because of your king which ye shall have chosen you: and the Lord will not hear you in that day." Nevertheless the people refused to heed the voice of Samuel and the injunction of Jehovah and insisted upon a king, "That we may also be like all the nations: and that our king may judge us, and go out before us, and fight our battles." And the Lord said unto Samuel, "Hearken unto their voice, and make them a king." Samuel chose Saul, and convened the people at Mizpeh. Introducing Saul he said, "See ye him whom the Lord hath chosen, that there is none like him among all the people?" And all the people shouted and said, "God save the king." Thus, around 1050 B.C., ended the Hebrew commonwealth and began what was in effect a Hebrew monarchy.

Historians are not altogether in agreement as to the significance that should be accorded this change. Viewed in perspective, it would appear to have been a rather natural development, arising out of the realization, enforced by centuries of experience, that a group of individual tribes could not sustain themselves against continuous aggression without a more firmly administered and stabilized central government than the system of improvised judges had made possible. Nevertheless, it has been viewed with regret by lovers of democracy. In a sermon delivered in 1775, Samuel Langdon, president of Harvard College, said: "The Jewish government, according to the original constitution which was divinely established, if considered merely in a civil view was a perfect republic. And let those who cry up the divine right of kings consider that the form of government which had a prior claim to divine establishment was so far from including the idea of a king that it was a high crime for Israel to ask to be in this respect like other nations, and when they were thus gratified it was rather as a just punishment for their folly." Oscar S. Straus points out in this connection that the Hebrew commonwealth was not subverted by force nor by the tricks or cunning devices of unscrupulous leaders, as was the case with the Grecian and Roman Republics, but by the people exercising their democratic prerogative, the right of choice to set up over themselves such form of government as they might elect.

Saul possessed the military ability that the times demanded but his career was marked by an insane jealousy of David, his son-in-law, and by refusals to obey the will of Jehovah, which ultimately brought him to a sad end. One of his aberrations involved his consultation, in disguise, of the witch of Endor. In his final battle "the Philistines followed hard after Saul, and after his sons, and the Philistines slew Jonathan, and Abinadab and Malchishua, the sons of Saul." Saul then killed himself by falling on his sword. "So Saul died for his transgression which he had committed against the Lord, even against the word of the Lord, which he kept not, and also for asking counsel of one that had a familiar spirit, to enquire of it: And enquired not of the Lord: therefore he slew him, and turned the kingdom over to David, the son of Jesse."

When David heard of the death of Saul and Jonathan he lamented in the Song of David: "Saul and Jonathan were lovely and pleasant in their lives, and in their death they were not divided; they were swifter than eagles, they were stronger than lions. How are the mighty fallen in the midst of the battle."

David was a strong king. He solidified the government and broke the Philistine yoke by wars of extermination against the surrounding peoples. He captured Jerusalem, and dwelt therein and established friendly relations with the Phoenicians.

Solomon. David was succeeded by his son, Solomon, about 970 B.C. In Gibeon, where Solomon had gone to sacrifice, the Lord appeared to him in a dream by night and said, "Ask what I shall give thee." And Solomon said, "Give therefore thy servant an understanding heart to judge thy people, that I may discern between good and bad: for who is able to judge this thy so great a people." This so pleased the Lord that he replied, "Lo, I have given thee a wise and understanding heart, so that there was none like thee before thee, neither after thee shall any arise like unto thee." We are told that Solomon's wisdom did indeed exceed the wisdom of all the children of the east country, and all the wisdom of Egypt, and his fame was in all nations round about. "He spake three thousand proverbs and his songs were a thousand and five. And he spake of trees, from the cedar tree that is in Lebanon even to the hyssop that springeth out of the wall; he spake also of beasts and of fowl, and of creeping things, and of fishes. And there came of all people to hear the wisdom of Solomon, from all kings of the earth, which had heard his wisdom."

The quality of his wisdom is commonly exemplified by his decision in the case of two harlots, each of whom claimed to be the mother of the baby which, with them, was before him:

And the king said, Bring me a sword. And they brought a sword before the king. And the king said, Divide the living child in two, and give half to the one, and half to the other.

Then spake the woman whose the living child was unto the king, for her bowels yearned upon her son, and she said, O my lord, give her the living child and in no wise slay it. But the other said, Let it be neither mine nor thine, but divide it.

Then the king answered and said, Give her the living child, and in no wise slay it: she is the mother thereof.

But the record raises grave question as to the broader aspects of Solomon's wisdom. He maintained a lavish court. He made a great throne of ivory and overlaid it with the best gold; there was not the like in any kingdom. All King Solomon's drinking vessels were of gold; none was of silver: it was nothing accounted for in the days of Solomon. For the king had at sea a navy of Tarshish, with the navy of Hiram: once in three years came the navy of Tarshish, bringing gold, and silver, ivory, and apes, and peacocks. And the king made silver to be in Jerusalem as stones, and cedars made he to be as the sycamore trees that are in the vale, for abundance. And Solomon had horses brought out of Egypt, and linen yarn. So King Solomon exceeded all the kings of the earth for riches and for wisdom. Moreover he instituted a lavish building program, including not only a temple for the ark of the covenant but a personal palace and other structures. As a result of such policies, the lot of his Hebrew subjects was not an easy one. "Solomon had twelve officers over all Israel, which provided victuals for the king and his household: each man his month in a year made provision." Thus, each man worked one month of a year for the king's establishment. But this was not all. He instituted what was in effect a system of forced labor. "And King Solomon raised a levy out of all Israel: and the levy was thirty thousand men. And he sent them to Lebanon, ten thousand a month by courses: a month they were in Lebanon, and two months at home: and Adoniram was over the levy." Debts were incurred to Hiram, the Phoenician king, which had to be liquidated by Solomon's turning over to Hiram twenty cities in the land of Galilee.

In the latter part of his reign Solomon's morals sank to a low ebb.

"But King Solomon loved many strange women, together with the daughter of Pharaoh, women of the Moabites, Ammonites, Edomites, Zidonians and Hittites: of the nations concerning which the Lord said unto the children of Israel, Ye shall not go in to them, neither shall they come in unto you: for surely they will turn away your heart after their gods: Solomon clave unto these in love. And he had seven hundred wives, princesses, and three hundred concubines: and his wives turned away his heart. For it came to pass when Solomon was old, that his wives turned away his heart after other gods: and his heart was not perfect with the Lord his god." The Lord stirred up adversaries to Solomon, and his last days were filled with trouble.

The Kingdom Divided. When Solomon died about 953 B.C., his son Rheoboam, who succeeded him, was asked to lighten the burdens to which the Israelites had been subjected. The old men of Solomon's court advised him to accede, but the young men advised otherwise. "And the king answered the people roughly, and forsook the old men's counsel that they gave him: and spake to them after the counsel of the young men, saying, My father made your yoke heavy, and I will add to your yoke: my father also chastised you with whips, but I will chastise you with scorpions." So Israel rebelled against the house of David unto this day.

In consequence, the kingdom was divided. Only the tribes of Judah and Benjamin followed Rheoboam. The other tribes set up a new kingdom, north of Jerusalem, with Jereboam as king. The latter kingdom, with Samaria as capital, was known as the Kingdom of Israel; the kingdom of which Jerusalem remained the capital was known as the Kingdom of Judah. As we have seen, in 722 B.C. the Assyrian king, Sargon, captured Samaria and carried away the flower of the Israelites. As we have also seen, in 586 B.C., Nebuchadnezzar, the king of Babylon, captured and destroyed Jerusalem, looted the temple of its sacred vessels, and carried the people into the Babylonian captivity. In 538 B.C., Cyrus the Great defeated Nebuchadnezzar and captured Babylon. The Book of Ezra describes how Cyrus permitted and cooperated in the repatriation of the captives, the rebuilding of the temple, and the restoration of the sacred utensils which Nebuchadnezzar had pilfered. His successors, Darius and Artaxerxes, carried forward the same friendly policy.

The land came under the Macedonian Empire in 332 B.C. In 301 B.C. Ptolemy Soter, king of Egypt, carried off 100,000 of the people to Alexandria and Cyrene. They were given equal rights with the Egyptians. The Greek translation of the Old Testament known as the

Septuagint was made by them. After a century of Egyptian rule Palestine was conquered by Syria. Antiochus, a Syrian ruler, made the temple at Jerusalem a temple of Jupiter. Under the Maccabees the Syrians were driven out. Jerusalem was captured by Pompey in 63 B.C. Antipater, made procurator by Caesar, was poisoned, and was succeeded in 37 B.C. by his brother, Herod. Herod's grandson, Herod Agrippa, was made ruler by the Emperor Claudius, and obtained for the Jews the right of Roman citizens. But there was rebellion against Roman occupation. In 70 A.D. Jerusalem was captured by Titus, son of Emperor Vespasian. He killed or drove into permanent exile hundreds of thousands of the people, destroyed the temple, and carried its sacred utensils to Rome as trophies of war. Not until May 15, 1948, did Israel again become an independent nation.

The Hebrew Judicial System. We have already noted the nature of the Hebrew government, including its judicial system, in its earlier period. The Sanhedrin, or council of seventy, around which centered the judicial system in later eras, can be traced to an early date. Whether it had its origin in Jethro's advice to Moses, or came into being somewhat later, is a matter concerning which biblical expositors are divided. That a permanent national senate was early created is maintained very generally by Jewish writers, as well as by such scholars as Sidney, Grotius, and Selden. The former claim that this senate continued with but short interruptions until the Babylonian Captivity, and was revived and reorganized on more definite principles after the return of the Jews to Jerusalem thereafter. Some writers even go so far as to deny that this council of seventy was a legislative body, and claim that it was purely judicial. However, Oscar S. Straus concluded that although its chief functions were legislative, and it occupied the same position in the frame of government as the Senate of the United States, yet it was at the same time a high court of justice, the legislative and judicial departments being united as in the English House of Lords.

In any event, around 200 B.C. we find in Israel a legal system in which the governmental authority in all its aspects was vested in a tribunal known as the Great Sanhedrin. Sitting in Jerusalem, this tribunal had a membership of seventy-one judges, the number being derived from the court's prototype, the assembly of seventy elders that Moses gathered about him, he himself constituting the seventy-first. All had to be men of irreproachable character, fine discrimination and balanced judgment. Although graduation from a school of religious law was an element of qualification, they came from all callings and were not compensated. The Great Sanhedrin was the legislature as well as the supreme court. It not only determined the law but formulated it.

There were also other courts. Courts of the Lesser Sanhedrin, composed of twenty-three members, sat in the remaining lesser cities. Every town had a Beth Din, a court dealing with minor cases, which held sessions at the gates. It was composed of three judges.

That the Beth Din, also, was of ancient origin, is indicated by the manner in which Absalom arrogated the judicial technique to promote his conspiracy against his father, David:

And Absalom rose up early, and stood beside the way of the gate: and it was so, that when any man that had a controversy came to the king for judgment, then Absalom called unto him, and said, Of what city art thou? And he said, Thy servant is of one of the tribes of Israel.

And Absalom said unto him, See, thy matters are good and right; but there is no man deputed of the king to hear thee.

Absalom said, moreover, Oh that I were made judge in the land, that every man which hath any suit or cause might come unto me, and I would do him justice!

And it was so, that when any man came nigh to him to do him obeisance, he put forth his hand and took him and kissed him.

And on this manner did Absalom to all Israel that came to the king for judgment; so Absalom stole the hearts of the men of Israel.

It has been noted that the Beth Din of even the lesser cities was composed of three judges. Originally, no court could consist of a single judge; three was the minimum. A single intelligence acting judicially would have been regarded as a usurpation of divine prerogative. In a single sentence from Pirke Aboth IV, 8, the Hebrews found their support for this rule: "Be not a sole Judge, for there is no sole Judge But One."

The profession of the law was no part of the judicial system of the Hebrews. There were no advocates in the sense that lawyers serve as such in modern times. In criminal cases the sole prosecutors were the witnesses who appeared against the accused. It was the judges who performed all the duties that fall within the province of the present-day attorney and counselor-at-law. The judges were the defenders, as well as the judges of the accused. Not until the later period of the Roman Republic did lawyers, as we know them, appear upon the scene.

The Books of Hebrew Law: The Torah. The coming to an end of the Hebrew state by no means signified the end of Hebrew law as such, but it did stop its progressive· development. There was no natural development of the Biblical legal system after the Roman conquest because the people who lived by it lost their national character. The evolution of that system had been greatly delimited eight centuries earlier by the Assyrian conquest of northern Israel, conducted by Shalmanezzer and Sennacherib, and was crippled in the sixth century B.C. by the Babylonian conquest under Nebuchadnezzar; it was cut short almost completely by the destruction of the Hebrew Kingdom. Nevertheless, the content of Hebrew law remained as a guide for the Hebrew people, and as a permanent influence upon all law to come. To say nothing of its other elements, the principles of the Ten Commandments are at the very heart of any legal system based on justice. Woodrow Wilson said that the laws of Moses as well as the laws of Rome contributed suggestions and impulse to the men and institutions which were to prepare the modern world. If we could have eyes to see we should discover how very much beside religion we owe to the Jews.

The Ten Commandments were of course basic in their coverage, but rules prescribing the detail of human relationships in their constantly developing ramifications could not before the Christian era be condensed into a few sentences any more than they can be now. We have seen that Hammurabi's Code incorporated the equivalent of twenty thousand English words. And so the Hebrew law went much beyond the Ten Commandments. The first five books of the Old Testament, sometimes referred to as the Pentateuch or Torah, are a rich repository of the detailed law of the time with which they dealt, and constitute a fundamental portion of the subsequent Hebrew law.

Speaking of the nature and content of this body of law, Rabbi L. Elliott Grafman states that it makes no such distinctions between civil, criminal and ecclesiastical laws as are to be found in later systems of jurisprudence. For there was for the early Hebrews no difference between their rights as citizens of the state, their duties to the state, infractions of which would amount to crimes punishable by the state, and the regulation of matters concerning religion. Jewish law did not distinguish between the obligation to do right by man respecting his person and property, and the obligation to do right by God by customary devotion and sacrifice. All such duties were equally sacred, having identical sanction in the accepted "command of God." One body of rules or customs sufficed to regulate them all.

That Hebrew law originated in earlier custom was recognized by Scripture writers. The Book of Genesis (as also Judges) describes a condition of society in which "every man did what seemed right in his own eyes." They were then a nomad people; the family was the unit of society. The customs allude principally to the family relations, to simple trade between families or tribes, and to regulation of the chief occupation, pasturage. Custom concerned itself that early with the relations of husband and wife, parent and child; it dealt with family property, including slaves, and regulated the rights and duties of kinsmen to one another.

When a well defined legal system or code developed, it dealt variously with these ancient patriarchal customs. Some were preserved and given the sanction of law; some were abolished and others were modified. This is evident even to the layman from a study of the text which comprises the Torah. Many a pronouncement or prohibition serves to establish contemporary existence of the very custom to which it refers. Other customs are neither mentioned nor suggested by the Torah, but persisted as part of the unwritten or "oral" law under the Talmudic period when they were committed to writing. The antiquity of this oral law is attested by various Jewish authorities, on grounds similar to those by which the origin of the English common law is often explained. As Sir Henry Maine points out, the law was early held to have existed, from time immemorial, in the breasts of the judges (so also the Roman praetors) awaiting the case in which it was to be first enunciated and applied.

The Torah, as finally evolved, contains codes of law on various subjects, in the form of a series of statutes and ordinances succinctly expressed—the first law in the modern sense, written by the authority of a lawgiver. Legislating for a stage of society higher than that of the nomad, it is intended for a people largely devoted to agriculture. It knows little of commerce or contract in the modern sense; its regulations are comparatively primitive, expressed in terse sentences and with little comment. The simplicity of Biblical law is perhaps its most striking characteristic. This is best illustrated by the fact that it is contained in some fifteen chapters, and in some of these consists of but a few verses. The bulk of its civil law comprises two codes dealing with slaves, land, inheritance, pledges, interest on loans, bailments, torts, marriage and divorce and legal procedure. The constitution of the courts and their jurisdiction is treated in Exodus 18 and Deuteronomy 17. Leviticus 25 and Deuteronomy 15 contain laws of the jubilee, of the Sabbatical year (land tenure) and ransom. Leviticus 19 treats of the poor laws, and Numbers 27 and 36, of the laws of inheritance.

The Daughters of Zelophehad. The incident of the daughters of

Zelophehad seeking to inherit is illustrative of the content of this law of the Torah and indicative of its divine origin:

Then came the daughters of Zelophehad.

And they stood before Moses, and before Eleazer the priest, and before the princes and all the congregation, by the door of the tabernacle of the congregation, saying,

Our father died in the wilderness, and he was not in the company of them that gathered themselves together against the Lord in the company of Korah, but died in his own sin, and had no sons.

Why should the name of our father be done away from among his family, because he hath no son? Give unto us therefore a possession among the brethren of our father.

And Moses brought their cause before the Lord.

And the Lord spake unto Moses, saying,

The daughters of Zelophehad speak right: thou shalt surely give them a possession of an inheritance among their father's brethren; and thou shalt cause the inheritance of their father to pass unto them.

However, as the Scriptural narrative discloses, this was not the complete statement of the law with regard to the rights of daughters to inherit as it finally developed. Such right was subsequently conditioned upon their marrying within their own tribe so that outsiders would not acquire rights to property therein.

In commenting on this a Hebrew scholar has said that later Jewish history brought further changes in economic and social conditions and with them came further reforms and adaptations of the law. The Jews lost their ties with the soil of their homeland. The geographical and ethnical division into tribes lost its practical importance and eventually also its ideological significance. It could no longer serve as a basis for rules of inheritance, nor could it sustain statutory limitations of the freedom to marry, such as that indicated above. In later Jewish sources, the succession of daughters in the absence of sons is, accordingly, no longer conditioned on their refraining from marrying outside their tribe. Moreover, even where both male and female issue survived the deceased, it was felt that the position of sisters vis-a-vis their brothers ought to be improved. Various devices were gradually introduced to that effect. At first certain marital and testamentary provisions in favor of daughters became customary: later such provisions became rules of law and were extended to cases of intestacy. The basic rule of discrimination in favor of male issue—a rule so well known to many legal systems—was, however, maintained. It is still one of the characteristic features of Jewish succession law.

The Talmud. As we have noted in previous connections, no code of

law can be formulated which is so inclusive as to detail that it will
cover all possible situations that may arise after its promulgation.
There arises a need for supplementation and interpretation. So it was
with the Pentateuch, or Torah, and the need was especially urgent
after the Hebrew people were driven out of Jerusalem and forced to
seek refuge where they might find it. Forced to conform their lives
to the customs of strange lands, they needed the sustenance of a vital
statement of their own faith. So in the early centuries of the Christian era Jewish scholars formulated interpretations of the Mosaic law
which were embodied in a volume of six books known as the Mishnah,
compiled about 200 A.D., and the Gemara, or commentary, compiled in the succeeding centuries. These constituted the Talmud, not
only a guide for legal conduct, but also for religious observances and
other matters which we would not think of as being in the realm of
strict law. These Jewish works on law, known as the Mishnah
and Talmud, deal voluminously with Biblical law and may be compared with the cases, opinions, arguments and citations of authority
known to modern law. The Talmud is mainly engaged with dis-
cussions of the law—civil and ritual—as developed from the second
century before the Christian era to the sixth century of the present
era. Thus covering eight centuries of compilation and codification,
it includes adaptations, innovations and modifications of the Biblical
laws. It evaluates mores, discourses in homilies, makes ethical pronouncements, and recites opinions which, like modern cases, set legal
precedents for later generations. Like equity jurisprudence, it seeks
to apply the spirit—back of the letter—of the law, and proffers
maxims which shall guide adjudications rather than supplant them.

There is a definite characteristic which permeates the entire Talmudic doctrine. This is its constant stress of human values. Its
concern is with the rights of *man* rather than with rights of property.
Like the Bible, on which it is predicated, it deals *primarily* with laws
governing men and only *incidentally* with laws governing property.
Perhaps because it is a pulsating ethical system rather than a cold legal system, most legal historians have passed it by. And yet, ironically enough, the epithet "legalism" has ignorantly, but frequently,
been applied to the Hebraic code. The student of that code will find
that it places ethics upon the highest conceivable plane, terming justice a mere corollary, necessary for its attainment. That "the laws
were made for man and not man for the laws" is ever reflected in the
Hebraic laws themselves.

The principle of justice—as Talmudic writers and sages morally sensed it—may be epitomized in the following illustrative maxims: "Thy neighbor's property must be as sacred to thee as thine own." "Thy neighbor's honor must be as dear to thee as thine own." "Whatever would be hateful to thee, do not unto thy neighbor" (a quotation from Hillel who lived two generations before Jesus). "To break a verbal agreement, though it be legally not binding, is a moral wrong." "Deception in words is as great a misdemeanor as deception in money matters." "Man's salvation depends not on the acceptance of certain articles of belief, nor on certain ceremonial observances, but on that which is the ultimate aim of religion, namely morality, purity of heart and honesty of life." "Human society rests on three things—on justice, on truth, and on peace."

Throughout the later periods of Hebrew history, after the Jews were scattered throughout the world, other commentators maintained the traditions of Hebrew law and added to its content. Among these was Moses Maimonides, a descendant of Rabbi Judah, compiler of the Mishna, who was born in Cordova, Spain, in 1135. He fled from Spain to Cairo, in Egypt, from fanatacism and persecution. There he studied science and the Greek and Chaldean languages. His first commentary was upon the Mishnah. Later he authored Mishnah Torah, the "Second Law"—simplifying the Talmudical rules and traditions, making them clear to the comprehension of all. He also wrote many philosophical treatises leveled against atheism, and designed to prove that God created the world from naught, and finally gave to the world his great work, Moreh Nebuchim—"Guide of the Perplexed."

The Mosaic statutes are but the roots from which a rich outgrowth of post-biblical Jewish law organically developed itself. One visiting a library of Jewish law will find hundreds of volumes dealing with its various aspects.

It has been said, with reason, that so little has been known by non-Jews about the Talmud, even by jurists, scholars and men of literature, that it has never been given its proper niche in legalistic philosophy. Yet it is to the Mosaic Code what the decisions of the United States Supreme Court are to the provisions of the federal Constitution.

Hebrew Law Today—The London Beth Din. At a meeting of the Society of Jewish Jurisprudence in London, Justice Gad Frumkin of the Supreme Court of Palestine pointed out that Jewish law in general has never ceased to have practical application in many parts of Europe where Jews resort to Rabbinical courts. Although the recognition by the Roman government of Jewish Rabbinic authority fluctuated greatly, this did not diminish the prestige and influence of the Beth Din, which weathered the persecutions of Hadrian with his edict against the ordination of Rabbis competent to act as judges. The Jews of England in the pre-expulsion period, before 1290, were allowed some home rule in religious matters. There was always a qualified autonomy of the Jewry. Separate jurisdiction of the Jews *inter se* was confirmed by public charter in the reign of King Richard I, and reenacted in the following year. It was ordained that all differences which did not concern the pleas of the Crown should be determined by themselves according to their own law. This privilege necessitated Jewish tribunals, and they did exist.

The jurisdiction and procedure of the modern London Beth Din has been interestingly described by Dayan Dr. Feldman. The London Beth Din, or the Court of the Chief Rabbi, is the recognized Jewish Court, functioning not alone ecclesiastically but also in a judicial and advisory capacity. It deals with matters affecting members of the Jewish community who seek remedy, advice and help. Judges in the government courts of London have referred to it in appreciative terms. The Chief Rabbi is its president. The members are designated as Dayanim, a Hebrew-Aramaic title. It holds its sessions five days of the week, dispensing justice and promoting peace, giving rulings on ecclesiastical and ritual Jewish law, advising and helping individuals and congregations in the Metropolis, the Provinces and the scattered communities of the British Empire, and exchanging views in Jewish religious questions and problems with the recognized rabbinical authorities in other lands.

The magisterial function of the Beth Din comprises cases between husband and wife, parents and children, and neighbors who are unfriendly; cases of slander, vulgar abuse and common assault. Other cases concern master and workman, landlord and tenant, vendor and purchaser, claims for commission, questions of inheritance, and breach of promise. Of the master and workman cases, many touch the relationship between employees and Jewish institutions. English magistrates often advise Jewish litigants to apply in the first instance to the Beth Din, feeling that the religious atmosphere where the Dayanim understand the psychology of the Jewish people and can make a cogent appeal not to profane the Divine Name would prove more effective in disposing of such cases to the mutual advantage of the parties concerned and the general social well being. There are no costs in the Beth Din; the expense is borne by the United Synagogue.

Lawyers are not encouraged to participate. Obedience to Beth Din judgments is enjoined by the Torah.

No hearing with a view to decision takes place in the Beth Din without both parties present. This is in accordance with the provision of Deuteronomy: "Then both men between whom the controversy is shall stand before the Lord, before the priests and the judges." As Dayan Dr. Feldman emphasized, the rendition would be "shall stand *Lifne Elohim*"—before the Lord. Elohim, in Jewish interpretation, is a name of God as reflecting the attribute of justice; and in the text quoted, as in many other injunctions in the Bible, the term Elohim is taken to comprehend also the judges. For, in Jewish teaching, human judges, by administering the law in accordance with the principles of right, are regarded as co-workers with the Divine Being in maintaining the moral foundations—Truth and Justice—upon which the world rests.

Neither the parties nor the witnesses are sworn. Litigants and witnesses, no less than others, are under a religious obligation and a standing oath. "Thou shalt not bear false witness against thy neighbor." "If a soul sin, and hear the voice of swearing, and is a witness, whether he has seen or known of it, if he do not utter it, then he shall bear his iniquity." If these Divine injunctions do not serve, there is no guarantee that human conduct will prove effective. Jewish law disqualifies as witnesses persons who have been guilty of an offense involving violence or unlawful acquisition.

Yosher, or "Equity." In its decision the Beth Din aims at *Yosher,* or equity. This is implicit in the injunction: "And thou shalt teach them ordinances and laws, and shalt shew them the way wherein they must walk, and the work that they must do." The principle calls for acting beyond the line of justice or strict law, of avoiding taking utmost advantage of the letter of strict legality. Jerusalem, the Rabbis pointed out, was destroyed because in the administration of justice they adhered too closely to strict discipline and disregarded the principles of *Yosher. Yosher* and the concomitant principle of *Pesharah* (splitting, compromise or adjustment), which is built on *Yosher,* have thus played an important part in the administration of justice in Jewish courts throughout the ages. The exercise of *Yosher* is also enjoined by other passages of the Old Testament: "And thou shalt do that which is right and good in the sight of the Lord." "That thou mayest walk in the way of good men, and keep the paths of the righteous." "Withhold not good from them to whom it is due, when it is in the power of thine hand to do it." "These are the things that ye shall do: speak ye every man the truth to his neighbor; execute the judgment of truth and peace in your own gates."

Jews Return to Palestine. In the decades preceding World War I, Palestine was a neglected province of the Ottoman Empire, its natural resources debilitated by centuries of abuse. Other aspects of the land were of far greater consequence. Within its physically wasted boundaries were the spiritual shrines of three of the world's great religious faiths. Christian pilgrims knelt at the Tomb of Christ within the Church of the Holy Sepulchre at Jerusalem, and at the Grotto of the Manger in near-by Bethlehem. Jews embraced the Wailing Wall, remnant of the Second Temple, destroyed by the Roman Titus in 70 A.D. Palestine had been the home of Abraham, Islam's first Prophet, to say nothing of the succeeding Islamic Prophets, including Jesus Christ, and Muslims worshipped at the Sacred Rock enshrined on the Mosque of Omar, from which Mohammed reputedly ascended to Heaven.

The Jews, to whom the country had been a homeland in Biblical times, had been driven away and scattered throughout the world, as we have seen. But never did the dream of coming back completely die. From the sixteenth century on there was a noticeable return of Jews to Palestine. A trickle at first, persecution in Russia and other places initiated a flow of refugees which grew at a modest rate. The nineteenth century witnessed the formation of the World Zionist Organization, which promoted a program of Palestinian resettlement. The twentieth century found the country occupied by many thousands of Jews, of all types and backgrounds, from peasants to intellectuals. Having in common the desire for a free way of life, and the willingness to work for it, they revitalized the country by reclaiming wasted swamps and worn-out land, building livable homes and organizing enterprises which put in motion the wheels of trade. At what turned out to be a strategic juncture in world history they had demonstrated that the dream of a modern Jewish homeland could be made a practical reality in Palestine. To be sure, Arabs had long been living in Palestine, and they continued to live there. But as the Jews settled there no untoward communal incidents developed, and the two peoples went on living together peacefully, just as Hindus and Muslims were normally wont to do in the villages of India.

The Balfour Declaration. On November 2, 1917, Lord Balfour wrote to Lord Rothschild a letter in which he stated:

I have much pleasure in conveying to you, on behalf of His Majesty's Government the following declaration of sympathy with Jewish Zionist aspirations which have been submitted to, and approved by, the Cabinet.

His Majesty's Government view with favor the establishment in Palestine of a national home for the Jewish people, and will use their best endeavors to facilitate the achievement of this object, it being clearly understood that nothing shall be done which may prejudice the civil and religious rights of non-Jewish communities in Palestine, or the rights and political status enjoyed by Jews in any other country.

I should be grateful if you would bring this declaration to the knowledge of the Zionist federation.

As later events have disclosed, this letter, which became known as the Balfour Declaration, turned out to be one of the most important documents of modern history, for it was the basis of what subsequently became the State of Israel. In a recent analysis of the matter, Sol M. Linowitz pointed out that for over thirty-nine years English, Arabs and Jews alike have indulged in partisan research and interpretation of this document and its genesis. The most significant and incontrovertible fact is, however, that by itself the Declaration was legally impotent. For Great Britain had no sovereign rights over Palestine; it had no proprietary interest; it had no authority to dispose of the land. The Declaration was merely a statement of British intentions and no more.

The Arab leader, Sherif Hussein, was assured that Jewish settlement in Palestine under this Declaration would be allowed only as it would be consistent with Arab freedom. At that time there were only about 65,000 Jews in the country.

The Palestine Mandate. In the peace settlement that followed World War I, Great Britain was awarded a mandate over Palestine which was confirmed by the League of Nations. The true importance of the Balfour Declaration, according to Linowitz, lay in the fact that the Preamble to the Palestine mandate issued in 1922 specifically recited that Great Britain as mandatory was to be responsible for putting the Declaration into effect. Significantly, it stated that recognition had thereby been given to the "historical connection of the Jewish people with Palestine and to the grounds for reconstituting their national home in that country." The mandate was accordingly set up to effectuate these purposes, and Great Britain as mandatory assumed the obligation of exercising the mandate in accordance with the precise terms of the Balfour Declaration.

The mandate device used by the Allied Powers in the Covenant of the League of Nations was an innovation in international law. While President Wilson and General Smuts had conceived of the mandate as a trust arrangement, the other powers had accepted their mandatory roles as a convenient manner of obtaining desired territories. It was, therefore, hardly surprising that the administration of the various mandates was inevitably molded to the political aims of the mandatories.

The touchstone for an analysis of what was sought to be achieved and the method for its attainment lay in the words "Jewish national home." Borrowed from the original Zionist platform at Basel, the words "national home" were novel in the field of international law. By the application of established principles of legal construction the intended meaning could be readily ascertained: the establishment of Palestine as a place to which Jews could emigrate with the understanding that if such immigration should prove to be large enough, a predominantly Jewish state or commonwealth would come into existence. Lloyd George, President Wilson and various others so understood the term, and their testimony offers an irrefutable "legislative history" of statutory meaning.

Over the years, however, both the British mandatory and the Arabs urged other interpretations designed to indicate a contrary policy. A 1939 White Paper restricted total future Jewish immigration to Palestine to 75,000; put rigorous restrictions on land purchase by Jews, and provided ultimate establishment of a Palestinian state with Jews as one-third minority. The Permanent Mandates Commission of the League unanimously held this White Paper to be inconsistent with the constant interpretation theretofore placed on the mandate.

Creation of the State of Israel. The termination of World War II disclosed great numbers of Jews who had survived the Nazi extermination procedures and brought to a head the problem of displaced persons. Great Britain had put into effect a quota system under which Jewish immigration into Palestine was limited to 1,500 a month. In 1945 President Truman requested British Prime Minister Atlee to open the gates of Palestine to 100,000 European Jews. Atlee countered with a suggestion to set up a joint Anglo-American Committee of Inquiry to visit Palestine and study the problem, with a view to making recommendations. Such a committee was appointed, and indorsed the proposal to send 100,000 Jews to Palestine, but attaching certain conditions. Without accepting the conditions President Truman renewed the demand upon Great Britain for the entry of the 100,000 Jews; he did this just before the Congressional elections of 1946.

In April, 1947, Great Britain passed the problem to the General

Assembly of the United Nations, which created a special committee to study the matter and make recommendations. After the committee had filed its report, recommending the partition of Palestine into two separate states, one Jewish and one Arab, neither including Jerusalem, which was to be placed under international administration, Great Britain renounced its mandate. On November 20, 1947, the United Nations General Assembly voted partition, to go into effect on May 15, 1948, on which date British troops were to leave the country.

May 15, 1948, came. In accordance with their previous assurances, the British left the country. There was a clear hiatus between governments. The Zionists proclaimed themselves to be the State of Israel, set up a provisional government that asserted jurisdiction over the territory partitioned to it, and began to function as such. The governments of the United States and of the Soviet Union at once extended recognition. The Arabs made no similar announcement as to their part of the territory, but marched their troops against Israel for the stated purpose of "restoring order" and setting up a government for an undivided Palestine. After several weeks of fighting, in the course of which their attacks were beaten back, they accepted a United Nations truce proposal. A final cease-fire was brought about over five months later.

In the course of all this some hundreds of thousands of Arabs were expelled from or voluntarily left the country, and became refugees. Some 170,000 Arabs remained, of whom about 70% are Muslims, 25% are Christians, and the remainder for the most part Druzes. Under the announced policy of the State of Israel of receiving all Jews who come, the Jewish population increased by more than a million within a few years and is still growing apace, with a present population of over 1,700,000 people.

Law in the Modern State of Israel. It might be thought that in the modern state of Israel, Hebrew law would be restored to an exclusive place. But any such impression can be only a passing one, for the elements militating otherwise are too profound to permit such a consummation. The situation has been described by Professor Benjamin Akzin, who has said that culturally, Israel represents a Western-type democratic and urban society in the midst of a rather patriarchal and rural Middle East. Ethnically, it is a society largely Jewish established in a territory which, in recent centuries at least, was predominantly Arab. Demographically, it is composed of several strata of inhabitants greatly differing from one another in religion, linguistic background, *mores* and—correspondingly—in inherited legal institu-

tions. Most of Israel's present population are comparatively new ar-
rivals, and their cultural integration is far from complete. From
the point of view of dominant social values, it is a welfare state placed
in a region in which social consciousness is perhaps as low as anywhere
on earth. By no means unimportant is the country's character as
central site of holiness for Christianity and Judaism, and as an object of deep veneration to Islam and two smaller denominations—
Bahaj and Druze; which helps to explain why large groups and political entities outside the state regard with jealous interest everything that occurs within its borders. And lastly, it will be well to
remember that the search for a better legal structure is taking place
while the state of war between Israel and every single one of its
neighboring states continues unabated.

As Uriel Gorney has pointed out, the first law enacted upon the
establishment of the State of Israel provided, *inter alia,* that "the
law which existed in Palestine" on the day of the establishment of the
state, May 14, 1948, "shall remain in force, insofar as there is nothing
therein repugnant to other laws and subject to such modifications as
may result from the establishment of the State and its authorities."
Similar provisions had been enacted by American states and by the
Irish Free State upon their secession from Great Britain. English
common law had first been introduced into Palestine in 1922 by section 46 of the Palestine Order in Council, an order which might be
considered the "constitution" of the mandatory government. This
section provided that so far as Ottoman and local laws "shall not
extend or apply," the jurisdiction of the civil courts "shall be exercised in conformity with the substance of the common law, and the
doctrines of equity in force in England, so far only as the circumstances of Palestine and its inhabitants permit and subject to such
qualification as local circumstances render necessary." It thus served
as a port of entry for many doctrines and principles of common law
and equity which have become firmly imbedded in the intricate pattern of Israel's legal system. The equitable doctrines of specific performance and equitable relief against forfeiture were introduced in
this way. On the other hand, adoption of the law of torts and the
doctrine of trusts was refused in the absence of express legislative
mandate. Among the important doctrines so introduced were *stare
decisis* and the related principle that an inferior court will follow
the precedents of a higher tribunal. The Palestine Supreme Court
thus held itself bound by its own decisions and those of the highest

British courts, and the lower district and magistrate's courts in turn by decisions of the Supreme Court.

The "Layers" of Israel's Law. Benjamin Akzin enumerates what he characterizes as the "principal layers" of Israel's authoritative legal material now in effect, as follows:

1. Statutory enactments of the State of Israel and regulations made pursuant to these enactments.

2. Quasi-statutory enactments of the period of British rule, 1918-1947, and regulations made pursuant to these enactments.

3. Ottoman law, such as was in force in Palestine on November 1, 1914. As a result of a series of enactments in the 19th and early 20th centuries, this material was overwhelmingly statutory in form; a large part of it was codified. As for the historical origins of its contents, the provisions of that law are taken partly from Moslem religious law, partly from Turkish and Arab customs, partly from later developments, and partly represent translations or adaptions from Western sources, chiefly French and German codes.

4. "The substance of the common law, and the doctrines of equity in force in England."

5. As far as Jews are concerned Jewish (rabbinic) law applies in matters of marriage, divorce and personal status. Developed from the Old Testament by centuries of theoretical writings and actual adjudication, the main body of that law has been set out in a succession of texts, most important of which are the Mishna (3rd century), the Babylonian Talmud (5th century), the Code of Maimonedes (13th century) and the Shulkhan Arukh (16th century).

6. As far as Moslems are concerned their religious law (sharyia), is decisive in matters of marriage, divorce and personal status. Developed from the Koran and early Islamic traditions, it had been laid down by scholars and judges of the succeeding generations, and has never been properly codified.

7. As far as certain Christian denominations are concerned (viz., Roman Catholics, Greek Orthodox, Armenians, Syrian Catholics, Chaldean Uniates, Greek Catholics, Syrian Orthodox and Maronites) Christian church law must be observed in matters of marriage, divorce, and personal status. In the case of Roman Catholics and the denominations affiliated with the Roman Catholic Church, this law has been elaborated in great detail, and, moreover, has been the subject of a comprehensive modern codification, with the code, the *codex iuris canonici*, in effect since 1918. The church law of the Eastern denomina-

tions, while equally based on the Holy Writ, apostolic tradition, and the decisions of the early synods, has not been properly codified.

8. As far as the Bedouin tribes in the southern part of the country, the Negev, are concerned "tribal custom, so far as it is not repugnant to natural justice or morality" is applicable. Palestine Order-in Council, 1922, Art. 45.

Problems of Codification. Not only does Israel lack a comprehensive constitution, but it lacks any formal constitutional document altogether; moreover, there is no discernible present-day trend to have one enacted. Whether or not a codification of the law should be attempted is a major issue. Akzin points out that any such attempt is bound to be attended with a basic controversy over terminology. Pride in a rich Hebrew terminology, found throughout two and a half millenia of a literature at once sacred and juristic, from the Old Testament onward, causes many participants in the drafting process to take a passionate interest in the choice of words and style. The struggle around a "national" terminology is perhaps fiercer than the struggle around "national" contents of the country's laws. Linguistic purists plead for the use of legal terms taken from ancient Hebrew literary monuments, even if their use in the original context was somewhat different from the meaning to be given to them now. Linguistic modernists of various schools of thought prefer to coin new and until their social acceptance, inevitably artificial terms, though in keeping with Hebrew grammar and phonetics. Still others are not averse to literally translating or simply transliterating foreign language terms borrowed from that language's cultural orbit.

A small staff working at Harvard University conducts research on topics designated by the Israeli Ministry of Justice; Israeli jurists engaged in codification projects visit the center for varying periods of time in order to pursue their work amidst the rich resources of the Harvard Law Library; and, in addition, the center acts as liaison agency with American specialists outside of Harvard, forwarding to them material for comments, arranging conferences, etc. This venture is interesting as a rather unique kind of "technical assistance," mobilizing in an organized and systematic way rich foreign resources for the benefit of the legal development of a far-off country. It may well have another result: because of the intimate and continuing contact between Israeli codifiers and American lawyers, American federal and state law may come to exercise in the future law of Israel a far greater influence than it would have had otherwise.

CHAPTER 11

CHRISTIANITY AND THE ROMAN CATHOLIC CHURCH

Christianity and Government. From the outset of our study we have noted the basic position of religion with relation to government and law. In substance, if not in full form, thus far the concept has remained in force that the law was of divine origin and that the rulers of the people were vested with priestly attributes. We come to the present point of discussion, therefore, familiar with the identification of law with religion, and with the concept of governmental action as divinely empowered.

Although this concept had its origin in the religions preceding Christianity, nothing in the record thus far would raise doubt about its carrying into the workings of the religion brought to the world by Jesus Christ. We have seen something of the influence which Christianity had upon Roman institutions and Roman law before the Roman Empire was divided. Christianity was just gathering its strength in these early centuries of the Christian era. It remains for us to sketch its progress through those which followed, in the course of which as corporately organized it gained and exercised at times the attributes of temporal as well as spiritual sovereignty, in the process developing a code of law covering the most intimate human relations and conduct.

Beginnings of Christianity. As we look at Christianity in its relation to law and legal institutions, we find it beginning with scattered groups of simple believers in the Gospel, associated in fellowship without professional ecclesiastical leadership. It passed through a later period when, although ecclesiastical magistrates had assumed priestly functions, the authority still remained in the general body of believers. Finally, it attained a state of close organization, with a clergy, separated from the people and forming a distinct body, in itself a society and with resources of its own, which governed not only itself but the whole body of the church, of which all were constituent parts.

The progress of ecclesiastical organization has been instructively traced by Guizot. In its infancy, Christian society presents itself as a simple association of men possessing the same faith and opinions, the same sentiments and feelings. The first Christians met to enjoy together their common emotions, their common religious convictions. At this time we find no settled form of doctrine, no settled rules of discipline, no body of magistrates. But the moment this society began to advance there gradually became moulded a form of doctrine, rules of discipline, a body of magistrates; of magistrates called elders, who afterwards became priests; of inspectors or overseers, who became bishops; and of deacons, whose office was the care of the poor and the distribution of alms. There was one prevailing character of this second epoch: it was that the power, the authority, the preponderating influence, still remained in the hands of the general body of believers. It was they who decided in the election of magistrates, as well as in the adoption of rules of discipline and doctrine. No separation had as yet taken place between the Christian government and the Christian people, and it was still the great body of Christian believers who exercised the principal influence in the society.

In the third period, all this was entirely changed. The clergy were separated from the people, and now formed a distinct body, with its own wealth, its own jurisdiction, its own constitution; in a word, it had its own government and formed a complete society of itself—a society, too, provided with all the means of existence, independently of the society to which it applied itself, and over which it extended its influence. This was the third state of the Christian church, and in this state it existed at the opening of the fifth century. As respects the relation between the clergy and the Christian in general, it was the clergy who governed, and governed almost without control. The Roman Catholic Church, thus established, has since continued as a great world institution.

The Roman Catholic Church. The Roman Catholic Church is grounded upon the injunction of Christ as expressed to Peter in the Book of Matthew: "And I say also unto thee, that thou are Peter, and upon this rock I will build my church; and the gates of hell shall not prevail against it. And I will give unto thee the keys of the kingdom of heaven; and whatsoever thou shalt bind on earth shall be bound in heaven; and whatsoever thou shalt loose on earth shall be loosed in heaven." Thus is Peter said to have been commissioned the first Pope and Bishop of Rome. The scope of the claim of the Church to supreme power was stated in 91 A.D. in the Decretals of Isidore, addressed by the Pope to the clergy, in which it was said: "Their duty is to obey you as they would God himself. And all princes, high or low, and other people, tribes and languages who do not obey shall be infamous, and shall be cast out from the Kingdom of God and the company of the faithful."

No attempt to chronicle the development of law and government, however brief, can ignore the part which this Church played both before the fall of the Western Roman Empire and thereafter, when Europe fell into a congeries of barbarian tribes and force became the law of last resort. As Lord Macaulay well said, it is better that mankind should be governed by wise laws, well administered, and by an enlightened public opinion, than by priestcraft; but it is better that men should be governed by priestcraft than by brute violence. The childhood of the European nations was passed under the tutelage of the clergy; the ascendancy of the sacerdotal order was long the ascendancy which naturally and properly belongs to intellectual superiority. The priests, with all their faults, were by far the wisest portion of society. If there were encroachments of ecclesiastical power on the province of the civil power, they produced more happiness than misery. In times when life and female honor were exposed to daily risk from tyrants and marauders, it was better that the precinct of a shrine should be regarded with an irrational awe than that there should be no refuge inaccessible to cruelty and licentiousness.

Church Law as State Law. The struggle of Christians and the Church to survive in the early centuries of the Empire is well known to all. Eventually, as we have seen, the persecutions ended. There was a dramatic background to the edict of Constantine, already referred to, making Christianity the religion of the state. Before he led his forces to the battle at Milvian Bridge in 312 A.D. there came to him a celestial vision of a cross above the setting sun, inscribed, "In this sign conquer." Under this standard he marched to victory. Another dramatic example of conversion, this time of a tribal ruler, is found in Clovis, leader of the Franks. In 496 A.D. in the course of a battle between his forces and the Alemanni, a Germanic tribe, after calling upon his own gods without apparent results he called upon Jesus Christ for aid and pledged that if he were granted victory he would be baptized "in thy name." Victory having came, he made good his pledge. Zealous to promote the faith of the Church he conquered the Burgundians and extended his realm to the Pyrenees. But the Empire had by then fallen into a collection of weak and disorderly states. Through conquest the power of the Church was in effect introduced, the civil ruler accepting the law of the Church and making it the law of his realm.

The State Punishes Heresy. The integration of the law of the

Church with that of the state is forcefully illustrated by the manner in which the state at this time dealt with heresy. Constantine called the Council of Nicaea, at which, as we have seen, a creed was adopted which the Emperor proceeded to enforce. In fact, he exiled to Illyria two bishops who dissented from it. As we have noted, in 438 A.D. Emperor Theodosius promulgated a code from which the power exercised by the Church throughout the Empire is evident. It provided: "We desire that all who are under the sway of our clemency shall adhere to the religion which . . . the blessed apostle Peter delivered to the Romans. According to the teachings of the apostles and of the Gospel we believe in one Godhead of the Father, Son and Holy Ghost, the blessed Trinity, alike in majesty. We ordain that the name of Catholic Christians shall apply to all those who obey this present law. All others we judge to be mad and demented; we declare them guilty of the infamy of holding heretical doctrine; their assemblies shall not receive the name of churches. They shall first suffer the wrath of God, then the punishment which in accordance with divine judgment we shall inflict." Continuing as to matters of heresy it was provided: "Whenever an assembly of Manichaeans is discovered, let their teachers be heavily fined. Those who are in attendance should be cast out from among their fellow men as infamous and discredited. The house or dwelling place in which their profane doctrines are taught should be confiscated by the government. Clerics adhering to the Eunomian or Montanist superstition shall be excluded from all intercourse with any city or town. We command that their books which contain the substance of their criminal teachings be sought out with the utmost care and burnt with fire under the eyes of the magistrates."

Privilege of the Clergy. The clergy were made a privileged class. Thus, by edict of Theodosius: "From public burdens and from every disquietude of civil office all clerics shall be free . . . we decree that all priests, deacons, subdeacons, exorcists, lectors and doorkeepers, likewise all who are in higher orders, shall be free from personal taxes." The clergy were to be tried only in courts set up and operated by the Church itself, and such courts were given jurisdiction of various other cases. There was significance, too, which will not be lost upon us in the present connection, in the vesting of the clergy with supervision over various governmental functions. Equally significant, perhaps, is the disclosure that the Emperor had a strong voice as to who should constitute the clergy. For it was provided that persons might not "join the order of the clergy easily or in too great numbers."

Ecclesiastical Wealth and Power. Impetus was given to the accretion of wealth by the Church by the edict that "Every one shall have the right, when he is dying, to leave so much of his goods to the Holy and Catholic Church." The governmental imprimatur was thus conferred upon a Christian principle which was imported into the Roman Law and in turn was incorporated in the body of our own law. As we know it, the doctrine applies to all charities and churches. At its inception, by force of circumstances the Roman Catholic Church alone was the beneficiary. That Church eventually became the holder of a large portion of the wealth of Europe. Centralization of the power of the Church in Rome was assured in 445 A.D. by a decree of Emperor Valentinian III, issued at the instance of Pope Leo the Great, declaring the power of the Bishop of Rome supreme, commanding that the Western bishops should accept the law as prescribed by the Bishop of Rome, and ordering that any bishop refusing to answer a summons to Rome should be forced to obey by the imperial governor.

Collaboration With the Rulers. The emperors having put the full force of governmental power behind the Church, Church and State became in effect an integrated partnership. We have noted the invasions which commenced during the latter part of the Fourth Century A.D., the result of which was the disintegration of the Western Empire around 476 A.D. At the time stable civil government in Rome and throughout the Empire ceased. The Roman Catholic Church, however, had gained the strength to stand and extend her organization throughout the troubled areas. We find Pope Gregory, chosen in 590 A.D., governing the City of Rome and exercising wide military and civil powers throughout Italy. As strong men arose, the Church followed the course of circumstances by collaborating with them and perhaps purporting to add to their increment of power, as in the case of Pippin. Charles Martel, a duke deputized by the king of the Franks, led the forces which repulsed the Mohammedan invaders at Tours in 732 A.D. The king was a figurehead. Pippin, Martel's son, assumed power. The Pope confirmed the action, anointed Pippin as king of the Franks, and enunciated an anathema of divine vengeance against whoever should attempt to supplant Pippin and his rule. To obey this temporal ruler was thus enjoined as a religious duty. The Lombardians in Northern Italy having threatened to take Rome and set up an independent Italian state, the Pope appealed to Pippin. Pippin mounted an expedition and conquered Lombardy, handing the Lombardian lands over to the Pope.

Death For "Unbelievers." The inseparability of the law of Church and state through this late period was emphasized by a decree of Charlemagne, Pippin's son, after he had subdued the Saxons in Germany. The decree provided the same death penalty for the one who "shall have shown himself unfaithful to the lord king" and the one who "shall have wished to hide himself unbaptized and shall have scorned to come to baptism and shall have wished to remain a pagan." Eating meat during lent was made a capital offense. However, the decree had a "saving" clause, to the effect that if one committing these crimes should "flee of his own accord to the priest and, after confessing, shall wish to do penance, let him be freed, on the testimony of the priest, from death."

Feudalism. As we have seen, in 800 A.D., at a service in St. Peter's in Rome, Pope Leo III crowned Charlemagne "Emperor of the Romans," and it was considered that the Roman Empire founded by Augustus had been reestablished. But the empire thus reestablished in form was not maintainable in substance. Centuries of disorder followed, witnessing, however, the interplay between temporal power and the power of the Church. During much of this succeeding period feudalism was the outstanding institution, filling the void of law ordinarily administered by organized government. Fuedalism was a way of life, embodying within itself what amounted to a private system of law, privately administered. Back of it was the primitive need for protection against local violence and the maraudings of predatory bands from a distance.

There was in the system an element of reciprocal duty and responsibility, that of the lord to administer the system and carry out its purposes and that of the vassal to render his individual services. As part of the transaction the lands were tilled. A complete body of property law evolved, under the working of which the fiefs, as the holdings of the vassals were known, could be transmitted to descendants of the vassals. The fatal weakness of the system was that there was no orderly governmental power to insure respect for the rules. Resort to arms to settle disputes was customary, with the result that turmoil in some degree was constantly present. In *The Federalist* this period of European affairs is referred to as the times of feudal anarchy.

In all of this the Church was directly involved, as it had come to hold a large proportion of the land, and Bishops were among the largest feudal lords. Thus responsibility settled upon the Church for maintaining order and administering the affairs of considerable areas of Europe and England. On the other hand, the Church was often in the position of vassal. This brought serious complications. The Catholic clergy could not marry and had no descendants to whom Church fiefs could be transmitted. Although it was the prerogative of the clergy of the diocese to choose ecclesiastical successors, feudal lords came to assume ecclesiastical powers by naming successor bishops and sometimes even investing them with the tokens of their spiritual authority.

Other serious problems also arose with relation to the clergy. Closely related to this practice of investiture was that of simony. Because of the vast property interests of the Church, spiritual responsibilities were only part of the ecclesiastical duties of the clergy, and the holders of office came into possession of fees in considerable amount. It is not surprising that Church offices were at times bought and paid for, and when this happened in the case of a bishop, the practice carried through to the clergy of the lower ranks and sometimes ended with money exactions from the parishioners whom it was their duty to serve.

Excommunication and Interdiction. In time the clergy began to disregard the injunction against marriage, and early in the eleventh century a Pope of Rome proposed to enter into matrimony. At this juncture Henry III of Germany took a hand, secured the resignation of Pope Gregory VI and brought about the election of another Pope whose first act was to crown Henry and his wife. This marked the high point of temporal interference with selection of the Popes. Shortly thereafter Pope Nicholas II issued a decree taking the choice out of the hands of the emperor and placing it in the hands of the Cardinals who represented the Roman clergy.

Gregory VII became Pope in 1073. He issued a statement called the *Dictatus* in which he asserted the authority of the Pope not only over Church but also over civil government. Not recognizing the *Dictatus,* young Henry IV retained as counselors persons whom the Pope had excommunicated and violated the Pope's injunctions against investiture. Gregory sent legates to Henry to charge him with crimes calling for excommunication and removal from royal position unless he recanted. Henry summoned a council of German bishops, which declared Gregory deposed. Gregory replied by declaring Henry accursed and excommunicated. Henry repented, but having violated his promises was again excommunicated. This time he invaded Rome and civil war followed. Some of the problems of conflict were compromised later by the Concordat of Worms.

The power of the Church was further vigorously asserted by Pope Innocent III, who brought the temporal power of the papacy to a high point. In 1205 the monks of Canterbury, England, had chosen an archbishop without consulting King John. John forced another election to make his treasurer archbishop. Innocent rejected both and ordered the election of his own choice. John drove the monks out of Canterbury. Innocent placed England under the interdict, closing all churches, excommunicating John, and threatening to make Philip Augustus of France king of England. John gave in to Innocent in 1213, acknowledging himself to be a vassal of the Pope, handing England over and receiving it back as a fief and agreeing to send an annual payment to Rome. Closer to home, the Pope placed France under an interdict until Philip Augustus gave up his second wife. Rival kings arose in Germany, both bidding for Innocent's support. Innocent chose Otto, but in 1212 repudiated him in favor of Frederick II.

Innocent III also instituted inquisition by officials, perfecting the procedure in a decretal of the Fourth Lateran Council of 1215-1216. Under it an official, by virtue of his office (*ex officio*), had power to make a person before him take an oath to tell the truth to the full extent of his knowledge as to all things he would be questioned about. In practice this *inquisitio,* one of the forms of action set up by Innocent III, became the invariable rule. Under it the inquisitor, without denunciation by any other person, cited a suspect, having him imprisoned if necessary. This system spread throughout Christendom and to the organs of the state on the mainland of Europe, beginning in France. The English people resisted the oath *ex officio*, as the inquisitional procedure came to be designated, precisely because it was inquisitional.

The Crusades. In our glance at the power of the Church in those times we must not overlook the Crusades, which involved a constant collaboration of ecclesiastical and temporal power. Addressing the Council of Clermont, France, in 1096, Pope Urban II urged knights and soldiers of all ranks to enter upon the road to the Holy Sepulchre at Jerusalem, wrest the land from the wicked race and subject it to themselves. He promised that the journey should take the place of all penance for sin. When he had concluded it is said that all present exclaimed, "It is the will of God," which the Pope declared should be the rallying cry of the Crusaders. Later the Church asserted its authority by declaring that those who with a pure heart undertook the journey were relieved from payment of interest on their debts; their wives, children and property were put under the protection of the Church, and any one interfering was excommunicated.

Soldiers of the First Crusade under Godfrey reached Jerusalem in 1099, massacred the inhabitants, took possession of the city and set up a Latin kingdom. It did not last. Waves of succeeding Crusaders, composed of rulers, common people and even children, poured to the East, but after two centuries of decisive reverses the undertaking was abandoned.

Church Power Challenged. We have already noted that the assertion of full power by the Church met with frequent challenge upon the part of temporal rulers. Though sometimes yielding for the moment, the Church insisted upon its supremacy. It might be said that it attained its highest point of recognized assertion of temporal power under Pope Innocent III, to whom we have referred above in relation to King John of England. Within less than a century the tide had turned. Pope Boniface protested the action of Philip the Fair of France in levying taxes on estates of the clergy, and made certain demands of Philip. Instead of acceding, Philip sent an adviser with a bodyguard to Italy. As Boniface was excommunicating Philip the soldiers broke into the papal palace and insulted Boniface, who died shortly thereafter. Philip then succeeded in having Clement V, Archbishop of Bordeaux, named Pope. Clement took up residence at Avignon, France, and until 1377, during the period known as the "Babylonian Captivity" of the Church, the Popes were all Frenchmen and France was the seat of the Papacy. After it was restored to Italy the Church went through a period of forty years, referred to as the Great Schism, during which rivals claimed the Papacy. The Council of Pisa attempted to solve the difficulty by deposing two rivals and electing another. Matters were not finally adjudicated until the Council of Constance in 1415.

Prelude to the Reformation. We have already noted the collaboration of Church and state in the various aspects of law and order, and have seen that the power of the state was thrown behind prosecutions for heresy. For a thousand years, in fact, the supremacy of the Church in matters of conformity was implemented by the state. As we have seen, the Theodosian Code required all to be Catholic Christians, and the centuries following witnessed a continuing campaign by Pope and kings. In 1166 Henry II of England ordered that any dwelling which housed heretics should be burned. In 1194 the king of Aragon ordered that any one listening to the Waldensians should be punished for treason. Pope Innocent preached the Albigensian Crusade in Southern France in 1208. and an army under Simon de Montfort invaded the region and killed many people. This was followed up in 1229 by the organization, under the orders of an Ecumenical Council, of an Inquisition at Toulouse, France. To insure thoroughness Pope Gregory IX did not entrust it to the local clergy but ordered it to be conducted by Dominicans. This was only one of such courts created by the Pope in Spain, Italy, Poland, Germany and England.

Those who confessed the error of their ways before these inquisition courts were received back into the Church, but were sentenced to life imprisonment. Those who would not recant were turned over to the state for punishment. Death was the penalty, but Church law would not permit the Church itself to inflict it. Burning at the stake was a common end.

The Burning of John Huss. One of the best known episodes of these times centers around John Huss, a teacher of the University of Prague, who believed and taught that everybody should understand the Bible for himself and that Christians should not be forced to obey those who were living in sin. He was ordered to appear before the Council of Constance in 1415. He came under a safe-conduct issued by Emperor Sigismund, in which the Emperor ordered that no violence be done him and that he be allowed to leave Constance whenever he wished. Nevertheless he was arrested, imprisoned and tried for heresy. The Council refused to recognize the safe-conduct on the specious ground that heretics were "outside the king's jurisdiction," and that no pledge prejudicial to the Catholic faith could be observed. Having been found guilty by the Council, he was turned over to the civil government. Apparently yielding to the assertion of higher power by the ecclesiastical Council, this government burned him at the stake. History affords no more emphatic demonstration of the supreme power asserted by the Church over life itself during the many centuries of ecclesiastical ascendancy.

But although thousands of individuals were thereafter subjected to Inquisition procedures, the power thus asserted had reached its climax. Weaknesses in the ecclesiastical structure had already been manifested in the Babylonian Captivity and the Great Schism. The same Council of Constance that condemned John Huss had on its agenda the consideration of abuses, remedial action on which held favorable implications for the future. The success of the movements led by Calvin, Zwingli and Luther opened the way to a modicum of "safety in dissent."

Luther and the Protestant Reformation. Of far-reaching impact was the Protestant revolt led by Martin Luther. Having thrown into a bonfire the Papal Bull *Exsurge Domine* which condemned him, he found himself excommunicated by Pope Leo X, who requested Charles V, newly crowned Roman Emperor, to enforce the order. Charles obediently issued the Edict of Worms, which declared Luther an outlaw, forbade giving him food or shelter and proscribed any reading of his writings of affirmance of his opinions. But friends concealed Luther and the Edict was a dead letter. The Protestant revolt which followed had widespread repercussions. The power of the Roman Catholic Church was widely and successfully challenged. By the Peace of Augsburg in 1555 each German prince was given liberty to choose between the Catholic Church and the creed embodied in the Augsburg Confession. But everyone was to conform to the choice of his particular state, or leave. Thus, although the necessity of conformity was abated at the top level the conscience of the humble individual was not protected, nor was relief accorded to the followers of Calvin and Zwingli. But the line was drawn between Catholicism and Protestantism, and whole nations swung away from the ancient faith.

The Church in England Under Henry VIII. England broke away from the Roman Catholic Church rather because of the matrimonial desires of Henry VIII than as a result of the influence of Luther or Calvin, or of any general sense of resentment against Catholic doctrine or practices. Henry was not an advocate of Protestantism as such. He had married Catherine, the widow of his older brother, under a Papal dispensation. When he appealed to Pope Clement VIII to annul the marriage so that he could marry Anne Boleyn, and the Pope refused, Henry defied the Papal authority, dissolved the monasteries and seized all Catholic Church property. In 1534 the English Parliament, declaring that the king was "the only supreme head on earth of the Church of England," vested him with the right to appoint all English prelates, and transferred the entire jurisdiction of the Catholic ecclesiastical courts to the courts of England. Every officer of England, lay and ecclesiastical, was ordered to renounce the authority of the Catholic Church, upon pain of being charged with treason. Many suffered death accordingly.

For the next generation the tables were turned. After Henry died his daughter Mary, who had been reared a Catholic, came to power. She married Philip II of Spain, a ruthless crusader for Catholicism, who promoted its cause on the Continent by sword and inquisition. Hundreds died in England for denying the teachings of the Catholic Church. But after Mary's death another of Henry's daughters, Elizabeth, became queen, and the tables were once again reversed. Parliament enacted the Supremacy Act, declaring her the head of the English Church and ordering all people to attend it. As a woman Elizabeth disclaimed a sacerdotal character, but in effect exercised the prerogatives of head of the Church of England.

Shortly after Elizabeth's accession in 1558 A.D. the Scottish Parliament, following the leadership of John Knox, abolished Catholicism, decreed death or banishment for all Catholics, and made Presbyterianism the state religion. Mary Queen of Scots, who had a claim to the English throne if Elizabeth died childless, was an ardent Catholic. However she was deposed as queen of Scotland rather because of matrimonial escapades with Lord Darnley and Bothwell than because of her religion. Fleeing to the court of Elizabeth, she there became the center of religious intrigue upon the part of Philip II and Catholics in England who hoped, through her, to restore Catholicism to that country. After nineteen years of virtual imprisonment Mary was executed. Philip's final attempt to restore the faith by invasion ended with the destruction of the Spanish Armada.

The Puritans. Thus far our attention with reference to England has been focused on the Roman Catholic Church and the Church of England which Henry VIII established. As indicated by the above reference to Presbyterianism in Scotland other groups had been developing in England and its contiguous areas. When James I, son of Mary Queen of Scots, came to the throne after the death of Elizabeth, he found in England, in addition to remaining Catholics, a strong group of Puritans.

As George Horowitz has pointed out, the Puritans were the chief group of non-conformists who suffered from prosecutions before Star Chamber and High Commission with their practice of compulsory oath and resulting self-incrimination, and it was they who led in curbing the pretensions of the Crown. In fighting the arbitrary exactions of Charles I and his tyranny they appealed to the Word of God as expressed in the Hebrew Scriptures. They opposed the law of that word to man-made laws: the civil law of the King's tribunals, or the canon law of the court Christian. In their eyes the canon law constituted mere human legislation, the work of popes, bishops, abbots or of church councils composed of such prelates and dignitaries. "God's law" meant to the Puritans primarily Scripture. They denounced church legislation, i.e., canon law, as being contrary to Biblical law; more exactly as contrary to the laws of the Old Testament, and thus rejected the procedure of Inquisition with its *jusjurandum de veritate dicenda* (oath to tell the truth) and the oath *ex officio mero*. To interrogate under oath religious and God-fearing persons like the Puritans as to possible offenses by themselves or others was obviously felt as a kind of torture.

The Puritans presented to the King what was known as the "Millenary Petition," seeking modification of the law and certain practices of the Church of England. Gaius Glen Atkins and Frederic L. Fagley, referring to the "momentous conclusions" of this petition, state that among other things it would eventually provoke civil war, mobilize Oliver Cromwell and his Ironsides, create a brief, strange, splendid Puritan Commonwealth in England and new Commonwealths in a new world—nothing of which could then be foreseen. Claiming that by divine right he could make any law he liked and was above the law, owing his power only to God, James denied the petition. Atkins and Fagley note that the King "heard the controversialists and contributed his own wisdom." He had nominated the disputants, and so predetermined the result. The Anglical side carried much the heavier weight of metal; batteries of bishops, and the favor of the King. The Puritans had only four disputants, whom the King sought to abash by majestic frowns, says Neal. Dale believes the deference of the bishops to have delighted and influenced the King, since his Scotch clergy had shown him no such deference. "One had told him that all Kings were the devils's bairns." How could he doubt the apostolic succession of a bishop in lawn sleeves "kneeling on the floor and declaring that there had been no such King since Christ's days," or the authority of an archbishop who assured him "that he had spoken with the special assistance of the Holy Ghost." Such disgusting obeisance hardly finds parallel in even that shown by the Roman senators to Emperor Theodosius, noted in our consideration of Rome.

Browneists and Congregationalists. Another group, modest in numbers, were known as Separatists or Browneists, the precursors of Congregationalists. They had fled to Holland in the reign of Elizabeth after passage of an act which prescribed imprisonment until conformity for all over sixteen years of age who refused for a month to attend divine service "as established by Her Majesty's Laws" or "denied Her Majesty's power in causes ecclesiastical." Those not conforming within three months should "abjure the realm" or die as felons without benefit of clergy. This group asked to be permitted to live in England, free from compulsion to follow "any remnants of papery and human tradition." This request, too, was denied, the formal reply formulated by the Doctors of Oxford referring to them as holding "pestilent and blasphemous conclusions." James said, "I shall make them conforme themselves, or I will harrie them out of the land, or else do worse."

The story of how the small group of Pilgrim Fathers got from the London Company a patent for lands and set sail for America in the Mayflower is known to every schoolboy. Landing on Cape Cod in 1620 after they had drawn up the Mayflower Compact as a basis for mutual association, under conditions of the greatest hardship they established themselves in the new land. They set up the first town meetings in America and later organized a representative assembly. Their church life was congregationally ordered in accordance with the principle, finding Scriptural basis in the words of Jesus Christ: "For where two or three are gathered together in my name, there am I in the midst of them." Under such concept each gathered group of Christians was itself a Church, fully autonomous in its own right as to matters of government and Christian conscience. Moreover, it became a fundamental principle of the Congregational order to hold sacred the freedom of the individual soul and the right of private judgment, and, in accordance therewith, to impose upon no member a binding statement of creedal belief.

The congregational form of church life has been an indigenous part of the American scene. Most noteworthy, indeed, is the creative part it has played in shaping many of the instruments of American freedom.

Conduct of the early town meeting was fashioned after the Congregational Church meeting. The Mayflower Compact, drawn up by the Pilgrim Fathers before they landed at Plymouth, was one of our first instruments of civil government, and of our emerging democracy. The constitutions of our several states show the handiwork of Congregational pastors, whose knowledge of government began with their first-hand contacts with democracy exercised in church life. Notable is the example of Connecticut's constitution, where Thomas Hooker of First Church, Hartford, was the formative influence.

In the course of time, of course, religious freedom was accorded in England. But not until the nineteenth century were English laws relaxed to permit Catholics and dissenters to hold public office or sit in Parliament.

The Canon Law. The development of the Roman Catholic Church was attended by a concurrent development of a body of law known as the Canon Law. It began as soon as there was need of a juridical order for the government of the Church, and this need arose not long after the advent of Christianity. Ecclesiastical Canon Law sprang up in consequence of the law-making powers of the Popes and the Great Councils of the Church.

At a very early date after the establishment of the Holy See pontifical laws began to issue from Rome in the form of Papal Decretals. The bishops, confronted by questions of discipline and other problems which arose in consequence of the growing religion, called upon the Pope for decisions, which took the form of Decretals and became Church Law. Councils issued decrees regulating doctrinal and disciplinary matters. In fact, practically everything done by the agencies of the Church, with its intimate dealings with the affairs of life, the extent of which we can well realize after sketching its activities through the centuries of Roman history, involved the making or application of Canon Law. In 1234 A.D. a comprehensive official body of Canon Law embodying its component elements was prepared under Gregory IX. There were subsequent codifications through the centuries, the latest being the Papal Code of 1917, in Latin text, known as the *Codex Juris Canonici*. It is divided into five parts, the first containing general rules; the second relating to persons; the third governing such things as the Sacraments, the authority of the Church, its benefices and temporal goods; the fourth dealing with procedure in the ecclesiastical courts; and the fifth with various crimes and penalties. We must include in the term Roman law a good deal of the Canon Law of the Church, and to do so is not misleading, because the Canon Law was profoundly influenced by the classics of the later Roman law.

Relation to Law of the State. It is understood, of course, that in the United States neither the Canon Law nor the law of any church can be the law of the land as such; that place is reserved for and rightly occupied by the law of the state. The principle was well expressed by the distinguished Roman Catholic layman, Alfred E. Smith, when campaigning for the presidency of the United States in 1928: "I summarize my creed as an American Catholic. I believe in the worship of God according to the faith and practice of the Roman Catholic Church. I recognize no power in the institutions of my Church to interfere with the operations of the Constitution of the United States or the enforcement of the law of the land. I believe in the absolute freedom of conscience for all men and in equality of all churches, all sects, and all beliefs before the law as a matter of right and not as a matter of favor. I believe in the absolute separation of Church and State and in the strict enforcement of the provisions of the Constitution that Congress shall make no law respecting an establishment of religion or prohibiting the free exercise thereof. I believe that no tribunal of any church has power to make any decree of any force in the law of the land, other than to establish the status of its own communicants within its own church. I believe in the support of the public school as one of the cornerstones of American liberty. I believe in the right of every parent to choose whether his child shall be educated in a public school or in a religious school supported by those of his own faith."

But in matters of faith and morals all Catholics, without distinction of race, nationality or rite, are bound by the authoritative pronouncement of the Holy See. There can be but one rule in these matters for all who belong to the Catholic Church. In short, within the realm of the Roman Catholic Church the Roman Catholic Canon Law is in full force, covering virtually all aspects of the personal life of its people, not only as to religious obligations but in such relations as marriage and divorce, parents and children, education, work and property rights. For example, under the rubric "Catholic Schools," the Canon Law provides: "Catholic children are to be educated in schools where not only nothing contrary to Catholic faith and morals is taught, but rather in schools where religious and moral training occupy the first place." Further: "Catholic children shall not attend non-Catholic, indifferent schools that are mixed, that is to say, schools open to Catholics and non-Catholics alike. The bishop of the diocese only has the right in harmony with the instructions of the Holy See, to decide under what circumstances, and with what safeguards to prevent loss of faith, it may be tolerated that Catholic children go to such schools."

Importance of Canon Law. Understanding, as we do, the vast power wielded by the Roman Catholic Church in Europe for a thousand years, we need no elaborate argument to convince us of the great importance of Canon Law as the developing body of legal principles that undergirded the Church's activities. We have noted the events in the course of which the successors of St. Peter claimed universal jurisdiction of law, not only over the Christian Church but also over temporal kings and princes. We have also noted expression of the claim in a communication of Pope St. Clement in the year 91, addressed to the clergy and later included in the Decretals of Isidore, in which it was said: "Your duty is to teach the people. Their duty is to obey you as they would God himself. And all princes, high or low, and other peoples, tribes and languages, who do not obey shall be infamous, and shall be cast out from the Kingdom of God and the company of the faithful." These words describe the church's domination over faith and morals as it was asserted for centuries. As we have noted, Constantine ordered the decrees of the Church to be enforced by officers of the state and that practice was followed to the extreme point of making the state responsible for executing the bloody ecclesiastical decrees of the Inquisition. During those periods when Church authority took the place of civil government the Canon Law was supreme. During the Middle Ages it formed, with Roman Law, the foundation of legal studies in the universities. Although, as we have seen above, it is in the United States fully subordinated to the law of the state, no student of our institutions would for a moment overlook the substantial contribution which it has made to the content of the body of state law under which we live, or its present effect upon members of the Catholic Church. Canon Law is practiced by a Bar which is older than the English and American Bars at civil law, the membership of which is regulated by the Church itself.

Roman Catholic Church Courts and Procedure. A booklet prepared by a group of Chicago lawyers for the general information of members of the Bar, and published by the Christian Family Movement, deals with the marriage laws of the Catholic Church and the procedure followed by Catholic Church Courts. It refers to some of the important provisions of the Code of Canon Law as they relate to marriage, and states that to administer Church laws respecting marriage, a system of courts has been established by the Code of Canon Law for the universal Church. These courts are instruments of the spiritual governing authority of the Church. Their jurisdiction is limited by the Canon Law of the Church (Canon 1553) to matters within the proper and spiritual sphere of the Church. For example, they do not undertake to decide property rights or other purely civil matters. Their decisions are binding on the parties in the forum of conscience. They have no civil effect.

In the Archdiocese of Chicago there are two courts. One is the Separation Court. This is concerned with petitions for permission to separate and live apart. Some involve a further request for permission to resort to the civil courts for separate maintenance or divorce.

The other court is called the Annulment Court. It is concerned with cases in which the validity of the marriage is in issue, or a dissolution of the bond of marriage is sought. In the Catholic Church there are only four instances in which the bond of a valid marriage may be dissolved: (1) unconsummated marriage; (2) the Privilege of the Faith; (3) unconsummated marriage where one of the parties thereafter takes solemn vows in a religious order; (4) the Pauline

Privilege. The Roman Court has jurisdiction of the first two grounds just mentioned but the cases go for decision directly to Rome for disposition by the Pope. The Defect of Form Court is concerned with cases of the attempted marriage of a Catholic by a ceremony other than that prescribed by the Catholic Church. The Documentary Court is concerned with cases which may be settled summarily upon the presentation of documentary evidence. In these cases a declaration of nullity is granted upon the showing of non-fulfillment of certain requirements of the Canon Law respecting marriage. The Tribunal Court is concerned with cases which require a full, formal trial for disposition. This court handles all cases involving matrimonial consent, and all cases involving impediments which Canon Law has forbidden to be handled in a summary process in the Documentary Court. Appeals are provided for to an Appellate Court, with right of ultimate appeal to the Rota in Rome. The decision of the Rota ends the case except for the right to re-open in the future upon a showing of new matter not presented originally, and for the right of any Catholic who feels aggrieved in his dealings with the Church to appeal directly to the Pope.

CHAPTER 12

ISLAM: TURKEY AND THE ARAB STATES

The Beginnings of Islam. About the year 570 A.D. there was born in Mecca, Arabia—a city lying on the trade route between the Mediterranean Sea and the Indian Ocean—one who was destined to promote throughout a large portion of the world a new way of life. That way of life was to inspire the Semitic peoples, intellectually alert and receptive as they were, to a religious fervor unique in history, carrying their armies, within a century of his death, to the west, through Egypt and the length of North Africa, up through Spain and almost to the gates of Paris. To the east the prophecies of this man were likewise to be carried, within the same period, to the Amu Darya River in central Asia, and, thereafter, sometimes by war and conquest and sometimes by peaceful penetration, through China, India and Indonesia to the Philippine Islands. The man was Mohammed. The way of life was Islam ("submitting oneself to God"), professed by him to have been revealed by the Angel Gabriel, and recorded in Islam's sacred book, the Koran.

Islam was and is a unique religion. Its sacred book, dealing not merely with questions of faith and morals but constituting also the primary sources of the juridical life of the Muslim world, is interpreted wholly by laymen. Islam is a layman's religion administered by laymen for laymen. It has no priests or sacerdotal class, no ordained ministers. Any Muslim of full age may validly lead in prayer whenever the faithful convene in their mosques or elsewhere. It knows no distinction between church and state. And without any lines between priest and layman, it recognizes no distinctions of class, race or color.

In the latter part of the sixth century A.D. the Arabian Peninsula, with its nomadic population, remained quite largely untouched by the civilizations of Greece and Rome, although it was the inheritor of the adjacent ancient civilization of Babylonia. There were Hebrew settlements in Arabia, including Mohammed's native Hijaz region, where the Jews were large landowners and traders. Christianity had been in the region, too, from the early years of the Christian era.

Paul's dramatic conversion on the road to Damascus and his lowering in a basket from the city wall to escape Jews seeking to kill him are dramatic incidents well known to Bible students. Differences of understanding had divided the Christians into the three groups of Nestorians, Monophysites and Greek Orthodox, which may still be found in the region. But such influence as Christianity might have gained had been halted; persecution by the Greeks, seeking conformity to the orthodoxy of the Catholic Church, had given it a bad name in the Arab world.

The Arabs in general continued their allegiance to the gods and goddesses of the Arab pantheon, who were presumed to reside in stones and trees. The rites in their honor involved pouring sacrificial blood on those objects, whereupon the ceremonial participants touched their hands or tongues to it. Injunctions of the polytheistic religion called for pilgrimages to the sacred shrines, the central place of pilgrimage being the Kaaba shrine in Mecca, the corner stone of which was said to have been brought from heaven by the Angel Gabriel.

The Prophet Mohammed. Mohammed was the posthumous son of 'Abd Allah, of the tribe of the Koraish, custodian of the Kaaba shrine. His mother died not long after his birth, and he was reared by his grandfather and an uncle. In his early life he was a shepherd.

However much the position of Mohammedan women was degraded by polygamy and concubinage, which were institutions subsequently approved by Mohammed, it is most interesting to note their status with regard to capacity to hold property and conduct business. This is revealed by the fact that after Mohammed attained majority he was employed by Khadija, a widow, to manage her camels in her trade with Damascus. In due course Mohammed married Khadija, and they had six children. From his daughter Fatima's marriage with 'Ali came a line of descendants regarded by one of the groups into which, as we shall hereinafter see, Islam became divided by schism, as the true heirs of the Khalifate, or ruling office of Islam.

Some fifteen years after his marriage, Mohammed felt himself to be inspired as a messenger of Allah, and his career as a prophet began. The Koran states that he sensed revelations from the one and only God, centering in the thesis that there was but one God and that Mohammed was His Prophet. This God was Allah ("The God"), who created heaven and earth in six days, and sits upon the throne, directing all things. Allah produced creation, and reproduces it, to reward those who believe and do good; the lot of unbelievers will be a scalding drink and painful doom. Allah is all-powerful, so completely so, in fact, that he is not bound by principles of consistency but can, at will, proceed arbitrarily. He is across an impassable abyss from humanity. Submission is exacted from all his creatures. Nevertheless, he is a "gracious and compassionate God," as evidenced by the fact that nearly all the suras, or chapters of the Koran, begin with the formula "In the name of Allah, the Gracious and Merciful."

Claiming no supernatural powers and living a simple life, Mohammed devoted himself to gaining adherents to this conception of deity, which in its departure from the pantheistic beliefs of those Arabs who had not embraced Judaism or Christianity was manifestly heretical. As the Koran says, by the setting star Mohammed does not err, nor does he speak of his own desire. He speaks what has been revealed to him by the Mighty Power. The Koran is from God through Gabriel; it is not the work of man. Why worship goddesses like Allat and Al'uzza and Manah? There are no goddesses. "Prostrate yourselves before Allah and serve him." Moreover, Mohammed did not claim that the revelations which came to him were new and original. They were but emphasized repetitions of revelations to the Prophets before him.

At first slowly, Mohammed nevertheless made progress in gaining adherents to his faith. Within a few years their numbers reached the point where the challenge to the national idols at the very Kaaba shrine itself no longer went unnoticed by the followers of the orthodox religion. They began to manifest their resentment against Mohammed by forceful means. But as subsequent events demonstrated, the period of Mohammed's persecution was short; the period of his triumph long-continued.

The Hejira. To escape the difficulties at Mecca, Mohammed and the followers he had gained fled for safety to the rival city of Medina, inhabited by members of the Yeminite tribe. For Muslims this "Hejira" in 622 A.D. marks the date from which subsequent events of their history should be reckoned.

At Medina, Mohammed found a favorable reception for his doctrines. The "Emigrants" who had fled with him from Mecca became the powerful hard core of the Medina community from which his influence radiated. The people of Medina had followed the Arab practice of leaving decisions of their disputes to their priests, or Kahins. As the professed messenger of God Mohammed soon became the one to whom these disputes were brought. The spiritual ascendancy which he thus gained rapidly acquired governmental significance. A constitution was adopted for Medina, providing that every dispute should be brought "before God and Mohammed." Medina became a political state for the promotion of Islam.

The ultimate step was to hold it to be the will of God that the faith of Islam should be promoted by force of arms. Consistent with this doctrine, Mohammed gave assurance that soldiers who died while upholding the cause of Islam would gain immediate entrance into a paradise which was described in the most alluring terms. It can hardly be questioned, however, that the prospect of sharing in booty played an important part in the motivation of the military recruits who rallied to his standard.

Conquest of Arabia. The military conquests of Islam began with violent harassment and looting by the "Emigrants" of the Meccan caravans. The Meccans did not at first comprehend the workings of a religion, the teachings of which impelled people to turn the sword of aggression against their own brethren. Taken at first by surprise, thereafter they undertook to provide military escorts for their caravans. But at the Battle of Bedr the Meccan convoy was defeated and its leaders were executed.

The Meccans were more successful at the Battle of Ohod. However, they failed to exploit their success by way of carrying through with their attack on Medina. Subsequently they were repulsed in the War of the Fosse. Several hundred male members of the Koraiza, an autonomous Jewish tribe living in Medina, who had made an underground alliance with the Meccans, were executed, one by one, in the market place of Medina. With the exception of one whom Mohammed took to wife, the Jewish women and children were sold into slavery.

Thereafter Mohammed led a military force against Mecca. He did not attack. Backed by this show of strength he negotiated a treaty by which the Meccans accepted Islam. The shrine of Kaaba was made the shrine of Islam. In quick succession the sheiks of Arabia, at their own request or by order of Mohammed, negotiated the acceptance of Islam for their tribes. Mohammed exacted of them the performance of the daily prayers, the payment of an alms tax, and the acceptance of Muslim law. Nonconforming Jewish leaders were assassinated, and the property of Jewish colonies was confiscated. Within seven years after Mohammed and his "Emigrants" had fled for their lives from Mecca, the whole of Arabia was under his control. Without any formal action in that regard, an Arab nation had come into being. With Mohammed as its temporal as well as spiritual ruler, it made rapid strides toward empire.

The Khalifates. Mohammed died in 632 A.D. Before his death he had designated his father-in-law, Abu Bakr, to take his place as Imam, or prayer leader. Abu was elected as first Khalif, or Successor. Taking hold with a strong hand, Abu announced that he would maintain a regime of justice. "He that is weakest among you shall be in my sight the strongest until I have vindicated for him his rights; but him that is the strongest will I treat as the weakest until he complies with the laws," he declared. Abu repressed the pretensions of several would-be prophet successors, and proceeded to carry through an expedition arranged by Mohammed, which brought under Islamic control territory along the Euphrates which Heraclitus, the Eastern Roman Emperor, had only shortly before regained from Persian King Chosroes II.

Under Omar, the second Khalif, the Persian Empire was destroyed. The old Semitic lands of Syria, Palestine, Mesopotamia and Babylonia were taken over, and Egypt was brought under control. To this end, the antipathy toward the Greeks or Christians in the territories involved, arising out of persecutions inflicted in the name of church orthodoxy, contributed in measurable degree.

Omar was assassinated. Before his death he had nominated six leading "Emigrants" to choose the Khalif from among themselves. Othman, a member of the leading family of Mecca, the House of Omayya, was selected. During Othman's rule rebellion broke out in Irak and other provinces, and eventually he was assassinated. There followed a schism in Muslim ranks, the effect of which may still be noted today. The rebels, commonly called the "Shiites" or partisans, regarded Ali, son-in-law of Mohammed, and his descendants, as the rightful successors of Mohammed. They named Ali as Khalif, announcing the doctrine that the Khalif, divinely descended from Mohammed, is possessed of powers derived from the Prophet himself, and therefore rates the same respect.

Ali set up the capital of Islam at Kufu, in Irak. Moawiwa, of the House of Omayya, governor of Syria, whose grandfather had led the Meccans against the forces of Mohammed in the Battle of Ohod, refused to recognize Ali as Khalif. Supporters of the House of Omayya, known as "Sunnis," or orthodox, holding that the Khalif holds office either by choice of the Muslim community or by designation of his predecessor, stood by Moawiwa. Because of the defection of the Kharijites, or dissenters, Ali's backers were not united. In the struggle which followed Moawiya's forces expelled Ali's governor from Mecca and took possession of all Muslim territory with the exception of Irak.

Pursuant to a plot concocted by the Kharijites, an attempt was made to assassinate Moawiya as well as Ali when they visited their respective mosques at Damascus and Kufa during the Ramadan fast. The plot succeeded as to Ali, but Moawiya, though wounded, recovered. The Shiite Muslims of Irak chose Ali's son, Hasan, as Khalif, but he abdicated, and in 661 A.D. Moawiya entered Kufa with his army, insuring his position as Khalif of the entire Islamic Empire. The capital was set up at Damascus. Thus was established the dynasty of the House of Omayya. It ended about a century later when the Abassids defeated the army of the Omayyad Khalif Merwan. As the aftermath of this defeat, Merwan was slain at the altar of a Coptic church where he had sought sanctuary.

With the institution of the Abassid dynasty by the installation of Abdallah, a grand-nephew of Mohammed, as Khalif, the capital was moved to Baghdad. Abdallah schemed to insure the continued supremacy of the Abassids. He issued a decree granting amnesty to all Omayyads who would acknowledge him as Khalif, and invited them to a banquet to celebrate the event. Some ninety of the leading Omayyads accepted the invitation. When all were assembled they were set upon by a body of armed executioners. All but one, Abd-al-Rahman, were killed. The one who ascaped, Abd-al-Rahman, later set up an Omayyad dynasty in Cordova, Spain. During the ninth and tenth centuries a peak of achievement in commerce, learning and arts was reached under the regime of the Abbasid Khalifs at Baghdad. The Abassid dynasty lasted, nominally, in the East, until Baghdad was captured and destroyed in 1258 A.D. by the Mongol invaders led by Jinghiz Khan.

Islamic Conquest and World Supremacy. Within a relatively short time after the death of Mohammed, as we have noted, the forces of Islam pushed into far-flung conquests. They conquered Syria, Palestine, Mesopotamia, Babylon, Persia and Egypt. Pushing on to the west, North Africa was conquered. Sicily was occupied. With the defeat of the Visigothic King Roderic at Xeres, and aided in considerable measure by the tacit approval of Spanish Christians who had been subjected to persecution by the Roman Church for alleged heresies, they conquered and took over Spain. Pressing across the Pyrenees, they surged over southern France. As we have seen, their penetration of Western Europe was halted only by the defeat of their hosts by the Franks under the command of Charles Martel at Tours, in 732 A.D.

As Islam swept through this vast area the Arabic language superseded Greek and Latin therein, and became not only the common medium of communication but also the language of culture throughout a large part of the world. The Greek philosophers became known to its peoples through the medium of Arabic translations. Such Arabic philosophers as Averroes brought permanent distinction to Islam scholarship. Art flourished in its highest forms. Literary works on philosophy, mathematics, astronomy, physics, geography, law and theology were the classics of the times. Abd-a-Rahman, who, as we have seen, escaped assassination in the East and came to Spain, where he set up an Omayyad dynasty, gave Spain an enlightened rule. Trade and agriculture flourished, and he employed the public revenues not only in maintaining a military force but also in constructing public works. Under him, the culture of the East combined with the Greco-Roman elements already present in Spain to achieve noteworthy results. Even after Islamic power began to wane, Cordova, in Spain, remained a brilliantly intellectual and artistic center. In the tenth century the University of Cordova, attached to the Mosque of Abderrahaman, and attended not only by Muslims but by Christian students as well, was the only university in Europe. The Alhambra, in Granada, was a masterpiece of Saracen architecture.

Nor was Islam static in the East, where, as we have already noted, it kept penetrating until it had made its way to the far reaches of the Orient, as evidenced today by its millions of adherents in Central Asia, Pakistan, India, the Malay Peninsula, Indonesia and the Philippines. Founded in 970 A.D. at the Mosque El Azhar at Cairo, Egypt, the world's oldest extant university has since constituted a center of Islamic scholarship. Islam in its relation to India and Hinduism has been accorded special consideration.

It has already been noted that in many of the areas to which the soldiers of Islam came their conquest was facilitated by readiness of the local Christians to accept their rule as a change from the persecution which had been inflicted by the Christian Church for alleged doctrinal aberrations. In other areas, particularly in the Far East, Islam was brought by individual missionaries who found in it for themselves sources of spiritual strength and undertook to pass it on to others. Those ascetically inclined and of philosophical bent, seeking individual realization of community with Allah, merged it with elements of mysticism to create the doctrine of Sufuism, which enhanced its appeal to many. In later centuries the efforts of individual missionaries were augmented by the organized activities of the Sufi brotherhoods.

All in all, Islam, with its synthesis of religion and law, was a dynamic force during the period from 800 to 1200 A.D. Through the time when Europe was shrouded in darkness, the world's intellectual and artistic interests flourished under the trusteeship of the Prophet Mohammed and his followers.

Islam As a State. Let us look more closely at the organized aspects of Islam as a state. We have seen that the Prophet was initially a religious leader. But even before he and the group of followers which he had acquired in Mecca fled to Medina, force of circumstances made it necessary that he exercise powers of leadership in a secular sense. Common religious belief makes for a common bond of opinion, but to live together people require more than agreement on broad religious concepts. Even within a strictly religious group there can be no escape from the necessity of government in some form. Where, as in the case of Islam, the religion purports to control all the activities of life, the governmental framework within which it operates must be correspondingly enlarged, with its boundaries extending beyond the religious domain and to the farthest reaches of the secular state. The more emphatically is this true where the religious group is not all-inclusive, but is only one group among others and under the necessity of maintaining itself by armed force. To live and grow it must possess and employ the attributes of a political organism. Such was the position of Islam.

In accordance with the common pattern disclosed by the procedures of the various early rulers of mankind, as we have thus far noted them, Mohammed assumed and exercised such power as he deemed essential to his purposes, supreme among which was promotion of the faith. Thereby he laid the foundation for the State of Islam. Himself defining the policies, he left to his lawyers the task of organizing the conquered lands. In this, his successors followed his example. Because Islam had no priesthood, this was inevitable: the transcendent role attributed to the Koran made of its expounders, the lawyers of Islam, the inevitable rulers of the Muslim world.

Upon this foundation the Khalifs built the state which, as we have seen, developed into the Islamic Empire. As supreme ruler, administering the law of Islam, the Khalif was at once high priest, ruler and judge. The administration of criminal justice was particularly within his personal province. He appointed the necessary agents to conduct the affairs of government, but their actions were subject in every

way to his approval. Of primary importance among his executive
duties was the administration of revenue and pensions. Every Muslim was compelled to pay an alms tax. Christians and Jews were
compelled to pay a poll tax, graduated in accordance with their
wealth. They also paid a land tax of contributions in kind, graduated in accordance with the amount produced on their land. Under
a plan initiated by Omar, each Muslim received an individual pension, originally in amount dependent upon the degree of relationship
with the family and tribe of Mohammed. This resulted in especially
handsome payments to the "Emigrants" and early adherents of Mohammed in Mecca and Medina. But something was provided for
every adult Muslim. In submitting to Islamic conquest and embracing the faith, conquered peoples found that they not only absolved
themselves from the payment of poll and land taxes, but that they
thereby qualified as beneficiaries of the taxes paid by others.

Provisions for judicial administration were not neglected. To administer justice the Khalif appointed judges known as Cadis, who
exercised thorough-going legal powers, and with growing professional
aptitude. The prescribed duty of the Cadis was to decide disputes
between persons; to enforce the execution of judgments rendered by
them; to name guardians for the administration of the estates of in-
competents; to administer religious endowments; to arrange marriages
for orphan girls who had no guardian, and to approve the execution
of wills. Although the Khalif concerned himself personally with the
determination of criminal cases, the Cadi was left to inflict the prescribed penalties upon those guilty of such crimes as religious heresy,
neglect of religious duties, refusal to pay taxes, murder, adultery
and theft. A court of appeal, of which the Khalif was presiding officer, was established to hear cases appealed from the Cadis.

Relation of Islam to Judaism and Christianity. It has been noted
that both Judaism and Christianity had a foothold in Arabia before
the advent of Islam. Mohammed had had personal contacts with
the peoples of both religions. He was familiar with the Scriptures,
as is evidenced by the fact that many portions of the Bible are to be
found in the Koran. It seems clear on the record that he rejected
Judaism and Christianity as true religions, but nevertheless employed
them as foundations upon which to build his own. He utilized them,
moreover, to point the divine finger at himself as the ultimate true
Prophet.

Mohammed's denial of Judaism and Christianity as true religions is
implicit in the Koran, the Sacred Book of Islam. Allah is the one

God. There is not any friend or helper but Allah. Whoever follows Allah finds his reward and shall have no fear. The Jews say that the Christians follow nothing, which is true. The Christians say the Jews follow nothing, which is true. Yet both follow the Scripture. Allah will judge them on the Resurrection Day. Mohammed has been sent with the truth.

In another part of the Koran Jesus is said to have prophesied the coming of Mohammed, Jesus the Son of Mary having stated that he was Allah's Apostle, confirming the revelation of the Old Testament, and bringing glad tidings of an apostle to come after him who would be Mohammed. Elsewhere it is pointed out that Abraham, Noah and other prophets were sent, but were not believed. Jesus was sent, but evil-doers remained. Finally came Mohammed, to provide a light wherein to walk. All believers should fear Allah and give heed to the words of his Prophet. Mohammed grounded himself on Abraham, already associated with the religion of the Arabs, and asserted the position of voicing Allah's ultimate revelation.

From a point of view transcending national boundaries, under Islamic doctrine all believers lived together as brothers, not as citizens owing political allegiance to independent nations but rather as people of "one world," recognizing Allah as the supreme power and ruler. The Muslims strove, accordingly, to make Islam the universal religion, to the presumed end that such universal brotherhood might be attained.

A "Crazy Quilt" of Legal Systems. But in spite of the far-flung campaign of conquest initiated by the rulers of Islam, presumably to attain this end, in the perspective of history it does not appear that Muslim ecumenicity, as such, was the real desideratum. In the mention of the special taxation of Jews and Christians we have gathered that throughout the Islamic Empire there remained groups whose members did not profess Islam, were not compelled to profess Islam, and who paid financial tribute because they did not. As far as these non-believing groups were scriptuaries, that is, Jews, Christians or Sabians, they were permitted to continue the exercise of their own religion, including application of their own laws in their own courts. Out of these privileges there developed in the period of the Ottoman Empire the *millet* system which still survives, though in a reduced form, in the present day structure of courts in the Christian and Jewish communities in all Arab states except certain of those in the Arab Peninsula where there is no significant indigenous non-Muslim population.

The situation has been clearly explained by Judge Pierre Crabites. "Visualize," he declared in 1925, "a crazy quilt and you have drawn a mental picture of the Egyptian legal system," adding that it was an evolution, surcharged with history, crystallizing "the genius of Islam." Under analysis its texture becomes a Rosetta stone which will help to decipher the mystery of the East. Symbolic of the policy to be initiated when the Ottoman Turks came to power was the action of the Ottoman Muhammad, who led the Turkish forces that captured Constantinople in 1453, when he entered the Cathedral of Saint Sofia and saw a fanatical Muslim destroying its mosaics. The despoiler was executed on the spot. A large proportion of the people had fled the city. The Patriarchate of Constantinople had been vacant for two years. Sultan Muhammad issued a firman, assuring all Greeks who had fled and who would return that their property would be protected and that they could freely exercise their religion. He ordered the Greek leaders to choose a Patriarch. The Monk Gennadius was chosen. Muhammad bestowed a scepter on him and assured him of enjoyment of all the rights and privileges of his predecessors. Joachim, Armenian Bishop of Brousa, Asia Minor, was ordered to return to Constantinople with his colony, and Moche Capsali was recognized as the head of the Jewish community.

Judge Crabites pointed out that Muhammed carried out this policy because he wanted to organize his foreign population into distinct compact and homogenous communities. "In the old days when the Star and Crescent were in the ascendancy, the sagacious Islamic leaders were delighted to have these foreign communities in their midst because they were the geese who laid the golden eggs," said Judge Crabites. The Muslims were fighters, and neither tradesmen, money makers nor taxpayers. Their "Little Armenia," their "Little Jerusalem" and their "Little Greece" supplied the money. Everybody was happy: The Turk, because he could fight without bothering about budgets. The Christians and Jews because they could make money and pay out just enough to keep the Turk fighting and therefore uninterested in money making.

These three non-Muslim communities which Sultan Muhammed thus established eventually grew in Egypt to thirteen: (1) Greek Orthodox; (2) Greek Melkite Orthodox; (3) Maronite; (4) Gregorian Armenian; (5) Catholic Armenian; (6) Syrian Jacobite; (7) Orthodox Coptic; (8) Catholic Coptic; (9) Orthodox Chaldean; (10) Catholic Chaldean; (11) Protestant; (12) Orthodox Jews; (13) Caraite Jews. Each had its own judicial system and its own judges and applied its own law, carrying things so far that not all used the same calendar, some applying the Gregorian and others either the Julian, Coptic, Jewish or Arabic, as the case might be.

The Nature of Islamic Law. With the understanding that because of the considerations of which we have just spoken Islamic law applied only to those who embraced the faith of Islam, let us glance further at its nature. We have already referred to Allah, the God of Islam, the concept of whom was obviously calculated to determine the scope and content of Islamic law. Allah revealed that law to Mohammed, and Mohammed transmitted it to the Muslim community. In his final address to an assembly of his believers, after uttering a specific exhortation to good living, Mohammed concluded: "I have revealed all. I leave you a law which will forever preserve you from error if you steadfastly adhere to it—a clear and positive law, the book of God and the example of his Prophet."

As Mohammed thus said, he presented to his followers a law, or Sharia, as it is called, which embodied a complete guide to life. Because of its theocratic foundation, therefore, it was all-pervasive. Incorporating the elements of secular law as well as of religious obligation, because it bore the authority of divine inspiration it was not only unchallengable, but also immutable. The government might fall, but the law in all its divine majesty remained. Applying directly to every Muslim, it bound believers, even though they resided outside Islamic territory. Thus it constituted a powerful force which gave all Muslims, everywhere, a sense of something more than mere abstract spiritual unity.

The Five Basic Prescriptions. The heart of Islamic law as it governs the personal life of the individual is found in five simple, readily understandable prescriptions. The first of these is to believe. One obeys this prescription and becomes a Muslim by professing "There is no deity but Allah, and Mohammed is his Prophet." The second prescription enjoins regular prayer. From the minaret of each Muslim mosque the designated muezzin, five times daily, summons the faithful by calling, in a voice of entreaty: "God is great. There is no God but Allah. Mohammed is his Apostle. Come to prayer. Come to salvation. Allah is most great." Although the Koran does not specifically enjoin the five set times of prayer, or the genuflections involved in the ceremony, these disciplines have behind them centuries of immutable custom. If possible they are to be performed in a mosque, under the timing of the *imam*, or leader, but if this is not possible they are to be observed wherever the believer may be. They are to be preceded, moreover, by prescribed ablutions. "When ye rise up for prayer, wash your faces, and your hands up to your elbows, and rub your heads and your feet to the ankles. If ye do not find water, go to clean high ground and rub your faces and hands with it."

The third rule of conduct is almsgiving. Thus, by the Koran, God has created some men in such poverty and distress as to need the help of others. "What does that braggart man mean when he says, 'None shall prevail over me: I have and have scattered riches boundless.' Does he not know that there is a Divine eye that sees him? Have not We created him with a capacity of distinguishing between the two highways, that which descends towards evil, and that which ascends towards the good? This niggardly man, however, makes no attempt to scale the heights. What is it to ascend the upward road? It is to free the prisoner, to feed the hungry, to defend the orphan who is akin, and the unfortunate poor. Moreover, it is enjoined that men believe in Allah and His Prophet; that they encourage one another to be steadfast in the faith, exercising mutual sympathy."

The fourth rule of conduct is keeping the fast of Ramadan, which lasts a month. During the fast no one may eat, drink or smoke between sunrise and sunset. The use of pork is forbidden at all times. The fifth rule of conduct is making a pilgrimage to Mecca, at least once in a lifetime, and kissing the wall of the Kaaba.

Marriage and Family Law. Obviously a body of law undertaking to meet all the requirements of group life must carry far beyond such simple injunctions for personal conduct as we have just noted, the heart of Islam though they may be. It has already been indicated that Islamic law in fact covered the entire field of law and government, and its broader content has been to some extent suggested by the previous references to judicial administration. Further illustrative of its comprehensive scope are its provisions relating to marriage and the family.

Thus, we find in the Koran the adjuration not to wed idolatresses until they believe, and not to give daughters in marriage to idolaters until they believe. Marry two or three or four of the women who seem good, but only one if it is feared that justice cannot be done to so many. Give to the women so married their marriage portions unless of their own accord they remit it. Rights to inherit property are dealt with in some detail. The degrees of relationship which constitute a bar to marriage are dealt with.

Men are stated to be in charge of women, because Allah so ordered, and good women are obedient. A husband may divorce his wife on any grounds, but a wife has no such right. Those who forswear their wives must wait four months. If they change their minds, Allah is forgiving; if they decide upon divorce, Allah is knowing. Women who are forsworn shall wait for three monthly courses. It is unlawful for them to conceal that which Allah has created in their wombs if they are believers, and if they desire a reconciliation their husbands should take them back in that case. When men put away women they should reckon the period and not expel them from the house during the period unless they are openly immoral. When they have reached their term, take them back in kindness or part from them in kindness and call as witness two just men.

The rewards for observance of Allah's law in these and in all respects are most alluring. By the promise of the Koran, all who believe in Allah and his Prophet shall be admitted hereafter into delightful gardens. They shall repose forever on couches decked with gold and precious stones, supplied with luscious drinks and fruits of their preference. With them shall be damsels of unsurpassed beauty, with large black, pearl-like eyes.

We have already seen how the promise of a glamorous future life led men to enlist in the military ranks of Islam and offer their lives in combat. It is important to note that the emphasis of Muslim law was upon the individual and his direct relationship to God. Before Allah, all were equals. No priest or clergyman, no man-administered sacrament, stood between him and Allah, even in a formal sense. As was made clear at the outset, when Mohammed and his "Emigrants" attacked their brethren of Mecca, family ties were absolutely subordinated to religious obligation. The extent to which this carried is evidenced by the denunciation in the Koran of Mohammed's uncle, Abu Lahab, who with his wife had rejected the Prophet: "Abu Lahab's power will perish, and he himself will perish. His wealth will not avail him, nor all that he has gained. He shall be thrown into the fiery flames. His wife, carrying wood for fuel, will have a noose of palm-tree fibre twisted around her neck."

The Koran. Islam's Basic Scripture. Let us look more closely at the Koran, from which we have been quoting, and which, as it has been indicated, is Islam's basic scripture. It enunciates, in general terms, Islam's basic law.

When Mohammed was not leading his forces in battle or absorbed by his spiritual communion with the Archangel Gabriel who brought the Koran to him piecemeal from heaven, he sat under a tree and settled the disputes which arose among his followers. In thus acting as an arbiter he did not impose his own opinion but merely applied to each concrete case a text of the Holy Book.   If there were no verse of the Koran applicable to the cause before him, the Prophet frankly told the litigants that in the light of present knowledge he could not pass upon their dispute, but that he would hold the matter under advisement until Gabriel brought him a ruling from On High.   This procedure trained True Believers to look to the Koran for everything.

As long as Mohammed was living his utterances, thus grounded and inspired, constituted the law in terms of its application.   At his death no more "law" was forthcoming from his living lips, by way of application of the Koran.   But under the conception of Islam this did not matter.   It was conceived that all truth had been divinely revealed to the Prophet in his lifetime, and had been recorded by him in word and deed.   In other words, he left behind him a system of law, good for all time to come, available for his followers to understand and utilize as he would have done.

Manifestly a legal system, so conceived, was a static one, by hypothesis beyond the possibility of being changed by the modification of old rules and the addition of new ones and thus without the qualification that a legal system must have if it is to accomplish the purpose of successfully regulating the changing relations of men in a changing society.   In spite of the expedients adopted to make it adaptable to the needs of the people governed by it, its rigidity has operated as a constant brake on Muslim progress.

The Koran itself was immutable.   By Muslim belief it existed before the Creation on the "Preserved Tablet" brought by the Angel Gabriel from the highest to the lowest heaven, and from thence dictated to Mohammed.   As stated in the Koran itself, "We have brought down to Mohammed the Koran on the Night of Power.   This one Night of Power is better than a thousand months.   On that night Gabriel and the angels descended and revealed to our Prophet all the words of the Koran."   It did not exist as a whole until after Mohammed's death.   It had been transcribed on palm leaves, stones, and the shoulder-blade bones of animals.   Without apparent scheme or plan, so far as arrangement was concerned, it was a compilation of haphazard utterances dealing with many things.   Khalif Omar caused to be made three originals of the text, which were never thereafter varied.

The Koran is not, of course, a law code in the modern sense.   It contains legal precepts intermingled with utterances of a purely religious kind.   Nor does it cover all fields of law.   Thus, in the very early days of Islam, there was still a field for the application of the customary law of the Arabs, which had governed the traders of Mecca, the farmers of Medina, and the nomads of the desert before the advent of the Prophet. And in those regions which were subjected to Islamic power by conquest it was not practicable or possible to fully supersede the local customary law by the Islamic Sharia, even as to all those who embraced Islam. So to a considerable extent such local law was left in force, even as local custom was recognized as law by the Hindu Laws of Manu in India.

In short, Mohammed did not leave, in the Koran, a body of written law comprehensive enough to meet the needs of even the primitive society of the seventh century A.D. As Judge Crabites emphasized, the Prophet himself did not always find in the text of the Koran the direct solution to the problems which he undertook to resolve. To satisfy the concept that all law came through and from what had been revealed to the Prophet it was necessary from the outset to reach beyond the Koran for sources directly identified with it and the Prophet. So it was that resort to the Koran was supplemented by reference to three other sources: the Tradition, or Sunna; the Unanimous Concordance, or Ijma; and Analogy.

Tradition, Or Sunna. Mohammed's conduct was conceived to have been divinely regulated. Consequently, not only what he said but also what he did was held to have been divinely inspired. We have just noted how in the course of his prophetic career he at times acted as judge of his people. In this connection he had decided a great many questions, dealing not only with personal relations but also with matters as far removed as the disposal of booty and prisoners of war acquired by conquest. All of his decisions were received as binding commands of heaven. Even the casual events of his daily life were made the basis for doctrines of momentous importance.

All of these decisions and incidents were preserved by tradition, each handed down in the form of a short statement known as a "hadith," purportedly narrated by some one who had heard the Prophet speak in that particular connection. As time went on these hadiths multiplied to a fantastic degree, to the number, it has been said, of some six hundred thousand. The most of this vast number were not regarded as authentic. After some generations those that could pass the test of Muslim jurisconsults, to the number of some seven thousand, were reduced to writing, and six of the collections thus made are generally accepted as authentic.

Unanimous Concordance. The four immediate successors of Mohammed followed his example in disposing, as chief judges, of a great number of litigious cases. Omar, as well as Abu Bakr, used to assemble for conferences, on such occasions, a council of the faithful. These considered the issue in the light of the words and acts of the Prophet in similar situations as narrated by those who remembered them. The concordances of opinion thus arrived at, or *ijmas,* became a further fountain of jurisprudence of great importance. It was by such means that Omar obtained a ratification of his determination not to distribute all the lands of Syria as spoils to his victorious soldiers, but to leave them in the hands of their Christian occupants, subject to a Kharaj exceeding the tithe payable by Muslims, and dedicated to the usages of Islam. The practice of obtaining enlightenment as to the law by the means of Ijmas continued for three generations.

A similar practice was followed during the same period by officials who exercised the judicial function in remote parts of the Muslim realm. Accordingly, judges in Syria, Northern Africa and Persia decided all new cases as best they could according to their knowledge of the Koran and the Tradition, using their discretion where the law was silent. Those judges who had seen the Prophet, and the contemporaries of those judges, were considered to have a good knowledge of the Koran and the Tradition. Because they lived with the Prophet or with his companions they were deemed to know exactly the meaning of the legal texts and could authoritatively interpret and apply them. The cases that were decided in that period without dissent are considered as authoritative binding law, and were said to have been decided by Unanimous Concordance.

Analogy or Qiyas. From the beginning of the second century of Islam the learned legal scholars known as "ylema," and upon whose thorough education in the law great stress was laid, were called upon to compile the tradition and to explain as well as to interpret the Koran. But issues were presented which did not lend themselves to resolution by clear statement of the Koran or even Tradition, and for which there was no precedent of Unanimous Concordance. With the sudden expansion and development of the Islamic Empire, the civil and commercial relationships, vast and complex, revealed numerous lacunae in the law. And so Analogy, or *qiyas,* came into play—the application to a new problem of the principles which had been declared applicable to a previous similar problem. To facilitate the process, the ylema set themselves to a careful study of the causes and circumstances of the revelation of each text in the Koran and the

Tradition, deducing from them the underlying legal principle, which might be applied to all similar cases by Analogy.

Such a process opened the way to divergencies of opinion, which in due course manifested themselves. In consequence there developed in Sunni Islam four schools of law, fundamentally similar but with some differences of detail, each bearing the name of its distinguished exponent—Abu Hunifa, Ash-Shafi, Ibn Malek and Ion Hanbal. In time each school became in turn subdivided by divergencies among the disciples of each of these exponents. Through fear of future abuse of the process, about the end of the third century of Islam it was decided to restrict jurisprudence to the more accepted solutions of any of these four schools. With this decision all further development of the Sharia, or Sunni law, was arrested, the result being that it stands today about where it was when expounded ten centuries ago.

But this closing of the gate of interpretative analogy was not recognized by the Shiites, for readily understandable reasons. We have already noted that under their belief the Khalif is the divine successor of Mohammed. It follows that, as such, he possesses the same full power of declaring the law, untrammeled by previous interpretations. Under this conception the result reached is somewhat the same as that attained under the workings of the English and American common law, which the court declares and applies on the basis of reason and justice as of the present time.

Rise of the Ottoman Turks. Before passing on from Islam, brief comment should be made as to the waning of the Islamic Empire, its absorption by the Ottoman Turks, and the recent renaissance of the Arab nations following the dissolution of the Ottoman Empire.

Islam's western extremity, Spain, began to crack under the pressure of growing strength of the Christian Church in the eleventh and twelfth centuries A.D. The fervor of the Crusades had been transmitted to the Church in that country, creating a steadily growing menace to Muslim tenure. In 1236 Cordova was taken by the Christians, and in 1248 Seville fell. Although Granada remained in Muslim hands for more than a century thereafter, Islamic influence on the Continent had become a matter of past history.

In the East there was manifested the phenomenon so inexorably demonstrated in the history of great empires: conquests which bring easy wealth, with its corollary debilitating luxuries, nourish within themselves the elements of political as well as spiritual decadence. Islam's own men laid down their arms and left the soldiering to mercenaries, imported from the Turkish tribes of central Asia. As the physical and moral fibre of their masters weakened, that of these hirelings strengthened. Eventually they became the masters, taking over the government itself. Islam, maintained in form, degenerated to a shell.

We have already seen that in 1258 A.D. the Mongol armies of Jinghiz Khan captured and destroyed the capital city of Baghdad. Hundreds of thousands of people were massacred. Aleppo, in Syria, was likewise destroyed, and its people killed. Still later, Tamerlane destroyed Damascus. Egypt was saved from heathen destruction only by the military power of the Mamluks, the imported mercenaries who had seized control. The Islamic Empire, as such, came to an end.

In the areas seized by the Mongols the temporal power of Islam was crushed, but it would be too much to say that its spiritual aspects were altogether subdued. Sufuism had been strong, and continued to live, and the culture of Persia continued to find expression in the arts. And even as the barbarian conquerors of Rome acquired the culture of those whom they conquered, so in time were the Mongol hordes uplifted by their Islamic heritage.

As the star of the Islamic Empire began to set, that of the Ottoman Turks, driven from their homes in central Asia by the Mongols, had begun its rise. Although not Arabs, they had embraced the faith of Islam. With the military vigor of a new people on the march they began conquests which, within three centuries, brought under their control, with the exception of such countries as Morocco, virtually all that remained of what had been the Islamic Empire. Having solidified themselves in Asia, they succeeded in completing an undertaking at which Islam had failed in 677 and again in 718 A.D.— the invasion of Eastern Europe. Aided by the resentment felt by Arab Christians who had been persecuted by the Greek ecclesiastical officialdom for alleged non-orthodoxy, and who were disposed to accept Turkish rule rather than continue under that of their ecclesiastical oppressors, they made their way to the Bosporus and, in 1360, gained a foothold in Europe by capturing Adrianople. We have already noted how, in 1453, they captured Constantinople.

In one sense at least Islam was not critically affected by the demise of the Islamic Empire. The Turks had accepted it as a religion. With official approval of the Ottoman rulers it continued on, but without the organic identity with the state conceived by the Prophet and the earlier Khalifates. Provision was made for a religious chief, however, known as the Shaikh al-Islam, or Chief Mufti of Constantinople. Thus Islam remained a power in itself in the conduct of public affairs.

Not for long was the Ottoman rule beneficent. In the matter of taxation, among others, it was harsh and oppressive. As stated in the Federalist, in the Ottoman Empire the sovereign, though in other respects absolute master of the lives and fortunes of his subjects, had no right to impose a new tax. The consequence was that he permitted the bashaws or governors of provinces to pillage the people without mercy; and, in turn, squeezed out of them the sums of which he stood in need. So harsh and corrupt did the government become that to the oppressed Arab peoples the very idea of government became anathema. Smarting under their wrongs, these peoples looked forward to the day when the Ottoman overlords could be overthrown, once and for all.

Development of the "European Concert." In its turn the Ottoman power waned, in part because any regime which depends for survival upon sheer force cannot permanently withstand the stresses of time, but also because of external developments affecting the whole world. Islamic prosperity was intimately identified with the operation of the great land trade routes between East and West, to which we have already referred. Such transport was slow and expensive, complicated by constant brigandage. Under the Ottomans, high tariffs were imposed. A probing for ocean routes had been going on. Vasco de Gama, who sailed around Africa in 1497, opened a new way that soon carried most of the trade, leaving only a trickle for the overland route. The impact upon the previously prosperous Islamic areas was thoroughly demoralizing, materially and spiritually.

At the same time the nations of Western Europe were coming to maturity and were becoming concerned about relations with the East. Hanging like a pall over the Chancelleries of Europe lay the eternal Eastern Question, the problem of finding a *modus vivendi* between the decaying empire of Turkey and its Christian subjects and neighboring states. Alexander I prevented this question from coming up for settlement at the Congress of Vienna, Russian prospects as a residuary legatee upon the death of Turkey being far too good to make the question one which Russian public opinion would wish to have discussed as a problem affecting all the European powers. As the horizon grew dark with complications, all Europe gradually came to the conclusion that the only way out lay in cooperation and in joint discussion. Collective authority in dealing with the disintegration of Turkey was exercised tentatively after 1826, systematically after 1856, when in the Treaty of Paris, which ended the Crimean War, the Signatory Powers undertook to respect the territorial integrity of the Ottoman Empire and to consider as a matter of general interest—and of mutual discussion—any act which might infringe it. Since the ratification of this clause, which was repeated in a stronger form in the Treaty of Berlin (1878), the method there laid down was applied successively to Greece, Egypt, Syria, to the Danubian principalities, and the Balkan peninsula generally, to certain other of the European provinces of Turkey and Russia, and to the treatment of Armenians. Of all the avenues leading to the realization of a League of Nations, the employment of the European Concert, sanctioned by the penetrating intellects of Bismarck and Cavour, not to mention others, was not the least important.

"Capitulations"—Consular and Mixed Courts. Out of the diplomatic contacts between the Eastern European nations and the Ottoman Empire came the system of "capitulations" and foreign consular and mixed courts, by virtue of which citizens of other countries enjoyed certain special privileges on Muslim soil.

It is true that from one point of view these things were mere reflections of Islamic logic. From what has been said it is clear that in dealing with Islamic law we are faced with certain seemingly immutable considerations, dictated by the tenets of Islamic religion. Islamic law, at once religious and secular, is basically religious. Because it is, it can have application only to professors of the faith of Islam. Non-professors cannot live under Islamic law, but must be ordered under another law appropriate to them. In consequence, as we have seen, Jewish and Christian communities were allowed to live by their own law. And in the course of time there arose in the course of trade with Greek and Roman cities contacts with other peoples outside the Muslim realm which by the same logic called for the recognition and application of a law appropriately personal to them.

Logically, therefore, citizens of other nations who did not profess adherence to Islam could be held to be outside the operation of Muslim law. But in this case they owed political allegiance to other sovereignties, and the grant of such privilege to them was a pragmatic reflection of the superior power which their countries were in position to assert.

The grant of such privileges was not in terms of surrender. The "diplomas" or "capitulations" were so called, not because of implied surrender, but because they were divided into articles, or capitulae.

Originally they were granted to European traders. Under the Ottoman Empire they were widely extended, and in the nineteenth century capitulations were granted to the United States. Under Sultan Suleiman the Magnificent, France was given the right to appoint consuls in Ottoman territories, with jurisdiction over French subjects in all civil and criminal matters, according to their own laws. England and other nations were in due course granted similar privileges. The consular courts established under these agreements were judicial tribunals, proceeding as such, with a system of appeals culminating, in the cases of England and France, in a high appellate court of the home country.

In 1875 the Mixed Tribunals or Courts of Egypt were established, with courts of first instance at Cairo, Alexandria and Mansouran, and an appeals court at Alexandria. Egypt and all nations which had been granted capitulations were represented by member judges. These courts were granted jurisdiction over all suits between foreigners and Egyptians, between foreigners of different nationalities, and between foreigners of the same nationality if the action were one affecting real estate. Obviously, the Mixed Courts did not replace the consular courts, in so far as criminal and civil matters involving only their own nationals were concerned.

Describing the Mixed Courts and their functioning, Judge Pierre Crabites said that Sir Maurice Amos, former adviser to the Egyptian Ministry of Justice once told him that the Mixed Courts were, with the exception of the Roman Catholic Church, the greatest international organization in the world.

Arab Renascence. The invasion of Egypt by Napoleon at the dawn of the nineteenth century sparked a stirring of the decadent ambitions of the Arab peoples, turning them into channels of Arabic nationalistic aspiration which in recent years came to run at full stream and are presently overflowing.

The immediate urge was to throw off Ottoman rule. However, the feeling was by no means confined to their Ottoman overlords. Through the system of capitulations and consular and Mixed Courts of which we have been speaking, the Arabs had become unpleasantly conscious of the hands of European nations in their affairs. As they turned their glance backward they noted that for many centuries, in fact, they had been pressured by such outside nations. In the days of the Crusades they had sustained military attack, and since then France had asserted the prerogative of protecting Christians of the Near East. More recently, as we have seen, Napoleon led the soldiers of

France into Egypt. Succeeding events further dramatized the interference by outsiders. In 1860 French soldiers entered Lebanon to protect Christians of the area from massacre by the Druzes, a fanatical Islamic sect. In 1830 France seized Algeria, and in 1881 took over Tunisia. In 1911, as one of the results of the war with Turkey, Italy took over Libya.

Events in Egypt. Egypt, particularly, merits further consideration in this connection. Mohammed Ali, commander of a division of Albanian soldiers sent to Egypt by the Sultan of Turkey to drive out Napoleon, stayed on in that country and so ingratiated himself that the people proclaimed him Pasha of Egypt. The Sultan confirmed the action. Thereupon Mohammed Ali liquidated the Mamluks who had been ruling Egypt under the Ottomans, organized an army of Egyptian fellaheen, or peasants, and started on a program of conquest which carried the Egyptian forces into Arabia, Syria, Palestine and Greece, and projected a challenge to the Ottoman Empire itself. Becoming alarmed, the European powers forced Mohammed Ali to withdraw his forces into Egypt. In consideration, however, Turkey was forced to grant a large measure of autonomy to Egypt, and rule was made hereditary in the family of Mohammed Ali. Thus, in 1841, Egypt gained virtual independence from the Ottoman Empire.

But Turkey's concession by no means solved the problems raised by Egypt's incubating aspirations as affected by her contacts with outside powers. The interest of Great Britain and France became focused on Egypt through the Suez Canal project, completed in 1869, under a concession granted by the Egyptian Khedive. French interests bought 51% of the stock, the Khedive 44%, and individual investors the remainder. The concession was to expire in 1968. In 1875 the Khedive was in financial difficulties. Great Britain bought his holdings, thus giving that nation a monetary as well as a strategic interest in the canal. By this time, as we have seen in our consideration of Hinduism and India, the canal was manifestly a vital link in Great Britain's life-line to India, where she had yet to bring about stability following the Indian Mutiny of 1857. But Egypt owed still other debts to the European powers. They brought pressure upon the Turkish Sultan to utilize his nominal control over Egypt to depose the Egyptian ruler and install another one through whom the financial affairs of that country could be controlled to their advantage.

It seemed to the Egyptians that other foreign powers were about to take them over. By way of reaction, under Colonel Ahmed Orabi they revolted, and seized Alexandria. With the motive of quelling the attendant disorder, British troops landed and occupied the city. Thus began a British occupation which came to extend to the whole of Egypt, including the Canal Zone and the Sudan. In the latter country a condominium was set up between Great Britain and Egypt, which lasted until the assassination of the British governor-general in 1924, at which time Great Britain asserted complete control.

In 1904, by treaty, Great Britain recognized the dominant position of France in Morocco, in consideration of the recognition by France of Great Britain's dominant position in Egypt. In 1909 Great Britain proposed that the Suez Canal concession be extended forty years from its expiration date in 1968, but Egyptian resistance was so strong that the matter was not pressed. During the period of occupation the Egyptian government formally ruled the nation—subject, however, to policies imposed by Great Britain. On the whole the influence of British law and administration was salutary, and had a great influence on Egyptian institutions. Nevertheless, nationalistic feelings increasingly manifested themselves. During the period of World War I it was necessary to impose martial law to insure the safety of the area as the Middle East center of Allied military forces. Following the war, in 1922, Egyptian independence, with certain rights reserved, was granted by Great Britain. Egyptian agitation continuing, a treaty was negotiated in 1936 further easing the British controls.

World War II brought full military occupation back to Egypt, with all its unpleasant manifestations. When it was over Egypt vigorously reasserted its demands for the withdrawal of British troops and for complete independence, buttressing its position upon the "free world" war slogans of Great Britain and the United Nations. In 1947 the Security Council of the United Nations failed to act on the charge presented by Egypt that the presence of British troops on Egyptian soil was an infringement upon Egyptian dignity and contrary to the United Nations charter. In 1951, Egypt denounced the 1936 treaty, declaring it to be no longer binding. Stung by the defeat of the Arab coalition by the army of Israel, and following a period of popular disorders, on July 26, 1952, the army, headed by General Naguib, forced King Farouk to abdicate and took control of the government. General Naguib was succeeded in turn, following another military coup, by Colonel Gamel Abdel Nasser. Colonel Nasser's strength was symbolized by his decree outlawing the powerful Muslim Brotherhood.

Following the withdrawal of British troops from Suez, in accordance with the treaty of 1936, on July 26, 1956, Colonel Nasser seized and nationalized the canal. How the joint military effort of Great Britain, France and Israel to oust the Egyptian forces from possession prior to the expiration of the original contract date of 1968 was brought to an end by action of the United Nations is a matter of current historical knowledge.

Events in Other Islamic Nations. The outbreak of World War I in 1914 found the Ottoman Empire on the side of the German Hohenzollerns. This presented a difficult dilemma to the Arabic nations, who were religiously of the same faith as that espoused by the Turks, but who resented the Turkish rule. In the rest of them, as in Egypt, nationalistic emotions had been steadily growing. Representatives of Great Britain negotiated with Sherif Hussein, of Mecca, the Arab leader, to revolt, agreeing in consideration to recognize Arab independence in Syria, Trans-Jordan, Irak and the Hejaz region of Arabia. Whether Palestine was included in the area has remained a disputed point.

The Arabs of these regions did revolt, thereby contributing materially to Allied victory. They came to the Peace Conference at Versailles, expecting to be rewarded in terms of independence. But at the Peace Conference previous secret treaties were disclosed whereby France was to have a mandate over Syria and Lebanon, and Great Britain was to have mandates over Palestine, Trans-Jordan and Iraq. These mandates were confirmed by the League of Nations in 1919. There was forceful resentment, and it brought results. With reservations as to military bases, Lebanon was declared a republic in 1926, and Syria in 1930. In 1941 Great Britain and the Free French declared both countries to be free and independent, and in 1945 they declared war on Germany and Japan.

As a result of the forceful Arab leadership of Emir Feisal Iraq received from the outset of the British mandate a high degree of independence. Following upon a free election, supervised by the British, Feisal was proclaimed king. Events following the death of Feisal threw the country into turmoil. At the time of World War II an anti-British coup was staged, and German assistance was solicited. British troops took over, and the pro-German government fled the country. Subsequently a pro-British government came into power, and initiated an educational system and internal improvements calculated to lift the nation out of its backward state.

As to Iran, by which name ancient Persia is now known, during the centuries following its decline as a world power the country had a long history of government by hereditary rulers, unrestrained only to the extent that they respected the authority of the Mujtahideen—the religious leaders of the Shiites. In 1906 the people forced a constitution, and a national assembly. World War I found both Russia and Great Britain maneuvering for control. Russian ambitions were diverted, but those of Great Britain continued. Ousting the pro-British cabinet, Reza Khan seized the government in 1921 and asserted his power over the Mujtahideen. In 1925 he was named hereditary Shah. Islam was separated from the state, and a program of education was instituted. Review of British oil concessions was forced in 1933, leading to greater royalty payments and employment of more local people. British and Russian troops occupied the country when the Shah assumed a noncommital position in World War II. In 1943 Iran declared war on the Axis powers, and at the Tehran Conference Roosevelt, Churchill and Stalin issued a declaration recognizing the independence and sovereignty of the country.

As to the Ottoman Empire and the Turks, the Empire was of course ended by Allied victory in World War I. Out of the war came modern Turkey, shorn of territory, but independent and democratic. Under the leadership of Mustapha Kemal, known as "Ataturk," Islam was disestablished as a state religion and its polygamous practices were forbidden by law. Titles of rank, including those associated with religion, were abolished, and a comprehensive system of public education was instituted.

Present events centering around the Arab states mark them as one of the most explosive areas of today's world. The brief sketch of events hereinabove presented throws some light on why this should be. Creation of the state of Israel in the heart of the region added a further powerful factor to contribute to the difficulty. Further mention has been made of this in the chapter dealing with Judaism.

Recent Developments in Islamic Law. That in modern times there would be difficulty in adapting Islamic law to the needs of those subject to it is obvious from what has been said about its nature and doctrines. Ahmed Safwat said that in recent years the Mohammedan states have felt the fettering influence of Mohammedan law, in view of the orthodox theory that the body of such law, as expounded by one or the other of the four rites of which we have spoken, is obligatory in this sense, that the state cannot by legislation violate any of its accepted rules.

The pressure of events has been hard to withstand. Some of the Mohammedan states, by a bold attempt, separated the domains of civil and criminal law from the rule of Mohammedan law altogether. Foremost among them was Egypt, when in 1883 it recast its judicial system on the French lines. When the new codes of civil, commercial, criminal and procedural laws were promulgated it was considered expedient to attach to them a Fatwa—a statement by the Grand Mufti—to the effect that the new codes are not contradictory to Mohammedan law. In Turkey, criminal, commercial and procedural codes were enacted early in the latter half of the nineteenth century, based on the French codes. In both countries Mohammedan law is still applied to matters of personal status, including inheritance and *wakf* land and, in Turkey, to civil matters as well. The exigencies of modern civil and commercial life, the doctrine of liberty, and the studies in criminology, have compelled the Mohammedan states to depart from the strict rule of Mohammedan law and to legislate freely in these spheres.

After the end of World War I the establishment of British and French mandates in the Arab parts of the Ottoman Empire led increasingly to judicial reforms designed primarily to replace the antiquated Ottoman codes by enactments more adequate for modern needs. Thus, a modern code of contracts replaced the Ottoman code known as the Majalla in Lebanon; new laws of procedure were enacted as well as new penal legislation. Even where no comprehensive new codification of the law of contracts took place, the field of application of the Majalla was gradually restricted. The most radical reforms were undertaken in Turkey, under the leadership of Kemil Ataturk. There the system of law was completely westernized. The Majella was replaced by the Swiss Civil Code and Code of Obligations, which were enacted in their entirety, with only minor modifications. That meant a revolutionary step, since also the personal status law, until then the main preserve of Islamic religious law, was put under the rule of modern secular European legislation. None of the Arab states, however, has up to now gone as far as Turkey. Personal status law has remained under the rule of religious law, and personal status cases are still in the main decided by the courts of the quadis or the courts of the various non-Muslim religious communities.

Herbert J. Liebesny has commented perceptively upon the effect of nationalism on Islamic law. With the formation of national states within the territory of Islam, it was also inevitable that certain concepts should intrude, which may not be in full consonance with the original idea of equality of all Muslims in legal matters and the principles of personality of the law as applied to the community of Muslims. The modern national state is after all based principally upon the idea of the territoriality of the law and upon the idea of nationality in such a territorial state. The problems have been posed not infrequently in marital cases where change of religion was involved. Islamic law provides a relatively easy form of divorce through repudiation of the wife by the husband. Cases have arisen in various states where a husband embraced Islam and then divorced his wife through repudiation. Clearly, it would not be in the public interest, or for that matter in the spirit of religious tenets, to encourage the practice of a change in religion for the purpose of facilitating divorce procedures. The solution applied in such cases is illustrated by a recent Egyptian decision. In that case the court held that an Italian who had become a Muslim could not repudiate his wife on the basis of the principle that all Muslims are equal in the territory of Islam. Egyptian law, so the court stated, based itself upon the principles of private international law and the criterion of nationality. On this basis it was held that Italian law applied to the divorce proceedings. It is plain that this decision responds fully not only to the rules of present day conflict of laws as reflected in the new Egyptian Civil Code, but also protects the public interest.

Speaking generally, Egypt's civil law under Nasser continues to be patterned after the jurisprudence of England and France although Islam was proclaimed to be the religion of the state.

PART V: MAN HIS OWN LAWMAKER

CHAPTER 13

FROM THE HOHENZOLLERNS TO THE NAZIS

Man Makes Law "On His Own." We have now traced the progress of law and governmental institutions, including the Church, from early days of recorded history through the Middle Ages and up to the era when our country began, with the Pilgrim Fathers leaving England to escape the penalties meted out to dissenters from the ecclesiastical ukases of the time. As later pages will abundantly disclose, the content of our legal system and the nature of our governmental institutions are in large measure a heritage from England. The detailed course of their development before they reached our shores cannot be traced here. We will be fully enough occupied in dealing with them as they actually present themselves.

Before we focus our attention on law in the United States let us take brief note of another kind of law which has played a major role in modern times. At the outset of our study we emphasized the integration of law and religion. We have been witnessing the manifestation of this integration in the history of nations since ancient times. Making due allowance for pious dissimulation and hypocrisy in all its possible forms, it is clear on the record that the law was not regarded as a set of merely human edicts, but was related in peoples' minds to a higher power. We have noted the widest differences in religious concepts, but it has been apparent that, to this point, the peoples whom we have studied held to religious faiths, and those faiths have had in common that they have provided in substantial if not in full degree the law of life for their adherents. In the interest of orderly classification, we have drawn a line of differentiation only on the basis of the polytheistic or monotheistic foundation of these religions.

As we reach modern times, a further element of classification seems to be an inescapable necessity. In certain nations man has ceased to look to a higher source to inspire or suggest the content of his law, but has avowedly proceeded to make it "on his own." In these instances we cannot accept as an answer the asseveration that in so doing, he is doing no different from those who purported to act under higher auspices. Not all were hypocrites. In their invocation of the "law of necessity" and "master race" and "economic determinism," the Hohonzollerns and Nazis, and after them the dictators of the Iron Curtain nations, usurped the role generally before accorded to a Higher Reason as law-maker, assuming a role of personal infallibility not essayed by their predecessor Caesars.

The Rise of Prussia. For present purposes German history begins in the fifteenth century with the acquisition of power in Prussia by the Hohenzollerns. At the outset the Hohenzollern domain was only a small strip of territory, and so remained until the time of the Thirty Years' War, 1618-1648. From thenceforth Prussian expansion was rapid. Frederick I who came to power in 1713 ruled with a strong hand and built up one of the largest armies in Europe. Thus favored, his son, Frederick the Great, who became ruler in 1740, and who combined close attention to duty with military genius, proceeded with a record of military conquest against Russia, Sweden, France, Austria, Saxony and Poland, the results of which were to greatly enlarge the Prussian kingdom, and make it one of the great powers of the Continent. Development of military resources by universal service and other projects was made a primary policy. Under Bismarck, appointed chancellor by William I in 1862, Denmark was vanquished, and Prussia took over Schleswig-Holstein. Following a dispute with Austria over the disposition of this new province, Prussia defeated Austria in 1866 and went ahead to set up the North German Federation, in which its former German rival states joined.

With the military power and impetus thus gained, the defeat of the forces of Napoleon III of France at Sedan, in 1870, was easily achieved. France was invaded and, shortly thereafter, Paris surrendered. Cession of the French provinces of Alsace and Lorraine was exacted as part of the peace settlement. The German Empire was proclaimed on French soil, at Versailles, in January, 1871, with William I as its Emperor.

Prelude to World War I. By the end of the century Germany had become a highly productive, industrialized nation, jealous of other nations such as England, France and Russia which appeared to have superior geographical and territorial advantages as well as colonial possessions. Walter Hines Page, Ambassador to Great Britain, wrote to President Woodrow Wilson on September 6, 1914, that he recalled writing down in his diary, several years previously, the conviction that

Italy, France, Spain, Holland and England had each had its day of primacy in Europe and that Prussia would not content itself until it, too, had tried. As in the course of his ambassadorial duties he gained insight into the intricacies of international policies, this Prussian determination became clearer. The Prussian diplomacy had been, as he put it, "simply a lie," all bent on making ready themselves and on keeping other nations from getting ready. It involved a publicity campaign throughout the world, in the course of which the Prussian Foreign Office bribed or attempted to bribe citizens of other nations to affect public opinion in their countries. The "cult of valour"—a religion of military force—captured Prussia, scholars and all.

Such an attitude, reflecting the theories of Nietzche that might is right, that the Aryan race is a superior breed, and that Christianity is a weakness, found fertile soil. In "Thus Spoke Zarathustra," he said that God is dead. What are men to do? If they cannot become gods themselves, they ought to do the next best thing and become supermen. Blessed are not the peacemakers, but they who make war, for they shall be called not the children of Jahve but the children of Odin, which is greater than Jahve.

The Pistol Shots at Sarajevo. On June 28, 1914, while the Archduke Franz Ferdinand of Austria was riding with his Duchess in the course of a visit of state to Bosnia, a young Serbian student fired two pistol shots at the carriage. The first shot killed the Duchess, the second shot killed the Archduke. Thus, as subsequent events quickly confirmed, was ignited the conflagration of World War I.

The assassination was reasonably explainable on the ground of Austria's oppressive rule of Bosnia, and hostility to Serbia. Military action by Austria alone might have brought repercussions beyond the immediate parties, as the Russian ambassador at Vienna made it known that Russia would not be indifferent to forceful action against Serbia. But the denouement had far more inclusive ramifications. Henry Morganthau, United States Ambassador to Turkey at the time, told how he attended a requiem mass for the couple on July 4th following. He noted that Baron von Wangenheim, the German ambassador to Turkey was not present. Subsequently, in an hour of exultation over the early German victories, the Baron told Mr. Morganthau that after the Sarajevo incident he, together with most of the important German ambassadors, had been summoned to Berlin for an imperial conference with Kaiser Wilhelm, the heads of the general staff of the German army and navy, and the leading industrialists and financiers of Germany. The conference was held on July 5th. The Kaiser asked each German who was in a strategic position if he was ready for war. All replied in the affirmative, with the exception of the financiers, who said they must have two weeks to sell their foreign securities and to make loans. The conference adjourned as quietly as it had been convened.

On July 23, Austria served on Serbia a harsh ultimatum, demanding a reply two days later. On July 24, the Russian foreign minister told the Serbian ambassador at St. Petersburg that Russia would under no circumstances permit Austrian aggression against Serbia. Serbia rejected the ultimatum in part, but expressed a willingness to refer the matter to the Hague Tribunal or a conference of the great powers. On July 28 Austria declared war on Serbia. On July 30, Russia ordered general mobilization. Germany immediately sent an ultimatum to Russia demanding cessation of mobilization within twelve hours. Russia having failed to reply, on August 1 Germany declared war on Russia. France was asked to promise neutrality and to hand over certain military positions in token of such promises. Such promises not being forthcoming, on August 3 Germany declared war on France.

Germany demanded of Belgium that German troops be allowed to pass through Belgium to France. This would have constituted a violation of Belgium's neutrality as guaranteed by a treaty entered into by the European powers in 1839. But the move was taken by Germany advisedly. As the late Justice Jackson of the Supreme Court of the United States put it, in August, 1914, Chancellor von Bethmann-Hollweg stood before the German Reichstag at the beginning of a war in which Germany held every card but one. He confessed the lack of that one. He said, "Gentlemen, we are now in a state of necessity, and necessity knows no law. Our troops have occupied Luxembourg; perhaps they have already entered Belgian territory. Gentlemen, this violates the rules of international law. The wrong—I speak openly—the wrong that we now do, we will try to make good again, as soon as our military ends have been reached." King Albert of Belgium appealed to Great Britain for support, and when German troops entered Belgium on August 4, Great Britain declared war on Germany.

On August 15, Japan served an ultimatum on Germany to withdraw all German warships from Japanese and Chinese waters and to surrender the Kiaochow territory upon which Germany was constructing a naval base. Germany having failed to reply, on August 23 Japan declared war on Germany. Turkish warships having bombarded Russian ports on the Black Sea, on November 3 Russia declared war on Turkey. France and Great Britain followed with a similar declaration on November 5. At still later dates Bulgaria came in on the side of Germany, Austria and Turkey, and Italy on the side of the Allies.

United States Neutrality. These world-wide developments came as a great blow to the United States, for this nation had been making heroic efforts in the cause of peace. The scope of such efforts is indicated by reference to the plan officially proposed by the United States in 1913 by Secretary of State William Jennings Bryan, acting under the direction of President Woodrow Wilson. The plan, submitted to the representatives of all foreign nations in Washington, contemplated an agreement, to be entered into between the United States and all the other countries, severally providing for the investigation of all questions in dispute before war was declared or hostilities begun. It proposed a permanent commission, the composition of which was to be agreed upon between the contracting parties, and the duty of which it should be to investigate such dispute when diplomatic efforts failed; the investigation to be made as a matter of course, without the formality of a request by either party. This latter provision was intended to save either nation from being compelled to ask for an investigation at a time when excitement might make both parties hesitant to ask for an investigation lest the request be considered a sign of weakness. The report was to be made within a time to be fixed by the agreement. The parties reserved the right to act independently after the investigation was concluded. Practically all the nations, including Germany and Austria, accepted the proposal "in principle," and some South American countries had entered into formal treaties with the United States which embodied its provisions.

Insofar as the outbreak of war in Europe was concerned, any other position than that of neutrality upon the part of the United States was of course unthinkable. On August 4, 1914, President Wilson issued a proclamation declaring such neutrality. In later messages he appealed to the people to act and speak in the true spirit of neutrality, and to be neutral in fact as well as name. Two factors operated, however, to make impossible the maintenance of neutrality in sentiment, if not in act. One centered in the makeup of the American population of the United States, drawn, as it had been, in large part from the European nations involved in the conflict, the various elements of which felt a resurgence of sentiment for their fatherlands. The other developed out of the trade relations which the United States endeavored to maintain with the belligerents on both sides.

At the outset Great Britain set up a blockade against contraband goods headed for Germany. By Orders in Council the list of such goods was constantly enlarged. Eventually Great Britain undertook to seize as contraband practically all goods shipped to Germany, or even the neutral neighbors of Germany. Principles of international law requiring a blockade to be effective as to blockaded ports and requiring the search of neutral vessels on the high seas without seizure began to be violated. The operations of German submarines having made it impossible for British vessels to operate near German ports, they took to seizing neutral vessels hundreds of miles away and taking them to British ports for search. These actions created no small degree of resentment in the United States, leading to formal protests and to the proposal in Congress of retaliatory legislation which would have placed an embargo on munition shipments to Great Britain.

Unrestricted Submarine Warfare by Germany. With the announcement by Germany of a policy of unrestricted submarine warfare, violation of neutral rights by Great Britain became of no more than academic interest. On February 4, 1915, Germany announced that the waters surrounding Great Britain and Ireland, including the whole English Channel, were declared a war zone, and that on and after February 18, 1915, every enemy merchant ship found in the said war zone would be destroyed without its being always possible to avert the dangers threatening the crews and passengers on that account. The edict went on to say that even neutral ships were exposed to danger in the war zone, as, in view of the misuse of neutral flags ordered on January 31 by the British government and of the accidents of naval warfare, it could not always be avoided to strike even neutral ships in attacks directed against enemy ships. This was in violation of the principles of international law, making illegal the sinking of merchant vessels without warning and without regard to the safety of their passengers and crews.

Shortly thereafter American lives were lost on torpedoed ships. On May 7, 1915, the English liner Lusitania was torpedoed without warning near the coast of Ireland, with a loss of twelve hundred lives. Some one hundred were Americans. There was an immediate and strong reaction of anti-German sentiment. On May 10 President Wilson declared in a public address that "there is such a thing as a man being too proud to fight," and that "there is such a thing as a nation being so right that it does not need to convince others by force that it is right." But these and other incidents led to vigorous protests by the United States and to the exchange of many sharp diplomatic notes. President Wilson and other national leaders took a stand advocating preparation for war. In 1916 Congress enacted a National Defense Act providing for an increase in the land forces, and a naval appropriation bill providing for a navy comparable with that of Great Britain.

In January, 1917, President Wilson addressed the Senate, advocating that the United States guarantee any just peace that might be arrived at by international concert, and which was based upon the acknowledgment of the equality of all nations and recognition of the principle that governments derive all their just powers from the consent of the governed. He asserted the belief that the only durable peace was a peace between equals, a negotiated peace, not one imposed by force— in short, a "peace without victory." The military situation in Europe at the time made this proposal apropos. Great Britain and her Allies issued a statement of their peace conditions. Germany made a response a week later, but two days thereafter came an announcement of renewed unrestricted submarine warfare. On February 3 the United States severed diplomatic relations with Germany. Several American vessels were torpedoed without warning. President Wilson asked Congress for authority to arm American merchant ships against submarines. While this proposal was pending there was made public an intercepted German dispatch, addressed to the German minister in Mexico, proposing to Mexico an alliance looking to a joint war against the United States unless the United States remained neutral.

"The Right Is More Precious Than Peace." Matters were brought to a climax on April 2, 1917, when President Wilson addressed a joint session of the U. S. Congress. He pointed out that vessels of every kind, whatever their flag, their character, their cargo, their destination, their errand, had been ruthlessly sent to the bottom by German submarines, without warning and without thought of help or mercy for those on board, the vessels of friendly neutrals along with those of belligerents. Even hospital ships and ships carrying relief to the sorely bereaved and stricken people of Belgium, though the latter were provided with safe conduct through the proscribed areas by the German government itself and were distinguishable by unmistakable marks of identity, had been sunk with the same reckless lack of compassion or of principle. "I was for a little while unable to believe that such things would in fact be done by any government that had hitherto subscribed to the humane practices of civilized nations." said he. "International law had its origin in the attempt to set up some law which would be respected and observed upon the seas, where no nation has right of dominion and where lay the free highways of the world. By painful stage after stage has that law been built up, with meager

enough results, but always with a clear view, at least, of what the heart and conscience of mankind demanded. This minimum of right the German government has swept aside under the plea of retaliation and necessity and because it had no weapons which it could use at sea except those which it is impossible to employ as it is employing them without throwing to the winds all scruples of humanity or of respect for the understandings that were supposed to underlie the intercourse of the world. The present German submarine warfare against commerce is a warfare against mankind."

In concluding his memorable message, President Wilson stated: "The right is more precious than peace, and we shall fight for the things that we have always carried nearest our hearts—for democracy, for the right of those who submit to authority to have a voice in their own governments, for the rights and liberties of small nations, for a universal dominion of right by such a concert of free peoples as shall bring peace and safety to all nations and make the world itself at last free. To such a task we can dedicate our lives and our fortunes, everything we are and everything we have, with the pride of those who know that the day has come when America is privileged to spend her blood and her might for the principles that gave her birth and happiness and the peace which she has treasured. God helping her, she can do no other."

On April 4, 1917, the Senate adopted a resolution declaring that a state of war existed against Germany. A similar resolution was passed by the House of Representatives on April 6, and on the latter date the President proclaimed the war, making it truly World War I. America threw her full might into it. Before it was over, more than two million American soldiers saw military service in France.

Deportation of Women and Girls From Lille. Although offenses against humanity reached an undoubted climax under the Hitler regime, the war against the Allies conducted by the Hohenzollerns was not without its unsavory aspects in that regard. An example was the deportation of women and girls from Lille, Roubaix and Tourcoing in 1916. In a documented Note to the Diplomatic Representatives of the French Republic under date of July 25, 1916, Foreign Minister Briand described the occurrences. The deportation was based on an order of the German Commandant at Lille, April 1916, stating as follows: "The attitude of England makes the provisioning of the population more and more difficult. In order to relieve the distress, the German Government has recently asked for volunteers to go to work in the country. This offer has not had the success anticipated. Consequently the inhabitants will be evacuated by order and removed to the country. Each evacuated person will be allowed 30 kilogrammes of luggage, which it would be well to prepare immediately. I therefore order as follows:—Pending further orders, no person shall change his residence. No person may be absent from his declared legal residence between the hours of 9 P.M. and 6 A.M. (German time) unless he is in possession of a permit. Since this measure cannot be recalled, it is in the interest of the population itself to remain calm and obedient."

By way of protest Monseigneur Charost, Bishop of Lille, addressed to General von Graevenitz a communication in which he said:

"It is my duty to bring to your notice the fact that a very agitated state of mind exists among the population. Numerous removals of women and girls, certain transfers of men and youths, and even of children, have been carried out in the districts of Tourcoing and Rubaix without judicial procedure or trial. The unfortunate people have been sent to unknown places. Measures equally extreme and on a larger scale are contemplated at Lille. You will not be surprised Monsieur le General that I intercede with you in the name of the religious mission confided to me. That mission lays on me the burden of defending, with respect but with courage, the Law of Nations, which the law of war must never infringe, and that eternal morality, whose rule nothing can suspend. It makes it my duty to protect the feeble and the unarmed, who are as my family to me and whose burdens and sorrows are mine.

"You are a father; you know that there is not in the order of humanity a right more honorable or more holy than that of the family. For every Christian the inviolability of God who created the family attaches to it. The violation of family rights is doubled by a violation of sacred demands of morality. Morality is exposed to perils, the mere idea of which revolts every honest man, from promiscuity which inevitably accompanies removals *en masse,* involving mixture of the sexes, or, at all events, of persons of very unequal moral standing. Young girls of irreproachable life—who have never committed any worse offense than that of trying to pick up some bread or a few potatoes to feed a numerous family, and who have, besides, paid the light penalty for such trespass—have been carried off. I am speaking of what I have seen and heard. I have faith in the human conscience and I preserve the hope that the young men and girls of respectable families will be restored to their homes in answer to the demand for their return and that sentiments of justice and honor will prevail over all lower considerations."

Unfortunately Monseigneur Charost's faith and hope were not vindicated in this instance. Some 25,000 French citizens were deported; those designated at Lille were given an hour and a half to make preparations for departure.

Abdication of the Kaiser—The Armistice—Treaty of Versailles. In the late summer of 1918 the tide turned decisively against Germany. Marshal Ludendorff's great drives on the Western Front were repulsed. Soldiers of the United States proved their mettle at Cantigny, Belleu Wood, St. Mihiel and the Argonne. German sailors at the great Kiel naval base mutinied. Internal disorders developed. On November 9 Prince Maximilian who had been serving as Chancellor was forced out and Friedrich Ebert, a Socialist, took over the portfolio. On November 10, Kaiser Wilhelm abdicated and fled ignominiously to the Netherlands. Austria and Bulgaria had already surrendered unconditionally. At five o'clock in the morning of November 11, 1918, in a railway car in the Compiegne Forest, German delegates signed the Armistice that at eleven o'clock that same day brought to an end the fighting in World War I.

In accordance with the Treaty of Versailles, which was worked out between the Allies in 1919, and which by the terms of its preamble purported to replace the state of war by a "firm, just and durable peace," Germany signed a blank reparations check and was reduced to a state of military and economic impotence.

The Weimar Republic and Its Constitution. On January 19, 1919, an election was held to choose members of a German national assembly. The assembly met at Weimar on February 6; five days later it elected Friedrich Ebert President of the Republic. Ebert announced himself as the "authorized representative of the entire German people." The assembly adopted a constitution which became effective August 11, 1919.

In the light of the previous history of Germany, and of that which was shortly to follow, the provisions of this constitution of the German Reich are indeed noteworthy. Its very first article provided: "The German Reich is a Republic. The state power is derived from the people." Article 4 provided: "The generally accepted rules of international law are to be considered as binding integral parts of the law of the German Reich." The Reich was declared to have exclusive legislative competence for certain stated matters, others being left to the German Member States (Lands). Article 17 provided that each Land must have a republican constitution; that the people's representatives must be elected by universal, equal, direct and secret ballot by all German men and women in conformity with the principles of proportional representation. The government of the Land must enjoy the confidence of the people's representatives.

Most noteworthy were the constitution's Bill of Rights provisions relating to the individual person. Thus, article 109 provided: "All Germans are equal before the law. In principle men and women have the same civil rights and duties. Public-legal privileges or disadvantages of birth or of rank are to be abolished. Titles of nobility shall be regarded merely as part of the name, and may no longer be bestowed. Orders and decorations may not be conferred by the state." Article 111 stated: "All Germans enjoy liberty of travel and residence throughout the whole Reich." Article 114 provided: "The freedom of the person is inviolable. Curtailment or deprivation of personal freedom by a public authority is only permissible on a legal basis." Article 115 provided: "Every German's home is his sanctuary and is inviolable. Exceptions may only be made as provided by law." Article 117 stipulated: "The secrecy of letters and all postal, telegraphic and telephone communications is inviolable." Article 118 provided: "Every German has the right, within the limits of the general laws, to express his opinions freely in speech, in writing, in print, in picture form or in any other way."

Thus was Germany apparently thoroughly democratized. Moreover, the Weimar Republic developed social security to a high degree, including unemployment insurance and old age and sick benefits. Labor unions were strong and flourishing, and the right to collective bargaining was unquestioned.

The Treaty of Locarno. The harsh experiences of World War I put the peoples of the world in the frame of mind that future war was something to be avoided. In his opening statement at the Nurnberg Trial of Nazi war criminals, Sir Hartley Shawcross, British Attorney General and Chief Prosecutor for the United Kingdom, pointed out that adoption of the Covenant of the League of Nations along with the Treaty of Versailles was followed by a series of treaties—numbering nearly one thousand—of arbitration and conciliation embracing practically all the nations of the world. The Treaty of Locarno, of October 16, 1925, between Great Britain, France, Belgium, Italy, and Germany, was more than a treaty of arbitration and conciliation. Subject to clearly specified exceptions of self-defense in certain contingencies, it was a general undertaking in which the parties agreed that "they will in no case attack or invade each other or resort to war against each other." This constituted a general renunciation of war and was so considered in the eyes of jurists and of the public opinion of the world. It was regarded as the corner stone of the European settlement. No jurist of authority, and no statesman of responsibility, would have associated himself, subsequent to the Locarno Treaty, with the assertion that, at least as between the parties, war remained an unrestricted right of sovereign states. Germany was a party to this Treaty.

The Kellogg-Briand Pact. Of still broader significance and appliction was the General Treaty for the Renunciation of War approved on August 27, 1928. It is also known as the Pact of Paris and the Kellog-Briand Pact. It provided:

Deeply sensible of their solemn duty to promote the welfare of mankind:

Persuaded that the time has come when a frank renunciation of war as an instrument of national policy should be made to the end that the peaceful and friendly relations now existing between their peoples may be perpetuated:

Convinced that all changes in their relations with one another should be sought only by pacific means and be the result of a peaceful and orderly progress, and that any signatory power which shall hereafter seek to promote its national interests by resort to war should be denied the benefits furnished by this Treaty;

Hopeful that, encouraged by their example, all the other nations of the world will join in this humane endeavor and by adhering to the present Treaty as soon as it comes into force bring their peoples within the scope of its beneficent provisions, thus uniting civilized nations of the world in a common renunciation of war as an instrument of their national policy.

Article I

The High Contracting Parties solemnly declare in the names of their respective peoples that they condemn recourse to war for the solution of international controversies, and renounce it as an instrument of national policy in their relations with one other.

Article II

The High Contracting Parties agree that the settlement or solution of all disputes or conflicts of whatever nature or of whatever origin they may be, which may arise among them, shall never be sought except by pacific means.

This pact was silent on the subject of the right of self-defense. The question was raised, however, and, following the lead of the United States, the signatory nations appended a series of notes which declared in more or less similar language that the "inherent" right of self-defense was unimpaired by the Treaty.

In 1939 this Treaty was binding upon more than sixty nations, including Germany. Whatever the position may have been in 1914 or 1918, Sir Hartley Shawcross argued that no international lawyer of repute, no responsible statesman, no soldier concerned with legal use of armed forces could doubt that with the pact of Paris a war of aggression was contrary to positive international law.

Other Non-Agression Pacts. Germany was bound, not only by these treaties which we have just mentioned, but also by others made concurrently with Belgium, Poland, Czechoslovakia, Denmark, the Netherlands and Luxembourg. On October 16, 1925, Germany entered into treaties with Belgium, Poland and Czechoslovakia by which it was agreed that all disputes of every kind between the respective countries which it might not be possible to settle amicably by the normal methods of diplomacy should be submitted either to an arbitral tribunal or to the Permanent Court of International Justice. Similar treaties were entered into by Germany with the Netherlands on May 20, 1926, and with Denmark on June 2, 1926. On September 11, 1929, Germany signed a similar treaty with Luxembourg.

On January 26, 1934, Germany entered into a treaty with Poland in which it was stated that under no circumstances would the parties proceed to use force for the purpose of settling disputes. On May 31, 1939, Germany had entered into a treaty of nonagression with Denmark, agreeing that the two countries should "in no case resort to war or to any other use of force against the other." Four months later, on September 25, Germany and Russia entered into a non-aggression treaty by which "the two contracting parties undertake to refrain from any act of violence, any aggressive action, or any attack against one another, whether individually or jointly with other powers."

Advent of the Nazi Party. In such an atmosphere, and confidently relying upon such positive accretions to the body of international law, the peoples of the free nations looked forward to the era of permanent peace for which World War I presumably had been fought. In those nations a spirit of pacifism, vigorously promoted by various churches, gained complete ascendancy. It was anticipated that with the abdication of the Hohenzollerns, Germany, as a member of the family of democratic nations would cease to be a menace to the world.

But such hopes and expectations for peace rested on a foundation of sand. In his opening statement to the International Military Tribunal, created to try Hermann Goering, Rudolph Hess, Joachim von Ribbentrop, Julius Streicher and other Nazis for war crimes, Robert H. Jackson, United States chief of counsel in the preparation and trial of the case pointed out that the Germans of the 1920's were a frustrated and baffled people as a result of defeat and the disintegration of their traditional government. The democratic elements which were trying to govern Germany through the new and feeble machinery of the Weimar Republic got inadequate support from the democratic forces of the rest of the world. When world-wide depression was added to her other problems, she was faced with urgent and intricate pressure in her economic and political life. The setting was favorable for a program of force, administered by desperate men. Such a program was not long in manifesting itself.

On January 5, 1919, not two months after the conclusion of the Armistice which ended World War I, and six months before the signing of the Peace Treaties at Versailles, there came into being in Germany a small political party called the German Labor Party. On September 12, 1919, Adolph Hitler became a member of this party. Hitler was born in Austria, the son of an obscure Austrian official. As a young man he worked as a draftsman, with a record of inability to hold a job. In 1912 he went to Germany, and served in the German Army in World War I, attaining the rank of corporal. By enlistment in the German army he had forfeited his Austrian citizenship and he was not a citizen of Germany when he commenced his machinations there.

At the first public meeting, held in Munich on February 24, 1920, he announced the party's program. This program remained unaltered until the party was dissolved in 1945. It consisted of twenty-five points; the following five are of particular interest here:

Point 1. We demand the unification of all Germans in the Greater Germany, on the basis of the right of self-determination of peoples.

Point. 2. We demand equality of rights for the German people in respect to the other nations; abrogation of the peace treaties of Versailles and Saint Germain.

Point 3. We demand land and territory for the sustenance of our people, and the colonization of our surplus population.

Point 4. Only a member of the race can be a citizen. A member of the race can only be one who is of German blood, without consideration of creed. Consequently no Jew can be a member of the race.

Point 22. We demand abolition of the mercenary troops and formation of a national army.

On July 29, 1921, the party name was changed to National Sozialistiche Deutsche Arbeiter Partei, (hereinafter referred to as the Nazi Party) and Hitler became its head. The same year there was organized Die Sturmabteilungen or SA, an organization of young "Storm Troopers," ostensibly trained to protect Nazi party members from attack by rival political parties and to preserve order at Nazi Party meetings; their real mission was to make the Nazi Party master of the streets. In March, 1923, Hermann Goering was appointed head of the SA.

"The Fuehrer is Always Right." No paraphrase of the nature and organization of the Nazi Party could possibly portray it more effectively than the official Organization Book of the NSDAP: "The Party

was created by the Fuehrer out of the realization that if our people
were to live and advance towards an era of prosperity they had to be
led according to an ideology suitable for our race. Therefore the
Party comprises only fighters, at all times prepared to assume and
to give everything for the furtherance of the National Socialist ideology. The NSDAP as the leading element of the German people
control the entire public life."

It was further pointed out: "The Party as an instrument of ideological education must grow to be the leader corps (Fuehrerkorps) of the
German nation. The basis of the Party organization is the Fuehrer
thought. The public is unable to rule itself either directly or indirectly. The man best suited for the job will be a Fuehrer. He
will be carried by the confidence of the people. All Political Di-
rectors stand as appointed by the Fuehrer and are responsible to him.
They possess full authority towards the lower echelons. In choosing
the Political Director the main consideration will be to put the right
man in the right place. With the Political Director we are building
the political leadership of the state."

With regard to the duties of Party members, the Organization Book
provided: "The commandments of the National Socialists: The Fuehrer is always right. The program be your dogma: It demands your
utter devotion to the movement. Right is, what serves the movement
and thus Germany which means the Nation."

Packed with implication is the provision for the oath of the Political
Director: "The Political Director is sworn in yearly. The oath is
worded as follows: 'I pledge eternal allegiance to Adolph Hitler. I
pledge unconditioned obedience to him and the Fuehrers appointed
by him.' The PD is inseparably tied to the ideology and organization of the NSDAP. His oath ends only with his death or with his
expulsion from the Nationalist Socialist Community."

In his opening statement to the International Military Tribunal at
Nurnberg Justice Robert H. Jackson, Chief of Counsel for the United
States, was well warranted in saying that the Fuehrer shaped the
collective will of the people within himself, enjoying the political
unity and entirety of the people in opposition to individual interests.
He was held to unite in himself all the sovereign authority of the
Reich; all public authority in the state was derived from the authority of the Fuehrer. To designate the character of the political authority correctly it was necessary to speak not of the state's authority
but of the Fuehrer's authority. The state did not hold political authority as an impersonal unit; received it from the Fuehrer as the

executor of the national will. The authority of the Fuehrer was not limited by checks and controls, by special autonomous bodies or individual rights; it was free and independent, all-inclusive and unlimited.

The highest repository of this supreme authority, Hitler once said: "Always before God and the world, the stronger has the right to carry through his will." Dr. Hans Frank, writing in the *Journal of the Academy for German Law*, declared: "The National Socialist State is a totalitarian state. As a totalitarian state, it makes no concessions to criminals; it does not negotiate with them, it stamps them out."

In such an environment, one is not surprised to learn to what extent judicial proceedings in the German courts of that day were a travesty. In each sitting of a court where cases with "political" aspects came up —and almost any case was susceptible of presenting such an aspect— agents of the Gestapo were present. If a sentence was not satisfying to them, they stepped in, arrested the person involved before the eyes of the judges, and corrected any sentence by means of the concentration camp. The most famous case of that sort was that of Pastor Niemoeller who was acquitted by the court before which he was tried, but taken to a concentration camp after the acquittal became effective.

The Beer Cellar Putsch. On the night of November 8, 1923, Hitler and his Nazi cohorts attempted to gain control of the German government by force. Bavarian Prime Minister von Kehr was addressing a meeting in the Burgerbraukeller in Munich. Hitler and other Nazis appeared, supported by storm troopers. Hitler fired a shot and announced that a nationalist revolution setting up a dictatorship had taken place. Hitler demanded of von Kehr that Bavaria join in a march on Berlin.

There followed a conference, after which von Kehr and others announced they would cooperate with Hitler. A provisional government was established with Hitler as Chancellor and General Ludendorff as Leader of the National Army. But during the night von Kehr alerted the police and government troops. When Hitler, Ludendorff and their supporters attempted to march into the center of Munich the next afternoon they were met by police. Shots were exchanged and men on both sides were killed. Hermann Goering was wounded, the Putsch was broken up, the Party was declared illegal and its leaders, including Hitler, were arrested. Hitler and others were tried for treason, and convicted. Hitler was sentenced to five years' imprisonment but served only a few months of the term.

The Political Rise of Nazism. In 1925, after Hitler's release the Schutzstaffel, or SS, was created, nominally to act as Hitler's body-guard, but in reality to terrorize political opponents. The Party was reorganized, and greatly extended its activities throughout Germany, paying particular attention to the training of youth in the ideology of National Socialism. The first Nazi youth organization had come into existence in 1922, and in 1925 the Hitler Jugend was officially recognized by the Party.

In 1927 Hitler's book *Mein Kampf* was published. Amplifying the basic party principles it became the Nazi statement of faith and was blasphemously called "the Bible of the German people." It contemplated Nazi Germany as a "Third Reich." From the days of Charlemagne, German emperors had succeeded to the power of the emperors of Rome, so the Roman Empire was the "First Reich." The Second extended from the advent of the Empire in 1871 to 1918.

Throughout this period the growing resources of the Nazi Party were employed to win political support from the German people. Elections were contested both for the Reichstag and the Landtage. The Party effort met with growing success. In May, 1928, it received 2.6% of the total vote and obtained 12 out of 491 seats in the Reichstag. In January, 1929, Hitler appointed Heinrich Himmler as Reichfuehrer SS with the special task of building the SS into a strong but elite group which would be dependable in all circumstances. In 1930 the Party polled 3% of the total vote and won 107 out of 577 seats. In 1932 it received 37.3% of the vote and won 230 out of 608 seats.

Justice Jackson said that during this period there were two governments in Germany—the real and the ostensible. The forms of the German Republic were maintained for a time, and it was the outward and visible government. But the real authority in the state was outside of and above the law and rested in the leadership corps of the Nazi Party.

In January 1933, Hitler became Chancellor of the German Republic. Less than a month later the Reichstag building was set on fire. The burning of this symbol of free parliamentary government was so providential for the Nazis that it was believed they staged the fire themselves. But the Nazis immediately accused the Communist Party of instigating and committing the crime. On the morning after the fire Hitler obtained from aged President von Hindenburg a Presidential Decree suspending the provisions of the Bill of Rights of the Weimar Constitution.

In commenting upon these developments, Sir Edwin S. Herbert pointed out that we have to learn that the so-called "democratic" idea is capable of becoming at least as heavy a tyranny as the rule of kings, or aristocrats, or dictators, and that in some totalitarian countries this conception of a fleeting majority's will as being in itself just has been the means of establishing the tyranny. "We all hated the tyranny of Hitler. Let us not forget that he obtained a majority in the Reichstag by constitutional means, and relied upon a majority throughout. It was his treatment of minorities that was shocking to us. Was that treatment just because they were minorities? Have Jews no rights because they are few? Should you have the right to persecute Christians because most people do not go to church? Of course we will all answer no. If we do we must remember that we are rejecting, as the common law man rejects, the will of the majority as the final criterion and admitting that for a law to be just it must be judged by some other standard: that the majority ought not to use its power unjustly."

Germany Becomes a Nazi State. Having attained a position where he could wield unlimited personal power, Hitler lost no time in exercising it. Sinister developments followed, initiated by a first ruthless purge of political opponents. In a speech at Frankfort am Main on March 3, 1933, Hermann Goering, Chief of the Storm Troopers, declared: "Fellow Germans, my measures will not be crippled by any judicial thinking. My measures will not be crippled by any bureaucracy. Here, I don't have to give justice, my mission is only to destroy and exterminate, nothing more. The struggle to the death, in which my fist will grasp your necks, I shall lead with those down there—those are the Brown Shirts."

On March 24, 1933, an act declaring absolute legislative power in the Reichstag, even to the extent of deviating from the Constitution, was enacted. A month later Hitler ordered Robert Ley "to take over the trade unions." At about the same time Hermann Goering founded the Gestapo as a secret police and confided to the deputy leader that its main task was to eliminate political opponents of National Socialism and Hitler.

From March until October, 1933, the Nazis arrested, mistreated and killed numerous politicians, Reichstag members, writers, physicians and lawyers. The people killed belonged to various political parties and religious faiths, such as Democrats, Catholics, Communists, Jews, and pacifists. The killings were usually camouflaged by such utterances as "killed in attempting to escape," or "resisting arrest." It is estimated that during this first wave of terror conducted by the Nazis, between 500 and 700 persons died.

In July, 1933, a law was passed declaring the NSDAP to be the only political party and making it a crime to form or maintain any other. In a speech on July 6 Hitler said: "The political parties have finally been abolished. This is a historical occurrence, the meaning and implication of which one cannot yet be fully conscious of. Now, we must set aside the last vestige of democracy, particularly the methods of voting and making majority decisions which today are used in local governments, in economic organizations and in labor boards. The Party has become the state. All power lies with the Reich authorities."

Dr. Frank, leader of the German Jurists, summed it up in a radio speech on March 20, 1934: "The first task was that of establishing a unified German state. It was an outstanding historical and juristic-political accomplishment on the part of our Fuehrer that he reached boldly into the development of history and thereby eliminated the sovereignty of the various German states. At last we have now, after 1000 years, again a unified German state in every respect. It is no longer possible for the world, based on the spirit of resistance inherent in small states, which are set up on an egotistical scale and solely with a view to their individual interest, to make calculations to the detriment of the German people. This is a thing of the past and for all time to come. As a leader of the German Jurists, I am convinced that together with all strata of the German people, we shall be able to construct the legal state of Adolph Hitler in every respect and to such an extent that no one in the world will at any time be able to dare to attack this legal state as regards its laws."

Blood Bath Procedures. Through what has become known as the "Roehm Purge" or the "blood bath," the methods which Hitler and his immediate associates were ready to employ to strike down all opposition and consolidate their power was clearly revealed. On June 30, 1934, Roehm, the Chief of Staff of the SA since 1931 was murdered by Hitler's orders, and the "Old Guard" of the SA was massacred without trial and without warning.

The policy of these bloody episodes was stated by Heinrich Himmler, Deputy Leader of the Prussian Secret Police, who said: "We are confronted with a very pressing duty—both the open and the secret enemies of the Fuehrer and of the National Socialist movement and of our National Revolution must be discovered, combatted and exterminated. In this duty we are agreed to spare neither our own blood nor the blood of anyone else when it is required by our country." Making a formal report of the matters to the Reichstag on July 13, 1934, Hitler said: "The punishment for these crimes was hard and severe. There were shot 19 higher SA (Storm Trooper) leaders, 31 SA leaders and SA members and also 3 SS leaders as participants in the plot. Also 13 SA leaders and civilians who tried to resist arrest and were killed in the attempt. Three others committed suicide." In this same speech Hitler boasted that he had given the order to shoot the principal traitors.

Further Measures of Control. Following these earlier events of the National Socialist regime, the Nazi program to take over Germany completely rapidly gained momentum, extending through all segments of the population, young as well as old.

From 1933 to 1939 an extensive indoctrination in the principles of Mein Kampf was pursued in the schools and universities of Germany, as well as by Hitler Youth and amongst the German population as a whole. A copy of the book was officially presented to all newly married couples in Germany. Measures were taken to staff the schools with teachers who taught the Nazi creed. A number of agencies were set up whose duty it was to control and influence the press, radio, films and publishing firms in Germany, and to supervise entertainment and cultural and artistic activities. All these agencies came under the ministry of the People's Enlightenment and Propaganda.

The nation teemed with military activities. Under the disguise of compulsory labor service, camps, essentially military in character, were established all over Germany. When conscription went into effect in 1935, through the medium of these camps it was possible for Germany to muster a trained army of around 3,500,000 men, which formed the nucleus of the future army of aggression. The Hitler youth, which included boys from 14 to 17, were everywhere in evidence. Under the direction of uniformed leaders they were schooled in the field in military maneuvers. The Deutsche Jungvolk—boys from the ages of 6 to 14—were likewise in evidence everywhere. They engaged in military exercises in the school yards during recesses, particularly throwing hand grenades, and in large numbers engaged in military maneuvers like their older brothers.

The Christian Churches of Germany were under attack from the outset of the Nazi regime, but the procedure was more slow and

subtle. The Nazi position was stated in an official letter by Martin
Bormann to Alfred Rosenberg that "the Christian religion and National Socialist doctrines are not compatible." Eventually, in 1941,
a decree was issued stating that "For the first time in German history
the Fuehrer consciously and completely has the leadership in his own
hand. With the Party, its components and attached units, the Fuehrer has created for himself and thereby the German Reich Leadership, an instrument which makes him independent of the Treaty.
More and more the people must be separated from their churches
and their organs, the pastor. Never again must an influence on leadership of the people be yielded to the churches. This influence must
be broken completely and finally. Only the Reich Government and
its direction by the Party, its components and attached units, have a
right to leadership of the people."

The "Master Race" Concept. Conspicuous among the activities of
the Nazis as they tightened their stranglehold upon Germany was
their implementation of the "master race" concept which, as we have
seen, was inherent in their party ideology. The second chapter of
Mein Kampf was dedicated to the doctrine of Aryan superiority
over all other races, and the right of Germans by virtue of this superiority to dominate and use other peoples to their own ends.

The Jews, who were considered to have no right to German citizenship, were held to have been largely responsible for the troubles with
which the nation had been afflicted following World War I. According to Nazi Alfred Rosenberg: "A new faith is arising today: the
myth of the blood, the faith, to defend with the blood the divine essence of man. The faith, embodied in clearest knowledge that the
Nordic blood represents that mysterium which has replaced and overcome the old sacraments. The new thought puts folk and race higher
than the state and its forms. It declares protection of the folk more
important than protection of a religious denomination, a class, the
monarchy, or the republic; it sees in treason against the folk a greater
crime than treason against the state."

With the coming of the Nazis into power, persecution of the Jews
became official state policy. On April 1, 1933, a boycott of Jewish
enterprises was approved by the Nazi Reich cabinet, and during the
following years a series of anti-Semitic laws were passed, restricting
the activities of Jews in the civil service, in the legal profession, in
journalism, and in the armed forces. In September, 1935, the so-
called Nurnberg Laws were passed, the most important effect of which
was to deprive Jews of German citizenship. In this way the influ-

ence of Jewish elements on the affairs of Germany was extinguished, and one more potential source of opposition to Nazi policy was rendered powerless.

Addressing the German people by radio, Dr. Frank, leader of German jurists, declared: "The second fundamental law of the Hitler Reich is racial legislation. The National Socialists were the first ones in the entire history of human law to elevate the concept of race to the status of a legal form. The German nation, unified racially and nationally, will in the future be legally protected against any further disintegration of the German race stock."

Extermination of the Jews. The "master race" doctrine found a logical objective in a policy that did not stop short of physical extermination. Stating in a deposition at the Nurnberg Trial that the "final solution" of the Jewish question meant the complete extermination of all Jews in Europe, Rudolph Hoess, Commandant at Auschwitz, admitted that he had been constantly associated with the administration of concentration camps since 1934, serving at Dachau and Sachenhausen until 1940, when he was appointed Commandant at Auschwitz. He estimated "that at least 2,500,000 victims were executed and exterminated there by gassing and burning, and at least another half million succumbed to starvation and disease." This figure represented about 70% to 80% of all persons sent to Auschwitz as prisoners, the remainder having been selected and used for slave labor in the concentration camp industries.

Mass executions by gassing commenced during the summer of 1941 and continued until the fall of 1944. Hoess testified that he was "ordered to establish extermination facilities in Auschwitz in June, 1941. At that time there were in the general government three other extermination camps, Belzek, Treblinka and Wolzek." Testifying further, Hoess said: "I visited Treblinka to find out how they carried out their exterminations. The Camp Commandant at Treblinka told me he had liquidated 80,000 in the course of one half-year. He was principally concerned with the liquidation of the Jews from the Warsaw ghetto." Hoess went on to describe the improvements that he made at Auschwitz. He introduced the new gas, Cyclone B, which "took from three to fifteen minutes to kill the people in the death chamber, dependent upon climatic conditions. We knew when the people were dead because screaming stopped. Another improvement we made over Treblinka was that we built our gas chambers to accommodate 2000 people at a time, whereas at Treblinka their ten gas chambers only accommodated 200 people each."

In his further testimony Commandant Hoess went on to describe the selection of the victims from the daily transports that arrived: those who were fit for work were sent into a camp; others were sent immediately to the extermination plant. "Children of tender years were invariably exterminated since, by reason of their youth, they were unable to work. Still another improvement we made over Treblinka was that at Treblinka the victims almost always knew they were to be exterminated and at Auschwitz we endeavored to fool the victims into thinking they were going through a delousing process; very frequently the women would hide their children under their clothes, but of course when we found them we would send the children to be exterminated. We were required to carry out these exterminations in great secrecy, but of course the foul and nauseating stench from the continuous burning of bodies permeated the entire area and all the people living in the surrounding communities knew that exterminations were going on at Auschwitz."

Reassertion of Military Power. As we reach the point of considering the era of far-reaching Nazi aggression and conquest anticipated by the events of which we have been speaking, whereby the Nazi's took control of Germany, we may appropriately refer back to the previously mentioned program of Nazi principles. That program, we recall, embodied as main elements the overthrow of the Treaty of Versailles, the recoupment by Germany of all that was lost by that Treaty, and the acquisition of German "lebensraum," regardless of national boundaries. In Mein Kampf Hitler said that "the soil on which we now live was not a gift bestowed by heaven on our forefathers. They had to conquer it by risking their lives. So also in the future our people will not obtain territory, and therewith the means of existence, as a favor from any other people, but will have to win it by power of a triumphant sword."

In a preceding section reference has already been made to the military activities with which Germany teemed after the Nazi accession. Even before that, the armament industry had secretly laid plans for German rearmament. Gustav Krupp von Bohlen wrote that it was one great merit of the German war economy that it did not remain idle through the "bad" years of 1919 to 1933, even though its activity could not be brought to light, for obvious reasons. "Through years of secret work, scientific and basic groundwork was laid in order to be ready again to work for the German armed forces at the appointed hour, without loss of time or experience."

In October 1933, Germany withdrew from the International Disarmament Conference and League of Nations. On May 12, 1934, Erich Raeder issued the Top Secret armament plan for what was called the Third Armament Phase. This contained the sentence: "All theoretical and practical A-preparations are to be drawn up with a primary view to readiness for a war without any alert period." A month later Raeder had a conversation with Hitler in which Hitler instructed him to keep secret the construction of U-boats and warships over the limit of 10,000 tons being undertaken. In 1935 the Nazi government decided to take the first open steps to free itself from its obligations under the Treaty of Versailles. On March 10, 1935, Hermann Goering announced that Germany was building a military air force. Six days later a law instituted compulsory military service and fixed the establishment of the German army at a peace time strength of 500,000 men.

Emboldened by the progress defiantly achieved in these regards, and unchallenged by France or Great Britain, which nations, either singly or jointly, could at that stage have nipped the Nazi conspiracy in the bud, on March 7, 1936, Hitler notified the governments of Great Britain, France, and Belgium that Germany did not consider herself bound by the Locarno Treaty of 1925, and ordered his forces to reoccupy and fortify the Rhineland.

The Oblivious Democratic Nations. The democratic nations seemed oblivious to these far-reaching, momentous and significant developments. James F. Byrnes, then a Justice of the Supreme Court of the United States, described his impressions of a trip to Europe in 1937. In France he found a bitter conflict between capital and labor. Neither side would make concessions. They were so busy fighting each other that they made no preparations to defend themselves against Hitler. In Germany he attended the Nazi Party Congress at Nurnberg, seeing there the greatest military display he ever witnessed. In Berlin, he witnessed the first blackout; no nation threatened but they rehearsed. From Munich to Bremen, Germany was an armed camp. Soldiers marched everywhere, singing always, "Germany Over All." Government officials, laborers talked only of war: the officials with confidence, the citizens with fear but with faith in their Fuehrer.

On the day of his arrival in England Justice Byrnes witnessed a parade. There were several thousand marching. They carried banners "Peace on Earth" and "We Did Not Raise Our Boys For Cannon Fodder." As Justice Byrnes observed: "While the British prayed earnestly, the Nazis prepared feverishly. Those Britons were precisely like the God-fearing, peace-loving people of America. Because they wanted to make war on no nation, they could not believe Hitler would make war on them." How wrong they were was soon evident.

The Axis Pacts. As the Nazis were completing their hold on Germany, they proceeded to strengthen their position externally by forming alliances with other totalitarian nations. On November 25, 1936, Germany and Japan signed an Anti-Comintern Pact, by the terms of which they expressed a desire to cooperate against communist activities and undertook to keep each other informed concerning the activities of the Third International, to consult upon the necessary defense measures, and to execute these measures in close cooperation with each other.

In 1936 Germany recognized the Italian conquest of Ethiopia, brought about by the Italian dictator, Mussolini. In September, 1937, Mussolini visited Hitler in Germany. Statements were issued proclaiming their solidarity of purpose. Mussolini approved the right of Germany to colonies, and joined in the German-Japanese Anti-Comintern Pact. Mussolini acquiesced in the German annexation of Austria and the invasion of Czechoslovakia, which we shall presently note. On May 22, 1939, Germany and Italy entered into a ten-year military alliance.

On September 27, 1940, Germany, Italy and Japan signed a ten-year Tripartite Pact stating: "The Governments of Germany, Italy, and Japan, consider it as a condition precedent of lasting peace that each nation of the world be given its own proper place. They have therefore decided to stand together and to cooperate with one another in their efforts in Greater East Asia and in the regions of Europe wherein it is their prime purpose to establish and maintain a new order of things calculated to promote the mutual prosperity and welfare of the peoples there concerned." The Pact further provided that Japan recognized and respected the leadership of Germany and Italy in the establishment of a new order in Europe, and that Germany and Italy recognized and respected the leadership of Japan in the establishment of a new order in Greater East Asia. The three powers agreed to assist one another with all political, economic and military means if one of them was attacked by a power not then involved in the European War or in the Chinese-Japanese War.

Annexation of Austria. Emboldened by their rearming successes and by their unchallenged reoccupation of the Rhineland, the Nazis proceeded with previously laid plans to annex Austria. For a number of years the Nazis in Germany had been cooperating with their counterpart National Socialists in Austria with that ultimate object. On July 25, 1934, the Austrian Nazis staged a putsch which achieved the assassination of Chancellor Dollfus but failed to give them control of the government. Their party was outlawed, but with the support of the German Nazis it continued its illegal activities under cover of secrecy. Resulting "incidents" were seized upon by Hitler as an excuse for interfering in Austrian affairs. Austrian Chancellor Schuschnigg was persuaded by Franz von Papen to seek a conference with Hitler, which took place at Berchtesgaden on February 12, 1938. Dr. Schuschnigg was threatened by Hitler with an immediate invasion of Austria. Schuschnigg finally agreed to grant a political amnesty to various Nazis convicted of crime, and to appoint the Nazi Seyss-Inquart as Minister of the Interior and Security with control of the police.

On March 9, 1938, in an attempt to preserve the independence of his country, Dr. Schuschnigg decided to hold a plebiscite on the question of Austrian independence, which was fixed for March 13, 1937. On March 11, Hitler sent an ultimatum to Schuschnigg that the plebicite must be withdrawn. Goering supplemented the ultimatum by a series of demands upon the Austrian government. After Schuschnigg had agreed to cancel the plebicite, Hitler demanded that he resign and that the Austrian Nazi Seyss-Inquart should be appointed Chancellor. Schuschnigg resigned, and Seyss-Inquart was appointed. Hitler had already given the final order for German troops to cross the border at dawn on March 12. Goering directed the German embassy in Vienna to have Seiss-Inquart send a telegram to Hitler in accordance with a copy provided, requesting that German troops be sent into Austria. Seiss-Inquart did not send the telegram. German troops marched in without resistance, and the telegram which Goering suggested but which was never in fact sent was quoted to support the German claim that Seiss-Inquart had requested the German troops to prevent disorder.

On March 13 Hitler assumed office as Chief of State of Austria, and took command of its armed forces. By a law of the same date, Austria was annexed to Germany.

Occupation of Czechoslovakia. Simultaneously with the annexation of Austria Hitler gave assurances to the Czechoslovak government that Germany would not attack that country. But within a month specific plans were laid for attacking Czechoslovakia. Preparations were made to launch an attack not later than October 1,

1938. The plan embodied the creation of an "incident" to justify attack. The decision was to launch a military attack only after a period of diplomatic squabbling which, growing more serious, would lead to the excuse for war, or, in the alternative, to unleash a lightning attack as a result of an "incident" of German creation. Consideration was given to assassinating the German ambassador at Prague to create an appropriate incident. By September 3, 1938, the plans were ready, and it was decided that all troops were to be ready for action on September 28, 1938.

Throughout the same period, Germany was agitating the minorities question in Czechoslovakia, and particularly in the Sudetenland, leading to a diplomatic crisis in August and September, 1938. Germany threatened war. A "peace in our time" diplomatic conference was assembled at Munich. The United Kingdom and France concluded a pact with Germany and Italy at Munich on September 29th, involving the cession of the Sudetenland by Czechoslovakia to Germany. Czechoslovakia was compelled to acquiesce. On October 1, 1938, German troops occupied the Sudetenland. On March 15, 1939, in violation of the Munich Pact itself, German troops seized and occupied the major part of Czechoslovakia not ceded to Germany by the Munich Pact.

Invasion of Poland. Poland was next on the list. It was recognized that Poland would fight if attacked, and that a repetition of the success against Czechoslovakia without war could not be expected. Accordingly, it was determined that the problem was to isolate Poland and, if possible, prevent a simultaneous conflict with the Western Powers. Nevertheless, it was agreed that England was an enemy to German aspirations, and that war with England and France would eventually result. In such a war it was determined that England must be quickly overwhelmed. It was thereupon determined immediately to prepare detailed plans for an attack on Poland at the first suitable opportunity, and thereafter for an attack on England and France, together with plans for the simultaneous occupation by armed force of air bases in the Netherlands and Belgium.

Accordingly, after having denounced the German-Polish Pact of 1934 on false grounds, Hitler proceeded to stir up the Danzig issue, to prepare frontier "incidents" to justify the attack, and to make demands for the cession of Polish territory. Upon refusal by Poland to yield, he caused German armed forces to invade Poland on September 1, 1939, danger of interference by Russia having been forestalled by the nonaggression pact of August 23, hereinafter further mentioned. This precipitated war with Great Britain and France.

Invasion of Norway, Belgium, the Netherlands, Luxembourg. In the early hours of April 9, 1940, without any warning and without any declaration of war, with the collaboration of Major Quisling, who had been negotiating with the Nazis, German war vessels disembarked 10,000 German soldiers at the strategic Norwegian ports while airborne troops were landed near Oslo and Stavenger.

On May 10, 1940, German forces invaded Belgium, the Netherlands and Luxembourg. Thus was achieved a threat which it was later ascertained had been made by Hitler in a conference on May 23, 1939, in the course of which he had said that the Dutch and Belgian air bases must be occupied by armed force, and that declarations of neutrality must be ignored.

Invasion of Greece and Jugoslavia. On August 12, 1939, Hitler had a conversation with Count Ciano of Italy and Joachim von Ribbentrop at Obersalzberg. "Generally speaking," he told them, "the best thing to happen would be for the neutrals to be liquidated one after the other. This process could be carried out more easily if on every occasion one partner of the axis covered the other while it was dealing with the uncertain neutral. Italy might well regard Yugoslavia as a neutral of this kind." This observation was made only two months after Hitler had given assurance to Yugoslavia that he would regard her frontier as final and inviolable. On October 28, 1940, Italy invaded Greece, but the military operations met with no success. Plans for the invasion of Greece and Yugoslavia proceeded thereafter under Hitler's direction. On April 6, 1941, German forces invaded Greece and Yugoslavia without warning and Belgrade was bombed by the Luftwaffe. So swift was this particular invasion that there had not been time to establish any "incidents" as a usual preliminary, or to find and publish any adequate "political" explanations. However, as the attack was starting, Hitler proclaimed that the attack was necessary because the British forces in Greece (who were helping the Greeks to defend themselves against the Italians) represented a British attempt to carry the war to the Balkans.

Invasion of Russia. The final big act of World War II was initiated by Germany with the invasion of Russia on June 22, 1941, without any declaration of war. This was in violation of a non-aggression treaty negotiated by von Ribbentrop acting for Germany and Molotov for Russia, which became effective on August 23, 1939. By the terms of this treaty, which was to continue fourteen years, the contracting parties undertook to refrain from any act of violence or aggressive action or attack against one another, and agreed to clear away disputes or conflicts "solely by means of friendly exchanges of views, or if necessary by arbitration commissions." But Hitler was not a man to be hampered by scruples. As invasion of Russia got under way he said, "I have decided to give the fate of the German people and of the Reich and of Europe again into the hands of our soldiers."

Nazi War Brutality. Referring to the injustices perpetrated upon the Filipinos by the Japanese in the course of the war in Asia, U. S. Supreme Court Justice Frank Murphy declared: "That there were brutal atrocities inflicted upon the helpless Filipino people, to whom tyranny is no stranger, by Japanese armed forces, is undeniable. Starvation, execution or massacre without trial, torture, rape, murder and wanton destruction of property were foremost among the outright violations of the laws of war and of the conscience of a civilized world." One who has reviewed the evidence assembled for the Nurnberg Trial would find Justice Murphy's language fully applicable to Nazi Germany's conduct of the war in Europe. Because there was also involved in the Nazi war the "master race" concept, the evidence would support even stronger language with relation to Germany. In their manifestations the Nazi procedures ran the gamut from the impressment of millions of people into slave labor, through the use of Jews and prisoners of war as "guinea pigs" for medical experimentation, to the physical liquidation of millions.

Summarizing the evidence as to slave labor at the Nurnberg Trial, Sir Hartley Shawcross, Chief of Counsel for the United Kingdom, revealed that by the end of 1943 more than five million men, women and children were working as slave laborers in the Reich, and including prisoners of war the number was around 7,000,000. Millions of men and women were taken from their homes by the most brutal methods, transported in all weathers in cattle trucks from every quarter of Europe, employed on farms and in factories throughout the Reich, frequently under abominable conditions. Children were taken from their parents, many to remain for their lives, orphans not knowing their identity or true names; taken away before they were old enough to remember the place from which they came.

The point of view of administrators of the program finds exemplification in a speech of Heinrich Himmler, Reichsfuehrer-SS at Kharkow, April 1943, in which he said: "Whether 10,000 Russian females fall down from exhaustion while digging an anti-tank ditch interests me only in so far as the anti-tank ditch for Germany is finished. When somebody comes to me and says, 'I can't dig the anti-tank ditch with women and children, it is inhuman, for it would kill them,' then I have to say that you are a murderer of your own blood because if the anti-tank ditch is not dug, German soldiers will die and they are the sons of German mothers. We must realize that we have 6-7 million foreigners in Germany. Perhaps it is even eight million now. We have prisoners in Germany. They are none of them dangerous so long as we take severe measures at the merest trifle."

Dr. Apolinary Gotowicki, a Polish doctor who attended some 1800 Russian prisoners at the Krupp works in Essen, affirmed at the Nurnberg trial: "The floor was cement and the paillasses on which the people slept were full of lice and bugs. Even on cold days the room was never heated. It was impossible to keep the place clean because of overcrowding. Every day at least ten men were brought to me whose bodies were covered with bruises on account of the continual beatings with rubber tubes, steel switches or sticks. The people were often writhing with agony and it was impossible for me to give them even a little medical aid. I had scarcely any medical supplies. It was difficult for me to watch how such suffering people could be directed to do heavy work. Dead people often lay for two or three days on paillasses until their bodies stank so badly that fellow prisoners took them outside and buried them somewhere. I was a witness during a conversation with some Russian women, who told me personally that they were employed in Krupp's factory and that they were beaten daily in a most bestial manner. Their clothing was ragged and torn and on their feet they had rags and wooden shoes. The food consisted of a watery soup which was dirty and its terrible smell would be noticed from a distance. The conditions lasted for years, from the beginning until the American troops entered."

The inmates of concentration camps were subjected to medical experiments of various kinds. At Dauchau in August, 1942, victims were immersed in cold water until their bodily temperature was reduced to 28 degrees Centigrade, when they died immediately. Other experiments included high-altitude experiments in pressure chambers, experiments to determine how long human beings could survive in freezing water, experiments with poison bullets, experiments with contagious diseases and experiments dealing with the sterilization of men and women by X-rays and other methods.

Extermination of the German Infirm. The Nazi policy of brutality and extermination was not confined in its application to Jews and the nationals of other countries. Evidence introduced at the Nurnberg

Trial indicated that it was applied to members of the Aryan race who had become too infirm or aged to labor for the state. It will be unnecessary to comment by way of amplification upon the following letter, written by Dr. Wurm, of the Wuerttemberg Evangelical Protestant Church to the Reich Minister of the Interior, Dr. Frick, under date of September 5, 1940: "On the 19th July I sent you a letter about the systematic extermination of lunatics, feeble-minded and epileptic persons. Since then this practice has reached tremendous proportions; recently the inmates of old-age homes have also been included. The basis for this practice seems to be the opinion that in an efficient nation there should be no room for weak and frail people. It is evident from the many reports which we are receiving that the people's feelings are being badly hurt by the measures ordered and that a feeling of legal insecurity is spreading which is regrettable from the point of view of national and state interests. If the leadership of the state is convinced that it is a question of an inevitable war measure, why does it not issue a decree with legal force, which would at least have this good point that official quarters would not have to seek refuge in lies? But if—as can be assumed with certainty—Germany is in a position to feed these members of the nation as well, why then these rigorous steps? Is it necessary that the German nation should be the first civilized nation to return, in the treatment of weak people, to the habits of primitive races? Does the Fuehrer know about this matter? Has he approved it? I beg you not to leave me without a reply in this tremendously serious matter. Heil Hitler. Yours faithfully, (Signed) Dr. Wurm."

Pearl Harbor. After the consummation of the Tripartite Treaty of November 27, 1940, Hitler urged Japan to attack British possessions in the Far East. On April 4, 1941, the Fuehrer told Matsuoka, the Japanese Foreign Minister, in the presence of von Ribbentrop, that Germany would "strike without delay" if a Japanese attack on Singapore should lead to war between Japan and the United States and stated that should Japan become engaged in a war with the United States, Germany would join the war immediately. A few days later Japanese representatives told Germany and Italy that Japan was preparing to attack the United States, and asked for their support. Germany and Italy agreed to render it, although in the Tripartite Pact they had undertaken to assist Japan only if Japan were attacked.

On December 7, 1941, in the course of diplomatic negotiations with the United States, Japan attacked Pearl Harbor, and also the possessions of the British Commonwealth of Nations, France and the

Netherlands in the South Pacific. Germany declared war on the United States on December 11, 1941.

The Victory of Moral Force. It is unnecessary to deal further with the details of World War II. One by one the totalitarian regimes of Germany, Italy and Japan were brought crashing to earth. The late Justice Robert H. Jackson of the Supreme Court of the United States summed it up well in an address to the American Society of International Law. Referring to Germany's actions in both World Wars, he said that by every calculation based on naked force Germany should be sitting astride the world. "But lawlessness, violations of what plain people think of as 'rights'—rights of minorities, rights of individuals, rights of nations—have twice roused moral forces which have supplied the military force to undo German might. Nothing disintegrates power like lawlessness, nothing makes force so effective as the sentiment of people that it is somehow defending the right and is exercised in harmony with the higher moral values." Looking to the future, Justice Jackson said "that we may go forward on the assumption that reason has power to summon force to its support, confident that acceptable moral standards embodied in law will so appeal to the better natures of men that somehow they will ultimately vouchsafe the force to make them prevail."

Moral Renascence in Post-Hitler Germany and Revival of Natural Law. Professor Gottfried Dietze has recently written of what he has termed "a fundamental re-orientation of juristic thinking in Germany, characterized by a farewell to positivism and a revival of natural law," which has come about within the past decade. It marks the end of a development that started in the early nineteenth century and reached its climax under Hitler. Ever since Savigny, in his famous answer to Thibaut's plea for the codification of German law, sounded a warning on the danger of such codification, German legal thinking followed the road to a legalistic positivism which became more and more a road to serfdom. In 1854 the Romanist Windscheid said in his university address at Greifswald that there was no such thing as an absolute law and that the dream of natural law was over. In the following decades, positivism became so firmly entrenched in Germany that toward the end of the century Bergbohm could, without fear of criticism, proclaim that "from the point of view of juridical positivism every law, even the most base legal norm, must be recognized as binding, as long as it came about in the prescribed forms." This remained the prevalent view in the days of the Empire, the Weimar Republic, and the Third Reich. For generations, German jurists accepted whatever law was made by the lawmaker. Its interpretation became a mere "art" or "technique."

The reaction was a revolt against juridical positivism through a revival of natural law as a safeguard against acts of the legislature, in its capacity of constitution-maker as well as in that of ordinary lawmaker. A recognition of natural law amounts to an evaluation of positive law. Consequently, judicial review was introduced as a means for norm-evaluation. The judges, having suffered qualms of conscience in the Third Reich for their application of terror law, were anxious to prove their farewell to a positivism that had assumed barbaric proportions in the previous years. Contrary to all accepted practice, they claimed the right of judicial review. They also gave that right a broad scope. Decrees and statutes were declared void not only for being unconstitutional, but for being incompatible with natural law. Following this general wave of natural law, new constitutions were adopted by the Germans on both the state and national levels, which contained strong elements of natural law and provided for judicial review. In view of the transmutation of natural law into some constitutional norms and not into others, judicial review soon assumed proportions that even its advocates in the past decades had never dreamed possible. It was soon claimed that the judges could not only review a statute for its constitutionality, but also the compatibility of constitutional norms with those "superior" constitutional norms that contained natural law. Closely tied up with the compatibility of constitutional norms with natural law, that issue became one of the most fascinating juristic phenomena of recent years. It reflects the German jurists' farewell to a positivistic tradition in which most of them had been brought up.

Illustrating the working of the natural law concept as thus recognized, Professor Dietze recited the decision of the Amtsgericht Wiesbaden in which a Jewish woman sued for the restitution of her dead parents' furniture. Defendant, having bought the furniture at a public auction, claimed property rights. The court was concerned with the question whether the Nazi government acquired property on goods sold to it under laws providing for a discriminatory treatment of Jewish property. The question was answered in the negative on these grounds: "According to natural law there exist human rights which are immune even from an infringement by state legislation. These rights are so immanent of man that their abolition would constitute the destruction of the spiritual and moral nature of man. One of these rights is the right of property. The state can never totally deny to any man or group of men who have done no wrong the right to possess private property. Therefore, the laws confiscating Jewish property are incompatible with natural law and were void the very moment they were promulgated."

After stating other cases by way of example, Professor Dietze pointed out that the significance of these decisions lies in the fact that decrees and statutes were not judged by some superior positive law, but by supra-positive or natural law.

The continuation of German juristic thought and action on this high plane is calculated to write a chapter in German history that will do much to make amends for the sordid misdeeds of the Hohenzollerns and Nazis.

CHAPTER 14

SOVIET RUSSIA AND THE IRON CURTAIN

Peter the Great and Lawyers. As is amply evident, justice in Russia, whether before or after the Soviets, has involved points of view foreign to those of England and the United States. Russia has never known a free government. Whether under the Czars or under the Bolsheviks, there has been no system under which the individual could challenge in an independent tribunal the legality of the acts and decisions of those in charge of the administration of the law.

Justice Elwyn Shaw, a member of the Supreme Court of Illinois, once told of a visit by Peter the Great to England, in the course of which he observed the procedure in English courts. He noted that barristers on each side of controverted matters were permitted freely to present the contentions of their clients in the way most favorable to them. His reaction was against this procedure. He remarked that such a system would prove dangerous to his absolute power, that there were only two lawyers at his court, and that as soon as he returned to Russia he would behead one of them.

Peter the Great was probably lacking in the more refined qualities displayed by some of the later Czars. Thus, Czar Nicholas I engraved in letters of gold on a wall of the Imperial Palace at St. Petersburg the poem "Mortality," by William Knox, said to have been the favorite poem of Abraham Lincoln. Perhaps more apropos in relation to those exercising power amidst the machinations of the Communist regime to come, its first stanza was as follows:

O why should the spirit of mortal be proud!
Like a fast flitting meteor, a fast flying cloud,
A flash of the lightning, a break of the wave—
He passes from life to his rest in the grave.

The Revolution of 1917. The aspect of Russian history that concerns us here commenced with the Revolution of 1917. To fully understand that event it is necessary to have in mind that although all revolutions are presumably aimed at overthrow of the existing government and the setting up of a new regime, not all revolutions

have gone so far as to seek the overthrow of the whole body of existing law as well. Thus, the purpose of the American Revolution was
to cast off the yoke of the English king and install a government representative of the people. There was no desire whatever to rid the
Colonies of the Common Law of England. To the contrary, the purpose of our forefathers was to overthrow British rule to the end that
they might enjoy the rights of free Englishmen as embodied in the
Common Law of England, but which had been denied them through
its perversion by an arbitrary English king.

Overthrow of All Existing Law. The purpose of the Russian Revolution of 1917 was to overthrow not only the Czarist government but
all existing Russian law as well. There is no question but that Russia
had a background of personal dictatorial justice that was at times
ruthless, the working of which was associated with such characters
as Ivan the Terrible. The episode of Peter the Great, narrated by
Justice Shaw, throws light on the lack of regard in Russia for procedures regarded by us as fundamental to justice. It may also be
conceded that abuses of administration existed until the period immediately preceding the Revolution of 1917.

But, however prostituted by its administration, for nearly a century
Russia had a comprehensive code of law, framed originally by a commission of distinguished jurists assembled by Count Michael Speran-
sky. Samuel Kucherov said that the Judicial Reform of 1864 put the
administration of justice in Russia on a modern and democratic basis.
The law contained basic elements of Eastern Christianity and
Byzantium culture, adapted to Slavic life and customs. As such we
would understand it to embody concepts of justice which had been
in the making for centuries. As Lord Bryce pointed out in 1901, the
law of Russia was originally Slavonic custom and was influenced to
some extent by the law of the Eastern Roman Empire, whence Russia
took her Christianity and her earliest literary impulse. While retaining in many points a genuinely Slavonic character, and of course
far less distinctively Roman than is the law of France, it drew so
much, especially as regards the principles of property rights and contracts, from the Code Napoleon, and to a less degree from Germany,
that it could be described as being Roman at the second remove, and
reckoned as an outlying and a half-assimilated province, so to speak,
of the legal realm of Rome.

Within a month after the Bolsheviks had seized power they abolished the Czarist courts and set up new ones. They made "revolutionary legal conscience" the standard of determination, forbidding

the new courts to refer to the Czarist laws. A succession of administrative decrees abolished such pre-revolutionary institutions as ecclesiastical control of family relations, private trade and commerce,
private property in land and the means of production, and rights of
inheritance. The astounding concept of criminal liability which was
introduced was expressed by Lacis, an associate of Lenin, who said:
"We don't liquidate individuals. We are liquidating a class. When
prosecuting some one, do not be concerned about proofs of their
criminal activity or the testimony of defendants. Their fate is already predetermined through their relations to a class and through
the education which they received."

Back of all this was of course the peculiar nature of the Soviet
Revolution, which was not at all concerned with law in the sense of
an instrumentality for doing justice between individuals, or between
individuals and their government, but with promoting a unique theory
of social relationship. Marx and Engels provide the key to understanding. They were not interested in justice in the sense that it was
expressed in the Code of Hammurabi, the Law of Moses, the Code of
Solon, the Twelve Tables of Rome, the Corpus Juris of Justinian, the
Canon Law of the Church, or the Common Law of England and the
United States, or even in the more fundamental sense of coming from
human reason or Divine guidance. Their only concern was to promote the Marxian doctrines of economic determinism.

No "Law" or "State"? Implicit in the Marxian theory as implemented by the Revolution of 1917 was the concept that there would
evolve a state of society in which there would be no state in the governmental sense, and no body of law as conceived by jurists since
time immemorial. The state, in fact, would have to go in order to
achieve this latter desideratum. As Lenin said, "While there is a
state, there is no freedom; when there is freedom there will be no
state." E. B. Pashukanis, once regarded as the leading Soviet jurisprudential authority, wrote in "General Theory of Law and Marxism"
that law was a typical product of bourgeois economics and culture;
that any attempt to develop an original type of proletarian law was
doomed to failure, and that with the attainment of a Marxian state
law would die out.

The scheme got under way through grandiose planning, which, conceived as an inherent manifestation of a classless society, universally
subscribed to and participated in whole-heartedly by every person,
was expected to replace the state and law. That subsequent events
in Russia have belied the theory, in spite of the attempted "iron cur-

tain" of secrecy as to Soviet internal affairs, is too well understood to require more than passing comment. Nothing better dramatizes it than the spectacle of jurist Pashukanis finally turning against his previous work and characterizing it as "a muddle from beginning to end." This retraction did not save him. In 1937 *Pravda*, the official organ of the Communist Party, denounced him as a traitor and enemy of the people, and he thereafter dropped from sight. In the words of Dean Roscoe Pound: "The professor is not with us now. With the setting up of a plan by the present government in Russia, a change of doctrine was called for and he did not move fast enough in his teaching to conform to the doctrinal exigencies of the new order. If there had been law instead of only administrative orders it might have been possible for him to lose his job without losing his life."

As we have already seen, the instinct for order for which law provides the implementation, is deep in human nature. It provided the driving force to start mankind on the road to civilization, and is inescapable from any concept of civilization yet grasped by man. In spite of all the theoretical planning it soon became apparent that such problems of every-day life as family relations, trade and commerce, contracts, housing, land use, tort liability and crimes still remained and demanded solution, and that it was necessary to have and to administer rules of conduct to take care of them. A criminal code was promulgated in 1922, an outstanding feature of which was an article permitting a court to punish an action which it deemed "socially dangerous," even if no other article of the criminal code made it a crime. By 1936 it was officially recognized that the Marxist conception of a classless society without state or law was not possible of achievement. A Soviet Constitution—a basic instrument of law and government—was adopted, defining the Soviet Union as "a socialist state of workers and peasants."

Certainly there was "very much" of a state in Russia after twenty years, and, along with it, a demonstrated need for a complete system of law. Without any regard for the niceties of dialectical materialism theories the Soviets tailored a legal system to fit their purposes.

A System of "Parental Law." The Soviet legal system has been characterized as a system of "parental law," in which people are treated not as independent possessors of rights, but as immature, dependent youths who must be guided, trained and disciplined in their consciousness of rights and duties, and for whom rights are also gifts. This concept serves to explain the dualism of law and terror in the total state. Both law and terror are instruments through which the state accomplishes its objectives. Terror serves as an instrument of political and ideological discipline; law serves as an instrument of moral and socal discipline, a means of promoting a sense of responsibility, a proper balance between inventiveness and restraint in the exercise of industry, initiative, honesty and other "legal" virtues. The Soviet system is dangerous, not because it is lacking in law and justice, but rather because it is developing a new type of law which, while helping to satisfy men's needs for justice in their personal and social relations, is reconcilable with political and ideological tyranny.

"Force" Law in Action. Analysis of the rather muddled theorizing of the Soviets reveals, therefore, that if they were originally consistent in their ideas about a "stateless" and a "lawless" society, such ideas gave way to the discovery that "law" was an indispensable adjunct to the promotion of their ends by force. Lenin had recognized this when he uttered the well-known epigram, "law is politics," and so had Stalin when in 1934 he said that it is necessary to have political power as a lever of change. Andrei Vyshinsky, admitting the presence of a class society and saying that law can never be anything but the will of a ruling class, defined law as the totality (a) of the rules of conduct, expressing the will of the dominant class and established in legal order, and (b) of customs and rules of community life sanctioned by state authority—that application being guaranteed by the compulsive force of the state in order to guard, secure, and develop social relationships and social orders advantageous and agreeable to the dominant class.

The economic and military strength of the Soviet state today stands in testimony to the effectiveness of this driving force. Illustrative of its workings, bringing about not only physical results but also the adaptation of the spiritual side of the people, is the publication *Izvestia's* reference to measures to still further consolidate collective farms, involving resettlement of farm families, as "strengthening of socialist discipline, fostering of communism in the soul of the peasant and the transformation of his psychology."

Certainly there is in operation in Soviet Russia a system of law, in many respects highly specific. Government regulations cover in minute detail matters of business practice and procedure which under other governments are left to private control. To the extent that it deals with the personal and social relations between man and man Soviet law now covers some aspects of life in a manner perhaps differing in detail rather than substance from the law under which we live.

But the distinctive thing is that all Soviet law is "force" law in the sense that all of it is pointed to promote the policy of the Soviet state. The first article of the Civil Code provides, significantly, that "civil rights shall be protected by law except in instances when they are realized in contradiction with their socio-economic purpose." Contracts may be voided if the court finds that when made they involved a "disadvantage to the state." The courts are without independence; the judiciary is completely subject to the will of the principal body of the state, the Supreme Soviet of the Union. In fact, the courts are made educational appendages of the state, subjected by the Judiciary Act of 1938 to the injunction that "by all their activities the courts shall educate the citizens of the Union of Soviet Socialist Republics in the spirit of devotion to the Motherland and the cause of socialism."

Dictatorship Control. The Soviet government is controlled and directed by a highly centralized dictatorship. A small group of leaders at the top exercises minute control over all aspects of political, economic and cultural life. Acting in the name of the Communist Party, these leaders issue elaborate instructions in all fields of activity. They enforce these instructions through the state administration, the party apparatus and the secret police. It is not claimed otherwise. Dean Roscoe Pound has called attention to a text book on administrative law issued in 1945 and which states that "Comrade Stalin teaches that the Communist Party directs the government machinery. The Communist Party through its members working in the government agencies guides their work and directs their activities." Dean Pound concludes that writers have not hesitated to say that resolutions of the central committee of the party may be "both directives and Soviet law," and he adds the documented observation that although Soviet policy is proclaimed to be a regime of control by the toilers it is actually one of control of the toilers by an office-holding class.

Perhaps no clearer example of the difference between the Soviet and the American concepts of law and government could be cited than the one stated by Justice Robert Jackson, who headed the staff of American lawyers which joined with the lawyers of England, France and Russia in prosecuting the Nazi war criminals at Nurnberg. At the beginning of negotiation of the agreement of London which provided for the trial, the Soviet delegation, with utmost frankness, said they saw no need for an independent judicial judgment as to the guilt of the war criminals because Churchill, Roosevelt and Stalin, as heads of state, had declared them guilty, and all that was needed from the judicial tribunal was to fix the punishment.

Law As Politics. Inevitably we come back to the Soviet thesis that law is politics. Within the narrowly circumscribed areas to which he is confined the Soviet citizen is always treading perilously near the political line, crossing of which is instantly punished. The most elaborate code of judicial procedure would become meaningless if ordinary procedures may be suspended whenever political issues are involved. And such is true in Soviet Russia. Almost anything involves a political issue, where all conduct is geared to the policy of the state, and the Special Board of the Ministry of Internal Affairs is authorized to try in secret persons who are charged with being "socially dangerous," and to exile them to labor camps.

Ironically enough, even those highest in the "state" itself are not immune from arbitrary power. Lucid confirmation of this was provided for the world in the revelations made by Nikita Khrushchev before the Twentieth Party Congress in Moscow, February 25, 1956. In the course of this lengthy diatribe he referred to Stalin as ignoring the "norms of party life," in the course of which "ignoring" he was responsible for "mass repressions" against the delegates to the Seventeenth Party Congress and against members of the Central Committee elected at that Congress. "And," said Khrushchev laconically, "it was determined that of the 139 members and candidates of the party's Central Committee who were elected at the Seventeenth Congress, ninety-eight persons, i.e. 70%, were arrested and shot." The Khrushchev speech was replete with narration of repulsive Soviet practices. Opinions of the outside world as to the barbarity of Soviet law and judicial procedure were confirmed by his conclusion that "many thousands of honest and innocent Communists have died as a result of this monstrous falsification of such 'cases,' as a result of the fact that all kinds of slanderous 'confessions' were accepted, and as a result of the practice of forcing accusations against ones self and others."

It would be a mistake to conclude that the Soviet jurists have altogether abandoned the idea of Marx that the law will ultimately wither away in a classless state. Stalin said in his Report to the Eighteenth Party Congress that as long as the Soviet Union is threatened by "capitalist encirclement," there can be no thought of abdication of state law or power. If for no other reason, it is indispensable as a defense against capitalist subversive activities. But as soon as the "capitalist encirclement" has been broken, there will be no need for coercive public authority in Russia. However thoroughly some aspects of Stalinism have been downgraded, it is doubtful if this expression of highest-level Soviet policy has been affected. From the standpoint of a world premised on "peaceful coexistence" its implications are not reassuring. Communism has thrived on war. The Soviet Revolution of 1917 easily penetrated the vitals of Czarist Russia, weakened by German invasion in World War I. However great the Soviet losses in World War II, it emerged with all strength necessary to bring into the Soviet orbit a surrounding ring of the nations of Europe and to take, with confidence, a position in defiance of the Free World.

"Scientific Genius and Political Primitivism." Referring to Russian achievement in launching the first earth satellite, Harrison E. Salisbury pointed out that behind it was an anachronistic combination of scientific genius and political primitivism that poses a threat not only to the existence of the Western world but to that of the world itself. The Soviet Union has no viable structure of government. It is ruled today essentially as it was at the time of Ivan the Great. The Soviet state is not quite so advanced a governmental structure as was that of France under Louis XIV or England in the time of Charles I. Russia's greatest progress has been made under a succession of dictators— Ivan the Terrible, Peter the Great, Katherine the Great, Stalin—autocrats everyone. Each held power by any means. None was a stranger to murder. Each brought Russia to a new pinnacle of achievement and power.

The inadequate political structure of the Soviet Union is a striking anomaly in contrast with the amazing technical achievements in that nation. It inevitably raises the question of how so retrogressive a political state could achieve so vast a measure of scientific progress. The answer is not simple. But one thing is certain. There is no necessary correlation between political maturity and technical progress.

Lawyers and Courts in Soviet Russia. At the outset, we noted the reaction of Peter the Great to lawyers. Such change as may have come about in this regard appears to be due to the fact that under the Soviet order they can be used to assist the implementation of Soviet policy. Recently, the president of the American Bar Association visited the Soviet Union. After his return he said: "There I found that lawyers had descended to a low ebb, indeed. They have been shorn of every vestige of independent thought and action. In the Soviet the lawyers are required to be members of a union and a union composed not only of lawyers, but a union known as an installation which is an installation of government workers. All the people who work for the government are members of that union or installation. That installation is controlled by a Presidium, just as the whole Soviet Republic is controlled by a Presidium, a few men. And the membership of that Presidium are controlled by the Communist Party, just as the governing rulers are controlled by the Communist Party. So you can see to what extent they have down-graded the lawyers of Russia. I estimate that in the whole Soviet Republic today there are only approximately twelve thousand lawyers to serve a population of approximately two hundred million."

Following a tour of duty with the American Relief Administration from September, 1921, to May, 1922, during the activities of which 1,400,000 Russian adults and children were fed with American food, Will Shafroth wrote of his observations. He reported that with the Revolution of 1917 the former judicial system and body of existing law was swept away as though they were rooted up and carried off by a flood. Following the first revolutionary tribunals, so-called People's Courts were established. The Communist Party program expressed the policy back of these courts. It said in this regard: "Proletarian democracy, taking power into its own hands and finally abolishing the organs of domination of the bourgeoise—the former courts of justice—has replaced the formula of bourgeois democracy, judges elected by the people, by the class watchword; the judges must be elected from the working masses and only from the working class. The Soviet government, abolishing all the laws of the overthrown governments, commissioned the judges elected by the Soviets to carry out the will of the proletariat in compliance with its decrees, and, in cases of absence or incompleteness of decrees, to be guided by socialist conscience."

By decree of the All-Russian Central Executive Committee in 1923, these People's Courts were continued as the foundation of the Russian court system. Their jurisdiction is similar to justice of the peace courts in the United States. They are presided over by one permanent judge, elected by the provincial executive committee for a term of one year; beside him on the bench sit two people's assessors who are simply working citizens called for this duty six days a year in the same way that our citizens are called for jury service, except that they are chosen from a picked list. A majority of these three decide the case. The People's judge can be dismissed at any time by the Executive Committee. The qualifications of the people's judges are very simple and shed considerable light on the kind of justice which is dispensed in their courts; any one who has not been convicted by a court of law, and who is qualified to vote and has not less than two years' experience of responsible political work in the worker's or peasant's public, industrial or party organizations or not less than three years experience of practical work in a Soviet judicial institution in post not lower than examining magistrate may be a People's judge. The People's assessors who sit with the judges are chosen 50% from industrial workers, 35% from villages and rural districts and 15% from local military units. In selecting the names to be put on this list of assessors the decree specifies that the work shop committee and other organizations which choose them shall proceed "taking into consideration their political development."

The provincial courts are set up along the same lines, and may be compared with our circuit or district courts. They control the work of the People's Courts in their territory. They also hear appeals from them, with original jurisdiction in the larger cases. The supreme Court of the Soviet Republic has jurisdiction over appeals from the provincial courts and original jurisdiction over cases of state importance. It also has supervision over all courts. Its members are appointed by the Presidium of the all Russian Central Executive Committee, and can be recalled or suspended by this Committee. People's assessors also take part in the proceedings of this court, but here they are special assessors, appointed from among the higher officials of the government.

Operations in Czechoslovakia. After World War II, under the guise of insuring its own security and without regard to treaty obligations to its former allies, the Soviet government seized control of its border nations in Eastern Europe and vested power in local puppets who would keep step with their Soviet masters. As a matter of course the law and legal procedures of the nations thus pulled behind the "Iron Curtain," were geared to the authoritarian techniques established in Russia.

Noteworthy in this connection was Czechoslovakia. In no sense was it a nation before World War I. Up to that time its Slavic peoples were among the subjects ruled by the Habsburgs. But there were kindred peoples in Russia; during World War I thousands of Czechoslovaks impressed into service by the Austrian Emperor deserted to the Russians. The Czechoslovak nation had its beginnings in the fighting divisions composed of these men under the leadership of Dr. Thomas Masaryk. Until the Russian debacle in 1917 they rendered great service to the Allied cause. After the Russian peace with Germany they were ordered to disband and submit to Russian orders. Refusing to do so, they fought their way some six thousand miles across Russia, from Kiev in the Ukraine to Vladivostok on the Pacific.

In the course of events there was established a Czecho-Slovak National Council with Dr. Masaryk as President. The Council was obviously without a country, but at Paris, in October, 1918, it issued a proclamation of national independence. By formal announcement of Robert Lansing, Secretary of State of the United States, the Czecho-Slovak National Council was recognized as a *de facto* belligerent government and the United States entered into formal relations with it for the purpose of prosecuting the war. On November 14, 1918, a provisional assembly of the National Council proclaimed the Republic of Czechoslovakia. Dr. Thomas Masaryk was named President and Dr. Eduard Benes Foreign Minister. The nation was represented at the Versailles Peace Conference. Early in 1920 a constitution was adopted, modeled after the constitutions of the United States and France, and providing for a parliamentary regime with separation of powers. Thus Czechoslovakia came into national existence with the strongest of ties, sentimental and political, with the Western democracies, and, until Munich, looked to the free nations which had sponsored it as staunch friends and protectors.

The Czechoslovak System of Justice. Eduard Taborsky, a former aide to Benes, has described the system of justice of Czechoslovakia as it was prior to World War II, and immediately thereafter. It provided for four tiers of courts having general jurisdiction over civil and criminal matters. The judges, all of whom had to have a law degree and pass a special judicial examination, were appointed by the President of the Republic and the cabinet for life. They enjoyed as complete a security of tenure as judges anywhere in the world. They were bound by law and had both the right and the duty to deny validity to any government ordinance (executive order) in conflict with an Act of Parliament. They had, however, no power to question the constitutionality of duly enacted laws. Judicial review of legislation was reserved exclusively for a special Constitutional Court, and could be exercised on a very limited scale only. There was a jury system, which was used in criminal trials for felonies punishable with a minimum penalty of five years in the penitentiary.

Protection against unlawful acts of the administration was afforded, not by the ordinary courts, but by a special Administrative Court, composed of experts in public law and administration appointed for life by the President of the Republic. Acting under the same guarantees of complete independence employed by the judges of the Supreme Court, the judges of the Administrative Court became intrepid protectors of individual rights on the part of any government agent, from the President of the Republic down to the village constable, thereby exercising a function similar to that performed by the French Conseil d'Etat.

In 1945 the judicial system was restored essentially in the form in which it had existed before the war. The Communist leaders had correctly anticipated that any restoration of the prewar judiciary would only make the fulfillment of their plans more difficult. For that reason they quite assiduously claimed the Ministry of Justice for the party during the strenuous negotiations between them and the leaders of democratic parties in Moscow in March, 1945. Their failure to get this post was one of the few setbacks they suffered in their early bid for power. When the public prosecutors began to demand, and the courts to mete out, jail sentences against Communist commanded policemen for having exceeded their authority, and when, in addition, the Administrative Court even went so far as to throw out as illegal some of the confiscatory measures taken against private property by Communist-directed local authorities, the Communists erupted.

Death-Knell of a Free Judiciary. After the end of World War II Czechoslovakia, under the leadership of Jan Masaryk and Dr. Benes, attempted to resume its course as a free and independent nation. It was not allowed to do so. In February 1948 the government was seized via a Communist coup. Jan Masaryk's dead body was found in the courtyard of his Ministry building, and, although Dr. Benes was nominally allowed to stay in office he resigned shortly thereafter, a broken man.

The events of February, 1948, as Taborsky has pointed out, rang the death-knell of a free and independent judiciary in Czechoslovakia. The Communist leader Klement Gottwald, having finally forced President Benes into submission, triumphantly announced to the gathering of his followers awaiting him in Prague that the Ministry of Justice would be taken over by Alexei Cepicka. The choice of the most rabid of the younger Communist generation to succeed the judicious Drtina was a perfect symbol of the changes to come. A colossal purge was immediately carried out in the Ministry of Justice, on all levels of the judiciary and the public prosecution. When it was finished, the backbone of the pre-Communist judicial system was broken and its whole character defaced almost beyond recognition. "Almost overnight the independence of the judiciary was done away with, and what had once been the staunch guardian of individual rights and freedom was turned into a tool of coercion and subjection."

Indicating that in the hands of tyrants the finest code of law and procedure offers little or no protection, and that in the last analysis the administration of justice becomes what its administrators make it, Professor Taborsky points out that all this was achieved without any change in the structure of the judiciary, and without formal amendment of the rules of procedure or the canons of substantive law.

Courts Must Pursue the Communist Line. Formal changes to bring the judicial system into word conformity with Communist principles of ideology and organization followed. The aims are apparent from statements made by Alexei Cepicka, Communist Minister of Justice, who told the National Congress of Czechoslovak Lawyers: "The starting point for the solution of all legal questions is Marx-Leninism, which enables us to express in a precise and understandable way legal conceptions which the bourgeois legal science sought to obscure." With further reference to the purposes sought to be achieved Cepicka emphasized primarily the need to strengthen the "people's democracy" and "socialist legality," while relegating to third place the need of "legal security of the workers."

Cepicka's successor as Minister of Justice told the National Conference of the Presidents of the Courts and public prosecutors: "In the struggle for the socialist rebuilding of the villages, the prosecutors and the judges have the task to protect the agricultural cooperatives, to prosecute the saboteurs, to hit hard the village bourgeoise. The trials in the villages must become effective means to convince the broad masses as to who is the sworn enemy of their interest. The proceedings against the saboteurs found among the village rich and their associates have a great political importance. The courts must be prepared and take advantage of every means suitable to unmask the true face of the village rich . . . in reaching decisions they have to consider the class character of the accused and the threat that his act represents for the community. The basic task of the judiciary in connection with the building of socialism is to pursue consistently the general line of the Communist Party of Czechoslovakia."

Within a few years the whole edifice of the Czechoslovakian legal system had been leveled to the ground and a new structure erected on its ruins, bearing the label "Prefabricated in Moscow."

Will Totalitarianism Rationally Disappear? In a most interesting study Zbigniew Brzezinski has recently dealt with the possibility that totalitarianism in its modern Iron Curtain form may disappear, not by forceful overthrow, but by a process of natural evolution. It could be argued, and some have, that Soviet totalitarianism, the most advanced totalitarian society of our age, is now entering upon a new stage of development, the character of which will be determined by the industrialized nature of the Soviet economy. This analysis, partaking somewhat of a material determinism, stresses the incompatabilities between totalitarianism and the requirements of a modern, industrial and hence also bureaucratic order. Noting that totalitarianism in the past has seemed largely irrational, it argues that the rationalistic routines of the indispensable managers of the industrial society will necessarily transmit themselves to the totalitarian leadership and gradually effect a fundamental transformation of the system itself. This transmission will be aided by the fact that the totalitarian movement has become highly bureaucratized and therefore shares in many of the operational patterns associated with running the industrial machine.

The argument proceeds that as stability, predictability and overall rationality set in, fear, terror and arbitrariness will fade. Mass enthusiasm and passionate unanimity will give way to disagreements on matters of expertise, and hence also on policy. Policy discussion will then become genuine arguments on alternate courses of action; selection will be made on the basis of rational (technical, objective assessments of the implications of perceived reality) considerations without violent (hence arbitrary and fear-inspiring) consequences for those whose arguments did not prevail. This, together with the growing stability of various privilege groups, will in turn lead to a form of pluralism, suggestive of the existing democratic systems. Democracy, even though likely a curtailed one, will enter by the back door. Such is the thesis propounded by Isaac Deutscher in his book *Russia: What Next.*

The Answer Appears to be "No." Brzezinski points out that the institutionalized revolution which still characterizes the existing totalitarianisms will inevitably slow down in the future, but by then it will be involved in an economic commitment which also has its own political logic. The totalitarian economy has been developed in Russia over the last thirty years in keeping with plans oriented to a final (if not yet defined) goal. It is thus a goal-oriented economy, the goal being communism. That this goal needs more definite formulation is, for our purposes, irrelevant. The important thing is that those in charge of the Soviet society have assumed that economic and social development in all its aspects can be purposefully steered by man in the direction of an ideal solution. This produces consequences not only economic but also political. It makes little political difference whether the range of man's alternatives is limited by uneducated revolutionaries or by scientific Ph. D.'s, once the entire economy is subjected to a process of human engineering oriented on a goal which cannot be questioned. As long as the party continues to hold its successful grip on the instruments of power, we can expect it to continue stressing first the long-range goals of an ultimate utopia, and then the consequent sacrifices to achieve them. The rationalist tomorrow, if it ever comes, will therefore not be an introduction to a democratic form of government, but rather a stage in further totalitarian revolution, accentuating rationalist features present from the start and minimizing some of the irrational outbursts already noted.

CHAPTER 15

THE ROLE OF RED CHINA

Patriarchal Despotism in Ancient China. China is a country whose people have not had the experience of being swept and dispossessed by conquering hordes. It was invaded by Jinghiz Khan and Kublai Khan, but its ancient stock was not destroyed, and the Manchu conquest which brought about a change of rulers did not greatly affect the people. Its history, commencing around 2500 B.C., is in the main one of rising and falling dynasties, few of which lasted more than two centuries. Government in the nature of a patriarchal despotism marked its beginnings and continued until modern times. The theory was simple. The country was divided into provinces, each ruled by a viceroy, all-powerful save as he was subject to the emperor. Strong emperors held these viceroys to a high degree of responsibility for the welfare of their people, and for appropriate contributions to support the central government. Failure to suppress crime or rebellion meant removal from office or perhaps the receipt from the emperor of a silken cord which indicated to the recipient that it was his ordered privilege to commit suicide.

A Country of Contradictions. From the standpoint of law and its administration China has been a country of contradictions. From early centuries the theoretical plane appears to have been a high one. An ancient king proclaimed: "The great God has conferred on the people a moral sense, compliance with which would show their nature invariably right. To cause them tranquilly to pursue the course which it indicates is the task of the sovereign." Thereby was recognized a concept of unwritten natural law, finding its essence in the general moral insight of the individual, similar to the corresponding natural law concept of later Greek and Roman legal philosophers. The responsibility for making it the instrument for justice was laid upon the rulers. Administered by educated, high-minded men, cognizant of the customs and standards of the people of the period, such a system was capable of working well. At times it would appear to have done so.

Nevertheless, under the conditions presented theory could not consistently meet the test of practice. The course of justice was a turbulent one. The rise, disintegration and fall of dynasties was attended with periods of violence and chaos, taking toll of millions of lives. The poverty of the masses, living in a condition almost always approaching if not attaining filth, was punctuated by oppressive practices upon the part of their superiors. A system based on natural law concepts can succeed only on the basis of a vital religious belief. This the masses of Chinese people did not have. Not all Chinese who came to power were high-minded; not all the high-minded were strong enough to rule where in the nature of things only strong-man government could succeed. The period of some five hundred years immediately preceding the birth of Confucius in 550 B.C. is probably typical of much that went before. In the absence of strong central authority, the country was much of the time in a state of unrest, crime and warfare between the provinces.

It was not that China was without a coherent system of law. There is little question that the Chinese people possessed a complete system of law, ethics and politics long before the origin of the English common law. In 2500 B.C., the existent system of law was so well adapted to the needs of the people that, ten centuries later, codification of the law involved simply detailed compilation. The modern character of the legal system in force during the reign of Emperor Shun (2255-2205) B.C.) is indicated by a statement attributed to the Emperor to the effect that "the ultimate purpose of penal laws is not so much punishing guilt as lifting the people above the necessity of punishment." Nevertheless, penalties were severe. Successive compilations of these codes contained provisions which bear a striking resemblance to the modern rule of reasonable doubt and the privilege against self-incrimination.

The code on which the Chinese criminal law was founded, before adoption of the Provisional Code of 1911, was originally published during the Tang dynasty (518-907 A.D.). That code formed the basis of the Ta Ching Lu Li, the famous Manchu Code of the seventeenth century, which continued in effect until displaced by the Provisional Code, the direct forbear of the Chinese Criminal Code of 1935. The form of punishment in effect until comparatively times was corporal in character. Imprisonment was not regarded as a punitive measure and prisons were used exclusively for criminals awaiting trial. The punishments in effect just before the adoption of the Provisional Code included imprisonment and omitted the maiming which was an essential part of the older forms of punishment. During that period, the penalties inflicted were (1) slicing to pieces until death (the so-called lingering death), (2) decapitation, (3) strangulation, (4) transportation for life or for a term, (5) penal servitude, (6) imprisonment, (7) the cangue, a heavy wooden collar, (8) application of the bamboo, (9) branding, and (10) fines imposed by way of commutation. Torture was an integral part of the administration of justice. Two legal forms of torture were recognized, one resembling the old Scotch Boot, the other a finger compressor. The Chinese courts paid little attention to the direct statement of the witnesses. The duty of the judge was to "wring the truth" out of those brought before him. There was no legal profession. The entire conduct of the examination and trial was in the hands of the judge.

The Paternal Power as Law. The paternal power has been traditionally the fundamental principle of Chinese law and Chinese government. "We may lay it down as an axiom," says Gardner, "that law in China is derived from evolution or by fictions from the necessary authority of adults over their progeny." The law upon the subject of the paternal power bears the imprint of primitive society, and has undoubtedly existed in substantially the form demonstrated in modern times for hundreds or thousands of years. With the Chinese law we are carried back to a position where we can survey, so to speak, a living past, and converse with fossil men.

"Of the 3000 crimes," says Confucius, "included under the five heads of punishment, there is none greater than disobedience to parents." This precept of philosophy was embodied in the seven penalties of the penal code. Under the Ta Ching Lu Li, children disobeying the commands of their parents or paternal grand-parents were punishable by one hundred blows.

The emperor was regarded in a double aspect. On the one hand, he was regarded as the son of Heaven, empowered by the Supreme Being to rule. On the other hand, he was the father of the people, responsible for their conduct and welfare. In him were vested all powers of government, legislative, executive and judicial. So long as matters went well, he was regarded as being under the favor of Heaven. When they did not go well, it was conceived that Heaven had withdrawn its favor.

Ancestor Worship. Ancestor worship, the original religion of China, was adopted by the creeds of Lao Tze, of Confucius, and of Buddha, and became almost the principal part of these beliefs. "The worship of ancestors," says Edmund Taylor, "begun during their life, is not interrupted, but intensified, when death makes them deities. The Chinese, prostrate bodily and mentally before the memorial tablets which contain the souls of his ancestors, little thinks that he is all the while proving to mankind how vast a power unlimited filial obedience prohibiting change from ancestral institutions may exert in stopping the advance of civilization."

Confucius and His Teachings. The teachings of Confucius fundamentally incorporated the general pattern of Chinese life as it had long been conceived. Not claiming to be a prophet or to have supernatural knowledge, but claiming only the sanction of reason and experience, he laid emphasis upon man in his relation to his family and the past. Society was an ordinance of heaven, made up of five relationships: ruler and subject, husband and wife, father and son, elder brothers and the younger, and friends. As to the first four, the first named ruled "with righteousness and benevolence," and the other submitted. The mutual promotion of virtue was the guide between friends. With confidence in men, and with past examples of good rulers, Confucius undertook to inspire the rulers of the day to meet their responsibilities to a degree that their predecessors had not. His efforts fell upon deaf ears. His character, and his experiences, will stand rather close comparison with those of Socrates, although he was not subjected to so tragic an end.

An anecdote related of Confucius is that when he and some of his disciples were on a journey they passed Tai Mountain, where they saw a woman weeping at a grave. Confucius sent one of them to ask the reasons for the woman's grief. She said: "My husband's father was killed here by a tiger and my husband also, and now my son has met the same fate." They asked her why she did not leave the ill-fated spot and she replied that in her village there was no oppressive government. Confucius was deeply impressed by the answer. "Remember this, my children," he said to his companions, "oppressive government is fiercer and more feared than a tiger."

Following the death of Confucius, his teachings began to gain influence and in succeeding centuries they came to be accepted reverentially as authoritative guides. In the thirteenth century A.D. the Tartar Kublai Khan, who had conquered China, issued a decree proclaiming that the law of Confucius was a law destined to govern all generations, and that all should conform to its divine behests. In such an atmosphere institutions of higher learning were established. Knowledge of the Nine Classics, five of which had been edited by Confucius and the other four of which bore the impress of his teachings, became the basis for examinations under which all aspirants to government employment must qualify. Millions pored over them. The high principles stated therein operated as a measurable check on despotic government.

But the philosophy of Confucius, however moral, was at best a static one. It negatived the dignity of the living individual soul and did not encourage independence of thought. Based on reverence for the family and invoking reverential respect for the institutions of past generations, it foreclosed adequate consideration of the present with relation to the future. As we have already indicated, it restrained the progress of civilization.

Corruption in Government. At best, the Confucian philosophy was an inadequate guide for a great nation, faced with a multitude of concrete practical problems of human relations. In the hands of men without moral convictions it meant nothing. In the course of events governmental administration fell largely into the hands of such men. The whole theory of their procurement fell down as government finances ebbed low and offices were in effect sold. Within each province there grew up a powerful bureaucracy, on the whole underpaid, thus putting a premium on illegal exactions and bribery. Extortion was promoted by the system prevailing under which suitors seeking to assert legal rights were compelled to pay fees to all the functionaries involved in a hearing of the matter. As in all authoritarian regimes the ruler himself, or through subordinates responsible to him personally, dispensed justice, along with the exercise of all other governmental functions. Under many governors the procedure was not, to say the least, refined. Witnesses were tortured, punishments were extreme. The dignity of death by strangulation was reserved for offenders of high rank, those of lower status being executed by decapitation, or cutting to pieces on a cross.

The Ultimate Reaction: A Republic. China began to awaken as a result of Western contacts during the nineteenth century. A treaty between that country and the United States was negotiated in 1844. Traders and missionaries followed, and acquainted the Chinese with Western ways. Not all Chinese took to this kindly. In 1900 a fanatical group known as Boxers, determined to drive all "foreigners" from China, staged an attack on foreign legations in Pekin. The German and Japanese ministers were killed. Only prompt and forceful joint military action by the various powers, including the United States, prevented greater disaster. As it was, thirty-five adult Protestant missionaries, fifty-three children, a number of Roman Catholic priests and thousands of Chinese Christians were tortured and killed. Among the results was the further penetration of Western ways into China.

Under the impetus of the educated classes the emperor was overthrown and a republic set up. By the constitution it was provided that the sovereignty of the Republic of China was vested in the entire people, and that all citizens of the Republic of China should be equal before the law, without distinction of sex, race, religion or class.

Thus, out of the travail of centuries finally came an enlightened government, destined unhappily, to go down under the stress of world war and communist machination before it had real opportunity to organize itself.

Communism Takes Over. The story of how Communism took over in China is so recent as to be a matter of considerable current knowledge; present purposes do not necessitate its recital here.

The People's Republic of China adopted its first constitution in 1954. Referring to it, Tao-Tai Hsia has said that the present political, social and economic arrangements in effect on the Chinese mainland are the dynamic expression of communist jurisprudence as formulated in this basic document: the constitution is a legal mirror reflecting the changing reality in the state. Laden with dialectics and pretense of democracy, it bears strong resemblance to its Soviet prototype. In contrast to the pre-communist constitutions of China, which are variously branded by the Chinese Communists as capitalistic, bogus, and reactionary, the new constitution is designated as "people's democratic" and a basic law of socialist character. These designations derive from the theory that a "people's democracy" is a form of proleteriat dictatorship in an intermediary stage towards complete communization. In line with this policy, Article 4 provides that "the people's Republic of China, relying upon the state organs and social forces, through socialist industrialization and socialist reform, guarantees the gradual elimination of the exploitation system and the establishment of a socialist society."

A Basic Instrument of "Class Justice." The 1954 constitution of Red China, therefore, is obviously a basic instrument of the "class justice" espoused by the Chinese Communist leaders. In discussing the strengthening of the apparatus of the people's state Mao Tse-tung declared: "The army, police, and courts of the state are instruments by which classes oppress classes. To the hostile classes the state apparatus is the instrument of oppression. It is violent, and not 'benevolent.' We decidedly will not exercise benevolence towards the reactionary acts of the reactionaries and reactionary classes. Our benevolence applies only to the people, and not to the reactionary acts of the reactionaries and reactionary classes outside the people." In accordance with this view, proletarian class justice is specifically emphasized by the constitutional language, "the People's Republic of China safeguards the people's democratic system, protects the security and rights of the citizens, suppresses all treasonable and counterrevolutionary elements."

The "Rights" and Duties of the People. Ironically enough, the new constitution of Red China provides that every citizen enjoys "freedom of thought, speech, publication, assembly, association, correspondence, person, domicile, moving from one place to another, religious belief, and the freedom of holding processions and demonstrations." In spite of this, indoctrination has taken the place of liberal education; news and other forms of public information have given way to propaganda; and both genuine freedom of thought and action are denied to the individual. But, as a Chinese Communist theorist has said, the rights enjoyed by the citizen are "determined by the state system and social structure." And it must be kept in mind that in a communist country the individual is subject to the state power and its elaborate apparatus. The duties prescribed by the constitution are understandable. They are "to defend the fatherland, to observe the laws, to maintain labor discipline, to protect public property, to perform public and military services, and to pay taxes."

Confiscation Without Indemnity. The constitution of 1954 provides that the state shall protect the land ownership and other properties of the peasants "in accordance with the law." However, it is emphasized in the same article that the state shall adopt a policy of restriction and gradual elimination of the rich peasant economy. Ownership of the means of production and other capital investments are also declared to be protected "in accordance with the law." This is illusory, since it is provided that the state prohibits all unlawful actions of capitalists that undermine the public interest, disrupt the economic order of society, and hamper national economic planning. For a long time the government has been confiscating the property of capitalists without any indemnity, on the basis of any of its own picked charges. The Chinese Communist leaders, like Lenin during the New Economic Policy of early Soviet Russian days, found the capitalist technique useful in the strengthening of bolshevism and the eventual destruction of capitalism itself. Using this approach, a policy of utilization, restriction and transformation toward capitalist industry and commerce is expressed in the constitution. Legal income, savings, individual ownership of homes and other means of livelihood are still recognized.

However, in relation to the above guarantee, a threatening tone pervades the provision that the use of any forms of private property to undermine the public interest is prohibited. The guarantee of private property is further restricted by the provision that lands and other materials are subject to requisition or nationalization in the public interest. Like similar provisions in the constitutions of other communist states, the legal guarantee of inheritance is limited only to "personal" property.

No Institutionalized Checks on Supreme Power. The structure of government, established by the new basic law, models itself on that of the Soviet Union. The power of the people, in theory, is exercised through their duly elected organs, the All-China People's Congress and the people's congress at lower levels. Mao Tse-Tung made it clear in his article "On the People's Democratic Dictatorship," that the "democratic centralism" he advocates means that the power arrangement is actually pyramidal and the authority is highly concentrated at the top. Such outward forms of "democratic" assemblies provided for in the constitution tend inevitably to become merely ritualistic, and not institutions of genuine democracy. At present, as admitted by Liu Shao-chi in his report on the draft constitution, universal, equal and direct suffrage has not yet been practiced. Landlords and political undesirables are deprived of their right to elect and be elected. In most basic-stratum elections, the method of voting is by a show of hands at a public meeting. Although the All-China People's Congress is theoretically "the supreme organ of the state power," the fact remains that the supreme power is in the hands of Mao and his colleagues and is not subject to any institutionalized checks as practiced in the Western democracies.

The Judiciary of Red China. The judiciary of Red China is an auxiliary and not an independent branch of the government. As provided for in the new Constitution, it is represented by the People's Supreme Court, the local people's courts at various levels, and the special courts. According to the law of the Organization of the People's Court, adopted by the All-China People's Congress in 1954, the local people's courts are composed of basic-stratum people's courts, intermediate people's courts, and high people's courts. Special courts, similar to those of the Soviet Union, include military tribunals, railroad-transport courts, and water-transport courts. The purpose of the people's courts is, as provided in the above law, to punish all criminals and to settle civil disputes through trial activities in order to (1) defend the people's democratic system, (2) maintain public order, (3) protect communal property, (4) guard the rights and legal interests of citizens, and insure the facilitation of transformation to a socialist state. It is also stressed that the entire activities of the people's courts are to be devoted to the education of the citizens, in order to make them "loyal to the fatherland and observe laws conscientiously."

The decisions and verdicts on cases tried for the first time by the local people's courts at various levels can be appealed by the parties or protested by the people's procurator in a higher court. There are no courts under the Chinese Communist judicial system designated solely for appellate functions. The case can go up only once for review by the court immediately higher.

The Supreme People's Court is the highest judicial body of the state and is charged with supervision over the judicial activities of the local people's courts, and also special courts. Similar to its counterparts in all countries of the Soviet bloc, it does not have the power of judicial review of legislation. The President of the Supreme Court is elected by the All-China People's Congress. The vice-president and other judges of the Supreme Court are appointed by the Standing Committee of the All-China People's Congress. To emphasize the essential oneness of the government, the Supreme Court is responsible to the All-China People's Congress and is required to report on its work to the People's Congress or its Standing Committee during the recess of the Congress.

"Decisions in Accordance With Governmental Policy." In all people's courts at various levels, except in cases specially provided for by law, people's assessors participate along with the judges. Pursuant to the law on the organization of the people's courts, people's assessors sit with regular judges and enjoy equal rights with them in all cases tried for the first time, except simple civil cases, unimportant criminal cases, and cases specially provided for by law.

There is a Committee on Trials in every people's court to see that all decisions rendered are in accordance with governmental policy. In the committee, experiences of trials are summarized, and serious and difficult cases and other questions relating to trials are discussed. The governmental policy is absolutely clear-cut. As recently stated by the State Department of the United States, the primary purpose of the Chinese Communists is to extend the Communist revolt beyond their borders to the rest of Asia and thence to the rest of the world.

The Procurator General: Supreme Law Officer. Under the new constitution of Red China the Procurator General of the People's Republic exercises the highest supervisory power over the execution of the law by various organs subordinate to the State Council and local state executive administrative organs, and individual officials and citizens. His supervisory competence is much broader than that of the Supreme Court, whose jurisdiction extends only over the judicial activities of all courts.

Like its counterpart in the Russian Government, the office of the Procurator General is highly centralized and entirely independent of local organs of power. The chief procurators on all levels are appointed by the Procurator General. He is, in theory, the only one who has procuratorial power. All other procurators can only exercise powers delegated to them by the Procurator General. The Procurator General is appointed by the All-China People's Congress for a term of four years. Like the President of the Supreme Court, he is responsible to the All-China People's Congress and its Standing Committee.

The duties of the local procurator's office on all levels and the special procurator's office are to see (a) that decisions, enactments and orders of the local governmental organs are in accord with the constitution as well as the decisions of the central government; (b) that individual officials and citizens observe laws; (c) that the judicial activities of courts are legal; (d) that investigative activities are carried out properly; (e) that decisions on criminal cases are correctly executed; and (f) that the activities of labor reform organs are carried out properly and legally. Moreover, the local procurator's office institutes criminal cases and prosecutes them. Important civil cases concerning the state's and the people's interests can also be instituted by the local procurator.

We may appropriately end our review of the Iron Curtain nations by emphasizing one clause of the preceding paragraph: "The duties of the local procurator's office are to see . . . (c) that the judicial activities of courts are legal." Words more emphatically descriptive of a regime of absolute judicial servility could not be easily found.

PART VI: CIVILIZATION UNDER THE COMMON LAW

Chapter 16

RIGHTS OF THE INDIVIDUAL

The Individual Comes Into His Own. Thus far in our study we have noted scant reference to individuals or the rights of individuals. This is not due to oversight. Through most of the centuries of civilization that we have sketched the individual was not in himself a factor. The extent to which he did not count in early epochs we have just seen paralleled in the Iron Curtain doctrines of today. This is true, moreover, even as to the nations of Continental Europe which are outside the Iron Curtain. Professor Gottfried Dietze has said that by the end of the Second World War the law had lost to most Europeans its quality as a Magna Charta for the individual. Under juridical positivism, it had increasingly become an expression of state authority, until under the dictatorships it degenerated into a means for the suppression of the individual. Under the slavery philosophy that has rather consistently prevailed somewhere throughout history and the conditions of physical turmoil that were never abated for long it could hardly be otherwise. The best that the individual could hope for was to rise or fall with his group; apart from it he counted for little.

From now on we are going to deal with the common law, and the common law system, distinctive—and this is said without intended disparagement of those who speak another tongue—of the English-speaking peoples. In a classic statement Judge Peter Grosscup stated that the progress of the English-speaking peoples to the highest form of civil and religious liberty is not adventitious or accidental, but is due to the ennoblement of the individual in the conceptions and practices of English law. We enter a truly new world when we commence our consideration of the common law as it arose in England and as it came to the shores of the United States with those who founded our nation, and was in due course woven into our governmental and jurisprudential fabric. Here, the individual comes into his own. It is recognized, as a matter of physical fact, that each

324

and every one of us came into being as an individual, and that each one of us, in accordance with nature's inexorable processes, will finally depart this physical life. But it is also recognized as what we may call a spiritual fact, that while each of us is here he is all-important, not only to himself but to his fellows. He has his own part to play, and he is entitled to play it. That there are scores of millions of Americans and billions of human beings throughout the world is beside the point. The individual is not indistinguishable in the mass; rather, the spotlight is on him.

Origin of Individual Liberty Concept. Over a century ago the distinguished French historian Guizot, tracing the origin of the individual liberty concept, pointed out that the rude barbarians of Germany introduced this sentiment of personal independence, this love of individual liberty, into European civilization. It was unknown among the Romans, it was unknown in the Christian Church; it was unknown in nearly all the civilizations of antiquity. The liberty met with in ancient civilizations is political liberty; it is the liberty of the citizen. It was not about his personal liberty that man troubled himself, it was about his liberty as a citizen. He formed part of an association, and to this alone he was devoted. The case was the same in the Christian Church. The feeling of personal independence, a fondness for genuine liberty displaying itself without regard to consequences, was unknown to the Romans and the Christians. Although it has received its distinctive recognition and development under our common law system, as Professor Guizot thus indicated there is nothing peculiarly modern about this concept of individual liberty. It was brought into our civilization by the "rude barbarians of Germany."

It would be difficult to find a better elucidation of it than the one expressed by Guizot. He pointed out that the first idea comprised in the word "civilization" is the notion of progress, of development. It calls up within us the notion of a people advancing, of a people in a course of improvement and melioration. The etymology of the word seems sufficiently obvious—it points at once to the improvement of civil life. The first notion which strikes us in pronouncing it is the progress of society; the melioration of the social state; the carrying to higher perfection the relations between man and man. It awakens within us at once the notion of an increase of national prosperity, of a greater activity and better organization of the social relations. On one hand there is a manifest increase in the power and well-being of society at large; and on the other a more equitable distribution of this power and well-being among the individuals of which society is composed.

But the word civilization has a more extensive significance than this, which seems to confine it to the mere outward, physical organization of society. Now, if this were all, the human race would be little better than the inhabitants of an ant-hill or bee-hive; a society in which nothing was sought for beyond order and well-being—in which the highest, the sole aim, would be the production of the means of life, and their equitable distribution.

Our nature at once rejects this definition as too narrow. It tells us that man is formed for a higher destiny than this; that this is not the full development of his character—that civilization comprehends something more extensive, something more complex, something superior to the perfection of social relations, of social power and well-being. All that we understand by the term civilization is not comprised in the simple idea of social well-being and happiness. If we look a little deeper we discover that, besides the progress and melioration of social life, another development is comprised in our notion of civilization—namely, the development of individual life, the development of the human mind and its facilities—the development of man himself.

The love of personal freedom of the Saxon conquerors of Great Britain was impressed upon the institutions they founded, or adopted, or modified. Learned investigators differ concerning the extent to which Roman law existed and prevailed at the time of the Saxon conquest, and the extent to which it was adopted or incorporated into the English laws, usages and institutions. But there is a universal assent to these propositions, viz., that the Saxon spirit of freedom was embodied in the various local courts; that it was in these popular tribunals that the principles of law and local government were cultivated and disseminated; that the Saxons breathed into the English government and institutions a spirit of equity and freedom which has never entirely departed from them; and that in the course of time the common law intertwined its roots and fibers inseparably into the constitution, polity, local, and municipal institutions, the civil and criminal jurisprudence, the family relation, and the rights of person and of property. So from an immemorial or early period the local territorial subdivisions of England, such as towns and parishes, enjoyed a degree of freedom, and were permitted to assess upon themselves their local taxes and manage their local affairs. The ratepayers were thus dignified by being an integral part of the communal life; the foundations of municipal liberty were laid; political power was decentralized; knowledge of the laws and reverence for and obedience to them were constantly taught by a participation in their administration and enforcement. This is exactly the opposite of the systems prevailing on the Continent, where the central power absorbs, governs, regulates everything, thereby destroying municipal freedom and the capacity to enjoy and exercise it, as well as the power to defend and preserve it.

As in the course of our further study we turn particular attention to our own law and institutions we will increasingly appreciate the extent to which our constitutional forefathers were cognizant of the individual's worth and dignity, how concerned they were with his spiritual as well as his physical freedom, and how effectively they laid the foundation to insure his future happiness as a citizen of the United States.

Brandeis, Wilson and Jefferson. No one has put the concept better than the late Justice Louis D. Brandeis of the Supreme Court of the United States. He noted that American ideals are the development of the individual for his own and the common good, the development of the individual through liberty, and the attainment of the common good through democracy and social justice. Our form of government as well as humanity compel us to strive for the development of the individual man. In so saying, Justice Brandeis was only repeating in somewhat different words the thought of Woodrow Wilson, who said that society is an organic association of individuals for mutual aid to self-development. The hope of society lies in infinite individual variety, in the freest play of individual forces; only in that can be found that wealth of resources which constitutes civilization with all its appliances for satisfying human wants and mitigating human suffering, with all its incitements to thought and spurs to action. The individual must be assured the best means, the fullest opportunities, for self-development.

Basic, of course, are the words of Thomas Jefferson, immortalized in the Declaration of Independence, that all men are created equal and endowed by their Creator with certain inalienable rights, among which are life, liberty and the pursuit of happiness. Granting that this inspired sentiment was not first pronounced by Jefferson, but as spoken by him was but an echo of such Roman jurists as Ulpian whose consciences, as we have seen, gave them insight into the eternal truths of natural law, as spoken by Jefferson for the first time in history the principle found itself in an environment in which it could live and thrive. And recently the Supreme Court of the United States summed it up succinctly in the statement that "equally manifest as a fundamental principle of a democratic society is political freedom of the individual."

Individual Rights Enumerated. What are the individual rights with which we are concerned? Every American is familiar with Jefferson's statement of rights as we have noted it above. In saying that "among" them are life, liberty and the pursuit of happiness, he did not purport to make an exhaustive enumeration. But he doubtless meant to employ those terms in a broad sense, and they may be taken as fairly inclusive of the whole field of individual human rights. Our purposes will be served to advantage by breaking down their implications into a little more detail and making a classification which will further their analysis.

The Right to Life. The right to live physically is manifestly the most basic of all rights. Other rights would be of less than academic interest to one without physical life. The right to life was stated at the outset of the United Nations Universal Declaration of Human Rights, and amplified in the European Convention for the Protection of Human Rights and Fundamental Freedoms. The right to be free from physical harm short of an act causing death is corollary to the right to life. Around this right and its corollary center those areas of our law relating to criminal homicide and civil actions for wrongful death, criminal assault in its various forms including mayhem and rape, and civil action to recover damages for personal injuries, both intentionally and negligently inflicted, in the great variety of situations under which they arise in modern life.

Property and Economic Rights. Basic to the exercise of the right to life is the right to hold property and to engage in economic activities related to gaining a livelihood. Around this right center those rather vast areas of the law which deal with the creation, enjoyment and transfer of interests in property, both real and personal; the making and enforcement of contracts; the formation and functioning of business and financial corporations; and the far-reaching processes of trade and commerce as they operate in today's complex society. Under this head falls logically, as a corollary, the relatively recent body of law involving the licensing and regulatory activities of our state and federal governments, and governmental programs of social security. It is, of course, interesting to note that the United Nations Universal Declaration of Human Rights contains no provision relating directly to property rights, although one of the rights stated is freedom to unite in the trade unions.

Spiritual Rights. Since under our conceptions "man does not live by bread alone," we have the third element of the classification as above stated—the right to live fully and freely in the spiritual realm. Around this right cluster some of the most enlightened constitutional guarantees, in the form of freedom of speech, freedom of the press and freedom of religion, as well as those segments of the common law which deal with such things as slander and libel and protection of the individual's right of privacy. For reasons primarily historical, because originally the law visualized only injury to tangible interests, writers and courts from time to time have referred to some of these essentially spiritual rights as "property" rights. But as long as they are protected their manner of classification is of secondary importance. In any event, they are appropriately considered apart from the general level of more mundane property interests.

Under the latter heading, too, may be brought the area of law which pertains particularly to family relationships. Family ties are not material. They are rather spiritual in the truest sense. We have seen this recognized in the Canon Law, which has properly held them to be within the province of the Church.

This statement of spiritual rights is substantially paralleled in the United Nations Universal Declaration of Human Rights. Freedom of thought, conscience and religion, freedom of opinion and expression, freedom of assembly, freedom of association, and right to marry and found a family are included there.

"Human" and "Property" Rights. The right to life is so fundamental that it is not open to question. In the United States the protection accorded spiritual rights by the Constitution is so inclusive as to remove such rights, also, from question. Perhaps in the nature of things, property rights are in a somewhat different category and may well be the subject of further comment before we pass on.

In recent years there have been controversies, sometimes vigorous, in the course of which persons emphasizing what they characterized as "human rights" have chided others not in full agreement with them —and incidentally our legal system and courts—for placing "property rights" above "human rights." So forceful have been such assertions at times that it would seem "property rights" have been relegated to a position of incompatibility with "human rights."

A moment's reflection will serve to convince, of course, that there is no basic incompatibility between "human rights," so called, and "property rights." The truth is, rather, that they are inseparable. We have material bodies and we live in a very material world. Our bare survival as human beings is conditioned upon possessing personally and being able to utilize freely such elementary items of property as food, and shelter from the elements in the form of housing and clothing. But the matter does not stop there. The voices which have been raised most strongly in insistence upon "human rights" have led the demand for universal participation in what we are wont to refer to as the "high standard of living" in America. Rising far above the level of the amount and quality of such food, clothing and housing as will suffice to sustain life, that standard has its present basis in such materialistic items of property, personally possessed and used, as automatically heated homes, electric and gas kitchens, frozen food lockers, radio and television sets, nylon hosiery and cosmetics, and automobiles which serve not only for quick and convenient transportation to and from work but also for pleasure tours on the long week-ends and regular paid-vacation periods now enjoyed by the masses. With the number of American families owning their own homes approaching 60% of the total in the surge of a sharply increasing trend, with 31,000,000 families in the United States owning automobiles, and with tens of millions of such other items as those just mentioned in use in homes ranging from rural farmsteads to city apartments and suburban mansions, it is commonplace that the personal ownership of "property" in abundance is the very foundation of the way of life which we today enjoy. And at the very heart of our free economic system is the production of "property" in its multitudinous forms, affording a livelihood to workers and remunerative employment of capital resources.

The Property Concept as Old as Civilization. The origin of the property concept was outlined by Sir William Blackstone in his Commentaries. He observed that in the beginning of the world, as we are informed by the Holy Writ, the Creator gave to man dominion over all the earth. The earth and all things therein are the general property of all mankind. It is reasonable to suppose that originally all was in common among men, and that every one took from the public stock to his own use such things as his immediate necessities required.

These general notions of property were sufficient to satisfy all the purposes of human life, and might perhaps still have answered them had it been possible for mankind to have remained in a state of primeval simplicity. But when mankind increased in number, craft and

ambition, it became necessary to entertain conceptions of more permanent dominion and to appropriate to individuals not the immediate
use only, but the very substance of the thing to be used. As human
life grew more and more refined, conveniences were devised to render
it more easy, commodious and agreeable; as habitations for shelter
and safety, and raiment for warmth and decency. But no man would
be at the trouble to provide either so long as he had only a usufruc-
tuary property in them, which was to cease the instant that he quitted
possession—if as soon as he walked out of his tent, or pulled off his
garment the next stranger who came by would have a right to inhabit
the one and to wear the other. In the case of habitations in particular, it was natural to observe that even the brute creation, to whom
everything else was in common, maintained a kind of permanent property in the dwellings, especially for the protection of their young; that
the birds of the air had nests and the beast of the field had caverns,
the invasion of which they esteemed a very flagrant injustice and would
sacrifice their lives to preserve them. Hence a property was soon
established in every man's house and homestead. And there can be no
doubt but that moveables of every kind became sooner appropriated
than the permanent substantial soil. To meet the need for food, eventually the art of agriculture developed, and by it was established the
idea of permanent property in the soil, vested in individuals.

In order to insure that property, recourse was had to civil society,
which brought along states, governments, laws, punishments and the
public exercise of religious duties. Thus connected together, it was
found that a part only of society was sufficient to provide, by their
manual labor, for the necessary subsistence of all; and leisure was
given to others to cultivate the human mind, to invent useful arts,
and to lay the foundations of science.

Continuous Recognition of Property Rights. Indeed, throughout
man's history under law to date, during which he has developed the
economic, educational and cultural institutions which have made for
the progress of civilization, "property rights" have been outstandingly
recognized and protected as a basic segment of "human rights." The
Decalogue itself bears witness to this. The Fourth Commandment
makes reference to "thy cattle." The Eighth Commandment adjures
"thou shalt not steal," and the Tenth Commandment "thou shalt not
covet thy neighbor's ox, nor his ass, nor anything that is thy neighbor's." Our Revolutionary forefathers were insistent upon the "essential natural right, that a man shall quietly enjoy, and have the
sole disposal of his property," and asserted that "the security of right

and property is the great end of government." As Roger Williams stipulated in the Acts and Orders agreed upon at the General Court of Election, held at Portsmouth, Rhode Island, in 1674, no one's property should be taken or molested "but by the lawful judgment of his Peeres, or by some known Law," for this, he declared, was end of the English common law. And, said he, the business of the state is civil justice, "which being of a materiall civille nature," has for its purpose the defense of persons, estates and liberties.

The Fifth Amendment to the Constitution of the United States placed property in the same category with "life" and "liberty" by providing that no person shall "be deprived of life, liberty or property without due process of law," and went on further to provide, "nor shall private property be taken for public use without just compensation." Following the Civil War, which we like to think of as having been waged for the vindication of human rights, there was adopted the Fourteenth Amendment, with its provision that "nor shall any state deprive any person of life, liberty or property without due process of law."

Recently the Supreme Court of the State of Washington has said that to own and manage property is a natural right. The Supreme Court of Illinois has said that the right of property is a fundamental right, and its protection is one of the most important objects of government. The Supreme Court of the United States has gone so far as to link together that "right of personal liberty" and "the right of private property" by saying that the right to make contracts for the acquisition of property partakes of the nature of each.

In the light of the foregoing considerations, any all-out disparagement of "property rights" is manifestly misplaced. There are, of course, many sharp restrictions on the use of property. The general welfare of all, and, in the last analysis, the personal welfare of the individual himself, forbids its uninhibited use. No principle is better settled than that there is no such thing as a right to own and use property in absolutely any manner that one desires: its owner and possessor is at all times limited by the condition that he cannot use it to bring injury or danger to his fellow citizens, or contrary to reasonable regulations laid down by law for the best interests of all. As the Supreme Court of Illinois has recently put it, every owner has the right to use his property in his own way and for his own purposes, subject only to the restraint necessary to secure the common welfare. This privilege was not created by the Constitution but existed before its adoption and is guaranteed by it. This privilege of a citizen to use his property according to his own will is both a liberty and a property right, subject always, however, to the police power of the state, under which new burdens may be imposed upon property and new restrictions placed upon its use when public welfare demands.

Property and Business in a Simple Economy. Granting the principle that "property rights" are an integral part of "human rights" to be grounded in sound moral and political theory as well as every-day practice in this country since Colonial days, any extreme complaints about putting "property rights" ahead of "human rights" may be largely discounted. We will be well advised, however, not to pass off such comments too superficially. Time may profitably be taken to scrutinize some of the developments which through the past century and a half have wrought great changes in our economic institutions and by their working have altered the relationship of "property" in many of its aspects to the life of the individual citizen. Here we may find, if not substantial justification for such asseverations as the above, at least a better understanding of the considerations which prompt them.

A visit to the unplumbed edifices which constituted the homes of Washington, Jefferson, Jackson and Lincoln, and to the primitive kitchens in which was prepared their daily fare, affords symbolic insight into the degree in which in the course of our history our manner of living has been made over. The change has been nothing short of revolutionary. For our present purposes, the most important thing to note is that as part of the process there have come fundamental alterations in the ownership of property as a tool of the individual to produce the elemental necessities of food, clothing and shelter. Not many generations back man had reached the stage of obtaining his food supply by applying his personal efforts to land in which he had some form of right; clothing came as a home-processed by-product of animals which he reared. To hold title in his own right to a piece of land upon which with his hands and the hands of his family a living could be produced represented fruition of one of the dearest hopes that a human being could entertain.

Fortunately for our forefathers individually, and for the welfare of our nation in its early period, from the outset America offered great opportunities in this regard. Hundreds of thousands of citizens left the relative security of the Atlantic Seaboard to strike into the vast wildernesses to the West, pushing farther and ever farther to acquire land of their own. It was to the great good fortune of these settlers and government alike that these lands were available, purchased from the Indians and made available to citizens as bounties for military service, under a general system of sales of small parcels with a low minimum price of $1.25 per acre, inaugurated in 1820, and under the Free Homestead Act of 1862. Following enactment of this latter Act, the lands beyond the Mississippi were partially peopled and the American economy strengthened by homesteading of approximately 90 million acres of land before the turn of the century. During the next few decades, an additional 175 million acres were transferred to homesteaders. In all, the Bureau of Land Management records show that title to about one billion acres of land in the United States has in the past been transferred by that agency, or its predecessors, to applicants under the public-land laws. As to the original ownership of these lands by the Indians, it has been said that practically all of the real estate acquired by the United States since 1776 was purchased not from Napoleon or any other emperor or czar but from its original Indian owners. After paying Napoleon fifteen million dollars for the cession of political authority over the Louisiana Territory, we proceeded to pay the Indian tribes of the ceded territory more than twenty times this sum for such lands in their possession as they were willing to sell. Whether the Indians received adequate remuneration remains to this day a much mooted question.

As the great areas of our nation became settled, agriculture developed; tools and wheeled vehicles came into growing use as aids to the cultivation of the soil and disposition of its products. Every few miles villages sprang up to serve the surrounding countryside. In these villages a blacksmith, operating with equipment decidedly primitive by modern standards, earned food, clothing and shelter for himself and his family by making and repairing such tools and vehicles and shoeing the horses which provided motive power for work and transportation. Another villager operated a grist mill to which farmers brought their grain to be ground into flour, paying for the service by leaving a part of it for the miller. On a similar basis another operated a molasses mill. Another supplemented his relatively leisurely activities as postmaster by stocking and selling such limited articles of merchandise as were available in those pioneer days. Such items as butter and eggs were brought in by neighboring farmers, who took their pay in sugar, coffee and calico. In timber country, small sawmills, set up in the woods, were the source of such lumber as was available.

In the communities of New England and elsewhere where manufacturing had its beginnings, the enterprises were individually financed and controlled, or were partnerships of local citizens. The use of the corporation as a business entity was originally restricted by government under the reasonably-grounded theory that it held a serious threat to the system of personal individual enterprise. Even as trade and commerce grew, stimulated by such inventions as the steam engine, the Bessemer process, the cotton gin, the reaper, the telephone and telegraph and other applications of electricity, accompanied by the growing penetration of the continent by railroads, the corporate form by which alone adequate capital could be provided for many enterprises was implemented by local entrepreneurs, to whose individual zeal many a village electric light plant, creamery, telephone system, carriage and wagon factory, harness works or other industrial institution stood as a tangible monument of local business attainment to which the eyes of the community were turned in pride.

There are Americans now living who can look back through the years to the days of which we have just been speaking and who pronounce them good, not only because the individual had it in his power to be so largely his own master, but for the broader reason that then and there were laid the foundations of true national strength. In these men and events is found exemplification for the "widespread belief" eloquently voiced by Justice Louis D. Brandeis of the United States Supreme Court that "the true prosperity of our past came not from big business, but through the courage, the energy and the resourcefulness of small men." We can be entirely safe in saying that to these men there was no line of demarcation between "human rights" and "property rights."

The Impact of Modern Forces. The days of "small men" were not to last. Their institutions, however bravely conceived and resourcefully administered, were doomed to undergo the changes inflicted by the passing of time and the inexorable material forces which accompanied it. We have already hinted at the business and technological development which picked up momentum and within a few decades was surging forward at a headlong pace, subjecting the individual proprietor in some fields to pressures against which he found it increasingly difficult to stand. The advent of the internal combustion engine, giving notice of the taking over of the automobile and mechanized farming, signaled the tapering off and ultimate passing of the horse and buggy age. After years of increasingly meager returns the village blacksmith closed his shop with its forge and simple tools. The stones of the local grain processor lay silent, yielding to the great mills of Minneapolis. The village hardware merchant, the proprietor of the "dry goods" store and the haberdasher, found their enterprises increasingly encroached upon by great mail-order establishments in Chicago, branches of which became accessible at the retail level throughout the United States as the automobile and hard roads came into their own; one after another the individual stores were closed. The village grocer found himself confronted by a large local unit of a chain of perhaps hundreds of other grocery stores, enjoying the advantage of a new building, large-scale purchasing power and almost limitless financial resources. Gradually the individual grocers succumbed. Thus, although no law of legislative or judicial origin purported to take from the local blacksmith, the miller and the merchant —symbolic of the individualistic business enterprise of the earlier days —the right to hold and use their business properties, they found themselves in the grip of economic forces whose workings were even more constant and inexorable than judicial decrees.

As and when the blacksmith, the miller and the merchant found themselves without ability to gain their livelihood by using tools and facilities that were their own, force of circumstances placed them in the position where they were in effect compelled to go to work for some one else, perhaps on the assembly line of an industrial city. Even though they found employment managing a local unit of an outside business the routine became impersonalized because they were operating under general orders from some one else and with property which did not belong to them.

In the case of the small community corporations to which reference has been made, as time went on their stockholders, personally directing their affairs, found themselves confronted by much more powerful corporate organizations, engaged in similar lines, with whose superior resources of research, production and salesmanship they could not cope. Our ideal was just as much one of economic freedom as of political freedom, and even at the time of adoption of the Federal Constitution Thomas Jefferson had complained of the omission of restrictions of monopolies. Opposition to monopoly began on the state level. Many states embodied provisions against monopoly, in one form or another, in their constitutions or laws. In 1890 Congress enacted the Sherman Anti-Trust Act applicable to interstate monopolies, which Chief Justice Hughes of the Supreme Court of the United States characterized as "a charter of freedom," going on to say that it "has a generality and adaptability comparable to that found to be desirable in constitutional provisions. It does not go into detailed definitions which might either work injury to legitimate enterprise or through particularization defeat its purposes by providing loopholes for escape. Its general phrases, interpreted to attain its fundamental objects, set up the essential standard of reasonableness." But whatever the purpose of such legislation, or its desirability, it did not stay the course of economic events. Whether making their power felt through superior competitive advantages, or by persuasive solicitation to submit to absorption, the larger enterprises, except in specialized fields, eventually took over. So strong and perhaps inevitable was the trend that however much the anti-trust laws may have accomplished in keeping open the field for competitors of the relative stature of Goliath, such laws appear, in retrospect, to have had little or no effect by way of preserving a way of economic life for the Davids. Here, as in many other connections, the limitations of the law become apparent. Before the impact of powerful custom or basic economic forces it can only bend or break.

Even on the farms of America, the changes were revolutionary. Those generations who with intense love of the soil had homesteaded the public lands passed away. Growing industrialization held out the increasing attractions of urban life, including short work weeks and minimized personal responsibilities. In consequence, the proportion in which American farms constituted the owner's home and were worked by owners steadly lessened, reaching the point where in some regions more than half of the farms are being worked by tenants. Even in the rich agricultural areas of the Middle West around half of the farms have come to be operated by tenants, and in the face of present trends doubt is frequently expressed as to whether what is sometimes referred to as the "family-size farm" can survive. Without security of tenure, it is difficult for a farm tenant, not having the incentive that goes with ownership of one's property, to look upon the soil he occupies for the time being as other than a transitory means of livelihood, here today and perhaps gone tomorrow.

Present Day Ownership and Usage of Property. Whatever may be said as to social attitudes, without property in the form of great factories and assembly lines, far-flung transportation systems, the assets of nation-wide trade and financial organizations and millions of pieces of paper in the shape of commercial instruments constantly circulating, there could not be production and distribution of the vast aggregate of goods to which we have referred above as being possessed and enjoyed by Americans in general. Property must have an owner. Enough has been said already to make understandable the rather complete extent to which large corporations have taken over in the field of business and industry. These corporations own, in large part, America's tools of manufacture, transportation and finance. Translating the situation into its lowest terms in the language of ownership, many millions of citizens, many thousands of charitable organizations and educational institutions, many scores and perhaps hundreds of trustees of pension funds hold the shares of stock in these corporations and therefore in the last analysis own these tools. But only in rare instances do they have adequate comprehension of the working of these tools. The ownership of the average shareholder is relatively so small as to make possible at most no more than an insignificant impact, individually, upon the corporate affairs.

Moreover, as has already been said, between the stockholders and the men and women who actually operate the factory assembly lines, the rolling and flying stock of transportation and the business machines in the counting houses, there lies an insulating layer of "management." "Management" has been a concomitant of growth of corporate size to the point where the stockholders as the owners of the business could not sufficiently grasp and deal with the problems involved, and consequently found it necessary to employ professional business experts to devote full time to supervision of the corporate operations. Though these managers operate the business, they may not own so much as a single share of stock in it. Thus, we have not only the actual operations of the tools by millions of workers who have no proprietary interest in the facilities, but also the actual direction of the whole process by one who commonly has no more legal ownership in the facilities than the workers whom he has authority to employ and discharge. To the millions of stockholders, as to the landlords of farms tenanted by others, property ownership comes to be a rather impersonal thing, tending to become without relation to pride of product or any feeling of the warranted satisfaction that normally accompanies personal production of something that adds to the world's comfort, convenience or happiness.

From the foregoing analysis it is evident that we have passed from a stage of society in which the individual's ability to earn a living was dependent upon his acquiring for himself the tools and facilities—and in which as a matter of course he made it his business to acquire them —which he employed in the process, to one in which a majority of our citizenry, realizing that for them this is no longer possible, tend to develop the feeling that the responsibility for providing such necessary tools and facilities rests upon others, and take such provision pretty much for granted. Here is the key to a possible profound change in the point of view as to property and property rights, carrying with it trends calculated to modify if not alter the conceptions of property law which were held in an earlier day. It is one thing for property in pretty much all its forms to be owned by individuals directly, and used by them personally. Under such a regime "property rights" were indissolubly identified with the individual's means of livelihood, universally recognized as meriting the fullest protection of the law. It is another thing for the overwhelmingly great segment of "property" which is today employed for production and distribution to be provided by absentee owners, commonly corporate, whose identity is sensed only remotely, if at all. Where the owner and user were the same, and the ownership of property was tied in with earning the wherewithal with which to live, there was no possibility of a clash of interests and no question about "property rights" being fully identifiable with "human rights." But under a regime where the user has no direct property right in the tools and facilities with which he works for his livelihood, and may even have a sense of resentful frustration because of that fact, and the provider of such tools and facilities depends for livelihood upon financial return from the capital investment therein, the stage is set for controversy.

Certainly there is a school of thought which draws a sharp line of demarcation between "human rights" and "property rights," excluding from the category of "human rights" all property interests which are not personally and intimately identifiable with the high standard of living of which we have spoken; retaining as assimilable to "human rights" only those "property rights" associated to make life in the home and in leisure time more comfortable and pleasant. Carrying the analysis through, the owner of the property used for production and distribution is alleged to have only a "property right," whereas the operator of the facilities is allegedly in position to assert, in economic controversies, a "human right."

Once the elements involved are understood, a conclusion as to "human rights" and "property rights" terminology is perhaps not particularly important. If the concept identifying "property rights" with "human rights" remains applicable, the situation involves only a potential conflict over the "human rights" of two groups of citizens. This concept must govern, at least in some degree, because such conflict as there is revolves, in the last analysis, around who shall receive "how much" in the way of prosperity; the employee group asserting its claim to be able to enjoy more abundant "property rights" in the form of such various adjuncts to a high standard of living as have been suggested, "guaranteed" in so far as possible by contractual expedients, and the owners of the tools and facilities insisting upon recognition of their "property rights" in the form of what they regard as an adequate return from their property which provides the economic sinews of the enterprise, and upon the profits for which they are dependent for their livelihood. The owners would of course insist, also, that the return should be sufficient to permit of plowing back into the business the wherewithal for expansion, which would in turn provide employment for the more workers to come. And in the present era, around half of the net income goes for the payment of federal income tax, save for the smaller corporations.

The Stake of All Citizens in Property and Business Law. Coming, as we must, to the conclusion that property ownership is common to practically all citizens, whatever may be the semantics of classification there is no question but that all look to the law and depend upon its principles and procedures to protect their ownership and enjoyment of their homes and possessions of whatsoever nature. The legal interests of the small home-owners are identifiable in their working with the basic principles of law which operate to protect the interests of the owners of the property which they operate on assembly line or in office. In short, whatever weight may be given to the idea that in our present society there is a clash between "human rights" and "property rights," the fact remains that all citizens, whatever may be their economic classification, have a stake in a body of law which protects the individual's right to own and use property in accordance with his desires, subject only to such restraint as the greater good of all finds it essential to impose.

The Problem of Reconciliation of Interests. Early in our study, when we were considering the law of ancient Egypt, we referred to the perpetual problem of the law by way of making accommodation between the conflicting interests of human beings. The problem becomes more intensified with the increasing recognition of the rights of the individual.

We start with the obvious premise that these basic rights of each individual should be respected and that he should be given the utmost opportunity to develop those qualities of learning and character that are conducive to what we sometimes refer to as the good life. Our form of government, our law and our political and social policies are pointed in that direction. But the end sought is not easy of attainment. As we have seen, if there were only one human being on earth, because his conduct could be of no concern to any one else he could follow fully his own devices in all the affairs of life. With each individual living in a world of other individuals, the conduct of each impinges on his neighbors. The conduct of groups of individuals impinges on other groups, and the conduct of nations on other nations.

From the first the problem has been to reconcile the interest of the individual with the interests of his fellows. In a simple society this was difficult enough. The problem has grown increasingly perplexing with the developing complexities of economic and social organization. We have reached the point where we must face it in the light of such challenging conclusions as Father De Chardin has recently expressed in a UNESCO symposium. Because of the rapid increase of economic ethnic and social ties, said he, the individual is drawn in an irresistible process directed toward the establishment on earth of an independent organo-psychic system, and whether we like it or not, humanity is totalizing itself. In our time, he further stated, the emphasis of the need of a new definition of the rights of men must be no longer as hitherto, to secure the greatest possible independence for the human unit in society, but to lay down the conditions under which the inevitable totalization of humanity is to take place in such a way as not to destroy but to enhance in each of us not independence but— what is quite a different thing—the incommunicable uniqueness of the being within us.

Whether or not it be felt that Father De Chardin is unduly pessimistic for the future of the individual, the fact remains that since the day of Magna Charta our law has devoted itself to this task of adjusting the interests of individuals. Fittingly, indeed, the American Bar Association, in July, 1957, erected at Runnymede a monument bearing the inscription, "To commemorate Magna Charta—Symbol of Freedom Under Law." As our law's ultimate concern has been, so will it continue to be to safeguard the rights of the individual citizen, holding all of equal dignity and limiting the exercise of these rights only in the demonstrated interest of the common good.

Safeguarding Individual Rights. Inasmuch as the major concern of our law and government is with individual rights, we may well concentrate our further studies on a consideration of their safeguards. In large part that is what we will be doing. Before passing on, however, something more may appropriately be said as to the general source of these rights from the historical point of view. And to promote better understanding of the significance of future references to "common law rights," "statutory rights," and "constitutional rights," there should be a brief explanation of how in accepted usages and customs of the people and apart from legislative statutes the English common law began, how legislative statutes from time to time amended it and introduced new rights, how it was brought to our country by the American colonists, and how the framers of our Federal Constitution and of the constitutions of the several states incorporated many of its basic principles into the supreme law of the land. This will be attempted in the chapters which follow.

CHAPTER 17

NATURE AND SOURCES OF THE COMMON LAW

Immutable Principles of Justice Translated into Experience. James Madison once said that with little regard to precise meaning the common law has been called our birthright. Actually our birthright is from a much higher source than the common or any other human law. In the words of the Supreme Court of the United States, the cardinal principles of justice are immutable. These principles inhere in the very idea of free government, and are incapable of impairment by legislation or judicial decision.

The common law has come about as men have translated these immutable principles of justice into the language of every-day experience, working against the handicap that makes men fallible. Nevertheless, while our legislators no longer claim divine sanctions for their enactments and our judges no longer claim that their decisions are divinely inspired, the law is still something more than a mere matter of mundane being. Lord Macmillian has recently quoted with approval Edward Jenks' provisional definition of law as the force or tendency which makes for righteousness. The conventional boundaries which are drawn between things human and things divine are after all only the expedients of convenience. Although law and religion have severed their original conjunction, we cannot by our divisions destroy the essential unity of man's nature. So long as we believe that man is spirit as well as matter, so long as we believe that peace, order and good government concern our souls as well as our bodies and our estates, the law will continue to possess for us a certain divinity and a certain authority derived from higher sources than the statute books or the volumes of the law reports. Justice can never shed her majestic and godlike attributes, no matter what humble details she may condescend in the regulation of the affairs of our daily lives.

Athena, it would seem, sprang from the head of Jove of full physical stature and completely armed and endowed for either active service in war or council in peace. But it is unnecessary to say that the common law of England had no such marvelous and instantaneous origin. It was the growth of many centuries—centuries of actual conflicts and

343

contentions, not only between government, as such, and the people, but also between the people themselves. It was the product of experience and of knowledge derived from experience. As Justice Harlan F. Stone has pointed out, it was characterized by its development of law by a system of judicial precedent, by its use of the jury to decide issues of fact, and by its all-pervading doctrine of the supremacy of law—that the agencies of government are no more free than the private individual to act according to their own arbitrary will or whim, but must conform to legal rules developed and applied by courts.

Common Law the Beneficiary of Earlier Civilization. No student of jurisprudence would be so superficial as to overlook the indebtedness of the common law to the civilizations which preceded its advent. At the very outset of our study we acknowledged our indebtedness in this regard, and in the present connection it must be emphasized again. The English obligation was acknowledged by Sir William Holdsworth when he said: "We have received Roman law; but we have received it in small homeopathic doses, at different periods and as and when required. It has acted as a tonic to our native legal system, and not as a drug or poison. When received it has never been continuously developed on Roman lines. It has been naturalized and assimilated; and, with its assistance, our wholly independent system has, like the Roman law itself, been gradually and continuously built up, by the development of old and the creation of new rules to meet the needs of a changing civilization and an expanding empire."

Rather than to attempt to trace the relationship of the past to the common law of today a chart is appended, with the thought of portraying graphically the relation of the common law to the various elements and institutions which have contributed to fill its reservoir through the centuries of its development.

The Common Law Not Legislatively Enacted. The basic characteristic of the English common law is that it was not and is not dependent for its existence or recognition upon enactment by any legislative body. Rather, the common law antedates formal legislatures as instruments of government. As was pointed out at the outset, human beings cannot live together without law. As they came together in some sort of a state of civilization, rules of conduct became essential. By gradual acceptance such rules came into existence, developing and changing in accordance with the pressures of circumstances and the ideas of the people. Thus were formed the "customs" of which we have been speaking in past connections, and which, as we

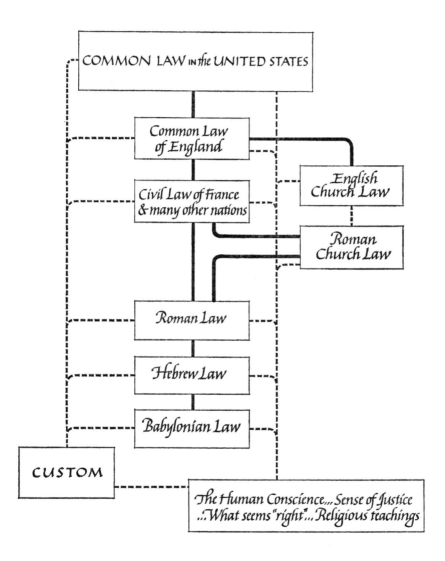

have seen, have played a part in all systems of law. But under the common law of England they were characterized by being accorded a fullness of sway, and were not always threatened by the despotic whims of rulers who made law a means to the end of their own personal aggrandizement.

At any rate, here was "law"—rules which regulated conduct—and which existed before the race had the capacity or the facilities to put it into written form. For the double reason that it was not formally codified, and that it regulated human conduct before the race got around to creating legislative assemblies in the formal sense, it could not by any stretch of the imagination be called "statute" law.

Here we have the real key to understanding of what we mean by the "common law" as an ultimate concept. Under this concept, rules of conduct, regulating the relationships between men, are not in any sense dependent upon formal legislative enactment. As the term "common law" implies, it is composed of rules "common" to the social group. It is a law arising directly out of the experience of people as they lived with each other and carried on the various activities of life, social and commercial. From generation to generation its elements have been passed along as a cumulation of human experience and conclusions, with roots in many sources. The Supreme Court of Errors of Connecticut was not far from the mark when it defined the common law as the prevailing sense of the more enlightened members of a particular community, expressed through the instrumentality of the courts as to those rules of conduct which should be definitely affirmed and given effect under the sanction of organized society, in view of the particular circumstances of the time, but with due regard to the necessity that the law should be reasonable, and hence that its principles have permanency, and its development be by an orderly process.

Recognition and Application of the Common Law. From what has been said thus far with particular reference to the nature of the common law, it sounds, perhaps, like a somewhat vague and undefined thing. How are the rules "which should be definitely affirmed and given effect under the sanction of organized society" to be recognized? How are they to be promulgated? Presumably, under our concepts every one is entitled to know them. If they are not to be found primarily in statute books, how can they be ascertained?

The answer is indicated by the above statement that they are "expressed through the instrumentality of the courts." To get an idea of the working of our common-law courts in England and the United

States, let us go back a century or so in point of time, and imagine ourselves in an English courtroom. The judge is hearing a case in which Cratchit is suing Chuzzlewit for the price of a cow. Cratchit's testimony is that Chuzzlewit bought a cow off him, and promised to pay for her an agreed sum on May 1st thereafter. May 1st came and went; Chuzzlewit did not pay and still has not paid. Chuzzlewit's testimony is that after the cow was delivered to him and while he was driving her to his own pasture, she slipped into a pond along the road-side and she was drowned; therefore, being without any benefit by the transaction he should not have to pay. There is no statute prescribing any rule to settle the matter, yet it is an event of everyday life calling for solution by legal processes. In dealing with it the English common law judge is right at home. He knows it to be the consensus of the community that agreements should be lived up to; such is right and just. It seems right and just, furthermore, that inasmuch as Chuzzlewit received delivery of the cow in good order, he should take the risk thereafter, so he rules that Chuzzlewit must pay.

Let us suppose, on the other hand, Chuzzlewit's testimony to be that when he bought the cow he said to Cratchit, "Do you warrant her to be in good health?" and that Cratchit responded, "I do," and that the next day after he got the cow home she collapsed from a pre-existing infection and shortly thereafter died. The judge, being satisfied that the fact was as thus testified to by Chuzzlewit, rules that there was a breach of warranty by Cratchit which absolves Chuzzlewit from any obligation to pay. This, again, is right and just.

In this rather crude example we have an illustration of the common law in action and a basis for understanding how it developed and was declared. Through the centuries the courts of England were called upon to deal with the disputes and misunderstandings of the times. Out of their adjudications, recorded in judicial records and ultimately put in printed form, came a steadily broadening body of principles relating to the rights and obligations of men in the affairs of life.

An "Unequalled Treasure of Instances." James Bryce summed up the inherent vitality of the common law when he pointed out that the merits of our English case law system were considerable. It is an abiding honor to our lawyers and judges to have worked it out with a completeness and success unknown to any other country. They have accumulated in the reports an unequalled treasure of instances, conjunctions of circumstances raising points of law, far more numerous than the most active intellects could have imagined. These points have been argued with the keenness which personal interest supplies, and decided under that sense of responsibility which the judge feels when he knows not only that his judgment is to determine the pecuniary value or social protection of suitors, but also that it is to constitute a rule which will be canvassed by the bench and bar and find its place in volumes that will be studied long after he has quitted this mortal scene. There is practicability about English case law, a firm grasp of facts and reality as well as a richness and variety, which cannot be looked for in legal treatises composed even by the ablest and most conscientious private persons, who writing in their studies have not been enlightened by forensic discussion, nor felt themselves surrounded by the halo of official dignity. If the treatises of the great Roman jurists do to a large extent possess these same merits, it is because they were, in a measure, public officers, and because much of the law they contain arose out of concrete cases.

The Common Law in America. When our English forefathers came to America they brought with them, as a matter of course, the common law. They expected that its salutary principles would be accorded full recognition in the new world, as is evidenced by the Declaration of Rights of the Continental Congress in which it was asserted that "the respective colonies are entitled to the Common Law of England."

In accordance with the principles of the common law itself, no legislative pronouncement that it was in effect was essential to its institution by our forefathers as the guide for their relationship with each other in the new land. But to this day there are legislative enactments on the statute books of many of our states evidencing its formal recognition. The Illinois statute is typical. It provides:

"The common law of England, so far as the same is applicable and of a general nature, and all statutes or acts of the British Parliament made in aid of, and to supply the defects of the common law (with certain named exceptions), shall be the rule of decision, and shall be considered in full force until repealed by legislative authority."

To all intents and purposes, then, our legal history began with that of the mother country. The rights which are ours today had their inception in the English law of centuries ago. Even in recent years the courts of America have found it necessary at times to examine the laws and constitutional principles of England which were very old when the federal convention met in Philadelphia in 1787.

"No Wrong Without a Remedy." From now on we will find a sharp departure from the kind of law and legal institutions which have been depicted in the earlier portion of this work. From the ancient days, to the present as we have noted it in the Iron Curtain nations, we

have found law to be in large part a rule of conduct laid down and enforced by despotic ukase. That the source of the ukase was sometimes ecclesiastical rather than secular in no way mitigated its impact. We have seen that from time to time there were written codes which, by introducing some certainty of content so that it could be known what the law was, made for a somewhat better measure of justice. Out of Rome there came eventually Roman Law, a codification which has met exacting tests as a system of formal written law, and which as we have seen is in force throughout much of the world today. But in all this there has been nothing like the Anglo-Saxon system of common law, the crowning excellence of which is that under its conceptions "there can be no wrong without a remedy." To this basic concern of the common law may be traced such constitutional provisions as that in the Bill of Rights of the Constitution of Illinois, which states that every person ought to find a certain remedy in the laws for all injuries and wrongs which he may receive in his person, property or reputation; he ought to obtain, by law, right and justice freely, and without being obliged to purchase it, completely and without denial, promptly and without delay.

A Boundless Reservoir of Rights. The common law, so conceived, might be thought of as a boundless reservoir of individual rights from which the courts of our states may freely draw for their decisions. Sir Maurice Sheldon Amos indicated its broad expanse when he said that the common law displays throughout the marks of its origin in the system of government administered in the Middle Ages at Westminster, a system in which judicial procedure played so large a part. The common law speaks to us of the High Court of Parliament, of sheriffs, of grand juries and their presentments, of coroners and their inquests, of the prerogative writs of habeas corpus, quo warranto, mandamus, prohibition, and certiorari, of petitions of right, of the Attorney General and the informations he may file, of the fiats he may refuse, and of the *nolle prosequis* he may enter; and it speaks to us of the chancellor and the jurisdiction he exercises.

Common Law Under Our Federal System. In making the broad generalization that the people of the United States live under the common law system, and that the common law itself prevails in so far as constitution or statute states no other applicable rule, there are some considerations which we must have in mind that do not have application to the common law as it is known in England.

One of these considerations relates to our federal form of government, under the operation of which governmental powers are divided

between the federal government and the several states. As we have
just seen, the English Colonies followed the common law, and in general it has been carried through and is a part of the law of the several
states. But state law is one thing; federal law is an entirely different
matter. We did not start as a federal government, and when the
federal government was established the common law did not become
a part of its body of law. As Justice Brandeis observed in the famous
case of *Erie Railroad Co. v. Tompkins* there is no federal common law.
We can understand the significance of this by glancing at the operation
of the courts of the United States Government. Inasmuch as there
is no federal common law, it follows that the law of the federal government which they apply is to be found in statutes or the federal
constitution. In other words, all federal law is constitutional or
statutory, with the Congress of the United States supplying the statutes.

But not all the law which the United States courts are vested with
jurisdiction to apply is federal law. Section 2 of Article III of the
Constitution vests the United States courts with jurisdiction of cases
between citizens of different states, subject only to the requirement that
a certain money amount (now $3,000) be involved. This means that
if a legal controversy arises between a citizen of Illinois and a citizen
of Connecticut, say, suit may be brought in a United States court in
either Illinois or Connecticut. It is not necessary that an issue involving federal law be involved. It may be a simple automobile accident
case, or dispute over an insurance policy, involving only principles of
the common law. In accordance with the rule laid down in *Erie Railroad Co. v. Tompkins* the United States court will here apply the substantive common law rules of the state in which it sits. For enlightenment as to those rules it looks to the decisions of the highest court
of that state. If it finds no decision in point, it, itself, will adopt as
its guiding rule of law such principle as a court of that state would, in
its best judgment, adopt if it were dealing with the same case.

In the chapters which follow we will take note of some of the main
elements of the common law from the standpoint of its substantive
content, and also of its workings as a fully-rounded system of jurisprudence.

Roman and Civil Law Elements in American Law. There is another consideration to be taken into account before we proceed to take
note of some of the main elements of the common law from the standpoint of its substantive content and of its workings as a fully-rounded
system of jurisprudence. That relates to the influence of the Roman

and civil law in certain portions of the United States, to which we have already made brief reference in our discussion of Roman law.

It is a matter of historical fact that certain areas of our country were not primarily under the prior influence of English colonists, as was true along the Atlantic Seaboard. Louisiana was settled by the French about 1700, and was later ceded by France to Spain, under whose rule it remained until shortly before it became a part of the United States in 1803. The law instituted by both regimes was essentially Roman Law, Spanish Law being essentially Roman and the Civil Code of France being based directly upon Roman Law. Much of the Southwest was originally a province of Mexico and a Spanish possession, the law of which was also the law of Spain. In these areas, therefore, the common law of England was not originally in force. As students of jurisprudence we would reasonably expect that the law under which the people lived would not change abruptly with the advent of a new government, and, in so far as it pertained to rights in property and commercial practice, very slowly if at all.

Understanding that revolutionary upheavals such as we have glanced at in Russia and China may bring a whole legal system crashing to earth, such consequences are not a concomitant of relatively peaceful transitional change. The story of Bogigish would tell us that, and our expectation is borne out as to such states as Louisiana, Texas, California, New Mexico, Arizona and Nevada, where the system of community property, indigenous to the Roman Law, has continued in effect to the present day. This came into the Roman Law through introduction by the Visigoths, who, as we have noted, invaded Spanish and French areas of the Roman Empire in the early part of the Fifth Century A.D. In the wake of the decay of the Roman Empire in the fourth and fifth centuries, the advancing Visigoths carried with them into Spain the custom of a marital community of goods, and as early as 693 A.D. this custom had been reduced to written form in the Visigothic Code or Fuero Juzgo. Later Spanish codes dealt with community property in greater detail, so that at the time of the Spanish colonization of Central and North America it formed a comprehensive system, which was subsequently adopted by those states and Latin American countries that were formerly Spanish possessions. Texas, after achieving its independence from Mexico, retained in large part the community property system of Spain and Mexico, with the basic idea of a marital partnership and with the Spanish definition of separate and community property.

An extended consideration of the difference between the community property system of the Roman law and the common law property system is not called for here. Suffice it to say that under the common law of marital rights the wife has a dower interest in all real estate owned by her husband during the marriage, giving her the right at his death to one-third of such real estate for as long as she lives. The husband has an estate of curtesy in all real estate owned by his wife during marriage, giving him the right to all of it, after her death, for his lifetime, provided issue was born alive. Statutory modifications have assimilated curtesy to dower and altered the common law rule in detail, but in substance it remains the same in that either spouse has a contingent interest, usually one-third, in all real estate owned by the other during marriage, such interest being held for the life of the survivor.

Under the community property system, on the other hand, the spouses may hold separate and apart from each other real estate owned individually at the time of marriage, and property acquired after marriage by gift, devise or descent. However real property otherwise acquired during marriage belongs, as it is expressed, to the "community," the idea being that whatever is acquired by the efforts of either husband or wife belongs one-half to each.

Understandably, then, allowance must be made for the presence of some substantive elements in the body of our American law which vary from the common law. This is altogether compatible with the working of the common law system, with its accepted principle that because of diversity of local conditions some diversity of rule of law as between states is to be expected and may be highly desirable. Our states have been regarded as individual laboratories for experiments in law making. Of major importance is the fact that the basic procedural principles of the common law are in force in all states, those of the Southwest included. The operation of our federal system with its basic common law procedures in the federal courts has promoted uniformity. It may accordingly be said that the common law prevails generally throughout the United States.

Where Today's Common Law Is Found. It was stated hereinabove that the common law is sometimes referred to as the "Unwritten Law." In its early stage, when people were none too literate and there was no way of keeping adequate records there was accuracy in such a characterization. But today, having it in mind as that segment of our body of law declarative of rights which are not specifically set forth in constitution or statute, it no longer remains unwritten, save in so far as it remains to be determined in application to the constantly developing new situations and conditions which are a part of life itself. As we realize, there will always be a time lag in this connection, but the main body of the common law is now in print, to be found in the thousands of volumes of printed opinions of the highest courts of our states, and in the opinions of the United States courts and the Supreme Court of the United States. The process of "finding" it there is of course a technical one, the acquisition of proficiency in which involves one of the most important phases of a lawyer's education.

In the following chapters we will glance at the actual content and working of the common law as it performs its function of vindicating the rights of the individual and, in the process, weighs in the balance the interests of his fellows.

CHAPTER 18

COMMON LAW LIABILITY FOR INTENTIONAL WRONGS

The General Principle. A characteristic of the common law is that through the operation of a few basic rules of conduct, developing through the processes that we have just been sketching, it provides a basis for solving the great body of controversies that accompany living in a civilized society which recognizes the rights of which we have spoken in a preceding chapter.

For example, one of these basic rules that developed at common law was that there was a cause of action whenever one person did damage to another wilfully and intentionally, and without just cause or excuse. Here is a broad principle, indeed, which has found application in many detailed connections, at some of which we shall glance.

Assault and Battery. Assault and battery provides a clear-cut example of intentional injury, for which the common law provided recovery. The terms "assault" and "battery" are commonly linked together, and in practice quite generally belong together, as more often than not an assault includes a battery. They are, however, distinct. A battery, as the term implies, involves actual physical contact. An assault does not. An assault is committed by A if by a menacing act he creates in B a reasonable apprehension of physical injury. To illustrate, if A points a gun at B in a threatening manner it is an assault, and it is an assault even though the gun was not loaded if B had reasonable cause to believe it might be. If A throws a missile at B and hits him it is a battery; if he misses, it is an assault. The common situation is, of course, where A attacks B with fists or weapon and physically injures or kills B, in which event both assault and battery are committed.

In such situations, unless A can prove some just cause or excuse to warrant his action he is liable to respond in damages to B. Under some circumstances a person is warranted in using physical force to protect himself, and, if so warranted, he cannot be held liable for assault and battery. This principle is well illustrated by the case of *Burdon v. Wood.*

Zola Burdon, widow of Robert Burdon, brought suit on the death statute for alleged wrongful killing of Robert. To Zola's complaint the defendant, Clarence Wood, filed an answer admitting the killing but asserting that he acted in self defense. The evidence at the trial was that Robert was a bartender, employed at a roadhouse in Henderson County, Kentucky, of which Clarence had been the manager. Robert's working hours were from 6 p.m. to 2 a.m. On the evening prior to the shooting Clarence and his wife with other friends visited roadhouses in the vicinity. Clarence lived in a trailer parked behind the roadhouse which he managed and where Robert worked. Returning from going the rounds on the night in question about 2 a.m., he retired in the trailer. About 7:30 he heard an argument going on in loud tones in the barroom. He went in there and found Robert, who had remained drinking after his shift at 2 a.m., standing behind the bar and arguing with another employee. The day bartender was at work behind the bar, filling an icebox with cokes. Clarence passed behind the bar to go to the water cooler for a drink, and as he passed Robert he admonished him to quit arguing. After getting the drink he returned past Robert, who was renewing the argument; in a sharper tone he told him to quit arguing and go home. Robert retorted that he did not have to take orders from anybody, that he would do as he "damned please," and that he would blow the "damned brains out" of Clarence. Thereupon Robert pulled his gun and fired a shot at Clarence, which missed. Instantly, Clarence pulled his gun and fired from the hip at Robert. One shot went through Robert's head, and shortly thereafter he died.

Self-Defense. At the close of all the evidence in the Burdon case, counsel for Clarence, the defendant, made a motion for a directed verdict. This is a procedural motion, generally made by defendants' counsel at this stage of the trial. Its legal effect is to raise the point that even though all the evidence adduced by plaintiff be conceded to be true, even looking at the matter most favorably from plaintiff's standpoint he has not made out a "case" upon which he is entitled to recover against defendant. Therefore, defendant is asking the trial judge to "direct" the jury to bring in a verdict for defendant, not submitting the evidence to them for their deliberation and finding, because there is not before the court sufficient evidence upon which any verdict for plaintiff could reasonably be postulated. In the Burdon case, the trial judge overruled the motion and let the case go to the jury. The jury brought in a verdict for Zola and awarded her damages. Counsel for Clarence appealed from the judgment on the verdict, contending that the trial court erred in not granting defendant's motion for a directed verdict.

The Court of Appeals, sustaining this contention, reversed the judgment. The Court of Appeals agreed that upon a showing that Clarence shot and killed Robert, a prima facie case of wrongful death was made out, and it then became the duty of Clarence to justify the killing. In his answer Clarence denied that his act was wilful, wrongful, grossly negligent or without provocation, as alleged in plaintiff's complaint. He alleged that he shot Robert in self defense. The law of self-defense applicable to the defense of one's person may be stated thus: If one is in a place where he has a right to be and is himself without fault, and he is assailed by another armed with a deadly weapon, he may repel force with force without retreating, even to the point of taking his assailant's life, if he believes and has reasonable cause to believe that he is in danger of losing his life or of suffering great bodily harm at the hands of his assailant.

The Court of Appeals pointed out that Clarence was president and general manager of the corporation which owned the roadhouse and had a right to be in the barroom. His admonition to Robert to cease quarreling and go home because the employees had to get along together was not a wrongful act but was in keeping with his duty as manager. The only inference possible from the evidence was that Robert, who had been drinking and quarreling, assaulted Clarence in anger with a deadly weapon. Clarence repelled the assault without retreating, as he had a right to do. The Court said it did not think that reasonable men could disagree with the proposition that Clarence had reason to believe that his life was in danger or that he was in danger of receiving great bodily harm at the hands of his assailant. No one could have stood in the shoes of Clarence at that moment without fearing death or great bodily harm. When Clarence fired, he had a right to act upon the appearance of things which could not spell anything but great danger to his person. Concluding that the trial court should have granted the motion for directed verdict, the Court of Appeals entered an order of reversal.

False Imprisonment. Another specific example of intentional wrong, remediable under the common law, is false imprisonment, which is the unlawful restraint of a person contrary to his will. The restraint need not necessarily be effected by physical contact; any demonstration of physical power which to all appearances can be avoided only by submission, operates to constitute an imprisonment. Moreover, restraint by fear of a personal difficulty may amount to false imprisonment.

An illustrative case is *Jacques v. Childs Dining Hall Company*. Plaintiff Bessie Jacques, with her aunt, entered a crowded Childs restaurant. Bessie was served, but her aunt did not eat anything and was not at the table with her. There was only one check, which Bessie paid, as they went out together. Just before they went out of the door a bell rang, and the cashier motioned Bessie to come back. The cashier demanded payment for the aunt, and, not accepting Bessie's explanation, summoned the head waiter. The latter said to Bessie, "come with me," and conducted her to the rear, where the waitress who served Bessie and the manager were brought into the interview. In the meantime the cashier mixed up the check. After about a half hour the manager informed Bessie "you may go now."

Bessie brought suit against the Childs Dining Hall Company for false imprisonment and a jury brought in a verdict for her under instructions by the trial judge as to the law. The Supreme Judicial Court of Massachusetts sustained the judgment. It was a question of fact, declared the court, whether Bessie's detention, caused solely by the inattention and carelessness of the cashier, was, under all the circumstances, unreasonable, or for an unreasonable time. There was ample evidence to support the verdict. As to the argument that there was no interference with Bessie's freedom, the court pointed out that her honesty and veracity had been openly challenged. If she had gone out before exoneration, her departure might well have been interpreted by the onlookers as an admission of guilt. In effect, then, she was restrained, and this amounted to arrest.

Libel and Slander. In primitive society, one who told A that B had committed some crime, or otherwise defamed B to A, ran only the risk that B would seek him out and undertake to "settle accounts" with his fists or a club. To the extent that A was willing to take this risk he might be said to have enjoyed the privilege of full "freedom of speech." It is interesting to note that some of the earliest developments of the common law were along the line of curtailing this "freedom" by providing a legal remedy for one who was made the subject of defamatory statements, and since then, speech has only been "free" to the extent that it does not defame others.

That custom played a part in this development is indicated by ancient English records recently quoted by Richard C. Donnelly. Thus, as of the year 1291, in Ipswich, it was the custom of the "aforesaid town" that if any one in the said town falsely or maliciously slanders another in the public market place or openly before the people, accusing him of larceny, robbery, treason, forgery or other crime, by which he may be injured or suffer damages, or may be humiliated or robbed of his honour, "he who is thus slandered shall have his recovery by gage and pledge before the bailiffs of the said town against the slanderers."

In fact, as Donnelly pointed out, defamation was one of the most common torts brought before the local courts in the Middle Ages. Shame was keenly felt, and the courts gave the offense a generous scope. Accusations of crime and sexual immorality were common types of statements for which actions were brought. Thus, one of the Pleas of the Manor of the Abbey of Bec in 1249 discloses that "Adam Moses gives half a sextary of wine to have an inquest as to whether Henry Ayulf accused him of the crime of larceny and used opprobrious and contumelious words of him. Afterwards they made accord and Henry finds security for an amercement. Fine, 12d." An unusual case of set-off appears in the records of the Court of the Bishop of Ely at Littleport in 1321: "It is found by inquest that Bohese Bindsboro called Ralph Bolay thief and he called her whore. Therefore both in mercy. And for that the trespass done to the said Ralph exceeds the trespass done to the said Bohese, as has been found, therefore it is considered that the said Ralph do recover from the said Bohese 12d. for his taxed damages." In the early law, no distinction was made between spoken and written words as the basis for liability.

The modern rule as to whether words are defamatory is that published words are defamatory if they tend to injure one's reputation in the community, and to expose him to hatred, ridicule or contempt. A broad field is thus opened. Obviously, it is not necessary to call one a thief, or to assert that he has been guilty of crime, to open the way to liability for a defamatory statement. Today, it is defamatory to call another a Communist. As Judge Fuld of the New York Court of Appeals declared in *Mencher v. Chesley,* today and in the recent past—whether or not communism stands for violent overthrow of government—it is undeniable that for communism and its adherents and sympathizers there has been widespread public aversion. Evidence of that antipathy is found not only in public opinion polls and in other studies, but also in legislation and executive orders enacted and promulgated during the past several years which subject Communists and their affiliates and sympathizers to loss of public office and private position, and in some cases, even to deportation proceedings. Accordingly, having regard for the current public attitude—transitory though it may be—the courts have held that a false charge that one is a Communist is basis for a libel action. And it is of little moment whether the statement describes one as a Communist or as one having communistic sympathies and affiliations, for any difference is one of degree only.

Difference Between Libel and Slander via Radio and Television. Traditionally, the distinguishing characteristic of a libel has been its expression in some permanent and visible form, such as writing, printing, pictures or effigies, whereas a slanderous statement is made in spoken words or in some other transitory form, whether visible or audible, such as gestures or inarticulate but significant sounds. At earlier stages of our law the same general principles were, as we have noted, applicable to both libel and slander. In later times there developed a broader liability for libel than for slander, the primary reason assigned by the courts being the greater capacity for harm that a writing is assumed to have because of the wide range of dissemination consequent upon its permanence of form. In the case of libel, it is presumed as a matter of law that the one defamed has sustained damage, and no special damage need be averred or proved. But in the case of slander, outside of certain limited catagories there can be no recovery without establishing that actual damages were sustained.

With the advent of radio and television this distinction between libel and slander became of vital importance. Here, indeed, were agencies not envisioned by even the most profound legal scholars who dealt with the law of libel throughout its history until very recent times.

Assuming that someone makes a defamatory utterance in the course of broadcasting, it would seem at first blush that we have a case of slander—the spoken word—rather than libel. If so, the distinction between libel and slander as we have heretofore considered it might become quite material in determining liability. Would it make any difference whether the broadcaster was speaking extemporaneously, or reading the remarks from a written manuscript?

The problem was involved in *Hartmann v. Winchell*, in which George Hartmann sued Walter Winchell for defamation in a New York court. The defamatory words were read by Walter from a script into the microphone. The New York Court of Appeals said that although the words were defamatory and were spoken of and concerning the plaintiff, they did not defame him in his business or professional character; moreover, although the complaint alleged that "plaintiff suffered a loss of earnings of upwards of $7,000," this was not sufficiently specific to constitute an allegation of special damage. In other words, in accordance with the principles which we have hereinabove developed, the plaintiff did not state a cause of action in slander, and if Walter's utterances had to be construed as slander, George could not recover. However, the court said that when Walter read from a script he was in effect libeling rather than slandering George, and inasmuch as the words were libelous, George could recover without allegation or proof of special damages. By implication, at least, it would seem to follow that if the commentator merely spoke the words as he went along, they not having previously been put in written form, the speaking would be slander, only.

A number of states have undertaken to deal by statute with the matter of defamation by radio and television. An Illinois statute, for example, provides that libel by radio or television is a malicious defamation broadcast by means of what is commonly known as the radio or television, tending to blacken the memory of one who is dead or to impeach the honesty, integrity, virtue or reputation, or to publish the natural defects of one who is alive, and thereby to expose him to public hatred, contempt, ridicule or financial injury.

The Illinois statute further provides that every person, firm, corporation, or unincorporated or voluntary association owning or operating a radio or television station within the State of Illinois, which shall broadcast a libel by radio or television, as defined above, directly or indirectly, or by means of electrical or other form of transcription, and every person who shall maliciously and knowingly participate in the publication or the broadcast of such libel, shall be guilty of libel—provided, however, that

(a) No such person, firm, corporation, or unincorporated or voluntary association owning or operating a radio or television station in the State of Illinois, or employee thereof, shall be found guilty of libel for the broadcast of any defamatory matter of which such person, firm, corporation, or unincorporated or voluntary association or employee thereof had no advance knowledge or opportunity or right to prevent; and

(b) No such person, firm, or corporation, unincorporated or voluntary association, or employee thereof, shall be found guilty of libel for any statement uttered over the facilities of such station by any candidate for public office.

The Illinois statute further provides that every person convicted of libel by radio or television shall be fined not exceeding $500, or confined in the county jail not exceeding one year.

Necessity for "Publication." Thus far in our consideration of libel and slander we have dealt primarily with the question as to when matter is of such nature as to provide a basis for action, whether in libel for written words or pictures or in slander for spoken words. It is essential to emphasize the basic element of liability that libelous or slanderous words are not actionable unless they are "published." This is clear upon reflection. Let us assume that A and B are having a private conversation, with no one listening. If A says to B, "you stole my automobile," B's feelings may be deeply hurt but he has sustained no injury to his reputation at A's hands—or mouth. Hearing by some third person is essential to such injury. Likewise, if A writes a letter to B and says the same thing, there is no actionable libel. B has it within his power to keep all third persons from knowing the letter's content. If he takes it on himself to show the letter to others, he himself is responsible for whatever injury follows. Before liability for defamation can arise some third person or persons must have heard or read the slanderous or libelous words, and at the instigation of the person making the charge, not of the one who is the subject of the remarks.

To further illustrate the point, let us suppose that A, instead of writing the libelous letter to B personally, calls in his stenographer and dictates the letter. The stenographer takes down the dictation in shorthand. In transcribing her notes, the stenographer "reads" what she took down in her book. She is a third person, and the law says there has been publication of a libel. *Ostrowe v. Lee* involved a situation of this nature. Defendant composed a letter accusing plaintiff of the crime of larceny and dictated it to his stenographer, who transcribed her notes and wrote and mailed the letter. Justice Cardozo, later of the Supreme Court of the United States but then on the New York Court of Appeals, stated the well-known principle that a defamatory writing is not published if it is read by no one but the defamed. "Published it is, however, as soon as read by any one else," he said. "The reader may be a telegraph operator, or the compositor in a printing house, or the copyist who reproduces a longhand draft. The legal consequence is not altered where the symbols reproduced or interpreted are the notes of a stenographer." Concluding, he said that when one speaks of a writing in this connection, one does not limit oneself to writings in manuscripts or books. Any symbol suffices—pictures, hieroglyphics, shorthand notes—if only what is written is intelligible to him who reads. There is publication of a libel if a stenographer reads the notes that have been taken by another. However, there is in law no publication where the only communication of defamatory matter is by a husband to his wife.

This rule appears to have its foundation in the old common law principle that the husband and wife are "one."

Truth as Defense in Actions for Libel and Slander. The general rule of common law is that the truth is a complete defense in all civil actions for libel or slander. However, where the truth of the words is pleaded in justification, the burden of proving the issue is upon the defendant.

In criminal libel, which is further mentioned hereinafter, we strike a difference here. Having in mind that the object of the state in punishing libel criminally is to prevent a breach of the peace, it is evident that the publication of true matter might cause such breach as well as the publication of false matter. At common law, therefore, truth was not a defense in criminal actions. But this has been generally altered by statute, making the truth a defense to criminal libel where the publication can be shown to have been made for good motives and for justifiable ends. Such a provision is found in the Constitution of Illinois.

The Illinois statute dealing with libel by radio and television provides that in all prosecutions for libel by radio or television, the truth, when published with good motives and for justifiable ends, shall be a sufficient defense.

Privilege, Absolute and Otherwise. The general common law rule is that a communication made in good faith upon any subject matter in which the party communicating has an interest, or in reference to which he has a duty, public or private, either legal, moral or social, if made to a person having a corresponding interest or duty, is privileged. Under certain circumstances the statements are said to be absolutely privileged; under other circumstances the privilege is said to be only "qualified."

Let us consider first absolute privilege, which affords a complete defense. It falls under three heads: (1) A member of the legislature is not liable to an action of slander for words spoken in the discharge of his official duties, even though spoken maliciously. But this privilege is not extended to words spoken unofficially, though in the legislative hall and while the legislature is in session. (2) No action will lie for defamatory statements made in the course of a judicial proceeding before any court of competent jurisdiction. Everything that a judge says on the bench, or a witness in the box, or counsel in arguing, is absolutely privileged, so long as it is in any way connected with the inquiry. So are all documents necessary to the conduct of the case, such as pleadings, affidavits and instructions to jury and counsel. (3) All acts done in the honest exercise of military authority are privileged.

It is recognized that this rule should be confined strictly to cases in which the public service or the administration of justice require complete immunity; to legislatures in debate, judges and attorneys in the preparation and trial of cases, and to executive and military personnel within the duties of their offices. In such connections as these, the interests and necessities of society require that utterances or publications of individuals, even though false and maliciously made, shall be protected from all liability. Here the right of free speech is allowed to prevail over the right to reputation.

Qualified Privilege. We have already stated, in effect, the rule of qualified privilege in introducing the topic above. A publication is qualifiedly privileged if made in good faith on any subject matter in which the person communicating has an interest, or in reference to which he has a duty, if made to a person having a corresponding interest or duty, even though it contains matter which, without this privilege would be actionable, and although the duty is not a legal one, but only a moral or social duty of imperfect obligation. Absent the existence of malice, there is no liability on a qualifiedly privileged communication, and in such cases the burden of proof is on plaintiff to establish malice.

Accordingly, publications dealing with political matters, public officials or candidates for office are entitled to a measurable privilege because of the public interest involved. As to this class of publications, the law raises a prima facie presumption in favor of the privilege. A mercantile agency's credit report to an interested subscriber is qualifiedly privileged, and unless it is made in bad faith or for an improper purpose the fact that it contains erroneous unfavorable statements about the plaintiff does not make the agency liable.

Application of the principle of qualified privilege is further illustrated by *Slocinski v. Radwan.* Rev. Roman Slocinski, pastor of the Holy Cross Church in Manchester, New Hampshire (a church being described as an independent, self-governing corporation, with full power to hire and discharge its pastor) sued three of his parishioners—Radwan, Stec and Krolikowski—for slander. The plaintiff alleged that Radwan said of him: "He [meaning Rev. Slocinski] is stealing the church money; look out for the church money in the bank. He is not a bishop and not even a priest. When he went to Albany with the church committee to buy a bell he did not return with the committee, but he remained over in Albany and stayed with a woman."

The other defendants were alleged to have made other similar slanderous remarks. At the trial, the jury brought in a verdict for Rev. Slocinski, but the judgment entered on it was reversed by the Supreme Court of New Hampshire and the case remanded for a new trial. The Supreme Court said the trial judge had erroneously instructed the jury with regard to the matter of privilege. He had told the jury that because the statements made by the defendants accused Rev. Slocinski of criminal offenses they could not be privileged. These statements of the law were clearly erroneous. In the absence of malice, an utterance may be qualifiedly privileged even though it is not true and notwithstanding the fact that it contains a charge of crime. Nor is there any rule of law which limits the occasion when church members may, without liability for slander, discuss among themselves the qualifications of their pastor, to committee meetings or parish gatherings. If fairly warranted by any reasonable occasion or exigency and honestly made, such communications are protected for the common convenience and welfare of society, and the law has not restricted the right to make them within any narrow limits.

The defense of qualified privilege was also involved in *Broking v. Phoenix Newspapers,* in which the paper published a picture of a dead dog chained to a post, with a comment that the dog had died of heat, thirst and starvation while chained to the post, that the neighbors blamed its master for its death, and that the humane officers were looking for its owner. The dog's owner brought suit for $25,000 damages. In the absence of any showing of malice, a defense that the publication was one of public interest and thus qualifiedly privileged was sustained.

In the older cases the rule was stated to be that every sale or delivery of a single copy of a newspaper or magazine was a distinct publication, and a separate basis for liability. William R. Prosser has pointed out that such a rule is potentially disastrous today when some periodicals are distributed to millions of readers and single radio programs are heard by millions of listeners. The late Annie Oakley, famed in "Annie Get Your Gun," reported by the Associated Press to have been arrested as a drug addict, brought 50 different actions against as many newspapers, of which she won 48, with damages ranging from $500 to $27,500. Some of the most troublesome problems confronting the courts today are in this area of "multiple publication."

CHAPTER 19

COMMON LAW LIABILITY FOR NEGLIGENT WRONGS

General Principle. In the discussion immediately preceding we have been dealing with a variety of situations in which one man has intentionally done some act which has the result of bringing injury to another. We have seen that under such circumstances the common law has recognized a right in the injured party to reimbursement, in so far as possible, in the form of damages. Where it can be said that an injury was intentionally inflicted, there will doubtless be universal agreement that the common law principle as to liability is right and just.

We are now ready to consider another field, in which one man injures another, not intentionally, but as the result of carelessness. Here again the common law has provided a basis of legal principle, under the working of which negligent conduct has been held in a great variety of situations to constitute a basis for liability to those suffering injury in direct consequence. Generally speaking, one is responsible for the direct consequences of his negligent acts whenever he is placed in such a position with regard to another that it is obvious that if he does not use due care in his own conduct he will cause injury to that person. The rule follows from the principle that every person in his intercourse with his fellows owes to them certain natural inherent duties, of which all normal persons are conscious, among which is the duty of protecting life and limb against peril when it is in his power reasonably to do so.

Contributory Negligence. In this field, where plaintiff's reliance for recovery is not upon any intentional or wilful misconduct upon the part of defendant, but only upon defendant's negligence, there is a further element which must be taken into account. Plaintiff cannot recover unless he, himself, was exercising due care for his own safety. If he, himself, was "contributorily negligent," he is barred from maintaining suit. Defined in legal terms, contributory negligence is conduct on the part of the plaintiff which falls below the standard to which he should conform for his own protection and which is a legally contributing cause, cooperating with the negligence of the defendant in bringing about the plaintiff's harm.

The working of the contributory negligence principle is illustrated by *Dee v. City of Peru*, in which action was brought by the beneficiary of Joseph Dee against the city of Peru. Joseph was drowned when the car in which he was riding went off a bridge into the Illinois River at Peru, through an opening occasioned by the turning of the drawspan. The suit was based on the alleged negligence of the City in failing to have a proper gate or barrier and to give warning of the danger. The evidence was that a gate was up and was visible for at least 110 feet, but that the car in which Dee was riding was going 50 or 60 miles per hour and crashed through it. In holding that the trial court should have allowed defendant's motion for a directed verdict, the Supreme Court of Illinois said the law does not afford to one who so exposes himself to danger the privilege of recovering damages for an injury arising from his actions, which injury might have been avoided by the use of reasonable care for his own safety.

Another case illustrative of the operation of the contributory negligence rule to bar recovery is *New York Central R. Co. v. Stevens.* Stevens sued for damages sustained by being struck by a locomotive while walking between two switch tracks leading to the Willys plant where he was going to work, the use of this way by Willys employees having been known by the railroad company for some time. Hearing a locomotive coming on one track, Stevens stepped toward the other and was struck by another locomotive coming on it, allegedly without ringing a bell or giving warning. The fact was that if he had stayed in the middle of the tracks both would have cleared him. The Supreme Court of Ohio said there should have been a directed verdict for defendant, because on the facts Stevens was clearly guilty of contributory negligence.

Operation of Motor Vehicles. Having seen the general principle of the common law with regard to negligence, we will illustrate its application in some representative fields. Any one would know, of course, that automobiles had not been invented when the common law principle of negligent liability was originally recognized and declared. But when the motor vehicle came into use the rule was directly adaptable, and was applied as a matter of course. Thus, the Supreme Court of Illinois has said that every person who drives upon the public highway is under a legal duty to observe, in the control and management of his vehicle, the exercise of reasonable care to prevent injury to others. Speaking somewhat more specifically, the same court has said it has long been the rule in this state that the driver of a vehicle on a city street is charged with a duty to exercise reasonable care in the operation of his vehicle and to have his vehicle under such control as will enable him to avoid collision with other vehicles or pedestrians. He is charged with notice that pedestrians may cross the street over which he is driving, and other vehicles may be traveling over a cross street. He is also to anticipate that cars parked at the curb might turn into the street.

A major segment of our litigation today consists of lawsuits brought to recover damages for injuries allegedly arising from the negligent operation of motor vehicles. The general principle as to liability being as stated, the ultimate determination as to whether there was negligence on all the facts is one that falls to the jury to determine. It should be said, however, in a sense by way of anticipation, that the situation has been considerably affected by statutes which deal with the operation of motor vehicles and lay down certain specific requirements for their operation. Failure to comply with the statute is, in effect, negligence *per se*. For example, the statute prescribes that before a left turn is made the motorist shall get into a certain lane, and give a designated preliminary signal. If he fails to do so, and an accident results, his negligence is almost automatically established. But as a matter of fact, a jury hearing the case on the same facts, but with no such statutory provision in effect, would very likely find him guilty of negligence, simply because not to get into the proper position and signal for the turn amounts to "negligence" under modern driving conditions. In short, the motor vehicle statutes have in effect done nothing more than to codify in detail "good driving" principles to which a jury would hold drivers, even if there were no such legislation.

Rendition of Professional Services—Malpractice. The duty imposed on a physician or surgeon is to employ such reasonable skill and diligence as is ordinarily exercised in his profession in the same general neighborhood, having due regard to the advanced state of the profession at the time of the treatment. Where a physician or surgeon exercises such ordinary care and skill, keeping within recognized and approved methods, he is not liable for the result of a mere mistake or error of enlightened judgment. There is no responsibility for an error of judgment unless it be so gross as to be inconsistent with the degree of skill which it is the duty of every physician to possess. Malpractice, which presupposes failure to live up to these duties, consists of a negligent or unskillful performance by a physician of the duties which are devolved and incumbent upon him on account of his relations with his patients or of a want of proper care and skill in the performance of a professional act.

The working of the principle is illustrated by *Winstead v. Hildenbrand.* Winstead sued Dr. Hildenbrand for malpractice to recover damages for total blindness resulting from certain treatments for syphilis. Winstead had received seven injections of tryparsamide, an arsenical specific used in the treatment of cerebro-spinal syphilis. Subsequently he was referred to Dr. Hildenbrand for fever therapy treatments, with recommendation that the tryparsamide injections be continued. Dr. Hildenbrand began the fever treatments and continued the injections. He did not make an independent examination of Winstead's eyes, but relied upon an earlier examination at Georgetown Hospital. After the ninth treatment Winstead became ill and was removed to the hospital, where he was found to be blind. At the trial, expert witnesses for Winstead testified that while tryparsamide and fever cabinet therapy were being employed, a careful and close watch on the eyes should be kept. Dr. Hildenbrand had not kept such a watch, and it appeared that he was not expert in the use of tryparsamide. The court said a verdict of malpractice might reasonably be found from the evidence.

Operation of Business Property. Quite a large area of the law where the principle of negligence provides the criterion of liability is found in the operation of business property, to which the public is directly or impliedly invited. The general rule in this connection is that the operator is required to use reasonable care to make the premises safe for the business visitor, or to warn him of dangerous conditions or activities creating an unreasonable risk of which the operator knows or which with reasonable vigilance he could discover.

An example involving a store is provided by *Giacomuzzi v. Klein,* in which Mary Giacomuzzi went to Klein's cleaning and pressing shop to get a pair of pants her husband left to be cleaned. Mary had forgotten the receipt, and the clerk asked her to come back to the rear room to pick out the pants. While back there Mary fell down an open trap door which led to the basement and was severely injured. She brought suit to recover damages, and the Supreme Judicial Court of Massachusetts held the trial court had erred in directing a verdict for defendant, as there was ample evidence from which a jury might find for Mary. The defendant owed plaintiff the duty to exercise reasonable care to see that the premises were in a reasonably safe condition or at least to warn her of dangers which in the exercise of reasonable care she might not discover and of which the defendant knew or ought to have known. The court commented that while the opening was obvious to one who might look at the floor, it was somewhat concealed by clothes hanging on the racks, and the attention of Mary naturally would have been centered on the clothes.

In another situation Clara Cory sued Otto Ray to recover for injuries sustained on his premises where he conducted a bingo game. The property was a large, one-story building, reached by a drive constructed of level, crushed stone which extended to the entrance, which entrance was between 25 and 50 feet in width. The floor and entrance level was about four inches higher than the drive and was constructed of cement, so that the floor and drive were of about the same color and at night were hardly distinguishable from each other. On the night in question Clara, who had never been there before, was invited to play, and was transported to and from the place in one of the busses furnished free of charge for that purpose by the management. There were from 700 to 1000 players that night. About 11:30 it was announced that one of the last busses was leaving, whereupon Clara and many others arose and made for the entrance. While some two or three hundred people were surging along, she being caught in the midst, she came to the "step-down" to the drive, which she had not been able to see, and was thrown down and injured.

The Appellate Court of Indiana ruled the trial court had erred in directing a verdict for defendant. "It is the law that one who operates a place of public entertainment is required to use reasonable care to keep the place safe for patrons in attendance, and failing to do so may be held liable for injuries occasioned by his neglect," said the court. The court went on to say that while it may be true that to permit a crowd to assemble even to the point of overcrowding does not of itself constitute negligence, since crowds are a part of our everyday life in populous centers, and patrons of places of amusement must be held to assume the risk of the dangers normally attendant thereon, it must certainly be true that when there is a question of the suitability of the construction or arrangement of a public place of amusement, and such construction or arrangement is itself such as to suggest danger, and crowds are permitted to thickly pack and crowd, push and jostle each other there, the question as to whether the management has used reasonable care under all of the circumstances to keep the place safe for patrons in attendance is one for the jury to determine.

Attention has been called to the general principle that a person whose own negligent conduct has contributed to his injury is not in a position to recover. An illustration is provided by *Flanders v. Pailey,* in which Esther Flanders sued William Pailey, a beauty shop operator, for injuries allegedly sustained when Esther caught her foot in an electric cord and fell while mounting a roller machine used in slenderizing treatments. The Supreme Judicial Court of Massachusetts decided the trial court had rightly directed a verdict for the defendant. The electric cord was not located in any aisle, though it was on the floor and was in the path of one approaching the machine from the direction of the wall. While it was defendant's duty to use ordinary care to maintain his premises in a reasonably safe condition for the use of his customers and to warn them of any dangers that either were not known to them or were not obvious to an ordinarily intelligent person, defendant could rightly assume that Esther by reason of her previous visits (19 in number) was familiar with the premises, that she would exercise ordinary circumspection in walking to the roller machine, and that she would readily observe the presence of the cord.

Owners of Property Rented to Others. It has been noted that in the cases under consideration in the section just preceding the defendant was conducting a business, in the course of which he "invited" patrons to come to his establishment. Under such circumstances, the basic liability at common law for not using reasonable care to provide safe conditions is clear. In passing, mention may be made of the situation of the person who owns a piece of property but who does not operate a business on it or "invite" the public to enter it: if some one does enter and is injured as the result of some dangerous condition, may he hold the owner to liability? Generally speaking, and apart from the so-called "attractive nuisance" doctrine applying to young children, the answer is "no." The party who entered was probably a "trespasser," and there is no duty recognized at common law to make premises safe for trespassers. An exception is sometimes made in situations where the property owner has known of the trespassing and acquiesced in it, to the extent that affirmative action calculated to injure them should be avoided. An example is *New York Central R. Co. v. Stevens,* in which the knowledge of the railroad company that men walked along a certain track to go to work in an adjoining factory obligated the company to use care by warning of the approach of locomotives. In that case we saw, of course, that plaintiff was barred because of his own contributory negligence.

What of the liability of the owner of a piece of property who rents it to another? Here the common law has worked out principles which upon analysis are seen to be quite reasonable. A distinction is drawn on the basis of who is in possession and control of the area in which an injury arises. The general rule is that, in the absence of warranty on the part of the landlord that the premises are fit for the purpose for which they are let and in the absence of concealment or fraud by the landlord as to some defect, structural or otherwise, in the premises, the tenant takes them in whatever condition they may be, thus assuming all risk of personal injury from defects therein, and neither he nor his invitees can hold the landlord liable for personal injuries resulting from such defects. But on the other hand, it has long been the rule that the landlord is responsible for the safe condition of stairways and areaways used in common by all the tenants of a tenement building, on the theory that the landlord and not the tenant is in possession and control of these areas.

A somewhat unusual situation arising in the City of Baltimore demonstrated how a landlord may be held liable for not maintaining with reasonable care the portion of the premises over which he retains control. In *Maryland v. Manor Real Estate & Trust Co.*, Ella Anderson as the surviving widow of Evered Anderson brought suit against the United States Housing Authority and other named defendants to recover damages for the death of Evered. It appeared that the Housing Authority had taken over twenty-two three-story dwellings, 125 years old, located in Baltimore, in order to provide defense housing. The Authority divided each of the houses into six apartments. The houses were heated by furnaces in the basement, one for each group of four houses. All occupants had access to the basements for laundry purposes, and to deposit garbage in containers furnished by the landlord. During the period of government control the wooden floors of the basements were honeycombed with rat burrows, and garbage frequently overflowed the "dilapidated uncovered containers" and spilled upon the floor. Only one janitor and a helper were employed to service the more than twenty houses in the 600 and 700 blocks, only the helper working full time. "As a result of this deplorable situation, many large and bold rats, often four or five at a time, were observed in the cellars each time the tenants descended to dispose of their garbage and trash." The tenants complained to the agent, but to no avail. Anderson rented one of the apartments in the 600 block in February, 1946. He was taken ill with typhus on January 13, 1947, and died ten days later. The incubation period for endemic typhus is from four to twenty-two days. There was no evidence, nor contention, that Anderson was exposed to the disease at any other place than the cellar of the house, where he disposed of his garbage daily. Evidence was presented that typhus is transmitted by the bite of a flea from an infected rat.

The U.S. Court of Appeals held that the government Housing Authority could be held liable for Anderson's death, saying there could be no question as to its responsibility for the condition of the basements and its liability for the consequences of its neglect. Granting there was no covenant in the lease to make repairs, and no implied warranty that the house should be fit for habitation, the landlord's obligations are different in the case of multiple unit dwellings. Where he leases separate portions of the same building to different tenants, and reserves under his control the halls, stairways and other portions of the building, used in common by all of the tenants as means of access to their respective rooms or apartments, he is under an obligation to use reasonable diligence to keep the portions so retained under his control of the building in a safe condition and free from improper obstructions. This obligation of the landlord to the tenants of different parts of the same building of which he has kept possession for their common use is of the same character as that of any other owner of real estate, who permits or invites others to use it for a particular purpose, to keep it safe for those using it within the scope of the invitation. The court said there was sufficient evidence to sustain a verdict finding that Anderson's death resulted from the rat condition. As to the argument that Anderson assumed the risk of injury by remaining in the apartment after he discovered the condition, the court pointed out that "the Andersons were not entirely free to leave the premises because of the difficulty of obtaining living accommodations in 1946, which the Authority's enterprise was designed to alleviate." The tenants were entitled to exercise the right of occupancy conferred by their lease and to demand that the landlord perform the duty of keeping the reserved portion of the parmises in safe condition for their use.

The Obligation of Manufacturers. In an age like the present, with a vast variety of machines and manufactured products in use on every hand, including the four walls of the home, important legal questions turn on liability for injuries resulting from manufacturing defects. In this broad field the common law has satisfactorily operated.

Mention of modern cases illustrating the rule should be prefaced by reference to the old English case of *Winterbottom v. Wright,* in which suit was brought by the driver of a stage coach to recover for injuries sustained when the coach collapsed with a broken wheel, allegedly defective. Recovery was denied. The theory was that any duty to provide a safe wheel was owed only to the proprietor of the coach line, the driver's employer, and did not extend to some one else. Justice Cardozo, as a member of the New York Court of Appeals, provided an outstanding example of the manner in which the common law keeps apace of economic and social developments, in *MacPherson v. Buick Motor Co.*, decided in the year 1916, at a time when the motor vehicle was really superseding the "horse and buggy." In that case MacPherson was riding in a car manufactured by Buick and sold to him by a retail dealer. A wheel collapsed, and MacPherson was thrown out and injured. The wheel was made of defective wood and its spokes had crumpled. Buick had bought it from another manufacturer, but had failed to inspect it thoroughly before placing it on the car.

Manifestly, the issue in the MacPherson case was similar to that in the old English Winterbottom case—did the manufacturer owe a duty of care which extended to any one beyond the immediate purchaser, who was here the dealer? Speaking for the Court of Appeals, Justice Cardozo said the manufacturer was liable for negligence. "We are dealing now with the liability of the manufacturer of the finished product, who puts it on the market to be used without inspection by his customers," said Justice Cardozo. "If he is negligent, where danger is to be foreseen, a liability will follow. If the nature of a thing is such that it is reasonably certain to place life and limb in peril when negligently made, it is then a thing of danger. Its nature gives warning of the consequences to be expected. If to the element of danger there is added knowledge that the thing will be used by persons other than the purchaser, and used without new tests, then, irrespective of contract, the manufacturer of this thing of danger is under a duty to make it carefully." Justice Cardozo concluded: "Precedents drawn from the days of travel by stage coach do not fit the conditions of travel today."

Commenting on the MacPherson decision, Leon Green pointed out that the expansion and application of the negligence formula to the manufacturer, assembler and dealer is due largely to Judge Cardozo's masterly opinion in that case. He drew from many sources, but the core of his opinion is Brett's formula in another English case, *Heaven v. Pender*. Danger was taken as the starting point, as it is in all tort law. Danger imposed a duty of care—in that instance a duty to inspect. Foreseeability of danger and the exercise of reasonable care under all the circumstances was the measure of this duty to inspect, and where in doubt it was for the jury to make the ultimate determination whether the duty had been performed. Thus it was that a general formula was outlined that would care for cases as they arose, a process indicated that accommodated the infinite variations presented by the cases to arise.

A recent case illustrating the working of the principle in another connection is *Carter v. Yardley & Co.* Plaintiff Esther Carter bought at a retail shop in Boston a bottle of perfume manufactured by Yardley and sold by it to the retailer. When Esther used it, she suffered a second degree burn to her skin, and she brought suit against Yardley for damages. At the trial Esther's counsel introduced the testimony of two lay witnesses and one expert physician to the effect that each of them had applied to his or her skin perfume from the same bottle and that it had irritated and injured the skin. The jury brought in a verdict for Esther, and the Supreme Judicial Court of Massachusetts held that it was amply supported by the evidence. Assuming a duty of care, a finding of negligence in the manufacture and bottling of the perfume was proper if the jury found a greater likelihood that the harmful ingredient found its way into the bottle through want of care of the defendant than through excusable accident or the act of a stranger or some other cause for which the defendant would not be responsible. The defendant had full control of the manufacture of the perfume and the filling of the bottle. No examination of the contents of the bottle by any middleman or retailer was practicable. Esther was not required to prove that a majority of consumers would be injuriously affected. "It is enough if a sufficient number are susceptible so that a jury could reasonably say that the defendant ought to have known and recognized the danger of injury and ought to have guarded against it," said the court, stating and applying the basic principle of law, as follows: "In principle, a manufacturer or other person owning or controlling a thing that is dangerous in its nature or is in a dangerous condition, either to his knowledge or as a result of his want of reasonable care in manufacture or inspection, who deals with or disposes of that thing in a way that he foresees or in the exercise of reasonable care ought to foresee will probably carry that thing into contact with some person, known or unknown, who will probably be ignorant of the danger, owes a legal duty to every such person to use reasonable care to prevent injury to him."

Chapter 20

RIGHTS AND OBLIGATIONS ARISING OUT OF CONTRACT

The Nature of Contract Rights. Thus far in our consideration of the common law we have dealt with it as recognizing rights and liabilities arising out of circumstances attending what might in a sense be referred to as the casual relation of people to each other—circumstances not involving any promises or agreements to do or not to do anything. We have seen that simply because one person does something in a certain way under certain circumstances, rights may arise in others even though they did not know the other party and perhaps never saw him before the event in question. Under the elastic working of the common law a vast scope of human activity is regulated by "tort" law, as this area is called—"tort" coming from the French word meaning "wrong" and signifying a wrong not having its basis in any contractual obligation.

We will now take note of rights and obligations arising out of contract. Our common law follows the same general concept as the Roman law, that all obligations owe their origin either to the consent of the parties (contractus) or to injuries (delicta) done by one person to another, which give the injured party a right to recompense. Consent, as we deal with it, is evidenced by contract.

In fitting contract rights into the scheme of rights in general, Holland pointed out that the nature and scope of rights is fundamentally dependent upon the limited or unlimited extent of the person against whom the right is available. A right is available either against a definite person or persons, or against all persons indefinitely. A servant, for instance, has a right to his wages for the work he has done, available against a definite individual, his master. On the other hand, the owner of a garden has a right to its exclusive enjoyment, available against no one individual more than another, but against everybody. This distinction between rights has been expressed by calling a right of the definite kind a right *in personam,* a right of the indefinite kind, a right *in rem.* The use of these terms to distinguish between two classes of rights is of comparatively recent date, but is in harmony with their use by the classical Roman jurists as distinguishing between different classes of stipulations, pacts, actions, exceptions and edicts.

By far the most important class of rights *in personam*, as Holland further pointed out, are those arising from that particular species of act which is called a contract. Thus, if a man goes into a shop and buys a watch for ready money a contract has taken place. The watchmaker and his customer have united in a concordant expression of will, and the result has affected once for all their legal rights. The customer has, according to the English common law, become owner of the watch, the watchmaker of its price, and the transaction is at an end. But suppose that instead of the instantaneous sale of the watch, the agreement had been merely for its purchase at a future day. In this case there is also a contract, but the right to which it gives rise is not a vested right of ownership in the watch, but an outstanding or continuing right in the customer to buy it at the time and for the price agreed upon, with a correlative right in the shopkeeper to receive the price in due course. In the former case the contract has given rise to rights *in rem*, and in so doing its force is instantaneously spent. In the latter case the results of the contract are deferred. It produces merely claims or rights in personam, which continue to be operative until the thing agreed upon is performed.

By legal definition, a contract is a promise the performance of which the law recognizes as a duty and for a breach of which a remedy is given. A contract does not contemplate simply the act of promising, but obligations arising therefrom.

Historical Background of Contract Law. Contracts mark the progress of civilization. They are at the base of the stability of the present and the future. That the development of contract is an outgrowth of commercial and industrial enterprises involving greater anticipation of the future than is necessary in a simpler or more primitive economy, has been pointed out by Morris R. Cohen. In the latter the solidarity of relatively self-sufficient family groups and the fear of departing from accustomed ways limit individual initiative as well as the scope and importance of what can be achieved by deliberate agreements or bargains. In some respects, however, less developed societies resort more than we do to contracts or compacts and enforce promises that we no longer enforce. Thus they preserve peace not by organized police or standing armies, but by agreements like our present treaties of peace between nations; and promises to the gods, which are now matters of individual conscience, used to be enforced by the community as a whole because it feared the undiscriminating effects of divine wrath. It has been assumed since the days of Homer—it is involved in Montesquieu's story of the Troglodytes—that savage men make no compacts or agreements and do not attach importance to promises. This is a doubtful generalization, which modern anthropology does not confirm. Although commerce in its early stages was connected with war and piracy, the main importance of widening markets was to favor steady industry and reliance on promises as a basis for individual enterprise otherwise impossible. Thus it was that individual bargains or agreements necessarily received increased attention from the law. This can be found to have been repeatedly illustrated in the history of the ancient Jews, Greeks and Romans, and of mediaeval Europe.

Constitutional Recognition of Importance of Contracts. The important place that contracts had attained in the life of our people at the time that our national government was established is attested by the fact that it was written into the Constitution of the United States that no State shall pass any law impairing the obligation of contracts. In *Ogden v. Saunders,* Chief Justice Marshall held that we cannot look back to the history of the times when the august spectacle was exhibited of the assemblage of a whole people by their representatives in convention, in order to unite thirteen independent sovereignties under one government, so far as might be necessary for the purpose of union, without being sensible of the great importance of this provision. The power of changing the relative situation of debtor and creditor, of interfering with contracts, a power which comes home to every man, touches the interest of all, and controls the conduct of every individual in those things which he supposes to be proper for his own exclusive management, had been used to such an excess by the state legislatures, as to break in upon the ordinary intercourse of society, and destroy all confidence between man and man. The mischief had become so great, so alarming, as not only to impair commercial intercourse, and threaten the existence of credit, but to sap the morals of the people, and destroy the sanctity of private faith. To guard against the continuance of the evil was an object of deep interest with all the truly wise, as well as the virtuous of this great community, and was one of the benefits expected from a reform of the government.

Referring to the nature of the contractual obligation, as thus involved, Chief Justice Marshall contended that we must suppose that the framers of our Constitution were intimately acquainted with the writings of those wise and learned men whose treatises on the law of nature and nations have guided public opinion on the subjects of obligations and contract. "If we turn to those treatises, we find them to concur in the declaration that contracts possess an original intrinsic obligation, derived from the acts of free agents, and not given by government," he further declared. Nevertheless, he granted that the whole subject of contracts is under the control of society, and that the power of society over it lies in the state legislatures except in those special cases where, as by the constitutional provision here involved, restraint is imposed by the Constitution of the United States. If the legislative will be that certain agreements shall be in writing, that they shall be sealed, that they shall be attested by a certain number of witnesses, that they shall be recorded, or that they shall assume any prescribed form before they become obligatory, all these are regulations which society may rightfully make, and which do not come within the restrictions of the Constitution because they do not impair the obligation of the contract.

Forms of Contract and Sealed Instruments. In our consideration of Rome we have noted the formalities attendant upon the creation of certain rights. Formality is characteristic of much of the older law, and such was true of the early English law of contracts. Without the observance of certain formalities, no obligation arose. Of all-pervasive importance was the seal. Originally, this was of wax, with an impression upon it. As time went on wax fell into disuse; eventually, a scrawl, or even the word "seal" printed on the document, came to suffice.

As the law developed, the seal became unnecessary to sustain the enforceability of various contracts which embodied the other recognized essentials of contractual obligations. There arose the basis for classifying contracts into two divisions: formal, and informal. Sealed contracts were, and are, spoken of as formal; all others as informal, or simple contracts.

Today the seal does not exercise the practical importance that it did even a few decades ago. In some states it has been abolished, with the apparent result that instruments now executed therein in formal sealed manner would have no more force than informal contracts. Where the seal still has recognized usage, its main significance is to make unnecessary the presence of consideration to sustain the contract to which it is attached.

Contracts and the Statute of Frauds. Formal contracts are, perforce, in writing, and upon parchment or paper. In the nature of things there was, and is, no reason why other contracts could not be oral. The basic consideration is the expression of agreement. This is ordinarily arrived at by the spoken word. All that a writing can do is to evidence it in a permanent form.

Here is the key to what, since it originated in England in the reign of Charles the Second, has been known as the Statute of Frauds. It early became evident that a party to an oral contract was in position to perpetrate a fraud by denying his obligation, in which event the other party might have great difficulty in establishing it, if he could do so at all. The Statute of Frauds, then enacted by the English Parliament, in effect required certain described contracts to be in writing. The English statute became the model for similar enactments in the several American states.

The Illinois Statute of Frauds, which is typical, provides that no action shall be brought (1) whereby to charge any executor or administrator upon any special promise to answer any debt or damages out of his own estate, (2) or whereby to charge the defendant upon any special promise to answer for the debt, default or miscarriage of another person, (3) or to charge any person upon any agreement made upon consideration of marriage, (4) or upon any agreement that is not to be performed within the space of one year from the making thereof, (5) or upon any contract for the sale of lands or any interest in or concerning them for a longer term than one year, unless the promise or agreement upon which such action shall be brought, or some memorandum or note thereof, shall be in writing, and signed by the party to be charged therewith, or some other person thereunto by him lawfully authorized. The Uniform Sales Act provides that a contract to sell or a sale of any goods or choses in action of the value of $500 or upwards shall not be enforceable by action unless the buyer shall accept part of the goods or choses in action so contracted to be sold or sold, and actually receive the same, or give something in earnest to bind the contract, or in part payment, or unless some note or memorandum in writing of the contract or sale be signed by the party to be charged or his agent in that behalf.

Following a report of an English Law Revision Committee in 1954 Parliament virtually repealed the Statute of Frauds in the jurisdiction of its origin. Among the criticisms listed by the Committee were that the maturing of evidentiary and jury procedures had removed a basic reason for its original passage; the Statute was accused of promoting more fraud than it prevents, in that it barred good claims more often than it protected innocent persons; the classes of contracts covered were arbitrarily chosen and there was no reason for the exclusion of the many others if the basic philosophy was valid; the statute was out of step with the customs and practices of the business world; the statute yielded partial and lopsided operation, in that where A and B entered into a contract and A signed a memorandum but B did not, B could enforce the contract against A, but A could not enforce it against B; from a technical standpoint the statutory language was obscure and ill-drafted, and had fostered needless litigation.

Similar comment could be made as to the operation of Statutes of Frauds in the 49 American states. Business practice may of course be taken to substantiate the requirement of a writing in sales of goods of the value of $500 or upwards, as codified in the Uniform Sales Act. Except as the Statute of Frauds is, by its terms, applicable, oral contracts are enforceable to the same extent as written ones.

The Making of a Contract. It is commonly said that a contract is made by an offer and an acceptance of the offer: one party undertakes to perform a certain act if the other party will perform a certain act. Or, perhaps, one party undertakes to perform a certain act if the other party will promise to perform a certain act.

The simple illustration just given points to the fact that there are, basically, two kinds of contracts, which are known in the common law as "unilateral" and "bilateral." A unilateral contract is one in which the party making the offer receives an act, rather than a promise, as consideration. In a bilateral contract there are mutual promises, the party making the offer receiving, in consideration, the promise of the other party to do a certain thing. Thus, if A says to B, "I will pay you $500 if you paint my house," B accepts the offer by painting the house, and the consummation of the contract leaves A with the obligation of paying B the promised $500. On the other hand, if A says to B, "I will pay you $500 if you will promise to paint my house and have the job done by September 1st," the contract is consummated by B's promise to paint A's house and have the job done at the time stated in the offer. In the first case, B did not promise to paint A's house and was not under any obligation to do; if he did so, however, he accepted A's offer and A was obligated to pay him the promised $500. In the second case B did promise to paint A's house for $500 within the time stated; if he failed to carry out the promise he committed a breach of the contract and became liable to A for damages. If B fulfilled his promise, A became obligated to fulfill his promise to pay B $500 for the job.

A recent succinct example of a unilateral contract is found in

Robertson v. United States, a case before the Supreme Court of the United States. The issue was whether Leroy J. Robertson was liable to pay federal income tax on $25,000 which he had received from Henry H. Reichhold, a philanthropist, as an award for the best symphonic work written by native-born composers of this hemisphere. Robertson claimed that the money was received as a gift, and was therefore not subject to tax. The government proposed to tax it as money received in the discharge of a contractual obligation. The Supreme Court upheld the government, saying that in a legal sense payment of a prize to a winner of a contest is the discharge of a contractual obligation. The acceptance by the contestant of the offer tendered by the sponsor of the contest creates an enforceable contract. The discharge of legal obligations—the payment for services rendered or consideration paid pursuant to a contract—is in no sense a gift. And where the payment is in return for services rendered, it is irrelevant that the donor derives no economic benefit from it.

In the business world bilateral contracts are legion, and take many forms. Typical are those in which one party promises to furnish certain goods or services and the other party agrees to pay therefor in a stipulated manner. Another common example is the land contract, by which one party agrees to convey a described lot or tract of land in consideration of the other party's promise to make payment in the manner specified.

It is, of course, to be understood throughout that only persons with legal capacity can bind themselves by contract. Because infants (at common law persons under 21 years of age), and insane and intoxicated persons are held to lack such legal capacity, their contracts are, generally speaking, voidable, with exception only for necessaries. At common law, married women were without capacity to contract, but in the period following the Civil War statutes in the several states, commonly referred to as Married Women's Acts, removed most of their disabilities. They have since been able to hold property in their own right and make contracts in their own behalf.

The Doctrine of "Consideration." It is a basic doctrine of the common law that informal contracts require "consideration" for their enforceability. To the uninitiated this may seem like the announcement of a simple rule, but few doctrines of the law have imported greater difficulty of application. The difficulty lies in the nebulous implications of the term "consideration." Professor John H. Moore pointed out that there is no clear consensus of authorities on what the term "consideration" has included through the five odd centuries of development of contract common law. Especially in this country at present there is a primary division among experts on what is the most convenient scope for the term.

The starting point of the courts in general has been the definition, well expressed in the English case of *Currie v. Misa,* that a valuable consideration, in the sense of the law, may consist either in some right, interest, profit or benefit accruing to one party, or some forbearance, detriment, loss or responsibility, given, suffered, or undertaken by the other. More succinctly, the principle is expressed by saying that any act which is a benefit to one party and a disadvantage to the other constitutes a sufficient consideration to support a contract. In the plainer language of every-day, the principle might be expressed by saying that there is consideration where a party performs some act which he is not legally bound to perform, or promises to perform some act which he is not legally bound to perform; or where a party is the beneficiary of an act, or the promise to perform an act, which would not otherwise lawfully accrue to him. Under such test there is no question about the presence of consideration in the "house-painting" example at which we have glanced hereinabove: B was under no legal obligation to paint A's house, or to promise to paint A's house, and A benefited by the act of B.

Those cases, too, are understandable, which hold that if one is already under a contractual obligation, a new promise to perform it is not consideration for another undertaking; that acts performed in the past are not sufficient to support a subsequent promise, and that merely moral obligations are not sufficient to make promises to carry them out binding in law. But there are many connections in which it is impossible to bring the result reached within the clear scope of formal definition. Exercising the freedom of approach and decision which is rightly theirs under our common law system, the courts have sought for, and have satisfactorily achieved, solutions to meet the problems encountered.

Out of the situation has come the "primary division among experts," above referred to by Edward Moore, as to the most convenient scope of the term "consideration." Under the apparent influence of the historical school of the nineteenth century the Restatement of the Law of Contracts by the American Law Institute and also the treatise on contracts by Samuel Williston use the word to denote only acts, forbearances, and so on, which are "bargained for and given in exchange"; and, since that meaning does not embrace all the phenomena of validation found in the cases, they treat as valid without consideration the remaining informal contracts recognized by the courts. However, there are able scholars in this field who would avoid the narrower definition used in the Restatement and in Williston, preferring to study all the observable types of validating facts, free of any assumptions reduced to definition. They would try to classify, under whatever heads usage might warrant, the various facts courts use as reasons for the recognition of contractual obligations. After research it might turn out that the term "consideration" would, under professional usage, include not only the present-exchange cases but also the past-requested act and the preexisting debt cases, the cases of new promise after discharge by bankruptcy or statute of limitations, other moral obligation cases, and so on, even possibly through the promissory estoppel cases. This conflict is sometimes spoken of as one of mere terminology, but perhaps it is hardly that; the former attitude assumes a continuing principle of consideration, and views the inconsistent decisions as presenting exceptions or anomalies. The latter group are realists.

Whatever the approach or the scope accorded to the term by way of definition, the general doctrine of "consideration" remains fundamental in contract common law.

Problems of Interpretation. Words constitute the only adequate medium for conveying thought and registering mutual intention. The course of civilization has been marked by their development in this regard. Contracts are created from words. However, at best words are an imperfect medium. Carelessly used, they can be an inaccurate and misleading medium. But this is not all. Frequently, parties making a contract do not incorporate words that deal with situations or contingencies that later arise in the course of its execution. Sometimes they do not even foresee these situations or contingencies. Ultimately the question arises, "what is the contract here?" If specific words are present, the court has something to work upon in a process of interpretation. If the situation or contingency is not covered by any words found in the contract itself, another approach is necessary.

As Justice Black of the Supreme Court of the United States recently declared, the cardinal rule in the interpretation of contracts is that the intention of the parties should be ascertained and enforced. Where the problem is one of determining the meaning of words actually used, aid is found in some fairly well-developed rules of interpretation. The surrounding circumstances, including expressions of the parties prior to the making of the contract, may be considered, as an aid in its interpretation, although what is known as the parol evidence rule forbids the introduction of any evidence that would add to or detract from the terms of a contract reduced to writing in final form. Usages of a trade or locality related to the contract will ordinarily supersede the popular meaning of words. Specific terms will ordinarily be held to qualify general language. Words of art, or words that have acquired a fixed meaning in the law, will usually be given their technical or fixed meaning.

Where no words specifically covering the point at issue are to be found in the contract, manifestly a different problem is presented. Feeling bound by what was to be found within the "four walls" of the contract as expressed in the words actually before them, the courts in earlier days labored mightily to attach to them the meaning necessary to cope with problems arising out of execution of the contract, but which, perhaps, the parties themselves had not foreseen when they made it. However satisfactory the result, the process by which it was reached was sometimes strained. In recent times the approach has come to be more realistic. It is now generally recognized, and admitted, that sometimes the parties have not, in terms, made a contract adequate for the contemplated purpose. When the court is confronted by such a situation, the best way out may be for the court to "make a contract" for them in whatever regard may be essential to a business-like and just solution of the problems.

Illustrative of the problem and the modern approach is the case of *Wood v. Lucy, Lady Duff-Gordon.* Lady Duff-Gordon was a fashion creator. Wood conducted a business adapted to the placing of her designs in the fashion trade. They entered into a written agreement whereby Wood was to have the exclusive right to place her designs on sale or license others to market them. In return Lady Duff-Gordon was to have one-half of "all profits and revenues" derived from any contracts Wood might make. This exclusive right was to last one year. When Lady Duff-Gordon proceeded to place her designs with others, Wood sued her for damages. Her defense was that the contract was void for want of mutuality and consideration because Wood did not "bind himself to anything," and did not specifically promise in the contract to place her designs.

The New York Court of Appeals upheld judgment for Wood. Judge Cardozo observed that it was true Wood did not promise in so many words that he would use reasonable efforts to place Lady Duff-Gordon's designs. "We think, however, that such a promise is fairly to be implied," said he. "The law has outgrown its primitive state of formalism when the precise word was the solemn talisman, and every slip was fatal. It takes a broader view today. A promise may be lacking, and yet the whole writing may be 'instinct with an obligation' imperfectly expressed." Judge Cardozo went on to point out the basis for "writing in" such a promise by Wood; he felt that the implications of a promise were evident in various circumstances. Lady Duff-Gordon gave Wood an exclusive privilege. She was to have no right for at least a year to market her own designs, except through the agency of Wood. The acceptance of the exclusive agency was an assumption of its duties. The terms of Lady Duff-Gordon's compensation were even more significant. Her sole compensation for the grant of exclusive agency was to be one-half of all the profits resulting from Wood's efforts. Unless he gave his efforts she would never get anything. Without an implied promise by Wood the transaction could not have such business efficacy as both parties must have intended that at all events it should have.

Another case illustrating the manner in which courts today proceed where the words of the contract do not suffice to provide the groundwork for adequate determination of the issue is *Sun Oil Co. v. Dalzell Towing Co.* Suit was brought by Sun Oil against Dalzell to recover for damages caused to Sun Oil's ship by Dalzell's allegedly negligent towage. The Sun Oil superintendent called Dalzell by telephone and requested that Dalzell take the "Sabine Sun" from one point to another. The Dalzell agent replied that they would take her about 1:30 P.M. This was all of the conversation which constituted the contract. Nothing was said about pilotage. The parties had done business before, and Dalzell had mailed to Sun Oil a printed document entitled "Pro Forma Towage Rates and Contract with Dalzell Towing Company." This stated that Dalzell was not liable for damages when their pilot was on a vessel making use of her own propelling power. However, the Sun Oil superintendent had not read this paper.

The court held that Sun Oil could not recover. It said that the Sun Oil superintendent's offer on behalf of Sun Oil, which Dalzell accepted, must be interpreted in the sense in which the party using the words should reasonably apprehend that they would be understood by the other party. Knowing that Dalzell had a schedule of rates and a pilotage clause, Sun Oil should reasonably apprehend that its telephone order for tugs would be understood by Dalzell as a request that they be furnished upon its customary terms as to rates and pilotage. The court below rightfully held that the contract between the parties included the pilotage clause as one of its terms. Whether the Sun Oil superintendent had actually read the paper, and whether it was in his mind when he telephoned the order for tugs for the Sabine Sea "is quite beside the point." The meeting of the minds of the parties to a contract is not determined by a subjective test.

The present day point of view of common law courts by way of in effect "making" a contract for the parties where circumstances call for such as the reasonable and just way to solve the problem is dealt with further in a later chapter.

Remedies for Breach of Contract. The most common remedy for breach of contract is a suit at law to recover the damages sustained. In determining damages many rules and refinements of rules are involved, and many difficulties are presented when it comes to making the necessary computation. The basic rule, however, was enunciated in the English case of *Hadley v. Baxendale,* in which the owner of a mill sued a carrier for negligently delaying delivery of a machine part. The miller contracted with the carrier to transport a broken part to another place, where it was to be used as a model for making a new part. The miller told the carrier that speedy delivery was essential, but did not tell him that the mill could not operate until the new part was had. The miller claimed damages for loss of profits while the mill was shut down. Such damages were denied by the court, which said that where two parties have made a contract which one of them has broken, the damages which the other party ought to receive in respect of such breach of contract should be such as may fairly and reasonably be considered either arising naturally, i.e., according to the usual course of things, from such breach of contract itself, or such as may reasonably be supposed to have been in the contemplation of both parties, at the time they made the contract, of the probable breach of it.

If the special circumstances under which the contract was actually made were communicated by the miller to the carrier, and thus made known to both parties, the damages resulting from the breach of such a contract, which they would reasonably contemplate, would be the amount of injury which would ordinarily follow from a breach of those special circumstances so known and communicated. But if these special circumstances were unknown to the party breaking the contract, he, at the most, could only be supposed to have in contemplation the amount of injury which would arise generally, and in the great multitude of cases not affected by any special circumstances, from such a breach of contract. All common law courts have followed this rule.

The remedy of specific performance of a contract may be had in a court of equity when the necessary elements of equity jurisdiction are present. Accordingly, specific performance may be had only when an action for damages at law would not be an adequate remedy, when the court can readily enforce a specific performance decree, and when the equities of the situation call for such action. The most common example of specific performance is found in the enforcement of contracts for the sale of land. The remedy of restitution, which, as the term implies, seeks restoration to the plaintiff of what he may have delivered to the other party who has breached the contract, is available where the subject matter is such that it may readily be restored.

Of considerable practical importance to today's citizens are the conditional sales contracts under which automobiles, household appliances and television sets are widely sold. Title remains with the seller until the last installment has been paid. Under the terms of such contracts, and in accordance with the law of many jurisdictions, if the buyer breaches his agreement by failing to make any payment when due the seller may himself repossess the article, declaring forfeited such payments as have been made. Or the contract may allow the seller, on breach by the buyer, to resell the article, credit the original buyer with the net proceeds of the resale and payments made before default, and hold him liable for the difference.

Within the past generation there has come into general usage in the United States a "declaratory judgment" procedure, by the operation of which courts may make a declaration as to the rights and duties of parties to a contract before actual controversy develops. This will be mentioned further in a later chapter.

CHAPTER 21

PROPERTY RIGHTS AND THE COMMON LAW

The Common Law of Property. We have already given consideration to property rights in their relation to the individual and to our economic way of life. We have just noted some of the basic principles of the law of contracts, which in itself is an important element of property law: under modern conceptions contract rights are property rights, and by the consensual process property rights are created and conveyed. And, as we have seen, many phases of obligation attending the use of property are involved when it is employed in a manner to bring injury to others. By the terms of the Fifth and Fourteenth Amendments one may no more be deprived of his property than of his life or liberty "without due process of law," but no one of these rights is absolute. In the interest of individual freedom itself the common law imposes limitations calculated to prevent the use of the contract process to promote unlawful ends, or the use of property in any form to bring injury to others.

The concept of property ownership being as old as the law itself, the common law holds nothing distinctive in this regard. Nor is there anything distinctive about its acquisition by inheritance, by will or by various forms of conveyance in the way of bargain and sale or gift. The Roman law classification of property into movables and immovables was followed by the common law classification of property into real and personal—real property being land and personal property whatever is not land.

A considerable portion of our law deals with these matters of acquisition and transfer of property, as well as the matter and scope of its usage, taking into full account the differences between realty and personalty. Much of our law of contracts and personalty traces to Rome. Our law of real property evolved from the feudal system of the Middle Ages, of which we have made mention elsewhere. In a number of our Southwestern and Pacific Coast States the community property system was, as we have seen, brought to this country by the French and Spanish, and retained after the governments established by them were superseded by governments under the aegis of the

United States. The developments in this field of property law have been in keeping with our conceptions of the ownership and use of property as related to our individual freedom and free economic enterprise. In such matters as evolving the principle that contractual rights, in the older law thought of as intangible, may acquire tangibility and a physical situs for jurisdictional purposes when manifested in such forms as negotiable instruments, warehouse receipts, bonds and stock certificates, it has kept well attuned to the requirements of trade and commerce in a free economy.

The American citizen finds assurance in the protection which the common law affords his property rights, along with his other rights, basically recognized, as we have seen, in the Fifth and Fourteenth Amendments to the Constitution of the United States, and in such state constitutional documents as that of Illinois, which provides that every person ought to find a certain remedy in the laws for all injuries and wrongs which he may receive in his person, property or reputation. Certainly the common law has manifested the resources to insure this end.

Chapter 22

CRIMES AND COMMON LAW

Crimes at Common Law. What we think of and refer to as Criminal Law is, historically at least, a basic segment of the English common law. The original concepts were that a crime is an offensive act, not against an individual who may be injured in consequence of it— although the right of such individual to maintain an action to recover damages for personal injuries was in no sense disparaged—but rather an offense against the state; and that no one can be found guilty of a crime unless its commission was instigated or accompanied by an "evil mind." As Marcel Frym has pointed out, our criminal law is based on the time-honored assumptions that human actions presuppose the formation of a conscious intent and that forming of an intent is exclusively a function of the human mind as a free agent. Roscoe Pound expressed this point by saying that historically our substantive criminal law is based upon a theory of punishing the vicious will. It postulates a free agent confronted with a choice between doing right and doing wrong, and choosing freely to do wrong. This "evil mind" concept had its basis in the Canon Law, and bore testimony to the influence of the Canon Law over the moral content of the common law.

These concepts— that crime is an offense against the state, and that to constitute it there must be present the element of "evil mind" or *"mens rea"*—were embodied in the common law, which comprehensively embraced the field and made criminal any and all acts so committed that menaced the public welfare.

Legislative Codification. The original concept of a crime as an offense against the state has remained throughout, emphasized by the fact that the field of criminal law has been covered almost completely by statutory enactments. Under our federal system there is no federal common law, with the consequence that crimes against the United States existed only as Congress enacted legislation defining them and providing for their punishment. But the several states began a process of restating common law crimes in statutory form, and this carried to the extent that in many of them the entire criminal law was eventually codified. This statutory activity was promoted by developments which made such old common law crimes as murder, rape, arson, burglary, robbery and treason insufficient to cope with wrong-doing in its modern ramifications, and called for amplification of their scope and application.

Statutory Multiplication of Crimes. The process of statutory dealing with crimes by no means stopped with the restatement or amplification of the common law of crimes. It has become apparent that there has come about a vastly enlarged category of crimes, rationalized by an enlarged concept of the place of the criminal process in our society. And along with this development there has been a concurrent depreciation of the element of the "evil mind" as an attribute of a crime.

The trend of events in this regard was summed up by Justice Robert H. Jackson of the Supreme Court of the United States in *Morissette v. United States.* Speaking for the Supreme Court in that case, Justice Jackson referred to the century-old but accelerating tendency, discernible both in the United States and England, to call into existence new duties and crimes which disregard any ingredient of intent. The industrial revolution multiplied the number of workmen exposed to injury from increasingly powerful and complex mechanisms, driven by freshly discovered sources of energy, requiring higher precautions by employers. Traffic of velocities, volumes and varieties unheard of came to subject the wayfarer to intolerable casualty risks if owners and drivers were not to observe new cares and uniformities of conduct. Congestion of cities and crowding of quarters called for health and welfare regulations undreamed of in simpler times. Wide distribution of goods became an instrument of wide distribution of harm when those who dispersed food, drink, drugs, and even securities, did not comply with reasonable standards of quality, integrity, disclosure and care. Such dangers have engendered increasingly numerous and detailed regulations which heighten the duties of those in control of particular industries, trades, properties or activities that affect public health, safety or welfare.

"Public Welfare Offenses." Justice Jackson went on to say in the *Morissette* case that while many of these duties are sanctioned by a more strict civil liability, lawmakers, whether wisely or not, have sought to make such regulations more effective by invoking criminal sanctions to be applied by the familiar technique of criminal prosecutions and convictions. This has confronted the courts with a multitude of prosecutions, based on statutes or administrative regulations,

for what have been aptly called "public welfare offenses." These cases do not fit neatly into any of such accepted classifications of common law offenses, such as those against the state, the person, property, or public morals. Many of these offenses are not in the nature of positive aggressions or invasions, with which the common law so often dealt, but are in the nature of neglect where the law requires care, or inaction where it imposes a duty. Many violations of such regulations result in no direct or immediate injury to person or property but merely create the danger or probability of it which the law seeks to minimize.

In this respect, continued Justice Jackson, whatever the intent of the violator, the injury is the same, and the consequences are injurious or not according to fortuity. Hence, legislation applicable to such offenses, as a matter of policy, does not specify intent as a necessary element. The accused, if he does not will the violation, usually is in a position to prevent it with no more care than society might reasonably expect and no more exertion than it might reasonably exact from one who assumed his responsibilities. Also, penalties commonly are relatively small, and conviction does no grave damage to the offender's reputation. Under such considerations, courts have turned to construing statutes and regulations which make no mention of intent as dispensing with it and holding that the guilty act alone makes out the crime. The pilot of the movement in this country was a holding by the Connecticut court that a saloon-keeper could be convicted for selling liquor to an habitual drunkard even if he did not know the buyer to be such. Later came Massachusetts holdings that convictions for selling adulterated milk in violation of statutes forbidding such sales required no allegation or proof that defendant knew of the adulteration. After the turn of the Century, a new use for crimes without intent appeared when New York enacted numerous and novel regulations of tenement houses, sanctioned by money penalties. In answer to the contention of landlords that a guilty intent was essential to sustain a violation Judge Cardozo ruled for the New York Court of Appeals that the element of conscious wrongdoing, the guilty mind accompanying the guilty act, is associated with a concept of crimes that are punished as infamous, and that it was not an essential concomitant of lesser offenses.

Mens Rea as a Shifting Concept. The historical perspective of this development is apparent from the conclusion of Francis Bowes Sayre that *mens rea,* the mental factor necessary to prove criminality, has no fixed continuing meaning. The conception of *mens rea* has varied with the changing underlying conceptions and objectives of criminal justice. At the beginning when the object of criminal administration was to restrict and supplant the blood feud, the mental factor was of importance insofar as it determined the provocative nature of the offense; a malicious burning of another's dwelling house being far more provocative than an accidental one, judges must distinguish between malicious and accidental burnings. Under the dominating influence of the canon law and the penitential books the underlying objective of criminal justice gradually came to be the punishment of evil-doing; as a result the mental factors necessary for criminality were based upon a mind bent on evil-doing in the sense of moral wrong. Our modern objective tends more and more in the direction, not of awarding adequate punishment for moral wrongdoing, but of protecting social and public interests. To the extent that this objective prevails, the mental element requisite for criminality, if not altogether dispensed with, is coming to mean, not so much a mind bent on evil-doing as an intent to do that which unduly endangers social or public interests. As the underlying objective of criminal administration has almost unconsciously shifted, and is shifting, the basis of the requisite *mens rea* has imperceptibly shifted, lending a change to the flavor, if not to the actual content, of the criminal state of mind which must be proved to convict.

Insanity—The Rule of M'Naghten's Case. However much the "evil mind" aspect of the criminal law may have been subordinated with relation to the "public welfare offenses" that have crowded upon the scene in recent decades, it remains of prime importance in connection with what we would think of as the basic common law crimes, such as murder. It is recognized that if a person is so lacking in mental capacity that he is incapable of having the "evil mind" which is an inherent element of the crime of murder, or of some other crime with which he is charged and the commission of which involves a guilty mind, it follows that he should not be found guilty thereof. As a matter of principle it would be generally agreed that an insane person is lacking in that capacity of mind, and should not be convicted.

But when are we to say that a person is "insane," within the meaning of this principle? The answer still generally followed, in this country as well as in England, was laid down in the year 1843 by the Lord Justices of England in the famous *M'Naghten's Case.* M'Naghten attempted to kill Sir Robert Peel, Prime Minister of England, but by mistake shot and killed Peel's secretary. He was acquitted on the ground of insanity. In the supervening uproar the House of Lords, desiring clarification of the law as to what constituted insanity, submitted certain questions to the Lord Justices. Among the rules submitted in answer by the Lord Justices was the following: "To establish a defense on the ground of insanity, it must be clearly proved that, at the time of the committing of the act, the party accused was labouring under such a defect of reason, from disease of the mind, as not to know the nature and quality of the act he was doing; or if he did know it, that he did not know he was doing what was wrong." This remains the English view today. The "right and wrong" test thus stated was widely accepted. The Supreme Court of the United States recently said that knowledge of right and wrong is the exclusive test of criminal responsibility in a majority of American jurisdictions.

Is the Existing Test Obsolete? In the case of *Durham v. United* States, decided in 1954 by the Court of Appeals for the District of Columbia, the defendant was on trial for burglary. The defense asserted at the trial was that he was of unsound mind. Expert testimony by a psychiatrist was that he had a history of hospitalization for mental disorder, and that he was mentally unbalanced at the time of the alleged crime. But the testimony stopped short of an opinion as to whether defendant could distinguish between right and wrong at the time the crime was committed. The trial judge rejected the defense, and he was convicted. The Court of Appeals, holding that the M'Naghten test should be abandoned, reversed, and declared the rule it held applicable to the case at bar and future cases "is simply that an accused is not criminally responsible if his unlawful act was the product of mental disease or mental defect."

A representative appraisal of the *Durham* case was made by the Supreme Court of Illinois in *People v. Carpenter,* in which the court sustained the conviction of defendant for murder. Counsel for defendant contended that the trial judge should have recognized the *Durham* case as persuasive authority, and should have instructed the jury in terms of the rule stated in that case rather than in accordance with the *M'Naghten* rule. The court said the *Durham* case aroused a great deal of interest and has been commented upon extendedly, but that it did not believe the *Durham* type instruction would be an improvement." It quoted the observation of a commentator, who concluded that *"Durham* then puts forth, in my opinion, a legal principle beclouded by a central ambiguity, both unexplained and unsupported by its basic rationale." The court also quoted Judge Learned Hand, who said: "I have read the opinion that you mention, and perhaps it is all that can be said; but, frankly, it did not seem to me to give us any guidance that perceptibly would help." The Illinois court then referred to the instruction, based on the *Durham* case, requested by counsel for defendant but refused by the trial court, and the instructions, based on the *M'Naghten* rule, which the trial court gave, and said: "From the substantive standpoint there does not seem to be any significant difference, especially as the instructions would be understood by the ordinary jury. Both tests recognize that criminal responsibility must take account of impairment of the will, as well as impairment of the intellect. And, if anything, the given instructions are the more explicit, articulate and useful."

Although it is doubtful whether the *Durham* case has brought about any innovation, students of criminology have regarded it as of great significance. In this connection, Harry Kalven, Jr., commented: "When so basic a rule which has survived so much criticism for so long a time finally falls officially, we sense that a great event in law has taken place. And it remains a great event even though there be disagreement as to how much difference this change of wording in the test for insanity makes, and even though there be not a little skepticism as to whether the change makes any difference in the outcome of cases."

Individualization of Punishment. Judge Leon R. Yankwich has recently said that the most intelligent advance in the realm of penology in the last half century is individualization of punishment, achieved through the indeterminate sentence, parol and probation. It may be expected that judges will tend to confine themselves to the determination of guilt, leaving the disposition of the offender, within very wide limits, to the efforts of a scientific group (the treatment tribunal or whatever it may be called) which will have in mind not only the constitutional guarantees, but also the welfare of society. Basically important procedural aspects of criminal law are considered in the chapter which follows.

Chapter 23

PROCEDURAL ASPECTS OF THE COMMON LAW

Substantive and Procedural Elements. Our body of law is made up of two broad elements, the one commonly referred to as substantive, the other as procedural. The substantive element relates to fundamental rights of person and property; the procedural element to the processes by which those rights are administratively and judicially enforced.

Thus far in our analysis of the content of the common law we have been dealing in the main with its substantive content. Before passing on, it is essential to take note of its procedural side. In all probability the reader has already formed the impression that substantive rights, however fully recognized, would be of little value or avail were there not available procedural processes to vindicate them when they are drawn into question. Pregnant with forceful implication are the words of Justice Oliver Wendell Holmes: "Legal obligations that exist but cannot be enforced are ghosts that are seen in the law, but that are elusive to the grasp." Justice William O. Douglas, a later member of the Supreme Court of the United States, observed: "It is not without significance that most of the provisions of the Bill of Rights are procedural. It is procedure that spells much of the difference between rule by law and rule by whim or caprice. Steadfast adherence to strict procedural safeguards is our main assurance that there will be equal justice under law."

Rights "Wrenched from the King." We cannot here undertake to detail the development of the procedural side of the English common law. At the outset, by force of circumstances it was limited in its processes and rigid in its forms. But as the concept of substantive rights expanded, and as recognition of those rights was brought about —in large measure by forcing recalcitrant monarchs to accede to them —the procedural element of the law kept fair pace. The process was well expressed by Kipling:

> All we have of freedom, all we use or know—
> This our fathers bought for us long and long ago.
> Ancient Right unnoticed as the breath we draw—

> Leave to live by no man's leave, underneath the Law.
> Lance and torch and tumult, steel and gray-goose wing
> Wrenched it, inch and ell and all, slowly from the King.

Out of the pressures came equity as a separate segment of jurisprudence, which will be considered in a later chapter. But there were profound developments in the English procedural law itself. Thus, the grand jury came to be an institution that protected against tyranny, the right to be free from self-incrimination came into recognition by way of reaction to ecclesiastical inquisition, the right to trial by jury developed, and the high prerogative writ of habeas corpus was employed as an instrument to free men from unlawful detention of their persons.

The Constitution and the Bill of Rights. In the United States the groundwork of the procedural element of our law was established in the Constitution, particularly in the Bill of Rights, by drawing upon such developments of the English common law as those to which we have just alluded.

Thus the Fourth Amendment provides that the right of the people to be secure in their persons, houses, papers, and effects, against unreasonable searches and seizures, shall not be violated, and no warrants shall issue, but upon probable cause, supported by oath or affirmation, and particularly describing the place to be searched, and the persons or things to be seized.

The Fifth Amendment stipulates that no person shall be held to answer for a capital, or otherwise infamous crime, unless on a presentment or indictment of a grand jury, except in cases arising in the armed forces, when in actual service in time of war or in public danger; nor shall any person be subject for the same offense to be twice put in jeopardy of life or limb; nor shall be compelled in any criminal case to be a witness against himself, nor be deprived of life, liberty or property without due process of law; nor shall private property be taken for public use, without just compensation.

The Sixth Amendment provides that in all criminal prosecutions the accused shall enjoy the right to a speedy and public trial, by an impartial jury of the state and district wherein the crime shall have been committed, which district shall have been previously ascertained by law, and to be informed of the nature and cause of the accusation; to be confronted with the witnesses against him; to have compulsory process for obtaining witnesses in his favor, and to have the assistance of counsel for his defense.

The Seventh Amendment stipulates that in suits at common law, where the value in controversy shall exceed twenty dollars, the right of trial by jury shall be preserved, and no fact tried by a jury shall be otherwise re-examined in any court of the United States than according to the rules of the common law. By the Eighth Amendment it is provided that excessive bail shall not be required, nor excessive fines imposed, nor cruel and unusual punishments inflicted.

We start with the understanding that these constitutional provisions embody basic concepts which in themselves are, for us, immutable. As such, they are not amenable to "development" or alteration in any manner, shape or form. Judge Leon Yankwich has said that as we sum up the antecedents of the Bill of Rights, we find in them the desire to limit sovereign power, and, at the same time, to insure to the individual citizen certain rights and privileges which he can assert against the sovereign, be he a constitutional monarch, a legislative body, or a constitutional majority. And implicit is the idea, fundamental to all Anglo-American political theory, that the government be one of laws rather than one of men. This flows directly from the due process clause of the Fifth Amendment and is still at the heart of our system of free government.

Pointing out that modern students of political science consider the doctrine of limited sovereignty the basis of free government, Judge Yankwich recently quoted Hans Kelsen as saying that government by a majority, so characteristic of democracy, differs from every other government because, by its very nature, it not only recognizes opposition—the minority—but also protects it politically, by guarantees of fundamental rights and liberties, and through proportional representation. "The right to dissent and to oppose the state are of the very essence of the democratic process," concluded Judge Yankwich. "It flows from the limitation of sovereignty and the recognition of rights in the individual."

Without thought or intention of minimizing any one of the guarantees of the Bill of Rights—all of which are in effect duplicated in the constitutions of the several states—special mention will be here further made of only two of them: due process of law, and the right to trial by jury.

Due Process of Law Via the Fifth and Fourteenth Amendments.
Thus far we have mentioned only the Fifth Amendment provision as to due process of law, which by its terms protects the person only against action by the federal government. The Fourteenth Amendment, enacted following the Civil War, provides that no state shall deprive any person of life, liberty, or property without due process of

law. Thus there is at present a constitutional guaranty against both federal and state governments.

In considering the due process guaranty we are necessarily concerned with the definition of the several terms employed. What is "life"? What is "liberty"? What is "property"? What is it to "deprive"?

Generally speaking, the citizen is entitled to have his own concept of these things. It is probably accurate. To be executed would be to be deprived of life. To be imprisoned would be to be deprived of liberty. To have one's property seized and taken away, or to be ousted from his home, would be to be deprived of property. Such concept affords a working start. But it is important and reassuring to note that it is not a static or circumscribed concept. The Supreme Court of the United States held in *Allgeyer v. Louisiana* that liberty means not only the right of the citizen to be free from the mere physical restraint of his person, as by incarceration, but the term is deemed to embrace the right of the citizen to be free in the enjoyment of all his faculties; to be free to use them in all lawful ways; to live and work where he will; to earn his livelihood by any lawful calling; to pursue any livelihood or avocation, and for that purpose to enter into all contracts which may be proper, necessary and essential to his carrying out to a successful conclusion the purposes above mentioned.

In the recent case of *Kent v. Dulles* the Supreme Court ruled that the right to travel is part of the citizen's liberty of which he cannot be deprived without due process of law.

It is noteworthy, of course, that the clause in question does not say, simply: "Nor shall any person be deprived of life, liberty, or property." If it did, the government could not, under any circumstances, execute a person convicted of murder. Nor could it incarcerate a robber or an arsonist, or take possession of a debtor's property to satisfy a claim for unpaid taxes. There may be "deprivation" of these things, but it must be in accordance with "due process of law."

What, then, is "due process of law"? We may well define it in the light of the purpose of the constitutional forefathers who built it into the fundamental law, and which, in general, has already been stated. More specifically, the object of the due process clause has been said to be to preserve the personal and property rights of a person against the arbitrary action of public officials. The wielding of official power under our system of government must be by procedure which will protect persons against the ills arising out of the whims and caprice of officials. The guaranty of due process of law requires that every man shall have the protection of his day in court and the benefit of the general law, a law which hears before it condemns, which proceeds not arbitrarily or capriciously but upon inquiry, and renders judgment only after trial, so that every citizen shall hold his life, liberty, property and immunities under the protection of the general rules that govern society.

In other words, as Justice Felix Frankfurter has pointed out, the due process clause embodies a system of rights based on moral principles so deeply imbedded in the traditions and feelings of our people as to be deemed fundamental to a civilized society as conceived by our whole history. Due process is that which comports with the deepest notions of what is fair and right and just. Due process thus conveys neither formal nor fixed nor narrow requirements. It is the compendious expression for all those rights which the courts must enforce because they are basic to our free society. But basic rights do not become petrified as of any one time, even though, as a matter of human experience, some may not too rhetorically be called the eternal verities. It is of the very nature of a free society to advance in its standards of what is deemed reasonable and right. "Representing as it does a living principle, due process is not confined within a permanent catalogue of what may at a given time be deemed the limits or the essentials of fundamental rights," according to Justice Frankfurter. "To rely on a tidy formula for the easy determination of what is a fundamental right for purposes of legal enforcement may satisfy a longing for certainty but ignores the movements of a free society. It belittles the scale of the conception of due process. The real clue to the problem confronting the judiciary in the application of the due process clause is not to ask where the line is once and for all to be drawn but to recognize that it is for the court to draw it by the gradual and empiric process of 'inclusion and exclusion.' "

Certainly much of the content of the "due process" guaranty as historically conceived might be thought of as embodied in the other portions of the Bill of Rights which we have stated hereinabove. Such practices as prosecution for capital or infamous crimes without indictment by a grand jury, or double jeopardy, or refusal to recognize the privilege against self-incrimination, or unreasonable searches and seizures, would constitute violation of Justice Frankfurter's category of rights that are "basic to our free society." The citizen finds satisfying reassurance in the realization that as of any given time the limits of the due process guaranty are not rigidly defined and that its boundaries extend well beyond the other specific protections enumerated.

A noteworthy example of the working of the due process principle is found in *Wong Yang Sung v. McGrath,* discussed in the chapter on Administrative Law.

Trial by Jury. If any one specific feature of our common law procedural system were to be chosen as distinctively outstanding, it would be the institution of trial by jury. In early times the English jury consisted of a body of neighbors, summoned by a public officer to give an answer to a question under oath. Originally the jury comprised witnesses largely under the control of the judge. In the course of time the jury assumed, and has since retained, the function of independent trier of the facts in suits at law, civil and criminal.

Recapitulating some of the history of the institution of trial by jury, the Supreme Court of the United States said in *Patton v. United States,* that trial by jury was regarded as a valuable privilege bestowed upon the person accused of crime for the purpose of safeguarding him against the oppressive power of the king and the arbitrary or partial judgment of the court. Thus Blackstone, who held trial by jury in both civil and criminal cases in such esteem that he called it "the glory of the English law," nevertheless looked upon it as a "privilege," albeit "the most transcendent privilege which any subject can enjoy." And Justice Story of the Supreme Court of the United States, writing at a time when the adoption of the Constitution was still in the memory of men then living, emphasized that when our more immediate ancestors removed to America they brought with them, as their birthright and inheritance, trial by jury as a part of that admirable common law which had fenced round and interposed barriers on every side against the approaches of arbitrary power. It is now incorporated into all our state constitutions as a fundamental right, and the Constitution of the United States would have been justly obnoxious to the most conclusive objection if it had not recognized and confirmed it in the most solemn manner.

Thomas Jefferson declared: "I consider trial by jury as the only anchor yet imagined by man, by which a government can be held to the principles of its constitution." Transplanted from English soil to our hemisphere, it has been characterized as perhaps the most cherished institution of the greatest exemplar of free and intelligent government that the world has ever seen.

Any further encomiums would be a work of supererogation. Having developed within the procedural structure of the English common law into the institution thus cemented into our constitutional structure, we look to it as a permanent guardian of our liberties. As we shall proceed to point out, other aspects of our procedural system should be, and have been, open to change, as change is needed to facilitate the vindication of the citizen's rights. The jury system, however, will go on as long as there is a free United States.

Habeas Corpus and Other High Prerogative Writs. We have already noted that the writ of habeas corpus was a development of the English common law. Like other rights of the individual which had a similar origin, it was embodied in the Constitution of the United States, not, however, in the Bill of Rights, but in the body of the document itself. By section 9 of Article I it is provided that the privilege of the writ of habeas corpus shall not be suspended, unless when in cases of rebellion or invasion the public safety may require it. The constitutions of the several states embody a similar provision.

Chief Justice Marshall held in *Ex Parte Watkins* that the writ of habeas corpus is a high prerogative writ, known to the common law, the great object of which is the liberation of those who may be imprisoned without sufficient cause. It is in the nature of a writ of error, to examine the legality of the commitment. English judges, being originally under the influence of the crown, neglected to issue this writ where the government entertained suspicions which could not be sustained by evidence; and the writ when issued was sometimes disregarded or evaded, and great individual oppression was suffered in consequence of delays in bringing prisoners to trial. To remedy this evil the celebrated Habeas Corpus Act of 1679 was enacted, for the purpose of securing the benefits for which the writ was given.

The writ, in its historic form, like that now in use in the United States courts, was directed to the disposition of the custody of the prisoner. It commanded the officer to "have the body" of him "detained in our prison under your custody," "together with the day and cause of his being detained," before the judge at a specified time and place "to do all and singular those things which our said chief justice shall then and there consider of him in this behalf."

We have previously noted the statement of Sir Maurice Sheldon Amos as to the place in the common law of such other high prerogative writs as quo warranto, mandamus, prohibition and certiorari. The importance of these writs, he pointed out, is that they constitute an important part of the machinery provided by the common law for government by judicial process, adding noteworthy elements of protection against arbitrary governmental action.

Chapter 24

EQUITY AND THE COMMON LAW

Equity and Its Place in the Common Law System. Thus far in our study of the common law system our discussion has been in terms of "law," and in terms of the "common law" in particular. In the last analysis our conclusions must necessarily be reduced to the common denominator of "law," which alone is the term that comprehends all the rules of conduct by which we live.

This being so, there may seem to be some incongruity about introducing into our agenda the term "equity," descriptive of a category of legal principles which in their application, when pertinent, have all the force of law, but which, nevertheless, are commonly thought of as constituting a distinctly separate system of jurisprudence. Why are not these principles just a portion of the "law" itself, to be dealt with on the same basis as all other legal principles? Why is it necessary to accord them distinct consideration?

From the standpoint of strict logic there should be no such necessity. But we are on notice that we cannot depend too much on logic, and here is indeed a situation where history rather than logic provides the answer. We have retained the impression that something in the nature of "equity" had a separate existence in the system of the ancient Hebrews, as well as that of the Romans, and are well prepared to be told that equity came into our system from a genesis altogether apart from that of the common law itself. In spite of the fact that threads of the common law and equity have become closely interwoven in our legal fabric, they are, historically, two different things. Viewed from that standpoint equity jurisprudence, as a separate system, administered by separate courts, not only in England but in some of the American states, is understandable. The statement of Section 2, Article III of the Constitution of the United States that "the judicial power shall extend to all cases, in law and equity," takes on real significance; and the Seventh Amendment, which provides that "in suits at common law" the right of trial by jury shall be preserved likewise becomes significant, because there never was, nor is there now, a right of trial by jury in equity cases.

Early Shortcomings of the Common Law. It has already been indicated that it is the nature of the common law to develop to meet the needs of advancing society, and that thesis will be further developed in the chapter which follows. Through enlightened exercise by the courts of the power to declare the common law by judicial decision, and by the supplementing statutes of our legislative bodies, basic principles of right and liability are promulgated in general accord with felt current needs. Inherent as is this operation in our common law system as we know it today, in its earlier history it was not thus manifested. Principles declaratory of rights were narrowly conceived and adhered to in a formalistic spirit of utmost rigidity. Persons who under what might be called the general conscience of those times had suffered wrong often found that no remedy was open to them. In the matter of recognition of the principle that if justice is to be achieved, not only must there be flexibility in the adapting of legal rules to individual cases, but also the molding of legal remedies to the needs of particular cases before the court, the early common law courts maintained a position of static indifference.

This early attitude has been well summed up by saying that the common law courts paid such deference to forms and precedents that they became slaves to them. Their jurisdiction was thus circumscribed. They adhered to certain precise writs and rigid forms of action which were not sufficiently comprehensive to enable them to give adequate redress in some cases of injustice and wrong, or to give any redress in many others. In short, there existed a situation in which, in all good conscience, wrongs were committed, and there was no recognized "law" under which they could be redressed.

It has been well said that whether the wellspring of equity be viewed as "natural justice," "higher ethical standards," or the like, we are inevitably led to philosophic inquiry as to the contents of such concepts as "justice," "morality," "good faith," "honesty" and "conscience"—ideas which mean much to thinking men of whatever age or station. These ideas are intuitively perceived by the great mass of men, and while it may be possible to go far in defining and ordering them in a philosophic system, the important point is that they are workable concepts even if not precisely defined. They are "felt necessities," to use the phrase of Oliver Wendell Holmes. And the people, not the judges, are the ones who first "feel" these "necessities" or moral aspirations. Under the common law system as it originated, the opportunity for translating these felt moral mandates into law was rigidly circumscribed by jurisdictional and procedural limitations. But even under that system new principles were planted and grew. The Chancellor was much more successful in improving the law, although in consulting his conscience and making his decree equivalent to *arbitrium boni viri*, he was subject to the criticism that equity varied with the length of the Chancellor's foot. The exercise of discretion necessarily injects a certain degree of uncertainty into the law, but if that is the price of progress, we must live with it.

It does not seem unreasonable to say that had the common law courts, from the outset, consistently adopted and exercised the policies which in recent generations they have recognized and followed, or had democratically based legislative action been then available, there never would have come about in the Anglo-American legal system a separate body of equity jurisprudence. Having in mind the considerations of which we have just been speaking, its presence as such a separate body can be accepted as a matter of course.

"Equity as Old as Aristotle." Because of the operation of the Greek legal system through assemblies of the people, with the result that the "law" was in large measure pragmatically made from case to case, they had no such problem as arises when a judicial tribunal is acting under narrower limitations. The Greek tribunals could, so to speak, do "equity" on the spot. The interesting thing for us to note is that they had the concept just as it appeared in the jurisprudence of the Hebrews and the Romans. The distinction between law and equity is not peculiar to the English legal system. The distinction is as old as Aristotle; and it was known in substance to the classical Roman lawyers and to the mediaeval canonists and civilians. Aristotle defines equity as "a better sort of justice, which corrects legal justice where the latter errs through being expressed in a universal form and not taking account of particular cases." And Grotius condensed this definition into a modern one: "Equity is the correction of the law, wherein by reason of its universality it is deficient."

Equity is based, as Lord Ellesmere declared in the *Earl of Oxford's Case*, on the fact that "men's actions are so diverse and infinite that it is impossible to make any general law which may apply with every particular act, and not fail in some circumstances." It is in fact a universal distinction. What is peculiar to England is the sharpness of the separation between the rules of law and equity. That phenomenon is due to the fact that the rules of law and the rules of equity were administered by distinct tribunals using a distinct procedure; and that in consequence two separate systems of rules grew up, which

occasionally conflicted with, but were often supplementary to, one
another.

"The Keeper of the King's Conscience." The historical reason for
this peculiarity of English law, according to Sir William Holdsworth, is the fact that when in the fourteenth century, as we have
seen, the rules administered by the common law courts had become
so rigid and technical that they failed to provide adequate remedies
for litigants, litigants who needed relief applied to the king, who referred them to his Chancellor, "the keeper of his conscience." The
Chancellor was the king's secretary. From the fact that this was
the practice of the king, litigants came in course of time to present
their petitions to the Chancellor directly, and thus gradually and at a
time which history cannot enable us to precisely fix, the Court of
Chancery came to be established.

Separate Courts of Law and Equity. The jurisdiction of the Court
of Chancery, then, was wholly extraordinary. Relief was afforded by
it only in those cases wherein the common law courts either could
give no redress at all, or could not give adequate redress; and any one
coming to chancery with a case which did not meet its extraordinary
jurisdiction, but which on the other hand could be adequately dealt
with by the common law courts, was dismissed for lack of jurisdiction. Thus was initiated what remains, to this day, a distinctive
feature of equity jurisdiction: one who has a sufficient remedy at law
cannot invoke the aid of equitable remedies.

It is evident, therefore, that there came to exist, side by side, two
kinds of courts—the common law courts, and the Court of Chancery—
each with a distinct jurisdiction; the test of chancery jurisdiction in
any given case being that the suitor could either get no relief at all, or
could not get adequate relief, in a court of common law. And, therefore, necessarily, there grew up not merely two distinctive systems of
practice in these courts, but also two distinctive systems of substantive
jurisprudence, that in the Court of Chancery being the system we call
"equity."

In the formation of the government of some of our states, such as
New York and New Jersey, these two distinct systems of courts were
given a place, and courts of chancery were clothed with the general
jurisdiction and powers of the high court of chancery in England.
Separate courts thus administered these separate systems of jurisprudence in such states until by later constitutional change the courts
of chancery were abolished and their jurisdiction and powers devolved upon other courts. From that time on the same court admin-

istered justice under both systems, but the systems themselves have maintained their identity and have continued to exist. In those states, such as Illinois, which never had separate chancery courts, the one court, from the outset, administered both systems. Although this was true in the United States courts, until recent times they operated under separate rules of law and equity procedure. Recent developments in this regard will be pointed out in the next chapter.

The Scope of Equity. From what has been said, the general scope of equity as providing relief for legal wrongs not otherwise redressable is clear. Supplementing, in a generalized way, this broad principle, it may be further said that equity is a system of positive jurisprudence, founded upon established principles, which can be adapted to new circumstances where a court of law is powerless to give relief. Equity is the correction of that wherein the law by reason of its universality is deficient.

Equity in the process of development has assumed the qualities of a composite system, expansive rather than abstract in relation to settled rules by which rights are measured and processes invoked—not always defined. The power of the chancellor and the processes of a court of equity must be equal to any emergency and portend to protect the poor and the rich alike, compel justice and right to every one in its hold. The cradle of equity is the power to afford adequate remedy where the law is impotent; it does not create new rights, but affords a remedy for existing rights. Every known step in the court of equity was born of some emergency to apply settled rules to new conditions. The entrances to the portals of equity are not branded, labeled or limited, nor has equity or its processes become static, but continues to grow, and if need be extend its borders so as to encompass any civil right of a pecuniary relation. A court of equity may contrive new remedies, the remedies at law being inadequate.

Cases Within Equity Purview Enumerated. However essential may be some understanding of the history of equity, with its explanation of the general scope of equity's application, a satisfactory grasp of its relation to our whole body of law is possible only through a partial enumeration of the types of cases which fall within as well as without its purview.

As to the cases which fall clearly into the field of law, and thus outside the scope of equity jurisprudence, criminal actions may be named as an outstanding example. Generally speaking, actions seeking only the recovery of money damages are distinctively actions at law. Such are the typical breach of contract and tort suits which make up a major portion of today's legal grist. Rights created by statute, such as arise out of workmen's compensation acts, are at law and not in equity. The whole field of Administrative Law is without its scope, save as its remedies may be invoked to restrain the improper exercise of administrative power.

A longer enumeration is called for when we come to equity. First, we may point to those actions wherein the equitable writ of injunction comes into play. Such are suits to enjoin unlawful picketing in labor disputes; suits to enjoin the unlawful maintenance of nuisances, and suits to enjoin action by administrative agencies which transcends the bounds of constitutional protection. Suits of this latter kind have been increasingly important with the rapid growth of the administrative process. Among other characteristic equity cases are suits for divorce and separate maintenance; suits for the specific performance of contracts; suits for the reformation, rescission or surrender of written instruments executed as a result of fraud or mutual mistake; suits arising from trusts express, constructive or resulting; suits between partners for accounting and to wind up partnerships; suits for the enforcement of liens created by mortgages or sales of land on credit; suits by wards against guardians, executors and administrators where an accounting is necessary; suits to have absolute deeds declared mortgages; suits to partition land; suits to remove clouds on title, and suits for the construction of wills and trusts.

Commenting with regard to the constitutional provision that jurisdiction of the federal courts shall extend to all cases in law and equity arising under the Constitution and the laws of the United States, *The Federalist* took up the question: what need of the word "equity"? What equitable causes can grow out of the Constitution and laws of the United States? There is hardly a subject of litigation between individuals, which may not involve those ingredients of fraud, accident, trust, or hardship, which would render the matter an object of equitable rather than of legal jurisdiction, as the distinction is known and established in several of the states. It is the peculiar province, for instance, of a court of equity to relieve against what are called hard bargains: these are contracts in which, though there may have been no direct fraud or deceit sufficient to invalidate them in a court of law, yet there may have been some undue and unconscionable advantage taken of the necessities or misfortune of one of the parties, which a court of equity would not tolerate. In such case, where foreigners were concerned on either side, it would be impossible for the federal judicatories to do justice without an equitable as well as a legal jurisdiction. Agreements to convey lands claimed under the grants of different states, may afford another example of the necessity of an equitable jurisdiction in the federal courts.

In view of what has been said, it is clear that attempting a full and complete enumeration of the cases in which equity jurisdiction exists would be not only impossible but out of order. The entrances to equity's portals "are not branded, labeled or limited," and the cases mentioned represent only some of the actions in which equity is most commonly invoked.

The Future of Equity. At the outset of this brief sketch of equity jurisprudence, mention was made of the apparent logical incongruity involved in a separate body of jurisprudence within a legal system conceived and presently operating under the theory that it possesses the capacity to make all necessary adaptation to the needs of the time. The historical explanation for such a system being apparent, the logical and even the practical necessity for its future continuance is not evident.

There is no doubt that in many of their aspects the differences between law and equity have, in recent years, become nebulous. As we shall point out in the next chapter, the procedural distinctions between law and equity have been in large measure eliminated. Distinctions having no more than historical basis will almost inevitably fade, albeit slowly. Such is proving the fact here. The opinion may be hazarded that in the course of time the distinctions between law and equity, already largely eliminated in practical application, will become so far obscured as to play no direct part in judicial procedure, except in so far as they involve such inherent historical qualities as the right or non-right to trial by jury. The most important aspect of difference is found in this latter, and its future will be largely dependent upon how immaculately the right to trial by jury is preserved as an integral feature of the democratic process.

CHAPTER 25

THE COMMON LAW'S CAPACITY FOR GROWTH

Aptitude of the English People. The subject matter of the preceding chapters having afforded some idea of the general scope and content of the common law, we may well commence further consideration of it by pondering the well chosen words of Lord Porter of the English House of Lords in the recent case of *Best v. Samuel Fox & Co., Ltd.:* "The common law is a historical development rather than a logical whole, and the fact that a particular doctrine does not logically accord with another is no ground for its rejection." The same thought was involved in the famous dictum of Justice Holmes that the life of the law has not been logic but experience, and that " . . . a page of history is worth a volume of logic."

The logical qualities of the English people are not disparaged by saying that the origin and satisfactory development of the common law was due in considerable measure to their aptitude to inaugurate and nourish such a system to maturity. The opinion has been expressed that the common law of England never could and never would have started in a community imbued with the principles, theories, manners and customs of either the Persian, Grecian, Roman, Aryan or Mohammedan nationalities. There was lacking in each and all of them those elements of a strong and vigorous individuality, a responsible personal humanity, which are the inspiring elements of the common law of England as it has come down to us. To the island of Britain, on which were already the high-spirited Celts, came the Angles, the Jutes and the Saxons, peoples who, measured in the standards of that day, were characterized by high regard for the sanctity of domestic relations, strict observance of individual obligations, and, what is particularly signficant, by a strong feeling of personal independence. Looking back through the centuries, it is evident that these peoples had peculiar aptitudes for laying the common law foundations and erecting the structure's framework.

Geographical Considerations. Geographical isolation also played its part in the development of the common law. The island of Britain was aloof from much of the turbulent succession of events on the

Continent of Europe during the centuries in which there was a physical struggle for territorial sovereignty with the aggrandizements incidental to such domination. Because the Romans occupied England for a considerable time we might expect to find some impress of the influence which, as we have seen, culminated eventually in their great system of Roman Law. But it appears that when the Romans left Britain about 450 A.D., their influence took its departure with them. No new customs, methods, usages, laws or language had taken root as a consequence of their sojourn.

In this environment the common law began. People were living in separated communities or separated petty kingdoms. We are already familiar with the need for accepted usages and modes of conduct among human beings who live together. Absent despotic interference by artificial ukase, modes of conduct will take the course of natural development. That was true here. Usages, geared to their needs and way of life, gradually crystallized in a natural manner and became recognized as establishing and regulating their rights and obligations. These customary usages were the "law," applied by early arbiters. Gradually, outside contacts began to play a part in social and trade relationships. There followed a correspondingly enlarged body of customary usages likewise recognized, the arbiter deciding each case upon the basis of such usages as seemed applicable or adaptable to the situation at hand. By such ruling he added a solidifying element to the usage and created a precedent for future cases of similar nature. We have already seen, in general, how the process operates and will note it further in the chapter on the place of judicial precedent.

Adaptability to Life of the People. Obviously, the common law was thus more than just "a law" or even a set of laws. In its working aspect it was from the outset rather a legal system, not only embodying rules of conduct applicable to particular situations but also containing within itself the means whereby those rules would be adapted to future situations, or new rules found and declared as changed conditions demonstrated themselves. The actual law emerging from the operation of such a system was as close to the people who lived by it as law could possibly be. The system itself well met the test implicit in the story of Bogigish, as told by Justice Brandeis.

Bogigish was a native of the ancient city of Tagusa off the coast of Dalmatia—a deep student of the law, who after gaining some distinction at the University of Vienna and in France became Professor at the University of Odessa. When Montenegro was admitted to the family of nations, its Prince concluded that, like other civilized countries, it must have a code of law. Bogigish's fame had reached Montenegro, for Ragusa is but a few miles distant. So the Prince begged the Czar of Russia to have the learned jurist prepare a code for Montenegro. The Czar granted the request, and Bogigish undertook the task. But instead of utilizing his great knowledge of law to draft a code, he proceeded to Montenegro, and for two years literally made his home with the people—studying everywhere their customs, their practices, their needs, their beliefs, their points of view. Then he embodied in law the life which the Montenegrins lived. They respected that law, because it expressed the will of the people.

In those times, centuries ago, the prolific methods of making and circulating records and information that are commonplace today were non-existent. Few could read or write; the art of printing was still in its infancy. The rules and regulations of conduct thus arising and crystallized by application were for long only matters of memory or tradition. But they had a living and a growing force. Such were the humble, "grass-roots" beginnings of the common law, which, understandably, is sometimes referred to as the "unwritten law."

Idea of Justice Is Evolutionary. As Judge William H. Hastie recently pointed out, observance of the idea of justice itself is evolutionary, as the development of thought in this very area shows. It was for a long time a postulate of American thinking about the legal order that the essence of justice was to be realized in the providing of a workable maximum of individual freedom in human community. Much has been written of the way in which such influences as the philosophy of the Enlightenment, the revolutionary origin of the United States and the pioneer and frontier character of our society in a continental vastness contributed to such thinking.

But, understanding this point of view, many of today's most observing and thoughtful men find it inadequate. They are impressed that among the twentieth century's most notable social phenomena have been the emergence and persistence and variety of human demands that society make greater affirmative provision for the well-being of its members. They find yesterday's view of justice deficient in its failure to take sufficiently into account, as Pound puts it, that "Men wish to be free, but they want much besides." So, in informed thinking, there is an observable trend away from the idea that justice consists of providing a workable maximum of individual freedom, and toward a more inclusive concept of reconciling and satisfying a great diversity of deserving but often conflicting human claims.

If such a concept be recognized—and to deny its potency today would be to deny reality—a legal system capable of implementing it must have more than static attributes.

Flexibility of the Common Law. Having in mind the rigidity of a code of written law such as the Law of the Twelve Tables of Rome, we can appreciate the advantage of a system of law which is not tied down to formalized statements of principle, and which does not have to rely for progress upon "interpretations" of such statements. It is impossible to emphasize too strongly the highly flexible element of the common law, clearly implicit in its nature as the "unwritten law." Referring back to Bogigish, we would at once say that whereas the Montenegrins thus began with a formal written code of law which well met their needs and purposes at the moment, they stood to be hampered by its formal rigidity as time went on and the conditions of life changed. Here we put our finger on the basic difference between our system of common law and the Roman Law. A formal code, purporting to state legal principles for the whole field of conduct, does not lend itself to ready adaptation to changed conditions.

The strength of the common law is found in the fact that it is not a rigid codified body. Though inherent in the system as an attribute of stability is the principle of following prior precedents, equally inherent is the principle that when conditions have so changed as to make adherence to precedents conducive to results that are not compatible with the new enlightenment, the courts have it within their power to declare new law. In the absence of constitutional inhibition—and it rarely enters in this regard—they are free to determine the law according to reason and justice, taking into account such past precedents as there may be in their relation to the usages of the day. Such approach is in accordance with what Paul Vinogradoff has characterized as the best traditions of the common law system—traditions bound up with a constant striving to extend substantial justice to litigants, and to take into account as far as possible not only technical formalities, but underlying ideas of right.

A century ago Chief Justice Shaw of the Supreme Judicial Court of Massachusetts, dealing with what was then a new instrumentality— a street car drawn by a horse—put the matter very well indeed. He declared it is the great merit of the common law that it was founded upon a comparatively few broad, general principles of justice, fitness and expediency. These remain fixed, and are generally comprehensive enough to adapt themselves to new institutions and conditions of society, new modes of commerce, new usages and practices, "as the progress of society and the advancement of civilization may require."

Capacity for Growth. A basic characteristic of the common law, then, is that it is not static, but is endowed with vitality and capacity for growth. It never becomes permanently crystallized but changes and adjusts itself from time to time to new developments in social and economic life in order to meet the changing needs of society. In a sense the law will always be behind the times, because before it changes or develops new rules the conditions requiring the modification must acquire some degree of permanency.

The lag, however, must not be too great. As was observed by Justice Brandeis, "Modification implies growth. It is the life of the law." And with poetic imagery Justice Cardozo gave the following expression to this thought: "The inn that shelters for the night is not the journey's end. The law, like the traveler, must be ready for the morrow. It must have a principle of growth."

A striking characterization of the judge in his relation to the common law was drawn by Justice Cardozo: "The judge is not to innovate at pleasure. He is not a knight errant, roaming at will in pursuit of his own ideal of beauty or of goodness. He is to draw his inspiration from consecrated principles. He is not to yield to spasmodic sentiment, to vague and unregulated benevolence. He is to exercise a discretion informed by tradition, methodized by analogy, disciplined by system, and subordinated to the primordial necessity of order in the social life." How under him the common law grows we will now see.

Right to Privacy. In the course of an earlier chapter of this book reference was made to the case of *Macpherson v. Buick Motor Company* in which the New York Court of Appeals discarded the doctrine growing out of an English case in which recovery was denied a stage coach driver for injuries sustained when a defective wheel caused the coach to crash, and held that an automobile driver injured when the car crashed because of a defective wheel, had a right of action under the common law. This landmark case may be readily supplemented by others of different nature, and of more recent date.

In 1890 Samuel Warren and Louis D. Brandeis, later Justice of the Supreme Court of the United States, wrote a very convincing article for the *Harvard Law Review* entitled "The Right to Privacy." They began by saying that the individual's right to full protection in person and in property is as old as the common law; but it has been found necessary from time to time to define anew the exact nature and extent of such protection. Political, social and economic changes entail the recognition of new rights, and the common law, in its eternal youth, grows to meet the demands of society.

Thus, in very early times the law gave a remedy only for physical interference with life and property. Then the "right to life" served only to protect the subject from battery in its various forms; liberty meant freedom from actual restraint, and the right to property secured to the individual his lands and his cattle. Later, there came a recognition of man's spiritual nature, of his feelings and of his intellect. Gradually the scope of these legal rights broadened; and now the right to life has come to mean the right to enjoy life—the right to be let alone; the right to liberty secures the exercise of extensive civil privileges; and the term "property" has grown to comprise every form of possession—the intangible as well as tangible.

Our survey of the law and its development as we have made it to this point has put us in position to thoroughly understand and appreciate these conclusions of Warren and Brendeis, and to go along with them as they further traced the development of the law. Thus, they continued, with the recognition of the legal value of sensations, the protection against actual bodily injury was extended to prohibit mere attempts to do such injury; that is, putting another in fear of such injury. From the action of battery grew that of assault. Much later came a qualified protection of the individual against offensive noises and odors, against dust and smoke and excessive vibration. The law of nuisance was developed.

All this we have noted, and we are prepared to follow these scholars as they proceeded to point out that regard for human emotions soon extended the scope of personal immunity beyond the body of the individual. His reputation, the standing among his fellow men, was considered, and the law of slander and libel arose. Man's family relations became a part of the legal conception of his life, and the alienation of a wife's affections was held remediable.

"This development of the law was inevitable," declared Warren and Brandeis. "The intense intellectual and emotional life, and the heightening of sensations which came with the advance of civilization, made it clear to men that only a part of the pain, pleasure and profit of life lay in physical things. Thoughts, emotions, and sensations demanded legal recognition, and the beautiful capacity for growth which characterizes the common law enabled the judges to afford the requisite protection, without the interpolation of the legislature."

General Nature of the Right. It might be said that the right of privacy takes up where rights arising out of the law of libel and slander leave off. From what has already been said it is evident that such law does not cover all the different things that people can write, say or do that may bring embarrassment or humiliation to a person. One can gravely wound the sensibilities of another without subjecting himself to liability under the law of libel or slander. The individual who desires to live quietly and perhaps in seclusion feels the need of protection from the written or spoken product of others on occasion, even though what they publish may be strictly factual and involve no particular moral reproach.

In the article to which we have already referred Warren and Brandeis stated that the intensity and complexity of life, attendant upon advancing civilization, have rendered necessary some retirement from the world, and that man, under the refining influence of culture, has become more sensitive to publicity, so that solitude and privacy have become more essential to the individual. They also said that the common law secures to each individual the right of determining, ordinarily, to what extent his thoughts, sentiments and emotions shall be communicated to others. Holding that the right of privacy was inherent in the common law, they concluded that the time had come for recognition of this right of privacy, as an independent right of the individual. In substance, they defined the right of privacy as the right to be let alone, the right to live in a community without being held up to the public gaze if one does not want to be held up to the public gaze.

The article was truly a landmark in the law because, however correct the authors were about the right of privacy being indigenous to the common law, not until the import of the article was judicially grasped did the courts accord to it effective recognition.

As it has been succinctly defined, judicially, actionable invasion of privacy is the unwarranted appropriation or exploitation of one's personality, the publicizing of one's private affairs with which the public has no legitimate concern, or the wrongful intrusion into one's private activities, in such manner as to cause mental suffering, shame or humiliation to a person of ordinary sensibilities.

Appropriation of Another's Personality. In accordance with the principles which have come to be recognized as protecting the right of privacy, one may not make an unauthorized appropriation of the personality of another, especially of his name or likeness, without being liable to him for mental distress as well as the actual pecuniary damages which such appropriation may cause. Thus, the right of a young woman to bring action for unauthorized use of her photograph in an advertisement promoting the sale of dog food has been upheld. A five-year-old child, whose picture was used without authority in connection with a jewelry advertisement, was held to have a right of action. A woman was also held to have a right of action against the proprietors of a dry goods store who caused moving picture films to be taken of her and used in a theatre to advertise their business. A photographer who had been employed to take a photograph of the corpses of plaintiff's children, who had been born Siamese twins, was considered in violation of plaintiff's right of privacy by making additional photographs from the negatives and having them copyrighted.

In *Melvin v. Reed* a cause of action was held to be stated in a complaint which charged the defendant with producing a moving picture of events in the unsavory past of the plaintiff. Eight years before, the plaintiff, at that time a prostitute, had been the accused in a sensational murder trial, had since married, reformed and faded from the public view. The picture not only was based upon the record of the trial, but went further and used the plaintiff's true maiden name. In another case of different nature, it was held that a lobbyist who unauthorizedly signed another's name to a telegram sent to the governor of a state urging him to veto a certain bill actionably invaded the latter's right of privacy.

In none of the above representative cases in which the right of privacy was recognized as the basis for judicial relief would there have been the necessary basis for a cause of action in libel or slander. In most of them the publication was not defamatory. Defenses of truth or privilege would have been available in others. Nevertheless, the hurt to the sensibilities of all the plaintiffs is obvious, and the courts recognized the right to its vindication.

Public Interest as a Limiting Element. Like all other rights, the right of privacy has its limitations imposed by the interest of the people as a whole. The right of the general public to the dissemination of news and information must be protected and conserved. Freedom of speech and of the press must be fostered. It follows that the right of privacy does not prohibit the publication of matter which is of legitimate public or general interest. At some point, the public interest in obtaining information becomes dominant over the individual's desire for privacy.

The leading case of *Sidis v. F-R Publishing Corporation* calls for consideration in this connection. William Sidis was the unwilling subject of a brief biographical sketch and cartoon printed in the *New Yorker,* on the basis of which he brought action for alleged violation of his right of privacy. In 1910 William was a famous child prodigy. His name and prowess were well known to newspaper readers of that period. At the age of eleven he lectured to distinguished mathematicians on the subject of four-dimensional bodies. When he was sixteen he was graduated from Harvard College amid considerable public attention. After that his name appeared in the press only sporadically and he sought to live as unobtrusively as possible.

The publication complained of appeared under the title of "Where Are They Now?" and the article on William was printed with a subtitle "April Fool." The author described William's early accomplishments in mathematics and the widespread attention he received, then recounted his general breakdown and the revulsion which he thereafter felt for his former life of fame and study. The unfortunate prodigy was traced over the years that followed, through his attempt to conceal his identity, through his chosen career as an insignificant clerk who would not need to employ unusual mathematical talent, and through the bizarre ways in which his genius flowered, as in his enthusiasm for collecting street car transfers and in his proficiency with the adding machine. The article closed with an account of an interview with William at his lodgings, "a hall bedroom of Boston's shabby south end"; the untidiness of his room, his curious laugh, his manner of speech, and other personal habits were commented upon at length, together with his interest in the lore of the Okamakammescett Indians. The subtitle "April Fool" was explained by the closing sentence of the article, quoting William as saying "with a grin" that it was strange, "but, you know, I was born on April Fool's Day." Accompanying the article was a cartoon showing the genius of eleven years lecturing to a group of astounded professors.

The United States Court of Appeals conceded that the *New Yorker* had a good defense. Pointing out that it was not contended that any of the matter printed was untrue, the court held there would have been no basis for a libel suit. The manner of the author was not considered unfriendly in that William was described as having a "certain child-like charm." But the court said that the article was merciless in the dissection of intimate details of William's personal life, containing elaborate account of his passion for privacy and the almost pitiable lengths to which he had gone in order to avoid public scrutiny. "The work possesses great reader interest for it is both amusing and instructive, but it may be fairly described as a ruthless exposure of a once public character, who has since sought and has now been deprived of the seclusion of private life," the court observed.

Taking up the discussion of the principles of law involved, the court said that all comment upon the right of privacy must stem from the famous article by Warren and Brandeis referred to above. The learned authors of that paper were convinced that some limits ought to be imposed upon the privilege of newspapers to publish truthful items of a personal nature. "The press is overstepping in every direction the obvious bounds of propriety and decency," declared Warren and Brandeis, "Gossip is no longer the resource of the idle and of the vicious, but has become a trade which is pursued with industry as well as effrontery. The intensity and complexity of life, attendant upon advancing civilization, have rendered necessary some retreat from the world, and man, under the refining influence of culture, has become more sensitive to publicity, so that solitude and privacy have become more essential to the individual; but modern enterprise and invention have, through invasions upon his privacy, subjected him to mental pain and distress far greater than could be inflicted by mere bodily injury."

Referring further to Warren and Brandeis, the court recognized that the interest of the individual in privacy must inevitably conflict with the interest of the public in news. Certain public figures, they conceded, such as holders of public office, must sacrifice their privacy and expose at least part of their lives to public scrutiny as the price of the powers they attain. But even public figures were not to be stripped bare. "In general, then," said Warren and Brandeis, "the matters on which the publication should be repressed may be described as those which concern the private life, habits, acts and relations of the individual, and have no legitimate connection with his fitness for public office. Some things all men alike are entitled to keep from public curiosity, whether in public life or not, while others are only private because the persons concerned have not assumed a position which makes their doings legitimate matters of public investigation."

The court felt that under the strict standards suggested by Warren and Brandeis, William's right of privacy had been invaded. He was neither politician, public administrator nor statesman. Even if he were, some of the personal details revealed were of the sort that Warren and Brandeis believed all men alike are entitled to keep from popular curiosity. But the court said it was not disposed to afford to all of the intimate details of private life an absolute immunity from the prying of the press. Every one will agree that at some point the public interest in obtaining information becomes dominant over the individual's desire for privacy. Brandeis and Warren were willing to lift the veil somewhat in the case of public officers. "We would go further, though we are not yet prepared to say how far," declared the court. "At least we would permit limited scrutiny of the 'private' life of any person who has achieved, or has had thrust upon him, the questionable status of a 'public figure'." Noting that William was once a public figure, the court commented that as a child prodigy he excited both admiration and curiosity. Of him great deeds were expected. In 1910, he was a person about whom the newspapers might display a legitimate intellectual interest, in the sense meant by Warren and Brandeis, as distinguished from a trivial and unseemly curiosity. His subsequent history, containing as it did the answer to the question of whether he had fulfilled his early promise, was still a matter of public concern.

In the conclusion of its well-reasoned opinion the court noted that it expressed no comment on whether or not the newsworthiness of the matter would always constitute a complete defense. Revelations may be so intimate and unwarranted in view of the victim's position as to outrage the community's notions of decency, but when focused upon public characters truthful comments upon dress, speech, habits and the ordinary aspects of personality will usually not transgress this line. "Regrettably or not, the misfortunes and frailties of neighbors and 'public figures' are subjects of considerable interest and discussion to the rest of the population," the court ruled. "And when such are the mores of the community, it would be unwise for a court to bar their expression in the newspapers, books and magazines of the day."

Fingerprints. Considerations of public safety are always paramount, and, like considerations of public interest, impose a limitation on the right of privacy. Accordingly it has been held that where a citizen is arrested and fingerprinted, although no charges are brought against him, the fingerprints need not be returned to him after his release; fingerprinting is considered to be proper police procedure in the administration of justice. And when a person is arrested and his picture hung in the "rogues" gallery, the court, for the same reason, can refuse to order his photograph returned to him after his acquittal. Nor can dissemination of fingerprints and photographs be enjoined where a citizen had been acquitted of the crime charged against him. The courts have held that when one enters into society he gives up a part of his natural liberty as the price of so valuable a boon. He obligates himself to conform to those laws which the community has thought proper to establish; otherwise there would be no security to any individual in any of the enjoyments of life. From this premise it has been reasoned that the retention and dissemination of the finger-prints were proper police protection that could not be enjoined.

Right of Recovery for Pre-natal Injuries. In 1921, in *Drobner v. Peters*, the New York Court of Appeals, the highest court of New York State, dealt with a case in which the plaintiff was a child who, through the negligence of defendant, had sustained injuries while he was still in his mother's womb. Following the precedent set by the opinions of the highest courts of several other states in which a similar issue had arisen, the New York court denied recovery, rationalizing its de-cision, as had the other courts, on the thought that until the child was born he had no separate existence of his own and his full rights as a human being sprang into existence only with his birth.

In 1951, in *Woods v. Lancet,* the same New York court was pre-sented with a case which, like the *Drobner* case, involved the right of an infant, after birth, to recover for tortiously inflicted pre-natal in-juries. A majority of the court voted to overrule the *Drobner* case, saying it would hardly be disputed that justice (not emotionalism or sentimentality) dictates the enforcement of such a cause of action. The trend of decisions of other courts, and the writing of learned com-mentators, in the period since *Drobner v. Peters* was handed down in 1921, is strongly toward making such a recovery possible. "The pre-cise question for us on this appeal is: shall we follow *Drobner v. Peters,* or shall we bring the common law of this state, on this ques-tion, into accord with justice," said Judge Desmond, speaking for the majority. "I think, as New York State's court of last resort, we should make the law conform to right."

To substantiate its position that recovery should be allowed, the court went on to say that *Drobner v. Peters* must be examined against a background of history and of the legal thought of its time and of the thirty years that had passed since it was handed down. When the *Drobner* case came before the court in 1921 there had been no decisions elsewhere upholding such suits. But since 1921, impressive affirmative precedents have been developed, in California, Ohio, Minne-sota, Maryland, Georgia and Canada. "What, then, stands in the way of a reversal here?" asked the court. "Surely, as an original proposition we would, today, be hard put to it to find a sound reason for the old rule." Of course, rules of law on which men rely in their business dealings should not be changed in the middle of the game; " . . . but what has that to do with bringing to justice a tort-feasor who surely has no moral or other right to rely on a decision of the

New York Court of Appeals?" Negligence law is common law, and the common law has been molded and changed and brought up to date in many other cases. "Our court said, long ago, that it had not only the right, but the duty, to re-examine a question where justice demands it."

The court then referred to Chancellor Kent, a distinguished New York jurist who more than a century ago stated that upwards of a thousand cases could have been pointed out in the English and American reports which had been overruled, doubted, or limited in their application, and declared that decisions which seem contrary to reason ought to be re-examined without fear and revised without reluctance, rather than to have the character of our law impaired and the beauty and harmony of the system destroyed, by the perpetuity of an error.

Hereinafter the point will be emphasized that within constitutional limits law can always be changed by legislative action. Certainly it would be within the proper and normal province of the New York legislature to enact a statute conferring upon unborn infants rights enforceable by them after birth. Two judges of the New York Court of Appeals dissented in *Woods v. Lancet,* the case we are now considering, on the ground that the court should not take it on itself to make the change, but that it should rather be left to the legislative branch of the government. But, as we are seeing, an inherent feature of the common law, as law in its historical origins and development "made" by judges, is the judicial power to effect change. In this connection the majority of the court in *Woods v. Lancet* referred to the decision of the Supreme Court of the United States in *Funk v. United States,* in which that court ruled that legislative bodies have the power to change old rules of law; nevertheless, when they fail to act, it is the duty of the court to bring the law into accordance with present day standards of wisdom and justice rather than with some outworn and antiquated rule of the past.

Finally, the court overruled the contention as to the great difficulty of proving the nature of the injuries and that they produced the defects discovered at birth. The court pointed out that every day in all trial courts and before administrative tribunals, particularly workmen's compensation boards, such issues are disposed of, "and it is an inadmissible concept that uncertainty of proof can ever destroy a legal right."

In *Amann v. Faidy* the Supreme Court of Illinois, which like the New York court had held that there could be no recovery on a basis of pre-natal injuries, reversed its former position, saying that upon a reappraisal of the question "we conclude that the reasons which have been advanced in support of the doctrine of nonliability fail to carry conviction." This case involved the further interesting element that the child, injured before birth, died after birth as a result of such injury, and the suit was by his beneficiaries to recover damages for his wrongful death. It is elsewhere pointed out that there was no right of action at common law for wrongful death, and that such actions are maintained under statutes which are now found not only in England but in all of our states. The Illinois death statute afforded a remedy for the liability which the defendant whose negligence brought injury to the child before birth was under, as a result of the reversal by the Illinois court of its former holding.

Right of Wife to Sue For Loss of Consortium. Another good illustration of the growth of the common law by way of adaptation to changing social concepts is found in the recent recognition of the right of the wife to sue for loss of consortium as a result of wrongful injuries to her husband. The right of consortium originated in the right of the husband to the domestic services of his wife, and he was allowed to claim damages for their loss when wrongful acts of defendants so incapacitated the wife that she was unable to perform them. Subsequently the term consortium was expanded in coverage to include, in addition to material services, the elements of companionship, love, felicity and sexual relations.

But whereas at common law the husband could recover damages for the loss of consortium of the wife, a wife could not at common law include loss of consortium as an element of the damages sustained by a wrongful injury to her husband. This was in spite of the fact, which we would now admit, that the injury to the wife from loss of consortium parallels the injury to the husband. His right to the conjugal society of his wife is not greater than her right to the conjugal society of her husband. Marriage gives each the same rights in that regard. Each is entitled to the comfort, companionship and affection of the other. And, we would add, as the wrongs of the wife are the same in principle, and are caused by acts of the same nature as those that injure the husband, the wife's remedy should parallel that of the husband. But the old common law did not see it this way.

In 1950 the United States Court of Appeals for the District of Columbia broke away from the old common law rule in this regard. In *Hitaffer v. Argonne Company* it allowed the wife, Lucia Hitaffer, to recover for loss of consortium because of injuries negligently inflicted upon her husband, Pierce. The court could not conceive of any reasons for denying the wife this right "for the reason that in this enlightened day and age they simply do not exist." The mediaeval concepts of the marriage relation to which other jurisdictions have reverted in order to reach the conclusion that the wife could not recover have long since ceased to have any meaning. The husband owes the same degree of love, affection and felicity to the wife as she to him. He also owes the material services of support, but above and beyond that he renders other services as his mate's helper in her duties, as adviser and counselor. "Under such circumstances," the court decided, "it would be a judicial fiat for us to say that a wife may not have an action for loss of consortium due to negligence." This decision has since been followed by the Supreme Court of Iowa in *Acuff v. Schmit.* That not all courts have done so in no way detracts from the force of the decision as an example of the adaptability of the common law to changed concepts, and the power of our courts to so declare and implement it.

Contract Law: "Primitive State of Formalism" Outgrown. The examples thus far cited to illustrate the growth of the common law have been of tortious injuries to the person or to the personality. The impression should not be gained, however, that its growth is in any sense confined to that area. The same phenomenon is readily observable in other fields, including that of contract law.

In a previous chapter reference was made to the case of *Wood v. Lucy, Lady Duff-Gordon,* in which Judge Cardozo, then on the New York Court of Appeals, declared that "the law has outgrown its primitive state of formalism when the precise word was the solemn talisman, and every slip was fatal." In that case the court, in effect, "wrote into" a written contract words of obligation which the parties themselves had not included, achieving, nevertheless, the result the parties would doubtless have reasonably contemplated. In an earlier period of the common law no court would have dared to do such a thing.

A recent English case, *British Movietonews Ltd. v. London & D. Cinemas, Ltd.,* is likewise instructive as to the realistically enlightened point of view that common law courts have come to entertain in dealing with contracts. By an agreement dated July 5, 1941, London film distributors agreed to supply their newsreels to exhibitors for showing at theatres at ten guineas per week, the agreement to be thereafter determinable by four weeks' notice. In 1943 the government issued Cinematograph Film Control Order 1943 in order to maintain supplies of raw film essential to the British war effort. In consequence of this the exhibitors and distributors made a supplemental agreement, reciting new terms necessary in the light of the Film Control Order. This provided that the supplementary contract "shall remain in full force and effect until such time as the said order is cancelled," but also that "all the conditions of the principal agreement shall remain in full force and effect in so far as the same are not excluded or varied hereby."

The Film Control Order was not cancelled. In 1946 it was continued in force—not for the purpose originally contemplated but "for the purpose of so maintaining, controlling and regulating supplies and services as to secure a sufficiency of those essential to the well-being of the community or their equitable distribution or their availability." In 1948 the exhibitors gave four weeks' notice to terminate the agreement and then ceased taking the films. The distributors brought suit, claiming that the exhibitors, whether taking the news-reels or not, must continue to pay the contract price until the Film Control Order was cancelled.

The court held that this claim could not be sustained. Lord Justice Denning pointed out that on the one hand the distributors pointed to the letter of the contract and argued that it governed the case. Since the words "during the continuance of the Cinematograph Film Control Order 1943" were plain enough they should be followed while the Order still continued. But, Lord Justice Denning pointed out, parties with their minds concerned with the particular objects about which they are contracting are apt to use words, phrases or clauses which, taken literally, are wider than they intend, or which cover situations which they never contemplated. Recognizing this fact, the court refused to apply them literally to an uncontemplated turn of events.

This does not mean, declared the Lord Justice, that the courts no longer insist on the binding force of contracts deliberately made. It only means that they will not allow the words in which they happen to be phrased to become tyrannical masters. The court qualifies the literal meaning of the words, so as to bring them into accord with the true scope of the contract. Even if the contract is absolute in its terms, nevertheless if it is not absolute in intent it will not be held absolute in effect. "The day is done," said the Lord Justice, "when we can excuse an unforeseen injustice by saying to the sufferer, 'It is your own folly. You ought not to have passed that form of words. You ought to have put in a clause to protect yourself.' We no longer credit a party with the foresight of a prophet or his lawyer with the draftsmanship of a Chalmers. We realize that they have their limitations, and make allowances accordingly."

Lord Justice Denning concluded that the parties could not have contemplated that the Order would ever last so long. It was an Order made in wartime to deal with war conditions, and they must have contemplated that it would be cancelled at or shortly after the end of the war. They could not have contemplated that it would be continued in peace time to deal with dollar shortages—certainly not that it would still be continuing five years after the war had ended.

Merger of Law and Equity. The importance of the procedural side of our common law system has already been emphasized. Over-emphasis is impossible. And it is essential to point out that developments in the law are not confined to the substantive law, but have been notably present in procedural methods.

In a preceding chapter we referred to the separate courts of law and equity and their separate procedures, which have characterized our system of jurisprudence historically. In some states, certain courts were set up for law cases only, and other courts for equity cases. In those states which did not go this far by way of separation, law and equity cases were docketed and tried separately under different rules of procedure. In the District Courts of the United States, until some twenty years ago cases on the equity dockets were governed by a special set of Equity Rules.

Such a separation operated in a manner well understood by all lawyers to impede and often frustrate the processes of justice. To-day, fortunately, the situation has changed. Practically all states have abolished separate courts of law and equity. Most states have abolished separate procedural rules for law and equity cases, and have merged law and equity procedure under one set of rules. The Federal Rules of Civil Procedure, which became effective in 1938, accomplished this result in the District Courts of the United States. Thus has been accomplished a procedural integration of these two great segments of our jurisprudence which makes not only for expedition but for the ready achievement of justice by direct rather than roundabout methods.

The important chapter in which these events of procedural progress were written was initiated in England by Jeremy Bentham, a student of Blackstone, whose activities resulted in what are known as the Hilary Rules of 1834. These Rules abrogated some of the uncertainties and shortcomings of the old system of pleading at law. In 1848 came the adoption of the Field Code in the State of New York. Not only did this lay the foundation for integrating law and equity procedure, to which we have hereinabove referred, but it introduced a number of simplifying and expediting innovations. In England, in 1852, came the Common Law and Equity Procedure Acts, introducing further reforms into law and equity pleading. The English Supreme Court of Judicature Act of 1873 consolidated the English courts and brought about the merger of law and equity procedure in that country. Commencing with Missouri in 1849 and California in 1850, the American states began adopting procedural codes based upon the Field Code of New York. A majority of them have since followed this direct lead. Illinois, among the latest, adopted the Illinois Civil Practice Act in 1933. Those states which have not followed the model of the Field Code as such have adopted procedural methods fairly comparable in scope and purpose.

As any student of the matter knows, these statutes and rules of procedure are by no means static. For the most part they were brought into being by committees of the organized bar. Having played a leading part in their original preparation, these professional organizations remain alert to scrutinize their working and to formulate such amendments as may seem desirable.

Procedures For Discovery Before Trial. One of the most noteworthy innovations of recent times is found in what is known as procedure for "discovery before trial." A frequently voiced criticism of the common law procedural system was that it lent itself too much to something in the nature of a game in which the respective participants sought—and in large measure were able—to conceal the facts of their cases until the time of trial. Then they would "spring" them by way of surprise. In the last analysis, no one would contend that the cause of justice is best served by such tactics.

Obviously, such practices could be curbed by providing a way whereby the respective parties could compel disclosure of the facts known to the other party, before trial. Not until recent decades, however, has procedure been provided to accomplish this purpose. Now it is in common usage. Perhaps the best model is found in the Federal Rules of Civil Procedure, of which we have already spoken. Twelve of the Rules deal particularly and specifically with various aspects of this matter. (Rules 26-37.) Any party may take the testimony of any person, including a party, by deposition, orally, or upon written interrogatories. Unless otherwise ordered by the court, the deponent may be examined regarding any matter, not privileged, which is relevant to the subject matter involved in the pending action. Production for inspection and copying of any designated documents, not privileged, which constitute or contain evidence may be ordered. In any action in which the mental or physical condition of a party is in controversy, the court may order him to submit to a physical or mental examination by a physician. A party may serve upon any other party a written request for the admission by the latter of the genuineness of any relevant document exhibited with the request. The Rules deal in detail with the consequences of failure to make discovery, providing effective sanctions.

Another one of the Federal Rules of Civil Procedure provides for what is known as a pre-trial hearing, in which the attorneys for the respective parties meet with the judge in informal conference to discuss, informally, the material aspects of the case. Points taken up at such a conference include the simplification of the issues, the necessity or desirability of amendments to the pleadings, the possibility of obtaining admissions of fact and of documents which will avoid unnecessary proof, the limitation of the number of expert witnesses, and such other matters as may aid in the disposition of the action. Following the conference, the judge enters an order reciting the action taken, which controls the subsequent course of the suit.

These processes not only eliminate the possibility of surprise at the trial, but work to simplify and expedite determination of the issues of the case.

The Declaratory Judgment. We have gained an understanding of our system of common law as one in which the law is made, basically, by the adjudication of actual cases. To a court is submitted a controversy between two or more parties. In the process of reaching a decision the facts are found, and to the facts thus found the rule of law determined to be applicable is applied. Such a process insures a careful, searching inquiry, with the court having in mind that it is not only making a just decision between the immediate litigants, in so far as such a decision is humanly possible, but that it is also establishing the rule applied as a precedent for future cases of similar nature. From time to time, of course, as we have seen, common law courts will break away from precedents which, in the light of new knowledge and altered social attitudes, are recognizably outmoded. Nevertheless, the force of judicial decision as precedent remains a basic characteristic of the common law and it is most desirable to maintain it as such.

This case-adversary system was embodied in the constitutional system of the United States. The grant of judicial power by section 2, clause 1 of Article III of the Constitution of the United States is of enumerated "cases and controversies." Referring to this provision, the Supreme Court of the United States held in *Muskrat v. United States* that the exercise of the judicial power is limited to "cases" and "controversies." Beyond this it does not extend, and unless it is asserted in a case or controversy within the meaning of the Constitution, the power to exercise it is nowhere conferred. In *Marbury v. Madison* a "case" was defined by Chief Justice Marshall as a suit instituted according to the regular course of judicial procedure. By cases and controversies are intended the claims of litigants brought before the courts for determination by such regular proceedings as are established by law or custom for the protection of rights, or the protection, redress, or punishment of wrongs. The term "case" implies the existence of present or possible adverse parties, whose contentions are submitted to the court for adjudication.

Under such a concept, strictly construed, it was necessary for a lawsuit to develop before judicial aid could be invoked to settle the matter. For example, let us suppose a case in which a contract is made between a designer and manufacturer of type, and a company which manufactures and sells monotype machines and matrices for use with such machines, whereby the designer grants to the manufacturer a right to manufacture matrices of all sizes of all the type faces designed by the designer, and the manufacturer agrees to pay a royalty for each matrix manufactured by it under the contract. No date is fixed by the contract for its duration, nor is any method prescribed for its termination. After a number of years one of the parties desires to terminate the contract, but the other does not. Under the traditional working of the law, the only way to determine the right to terminate the contract would be for the party desiring so to do to cease performing his agreement, thus bringing about a suit for damages by the other party. The matter of proving damages is, frequently, a difficult, elusive and unsatisfactory process, importing complexity and making for delay in a lawsuit involving it.

It is obvious that if it were possible to secure from a court, while both parties are still performing the contract, an adjudication as to the right to terminate it, much expense, to say nothing of delay and the inevitable acrimony that attends a contested adversary proceeding where there has been alleged breach of duty, would be avoided, to the benefit of both parties. Here is the place for the "declaratory judgment," and in view of the developments which we will now mention, it was possible to employ that procedure in *American Type Founders v. Lanston Monotype Machine Company.*

Declaratory judgment procedure was found in the Scotch law as far back as the sixteenth century. It was first introduced into English equity procedure by the Chancery Procedure Act of 1852. The English courts were hesitant to give the Act liberal construction, however, and it was not until 1883 that the Supreme Court of Judicature under its rule-making power promulgated Order XXV, Rule 5, a general authorization to render declaratory judgments.

As recently as 1928, and by no other a jurist than Justice Brandeis, it was said that "What the plaintiff seeks is simply a declaratory judgment. To grant that relief is beyond the power conferred upon the federal judiciary." Nevertheless, it came to be realized that the "case and controversy" requirement of the Constitution could be met by a procedure which, so to speak, anticipated the crisis which could be judicially ascertained to be in the offing, and which could render judgment beforehand declaring the rights and obligations of the parties. Before proceeding, it would be essential for the court to find that there were present the elements of "case and controversy" in the sense of a potential lawsuit, but, these being present, the court could render a declaratory judgment without exceeding its constitutional powers.

Accordingly, in 1934, Congress passed an act authorizing declaratory judgments in the federal courts. In its present form the act provides that in a case of actual controversy within its jurisdiction, except with respect to federal taxes, any court of the United States, upon the filing of an appropriate pleading, may declare the rights and other legal relations of any interested party seeking such declaration, whether or not further relief is or could be sought. Any such declaration shall have the force and effect of a final judgment or decree and shall be reviewable as such. The Supreme Court sustained its validity in *Aetna Life Insurance Company v. Haworth.*

The first declaratory judgment statute was passed in Michigan in 1919. The Uniform Declaratory Judgments Act was approved by the Conference of Commissioners on Uniform State Laws in 1922 and has since been adopted in substantially unchanged form in thirty-three states. Ten other states have enacted statutes similar either to the English Order XXV, Rule 5, or to the Uniform Act.

The declaratory judgment enables the courts to render final judgment between litigants, without attaching to that judgment a coercive decree for damages or injunction. Except for such coercive decree, the judgment differs in no essential respect from any other judgment between opposing parties. Its great advantage lies in the fact that it enables the issue to be narrowed and to be determined before breach or violence has occurred. It takes into account that people may have controversies as to their legal rights under a written instrument, or otherwise, which require settlement by a court prior to the irretrievable destruction of economic and social relations consequent upon a breach or violence, and that in many cases grave doubt or uncertainty as to legal relations may disturb the social equilibrium and require prompt judicial settlement. In an economic world held together by a network of long-term contracts and governmental regulation and control, it seems crude to insist that a dispute arising between parties can only be judicially settled if one or the other acts at his peril upon his own interpretation of his rights and takes the fatal plunge. Relations once destroyed by open breach can rarely be knit together again.

CHAPTER 26

THE FUNCTION OF STATUTES

Legislative Enactments as Part of the Common Law System. In the course of our previous discussion of *Woods v. Lancet* we anticipated the subject matter of the present chapter relating to the place of the legislative process as part of the common law system. As we have seen, in 1921 the New York court, confronted by a specific case in which an infant plaintiff sought damages for bodily injuries inflicted upon him before birth by defendant's negligent conduct, felt constrained to hold that there could be no recovery. Although the New York legislature might well have concerned itself with the situation thereafter, it did not do so. In 1951 the same court was confronted by a similar situation. In reversing its own former decision, in full accordance with the working of the common law system, it in no sense questioned the prerogative of the legislature to lay down the same rule of law by legislative enactment.

The Supreme Court of the United States ruled in *Munn v. Illinois* that a person has no property, no vested interest, in any rule of the common law. That is only one of the forms of municipal law, and is no more sacred than any other. Rights of property which have been created by the common law cannot be taken away without due process; but the law itself, as a rule of conduct, may be changed at the will, or even at the whim, of the legislature, unless prevented by constitutional limitations. "Indeed," said the Court, "the great office of statutes is to remedy defects in the common law as they are developed, and to adapt it to the changes of time and circumstances."

It is plain, therefore, that the particular function of statute law is to modify or add to the common law as it already exists. A legislative body is in position to deliberate over proposed enactments, and bring to bear more or less directly a considered opinion as to whether they should be embodied in the legal structure. Presumably, a legislature is more directly representative of public sentiment as a whole than any other part of the government, and in so far as law tends to go along with the feelings and mores of the times the legislature is well fitted to contribute to it.

Illustrations of changes of the common law by statute are legion. Of outstanding interest is the manner in which the disabilities of married women, inherent in the common law concept that the husband and the wife constituted a legal unity, were abrogated. As the Supreme Court of Illinois decided in *Snell v. Snell*, the contracts of married women, by the common law as it existed in England and in Illinois prior to the legislation on the subject, were absolutely void at law, and were equally so in equity, so far as imposing any personal obligation was concerned. But the law in respect of the rights and obligations of married women has undergone a radical change. By the acts of 1861, 1869 and 1874 married women were placed upon a common footing with married men in respect to all property rights, including the means to acquire, protect and dispose of the same. Another respect in which the common law disability of women has been radically altered by statute is found in the relation of women to jury service. Upholding an Illinois statute making women eligible for jury duty, the Supreme Court of Illinois said that until recent times woman was not thought to be on a parity with man, and it was considered that she did not possess those qualitative attributes that made her capable of exercising the right of suffrage or of rendering jury service. She was excluded from jury service on the false theory of economic, sociological and legalistic inferiority and not by any positive statement found in any of the constitutional provisions guaranteeing the right of trial by jury. But the legislature has the right to prescribe the qualifications of jurors, and legislation admitting women to service is not subject to constitutional objection.

A few further illustrations will suffice, in addition to the references already made from time to time in preceding chapters, to show the workings of the legislative process.

"Wrongful Death." Generally speaking, as we have seen, when circumstances called for legal relief in order to do justice to an injured person, courts operating under our English common law system provided it. Were it not for the considerations surrounding the difficulty of providing a remedy for the survivors of some one who has been killed, it would be more difficult than it is to realize that the common law, which we confidently trust to do justice, did not at any time recognize any right of action in tort to recover damages against a wrongdoer causing the death of a human being. In the leading English case of *Baker v. Bolton*, Lord Ellenborough, a distinguished English jurist, said that in a civil court the death of a human being could not be complained of as an injury. The reason for the

rule was said by Baron Parke, another distinguished English jurist, to be that in the eye of the common law the value of life was so great as to be incapable of being estimated by money.

Baron Parke's rationalization was of course too sweeping in the sense that it failed to recognize that although the spiritual values of a human life cannot be appraised in monetary terms, and the grief at its passing cannot be so measured, there is a direct relationship between a human life and its economic fruits which others of the family group have a right to share. When this became sufficiently apparent to the people of England, the English Parliament acted to supply the deficiency of the common law. In 1846 Lord Campbell's Act was enacted, providing as follows: "Whenever the death of a person shall be caused by wrongful act, neglect or default, and the act, neglect or default is such as would (if death had not ensued) have entitled the party injured to maintain action and recover damages in respect thereof, then and in every such case the person who would have been liable if death had not ensued shall be liable in an action for damages, notwithstanding the death of the person injured, and although the death shall have been caused under such circumstances as amount in law to felony."

Lord Campbell's Act also provided: "Every action shall be for the benefit of the wife, husband, parent or child of the person whose death shall have been so caused, and shall be brought by and in the name of the executor or administrator of the person deceased; and in every such action the jury may give such damages as they may think proportioned to the injury resulting from such death to the parties respectively for whom and for whose benefit the action shall be brought; and the amounts so recovered, after deducting the costs not recovered from the defendant, shall be divided among the aforementioned parties in such shares as the jury by their verdict shall find and direct."

American State and Federal Statutes. Here, as in many other connections, English statutory innovation was followed in America. Justice Cardozo of the Supreme Court of the United States summed it up by saying that the adoption of Lord Campbell's Act marks the dawn of a new era. In this country, statutes of substantially similar tenor followed in quick succession in one state after another till today there is not a state of the Union in which a remedy is lacking. Thus, in 1847 the New York legislature, acting the year following the enactment of Lord Campbell's Act in England, took action along this line. In 1853 the Illinois General Assembly followed suit. The Supreme Court of Illinois has referred to the Illinois statute as "substantially a copy of a statute of New York enacted in 1847, which latter statute is also a substantial copy of Lord Campbell's Act."

It is to be noted, however, that death statutes do vary somewhat from state to state in such details as the amount of damages recoverable, the party who should initiate suit, and the time within which suit must be brought.

The Congress of the United States, too, has enacted death statutes, effective in the fields in which under our constitutional system the federal government has power to legislate. This federal legislation relates particularly to (1) railroad workers employed in interstate commerce and (2) seamen, or persons killed on navigable waters of the United States. Thus, by the terms of the Federal Employers' Liability Act enacted in 1908 and constitutionally proper under article 1, section 8 of the Constitution of the United States which confers upon Congress power to regulate commerce among the several states, railroads are made liable for damages for the death of an "employee" engaged in interstate commerce where such death results from the negligence of the employees of the railroad, or by reason of negligent defect or insufficiency of its equipment.

By the Jones Act, enacted in 1915, and constitutionally proper under article 3, section 2 of the Constitution of the United States which extends the judicial power of the United States to all cases of admiralty and maritime jurisdiction, a right of action is given in any case where the death of a seaman results from personal injuries sustained in the course of his employment. By the Death on the High Seas Act, enacted in 1920 and constitutionally proper under the constitutional provisions just cited, and not limited to seamen, whenever the death of a "person" shall be caused by wrongful act, neglect or default occurring on the high seas beyond a marine league from the shore of any state or dependencies of the United States, action may be maintained against the vessel, person, or corporation which would have been liable if death had not ensued.

Modification of the Principle of Negligent Liability. As we have seen in our consideration of the principles of liability with relation to the operation of motor vehicles, the rule of the common law is that the operator is liable to third persons who are injured as a result of the negligence of the operator; such third person being assumed, of course, to have been without contributing fault himself. Supposing A to be the operator, under this common law rule A was liable to B, the driver of another car, who was injured as the result of

A's negligence. And under the same rule, if B, instead of being the driver of another car, was riding in the car with A at A's invitation, he could recover from A if he was injured as the result of A's negligence.

In the course of time it became apparent that the working of the common law principle in this latter situation was tending to be to the great disadvantage of A. As a generous gesture A would pick up hitch-hikers, who, when there was an accident of any sort would turn on A and ask heavy damages, which, under the ordinary principles of negligence, they were frequently able to establish. The result was that some years ago the state legislatures stepped into the picture and enacted what are commonly referred to as "guest-rider" statutes. The Illinois statute, a representative example, provides as follows: "No person riding in a motor vehicle as a guest, without payment for such ride, nor his personal representative in the event of the death of such guest, shall have a cause of action for damages against the driver or operator of such motor vehicle or its owner or his employee or agent for injury, death, or loss, in case of accident, unless such accident shall have been caused by the wilful and wanton misconduct of the driver or operator of such motor vehicle or its owner or his employee or agent and unless such wilful and wanton misconduct contributed to the injury, death or loss for which the action is brought."

The words that particularly strike our attention are "wilful and wanton misconduct"—there is to be no recovery unless the operator was guilty of wilful and wanton misconduct. This sounds like something more than ordinary negligence, and in truth it is, as we shall presently see. In *American Smelting and Refining Company v. Sutyak* the United States Court of Appeals dealing with the similar Colorado statute spoke of the evils which brought about the enactment of such statutes. The legislature undoubtedly appreciated the apparent injustice of holding the owner or operator of an automobile liable in damages for failure to exercise ordinary care toward one riding merely as a guest, said the court. It doubtless was considered unjust that one who accepts the kindness or hospitality of an owner or operator of an automobile in extending an invitation to ride should recover damages for personal injury unless it results from intoxication, gross negligence, or intentional wrong on the part of such owner or operator. "The plain intent of the statute is to prevent recovery by 'hitch-hikers,' 'bums,' and others invited by the owner or operator of the motor vehicle to ride as a mere generous gesture," said the court. "Its purpose is to deny recovery to those without moral right to recompense."

There are at least two important issues involved in the "guest statutes" such as the Illinois statute above. In the first place, there may be a question presented as to whether the injured rider was a "guest, without payment for such ride." A guest, without payment, can recover only if the operator was guilty of wilful and wanton misconduct, but under a proper construction of the statute, one who "pays" is not subject to this wilful and wanton limitation but may establish a case by proving that the operator was just ordinarily negligent. The case of *Connett v. Winget* is enlightening in this connection. Connett owned a house in Peoria and Winget was a real estate broker. Winget called Connett for the purpose of taking him some distance into the country and showing him a property which was for sale or trade. While Winget was driving, there was an accident and Connett was injured. Connett brought suit. Winget set up by way of defense that Connett was a "guest without payment for such ride," and that in consequence he, Winget, was liable only for wilful and wanton misconduct, which the facts did not establish. The Supreme Court of Illinois held that there was ample basis for finding that Connett was not a guest as defined by statute, because he was invited to go as a matter of business in which Winget, the operator of the car, was interested. The court said that if the carriage "confers only a benefit incident to hospitality, companionship or the like, the passenger is a guest, but if the carriage tends to promote mutual interests of both the person carried and the driver, or if the carriage is primarily for the attainment of some objective or purpose of the operator, the passenger is not a guest within the meaning of such enactments." The court referred to *Parrett v. Carothers*, holding that a prospective purchaser of real estate riding to view property which an owner is trying to sell is not a guest; *Thomas v. Currier Lumber Company*, holding that a prospective purchaser of lumber riding with a salesman of the lumber company was not a guest; and *Piercy v. Zeiss*, holding that a person riding with an insurance salesman to talk insurance was not a guest. Hence, in the case at bar, Connett did not need to establish wilful and wanton misconduct.

The other important question, which arises as of course if plaintiff was a guest within the statutory definition, is as to what is required to constitute wilful and wanton misconduct. *Stephens v. Weigel* is illustrative. The Illinois Appellate Court there said that although no specific rule can be promulgated to determine categorically what constitutes wilful and wanton misconduct, it is generally established that defendant must exhibit a lack of regard for the safety of others, and a conscious indifference to the consequences that might follow from his acts. In the case at bar, where the accident happened in 1947, defendant Charles Weigel was driving a 1933 Chevrolet sedan at night. Although his headlights cast a beam of only 11 to 20 feet ahead, he was traveling 50 to 60 miles per hour, despite admonitions to slow down. At a curve in the paved highway "he deliberately drove off the paved portion of the road onto the shoulder, though he admittedly was unable to see where he was going, since the lights of approaching cars blinded him. Without slackening his speed he drove blindly ahead on the shoulder for some 250 feet, until his car struck a telephone pole. The impact of the collision broke the pole in half, and threw all of the occupants of the car, including those in the back seat, out of the two-door sedan." Two of the passengers were guests, and were confined in the hospital for eight or ten weeks. The Appellate Court sustained verdict and judgment in their favor, saying that there was ample evidence of wilful and wanton misconduct upon the part of Weigel to support it.

In *Hollander v. Davis* the United States Court of Appeals decided that the conduct of the driver of an automobile in driving along a paved public highway in Florida at a speed of seventy miles per hour approaching a curve and attempting to pass other cars traveling in the same direction "rises above ordinary negligence." An automobile moving at seventy miles per hour is traveling at a speed of approximately 6,160 feet per minute, 103 feet per second, and where the driver of such car attempts to pass other cars on a curve and in so doing takes over and usurps the way of oncoming automobiles "he can be held by a jury to be guilty of wilful and wanton misconduct."

Sale of Intoxicating Liquor. Another situation in which the working of statutes to introduce new rights and obligations into the body of the law is well exemplified is in the field of sale of intoxicating liquor. By the common law it was not a tort to either sell or give away intoxicating liquor to "a strong and able-bodied man," and such act was not held to impose legal liability for damages upon the seller or donor of such liquor. But the legislatures of a number of states, including Illinois, have enacted statutes which have the effect of imposing liability upon those engaged in the liquor trade, under certain circumstances.

The Illinois statute, usually referred to as the "Dram Shop Act," provides: "Every husband, wife, child, parent, guardian, employer or other person, who shall be injured, in person or property, or means of support, by any intoxicated person, or in consequence of the intoxication, habitual or otherwise, of any person, shall have a right of action in his or her own name, severally or jointly, against person or persons who shall, by selling or giving alcoholic liquor, have caused the intoxication, in whole or in part, of such person; and any person owning, renting, leasing or permitting the occupation of any building or premises, and having knowledge that alcoholic liquors are to be sold therein, or who having leased the same for other purposes, shall knowingly permit therein the sale of any alcoholic liquors that have caused, in whole or in part, the intoxication of such person, shall be liable, severally or jointly, with the person or persons selling or giving liquors aforesaid." There are still further provisions which for present purposes it is not necessary to set out. A careful reading of the portion of the statute quoted will convey the impression that it is a very far-reaching and drastic enactment.

The working of the statute is illustrated by *Cox v. Hrasky*, in which Rosa Cox brought action against Louis Hrasky, Genofefa Hrasky, and Alvina Vicek, to recover damages to her means of support by reason of the killing of her husband, Mose Cox, by an intoxicated person. The Hraskys owned the building in East St. Louis in which was operated a tavern by their daughter, Alvina. A verdict for Rosa in the sum of $4500 was sustained on appeal. The facts were that Mose Cox and another man went to the tavern shortly after one Hill and others had arrived there. Hill and his party sat at one table, and Mose at another. After drinking whiskey and soda at the Hill table, Hill got up from his chair and as he did so a gun dropped from his pocket. Mose said in an ordinary tone of voice, "What did you drop there? You should be more careful or you will get in trouble." Hill picked up the gun, saying, "That's none of your business," and started shooting. Cox was hit several times and fell to the floor, dying in the tavern. Hill backed out of the door and ran down an alley. Later that night he was apprehended in St. Louis. In upholding the lower court judgment the Illinois Appellate Court said it was a question of fact for the jury whether the death of Mose was caused by Hills' intoxication and whether the intoxication was the result of the serving of liquor at defendant's tavern.

In *Haw v. 1933 Grill* Fred Haw was served liquor by the Grill and became intoxicated. He conducted himself in a boisterous manner and used profane language. Fred Belmont, one of the Grill's floor managers, remonstrated with him and told him he would be removed unless he behaved properly. Subsequently there was a scuffle between Haw and Belmont, in the course of which Haw was struck in the eye. The injury was so serious as to make him lose his job and expensive medical treatment was required. His wife, Carrie, was obliged to pay the bills for treatment. She brought suit against the Grill under the Dram Shop Act, and a judgment in her behalf was sustained, the Appellate Court over-ruling the contention that the Grill was not liable because Haw's injury was caused not by his intoxication but rather by assault by Belmont, who was sober. "While we have a third party, defendant's floor manager, inflicting the injury in this case, the defendant must be presumed to have foreseen that its act of selling the liquor to Haw might have produced or been followed by the altercation in which he was injured," said the court. "In view of the natural and logical sequence of the events leading up to Haw's injury and the fact that Belmont would not have struck him except for the manner in which he conducted himself as the result of his intoxicated condition, in our opinion such intoxication was a contributing factor and at least a proximate cause of the injury."

Circumstances of a somewhat different nature were involved in *Hyba v. Horneman.* Wilson Lowery had been served drinks at the Horneman tavern. That evening thereafter, while Mary Hyba was riding with him in his car as his guest there was an accident and she was killed. Alleging that Mary was killed in an accident caused by his intoxication, and that his intoxication was produced by Horneman, the parents of Mary brought suit against Horneman, and were held entitled to recover. Referring to statutes like the Illinois Dram Shop Act, the court said that the evident object is to punish those who furnish means of intoxication by making them liable in damages caused thereby. Such statutes are generally designed to embrace and include all injuries produced by the intoxication which legitimately result therefrom. "To maintain an action under the Dram Shop Act against the vendor of liquor, it is not necessary that action should also be maintainable against the intoxicated person," the court said. "There are many cases where suits result under such act based upon injury to means of support due to the husband's loss of earning power. It is sufficient if any person has been injured as provided by the act."

In other connections we have seen a principle in operation that a person who is himself at fault is barred from recovery. It has application here, also, and is illustrated in application by *Bennett v. Auditorium Bldg. Corporation.* Wilma Bennett brought suit against defendant to recover for damages sustained when she fell as a result of slipping on vomitus deposited by another patron of defendant's tap room. A verdict for $2500 in her favor was reversed by the Illinois

Appellate Court. The evidence was that Wilma had been spending the evening there, and had some drinks. The court said if Wilma became intoxicated and fell as a result she could not recover, and the verdict being against the weight of the evidence the case should be remanded for a new trial. If she herself had not been at fault she would have been in position to maintain action for injury based on the "result" of intoxication of the person depositing the vomitus, for which the tap room was responsible under the statute.

Abolition of Common Law Master and Servant Defenses. As a further present example of the working of the legislative process to alter principles which have developed at common law we may take the statutory abrogation of certain defenses interposable by the master—or employer to use the more modern term—to defeat actions for personal injuries brought by his servant.

It is a well-known rule of the common law that one who is himself contributorily negligent may not recover damages from another whose negligent conduct played a part in the injury. Negligence of the servant contributing to his own injury accordingly barred the servant from recovering from his master for injuries sustained by him in the course of his employment, and constituted a defense which the master could invoke. Another common law defense of the employer was assumption of risk. By this rule, the servant was held to assume the risks of dangers which ordinarily attend or are incident to the business in which he engages. True, it has always been held to be the duty of the master to use due care to provide safe instrumentalities for doing the work and not to expose the servant to perils or hazards which might be guarded against by proper diligence on the part of the master. But under the assumption of risk principle, the servant risked the dangers ordinarily incident to the business. And among these risks were included negligence on the part of fellow workmen.

The general purpose behind these rules of common law seems to have been to give maximum freedom to expanding industry. The assumption of risk doctrine in earlier years was attributed by the Supreme Court of the United States to a rule of public policy, inasmuch as the opposite doctrine would not only subject employers to unreasonable and often ruinous responsibilities, but would also encourage carelessness on the part of the employee.

The net result of the common law rules was that the master's obligation stopped when he had used reasonable care to provide working facilities in good condition. Assuming that he had met this obligation, if the servant sustained injuries while at work he could not recover against the employer if his own negligence had contributed to the injury. Even though he had not been contributorily negligent himself, because of the assumption of risk rule he could not recover if the injury was attributable to the normal operation of the business. Finally, the injured workman could not recover if his injury was caused by the negligence of a fellow workman.

Any one familiar with modern industrial plants and operations realizes the inevitability of some physical injuries, even at best. This was even more true before the advent of modern safety devices and precautions. The workman who was unfortunate enough to be injured found himself without the possibility of any effective recourse and had to sustain the loss himself.

Workmen's Compensation Acts. With the growth of social consciousness the undesirability, if not the injustice, of such a situation, became more and more apparent. The repercussions of workmen who were killed or disabled came to be felt by the general public, because provision had to be made to take care of their indigent dependents. And so came legislative action in the form of Workmen's Compensation Acts. The first Act was adopted in England in 1897. About ten years later our states began to adopt such acts, and they are now universal, covering major segments of employees in all the states.

Generally speaking, such statutes abolish all the above defenses which the employer had at common law. The net result is that a workman who sustains injuries which arise out of and in the course of his employment is automatically granted an award based on the extent of the injury received, or, if he was killed, his beneficiaries receive an award in stated amount. Speaking of the Illinois Workmen's Compensation Act, which is typical, the Supreme Court of Illinois decided in *Keeran v. P. B. & C. Traction Company*, that in its nature it was an entire departure from the common law in regard to the relation of master and servant. It does not rest on the theory of negligence, but on the theory that the injuries to workmen and deaths caused by accident in any business should be regarded as a part of the expense of the business and should be borne by the business. Under the Act, the amount which a workman may recover for a particular injury is fixed by law. He may recover this amount regardless of the cause of the injury, the fault of the employer, or his own negligence, so long as it arose out of and in the course of his employment. The court went on to say it is apparent that the legislature considered the law of negligence as applied to the relation of master and servant as unsatisfactory in its results and sought by this Act to secure to injured workmen and their dependents a more certain, prompt and inexpensive relief than the common law action affords, by imposing upon the employer, as incident to his business, the burden of providing for the loss sustained by his employees from accidental injuries received in his business according to a certain definite scale.

Federal Employers' Liability Act. The federal government has not stopped with workmen's compensation laws in the area where it has power to legislate, but has set up special statutes governing the master and servant relationship on interstate railroads. By the Federal Employers' Liability Act of 1908 it abolished the fellow-servant rule as to interstate railroads and employees, and took much of the force out of the contributory negligence rule by substituting a rule of comparative negligence. By a 1939 amendment the assumption of risk rule was entirely abrogated. It now provides that every common carrier by railroad while engaging in commerce between any of the several states shall be liable in damages to any person suffering injury or death resulting in whole or in part from the negligence of any of the officers, agents, or employees of such carrier, and that no employee shall be held to have assumed the risks of his employment in any case where such injury or death resulted in whole or in part from the negligence of the carrier's agents. "The result is an Act which requires cases tried under the Federal Act to be handled as though no doctrine of assumption of risk had ever existed," said the Supreme Court of the United States.

The Supreme Court recently summed up the situation by saying that the Act was enacted because the Congress was dissatisfied with the common law duty of the master to his servant. The statute supplants that duty with the far more drastic duty of paying damages for injury or death at work due in whole or in part to the employer's negligence. The employer is stripped of his common law defenses and for practical purposes the inquiry in those cases today rarely presents more than the single question whether negligence of the employer played any part, however small, in the injury or death which is the subject of the suit. The burden of the employee is met, and the obligation of the employer to pay damages arises, when there is proof, even though entirely circumstantial, from which the jury may with reason make that inference.

Illustrative of the extent to which the railroad employer's liability is held to carry under the legislation is *Webb v. Illinois Central R. Company,* in which evidence that a brakeman slipped on a cinder

about the size of a fist along the roadbed and fell, was held sufficient
to support a recovery for resultant injury to his knee, the Supreme
Court of the United States reversing the lower courts which had held
such evidence insufficient to take the case to the jury.   And a railroad employee who sustained a crushed leg when switching operations
caused the shifting of some steel plates in a gondola car which he
was at the moment using as a toilet was held to have sufficient evidence to sustain a cause of action against his employer.

The impact of the Federal Employer's Liability Act is greatly
strengthened by its relation to the Federal Safety Appliance Act.   As
far back as 1893, with the purpose of promoting the safety of the
public as well as that of railroad employees, Congress enacted statutes
prescribing various equipment for railroad cars and engines, such as
brakes and couplers, and providing penalties for violation.   Civil
lability in damages under the Federal Employer's Liability Act follows as a matter of course if the violation of the Safety Appliance Act
is a proximate cause of an employee's injury.

CHAPTER 27

ADMINISTRATIVE LAW

Importance of Administrative Law. We commenced our analysis of the common law by noting its advent and development in the form of a declaration of legal principles and their application by the courts. We have considered the function of statutes and constitutions, and have witnessed the coming of equity as, in effect, a supplementary element of common law jurisprudence. It remains to give consideration to an element of today's body of law that antedates the common law, and, though confined within the structure of our common law system, sometimes appears to be straining hard to burst the bounds. That element is Administrative Law.

No other arm of the law directly touches the citizen of the United States in as many aspects of his life as does Administrative Law. The quantity of the food that is raised to feed him, the content of the finished food product to the minutest detail, the cost of transporting it and the place where he must go to buy it, are subject to administrative regulation. Where he may build a home and the dimensions of his house in relation to the size of his lot; whether he may enter and continue to carry on a desired business or profession and the extent to which he may exercise his own initiative in conducting it; whether or not he is qualified, not only by technical ability but also in the ideological sense, to fill a government position; who shall provide him with the services of radio, television and air travel—all are within the presently accepted orbit of Administrative Law, and a bare beginning by way of reciting situations governed by its procedures.

The scope of Administrative Law, thus suggested in outline, is attested by the sheer mass of its physical volume. Its output threatens to inundate all other fields combined. Thousands of recording machines and typewriters, playing the lead, click continuously to transcribe the executive, legislative and adjudicative output of the congeries of administrative agencies in action. For, as the student of the subject knows, administrative agencies, within themselves, exercise executive, legislative and judicial functions. Every hour the sound of mimeographs, playing their part of the accompaniment, is heard in the land, their concentrated whir in the national capital being echoed from the seats of government of our several states and the islands of the sea. Printing presses of the government and of private loose-leaf services answer the cue to the bass section, adding their deep rumble to the administrative symphony. The scratching of a myriad of pens, signing and initialing administrative documents in their multitudinous forms, speaks from percussion desks. Critics with ears attuned to the earlier era of our jurisprudence when the law found relatively little application outside the courtrooms of the United States and the state governments, and from which courtrooms emerged accepted close harmonies, only, familiar to all members of the bench and bar, are wont to suggest that the present-day symphony, though perhaps acceptable in a modernistic sense, is cacophonous. But, beyond question, administrative law is here to stay, and to grow.

Administrative Law as Old as Government. Administrative law is as old as government itself. We have seen that when human beings began living together in society what we may call "law" began, because without some rules of conduct they could not get along with each other. From this point of view there was "law" before there was government. But when some ruler undertook to act in the sense of acting as a government, there was law in a further sense. Early rulers were autocrats. They "were" the law. As citizens of the United States we can understand the significance of saying that an autocrat combined in himself the three departments of government: the legislative, executive and judicial. There was no separation of powers. He "made" the law, he "executed" the law, or administered it, and he "interpreted" the law, as one of our courts might do. He combined all the functions in his own person, and the result was "administrative" law in an undiluted form.

As John Foster Dulles has pointed out, the administrative process is the oldest thing there is in the way of government. The simplest and most primitive organization of society involved the vesting, in a single person or group, of the entire authority of government. Our Anglo-Saxon history has involved the breaking away from this sort of thing. Through long experience and much struggle there has emerged in certain areas, a division of authority into parts independent of each other and checking each other. In this way, it was believed, the freedom of the individual could be insured as against the despotic tendencies of government.

Administrative Law being a concomitant of government as such, administrative processes have been with us since our earliest governmental beginnings. Administrative agencies were utilized by colonial legislatures and the first session of the First Congress enacted three statutes conferring administrative powers, which are antecedents of statutes still administered by two existing agencies. Of the approximately fifty existing agencies or subdivisions discussed by the Attorney General's Committee on Administrative Procedure in 1941, eleven trace their beginnings to a period prior to the close of the Civil War and only seventeen to the period from 1930 to 1940. From the beginning the administrative process has been utilized to limit discretion, to effectuate social legislation, to provide for continuity of attention and clearly allocated responsibility, or to provide for action which because of practical or legal limitations, neither the courts nor Congress could themselves handle.

In Illinois, for example, supervising the sale of liquor, inspecting of warehouses and of agricultural products and licensing of merchants, auctioneers and peddlers were functions of government as far back as 1845. In 1874, interestingly enough, county boards in Illinois were empowered to "grant licenses to keep so many dram shops in their county as they shall think the public good requires." Here, forsooth, was a "delegation of power" calculated to give some concern to the modern student of Constitutional Law, alert to the principle of separation of powers.

Recent Growth of Administrative Law. Although there is nothing new about Administrative Law as such, only in recent times has it known its major development. Justice Frankfurter has observed that there were births and deaths before there were vital statistics, and there was Administrative Law before Anglo-American lawyers had a name for it. But in its reach and amplitude what is now known as Administrative Law is a relatively modern phenomenon. This is particularly true with respect to those fields in which the regulatory power of the government, state and national, has been directed against economic enterprise. Apart from legislation touching the revenue, the public domain, national banks and patents, not until the Interstate Commerce Act of 1887 did Congress begin to place economic enterprise under systems of administrative control. Once begun, and stimulated by a sequence of political movements growing out of "crises" and "emergencies" in peace as well as in war, this movement has proceeded with cumulative momentum. Writing with prophetic vision, A. A. Berle reported in 1916 that public sentiment has become markedly in favor of expanding governmental controls over affairs once thought sacredly private. "There is a desire," said Mr. Berle, "even a clamor, for public regulation, state or national, in matters which before the Civil War the nation conceived concerned only the persons directly interested. More accurately stated, we have come to see that in most problems it is not a few people who are interested, but all the people."

Implementing Political Programs. That the administrative process lends itself directly to the implementation of political programs has already been suggested. In his message vetoing the Walter-Logan Bill in 1940, President Franklin D. Roosevelt declared: "The very heart of modern reform legislation is an administrative tribunal. A 'truth in securities' act without an administrative tribunal to enforce it, or a labor relations act without an administrative tribunal to administer it, or rate regulation without a commission to supervise rates, would be sterile and useless."

The political aspect of the administrative process was well illustrated by the examples thus cited by President Roosevelt. The Interstate Commerce Commission was created in 1887 as the result of public demand for curbing the exactions of the railroads. The Securities and Exchange Commission and the National Labor Relations Board came out of legislation following hard upon the depression of the early 1930's, in the course of which millions sustained great economic hardship. Pressures for a national policy supporting the unionization of labor became irresistible, and the great losses sustained by the "white collar" groups of the population through defaulted securities likewise gave impetus to legislation looking to the supervision of the nation's investment reservoirs. In the realm of agriculture, insistence upon financial relief brought about far-reaching administrative programs of subsidy and control.

But although much of the administrative activity of the federal government thus has a political tinge, perhaps the most of it involves only the routine functioning of essential governmental processes. Such could be said of the activities of the Treasury Department and the Internal Revenue Service under its jurisdiction, the State Department, the Department of Defense, the Post Office Department, the Department of the Interior, and the Department of Justice which administers, among other activities, the Immigration and Deportation Service. Certainly the Atomic Energy Commission was not brought into being to implement any particular political program and it is generally recognized that the Civil Service Commission is charged with administering government personnel affairs in such manner as to obviate political influence in that connection. And it can be said that, whatever may have been the background of the Interstate Commerce Commission, the Securities and Exchange Commission and the National Labor Relations Board, the passing of time and the standardization of procedures have removed much, if not all, of the political atmosphere from their operations. Administrative Law implements reform. As reform is accepted, it becomes routine.

The operation of the administrative process in the several states has been characterized by a routine rather than a political nature. There the process operates to carry out programs of maintaining institutions of various kinds, of carrying on public education, of highway construction and maintenance, of regulating public utilities and insurance companies, of licensing trades and occupations, of administering social security programs and workmen's compensation, and of collecting revenue. These activities are conducted in the main by a civil service personnel which continues through the regimes of changing state officialdom.

How an Administrative Agency Proceeds. It is obvious that the nature of administrative agencies will be as diverse as the activities of government which call for administrative action. But regardless of the function assigned, there are discernible broad similarities between all.

Thus, each agency is charged with doing a particular job. It is generally empowered to adopt rules and regulations, not only for its own procedure, but also by way of supplementing the broad grant of power under which it operates. In doing the job assigned it applies the statute and its rules and regulations. If its processes are resisted, there arises occasion for a hearing to determine their applicability. One sees here the operation of the legislative, executive and judicial functions. When the agency adopts rules and regulations, it "legislates." When in the process of doing its job it applies them, and the statute, it "executes." When it conducts a hearing to determine whether its action as applied to some party is lawful, it acts in a judicial capacity, for an administrative hearing, though without the formal setting of a courtroom, is conducted with the same respect for due process of law that is observed by a court, and in much the same manner, except that there is no jury, and the strict rules of evidence are not enforced.

The Administrative Process Illustrated. Because, as we have seen, the working of the administrative process is similar throughout all agencies, it does not greatly matter what one might be chosen by way of general illustration. The regulation of business being one of the characteristic functions of Administrative Law, and horse racing being nowadays legislatively treated as a business calling for regulation, a good example may be found in *Sandstrom v. California Horse Racing Board*, a case in which the Supreme Court of California was reviewing the action of the California Horse Racing Board, the administrative agency set up by the California legislature to carry out the purpose of the regulatory statute, which had suspended the license of a trainer. The issue was whether such suspension was lawful.

As we have noted, administrative agencies are commonly vested with power to adopt such rules and regulations as will facilitate the achievement of their purpose. The statute here provided: "The Board may prescribe rules, regulations and conditions consistent with the provisions of this chapter, under which all horse races, upon the results of which there is wagering, shall be conducted in this state." Pursuant to this authority thus conferred upon it by the legislature, the Horse Racing Board adopted several hundred rules and regulations. Among them was Rule 313 as follows:

"Equipment as prescribed by the California Horse Racing Board for the administration of saliva, or urine, or other tests, shall be required at all meetings. All horses will be subject to these tests or any other tests prescribed by the Board or ordered by the Stewards either before or after the race, or both. The trainer shall be the absolute insurer of and responsible for the condition of the horses entered in a race, regardless of the acts of third parties. Should the chemical, or other analysis of saliva or urine samples, or other tests, prove positive, showing the presence of any narcotic stimulant, chemical or drug of any description, the trainer of the horse may be suspended or ruled off, and, in addition, the Foreman in charge of the horses, the Groom signing the Pre-Race Examination slip and paddock certificate, and any person shown to have had the care or attendance of the horse, may be suspended or ruled off, in the discretion of the Board."

After a race at Del Mar Race Track, examination of one of the participating horses, "Cover Up," indicated the presence of a caffein type alkaloid. The Racing Board notified Sandstrom to appear before it at a hearing to determine whether his license should be revoked as the trainer of "Cover Up." No evidence was presented that Sandstrom either administered the stimulant or had any knowledge of it. Nevertheless the Board, after hearing the case, entered an order suspending Sandstrom's license for six months for violating

Rule 313. Other rules of the Board, of course, required all trainers to qualify for licenses in the first instance, in accordance with prescribed regulations, and made it unlawful for any one to act as a trainer without a license.

In what was done here by the Board we can see "legislative," "executive" and "judicial" action. In enacting its rules and regulations, including Rule 313, the Board "legislated." In making the tests prescribed by the rules it acted executively. In conducting a hearing to determine whether Sandstrom's license should be revoked it acted judicially.

The tests having demonstrated that a stimulant had been administered to "Cover Up," and there being no question about Sandstrom's being "Cover Up's" trainer, the ultimate issue of the case was whether the Racing Board had authority to enact a regulation making a trainer an absolute insurer of the condition of horses entered in a race, under penalty of having his license revoked if one of his horses was found to have been "doped," even though he had no knowledge of it. To deprive one of his means of livelihood is to come within the literal prohibition of the due process clause of state and federal constitutions, which provides that no one shall be deprived of life, liberty or property without due process of law. It has long been understood that the enjoyment by the citizen, upon terms of equality with all others in similar circumstances, of the privilege of pursuing an ordinary calling or trade, is a general part of his rights of liberty, and that the right to follow any of the common occupations of life is an inalienable right.

But the right to pursue a trade or calling as a part of liberty, like all other rights, is not an absolute. It may not be curtailed "without due process of law," but if "due process" is observed, it may be. The valid exercise of governmental power in the interest of health, safety, morals and general welfare—the police power—is consistent with due process of law, and governmental action so taken is unimpeachable. The California court held that Rule 313 was a proper exercise of the police power and therefore did not violate Sandstrom's constitutional rights.

"Rule 313 is designed to afford the wagering public a maximum of protection against race horses being stimulated or depressed by making the trainer the insurer of the horse's condition," said the court. "That the wagering public merits such protection is evident from the magnitude of its patronage. Revenue to the California Horse Racing Board at four per cent of the pari-mutuel wagers amounted to

$16,563,763 for the fiscal year 1945-46. Should responsibility be imposed only for actual guilty participation or culpable negligence, as petitioner contends, there would exist a possible field of activity beyond the affirmative protection thereby afforded to patrons of the pari-mutuel system. The recognized interest of the wagering patrons is sought to be safeguarded by Rule 313. The closer the supervision to which the trainer is held, the more difficult it becomes for any one to administer a drug or chemical to the horse. The exaction of the ultimate in that regard is justified by the peril to be avoided."

Judicial Review of Administrative Action. Although the horse trainer, Sandstrom, did not get relief in court in the case which we have just been considering, because the court held that the agency charged with administering the statute regulating horse racing had not exceeded its powers, he had the benefit of judicial review of the administrative action which deprived him of his license. One of the most vital issues in the field of Administrative Law is that of the scope of judicial review of administrative orders. Although some kinds of administrative orders—such as those of the Federal Veterans Administration and other agencies which administer legislation relating to bounties and pensions—are not judicially reviewable, generally speaking the right to such review is granted by statute. This is true as to most of the major agencies of the federal government, and is generally true as to the administrative agencies of the several states.

But, granted the right to judicial review of administrative action—which means that the record transcribed at the administrative hearing will be sent to the reviewing court for its scrutiny—what shall be the scope of that review?

If the administrative action appears to be violative of some constitutional right, the court should set it aside. There is no room for dissent from such a conclusion. But where, as is often or generally the case, the result is dependent on the finding of facts from evidence introduced at the hearing, what attitude is the court to take? Will it read the testimony as transcribed from the point of view of weighing the evidence "on its own," so to speak, and coming to its own conclusion on the facts, or will it do so in the frame of mind of sustaining the administrative findings if there is a reasonable amount of evidence to sustain them, even though it might not agree with the agency conclusion? Particularly, where the agency involved is one working in a field of specialized knowledge, such as the Federal Communications Commission, the Civil Aeronautics Authority, or the National

Labor Relations Board, where scientific or economic considerations are paramount, should the court defer to the presumed "expertise" of the agency?

Such questions are profound ones, reaching to the very heart of the administrative process. They were responsible for deep-seated differences of opinion within the legal profession, and those differences still remain. Pursuant to the conception of the administrative process as one associated with reform, those of more "liberal" persuasion stand for a minimum of judicial review, affording administrative agencies a wide scope of action, beyond the restraint of courts. Those who are impressed by the possibility of administrative action getting out of hand if not kept under fairly close judicial surveillance would recognize the right of courts, in the exercise of their judicial function, to set aside administrative action not supported by at least substantial evidence.

The Federal Administrative Procedure Act. Insofar as the federal field is concerned, the question of scope of judicial review was settled as to most situations by the enactment, in 1946, of the Federal Administrative Procedure Act, dealing in general, as its name implies, with the procedure of federal administrative agencies. By section 10(e) of that Act, so far as necessary to decision and where presented the court shall decide all relevant questions of law, interpret constitutional and statutory provisions, and determine the meaning or applicability of the terms of any agency action. It shall compel agency action unlawfully withheld or unreasonably delayed; and hold unlawful and set aside agency action, findings, and conclusions found to be (1) arbitrary, capricious, an abuse of discretion, or otherwise not in accordance with law; (2) contrary to constitutional right, power, privilege or immunity; (3) in excess of statutory jurisdiction, authority, or limitations, or short of statutory right; (4) without observance of procedure required by law; (5) unsupported by substantial evidence in any case subject to the operation of the Rules or statutes; or (6) unwarranted by the facts to the extent that the facts are subject to trial *de novo* by the reviewing court.

Judicial Function Not Abdicated. This section of the Administrative Procedure Act was before the Supreme Court of the United States in *Universal Camera Corporation v. National Labor Relations Board,* when it reviewed a judgment of the United States Court of Appeals enforcing an order of the National Labor Relations Board directing an employer to reinstate, with back pay, an employee found to have been discriminatorily discharged. Under the working of the Taft-

Hartley Act, judicial review by the United States Court of Appeals is in effect had when the Labor Relations Board, in accordance with the statutory procedure, petitions the court for enforcement of its orders. The Taft-Hartley Act itself incorporates the same "substantial evidence" test that we have noted in section 10(e) of the Administrative Procedure Act. The Supreme Court said that the provisions of both Acts were applicable, and that the standard of proof required of the Labor Relations Board by the Taft-Hartley Act was the same as that to be exacted by courts reviewing every administrative action subject to the Administrative Procedure Act. The question before the court is whether, on the record as a whole, there is substantial evidence to support the agency's findings.

The difficulty of defining what is meant by "substantial evidence" is at once apparent. The problem posed is one of the sort that taxes the capacity of the law to provide a specific, readily understandable, working rule. The Court well said in the *Universal Camera* case that a formula for judicial review of administrative action may afford grounds for certitude but cannot assure certainty of application. Some scope for judicial discretion in applying the formula can be avoided only by falsifying the actual process of judging or by using the formula as an instrument of futile casuistry. It cannot be too often repeated that judges are not automata. The ultimate reliance for the fair operation of any standard is a judiciary of high competence and character and the constant play of an informed professional critique upon its work. Since the precise way in which courts interfere with agency findings cannot be imprisoned within any form of words, new formulas attempting to rephrase the old are not likely to be more helpful than the old. There are no talismanic words that can avoid the process of judgment.

The Supreme Court was clear in its pronouncement, however, that some Courts of Appeals had not been exercising a properly inclusive scope of review. It said the Administrative Procedure Act and the Taft-Hartley Act direct that courts must now assume more responsibility for the reasonableness and fairness of Labor Board decisions than some courts have shown in the past. Reviewing courts must be influenced by a feeling that they are not to abdicate the conventional judicial function. Congress has imposed on them responsibility for assuring that the Board keeps within reasonable grounds. That responsibility is not less real because it is limited to enforcing the requirement that evidence appear substantial when viewed, on the record as a whole, by courts invested with the authority and enjoying the prestige of the Courts of Appeals. The Board's findings are entitled to respect; but they must nevertheless be set aside when the record before a Court of Appeals clearly precludes the Board's decision from being justified by a fair estimate of the worth of the testimony of witnesses or its informed judgment on matters within its special competence or both.

Judicial Review by State Courts. State courts have shown a disposition to exercise a closer scrutiny of administrative action than that evidenced by the federal courts, or prescribed by the "substantial evidence" rule of the Federal Administrative Procedure Act.

Thus, the Supreme Court of Illinois, reviewing the administrative order of a school district detaching certain territory from one district and adding it to another, the ultimate question being whether such action would be to the best interests of the schools of the area and the educational welfare of the pupils, recently said that the argument that the scope of review does not include a weighing of the testimony, and that an administrative order must be upheld "if based on evidence," was not applicable. The rule which accords a prima facie validity to administrative decisions does not relieve a court of the important duty to examine the evidence in an impartial manner and to set aside an order which is unsupported in fact. The court said it was unnecessary for it to advert to the dangers inherent in a relaxation of this function, which had recently been ably pointed out by George Winder. Referring to the Illinois Administrative Review Act, the court said that it does not require recognition of an order which is against the manifest weight of the evidence, nor does the law allow a stamp of approval to be placed on the findings of an administrative agency merely because such agency heard the witnesses and made the requisite findings.

Constitutional Right to Judicial Review of Administrative Action. We have already seen that provision for judicial review of administrative action is commonly made by statute or rule. But the fact that no such provision is affirmatively made is not necessarily conclusive against the right to invoke it. If a constitutional right has been infringed, the one injured has the right to judicial relief.

Such was the situation presented in the case of *Wong Yang Sung v. McGrath.* Wong Yang Sung, a native and citizen of China, was arrested by United States immigration officials on a charge of being unlawfully in the United States through having overstayed shore leave as one of a shipping crew. A hearing was held before an immigrant inspector who recommended deportation. The acting Commissioner approved, and the Board of Immigration Appeals affirmed. Wong Yang Sung then sought release from custody by *habeas corpus* proceedings in District Court for the District of Columbia, upon the sole ground that the administrative hearing was not conducted in conformity with certain provisions of the Administrative Procedure Act which prescribed certain requirements as to hearings. The Government admitted noncompliance, but asserted that the Act did not apply. The District Court, agreeing, dismissed the *habeas corpus* petition. Appeal to the Supreme Court followed.

The provisions which were not followed were declared by the Act to be applicable "in every case of adjudication required by statute to be determined on the record after opportunity for an agency hearing." The statute authorizing deportation did not "require" a hearing, although, as we have seen, one had been granted. It was argued, therefore, that the provisions of the Administrative Procedure Act were not applicable.

The Supreme Court rejected this contention. It pointed out that even though the deportation statute did not require a hearing, without such hearing there would be no constitutional authority for deportation. The constitutional requirement of procedural due process of law derives from the same source as Congress' power to legislate and, where applicable, permeates every valid enactment of that body. "It was under compulsion of the Constitution that this Court long ago held that an antecedent deportation statute must provide a hearing at least for aliens who had not entered clandestinely and who had been here some time even if illegally," said Justice Jackson, speaking for the Court. "The limitation to hearings 'required by statute' in the Administrative Procedure Act exempts from its application only those hearings which administrative agencies may hold by regulation, rule, custom or special dispensation; not those held by compulsion. We do not think the limiting words render the Administrative Procedure Act inapplicable to hearings, the requirement for which has been read into a statute by the Court in order to save the statute from invalidity. They exempt hearings of less than statutory authority, not those of more than statutory authority."

In short, the Court held that the Constitution demands a hearing in deportation cases. A person not accorded a hearing by the agency would have constitutional ground to seek judicial review, even though no statute or rule provided for it. The immigration Act would be unconstitutional except as it either provided for a hearing, or such requirement were read into it. By reading the requirement into it there was present the "adjudication required by statute" that made the provisions of the Administrative Procedure Act applicable.

The right to judicial review of unlawful administrative action, even though not provided for by statute, or even if purportedly denied, has long been recognized. In *Chin Yow v. United States*, the Supreme Court was reviewing the judgment of a lower federal court denying a petition for *habeas corpus* filed by a Chinese person seeking to enter the United States, and claiming to be a citizen by birth. Following an administrative hearing, he was ordered excluded, and his petition, which served the purpose of bringing the matter before the court, looking to judicial review, alleged that the hearing had been unfair because the agency had violated its own procedural rules. The Act of Congress governing immigration procedures purported to make the decision of the administrative officials in such matters "final," thus precluding judicial review. The Supreme Court reversed and upheld the right to maintain the petition for *habeas corpus*.

Speaking for the Court, Justice Holmes declared: "The decision of the Department is final, but that is on the presupposition that the decision was after a hearing in good faith, however summary in form. As between the substantive right of citizens to enter and of persons alleging themselves to be citizens to have a chance to prove their allegation, on the one side, and the conclusiveness of the commissioner's fiat on the other, when one or the other must give way, the latter must yield. In such a case something must be done, and it naturally falls to be done by the courts."

The Problem of "Finding" Administrative Law. It was the practice of the Roman Emperor Caligula to write his laws in small characters and hang them on places too high for the populace to read. Such a procedure evokes the condemnation of the American citizen, whose reactions are geared to principles of fairness inherent in the due process concept. Certainly, the Anglo-American system has never countenanced, much less promoted, hiding the law. Rather has it taken all reasonable ways to make it accessible to the public. To be sure, there have always been "gaps," not covered by statute or judicial decision: such are unavoidable in our system, or, for that matter, in any system of jurisprudence. The point is that under our common law system the fundamental sources of judicial decision and statute have traditionally been open to the view of all. In times past lawyers working with the materials customarily at hand in their office libraries, supplemented by occasional visits to the libraries of their bar associations, could proceed with considerable confidence, from one year's end to another, that they were not overlooking the basic authorities essential to well-reasoned determination of their problems.

Today, this situation no longer exists. It is essential to have in mind that the three routine sources which the common law lawyer in times past consulted to find the law governing the problem which concerned him—the constitutions of nation and state, the reports of opinions of the courts of last resort, and the statutes of nation and state—will not suffice in the modern practice of law. Abraham Lincoln and his contemporaries rode the prairie circuits of Illinois with law libraries adequate to meet all practical demands carried in their saddle-bags. Today, in the same predominantly rural counties their professional successors, even with all the advantages of speedy and capacious motor transportation, could not carry a complement of legal materials which would assure them of comprehensive access to the current law, because administrative regulations affecting various phases of agriculture, for example, might be changed any day in Washington by the cutting of a mimeograph stencil. The force of this statement will shortly become apparent, with consideration of the case of *Federal Crop Insurance Corporation v. Merrill*.

In this situation—one in which the lawyer is plagued with uncertainty as to just what the law is because under many circumstances he does not know where to find it and lacks the assurance that what he does find has not been superseded—lies one of the main weaknesses of the administrative process: a weakness which makes it vulnerable to legitimate criticism.

The "Hip-Pocket" Incident. Prior to the National Industrial Recovery Act of 1933 there had not been devised any standard or method of publishing the administrative regulations and decisions which constitute so large an element of Administrative Law. Such regulations and decisions, as we have noted in the *California Horse Racing Board* case, have the force of law, as much as do the statutes themselves. In those earlier days, some of the regulations issued by federal agencies were buried in the files of government departments. Some were held to be confidential and were not released. The practice as to printing and issuance of such as were published was not uniform. Even Presidential Executive Orders were not adequately promulgated. Presumably they were filed with the Department of State and published each year with the statutes at large. But this was not uniformly done. It was not uncommon for the White House to retain orders which it preferred to keep from public view. The Executive

Orders embodying the administrative "codes" prepared under the National Industrial Recovery Act were, in many instances, not even at the White House, but in the desk drawers of administrative officials. Professor Frank Newman has aptly reminded us that until the Federal Register Act was passed, the government was allowed to penalize citizens under rules whose existence was unproclaimed and whose text could be found only in the vaults of the Department of State.

The situation was brought to a head in rather dramatic manner when a test case involving the administrative "Petroleum Code" came before the Supreme Court of the United States. In the course of the oral argument of this "Hot Oil" or "Hip Pocket" case, as it is sometimes called, (*Panama Refining Company v. Ryan; United States v. Smith*) the Attorney General, challenged by questions of the justices, was compelled to admit that a regulation of the administrator upon which an indictment had been based could not be found in print. Counsel for the oil producers on trial charged that the only copy of this regulation he had ever seen was in the hip pocket of an agency representative in the oil fields. Whatever had been the original status of the regulation in question, it turned out that it had been eliminated by an Executive Order unknown to both prosecutors and the oil producers. As Louis L. Jaffe has stated, "the case exploded in the government's face," and those who heard and participated in the argument were struck by the eagerness with which the Court probed into the "unsavory story."

The Federal Register. A long needed publication, the *Federal Register,* came into being as an aftermath of the "Hot Oil" or "Hip Pocket" incident. In 1934 the Congress was distinctly alarmed by the incident in *Panama Refining Company v. Ryan,* when the Attorney General, arguing in the Supreme Court, admitted that the case had proceeded in the lower courts in ignorance of a technical though inadvertent revocation of the regulation upon which the prosecution was based. The Congress then passed the Federal Register Act.

The Federal Register Act provides that there shall be published in the *Federal Register* (1) all Presidential proclamations and Executive Orders, except such as have no general applicability and legal effect or are effective only against federal agencies or persons in their capacity as officers, agents or employees thereof; (2) such documents or classes of documents as the President shall determine from time to time have general applicability and legal effect; and (3) such documents or classes of documents as may be required so to be published by Act of the Congress: Provided, that for the purposes of the Act every document or order which shall prescribe a penalty shall be deemed to have general applicability and legal effect. By further provisions of the Act, there shall also be published such other documents or classes of documents as may be authorized to be published by regulations prescribed with the approval of the President, but in no case shall comment or news items of any character whatever be authorized to be published in the *Federal Register*. The Federal Administrative Procedure Act also contains certain provisions as to what shall be published in the *Federal Register*.

The *Federal Register* is published at Washington, D.C. daily, except Sundays, Mondays and days following official holidays, pursuant to the authority contained in the Federal Register Act and under regulations prescribed by the Administrative Committee of the *Federal Register*. Any one may subscribe to it. The price has been $15 per year. In the course of a year its bulk runs to 10,000 or more pages, printed three columns to the page. Some individual issues may contain 200 or more pages.

Thus the *Federal Register* contains "law in quantity." Even so, it is questionable whether it contains all that should be printed on its pages. Professor Newman has asked whether the *Federal Register* contains substantially all the rules that officials, lawyers and other specialists need. The answer, he said, is "no." Moreover, the *Federal Register* does not even contain the rules Congress has declared it should contain. Under the Federal Administrative Procedure Act the following kinds of rules are required to be published: (1) substantive rules adopted as authorized by law; (2) statements of general policy or interpretations formulated and adopted by the agency for the guidance of the public; (3) descriptions of central and field organization; (4) statements of the general course and method by which functions are channeled and determined. In addition, regulations promulgated under the Federal Register Act provide for the publication of rules prescribing a penalty or a course of conduct, conferring a right, privilege, authority or immunity, or imposing an obligation, and relevant or applicable to the general public, the members of a class or the persons of a locality.

After calling attention to the provisions of the Federal Administrative Procedure Act and regulations under the Federal Register Act, Frank C. Newman pointed out: "There are thousands of rules meeting these definitions—rules that create and interpret law, that state policy and that describe agency organization and procedure—which do not appear in the *Federal Register.*"

The same Act which established the *Federal Register* provided for the *Code of Federal Regulations.* This is a set of volumes in which the rules and regulations pertaining to each agency are brought together and published in code form, in broad arrangement corresponding to that of the federal statutes, with fifty titles paralleling those of the *United States Code.* That its content cannot be relied upon as permanent goes without saying. Any issue of the *Federal Register* may contain matter which supersedes or amends what has gone before. By a process of supplementation, however, it is kept up to date to the extent that circumstances permit this.

Citizens Are Charged with Knowledge of Content of the Federal Register. It is probably safe to say that the average citizen does not know that there is such a publication as the *Federal Register.* Nevertheless, in so far as his interests may be affected, he is held to knowledge of its content. This was established in an unmistakable manner in *Federal Crop Insurance Corporation v. Merrill.* In March, 1945, the Merrill brothers applied to their County Agricultural Conservation Committee, acting as agent for the Federal Crop Insurance Corporation, a United States Government corporation, for insurance under the Federal Crop Insurance Act to cover wheat farming operations in Bonneville County, Idaho. They informed the Committee that they were planting 460 acres of spring wheat and that on 400 of those acres they were reseeding winter wheat acreage. The Committee advised them that the entire crop was insurable, and recommended to the Corporation's Denver branch office acceptance of the application. The application was there accepted. That summer most of the Merrill brothers' wheat was destroyed by drought. They made application for payment of the anticipated insurance reimbursement. However, the Federal Crop Insurance Corporation denied the claim, calling attention to an agency regulation, issued in February of 1945, which stated that the term "wheat crop shall not include winter wheat in the 1945 crop year, and spring wheat which has been reseeded on winter wheat acreage in the 1945 crop year." This had been duly published in the *Federal Register.*

As the statute permitted, the Merrill brothers filed suit against the Corporation in the Idaho state court. That court allowed evidence to go to the jury that the Merrills had no actual knowledge of the regulation in question, insofar as it precluded insurance for reseeded wheat, and that they had in fact been misled by the Corporation's agent into believing that reseeded acreage was insurable. Judgment was entered on the verdict in their favor; the Supreme Court of Idaho affirmed. The Supreme Court of the United States, granting certiorari because the case involved "a question of importance in the administration of the Federal Crop Insurance Act," reversed the lower court's decision.

The Supreme Court decision was not unanimous. Speaking for the majority, Justice Frankfurter declared the Court took it for granted that the Merrills reasonably believed their crop was insured, and that recovery could be had against a private insurance company. But the Federal Crop Insurance Corporation was not a private insurance company. "It is too late in the day," the Justice explained, "to urge that the government is just another private litigant, for the purpose of charging it with liability, whenever it takes over a business theretofore conducted by private enterprise or engages in competition with private enterprise." He went on to say that whatever form in which the government functions, any one entering into an arrangement with the government takes the risk of having accurately ascertained that he who purports to act for the government stays within the bounds of his authority. And this is so, even though, as here, the agent himself may have been unaware of the limitations upon his authority. The Wheat Crop Insurance Regulations were binding on all who sought to come within the Federal Crop Insurance Act, regardless of actual knowledge of what was in the regulations or of the hardship resulting from innocent ignorance.

In his dissenting opinion Justice Jackson pointed out that it was early discovered that fair dealing in the insurance business required that the entire contract between the policyholder and the insurance company be embodied in the writing which passed between the parties, namely, the written application, if any, and the policy issued. "It may be well enough to make some types of contracts with the government subject to long and involved regulations published in the Federal Register," said he. "To my mind, it is an absurdity to hold that every farmer who insures his crops knows what the Federal Register contains or even knows that there is such a publication. If he were to peruse this voluminous and dull publication as it is issued from time to time in order to make sure whether anything has been promulgated that affects his rights, he would never need crop insurance, for he would never get time to plant any crops. Nor am I convinced that a reading of technically-worded regulations would enlighten him much in any event." Concluding, he said the government asked the Court to lift its policies out of the control of the states and to find or fashion a federal rule to govern them. "I should respond to that request," said he, "by laying down a federal rule that would hold those agencies to the same fundamental principles of fair dealing that have been found essential in progressive states to prevent insurance companies from being an investment in disappointment."

The logic of the situation is demonstrably on the side of the majority. Administrative regulations have the force of law. American citizens are presumably cognizant of the principle that ignorance of the law excuses no one. But the technical harshness of the result is emphasized by the fact that the regulations which specifically defined the various types of crop insurance that might be issued had remained unchanged, so far as wheat crops were concerned, for a period of nine years, and for the first time—for the single year of 1945, and in a single sentence—wheat crop insurance was restricted as indicated. As Urban Lavery pointed out, the farmers were thrown out of court by the Supreme Court of the United States because of that obscure and hidden change—"a change which obviously had escaped the attention of everybody, until the farmers' claim for loss reached the main agency offices in Washington."

The Danger Point. The Idaho wheat farmers whose experience with the workings of Administrative Law we have been considering were not deprived of their liberties. Only their pocket-books were affected, and that, only, after a thorough judicial review extending to scrutiny of the Supreme Court of the United States. It is true, of course, that administrative action may result in deprivation of liberty to the extent of imprisonment for contempt or for violation of a duly-promulgated administrative regulation having the force of law. But the significant thing is—and the significance of it cannot be over-emphasized—that such deprivation of liberty can thus far be ordered only by a constitutional court of our nation or our several states. An administrative tribunal has no penal power.

If the time should ever come when, as in Nazi Germany and Soviet Russia, administrative agencies of our nation and states assume to exercise criminal jurisdiction, the danger point will have been reached. The liberties of the individual will have been fatally jeopardized.

CHAPTER 28

THE PLACE OF JUDICIAL PRECEDENT

The Dilemma. We have already referred to the statement of Justice Holmes that a page of history is worth a volume of logic, and have thus been put on notice that logic is not the ultimate determining factor in our law. We are consequently prepared to find that our legal system embodies some anomalies. One of them has to be faced up to at this point. We have been laying much stress upon the capacity of the common law to change as occasion calls upon it to do so. It is certainly true that with relation to human progress the law must be readily amenable to change.

But, on the other hand, the citizen lives in the present. To fulfill his obligations to his family and his fellows he needs definite guidance for the immediate hour at hand. If the law is to fulfill its immediate present purpose it must provide stable rules of conduct, with knowledge of which the citizen is chargeable, and which he can ascertain with reasonable assurance that they constitute the measure of his responsibility. Where is he to find this stable guidance if the rules which govern his conduct are in constant jeopardy of change? Can he not rely on the decisions of the courts which have declared the law?

Here, indeed, is a dilemma. There is no escaping it. Nor does our legal system ignore or seek to avoid it. Perhaps illogically, but with commendable pragmatism, it recognizes that there must be both change and stability. With a mind open to change, it is recognized that until the need for change is convincingly manifested, it is essential that the judicial decisions of the day be accepted as at least prima facie guides of conduct for the present and the immediate future. Understanding, as we now do, that the body of common law has developed by a process of following precedent, or *stare decisis* as it is succinctly called, before we close our study it remains to deal a little more directly with this dilemma and to note how the Supreme Court of the United States has applied the *stare decisis* doctrine.

The Doctrine of Stare Decisis. The basis for the doctrine of *stare decisis* is found in the principle, now well understood by us, that under our common law system the decisions of our courts are the declared law, constituting the basic source of information as to what the law is. This is true whether the court was proceeding in the traditional common law manner in the absence of a governing statute, as it was doing in *Woods v. Lancet,* and *Hitaffer v. Argonne Company,* or whether it was applying a statute or dealing with a constitutional provision. In these latter situations the constitutional provision or statute has force only as thus construed, and that force can be understood only by reference to the judicial decision. We will have a further understanding of this after perusal of the chapter which follows, and which deals with the public school segregation case.

The considerations inherent in the *stare decisis* doctrine were brought out by Justice Frankfurter in *Helvering v. Hallock,* in which he declared the Supreme Court recognized that *stare decisis* embodies an important social policy. It represents an element of continuity in the law, and is rooted in the psychologic need to satisfy reasonable expectations. But *stare decisis* is a principle of policy and not a mechanical formula of adherence to the latest decision, however recent and questionable, when such adherence involves collision with a prior doctrine more embracing in its scope, intrinsically sounder, and verified by experience. Justice Brandeis dignified the doctrine on practical grounds by saying that *stare decisis* is usually the wise policy, because in most cases it is more important that the applicable rule of law be settled than that it be settled right.

Limited Applicability to Constitutional Issues. After the consideration which we will give in the next chapter to *Brown v. Board of Education,* we will become aware that the *stare decisis* doctrine has limited applicability to constitutional issues. The flexibility of our constitutional system is inherent in our theory of government. Our governmental scheme would be defeated by a strict application of the *stare decisis* principle to constitutional decisions. Justice Brandeis has forcefully pointed out that in cases involving the Constitution of the United States, where correction through legislative action is practically impossible, the Supreme Court has often overruled its earlier decisions. "The Court bows to the lessons of experience and the force of better reasoning, recognizing that the process of trial and error, so fruitful in the physical sciences, is appropriate also to the judicial function," said he.

Exemplification in the Professional Sports Cases. The working of the *stare decisis* doctrine and its recognition by the Supreme Court of the United States as an important attribute of our legal system was involved in the series of cases in which the Court had occasion to deal with the question as to whether professional sports are subject to the provisions of the anti-trust laws. In *Radovich v. National Football League* the Court held professional football to be subject to such laws. This was the latest of the series of cases. In 1922, in *Federal Baseball Club v. National League* the Court had held professional baseball not to be in interstate commerce and therefore outside the scope of the Sherman Antitrust Act. In 1953, in *Toolson v. New York Yankees,* also involving baseball, in spite of many demonstrated changed conditions it held by its 1922 decision in the *Federal Baseball Club case.* In the *Radovich* case it was urged upon the Court that the *stare decisis* doctrine "compelled" it to hold, in turn, that professional football "stood under the same umbrella" as professional baseball, and under those holdings was not subject to the sanctions of the Sherman Antitrust Act.

In justifying its refusal to apply the doctrine to professional football, as it had to baseball, the Court was at pains to explain why it had ruled as it did in the *Toolson* case. The Court stated it did this because it was concluded that more harm would be done in overruling the 1922 decision than in upholding a ruling which was at best of dubious validity. "Vast efforts had gone into the development and organization of baseball since that decision and enormous capital had been invested in reliance on its permanence," the Court observed. "Congress had chosen to make no change. All this, combined with the flood of litigation that would follow its repudiation, the harrassment that would ensue, and the retroactive effect of such a decision, led the Court to the practical result that it should sustain the unequivocal line of authority reaching over many years."

In other words, the Supreme Court applied the doctrine in the baseball case to the end of insuring property stability, even though the decision it thereby followed was of "dubious validity." But it refused to extend the application of the doctrine to professional football, as it had refused to extend it to boxing and the theatre upon the basis of a decision of "dubious validity," which the Court said it would not render if it were considering the question of baseball for the first time "upon a clean slate."

Thus, the *stare decisis* doctrine finds understandable usage where property rights are in effect established by judicial decision and no constitutional issue is involved. In the next chapter we shall see the limitations imposed upon it where the issue is one of constitutional interpretation.

CHAPTER 29

CONSTITUTIONAL EVOLUTION

Constitutions and Constitutional Change. Although, as we have seen, our basic rights long antedated the constitutions of our nation and the states, those constitutions are, emphatically, their present foundation.

Once written and adopted, constitutions cannot be altered as to text except as they are superseded in whole by repeal or amended as to specific provisions in accordance with the formal processes prescribed. The presence of the First Ten Amendments to the Constitution of the United States, adopted almost simultaneously with the Constitution itself, and of twelve subsequent Amendments, evidences the possibility of such changes in the fundamental law itself. In the realm of the states, not only are examples of amendment of existing constitutions abundant, but many examples can be found of repeal of existing constitutions and the enactment of new ones.

But such processes are, understandably, slow. In the meantime, public pressures, pointing to changing concepts of social and legal relations, may become cumulatively more insistent. The change sought seems perhaps in conflict with constitutional provisions, either as they stand in literal text or as they have been judicially interpreted at an earlier date. Events press hard for action.

Constitutional Interpretation. The answer to the problem thus presented is found in the nature of our constitutions, particularly that of the Constitution of the United States. The Supreme Court of the United States long ago pointed out that it was made for "an undefined and expanding future, and for a people gathered and foregathered from many nations and of many tongues." Chief Justice Marshall stated that "it is a *constitution* we are expounding." Referring to this statement, Justice Frankfurter added: "Not the least characteristic of great statesmanship which the Framers manifested was the extent to which they did not attempt to bind the future." In a recent pronouncement the Supreme Court declared that while the language of the Constitution does not change, the changing circumstances of a progressive society for which it was designed "yield new and fuller import to its meaning."

Our constitutional documents, then, are to be interpreted in the light of the "new and fuller" import of their meaning. Proceeding in this light, our legislators and courts alike have latitude to meet the demands of changing conditions. That the doctrine of *stare decisis*, hereinbefore considered, does not operate to impede this process, we shall proceed to see.

The Public School Segregation Case. The working of the principle of constitutional interpretation to bend the constitution to the concepts of the times was recently exemplified in the public school segregation case, *Brown v. Board of Education.* The issue was whether the provision of the Fourteenth Amendment to the Constitution of the United States that no state shall deny to any person within its jurisdiction the equal protection of the laws was violated by requiring negro children to attend public schools provided specially for them, it being conceded for the purposes of the case that such facilities were equal to those provided for white children. It is a matter of common knowledge that the Supreme Court of the United States held that such was a constitutional violation.

Up to the time of this decision it had been thought that a previous decision of the Court in the case of *Plessy v. Ferguson*, handed down nearly sixty years before, was decisive of the issue. The Plessy case involved a Louisiana statute, effective within the state, providing for separate but equal accommodations on railroads for the white and colored races, either by separate cars or by partitioned coaches, and empowered conductors to assign passengers to the place where each belonged. The Supreme Court said this violated neither the Thirteenth nor the Fourteenth Amendments. No involuntary servitude was involved within the Thirteenth Amendment. As to the Fourteenth, while its object was to enforce the absolute equality of the races before the law, in the nature of things it could not have been intended to abolish distinctions based on color, or to enforce social, as distinguished from political, equality, or a commingling of the races upon terms unsatisfactory to either. The Court concluded that when the government has secured to each of its citizens equal rights before the law and equal opportunities for improvement and progress, it has accomplished the end for which it is ordained and performed all of the functions respecting social advantages with which it is endowed. "Legislation is powerless to eradicate social instincts based upon physical differences, and the attempt to do so can only result in accentuating the difficulties of the present situation," the Court declared. "If the civil and political rights of both races be equal, one cannot be inferior to the other civilly or politically. If one race be inferior to the other socially, the Constitution of the United States cannot put them upon the same plane."

Following the *Plessy v. Ferguson* decision, the Supreme Court was frequently called upon to review cases in which, in consequence of state action, there was involved separation of the races in the fields of transportation, use of public facilities and public education. Where state legislation called for equal facilities, though separate, and such facilities were in fact provided, over a long period of years the decision in *Plessy v. Ferguson* was followed.

"Modern Authority" as to "Separate But Equal." In *Brown v. Board of Education* minors of the Negro race, through their legal representatives, sought the aid of the courts in obtaining admission to public schools of their community on a nonsegregated basis. In each instance they had been denied admission to schools attended by white children under laws requiring or permitting segregation according to race. This segregation was alleged to deprive them of the equal protection of the laws under the Fourteenth Amendment. The lower courts denied relief on the basis of the "separate but equal" doctrine.

On the appeal to the Supreme Court the cases were exhaustively briefed and had the unusual distinction of being argued orally at two terms of the Court. The Court finally disposed of them in a brief opinion, in marked contrast to its general run of thoroughly reasoned opinions of recent times, and obviously calculated to present the smallest possible target to external criticism, consistent with the accepted rule that a judicial opinion should openly deal with and rationally dispose of all the issues involved in the case.

Not questioning the "equal" element from what might be termed the physical point of view but reversing the lower courts, the Supreme Court held that the relief sought should be granted. It said that the purposes of the Fourteenth Amendment with regard to schools as disclosed by its history are, at best, "inconclusive," and that the Court could not turn the clock back to 1868 when the Amendment was adopted or to 1896 when *Plessy v. Ferguson* was written. It went on to say that to separate Negro children from others of similar age and qualifications solely because of their race generates a feeling of inferiority as to their status in the community that may affect their hearts and minds in a way unlikely ever to be undone. Segregation with the sanction of the law has a tendency to retard the educational and mental development of Negro children and to deprive them of some of the benefits they would receive in a racially integrated school system.

"Whatever may have been the extent of psychological knowledge at the time of *Plessy v. Ferguson,* this finding is amply supported by modern authority," observed the Court. "Any language in *Plessy v. Ferguson* contrary to this finding is rejected. We conclude that in the field of public education the doctrine of 'separate but equal' has no place. Therefore, we hold that the plaintiffs and others similarly situated for whom the actions have been brought are, by reason of the segregation complained of, deprived of the equal protection of the laws guaranteed by the Fourteenth Amendment." The Supreme Court did not purport to enforce its judgment requiring segregation, but delegated it to lower courts in the areas affected.

In commenting on the Court's decision, Robert J. Harris stated that instead of relying upon history, which in these cases would have been a slender reed unless the Court had invented a historical fiction, as it has done occasionally, and instead of invoking earlier precedents which could have provided strong support, the Chief Justice based his opinion upon the quicksands of social psychology reinforced by vastly changed conditions in education between 1868 when the Fourteenth Amendment was adopted and 1954 when these cases were decided. By all standards, however, the *decision* in the Segregation Cases was a great decision. The *opinion,* on the other hand, was not a great opinion. Indeed, after the exhaustive records compiled and the elaborate arguments adduced in briefs and supplements of counsel, the opinion was something of an anticlimax and did not reach the "height of this great argument" to assert equality before the law and to justify the ways of the law to man.

Critical Comment on the Court's Decision. In the technical usage of the law the term "authority" is ordinarily employed to denote reasoned judicial opinions, or, of course, applicable constitutional provisions or statutory enactments. It would accordingly be thought that when the Court in the Brown case referred to "authority" as supporting the findings regarding the effects of segregation, it meant legal authority in this accepted sense of the term. Such was not the case. In support of its statement the Court cited several psychological treatises, including Clark's "Effect of Prejudice and Discrimination on Personality Development" and Myrdal's "An American Dilemma." By thus premising its conclusion as to a departure from previous constitutional interpretation upon sociological opinion rather than upon a legal approach such as the Court had previously recognized and followed, involving a full weighing of the original intention, the Court made itself vulnerable to the strong volume of criticism which followed. Some one hundred members of the Congress of the United States issued a critical manifesto and pointed comment came from many quarters.

Among outspoken individuals was James F. Byrnes, a member of the Supreme Court of the United States who resigned in 1942 to become United States Director of Economic Stabilization and who later served thereafter in various governmental capacities, including Secretary of State of the United States and Governor of South Carolina. He chided the Court for ignoring the very principle that it had previously stated in the case of *Beauharnais v. Illinois.* In that case the Court ruled: "It is not within our competence to confirm or deny claims of social scientists as to the dependence of the individual on the position of his racial or religious group in the community." Mr. Byrnes felt the Court had disregarded the written Constitution and its own decisions and substituted for these a policy of its own, supported not by legal precedents but by the writings of sociologists, none of whom had testified in the trial court and whose opinions were not subject to cross-examination or rebuttal. He pointed out that Clark was an employee of the National Association for the Advancement of Colored People. Referring to Myrdal's *An American Dilemma,* he quoted therefrom a statement that the Constitution of the United States was "impractical and unsuited to modern conditions" and its adoption was "nearly a plot against the common people."

The conclusion of the Court that the purpose of the Fourteenth Amendment with regard to schools as disclosed by its history was "inconclusive," was directly challenged. For example, Ralph T. Catterall stated: "After thousands of hours of laborious research the facts of history were produced; they proved that nobody in 1868 expected the Fourteenth Amendment to abolish segregation. The facts of history were dismissed as irrelevant and immaterial." Alexander M. Bickel, law clerk to Justice Frankfurter at the time of the first argument, said: "The obvious conclusion to which the evidence, thus summarized, easily leads is that section 1 of the Fourteenth Amendment, like section 1 of the Civil Rights Act of 1866, carried out the relatively narrow objectives of the Moderates, and hence, as originally understood, was meant to apply neither to jury service, nor suffrage, nor antimiscegnation statutes, nor segregation."

But, as Charles Fairman has suggested, in the midst of all the criticism of the Segregation cases it is well to consider what the effect would have been had the Court reaffirmed the language of *Plessy v. Ferguson.* Doubtless the public reaction would have been less intemperate than that which we now experience, but the moral hurt would have been incalculably profound. Such a decision would have repudiated a current already running strong in American life.

However vigorous the criticism of the Court's decision, no one questions that it stands as interpretative of the present law of the land.

"The Challenge of an Enigma, the Mystery of a Miracle." In the pages immediately preceding we have seen the common law and legislative statutes, "in action." We have noted the relation of our Constitution to the common law system, and have seen that although the Constitution is a document stated in formal general terms, as the basic element of a system of law with the genius of adaptation to change it, too, is open to interpretative expansion.

It is therefore true that an English or American judge dealing with a case may find the law governing it in a statute book rather than in the reported decision of a court. If there is such an applicable statute it manifestly reflects an unmistakable pronouncement of the public's will as to the law that governs. Or the law that should be declared decisive may be found in a constitutional provision, perhaps of long standing literally, but calling for enlightened interpretation in relation to changing circumstances. That interpretation the court may proceed to make.

All in all, we have here something which has been well said to present to the philosophical scholar of human history the challenge of an enigma, the mystery of a miracle. Uncreated by regal fiat, it nevertheless vibrates with a life all its own; threatened with extinction by competing systems, Chinese-like it invariably absorbs the invader for its greater glory. The common law plunges its millenary roots into the era of feudal agriculturalism, yet it flourishes in the shadow of skyscrapers, and is fertilized by the black soot of steel mills. Changing and yet unchanged for a thousand years, hoary with age yet contemporaneous in effectiveness, it seems to defy the rhythm of growth and decay. It has produced no finer fruit than the constitutional system of the United States, embodying in clear-cut terms a full quota of individual spiritual rights and buttressing them and other basic common law and statutory rights with procedures insuring as adamant protection and vindication as appears humanly possible.

PART VII: EPILOGUE

CHAPTER 30

WHAT DOES THE FUTURE HOLD?

Beyond the Wide Horizons. The college student of the early 1900's who was referred to in the first paragraph of our study, and who has accompanied us through our consideration of law in its relation to civilization, is now approaching the mellowed maturity implicit in the age of three-score-and-ten years. Sharing with us the story of the millenia preceding his advent, he has himself played the role of an American citizen in the stirring events which have transpired during his lifetime.

We ask him if he has the answer to the question with which we started: "What does the future hold?"

"In my college days that question would have seemed easy to answer," he replies. "The theory then was that the human race was going forward by a process of peaceful evolutionary progression, slow, maybe, but sure. That would have been the outlook for the future. I anticipated making my way through the course of a relatively uneventful life in a relatively uneventful world. I soon found that this was not to be. We were made to realize how small the world had become. It has steadily become smaller, at a rate that we have hardly been able to sense. All the nations of the earth are within a few hours' reach of each other's doorsteps. I could go clear around the world in less time than it used to take me to go home from college. In today's atomic age international problems are as pressing as those down the street on which we live. We can sense them, but we do not know the answers. The solution lies somewhere clear out beyond the wide horizons. And there, we know only too well, lurks the grim specter of war, ever threatening the welfare of mankind."

The Consciences of Nations. The thing is to find a way to solve those problems without war, we suggest. And do we not have, to start with, International Law?

"Going back again to my college days, we thought International

474

Law would provide the solution," he says. "We know that society cannot exist without law, and International Law developed out of the realization that this principle applies to the relations between nations and their peoples, just as it does at lower group levels. Its principles and practices had been in process of development since the early days of recorded history. They had grown with the acceptance of the concept of natural law. Grotius marshaled them in a reassuring manner in his work *De Jure Belli ac Pacis,* which came out in 1625. By our time International Law had attained recognition as a branch of jurisprudence which could be looked to for the orderly regulation of international relations. As John Bassett Moore pointed out, in the works written and published in the sixteenth and seventeenth centuries we naturally find a blending of moral principles, as discovered by reason and revelation, with positive law and custom, of which the Roman civil law formed the chief source. This composite body of law was, under the comprehensive title of the law of nations, formally declared by the highest courts in England, in the eighteenth century, to be in its full extent a part of the law of the land, not by formal or statutory adoption, but by long recognition and observance."

It would seem to have been fitted right into our common law system, we observe.

"That is just what Professor Moore said," he replies. "International law formed a part of the common law and developed in the same way. And he went on to say that the United States, on declaring their independence, took the same position, which the executive, legislative and judicial authorities, federal and state, then and thereafter consistently maintained. In 1888 Sir Henry Maine, in summing up the attitude of the statesmen and jurists of the United States, said that they regarded International Law not as a body of rules that had become binding by legislative action, or as immemorial usage 'of which the memory of man runneth not to the contrary,' but as a main part of the conditions on which a state was originally received into the family of civilized nations; and that, if they were to formulate their view in their own way, they 'probably' would say that the state which disclaimed the authority of International Law would place itself 'outside the circle of civilized nations.' "

That would seem to have grounded International Law upon a strong foundation, we comment.

"Yes," he agrees. "According to Professor Moore, the sixty years following the close of the Napoleonic Wars were marked by a progressive development of International Law. The Treaty of Vienna of June 9, 1815, itself sought to establish rules that would liberalize international practices. Such were the rules designed to assure the free navigation of rivers which on their way to the sea washed in their navigable course the territory of two or more states. Concurrently with the extension of this enlightened principle the movement to exempt vessels on the high seas from visit and search in time of peace made triumphal progress. Especially striking was the progress made in liberalizing the rules of maritime warfare. When in 1898, the United States and Spain went to war, they immediately announced that they would observe the rule that free ships make free goods. The United States also stated that it would be its policy not to resort to privateering, and Spain made no attempt to resort to it. In 1899 the first peace conference was held at the Hague, initiated, ironically enough in the light of today's events, by the Czar of Russia. It was a constructive conference. A second one was held in 1907, resulting in a comprehensive convention for the pacific settlement of international disputes."

In the light of these things the events that preceded the entry of the United States into World War I came as a great surprise and disappointment, we say.

"The shock is still vivid," he replies. "We had built up great hopes for the processes of treaty making and arbitration of disputes between nations which were part of the structure of International Law. If all nations had been willing to live by it, I believe it would have done the job. But the Hohenzollerns taught us the unhappy lesson that International Law, as we knew it, means no more than what an aggressive nation chooses to make it. From the earliest times people have known that no law is self-enforcing, save as it may find sanction in the consciences of men. In the absence of an agency of governmental nature, vested with power to enforce it, International Law rests only upon the consciences of nations. Granted the free participation of all citizens in government, I believe there could be such a thing as a national conscience that would voluntarily accept standards of right and wrong as a guide for national action. But the Germany of the Hohenzollerns was not such a nation. How many such nations are there today? How many will there be tomorrow? Certainly it will be a long time before all nations have developed the moral sensibilities to possess and abide by true conscience. Until all have attained that point, one nation without moral scruples can upset the honest desires of all the rest."

It seems that way, we agree. In the meantime, what would apparently be needed is some form of governmental organization that can impose sanctions for disobedience of International Law.

"Yes," he says. "Let's pass over, for the moment, the question as to whether at this juncture we would be willing to join in such an organization. The idea is by no means a new one."

Had it been thought of before we went into World War I, we ask. *The League to Enforce Peace.* "Yes, it had been," he replies. "In 1915, after World War I was on in Europe, a group of distinguished Americans assembled at Independence Hall in Philadelphia to consider the matter. The chairman was William Howard Taft, former President of the United States who was later to become Chief Justice. Among those present were John Bassett Moore, A. Lawrence Lowell, John Grier Hibben, John H. Finley, Benjamin Ide Wheeler, Stephen S. Wise, Lyman Abbott, Oscar S. Straus, James Cardinal Gibbons and Washington Gladden. They agreed upon this statement of 'Warrant from History':

Throughout five thousand years of recorded history peace, here and there established, has been kept, and its area has been widened, in one way only. Individuals have combined their efforts to suppress violence in the local community. Communities have cooperated to maintain the authoritative state and to preserve peace within its borders. States have formed leagues or confederations, or have otherwise cooperated, to establish peace among themselves. Always peace has been made and kept, when made and kept at all, by the superior power of superior numbers acting in unity for the common good.

Mindful of this teaching of experience, we believe and solemnly urge that the time has come to devise and to create a working union of sovereign nations to establish peace among themselves and to guarantee it by all known and available sanctions at their command, to the end that civilization may be conserved, and the progress of mankind in comfort, enlightenment and happiness may continue.

Woodrow Wilson was then President of the United States, we remark.

"Yes," our student replies, "and this meeting was doubtless very close to his heart."

The League of Nations. As a matter of fact, this Philadelphia meeting was sort of a forerunner of the League of Nations, we observe.

"It was," he says, "after World War I that the League of Nations was set up. The Statement of Purpose at the outset of its Covenant was imposing:

The High Contracting Parties
In order to promote international cooperation and to achieve international peace and security

by the acceptance of obligations not to resort to war,

by the prescription of open, just and honorable relations between nations,

by the firm establishment of the understandings of international law as the actual rule of conduct among Governments, and

by the maintenance of justice and a scrupulous respect for all treaty obligations in the dealings of organized peoples with one another,

Agree to this Covenant of the League of Nations.

Inspiring as well as imposing, we observe. This dream of Woodrow Wilson deserved a better fate. Its history might have been very different had the United States joined in it rather than repudiating it.

"I will go beyond that and say I believe that we would not have had World War II and that the whole course of history in my time would have been different if we had gone into it," he says. "With the United States in it, there would have been a world-wide foundation upon which to build as time went on. Without the United States, or any other great power, in it, it would not work."

That was demonstrated by events, we comment.

"It was criticized from two opposite directions," he continues. "On the one hand it was attacked because to belong to it involved infringement of national sovereignty, on the other because it was too weak to achieve results. It failed for a combination of both reasons. The United States would not subscribe to even the small degree of infringement of sovereignty involved, and, as administered, the League was too weak to stop the aggressions of Mussolini and the Japanese war lords. Hitler was allowed to go his way, and World War II was on."

This trend of events was a great disappointment to a generation that had counted on victory in World War I and the League of Nations to solve the world's problems, we say.

"It is hard to express the disillusionment that we felt when we found we had been let down," he replies. "It was the greater because we had set our sights so high in World War I. Remember, we fought 'to make the world safe for democracy.' Newton D. Baker, who was Secretary of War during the conflict, and a great idealist, expressed it well. He said the greatest loss to mankind from the World War was not the vast destruction of property, impoverishing as that was, nor was it loss of human life, which of course was infinitely more pathetic and tragic, but it was the loss of faith among men all over the world. It has left in the minds of men everywhere a resolute doubt as to the capacity of man in any form of government, absolutist or free, to set up political institutions adequate for the safety

of mankind. If one seeks an explanation of the long-continued dominance of the handful of men in Russia, he will find it not in the sweet-
ness or attractiveness of the doctrines they teach, nor in the extent
of the physical power by which they seek to enforce their philosophy,
but in the despondency of the people to whom their mandates are addressed and in the belief that no other form of government can provide anything more safe and secure. Mr. Baker was speaking ten
years after the Armistice was signed in 1918, and he said that ten
years after the conclusion of a war which had in it the impulse to
make the world safe for democracy, we find a substantial part of the
world governed by dictators. These new autocracies were not set up
among savage or barbarous peoples, but rather in civilized nations
in all of which there has been aspiration for popular government and
in some of which substantial progress toward that end had been made
before the war. The reason for this must be that same loss of faith
in the solidity of humanly contrived political institutions."

When the sights were set at making the world safe for democracy
they were set too high, we observe.

"In the light of subsequent events they certainly were," he agrees.
"Looking at it in retrospect, we were a naive lot in 1917. But I
have had no regrets about that aspect of it. We had a tremendous
ideal for which to fight. The spiritual uplift it gave us made our
job in the trenches and dugouts of France a happier one than that of
our comrades of World War II—to hear them tell it. Having our
disillusioning experience in mind, they were matter-of-fact and realistic. They probably rate more credit than we do, because they did
their part without greater inspiration than comes from doing a dirty
job that had to be done all over again because the mess had not been
cleaned up right the first time."

The United Nations and Korea. All that is past history, of course,
we suggest. Pearl Harbor initiated great changes in the thinking
and attitude of the people of the United States. A fresh start has
been made with the United Nations. From the outset we have supported it, and even invited it to make its home with us. The grandson of the Senator who did perhaps the most to kill the League of
Nations, in so far as the United States was concerned, became the
effective ambassador of the United States to the United Nations.

"That is all true," he agrees. "And let's take a look at how it has
been doing the job. As Al Smith used to say when he was running
for President of the United States against Herbert Hoover, 'let's look
at the record.' Perhaps we can find some enlightenment as to whether

it is an effective instrument to promote true peace, and whether we would want to be in it if it had more power than it has now, and could exert physical sanctions on us against our will."

What particular aspects of the record provide enlightenment? we ask.

"Well, let's look at Korea," he replies. "After the shooting stopped in World War II, we started doing the same thing we did after World War I, demobilizing our military machine and heading back home to business as usual. 'Back to normalcy,' we called it in the nineteen-twenties. This time we have a United Nations to look after things, we thought. If nations did not get along together smoothly, some-how the United Nations would iron out the difficulty. But somehow it has not succeeded in doing the job. Only a few years went by be-fore the United States had a great army on the other side of the world, in Korea, fighting a bloody war—call it by any other name you will. As a result of Korean and Chinese aggression in Korea, the United States suffered 142,000 casualties. American soldiers who were unfortunate enough to be taken prisoners were put through tor-tures that those of us who had fought in what was a relatively more civilized war in Europe can hardly imagine. The United Nations was simply defied."

The use of force was contemplated in the set-up of the United Nations, and the forces which fought in Korea were under the United Nations flag, we observe.

"True," he agrees. "But American fighting men carried the main load of fighting and dying and being captured. And the United Na-tions flag was there only because the Soviet Union, which could have blocked its use, for reasons of pique was absent from the meeting of the Security Council which voted it. With all deference to the United Nations, its participation was more a formality than a matter of true substance. And with all the bloodshed, things are not settled there even now. The shooting could break out of an uneasy armistice any time."

The Two Kinds of Nations. We ask him what else he has in mind. "There is still more recent history," he replies. "Since World War II, the Middle East has been a trouble spot. Because the United Nations could not, would not, or did not act effectively there, only a few months ago we landed some 15,000 soldiers in Lebanon and alerted our military forces all over the world to a combat basis. This is drastic business. In Woodrow Wilson's day such an action would have been associated only with the malfunctioning of a diseased brain. Now we have done it. But we did not expect to have to do such things when we joined in support of the United Nations."

Probably not, we agree.

"That is not all," he continues. "It is not just a question of sending United States soldiers into war and military operations around the world. The failure of the United Nations to do the job is reflected in another way."

How is that? we ask.

"We have been made to realize that there are two very different kinds of nations in the world, and in the United Nations," he replies. "There are free, democratic nations, and authoritarian, Communist nations. It is interesting to speculate upon what Lincoln would say if he were here to draw conclusions from what he would see. He said that a nation could not exist half slave and half free; it is a little hard to believe that he would conclude that a world could do any better. Anyhow, the free nations have been driven to the conclusion that their interests were not adequately protected by the United Nations. Those interests are manifestly in common. So we find the United States a party to a whole series of treaties. In 1947 we entered into a treaty at Rio with the countries of South and Central America, whereby the signatory nations bound themselves to provide assistance to any one of them if assistance is requested to repel aggression. In 1949 we entered into the North Atlantic Treaty Organization, composed of the United Kingdom, France, Belgium, Norway, the Netherlands, Denmark, West Germany, Luxembourg, Italy, Portugal, Greece, Turkey, Iceland and Canada, in addition to our own country. This binds the members to aid any one of them subjected to attack. In 1951 we entered into a treaty with Australia and New Zealand, by the terms of which an attack against any one will be regarded as involving all. In 1954 the Southeast Asia Treaty Organization was set up at Manila. The signatories were the Philippines, Pakistan, Australia, Thailand, New Zealand, the United Kingdom, France and the United States. We were not signatories of the Baghdad Pact, which was signed in 1955 by Iran, Iraq, Pakistan, Turkey and the United Kingdom, but in the course of events following the revolution in Iraq the United States became virtually committed to the obligations of its members, to cooperate in mutual defense against aggression."

That, we comment, is a rather imposing lot of treaties, dwarfing in scope and content the puny efforts achieved by William Jennings Bryan in the days before World War I. And, after all, there is nothing inconsistent between them and the charter of the United Nations. It was designed to allow for agreements outside its immediate framework.

"Of practical necessity, perhaps, yes," he agrees. "But any one can realize that unless the United Nations keeps the real hold on the situation, its powers will fade out. I can enumerate still more treaties outside its framework to emphasize that it has not been able to handle the situation. In addition to these others, we have separate agreements providing for mutual assistance, with Japan, South Korea, the Philippines and the Republic of China."

We should not overlook the fact that it was through the intervention of the United Nations that the action begun by Great Britain, France and Israel, at Suez was stopped in 1956, we remind him.

"Nor should we overlook that about the same time as that the invasion of Hungary by Soviet Russian military forces was not stopped by the United Nations," he replies. "Soviet soldiers shot down Hungarians who were only demonstrating in their own country for the rights of free men. The Suez incident demonstrated that in free nations there is such a thing as a national conscience, which can hear the still small voice of right and wrong. The Hungarian tragedy demonstrated that there is no such thing in a nation actuated by a philosophy that the end justifies the means, and impelled by motives of communistic aggrandizement."

Perhaps the Hungarian tragedy also demonstrated that we have to approach international problems in terms of great realism, we suggest.

"Yes," he agrees. "And the realism tends to be so intense that it almost forecloses solving them on a basis of justice. Where can we hope to get, appealing to aggressor nations who will not listen to it?"

The Problem of Nationalism. Let us recapitulate a little, we suggest. We are agreed that the solution of world problems, as of all others, is to be found in law. We are further agreed that there must be some overall agency to enforce the law. The League of Nations was not set up to be an enforcing agency in any final sense; anyhow, it did not get a chance. The United Nations is a going concern, of which the nations of the world, great and small—with the notable exception of Red China to date—are members. Like the League of Nations, it has no power of sanctions. To date, its record of solving international problems is not impressive. Is the trouble simply that it does not have the power of sanctions, or what is it?

"Certainly we cannot expect law to be enforced without sanctions," he replies. "In a superficial sense, the absence of that power would explain the failure of the United Nations to accomplish more. But the seat of the difficulty is far deeper than that. It lies at the very heart of what makes up the United Nations—the nations that subscribed to its charter. After all, they are individual nations. The difficulty might be resolved into a single word: 'nationalism.'"

Nationalism has had an honorable place in history, we observe. Consider its workings in the origin of the United States, and throughout our history.

"It has had an outstanding place," he agrees. "It came about naturally enough. Sir Geoffrey Butler made a good explanation of its origin. He said mediaeval history treats of a Europe changing from a feudal organization to that of a number of contiguous nation states. The process, which was reluctant, was heralded and foreshadowed by the recrudescence in Italy of the city state. The Englishman and the Frenchman of the Middle Ages had much in common. Each was a member of the Catholic Church, each could pass from Oxford to Paris, thence also to Bologna, Salerno and elsewhere, but neither need violently change his habit of life nor his attitude toward it. Latin provided both with a common tongue in which they could express themselves and be understood. The line of demarcation between the nations was not deeply marked. When the Nation States of the Renaissance rose, all this was gradually changed."

There came about a consciousness of differences, we suggest.

"That's right," he says. "Sir Geoffrey proceeded to say that the Frenchman became a law unto himself. He began, for instance, to wish to see incorporated within the boundaries of France the inhabitants of the neighboring French-speaking duchies, the allegiance of whose rulers to the French king had till then been ill defined and a source of controversy. The cement that bound the kingdom together was in France, as in England mixed in the royal laboratory. The Frenchman lost touch with the Englishman or German. The Nation State was forced to deal with the Nation State. Their representatives met as strangers, and their differences, when they met, could no longer be regarded as the fascinating, if quaint, local divergencies which geographical distance had worked in the seamless garment of the body of the Church on earth."

In other words, we observe, today's world is made up of nations which have their own ideas of what is good for them—nationalistic aspirations shall we say—and they want to realize these aspirations.

The problem confronting us is one of creating a unified legal structure out of such diverse elements.

Political Science Drawing Boards. "Precisely," he says. "The political scientists have had this project on their drawing boards for a long time. With a piece of paper, a pencil and a moment's time I could reproduce the outline of their diagram. Its caption is "One World." In words, I would describe it as depicting a world government, of which all the nations of the earth are the constituent elements. It has a written constitution which sets up three departments—legislative, executive and judicial—and in appropriate terms prescribes the powers and duties of each along generally accepted lines."

We remark that this sounds very much like the constitutional system of the United States, which would be a worthy pattern for any government.

"It is obviously based upon the constitutional system of the United States, and as an American I can say no less than that our constitutional system is the most worthy pattern disclosed by history," he replies. "But after all, a garment, or a part of a machine or structure, must fit into place. It cannot be used everywhere, or by all. What the political scientist has to accomplish here is to draft a pattern that will fit a whole world, with convolutions and bumps that pretty well defy any sort of a fit.

The constitutional pattern of our government should go a long way, we insist.

"But a 'long way' is not enough," he replies. "When the political scientist starts filling in the detail of the pattern, he finds himself in difficulty induced by the nationalism of which we have been speaking. He is used to dealing with governments whose elements combine for some degree of constituent unity. By that I mean geographical contiguity and, in general, a common religious and political heritage; people speaking one tongue and with a common concept as to the ordering of life. When these elements are not present in proper coordination, the political scientist simply says, 'we cannot draft a plan for a nation here; there will have to be more than one.' We have noted a dramatic example of this when India recently became independent. There was geographical contiguity, and even racial identity, but because of the division created by religious differences two nations came into being instead of one—not only India, but Pakistan. Small wonder that the political scientists who have worked on the 'one world' project have been pretty much baffled when it comes to filling in the details."

We can see that, we say. They have to contend with the problem of scores of nations, large and small, scattered over the whole surface of the earth, physically separated by great oceans, speaking hundreds of different tongues, professing fundamentally divergent religious faiths, and living under national governments of great variety. Some are extremely poor economically, and largely illiterate. Only a few have a background of stable political experience.

"There is where the difficulty lies," he says. "Before we get through we are going to have to grapple with the question as to whether we would be willing to submit ourselves to a super-government attempted upon such a foundation. But first of all, the question is whether all these nations can be brought together for an all-inclusive common purpose, which certainly there must be if there is to be a world government. In the light of our experience to date, with its failure to achieve a satisfactory solution of international problems under the United Nations aegis, there is a lot of doubt whether there is such a common purpose at all."

World Government "In the Common Interest?" There must be an adequate common purpose, we insist, even though it may not have been adequately sensed by the nations of the world to date. Could we not proceed by setting up a world government on some such basis as that it is created to act for its constituent nations "in the common interest?" The "common interest" is a well-understood concept in the United States. It is at the heart of the police power doctrine that our government applies in dealing with the exercise of individual rights: in the common interest, individual rights must give way. Why would not it work in dealing with national rights: nationalistic aspirations must give way when they threaten the welfare of the international community?

"It is true that we understand the concept," he replies. "So might the other common law countries of the world. But elsewhere it is not accorded the connotation that we give to it. There is an old Nietzschean formula at large that says, 'What's good for me, that's what I call justice.' Now when we get right down to it, who is going to settle the question of what is in the common interest, and how, and when?"

We see the difficulty, we say. But can we not solve it by arriving at a formula of world-government objective that is more definite?

"Do you have one in mind?" he asks.

How about an objective of world-peace? we reply. All nations say they want peace. Why not take that, and build on it?

"The United Nations already has such a platform," he says. "The preamble is couched in terms of seeking peace:

We the peoples of the United Nations
Determined
    to save succeeding generations from the scourge of war, which twice in our lifetime has brought untold sorrow to mankind, and
    to reaffirm faith in fundamental human rights, in the dignity and worth of the human person, in the equal rights of men and women and of nations large and small, and
    to establish conditions under which justice and respect for the obligations arising from treaties and other sources of international law can be maintained, and
    to promote social progress and better standards of life in larger freedom,
And for these ends
    to practice tolerance and live together in peace with one another as good neighbours, and
    to unite our strength to maintain international peace and security, and
    to ensure, by the acceptance of principles and the institution of methods, that armed force shall not be used, save in the common interest, and
    to employ international machinery for the promotion of the economic and social advancement of all peoples
Have resolved to combine our efforts to accomplish these aims.

A cynic would be moved to characterize this as a masterful collection of pious platitudes, honored in the breach, we suggest.

"One could stop short of cynicism and yet say as much," he says. "Here all have joined in an expression of wanting peace. Do they, really? Have they all shown by deed, rather than word, that they do? If they had, perhaps the objective would have been attained and there would not have been a Korea and a Lebanon. But that is water over the dam. We have to take the world as we find it. Peace has not been enforced; the question remains whether it can be."

Peace could be enforced by invoking military sanctions upon any nations that threatened to break it, we suggest. Nations with militaristic aspirations would simply be curbed.

"It sounds simple when you put it that way," he says. "But is it that easy? We have to go behind the 'aspirations' that need curbing, and find out the 'who' and the 'how' and the 'when' of doing it.

What do you mean? we ask.

The United States As a Threat to Peace? "I will explain it this way," he replies. "Under the plan you are suggesting, a nation held to be demonstrating a threat to peace by a manifestation of militaristic aspirations would be restrained by military force. Somebody would have to interpret what is meant by a 'threat to peace,' and whether, in fact, the nation in question had acted to bring itself within that definition. Presumably that would be done by the personnel of the world government charged with that responsibility. Now let's get down to cases. Take our own nation, the United States. Can you conceive of it having militaristic aspirations, or being a threat to peace?"

No, decidedly no, we reply.

"But that does not settle the matter," he continues. "Under the proposal we are discussing, might it not be held that we are guilty of threatening the peace of the world, no matter how innocent we are?"

That could be, we admit. We see what is meant. As a matter of fact we sent our soldiers to Lebanon with the overall purpose of preserving the peace, and the Communist nations accused us of subverting it.

"Nor did they mince words about it," he says. "After the Russian Nikita Kruschev and Red China's Mao Tse-Tung had a secret four-day rendezvous in Peiping, they issued a communique saying: 'The aggressive imperialist block, headed by the United States monopoly groups, persistently opposes peaceful coexistence and cooperation, stubbornly refuses to ease international tension, obstructs a meeting of the heads of government of the big powers, and steps up preparations for a new war and threatens the peace and security of all peoples.' "

Several mouthfuls in one, we comment. Charges false in proportion to their vehemence, and to be written off as histrionics for home-town entertainment.

"No," he says. "Millions outside of Red China and Soviet Russia have believed them. And if we were subject to the sanctions of a world government, we would find out overnight that they packed more than gaseous bluff and bluster."

Peace at Any Price? The world being as touchy as it is, is it not for us, as a nation cherishing peace, to keep our policies within limits that will not cause offense to other nations? we ask.

"Taking your words for what they say, the answer is 'no,' " he replies. "You are talking the language of appeasement—the sort of thing that Chamberlin and the others indulged in at Munich when they sold Czechoslovakia down the river of 'peace in our time.' "

We agree that it did not work there, we say. But, after all, war is so great an evil that anything that seems calculated to obviate it is perhaps worth trying. The consensus seems to be that a third world war would wipe us out.

"If what you are saying is that we must have peace at any price, I do not go along," he says.

Did not Woodrow Wilson once say that there is such a thing as being too proud to fight? we ask.

"Yes," he admits. "But in the light of what happened afterward, I don't think he would have chosen those words as his distinctive spiritual legacy to mankind."

We remind him that the highest body of one of our religious denominations recently declared in effect that there are presently two alternatives: coexistence or extinction, and that survival involves adjustment to the aspirations of other nations pressing different ideologies.

"If that means abandonment of the aspirations of the United States to stand for right and justice, not only at home but throughout the world, come what may, I stop short of it," he says. "So far as I am concerned, the measure of right and justice here, as elsewhere, is found in the original source. A lawyer asked Jesus what he should do to inherit eternal life. Jesus asked him, in turn, what he found in the law. The lawyer replied that, among other things, it said: 'Thou shalt love thy neighbor as thyself,' and then went on to ask, 'And who is my neighbor?' Whereupon Jesus answered by telling the parable of the man who fell among thieves, who wounded him and left him by the wayside, half dead. A priest and a levite passed him by on the other side, but the Good Samaritan stopped, ministered to him, and saved his life. 'Which one of these three thinkest thou was neighbor unto him that fell among the thieves?' Jesus asked. When the lawyer replied, 'he that shewed mercy on him,' Jesus said: 'Go thou and do likewise.' "

In extending help, the good Samaritan does not appear to have faced any risk of personal violence or extinction, we suggest.

"What difference does that make?" he asks. "I cannot believe the doing of acts of mercy and justice are qualified by factors relating to the personal safety of the doers. The emphasis is on the spiritual; the physical is deprecated. 'Whosoever shall save his life shall lose it. For what is a man profited, if he shall gain the whole world and lose his own soul?' "

Perhaps we better get back to the ultimate difficulty that we have been skirting around, we say. There seems to be no way out except a structure of world government, with power of sanction over all nations. Without question this means a pretty complete surrender of national sovereignty.

"Let's face it," he says. "If there is to be a rule of world law, as such, there must be a world government with power to lay down the law, make a determination as to whether it has been violated, and enforce its decrees. This is not a new phenomenon. The world saw it centuries ago, in the Roman Empire. In our day such power was sought by the Hohenzollerns and Hitler and their satellites, Mussolini and the Japanese war lords. We have crushed that attempt, only to find that other nations who started out as our ostensible friends have stepped into the military boots of these dictators and are openly stating that they will overcome us."

Unite—and Trust? Perhaps the solution is for us and all other nations to unite in a world government, dedicated to keeping the peace, and trust to our control of it to turn its power against aggression, we suggest.

"Let's follow through on it," he says. "The United States would subscribe to some kind of a constitution for world government, whereby it, along with all other nations, would be bound by the sanctions such a government might undertake to maintain peace. Now what does it mean to 'maintain peace'? How is peace threatened? When is peace threatened? Who threatens peace? What is to be done about it? The way would be left open for the exercise of the most unbridled discretion upon the part of whoever was in control. We should find a sufficient lesson in our experience in Lebanon, and the charges made against us. Even within our own government we don't tolerate the delegation of power to the executive except as it is hedged about with definite standards by way of putting practical limitations on its exercise. Under the proposal here, we would be vesting in the administration of a world government powers so broad that we would not put them in the hands of a President of the United States, elected by ourselves. He, alone, cannot declare war. The very nations which would have as much part as ourselves in world government, and which have been at pains to demonstrate to the world that they regard us as imperialistic war-mongers, would sit in judgment on us, and have a part in enforcing judgment against us."

This would seem to call for the conclusion that we cannot afford to take such a chance, and that we could not in all good justice surrender our sovereignty to a world government, we observe. And if only a world government can lay down and administer a system of world law, we have reached an impasse which blocks the way to world peace.

"I have said that I don't regard 'peace' as necessarily the final and only answer to everything," he says. "The right is more precious than peace. But, even so, the impasse is not a permanent one."

A World Government of Free Peoples. We ask him to elucidate. "We are really getting to the heart of the matter," he says. "Only free peoples can cooperate fully together for the common good. As to peoples who are not free, we will have to get along with their rulers the best we can until such time as they become the masters of their own destinies as individual human beings. We are a free people. We intend to remain that way. The governments of free people can work together, in spite of the divergencies of policy and the difficulties of mutual understanding that even free governments will necessarily have. We have proved it with Great Britain and France in two World Wars, and in solving the problems of peace as they have affected us thereafter. When all nations of the earth are governments of free people, they can federate in some form of world government that will administer the principles of freedom in the interest of all, and truly serve the welfare of the human race. Until that time comes we will have to do the best we can with the United Nations as a cooperative enterprise, whether as it is or as it evolves in future years; standing firmly for its stated purposes whether others do or not.

The goal seems far removed in the future, we comment.

"That is true," he agrees. "In my college days we thought the millenium might not be far away. Events of my lifetime have dashed the dream, and sent us back centuries to the Middle Ages. Those of us who enjoy freedom should be eternally grateful for having been so born that it has come to us, as it has not to most of those now living on the earth. We should never cease praying and working that it may come to all. But universal freedom is almost certainly decades off, possibly centuries, possibly even millenia. We are not well qualified to see things in their true perspective. This old world has been going on for a long time. As far as we know, it will continue through infinity. Every human being who has been born has had to face the problem of physical survival. Every one who has attained maturity has had to meet problems of adjustment to his environment and to his fellows. So will it be with all future men. So has it been with nations. Governments have risen and fallen; from their remains new governments have risen, to fall again in turn. In political as in natural science, change is the law of life. Out of the process governments of free people will come. Even they will have problems of their own administration—and possibly of survivorship in relation to the peoples of outer space—that will seem no less imperious and worrisome to them than those about which we have been talking seem to us. But all peoples then will be able to devote themselves to their solution in the interest of free men.

The Spirit of Freedom Never Dies. The ending seems to be a happy one, but how can we be confident of it?

"I am as confident of it as I am conscious of speaking these words to you," he replies. "There is in man an indigenous yearning for freedom of his soul. The spirit of freedom never dies. If it is crushed in one man, it is born in another. It is true that life is so ordered that there is no such thing as gaining freedom for any man, or for all men, for all time to come. Free institutions, as institutions, are ephemeral. The flag of our country, the symbol of freedom, could disappear. But even if that sad consummation should come to pass, freedom, like truth crushed to earth, will rise again. Man will never cease his efforts to attain ordered liberty, and in the successful consummation of those efforts he will find earth's greatest reward."

REFERENCES

CHAPTER I

Roscoe Pound, Interests in Personality, 28 Harvard Law Review 343 (1915); A Survey of Social Interests, 57 Harvard Law Review 1 (1943).

Manuel du Droit Civil Suisse (Tome Premier) 47 (1922).

William Bondy, The Separation of Governmental Powers, V Columbia College Studies in Political Science, No. 2, p. 7 (1896).

Joseph Story, I Commentaries on the Constitution of the United States 193 (1833).

Hans Kelsen, The Law As a Specific Social Technique, 9 University of Chicago Law Review 75 (1942).

Paul Vinogradoff, I Historical Jurisprudence 84 (1920).

Joseph M. Snee, address at the Harvard Law School John Marshall Bicentennial Conference, printed in Government Under Law 91 (1956).

Woodrow Wilson, The State 668 (1889).

Andrei Vyshinsky, The Law of the Soviet State (1948).

John F. Kennedy, Congressional Lobbies, 45 Georgetown Law Journal 535 (1957).

United States v. International Union, 352 U.S. 567 (1957).

Robert H. Jackson, The Trials of War Criminals, 32 American Bar Association Journal 319 (1946).

Munroe Smith, A General View of European Legal History, 312 (1927).

Felix Frankfurter, concurring in Youngstown Sheet & Tube Co. v. Sawyer, 343 U.S. 579 (1952).

CHAPTER 2

Bess Furman, New York Times, October 27, 1957, Part 1, p. 84.

Huntington Cairns, Law and Anthropology, 31 Columbia Law Review 32 (1931).

Lord Macmillan, Address to Edinburgh Philosophical Institution, 50 Scottish Law Review 1 (1933).

E. Smythe Gambrell, The Challenge We Face, 24 Tennessee Law Review 632 (1956), quoting Jefferson.

M. Guizot, History of Civilization (3d Am. ed. 1882).

The Federalist, No. 37.

Estin v. Estin, 334 U.S. 541 (1948).

Abraham Lincoln, quoted by Felix Frankfurter, dissenting, in Kennecott Copper Corporation v. State Tax Commission, 327 U.S. 573 (1946).

CHAPTER 3

Genesis 11.

J. H. Hertz, Ancient Semitic Codes, 10 Journal of Comparative Legislation and International Law (3d ser. 1928) 207.

D. Oswald Dykes, The Code of Hammurabi, 16 Juridical Review 71 (1904).

Erwin J. Urch, Law Code of Hammurabi, 15 American Bar Association Journal 437 (1929).

Charles Sumner Lobingier, The Cradle of Western Law, quoting Lee, Historical Jurisprudence, 64 United States Law Review 8 (1930).

II Kings 15, 17.

Jonah 3.

Nahum 3.

Jeremiah 39.

Daniel 3, 5.

CHAPTER 4

Sir John Simon, Some Aspects of the Indian Problem, 16 American Bar Association Journal 648 (1930).

The Upanishads and Bhagavad-Gita.

The Laws of Manu.

Stanley Maron, Storm Signals in Pakistan, 35 Foreign Policy Association Bulletin 156 (1956).

James Bryce, Studies in History and Jurisprudence (1901).

Lawrence K. Rosinger, Restless India, Foreign Policy Association Headline Series No. 55 (1946), quoting Henry Lawrence.

London Letter, 31 American Bar Association Journal 265 (1945).

Life Around the World, United States News & World Report, November 5, 1948, p. 61; November 26, 1948, p. 62; January 21, 1949, p. 59; October 29, 1949, p. 38.

Sir Geoffrey Butler, Handbook to the League of Nations (1919).

Norman D. Palmer, Indian and Western Political Thought, 49 American Political Science Review 747 (1955).

The Marquess of Reading, Address to American Bar Association, 18 American Bar Association Journal 737 (1932).

Charles H. Alexandrowicz-Alexander, American Influence on Constitutional Interpretation in India, 5 American Journal of Comparative Law 98 (1956).

William O. Douglas, The Bill of Rights, Due Process and Federalism in India, 40 Minnesota Law Review 1 (1955).

A. M. Rosenthal, New York Times, May 18, 1958.

CHAPTER 5

Munroe Smith, The Unity of Western Civilization (1915).

Marion J. Bradshaw, Free Churches and Christian Unity, 115, 145 (1954).

Acts 14.

Plutarch's Life of Alexander.

Sir Geoffrey Butler, Handbook to the League of Nations (1919).

The Federalist, Numbers 6, 18, 38, 55

Julius C. Smith, Totalitarianism and Administrative Absolutism, 5 John Marshall Law Quarterly 202 (1939), quoting Fustel de Coulanges, Ancient City (1884) 250.

Edward Van Dyke Robinson, Division of Governmental Powers in Greece, 18 Political Science Quarterly 614 (1903).

C. H. McIlwain, quoted by Charles E. Wyzanski, Jr., Government under Law 481 (1956).

De Toqueville, Democracy in America, Vol. 2, p. 497 (1912).

Louis D. Brandeis, quoted by Paul A. Freund, Mr. Justice Brandeis: A Centennial Memoir, 70 Harvard Law Review 769 (1957).

St. John- Stevas, Obscenity in the Law.

Alexander Hamilton, quoted by Gottfried Dietze, Hamilton's Federalist, 42 Cornell Law Quarterly 307, 320n. (1957).

Francis Lieber, Civil Liberty and Self Government (3d ed. 1883).

Fred H. Blume, Human Rights and Property Rights, 64 United States Law Review 581 (1930).

George H. Smith, Right and Law (2d ed. 1887) 257.

A.H.F. Lefroy, Rome and the Law, 20 Harvard Law Review 606 (190).

Roscoe Pound, The Lawyer from Antiquity to Modern Times 29 (1953).

Plato's Phaedo.

Plato's Crito.

Plato's Republic.

Plato's Apology.

Proverbs 25

I Corinthians 4.

Edwin H. Corwin, The Higher Law Background, quoting Joubert, Pensees, 42 Harvard Law Review 149 (1928).

Judge Wilkin, dissenting, in Methodist Federation for Social Action v. Eastland, 141 F. Supp. 729 (D.D.C. 1956).

Romans 12.

Manson, The Laws of Plato, 9 Journal of Comparative Legislation (N.S. 1908) 55.

Sophocles' Antigone.

Judge Jerome Frank in Guiseppi v. Walling, 144 F. 2d 608 (2d Cir. 1944).

Massachusetts Constitution of 1780.

Marbury v. Madison, 1 Cranch 137 (1803).

Robinson, Division of Governmental Powers in Greece, 18 Political Science Quarterly 614 (1903).

Thomas E. Holland, Elements of Jurisprudence (13th ed. 1924).

Barna Horvath, Rights of Man, 4 American Journal of Comparative Law 539 (1955).

James Bryce, Studies in History and Jurisprudence (1901).

CHAPTER 6, 7, 8, & 9

Morey, Outline of Roman Law (8th ed. 1894).

Julius C. Smith, Totalitarianism and Administrative Absolutism, 5 John Marshall Law Quarterly 202 (1939).

Kocurek and Wigmore, Primitive and Ancient Legal Institutions (1915).

Marion J. Bradshaw, Free Churches and Christian Unity (1954), citing Josephus, Antiquities, and Nicene and Post-Nicene Fathers.

Brendan F. Brown, Jurisprudential Basis of Roman Law, 12 Notre Dame Lawyer 361 (1937).

Joseph Story, Commentaries on the Constitution of the United States, Vol. III, p. 660 (1833).

George Horowitz, The Privilege against Self-Incrimination, 31 Temple Law Quarterly 121 (1958), quoting Edmund M. Morgan.

Benjamin N. Cardozo in Palko v. Connecticut, 302 U.S. 319 (1937).

Rudolf Leonhard, The Science of Roman Law in America, 26 Harvard Law Review 389 (1913).

The Theodosian Code.

Fred H. Blume, Human Rights and Property Rights, 64 United States Law Review 581 (1930).

F. P. Walton, Growth of Commercial Law at Rome, 5 Juridical Review 332 (1893).

A. H. F. Lefroy, Rome and the Law, 20 Harvard Law Review 606 (1907).

Cato, quoted by Hessel E. Yntema, Roman Law, 35 Cornell Law Quarterly 77 (1949).

James Bryce, Studies in History and Jurisprudence (1901).

Joseph Story, Conflict of Laws 3 (7th ed. 1872).

Paul Vinogradoff, II Historical Jurisprudence 9 (1920).

M. L'Abbe H. Aragon, Histoire de Toulouse.

Genesis 27.

Deuteronomy 24.

1 Timothy 6.

Acts 22.

The Federalist, Nos. 34, 70.

Greenridge, Legal Procedure of Cicero's Time, quoted in Note, 3 Journal of Comparative Legislation (New ser. 1901) 144.

Kent's Commentaries (Holmes 12th ed. 1884).

Benjamin Cardozo, The Nature of the Judicial Process 143 (1921).

Munroe Smith, A General View of European Legal History (1927).

Austin, Jurisprudence, Vol. II (5th ed. 1911) 519: Vol. III, 591.

Hessel E. Yntema, Roman Law, 35 Cornell Law Quarterly 77 (1949).

St. John-Stevas, Obscenity and the Law 3 (1956).

Acts 17.

Trumbull, The Concept of Loyalty, 25 Chicago Bar Journal 439 (1954).

Justice Hugo Black, dissenting in Jay v. Boyd, 351 U.S. 345 (1956).

Zbigniew Brzezinski, Totalitarianism and Rationality, 50 American Political Science Review 751 (1956).

M. Guizot, History of Civilization.

Hurtado v. California, 110 U.S. 516 (1884).

Justinian's Institutes.

William Wirt Howe, Roman and Civil Law in America, 16 Harvard Law Review 342 (1903).

Hans Kirchberger, Significance of Roman Law, 1944 Wisconsin Law Review 249.

Charles Sumner Lobingier, Las Siete Partidas in Full English Dress, 15 American Bar Association Journal 365 (1929).

Roger Houin, Reform of French Codes, 4 American Journal of Comparative Law 485 (1955).

Robert L. Henry, Jurisprudence Constante and Stare Decisis, 15 American Bar Association Journal 11 (1929).

Blackstone's Commentaries (1827 ed.).

Pollock, History of the Law of Nature, 2 Journal of Comparative Legislation (N.S. 1900) 418.

Hugo Grotius, De Jure Pacis ac Belli.

Joseph M. Snee, Government under Law 96 (1956).

CHAPTER 10

Acts 7.

Genesis 8, 15.

Exodus 1, 3, 5, 14, 16, 18, 20, 23, 34.

Oscar S. Straus, Origin of the Republican Form of Government (1901).

Numbers 17, 27, 36.

L. Elliott Grafman, Influence of Mosaic Law, 2 John Marshall Law Quarterly 351 (1937).

Deuteronomy 32, 33.

Judges 4, 6, 7, 11, 12, 13, 14, 16, 17.

I Samuel 8, 10.

II Samuel 1, 5, 11, 15.

Samuel Langdon, quoted by Oscar S. Straus, Origin of the Republican Form of Government 120 (1901).

I Chronicles 10.

I Kings 3, 4, 9, 10, 11, 12.

Samuel Hirshberg, Jurisprudence Among the Ancient Jews, 11 Marquette Law Review 25 (1926).

Paul L. Ross, Lawyers and Judges in Hebrew Jurisprudence, 67 United States Law Review 19 (1933).

Woodrow Wilson, quoted by George Horowitz, The Privilege against Self-Incrimination, 31 Temple Law Quarterly 121 (1958).

The Talmud.

B. Felsenthal, Jewish Law, 8 Albany Law Journal 261 (1873).

Gad Frumkin, Address at Society of Jewish Jurisprudence in London, 161 Law Times 117 (1926).

Dayan Dr. A. Feldman, The London Beth Din, 41 Juridical Review 158 (1929).

Leviticus 5.

Proverbs 2, 3.

Zechariah 8.

Sol M. Linowitz, The Legal Basis for the State of Israel, 43 American Bar Association Journal 522 (1957).

Benjamin Akzin, Codification in Israel, 5 American Journal of Comparative Law 44 (1956).

Uriel Gorney, American Precedent in Israel, 68 Harvard Law Review 1194 (1955).

CHAPTER 11

M. Guizot, History of Civilization (3d Am. ed. 1882).

The Theodosian Code.

The Federalist, No. 17.

O. John Rogge, Compelling the Testimony of Political Deviants, 55 Michigan Law Review 375 (1957).

George Horowitz, The Privilege against Self-Incrimination, 31 Temple Law Quarterly 121 (1958).

Atkins and Fagley, History of American Congregationalism (1942).

Matthew 18.

Malcolm K. Burton, Destiny for Congregationalism.

Sir Maurice Sheldon Amos, Common and Civil Law in the British Commonwealth of Nations, 50 Harvard Law Review 1249 (1937).

Alfred E. Smith, quoted by Conrad Henry Moehlman, The Wall of Separation, 38 American Bar Association Journal 281 (1952).

Stanislaus Weywod, A Practical Commentary on the Code of Canon Law (1925).

Robert H. Jackson, dissenting, in Everson v. Board of Education, 330 U.S. 1 (1947).

Marriage Laws of the Catholic Church (Chicago 1953).

State v. McWhinney, 100 N.E. 2d 273 (Ohio 1950).

CHAPTER 12

Pierre Crabites, The Omnipotent Bar of Islam, 13 American Bar Association Journal 694 (1927); The Courts of Egypt, 11 Id. 485 (1925).

The Koran.

Herbert J. Liebesny, Religious Law and Westernization in the Moslem Near East, 2 American Journal of Comparative Law 492 (1953).

Sir Raymond West, Mohammedan Law in India, 2 Journal of Comparative Legislation 27 (1900).

Ahmed Safwat, the Theory of Mohammedan Law, 2 Journal of the Society of Comparative Legislation (3d ser. 1920) 310.

The Federalist, No. 30.

Sir Geoffrey Butler, Handbook to the League of Nations (1919).

CHAPTER 13

Walter Hines Page, Life and Letters (1925).

Great Events of the Great War (1920).

Robert H. Jackson, The Rule of Law among Nations, 31 American Bar Association Journal 290 (1945).

The Commoner (William J. Bryan, 1913).

Messages and Addresses of Woodrow Wilson.

German Documents, Annexe 1: The Deportation of Women and Girls from Lille (1916).

Documentary Evidence Prepared by the American and British Prosecuting Staffs for Presentation before the International Military Tribunal at Nurnberg, Germany, in the case of The United States of America, The French Republic,

The United Kingdom of Great Britain and Northern Ireland, and the Union of Soviet Socialist Republics *against* Hermann Wilhelm Goering, *et al.*, Vols. 1-8, and Supplementary Volumes A and B (1946).

David A. Simmons, Power in Government, 31 American Bar Association Journal 559 (1945).

M. A. Weightman, Self-Defense in International Law, 37 Virginia Law Review 1095 (1951).

Judgment of the International Military Tribunal, 20 Temple Law Quarterly 171 (1946).

Arno A. Herzberg, The Situation of the Lawyer in Germany, 27 American Bar Association Journal 294 (1941).

Sir Edwin Savory Herbert, The Common Law Man, 42 American Bar Association Journal 1019 (1956).

James F. Byrnes, The Lawyer in War Time, 28 American Bar Association Journal 453 (1942).

Frank Murphy, dissenting in Matter of Yamashita, 327 U.S. 1 (1946).

Gottfried Dietze, Constitutional Development in Post-War Germany, 42 Virginia Law Review 1 (1956).

CHAPTER 14

Julius C. Smith, Totalitarianism and Administrative Absolutism, 5 John Marshall Law Quarterly 202 (1939).

Elwyn Shaw, Address to Illinois State Bar Association, 4 John Marshall Law Quarterly 421 (1939).

"Mortality," quoted by Boyd, in Lincoln and the Influence of William Knox, 60 Lincoln Herald 12 (1958).

James Bryce, Studies in History and Jurisprudence (1901).

Roscoe Pound, quoted by Bernard Schwartz, reviewing Hans Kelsen, The Communist Theory of Law, 23 University of Chicago Law Review 354 (1956).

Harold J. Berman, Soviet Justice and Soviet Tyranny, 55 Columbia Law Review 79 (1955).

Roscoe Pound, Soviet Civil Law: A Review, 50 Michigan Law Review 95 (1950).

Robert H. Jackson, The Legal Profession in a World of Paradox, 33 American Bar Association Journal 24 (1947).

Harrison Salisbury, New York Times Nov. 10, 1957.

David F. Maxwell, Address to Tennessee Bar Association, 25 Tennessee Law Review 10 (1957).

Will Shafroth, The Judicial System of Soviet Russia, 12 American Bar Association Journal 795 (1926).

Eduard Taborsky, Administration of Justice in a People's Democracy, 49 American Political Science Review 402 (1955).

Jack Raymond, New Era in Europe, Foreign Policy Association Headline Series No. 122 (1957).

Zbigniew Brzezinski, Totalitarianism and Rationality, 50 American Political Science Review 751 (1956).

CHAPTER 15

George Sylvester, the Criminal Code of China, 69 United States Law Review 575 (1935).

Charles H. Huberich, The Paternal Power in Chinese Law, 14 Juridical Review 378 (1902).

Topics of the Times, New York Times, July 7, 1957, sec 4, p. 6.

Tao-Tai Hsia, The Constitution of Red China, 4 American Journal of Comparative Law 425 (1955).

Mao-Tse-tung, quoted from Brandt, A Documentary History of Chinese Communism (1952) by Hsia, supra.

Liu Shao-chi, Report on the Draft Constitution, quoted by Hsia, supra.

State Department, Memorandum of August 11, 1958, United States News and World Report August 22, 1958.

CHAPTER 16

Gottfried Dietze, Judicial Review in Europe, 55 Michigan Law Review 539 (1957).

Judge Peter Grosscup in United States v. James, 60 Fed. 257 (D. Ill. 1894).

M. Guizot, History of Civilization (3d Am. ed. 1882).

Judge John F. Dillon, Address to American Bar Association in 1884, reprinted 69 United States Law Review 355 (1935).

Louis D. Brandeis, Business, a Profession, 356 (1933).

Woodrow Wilson, quoted in Miami Laundry Co. v. Florida Dry Cleaning & L. Board, 119 A.L.R. 956 (Fla. 1938).

The Declaration of Independence.

Sweezy v. New Hampshire, 354 U.S. 234 (1957).

Coblentz and Warshaw, European Convention: Rights and Freedoms, 44 California Law Review 94 (1956).

New York Times, September 27, 1953, and October 4, 1953, stating figures on home and automobile ownership based on United States Census Reports and Automobile Facts and Figures.

Blackstone's Commentaries (Christian, Archbold and Chitty's ed. 1827) Book II, ch. 1, p. 1.

Exodus 20.

Andrew McLaughlin, Constitutional History of the United States (1935) 59, quoting from pronouncements of Samuel Adams and others.

Roger Williams, quoted in Fellman, Property in Colonial Political Theory, 16 Temple Law Quarterly 388 (1942).

State v. Boren, 20 A.L.R. 2d 798 (Wash. 1950).

Schiller Piano Co. v. Illinois Northern Utilities Co., 288 Ill. 580 (1919).

Coppage v. Kansas, 236 U.S. 1 (1914).

Trust Co. of Chicago v. City of Chicago, 408 Ill. 91 (1951).

United States Conservation Bulletin No. 40, Department of the Interior, 1951.

Felix S. Cohen, Original Indian Title, 32 Minnesota Law Review 28 (1947).

Louis D. Brandeis, dissenting, in Liggett Co. v. Lee, 288 U.S. 517 (1933).

Thomas Jefferson, quoted by Judge Leon R. Yankwich, 14 F.R.D. 199 (1953).

Chief Justice Charles Evans Hughes, Appalachian Coals v. United States, 288 U.S. 344 (1933).

De Chardin in Human Rights, Comments and Interpretations, A Symposium, edited by UNESCO, quoted in review by Serge L. Hughes, 24 St. John's Law Review 349 (1949).

CHAPTER 17

James Madison, Letter to Duponceau, quoted by Joseph M. Snee, Government under Law 113 (1956).

Holden v. Hardy, 169 U.S. 366 (1898).

Twining v. New Jersey, 211 U.S. 78 (1908).

Lord Macmillan, Address to Edinburgh Philosophical Institution, 50 Scottish Law Review 1 (1934).

Judge John N. Jewett, The Common Law.

Harlan F. Stone, The Common Law in the United States, 50 Harvard Law Review 4 (1937).

Sir William Holdsworth, History of English Law, Vol. 4, 293 (1924), quoted by Fins, Law of Blackstone and Justinian, 5 John Marshall Law Quarterly 53 (1939).

State v. Muolo, 118 Conn. 373 (1934).

II Bryce, Studies in History and Jurisprudence (1901).

Waters v. Gerard, 189 N.Y. 302 (1907).

Illinois Revised Statutes, Chap. 28, par. 1.

Andrew McLaughlin, Constitutional History of the United States 3 (1935).

Constitution of Illinois, Article II, sec. 19.

Sir Maurice Sheldon Amos, Common and Civil Law in British Nations, 50 Harvard Law Review 1249 (1937).

Erie Railroad Co. v. Tompkins, 304 U.S. 64 (1938).

David W. Purcell, Comparison of Community Property Systems, 34 Texas Law Review 1065 (1956).

CHAPTER 18

Skinner & Co. v. Shew & Co., (1893) 1 Ch. 413.

Burdon v. Wood, 142 F. 2d 303 (7th Cir. 1944).

Jacques v. Childs Dining Hall Co., 26 A.L.R. 1329 (Mass. 1923).

R. C. Donnelly, History of Defamation, citing Select Pleas in Manorial Courts, Seldon Society, 1949 Wisconsin Law Review 99.

Stanton v. Sentinel Printing Co., 84 N.E. 2d 461 (Mass. 1949).

Spanel v. Pegler, 160 F. 2d 619 (7th Cir. 1947).

Mencher v. Chesley, 75 N.E. 2d 257 (N.Y. 1947).

Hartmann v. Winchell, 73 N.E. 2d 30 (N.Y. 1947)

Illinois Revised Statutes, Chap. 38, par. 404.1 et seq.

Ostrowe v. Lee, 175 N.E. 505 (N.Y. 1931).

Springer v. Swift, 78 A.L.R. 1171 (S.D 1931)

Ogren v. Rockford Star Printing Co., 288 Ill. 405 (1919).

Mills v. Denny, 40 A.L.R. 2d 933 (Iowa 1954).

Faber v. Byrle, 25 A.L.R. 2d 1379 (Kan. 1951).

Utah State Farm Bureau Federation v. National Farmers Union Service Corporation, 198 F 2d 20 (10th Cir. 1952).

Watwood v. Stone's Mercantile Agency, 194 F. 2d 160 (D.C. Cir. 1952).

Slocinski v. Radwan, 63 A.L.R. 643 (N.H. 1929).

Broking v. Phoenix Newspapers, 39 A.L.R. 2d 1382 (Ariz. 1953).

Prosser, Interstate Publication, 51 Michigan Law Review 959 (1953).

CHAPTER 19

Skillings v. Allen, 5 A.L.R. 922 (Minn. 1919).

Katz v. Helbing, 62 A.L.R. 825 (Cal. 1928).

Wertz v. Lincoln Liberty Life Ins. Co., 17 A.L.R. 2d 629 (Neb. 1950).

Dee v. City of Peru, 343 Ill. 36 (1931).

New York Central R. Co. v. Stevens, 185 N.E. 542 (Ohio 1933)

Moran v. Gatz, 390 Ill. 478 (1945).

McHugh v. Audet, 72 F. Supp. 394 (D. Pa. 1947).

Giacomuzzi v. Klein, 88 N.E. 2d 548 (Mass. 1949).

Cory v. Ray, 55 N.E. 2d 117 (Ind. 1944).

Flanders v. Pailey, 71 N.E. 2d 112 (Mass. 1947).

Kline v. Rider, 73 N.E. 2d 378 (Oh. App. 1947).

Maryland v. Manor Real Estate & Trust Co., 176 F. 2d 414 (4th Cir. 1949).

Winterbottom v. Wright, 10 M. & W. 109 (1842).

MacPherson v. Buick Motor Co., 217 N.Y. 382 (1916).

Green, Strict Liability of Manufacturers, 24 Tennessee Law Review 928 (1957).

Carter v. Yardley & Co., 64 N.E. 2d 693 (Mass. 1946).

CHAPTER 20

Thomas Sanders, Introduction to Institutes of Justinian 44 (1876).

Thomas Erskine Holland, Elements of Jurisprudence (11th ed. 1910) 143.

Port Huron Machine Co. v. Wohlers, 221 N.W. 843 (Iowa 1928).

Bowman v. Obee, 290 Ill. App. 45 (1937).

Morris R. Cohen, The Basis of Contract, 46 Harvard Law Review 553 (1933).

Constitution of the United States, Article I, sec. 10.

Ogden v. Saunders, 12 Wheat. 213 (1827).

Illinois Revised Statutes, Chap. 59, pars. 1, 2; Chapter 121½, par. 4(1).

Note, English Law Reform Act, 1954, 40 Cornell Law Quarterly 581 (1955).

Robertson v. United States, 343 U.S. 711 (1952).

Currie v. Misa, (1875) L.R. 10 Exch. 153.

Schlatter v. Triebel, 284 Ill. 412 (1918).

Moore, Consideration in Contracts, 16 Tennessee Law Review 915 (1941).

Ryan Stevedoring Co. v. Pan-American SS Corp., 350 U.S. 124 (1956).

Wood v. Lucy, Lady Duff-Gordon, 118 N.E. 214 (N.Y. 1917).

Sun Oil Co. v. Dalzell Towing Co., 55 F. 2d 63 (2d Cir. 1932).

Hadley v. Baxendale (1854) 9 Exch. 341.

CHAPTER 21

Constitution of the United States, Fifth and Fourteenth Amendments.

Constitution of Illinois, Article II, sec. 19.

CHAPTER 22

Marcel Frym. The Criminal Intent, 31 Texas Law Review 260 (1953).

Roscoe Pound, Introduction to Sayre, Cases on Criminal Law (1927).

Morissette v. United States, 342 U.S. 246 (1952).

Francis Bowes Sayre, Mens Rea, 45 Harvard Law Review 974 (1932).

M'Naghten's Case, 10 Clark & Fin. 200 (1843).

Leland v. Oregon, 343 U.S. 790 (1952).

Durham v. United States, 214 F. 2d 862 (D.C. Cir. 1954).

People v. Carpenter, 11 Ill. 2d 60 (1957).

Herbert Wechsler, The Criteria of Criminal Responsibility, 22 University of Chicago Law Review 367 (1955).

Harry Kalven, Jr., Introduction to Insanity and the Criminal Law, 22 University of Chicago Law Review 317 (1955).

Judge Leon R. Yankwich, The Federal Penal System, 10 F.R.D. 539 (1949).

CHAPTER 23

Oliver Wendell Holmes in United States v. Thompson, 257 U.S. 419 (1922).

William O. Douglas in Joint Anti-Fascist Refugee Com. v. McGrath, 341 U.S. 123 (1951).

Rudyard Kipling, quoted in Editorial "The Old Issue," 32 American Bar Association Journal 850 (1948).

The Bill of Rights, and the Fourteenth Amendment.

Leon Yankwich, The Background of the American Bill of Rights, 37 Georgetown Law Journal 1 (1948).

Allgeyer v. Louisiana, 165 U.S. 578 (1896).

Kent v. Dulles, 2 L. ed. 2d 1204 (1958).

People v. Belcastro, 356 Ill. 144 (1934).

Durkin v. Hey, 376 Ill. 292 (1941).

Felix Frankfurter, dissenting, in Solesbee v. Balkcom, 339 U.S. 9 (1950).

Wolf v. Colorado, 338 U.S. 25 (1949).

Morris v. United States, 156 F. 2d 525 (9th Cir. 1946).

Patton v. United States, 281 U.S. 276 (1930).

Thomas Jefferson, quoted in Galloway v. United States, 319 U.S. 372 (1943).

Constitution of the United States, Article I, sec. 9.

Ex Parte Watkins, 3 Peters 193 (1830).

McNally v. Hill, 293 U.S. 131 (1934).

CHAPTER 24

Dalton v. Vandeveer, 29 N.Y. Supp. 342 (1894).

Philip A. Ryan, Equity: System or Process? 45 Georgetown Law Journal 213 (1957).

Sir William Holdsworth, Essays in Law and History 138 (1946).

Aristotle, Ethics, Book 5, chapter 10.

Baltimore & N.Y.R. Co. v. Bouvier, 62 Atl. 868 (N.J. Ch. 1906).

Earl of Oxford's Case (1615) 1 Ch. Rep. 1.

Harper v. Adamatz, 113 Atl. 2d 136 (Conn. 1956).

Bormann v. City of Richmond Heights, 213 S.W. 2d 249 (Mo. App. 1948).

Berdie v. Kurtz, 88 F. 2d 158 (9th Cir. 1937).

The Federalist, No. 80.

CHAPTER 25

Best v. Samuel Fox & Co., Ltd. (1952) A.C. 716.

Oliver Wendell Holmes in New York Trust Co. v. Eisner, 256 U.S. 345 (1921).

John N. Jewett, The Common Law.

Louis D. Brandeis, Address to Chicago Bar Association, quoted by Robert H. Jackson, The Product of the Present Day Law School, 27 California Law Review 635 (1939).

William H. Hastie, Government under Law 330 (1956).

Paul Vinogradoff, Historical Jurisprudence, Vol. I, p. 116 (1920).

Commonwealth v. Temple, 14 Gray 69 (Mass. 1859).

Benjamin N. Cardozo, quoted in Belt v. Hamilton National Bank, 108 F. Supp. 689 (D.D.C. 1952); Brooks Brothers v. Brooks Clothing, 60 F. Supp. 442 (D. Cal. 1945).

Macpherson v. Buick Motor Co., 217 N.Y. 382 (1916).

Warren and Brandeis, The Right to Privacy, 4 Harvard Law Review 193 (1890).

Cason v. Baskin, 30 S. 2d 635 (Fla. 1944).

Eick v. Perk Dog Food Co., 347 Ill. App. 293 (1952).

Munden v. Harris, 134 S.W. 1076 (Mo. App. 1911).

Kunz v. Allen, 172 Pac. 532 (Kan. 1918).

Douglas v. Stokes, 149 S.W. 849 (Ky. 1912).

Melvin v. Reid, 297 Pac. 91 (Cal. App. 1931).

Hinish v. Meier & Frank Co., 138 ALR 1 (Ore. 1941).

Sidis v. F-R Publishing Corp., 113 F. 2d 806 (2d Cir. 1940).

Bartletta v. McFeeley, 152 Atl. 17 (N.J. 1930).

Fernicola v. Keenan, 39 Atl. 2d 851 (N.J. 1944).

McGovern v. Van Riper, 43 Atl. 2d 514 (N.J. 1945).

Drobner v. Peters, 20 A.L.R. 1503 (N.Y. 1921).

Woods v. Lancet, 102 N.E. 2d 691 (N.Y. 1951).

Funk v. United States, 290 U.S. 371 (1933).

Amann v. Faidy, 415 Ill. 422 (1953).

Hitaffer v. Argonne Co., 183 F. 2d 811 (D.C. Cir. 1950).

Acuff v. Schmit, 78 N.W. 2d 480 (1956).

Wood v. Lucy, Lady Duff-Gordon, 118 N.E. 214 (N.Y. 1917).

Federal Rules of Civil Procedure.

Field Code of New York.

English Common Law and Equity Procedure Acts of 1852.

English Supreme Court of Judicature Act of 1873.

Illinois Civil Practice Act, Illinois Revised Statutes Chap. 110.

Constitution of the United States, Article III, sec. 2, clause 1.

Muskrat v. United States, 219 U.S. 346 (1911).

Marbury v. Madison, 1 Cranch 137 (1803).

American Type Founders v. Lanson Monotype Machine Co., 137 F. 2d 728 (3d Cir. 1943).

Note, Developments—Declaratory Judgments, 62 Harvard Law Review 787 (1949).

Louis D. Brandeis, in Willing v. Chicago Auditorium Association, 277 U.S. 274 (1928).

Federal Declaratory Judgment Act. 28 U.S.C. 2201 et seq.

Edwin Borchard, The Supreme Court and the Declaratory Judgment, 14 American Bar Association Journal 633 (1928).

CHAPTER 26

Woods v. Lancet, 102 N.E. 2d 691 (N.Y. 1951).

Munn v. Illinois, 94 U.S. 113 (1877).

Snell v. Snell, 123 Ill. 403 (1888).

People v. Traeger, 372 Ill. 11 (1939).

Baker v. Bolton, 1 Camp. 493 (1808).

Baron Parke, quoted in King v. Henkie, 80 Ala. 505 (1886).

Lord Campbell's Act, 17 Halsbury's Statutes of England, 2d ed. 4.

Benjamin N. Cardozo in Van Beek v. Sabine Towing Co., 300 U.S. 342 (1927).

Wilcox v. Bierd, 330 Ill. 571 (1928).

Federal Employers' Liability Act, 45 U.S.C. 51.

Mondou v. New York, N.H. & H. R. Co., 223 U.S. 1 (1912).

Jones Act, 46 U.S.C. 688

Panama R. Co. v. Johnson, 264 U.S. 375 (1924).

Death on the High Seas Act, 46 U.S.C. 761.

Echavarria v. Steam Navigation Co., 10 F. Supp. 677 (D.N.Y. 1935).

Illinois Revised Statutes Chap. 95½, par. 9-201.

American Smelting & Refining Co. v. Sutyak, 175 F. 2d 123 (10th Cir. 1949).

Connett v. Winget, 374 Ill. 531 (1940).

Parrett v. Carothers, 11 Cal. App. 222 (1936).

Thomas v. Currier Lbr. Co., 283 Mich. 134 (1938).

Piercy v. Zeiss, 8 Cal. App. 595 (1935).

Stephens v. Weigel, 336 Ill. App. 36 (1948).

Hollander v. Davis, 120 F. 2d 131 (5th Cir. 1941).

Cruse v. Aden, 127 Ill. 231 (1889).

Illinois "Dram Shop" Act, Ill. Rev. St. Chap. 43, par. 135.

Cox v. Hrasky, 318 Ill. App. 287 (1943).

Haw v. 1933 Grill, 297 Ill. App. 37 (1938).

Hyba v. Horneman, Inc., 302 Ill. App. 143 (1939).

Bennett v. Auditorium Bldg. Corp., 299 Ill. App. 139 (1939).

Tiller v. Atlantic Coast Line R. Co., 318 U.S. 50 (1943).

English and Illinois Workmen's Compensation Acts.

Keeran v. P.B.&C. Traction Co., 277 Ill. 413 (1917).

Rogers v. Missouri Pacific R. Co., 352 U.S. 500 (1957).

Webb v. Illinois Central R. Co., 352 U.S. 512 (1957).

Ringhiser v. Chesapeake & O. R. Co., 354 U.S. 901 (1957).

Federal Safety Appliance Act, 45 U.S.C. 1 et seq.

Baltimore & O. R. Co. v. Jackson, 353 U.S. 325 (1957).

CHAPTER 27

John Foster Dulles, Administrative Law—A Practical Attitude for Lawyers, 25 American Bar Association Journal 275 (1939).

Report of the Attorney General's Committee on Administrative Procedure, Summary, 27 American Bar Association Journal 143 (1941).

Walter F. Dodd, Appraisal of Illinois Administrative Procedure, 1949 University of Illinois Law Forum 181.

Illinois Revised Statutes of 1874, Chap. 43, par. 3.

Felix Frankfurter, Foreword to Report of the Attorney General's Committee on Administrative Procedure, 41 Columbia Law Review 587 (1941).

Stark v. Wickard, 321 U.S. 288 (1944).

A.A. Berle, American Administrative Law, 30 Harvard Law Review 430 (1916).

President Franklin D. Roosevelt, Message Vetoing the Walter-Logan Bill, 27 American Bar Association Journal 52 (1940).

Sandstrom v. California Horse Racing Board, 189 Pac. 2d 17 (Cal. 1948).

Allgeyer v. Louisiana, 165 U.S. 578 (1897).

Federal Administrative Procedure Act, 5 U.S.C. 1001 et seq.

Universal Camera Corp. v. National Labor Relations Board, 340 U.S. 474 (1951).

Oakdale Community Consolidated School Dist. v. County Board, 12 Ill. 2d 190 (1957).

Wong Yang Sung v. McGrath, 339 U.S. 33 (1950).

Chin Yow v. United States, 208 U.S. 8 (1908).

Federal Crop Insurance Corp. v. Merrill, 332 U.S. 380 (1947).

Louis L. Jaffe, Delegation of Legislative Power, 47 Columbia Law Review 561 (1947).

Frank Newman, Publication of Federal Regulations, 63 Harvard Law Review 929 (1949).

Panama Refining Co. v. Ryan, 293 U.S. 388 (1935).

United States v. Smith, 293 U.S. 633 (1935).

John H. Wigmore, The Federal Register, 29 American Bar Association Journal 10 (1943).

Federal Register Act, 44 U.S.C. 301 et seq.

Code of Federal Regulations (1949 Ed. and Title Revisions).

Urban Lavery, The Federal Register and the Need of Its Reform, 2 Lawyer and Law Notes 1 (1949).

CHAPTER 28

Woods v. Lancet, 102 N.E. 2d 691 (N.Y. 1951).

Hitaffer v. Argonne Co., 183 F. 2d 811 (D.D.C. 1950).

Helvering v. Hallock, 309 U.S. 106 (1940).

Louis D. Brandeis, dissenting, in Burnet v. Coronado Oil & Gas Co., 285 U.S. 393 (1932).

Brown v. Board of Education, 347 U.S. 483 (1954).

Radovich v. National Football League, 352 U.S. 445 (1957).

Federal Baseball Club v. National League, 259 U.S. 200 (1922).

Toolson v. New York Yankees, 346 U.S. 356 (1953).

United States v. International Boxing Club, 348 U.S. 236 (1955).
United States v. Shubert, 348 U.S. 222 (1955).

CHAPTER 29

Hurtado v. California, 110 U.S. 516 (1884).

Chief Justice Marshall in M'Culloch v. Maryland, 4 Wheat 316 (1819).

Felix Frankfurter, concurring in Youngstown Sheet & Tube Co. v. Sawyer, 343 U.S. 579 (1952).

Sweezy v. New Hampshire, 354 U.S. 234 (1957).

Brown v. Board of Education, 347 U.S. 483 (1954).

Plessy v. Ferguson, 163 U.S. 537 (1896).

Robert J. Harris, The Constitution, Education and Segregation, 29 Temple Law Quarterly 409 (1956).

Beauharnais v. Illinois, 343 U.S. 250 (1952).

James F. Byrnes, United States News & World Report, May 18, 1956, p. 50.

Ralph T. Catterall, Judicial Self-Restraint: The Obligation of the Judiciary, 42 American Bar Association Journal 829 (1956).

Alexander H. Bickel, The Segregation Decision, 69 Harvard Law Review 1 (1955).

Charles Fairman, The Supreme Court—Foreword, 70 Harvard Law Review 83 (1956).

Aronson, Mr. Justice Stone and the Common Law, 25 Cornell Law Quarterly 489 (1940).

CHAPTER 30

John Bassett Moore, Fifty Years of International Law, 50 Harvard Law Review 395 (1937).

League to Enforce Peace 3 (1915).

Newton D. Baker, Our Social Foundations, 15 American Bar Association Journal 463 (1929).

State Department Memorandum, Aug. 11, 1958, United States News & World Report, Aug. 22, 1958 p. 94.

Sir Geoffrey Butler, Handbook to the League of Nations (1919).

Rashba, Foreign Exchange Restrictions, 41 Michigan Law Review 1089 (1943).

Luke 10.

Matthew 16.

INDEX

ABRAHAM
call to Egypt, 28
Hebrew covenantee, 191
Islamic prophet, 212, 246
ADAMS, SAMUEL
"rebellion to tyrants," 193
ADMINISTRATIVE AGENCIES
See also Administrative Law
legislative, executive and judicial action, 450-452
no penal powers, 464
procedure, 450
ADMINISTRATIVE LAW
See also Administrative Agencies; Federal Register
absolutism in Rome, 171
as old as government, 447
citizens charged with knowledge, 462
Code of Federal Regulations, 462
constitutional right to review, 456
"expertise", 454
Federal Administrative Procedure Act, 454
"finding", 458, 459
Hammurabi, 30
"hip-pocket" incident, 459
implementing reform by, 449
importance, 446
judicial review, 453-456
licensing, 446, 451
limitations of delegation, 489
"orders" contrasted with law, 302
patents, 448
political aspect, 449
presidential executive orders, 459
recent growth, 448
regulation of business, 448, 451
regulations, 391; 450-452; 462-464
scope in states, 450
sources, 446, 447
state court review, 456
Veterans' Administration, 453
Walter-Logan Bill, 449
ADMIRALTY LAW, 436
ADOPTION, 31, 56, 82
AGRICULTURE, 15, 243, 333-337, 449
AKZIN, BENJAMIN, 215, 217
ALEXANDER THE GREAT, 102
conquers Egypt, 102
conquers Greece, 102
conquers Jerusalem, 102
consults Delphi oracle, 84
designated son of Zeus, 102
disintegration of empire, 103
invades Asia, 102
man of religion, 84
paves way for Christianity, 103
ALARIC, II, 177, 178
ALHAMBRA, 243
ALIENATION OF AFFECTIONS, 416
ALIENS, 138, 456, 457
Allgeyer v. Louisiana, 399
AMERICA
See also United States
common law in, 348
spiritual force of ideals, 23
AMERICAN LAW INSTITUTE
Restatement of Contracts, 382

AMERICAN REVOLUTION, 188
AMOS, SIR MAURICE S., 258, 349
AMPHICTYONY
Greek Council, 85
Hebrew Commonwealth, 197
ANAXAGORAS, 104
ANCESTOR WORSHIP, 316
ANONYMOUS INFORMATION
See also Secret Informers
condemned by Trajan, 165, 166
ANTHROPOLOGY, 21
ANTI-COMINTERN PACT, 289
ANTIGONE, 113
ANTI-TRUST ACT, 336
APOSTOLIC SUCCESSION, 231
AQUINAS, THOMAS, 188
ARABIA, 240
See also Arabs; Islam
ARABS
See also Islam
customary law, 251, 252
in Israel, 215
in Palestine, 212-214
religion, 238
renascence, 258
revolt in World War I, 261
ARGENTINA, 180
ARISTOTLE
See also Greece; Philosophy
clarifies concept of rights, 116
conception of freedom, 114
conception of natural law, 115, 182
elements of government, 115
equity, 116, 405
Rhetoric, 99, 101
slavery, acceptance of 114
ARIZONA
community property law, 351
ARSON, 391
ARTICLES OF CONFEDERATION, 86
ARYANS
See also Hinduism; India
gods as protecting color, 41
invasion of India, 39, 40
ASSAULT AND BATTERY
defined, 354
historical development, 416
laws of Manu provisions, 45
self-defense, 355, 356
ASSYRIA, 33, 34
See also Babylonia
ATHENS
See also Greece
constitution of Clisthenes, 91
destroyed by Xerxes and rebuilt, 92
Draco's Code, 89
early government, 89
Golden Age, 92
judicial system, 99, 101
procedure contrasted with Roman, 149
Pericles' funeral oration, 96
Plutarch on, 94
slavery, 98
Solon's Code, 89
war atrocities, 98
ATKINS, GAIUS GLEN
on Puritans, 231

ATLEE, PRIME MINISTER, 74, 214
ATOMIC AGE, 3, 12, 449, 474
ATTORNEY GENERAL'S COMMITTEE
on administrative procedure, 448
AUGSBURG CONFESSION
See also Reformation; Roman Catholic
Church
alternative choice of, 229
AUSTIN, JOHN, 151
AUSTRIA
adopts Code Napoleon, 180
annexed by Nazis, 289, 290
World War I ultimatum, 268
AUTOMOBILES
See Motor Vehicles
AVERROES, 243
AXIS PACTS, 289
BABYLONIA
See also Assyria; Hammurabi
Babylonian Captivity, 34
caste system, 31
conquered by Tiglath Pileser, 33
customs into Roman law, 150
early history, 28
final fall, 35
Hanging Gardens, 35
libraries and temples, 29
religion, 29
slavery, 95
Sumerian culture, 33
BAKER, NEWTON D., 478
BALFOUR, LORD, 212, 213
Beauharnais v. Illinois, 472
BELGIUM
adopts Code Napoleon, 180
invaded by the Hohenzollerns, 268
invaded by Nazis, 292
BELSHAZZAR, 35
BENES, EDUARD, 309, 310
BENTHAM, JEREMY, 427
BERLE, A. A., 448, 449
BHAGAVAD GITA
See also Hinduism
epic dialogue, 39
BIBLE
See also Christianity; Judaism; Septuagint
parts in Koran, 245
BICKEL, ALEXANDER M., 472
BILL OF RIGHTS
See also Constitution of the United States
and Amendments
bail, 398
confrontation by witnesses, 397
double jeopardy, 397
due process, 397
freedom of religion, 233
grand jury presentment, 397
limitations of sovereign power, 398
no cruel punishment, 398
no excessive fine, 398
"persons" protected, 138
procedural elements, 396
process to obtain evidence, 397
right to counsel, 397
self-incrimination, 397
taking private property, 397
trial by jury, 397, 398
unreasonable searches, 397
BISMARCK, 257, 266
BLACK, HUGO, 383

BLACKSTONE, WILLIAM
exposition of natural law, 182-186
on trial by jury, 401
origin of property concept, 330
BOGIGISH, 412
BOLIVIA
adopts Code Napoleon, 180
BOLOGNA
See also Roman Law
revival at, 178, 180
BOSE, SUBHAS CHANDRA, 69, 70
See also India
trial of partisans, 73
BOOK BURNING, 168, 222
BOXER UPRISING, 318
BRADSHAW, MARION J.
on Council of Nicaea, 170
on Paul, 84
BRANDEIS, LOUIS D.
Erie v. Tompkins decision, 350
on Bogigish, 412
on common law, 415
on declaratory judgments, 431
on right of privacy, 415
on stare decisis, 466
quotation from Pericles, 96
"resourcefulness of small men", 335
statement of American ideals, 327
BRAZIL, 178
BRITISH COMMONWEALTH
See also England
membership of, 75
BROWN, BRENDAN F., 121, 189
Brown v. Board of Education, 469-472
BROWNEISTS, 231
BRYAN, WILLIAM JENNINGS, 269
BRYCE, JAMES
on common law, 347
on East India Company, 54
on Greek civilization, 118, 119
on later Rome, 171
on Rome after division, 171
on Russian law, 300
on Roman conquests, 131
BUDDHISM, 47-50, 316
See also Hinduism; India
BURGLARY, 391
BURMA, 49, 50
BUTLER, SIR GEOFFREY, 483
BYRNES, JAMES, 288, 472
BRZEZINSKI, ZBIGNIEW, 311, 312
CAESAR, JULIUS, 144, 146, 157, 158
See also Roman Republic
CAIRNS, HUNTINGTON, 21
CALIFORNIA
community property law, 351
Spanish law in, 179
CALIGULA, 164, 458
CALVIN, JOHN, 228
CANON LAW
See also Christian Church Law; Roman
Catholic Church
application and scope, 234
Bar practicing, 235
Code of 1917, 233
crimes, 390, 393
denounced by Puritans, 230
family relationships, 329
importance, 234
origin, 232, 233

relation to state, 233
Roman law influence, 233
State of Israel, 217
CAPITULARIES, 180
CAPITULATIONS
Ottoman Empire, 257
CARDOZO, NATHANIEL
MacPherson v. Buick Motor Co., 373
on common law, 415
on contracts, 425
on criminal intent, 392
on ideal legal system, 147
on interpretation of contracts, 384
on libel, 361
on wrongful death, 435
CASTE SYSTEM OF HINDUISM
See also Hinduism; India; Manu, Laws of
continuing problem, 81
in Laws of Manu, 42, 47
origin, 40, 41
position of Brahmans, 42
relation to Muslims, 71
untouchables, 42
working of, 42
CATTERALL, RALPH T.
on Desegregation Case, 472
CAVOUR, 257
CHAMBERLAIN, NEVILLE, 487
CERTIORARI, 349
CEYLON, 49
CHARITIES, 223
CHARLEMAGNE, 171, 223, 224
CHARLES I, 306
CHILI
adopts Code Napoleon, 180
Chin Yow v. United States, 458
CHINA
See also Confucius; Red China
ancestor worship, 316
Buddhism in, 49
corruption in government, 315
legal system, 315
Manchu Code, 315
natural law, 314
Nine Classics, 317
paternal power, 316
patriarchal despotism, 314
penetration by Islam, 237
republic established, 318, 319
CHRIST, JESUS
Good Samaritan parable, 488
Islamic prophet, 212, 246
no approval of slavery, 137
trial of, 164
"what is man profited" 113, 488
CHRISTIAN CHURCH LAW
See also Canon Law
in State of Israel, 217
CHRISTIANITY
See also Canon Law; Church; Christians;
  Ecclesiastical Law; Roman Catholic
  Church
Arabia, 237, 238
as unifying force, 119
beginnings, 219
era of Roman persecution, 165
incompability with Nazism, 285
influence of Stoic philosophy, 118
influence on family law, 126
influence on natural law, 188, 189

relation to government, 219-223
relation to Islam, 245, 246, 253
Roman state religion, 84, 169, 221
way paved by Alexander, 103
CHURCH
See also Christians; Christianity; Ecclesiastical Courts; Religious Organizations;
  Roman Catholic Church
and state separation, 233
attacked by Nazis, 284, 285
early, 219, 220
no individual liberty in, 325
of England, 229, 231
CHURCHILL, WINSTON
Teheran Conference, 262
CICERO
See also Roman Republic; Roman Law;
  Rome
banishment from Rome, 146
betrayal and execution, 158
definition of natural law, 155
denounces slavery, 123
natural law exponent, 182
CITIZENSHIP
American rights without, 138
basis of Roman rights, 137, 138
education as basis, 104
Jews deprived by Nazis, 285
obligations in Athens, 90
CITY STATES, 28, 85, 118, 120, 483
CIVIL DISOBEDIENCE, 68, 69, 73, 141
See also Passive Resistance
CIVIL LAW
See also Code Napoleon; Codes; Roman
  Law
judges, 181
CIVIL SERVICE COMMISSION, 449
CIVIL WAR, 2, 94
CIVILIZATION, 3, 4, 174, 326, 327
CLIVE, LORD, 54
CLOVIS, 221
CODE NAPOLEON, 180-181
See also Civil Law; Codes: Roman Law
CODES
See also Code Napoleon; Legislation; Sta-
  tutes; Swiss Civil Code: Twelve Tables,
  Law of
codification in Israel, 218
contrasted with common law, 181
criminal, 390, 391
Dharma Sistras, 42
disadvantages of rigidity, 147
Draco's, 89
Egyptian Civil, 264
Field, 428
Lebanon, 263
Mediterranean maritime, 187
Manchu Code, 315
of Federal Regulations, 462
Papal of 1917, 233
Solon's, 89
Turkey, 263
United States Code, 462
COHEN, MORRIS R., 376
COKE, LORD
"law is above the king", 109
COMMON LAW
accessibility, 458
adaptability, 412
alienation of affections, 416

Amos' summary, 349
antedates legislatures, 344
application under federal system, 349, 350
comparison with Roman, 151
consortium, loss of, 424
contracts, adaptation to, 425
crimes, 390, 391
custom, 344, 346
defamation, 357, 358
elasticity contrasted with code, 147, 148, 181
ennoblement of individual, 324, 325
experience as source, 346
false imprisonment, 356, 357
flexibility, 414
geographical considerations, 411
growth of centuries, 343
historical development, 411
in America, 348
in "breast of judges," 206
in India, 64
in Palestine, 216
intentional wrongs, 354
malpractice, 367
nature summarized, 473
no federal, 350, 390
negligent wrongs, 365
"no wrong without remedy" 348, 349
nuisances, 416
original rigidity, 404, 406
overruling precedents, 423
pre-natal injuries, 422
property, 388
recognition, 346, 347
right of minorities, 282
Roman and civil elements, 350, 351
Roman law as tonic, 344
statutes making applicable, 216,348
statutory abolition of defenses, 442
Stone's characterization, 344
substantive and procedural, 396
time lag, 415
trial by jury, 397, 398
"unequalled treasure of instances" 347
unwritten law, 352
where found, 352, 353
wrongful death, 434
COMMUNIST PARTY, 304
See also Soviet Russia
COMMUNITY PROPERTY
right of spouses, 351, 352
CONCENTRATION CAMPS, 294
See also War Atrocities
CONFLICT OF LAWS
development by praetor peregrinus, 152
Egyptian divorces, 264
CONFLICTING INTERESTS
problem of the law, 27
CONFUCIUS
See also China
comment on crimes, 316
compared with Socrates, 317
on oppressive government, 317
static philosophy, 318
teachings, 317, 318
CONGREGATIONALISTS
flee to Holland, 231
Mayflower Compact, 232
polity, 232
CONNECTICUT, 232

CONSCIENCE
See also Reason; Religion; Truth
freedom of, 232, 233
guide for action, 113
key to natural law, 181, 182
supreme role of, 23
test of positive law, 155
CONSORTIUM, LOSS OF, 424
CONSTANTINE, 120, 169, 221.
CONSTITUTION OF THE U. S.
See also Bill of Rights; Constitutions; Police Power
as underwriting American way, 18, 19
established procedural safeguards, 397
habeas corpus, 402
interpretation, 468
limits governmental power, 14
natural law influence, 182
no impairment of contracts, 377
Public School Desegregation Case, 469
CONSTITUTIONS
See also Constitution of the U. S.
Connecticut, 232
Czechoslovakia, 309
India, 78, 79
none in Israel, 218
Pakistan, 80
Red China, 319
Roman Imperial, 166
Rome, no formal, 130
Soviet Russia, 302
Sparta, 86
CONTRIBUTORY NEGLIGENCE
bars recovery, 365, 366
CONTRACTS
adaptation to common law, 425
agency, 128
Babylonia, 29
bilateral and unilateral, 380
capacity to make, 381
consideration, 381-383
customary law in India, 57
declaratory judgments, 430
defined, 376
development of Roman law, 152, 153
early symbolism, 128
formal and informal, 378
freedom of, 399
Greeks, 377
Hebrews, 377
historical background, 376
in personam right, 376
interpretation, 383
Laws of Manu provisions, 45
making, 380
marriage as, 125
married women, 434
modern code in Lebanon, 263
nature of right, 375
no state may impair, 377
offer and acceptance, 380
remedies for breach, 386, 387
Romans, 143, 152, 377
seal, 378
Soviet law, 304
Statute of Frauds, 378, 379
CORDOVA, 243, 254
See also Islam
CORPORATIONS
early private, 335

inevitability of large, 337,338
management operation, 338
political expenditures, 16, 17
shareholders' ownership, 15, 338
CORPUS JURIS CIVILIS
See also Justinian; Roman Law
basic at Bologna, 178, 180
Imperial Constitutions, 176
Institutes, 176
Pandects, 126, 176
preparation, 176
CORWIN, EDWIN S., 114, 118
COURTS
See also Federal Courts; Judges; Trials
Czechoslovakia: Communist line, 311
Czechoslovakian Republic, 309, 310
Greece, 99-101
Nazi, 280
Red China, 321-323
Roman Catholic Church, 235, 236
Soviet Russia, 304, 307, 308
COUNSEL FOR DEFENSE, 397
COVENANT
Hebrew, with Jehovah, 191
CRABITES, PIERRE, 247, 252, 258
CRIMINAL LAW
Athens, 89
bail, 398
Babylonian, 32
Canon Law relationship, 390
China, 315, 316
codification, 390, 391
confrontation by witnesses, 397
Durham v. United States, 394
Eighth Amendment, 32, 398
elements of crime, 390
enlargement of category, 391, 392
evil mind, 390-394
federal, 390
Fifth Amendment, 397
fines and punishments, 398
Fourth Amendment, 397
grand jury, 397
Hebrew, 205
information and accusation, 397
Islamic, 244, 245, 263
jury, 397
Laws of Manu, 45
Lebanon, 263
mens rea, 390
M'Naghten's Case, 393
Muslim law in India, 57
objective, 393
process for witnesses, 397
punishment, 395
radio defamation, 360
Sixth Amendment, 397
"socially dangerous" offenses, 305
Soviet Russia, 301, 302, 305
Speedy and public trial, 397
tenement house regulations, 392
Turkey, 263
CRIPPS, SIR STAFFORD, 73
CROMWELL, OLIVER 231
CRUCE, EMERIC 187
CRUSADES
See also Roman Catholic Church
menace Islam, 254
"will of God", 226
CUNEIFORM WRITING

Babylonia, 28, 30
CUSTOM
defamation, liability for, 357
divine significance, 143
family, 124, 179
feudal system, 179
Hebrew law, 205, 206
Hindu and Muslin in India, 56, 57
in common law, 344, 346
Islamic law, 252
law for Spartan soldiers, 88
Laws of Manu, 43, 47
origin of lost, 21
Paris, 179, 180
Romans, 143
status, 179
Teutonic, 179
torts, 179
tribal, 85
tribal, Israel, 218
CZECHOSLOVAKIA
Communist seizure, 310
constitution, 309
former system of justice, 309, 310
occupied by Nazis, 290
present Communist judiciary, 310, 311
represented at Versailles, 309
Republic established, 308, 309
DALAI LAMA, 49
DAMAGES
against landlord, 370-372
alienation of affections, 416
assault and battery, 354
breach of contract, 386
difficulty of proving, 430
false imprisonment, 356
Federal Employers' Liability Act, 444
intoxicating liquor sales, 439, 440
libel and slander, 359
malpractice, 367, 368
negligent manufacturers, 372-374
negligent wrongs, 365
operation of business property, 368, 369
operation of motor vehicles, 366, 367
DARIUS, 35
DARK AGES, 171, 172
DEATH, WRONGFUL
assault and battery, 354, 355
Federal Employers' Liability Act, 436
High Seas Act, 436
Illinois Death Statute, 423, 424
Jones Act, 436
Lord Campbell's Act, 435
no common law action, 434
DEBTOR AND CREDITOR
Babylonia, 31
constitutional concern, 377
Greece, 89, 100
Laws of Manu, 45
Rome, 128, 141
DE CHARDIN, FATHER, 341
DECLARATION OF INDEPENDENCE,
187, 188, 327
DECLARATION OF RIGHTS, 348
DECLARATORY JUDGMENTS
advantage, 432
constitutional problem, 429, 430
England, 431
federal courts, 431
Uniform Act, 431

DEFAMATION, 358
See also Libel and Slander
DELPHI ORACLE, 84, 106
DEMOCRACY
See also Government; State
as totalitarian tyranny, 282
Athenian excesses, 94
fundamental principle, 328
law under, 13
Solon's concept, 90
working of Greek, 96-99
DEMOSTHENES, 117
DENNING, LORD JUSTICE, 426,427
DEPORTATION PROCEDURE, 456, 457
DE TOQUEVILLE, 95
DHARMA SISTRAS, 42
DIETZE, GOTTFRIED, 296, 324
DIVORCE
Babylonia, 31
Canon Law, 235
equity jurisdiction, 408
Hebrew law, 206, 217
Islamic law, 249, 250, 264
DOUBLE JEOPARDY, 397
DOUGLAS, WILLIAM O. 79, 396
DOWER RIGHT, 352
DRAMA, 95, 96, 113, 162
See also Antigone
Drobner v. Peters, 422
DUE PROCESS OF LAW
See also Procedure
business regulation, 452
defined, 399, 400
Fifth Amendment, 397, 398
Fourteenth Amendment, 398
relation to Roman law, 177
review of administrative action, 456, 457
DULLES, JOHN FOSTER, 447
Durham v. United States, 394
DYKES, C. OSWALD, 32
Earl of Oxford's Case, 405
EAST INDIA COMPANY
See also England; India
abuse by zamindars, 55
assumption of power, 53
corruption eliminated, 54
French challenge met, 54
granted charter, 52
impeachment of Hastings, 55
powers to crown, 59
regime of Bentinck, 55
regime of Dalhousie, 56
ECCLESIASTICAL COURTS
See also Canon Law; Christian Church
  Law; Roman Catholic Church
Canon Law, 233
England, 123
jurisdiction, 222
Roman Catholic Church, 123
torture to extort confessions, 123
EDUCATION
Aristotle's principles, 114
basis for citizenship, 104
Canon Law and, 234
India, 56, 62
Plato's principles, 110
EGYPT
autonomy from Turkey, 259
becomes Roman province, 158
Civil Code, 264

conquered by Alexander, 102
early civilization, 20
English troops withdrawn, 260
French legal system, 263
gods and goddesses, 20, 24
legal system, 247
Mixed Courts, 258
Napoleon's invasion, 258
occupation by England, 259, 260
persecution of Hebrews, 192
Pharaohs, 24-27
religious law, 21, 24
slavery, 26, 95
Suez Canal, 259
under Rome, 136
EIGHTH AMENDMENT
bail, 398
historical innovation, 32
punishment, 398
ELLESMERE, LORD
on equity, 405
EMPLOYERS AND EMPLOYEES
See Master and Servant
ENGLAND
See also British Commonwealth
Chancery Procedure Act, 431
Church of, 229, 231
cooperation with United States, 490
decentralization of power, 327
declaratory judgments, 431
Ecclesiastical Courts, 123
Hilary Rules, 427
House of Lords, 203
individual liberty concepts, 326
Inquisition courts, 228
international law recognized, 475
leaves Palestine, 215
lets Nazis proceed, 288
London Beth Din, 210
Middle East mandates, 261
Munich Pact, 291
occupies Egypt, 259, 260
pacifistic demonstrations, 288
Palestine mandate, 213
Procedure Acts, 428
Puritan Commonwealth, 231
relation to Israel, 213
religious disqualifications, 232
Roman law in, 189
Roman occupation, 412
Star Chamber, 230
Statute of Frauds repealed, 379
Suez Canal, 259
Supreme Court of Judicature Act, 428
under papal interdict, 226
withdrawal from Egypt, 260
EPICUREANS
pleasure highest good, 117, 118
EQUAL PROTECTION OF THE LAW
Fourteenth Amendment, 469
Indian Constitution, 80
School Desegregation Case, 469
EQUITY
"as old as Aristotle", 116, 405
constitutional jurisdiction, 403
elasticity of remedies, 407
future of, 409
"good faith" doctrine, 153
Grotius' definition, 405
Hebrew law, 211

historical development, 404
injunctions, 408
in Palestine, 216, 217
merger with law, 427
no jury trial, 403
praetorian edict equivalent, 151
relation to common law, 403
scope, 407
segment of English jurisprudence, 151
separate courts, 406
test of jurisdiction, 406
Erie Railroad Co. v. Tompkins, 350
EUROPEAN CONCERT, 256
FAGLEY, FREDERICK L., 231
FAIRMAN, CHARLES, 473
FALSE IMPRISONMENT, 356, 357
FAMILY
See also Family Law
customary law, 124
early self-help, 8, 9
unit of Hebrew society, 206
FAMILY LAW
barbarian, 179
Canon Law, 234
custom, 179
China, 316
early, 5
Hebrew, 206
influence of Christianity, 126
Laws of Manu, 43, 44
private nature of, 123, 124
Roman, 123
Roman Law of Twelve Tables, 144
Sparta, 88
FEDERAL   ADMINISTRATIVE   PRO-
   CEDURE ACT, 454, 457, 458
Federal Baseball Club v. National League,
   467
Federal Crop Insurance Corp. v. Merrill,
   462
FEDERAL COURTS
See also Courts; Judges; Supreme Court
   of the United States
jurisdiction, 350
when state law applied, 350
FEDERAL   EMPLOYERS'   LIABILITY
   ACT
abolished common law defenses, 444
recovery for death, 436
working illustrated, 444, 445
FEDERALIST
on Amphictyonic Council, 85
on equity, 409
on limitations of mental faculties, 26
on Roman Republic, 140
on Roman system, 147
FEDERAL REGISTER
See also Administrative Law
Act establishing, 460
content, 460, 461
FEDERAL RULES OF CIVIL PROCED-
   URE
law and equity merged, 427
preparation, 150
discovery before trial, 428
FEDERAL SAFETY APPLIANCE ACT
civil liability under, 445
FEDERAL SYSTEM
See also United States
common law under, 349

FELDMAN, DAYEN, DR.
on London Beth Din, 210, 211
FEUDAL SYSTEM
basis of customary law, 179
described, 224
FIFTH AMENDMENT
due process as to property, 332, 389
text, 397
FIRST AMENDMENT
freedom of press, 329
freedom of religion, 233, 329
freedom of speech, 329
right to petition, 16
FORCED LABOR
Hohenzollerns, 272, 273
Nazis, 293, 294
Romans, 137
Solomon, 201
Sparta, 87
FOURTH AMENDMENT
unreasonable searches, 397
FOURTEENTH AMENDMENT
due process as to property, 389
in Desegregation Case, 469
FRANCE
See also Napoleon
capitularies, 180
cooperation with United States, 490
defeat in 1870, 266
in Near East, 258, 259
in North Africa, 259
Islam repulsed, 242
law in New World, 180
Middle East mandates, 261
Pothier, 180
Roman law, 179
seat of papacy, 227
Suez Canal, 259
under papal interdict, 226
FRANKFURTER, FELIX
"Founders not imbued with cynicism", 19
on administrative law, 448
on constitutional interpretation, 468
on due process, 400
on *stare decisis,* 466
FRANK, JEROME, 114
FRANKLIN, BENJAMIN
"rebellion to tyrants", 193
FREEDOM, INDIVIDUAL
See also Individual Liberty
spirit of never dies, 491
FREEDOM OF THE PRESS
right of privacy, 420
spiritual right, 329
FREEDOM OF RELIGION
"equality of all beliefs", 233
Smith's statement, 233
spiritual right, 329
FREEDOM OF SPEECH
none in Greece, 107
spiritual right, 329
Socrates and, 105, 107
FRYM, MARCEL, 390
FUERO REAL, 178
GAIUS, 176
GALILEO, 104
GANDHI, MOHANDAS, 38, 66-67
See also India, Civil Disobedience
GERMANY
See also Hohenzollerns; Nazis; Prussia;

Weimar Republic; World War I; World
War II
inquisition courts, 228
legal positivism, 296
Nazis take over, 282
natural law revival, 296
non-aggression pacts, 277
recent moral renascence, 296
Roman law in, 189
GOOD SAMARITAN, 488
GURNEY, URIEL, 216
GOVERNMENT
See also Government of Laws; Nation;
State; World Government
absolutism in Rome, 171
administrative processes, 447
advent of, 8, 9
Aristotle's elements, 115
as implementer of law, 12
citizen deals at peril, 463
clash with individual interests, 27
evolution of Christian, 219, 220
feudalism supplanting, 224
identification with religion, 219, 223
individual citizen's responsibilty, 17
integration with law, 13
justice immutable in free, 343
Laws of Manu, 44, 45
Marxian theory, 301
Mayflower Compact, 232
of "groups", 15
of "laws", 114, 398
"of the people", 13, 14, 112
"personal": the despot, 14
personalized beginnings, 10
Plato's ideal, 109
power to make law, 13
purpose, 11
relation of Hinduism, 38
relation to religion, 22
Rome, not representative, 136
Soviet, not viable, 306
"strong man," 10
totalitarianism to continue, 311, 312
world, 11, 12, 484
GOVERNMENT OF LAWS
See also Government
concept from Aristotle, 114
political science fundamental, 398
GRAFMAN, L. ELLIOTT
on Hebrew Law, 205
GREAT BRITAIN
See British Commonwealth; England
GREECE
See also Alexander the Great; Aristotle;
Anaxagoras; Athens; Greek Law; Plato;
Socrates; Sparta
adopts Code Napoleon, 180
Alcibiades' exposition, 99
Amphictyonic Council, 85
art, 95, 100
city states, 85
Confederacy of Delos, 93
conquered by Alexander, 102
continuity of culture, 119
debt to, 103
Delphi oracle, 84
Draco's Code, 89
drama, 95, 96, 113
early history, 83

empire by chicanery, 93
equity, 405
incorporated into Rome, 154
invaded by Nazis, 292
medicine, 100
Olympic Games, 84
Pelopennesian War, 86, 97, 102
philosophy, 103
religion, 83, 84
slavery, 94
Solon's Code, 89, 90
Sophists, 104
Thirty Years Truce, 94
GREEN, LEON
on MacPherson case, 373
GREEK LAW
See also Greece
Babylonian content, 33
no heritage, 100
GROTIUS,
De Jure Pacis, 187, 475
on equity, 405
on natural law, 187
GROUPS, ORGANIZED
as the "people," 15, 16
pressure against government, 15
GUATAMA
See Buddhism
GUATAMALA
adopts Code Napoleon, 180
GUIZOT
on individual liberty, 325
HABEAS CORPUS
administrative review by, 457
function, 397
high prerogative writ, 349
Indian constitution, 79
nature of writ, 402
Hadley v. Baxendale, 386
HAGUE PEACE CONFERENCE, 476
HAMILTON, ALEXANDER, 97
HAMMURABI
See also Babylonia; Hammurabi's Code
creation of empire, 28
HAMMURABI'S CODE
compared with Corpus Juris, 177
discovery, 29
influence, 33
subject content, 30-33; 46
word content, 205
HAND, LEARNED, 394
HARRIS, ROBERT J., 471
HASTIE, WILLIAM H., 413
HASTINGS, WARREN
impeachment, 55
HATCH ACT, 17
HAYTI, 180
H-BOMB, 3
HEBREW COMMONWEALTH
See also Hebrews; Hebrew Legal System
amphictyony, 197
division of powers, 195
judges, 197, 198
period of, 194
termination, 199
HEBREW LEGAL SYSTEM
See also Hebrew Commonwealth; Hebrews
Beth Din, 204
Beth Din, London, 210
custom, 205

equity, 211
Gemara, 208
Lawyers, 204
Mishnah, 208
Pentateuch, 205
Sanhedrin, 203, 204
Talmud, 207, 208
Ten Commandments, 196, 205
Torah, 204-206
HEBREWS
See also Hebrew Commonwealth; Hebrew
Legal System; State of Israel
Aaron, 195
abduction by Ptolemy Soter, 202
Abraham, 191
Absalom, 204
as Roman slaves, 137
Babylonian Captivity, 34, 202, 203
covenant with Jehovah, 191
David, 200
Deborah, 197
early conflict with Islam, 240
exodus, 193
exiled by Titus, 203
family, 206
Gideon, 197
historical beginnings, 191
history, influence of, 193
Jereboam, 202
Jethrow, 195, 203
Jonathan, 200
Joseph, 137
Joshua, 195
kingdom divided, 202
kingdom established, 199
Rheoboam, 202
Sampson, 198
Samuel, 198, 199
Saul, 200
Scattered by Vespasian, 165
Solomon, 107, 200, 202
Slavery, 137
under Islam, 245
HENRY VIII, 229
HERBERT, SIR EDWIN, 282
HEROD, 203
HERESY
See also Inquisition
Punished by state, 221, 222, 227
HERTZ, RABBI J. H.
on ancient Semitic codes, 29, 30
HIGH COMMISSION
Puritan prosecution, 230
HILLEL, 209
HINDUISM
See also Buddhism; Caste System of Hin-
duism; India; Manu, Laws of
adoption, law of, 56
Aryan invasions, 39, 40
contrast with Islam, 52, 72
early tribal organization, 40
gradations of, 38
individual's relation to Brahman, 37
language, 79
nature worship, 40
not corporately organized, 47
pervasiveness of, 37, 38
relation to government, 38
scriptural basis, 38, 39
transmigration, 46

HISTORY
and anthropology, 21
chronicle of international failure, 8
chronicle of military force, 132
as record of civilization, 5
as record of injustices, 11
light shed by, 19
study of communities, 85
teachings as to man's nature, 19
teachings as to men of "brass", 110
HITLER
See also Germany
becomes chancellor, 281
Beer Cellar Putsch, 280
early life, 278
"eternal allegiance to", 279
liquidation of neutrals, 292
HOBBES, THOMAS, 188
HOHENZOLLERNS
See also Germany
acquisition of power, 266
deportation of women, 272
flout international law, 476
Kaiser abdicates, 274
HOLDSWORTH, WILLIAM, 344, 406
HOLLAND, T. E., 375
HOLMES, OLIVER WENDELL
"felt necessities," 404
"life of the law", 411
on due process, 458
on procedure, 396
HOMESTEAD ACT, 334
HONDURAS, 180
HOOKER, THOMAS, 232
HOOVER, HERBERT, 479
HOROWITZ, GEORGE
on Puritans, 230
HORVATH, BARNA
on Aristotelian justice, 116
HOUIN, ROGER
on Code Napoleon, 180
HOWE, WILLIAM WIRT
on Roman law, 177, 179
HUGHES, CHARLES E.
on anti-trust act, 336
"HUMAN RIGHTS AND PROPERTY
RIGHTS", 329, 339
HUNGARY
invaded by Soviets, 482
HUSS, JOHN, 228
HUSSEIN, SHERIF 213, 261
HYDERABAD
princely state, 59, 75
ILLINOIS
Administrative Review Act, 456
"certain remedy for wrongs", 349
Civil Practice Act, 150, 428
common law in, 348
radio defamation statute, 360
review of administrative action, 456
Statute of Frauds, 379
INDIA
See also Buddhism; Caste System of Hin-
duism; East India Company; Gandhi;
Hinduism; Indian National Congress;
Indian Republic; Manu, Laws of; Mus-
lim League; Nehru
Alexander's invasion, 49
Amritsar incident, 67
Aryan invasions, 39, 40

Asoka's conquest, 50
Atlee cabinet mission, 74
becomes independent, 75
Bose, Subhas Chandra, 73
constitutional government, 78-80
educational program, 56, 62
English courts and appeals, 58
English influence, 62
English language, 64
frontier security, 60
Government of India Act, 64
Gupta Dynasty, 50
habeas corpus, 79
Hindi language, 79
Hindus and Muslims, relations, 70
illiteracy, 65
Independence Act, 75
independent government, 74
Islam's gains, 51, 52
language difficulties, 64
law applied by English, 56-58
loyalty to England, 63, 64
Macaulay's Minute, 64
Mahrattas, 51
marriage, law of, 58
Muslim invasions, 50, 51
Muslim Mogul Dynasty, 50-52
Muslims, position of, 70
Mutiny of 1857, 59
National Congress and Muslim League,
    68, 69
penetration of Islam, 237
position in World War I, 63, 64
position in World War II, 72, 73
princes, 56, 59, 60, 75
Reading, Viceroy, 64
"region," not "nation", 37
rioting after partition, 78
Ripon, Lord, 61
Rowlatt Act, 67
Sikhs, 51
status of women, 80
Victoria crowned, 60
INDIAN NATIONAL CONGRESS
See also Gandhi; India; Muslim League
domination by Gandhi, 66
establishment of, 66
honeymoon with Muslim League, 67
opposes Government of India Act, 67
position in World War II, 73
schism within, 69
INDIAN REPUBLIC
See also India
separate nation, 484
INDIANS, AMERICAN, 4, 334
INDIVIDUAL DIVERSITIES, 109, 110
INDIVIDUAL LIBERTY
See also Freedom, Individual; Individual,
    Rights of; Liberty
advent, 25
Brandeis on, 327
concept unknown to Church, 325
concept unknown to Romans, 325
embodied in early institutions, 326
Jefferson on, 327
necessity, 10
not recognized by Plato, 113
suffrage essential to, 16
Wilson on, 327
INDIVIDUAL, RIGHTS OF

See also Man
constitutional protection, 398
enumeration, 328, 329
European Convention, 328
United Nations Declaration, 328
INDONESIA, 237
INHERITANCE
Babylonia, 31
India, 56, 57, 82
Muslim Law, 263
Laws of Manu, 45, 46
Rome, 128
Twelve Tables, 144
INJUNCTIONS
equitable remedy, 408
method of administrative review, 408
INNER TEMPLE
common law shrine, 29, 30
INQUISITION, 227, 230
INTENTIONAL WRONGS
assault and battery, 354
common law liability, 354
Demosthenes' concept, 117
false imprisonment, 356
libel and slander, 357
INTERNATIONAL LAW
and world government, 11
blockade, 270
development, 475
European Concert, 256
Grotius' contribution, 187
Hague Peace Conference, 476
Hohenzollern disregard, 476
League of Nations, 213, 275, 288, 477
Leage to Enforce Peace, 477
mandates, 213
maritime warfare, 476
natural law basis, 186, 475
navigation of rivers, 476
"necessity knows no law", 268
recognized in England, 475
recognized in United States, 475
Roman College of Heralds, 142
self-help, 11
Spanish-American War, 476
tendency to violate, 8
Treaty of Vienna, 475
INTERSTATE COMMERCE, 436
INTERSTATE COMMERCE COMMIS-
    SION, 448, 449
INTOXICATING LIQUOR
early regulation, 448
liability for sale, 392, 439
INVESTIA, 303
IOWA
wife's right to consortium, 425
IRAK, 261
IRAN, 261
IRISH FREE STATE, 216
ISLAM
See also Arabs; Islamic Law; Mohammed;
    Muslims
Abassid Dynasty, 242
arts and culture, 243
as state, 244
beginnings, 237
Cairo university, 243
conception of Allah, 238, 239
contrasted with Hinduism, 38, 52, 72
disestablished in Turkey, 262

INDEX

517

empire, 244
governing law, 244
governmental system, 244, 245
hejira, 239
in Pakistan, 77
jurisconcults, 252
khalifates, 241
lay religion, 237, 250
legal autonomy to others, 246-248
legal system, 244, 245
millet system, 246
Mogul Dynasty in India, 50-52
Omayyad Dynasty, 242
promotion by arms, 240
relation to Christianity, 245, 246, 253
relation to Judaism, 245, 246
religious autonomy to others, 246-248
repulsed at Tours, 223
scope of conquests, 237, 242
Shiites, 241
Spain, 242
Sufuism, 243
Sunnis, 241
waning of empire, 254
widespread Indian gains, 51, 52
ISLAMIC LAW
See also Islam ; Mohammed
Analogy, 253
custom, 252
criminal law, 263
divorce, 217, 249, 250, 264
effect of nationalism, 263
five basic prescriptions, 248, 249
hadiths, 252
ijmas, 253
Koran, 250
marriage, 217, 249
nature of, 248
recent developments, 262
State of Israel, 217
static characteristic, 251
Tradition, 252
Unanimous Concordance, 252, 253
women, 249, 250
ISOLATIONISM
abandonment of, 12
Pearl Harbor influence, 479
ISRAEL, KINGDOM OF
See also Hebrews
rebellion, 202
ISRAEL, STATE OF
See also Hebrews
Balfour Declaration, 212
codification of laws, 218
English quota system, 214
law, 205-208; 217, 218
no constitution, 218
Palestine mandate, 213
Palestinian resettlement, 212
partition of Palestine, 215
ISRAELITES
See also Hebrews ; Israel, State of ; Ten
Tribes of Israel
oppressed by Pharaoh, 26, 27
ITALY
See also Rome ; Mussolini
adopts Code Napoleon, 180
inquisition courts, 228
takes Libya, 259
JACKSON, ROBERT H.

law before government, 18
moral force versus Nazi might, 296
Nurnberg statement, 277, 279
on von Bethmann-Hollweg, 268
"public welfare" offenses, 391
JAFFE, LOUIS
on "hip-pocket" incident, 460
JAPAN
Anticomintern Pact, 289
Buddhism, 49
Pearl Harbor, 295
police informers, 168
Tripartite Pact, 289
war atrocities, 293
JEFFERSON, THOMAS
Declaration of Independence, 187, 188
liberty the gift of God, 23
on individual liberty, 327
on trial by jury, 401
Sidney's works, 193
JEHOVAH
Hebrew covenant with, 191
JENKS, EDWARD
definition of law, 343
JERUSALEM, 34, 102, 157, 165, 203, 212, 213, 226
JEWS
See also Hebrews
deprived of citizenship, 285
persecution of Nazis, 285, 286
JINGHIZ KHAN, 242, 255
JINNAH, MOHAMMED ALI, 71
See also India
JOHN, KING, 225, 226
JONES ACT, 436
JUDAH, KINGDOM OF, 34, 202
See also Hebrews
JUDAISM, 245, 246
See also Hebrews
JUDGES
See also Courts ; Trials
Cardozo on, 415
civil law, 181
common law, 181
Czechoslovakia, 309-311
Deborah, 197
Greece, 100
Hebrew Commonwealth, 197
modern Germany, 297
"not automata", 455
Nazi, 280
Red China, 321, 322
Roman, punishment for bribery, 145
Soviet Russia, 307, 308
sources of decision, 473
JURISCONSULTS, 154, 174, 178, 252
JURISDICTION
See also Courts ; Federal Courts
equity, 406
JURISPRUDENCE
See also Equity ; Law ; Roman Law
defined in Justinian's Institutes, 177
JURY, TRIAL BY
See Trial by Jury
JUS CIVILE, 150, 152, 153
JUS GENTIUM, 126, 152, 153, 173
JUS HONARARIUM, 150, 173
JUS NATURALE
See Natural Law
JUSTICE

Aristotle's concept, 116
changing concept, 413
equity, 404
Hastie on, 413
importance of procedure, 396
Justinian's Institutes, definition, 177
natural and conventional, 186
"one thing throughout world", 58
Plato's concept, 109
principles are immutable, 343
right of minorities, 282
Ten Commandments, 109
"What's good for me", 485
JUSTINIAN
See also Corpus Juris Civilis
comes to power, 176
orders Corpus Juris, 176
reconquers Italy, 171
KALVEN, HARRY
on M'Naghten's Case, 395
KASHMIR, 59, 75, 77
KELLOGG-BRIAND PACT, 276
KELSEN, HANS, 9, 13, 398
KEMAL, MUSTAPHA, 262
KENNEDY, JOHN F., 16
KENT, CHANCELLOR, 90, 423
Kent v. Dulles, 399
KIPLING, RUDYARD, 396
KNOX, JOHN, 230
KORAN
See also Islam; Mohammed
basic scripture, 250
content, 251
parts of Bible, 245
prophets, 246
revealed to Mohammed, 250, 251
rewards for observance, 250
source, 239
supplementation, 252
transcription, 251
KOREA
Buddhism in, 49
war in, 11, 480
KHRUSHCHEV, NIKITA
address to party congress, 305
castigates Stalin, 305
rendezvous with Mao Tse-Tung, 487
LABOR UNIONS
concentration of power, 17
political expenditures, 16, 17
pressure group, 15
LAISSEZ FAIRE
natural law and, 188
LANGDON, SAMUEL, 199
LANGUAGE
Arabic, 242, 243
as unifying force, 119, 484
difficulties in India, 64
Greek as universal, 103
Greek replaces Roman, 170
Hindi, 79
Sanskrit, 38, 41, 50
spread of Latin, 135, 136
Urdu, 76
LASKI, HAROLD J., 62
LAS SIETE PARTIDAS
See also Roman Law
content, 179
promulgation, 179
scope of coverage, 179

LAW
See also Civil Law; Common Law; Hebrew Legal System; Hinduism; International Law; Islamic Law; Natural
Law; Ottoman Law; Roman Law
"above the king": Coke, 109
accommodation between conflicting interests, 27, 89
administrative regulations as, 464
advent of, 5-8
American and Soviet concepts, 304
and state inseparable, 9
as politics, 304, 305
barbarian laws, 179
basis for social order, 4
common origin with religion, 21, 22
economic, 336
family, as private, 123, 124
federal, 350
feudalism, 224
force making for righteousness, 343
framework of freedom, 7
history as "borrowing", 18, 22
in animal kingdom, 6
influenced by culture, 189
"in small characters," 458
integration with government, 13
integration with religion, 265
"jungle", 6
knowledge of charged, 462
"made for man", 208
"makes the state", 94
merger with equity, 427
"necessity knows no law", 268
necessity of sanctions, 482
no federal common, 350
no Greek heritage, 100
originated before government, 18
Ottoman, 216, 217
private organizations, 15
problems as questions of degree, 27
reconciliation of interests, 340, 341
relation to military force, 132
relation to state, 9
social coercive technique, 13
source as human or divine, 26
Soviet, 303
Spartan soldiers, 88
State of Israel, 217-218
substantive and procedural, 396
territoriality, 264
LAW MERCHANT, 152
LAWRENCE, HENRY, 56
LAWYERS
See also Counsel for Defense
advent in Rome, 154
Canon Law Bar, 235
Greece, none, 100
Islamic, 244, 253
Russia, 299, 306, 307
LEAGUE OF NATIONS
See also International Law
arbitration treaties, 275
European Concert foreshadowing, 257
Hitler withdraws, 287, 288
mandates, 213
Middle East mandates, 261
no sanctions, 482
rejection by United States, 12, 478
statement of purpose, 477

LEAGUE TO ENFORCE PEACE, 477
LEBANON
codes, 263
declared independent, 261
entered by French, 259
Khrushchev and Mao Tse-Tung on, 487
United States soldiers in, 480
LEGISLATION
See also Codes; Statutes
ancient relation to religion, 87
by Roman emperors, 166
by Roman praetors, 150
Roman augur veto, 142
weakness of, 151
LEONHARD, RUDOLF
influence of Roman law, 189
LIBEL AND SLANDER
See also Defamation
by radio, 359
development of law, 416
difference between, 359
Egypt, 24
Laws of Manu provisions, 45
privilege as defense, 362
privilege, qualified, 363, 364
publication, 360, 361
truth as defense, 362
LIBERTY
See also Individual Liberty
advent of, 25
defined, 399
enlarging concept, 416
not absolute, 452
right to pursue trade, 452
LIEBESNEY, HERBERT J., 263, 264
LIFE, RIGHT TO
early limitations, 416
scope, 328
LINCOLN, ABRAHAM
circuit rider, 459
duty of government, 27
favorite poem, 299
Gettysburg Address, 13
"half slave and half free", 481
LINOWITZ, SOL, 213
LITERATURE
Babylonian, 28, 29
Egyptian, 20
Greece, 95
Islamic, 243
Roman Empire, 163
LLOYD GEORGE, 214
LOBBYING, 16
LOCARNO, TREATY OF, 275
LOCKE, JOHN, 115
LORD CAMPBELL'S ACT, 435
LOUIS XIV
government compared with Soviet, 306
"The State—It is I", 11, 13
LOUISIANA
adopts Code Napoleon, 180
community property, 351
French and Spanish law, 351
Las Siete Partidas, 179
LOUISIANA PURCHASE, 334
LUTHER, MARTIN, 228
LUXEMBOURG, 292
MACAULAY, LORD, 52, 62, 221
MACCABEES, 203
MACMILLAN, LORD, 21, 22, 58

MacPherson v. Buick Motor Co., 373
MADISON, JAMES, 343
MAGNA CHARTA, 341
MAIMONIDES, MOSES, 209
MAINE, SIR HENRY, 206, 475
MAITLAND, FREDERICK, 189
MAJESTAS, LAW OF, 164
MALPRACTICE
liability for, 367
MAMLUKS, 255, 259
MAN
See also Freedom, Individual; Individual
  Diversities; Individual Liberty
a political being, 10
capacity to set up institutions, 478
Neolithic, 21
spiritual urge, 6, 21
MANDAMUS, 349
MANDATES
See also League of Nations
Middle East, 261
MANU, LAWS OF
See also Caste System of Hinduism; Hin-
  duism; India
acceptance of, 47
ascribed origin, 42
content, 43-46
enunciation of caste system, 42
MANUFACTURERS' LIABILITY, 372-
  374
MAO TSE-TUNG, 487
See also Red China
MARATHON, BATTLE OF, 92
Marbury v. Madison, 114, 430
MARON, STANLEY, 52
MARRIAGE
Alexander's policy, 103
as contract, 125
Babylonia, 32
Breviary of Alaric, 178
Canon Law, 234
Hebrew Law, 206, 207, 217
Hindu Law, 58, 82
inter-caste prohibited, 41
Islamic, 245, 249
Manu, Laws of, 43, 46
Plato, community of wives, 110
Roman Canuleian Law, 146
Roman Law of Twelve Tables, 145
Roman slaves, 122, 123
Rome, 125, 127
Solon's Code, 90
Spartan, 88
MARRIED WOMEN
See also Women
Babylonia, 32
consortium, right to, 424
contracts, 381, 434
Laws of Manu provisions, 46
married women's acts, 381
Roman, 126
MARSHALL, CHIEF JUSTICE
"it is a constitution," 468
on contracts, 377
on habeas corpus, 402
MARX, KARL, 4, 301
MASARYK, THOMAS, 308, 309
MASSACHUSETTS, 114
MASTER AND SERVANT
See also Federal Employers' Liability Act;

Workmen's Compensation
common law defenses abolished, 442
Laws of Manu provisions, 45
MATHEMATICS
Babylonia, 29
Greece, 100
Islam, 243
MAYFLOWER COMPACT, 232
MEDICAL SCIENCE, 20 100
See also Physicians and Surgeons
MEIN KAMPF, 281, 287
M'Naghten's Case, 393
MENS REA
See Criminal Law
MESPOTAMIA
See Babylonia
MEXICO
adopts Code Napoleon, 180
German alliance proposed, 271
MILLENARY PETITION, 231
MINORS
incapacity to contract, 381
MOHAMMED
See also Arabs; Islam
death and succession, 241
early life, 238
hejira, 239
inspired, 238
revelation of Koran, 250, 251
MONGOLS
invasion, 255
MONOPOLY
early opposition to, 336
Sherman Anti-Trust Act, 336
MONTESQUIEU, 115
MOORE, EDWARD
on consideration, 382
MOORE, JOHN BASSETT
on International Law, 475
MOORE, JOHN H.
on consideration, 381
MORAL FORCE
victory of, 296
MORGENTHAU, HENRY
on Kaiser Wilhelm, 267
Morisette v. United States, 391
MOSAIC LAW
See Hebrew Law
MOSES
See also Hebrews
assembly of elders, 193, 203
colloquy with Jethrow, 195
confrontation of Pharaoh, 193
death, 197
flight to Midian, 192
life saved, 26
Ten Commandments, 196
MOTOR VEHICLES
guest-rider liability, 436-439
negligent liability, 366, 367
MOUNTBATTEN, LORD
succeeds Lord Wavell, 75
MUNICH
Czechoslovakia abandoned, 487
"peace in our time," 291
MUNICIPAL CORPORATIONS
autonomy in England, 326
Roman, 134, 168, 174
Munn v. Illinois, 433
MURDER

common law crime, 391
MURPHY, FRANK
on war atrocities, 293
Muskrat v. United States, 430
MUSLIM LEAGUE
See also India
honeymoon with National Congress, 67
organization, 70
MUSLIMS
See also Islam
contrasted with Hindus, 72
Indian, position of, 70
in independent India, 76
in Israel, 215
MUSSOLINI, 172, 289, 478
NAPOLEON
See also France
Code, 180
invades Egypt, 20, 258
NASSER, GAMEL ABDEL, 260, 261
NATION
See also Government; State
communist or free, 481
defined, 10
formation of, 186
importance of religious heritage, 484
problem of aspirations, 483
NATIONALISM
See also Nation; Patriotism
development, 483
effect on Islamic law, 263
NATIONAL INDUSTRIAL RECOVERY
ACT
executive orders, 460
NATIONAL LABOR RELATIONS
BOARD
"political" agency, 449
procedure, 454, 455
NATURAL LAW
"all men are equal", 187
American indebtedness, 187
basis of International Law, 475
between nations, 186
Blackstone's exposition, 182-186
China, 314
Cicero's definition, 155
concepts, 181, 182
Demosthenes' concept, 117
embodied in Aristotle, 115
Grotius, 187
incompatible with slavery, 137
influence on Christianity, 188, 189
influence on U. S. Constitution, 182
modern German jurists, 297, 298
physical nature, 6
Pound's comment, 155
reason and revelation, 184
revival in Germany, 296
Stoic, 118
universal law, 115
NAZIS
See also Hitler
abolish political parties, 283
advent, 277
Anti-Comintern Pact, 289
annex Austria, 289, 290
attack churches, 284, 285
Beer Cellar Putsch, 280
concentration camps, 294
conquered by moral force, 296

extermination of German infirm, 294
extermination of Jews, 286
"fuehrer always right", 278
gestapo, 280, 282
invade Poland, 291
invade Russia, 292
judicial proceedings, 280
master race concept, 285
medical experimentation, 294
Mein Kampf, 287
occupy Czechoslovakia, 290
party program, 278
private organization prohibited, 16
reassert military power, 287
rise of, 281
Roehm Purge, 283
slave labor system, 293, 294
take over Germany, 282
treaty with Russia, 292
Tripartite Pact, 289
war atrocities, 293
NEBUCHADNEZZAR, 34, 35
See also Babylonia
NEGLIGENCE
See also Common Law
contributory, 365, 366, 441, 442
general liability, 365
landlords, 370-372
malpractice, 367
manufacturers, 372-374
operation of business property, 368, 369
operation of motor vehicles, 366, 367
wilful and wanton, 437-439
NEHRU, JAWAHARIAL, 68, 73, 74, 81
NEHRU, MOTILAL, 68
NEOLITHIC MAN, 21
NETHERLANDS, 52, 180, 292
NEVADA
community property law, 351
NEWMAN, FRANK
on Federal Register, 460, 461
NEW MEXICO
community property law, 351
NEW SALEM
Lincoln's, 4
NICAEA, COUNCIL OF
See also Roman Catholic Church
creed promulgated, 169
enforcement of creed, 222
NICARAGUA
adopts Code Napoleon, 180
NIEOMOELLER, PASTOR, 280
NIETZCHE,
"God is dead," 267
"what's good for me," 485
NINEVEH, 34
NORTH ATLANTIC TREATY ORGANI-
ZATION, 481
NORWAY
invaded by Nazis, 292
NUISANCE
development of law, 416
NURNBERG TRIAL
Jackson's statement, 277, 279
Shawcross' statement, 275, 276, 293
extermination of infirm, 294
extermination of Jews, 286
medical experimentation, 294
slave labor, 294
OATH EX OFFICIO

See also Torture to Extort Confessions
inquisitional tool, 226
resisted by Puritans, 230
Ogden v. Saunders, 377
OLD TESTAMENT, 230
See also Bible
OLYMPIC GAMES, 84, 85
"ONE WORLD," 12, 103
See also World Government
ORDER
See also Law
basis of civil, 174
brought by Rome, 156
maintained by Church, 224
purpose of society, 10
natural law relation, 188
OSTRACISM, 92
OTTOMAN EMPIRE
See also Ottoman Law ; Turkey
capitulations, 257
European Concert, 256
harshness, 256
millet system, 246
Mixed Courts, 258
rise, 255
waning, 256
World War I, 261
OTTOMAN LAW
in Palestine, 216
in State of Israel, 217
origin, 217
PACIFISM
contributes to World War II, 288
PAGE, WALTER HINES
on German ambition, 266, 267
PAKISTAN
See also India
becomes independent, 75
constitutional difficulties, 80
one "ism" only, 77
riots after partition, 78
separate nation, 484
territorial division, 76
Panama Refining Co. v. Ryan, 460
PANDECTS
See Corpus Juris Civilis
PANDIT, VIJAYA
chief of Indian delegation, 80
PAPINIAN
See also Roman Law
Breviary Source, 178
Justinian source, 176
martyred, 167
praetorian prefect, 161
PARIS
See also France
Custom of, 179, 180
Treaty of, 257
PARKE, BARON
on wrongful death, 435
PASHUKANIS, E. B.
law a bourgeois product, 301
"not with us now", 302
PASSIVE RESISTANCE, 141, 146
See also Gandhi
PATRIOTISM
See also Nationalism
place in history, 11, 12
Patton v. United States, 401
PAUL, APOSTLE

"being reviled, we bless," 107
counsel to slaves, 137
conversion, 238
"God hath made of one blood", 165
"I was free born", 138
PEACE
"adjustment" or "extinction" 488
at any price? 487
League to Enforce, 477
purpose of society, 10
sanctions to enforce, 486
PEARL HARBOR
contrasted with Roman attacks, 142
initiates change of attitude, 479
PEOPLE
See also Government; State
groups, not individuals, 15
repository of power, 12, 13
PERICLES
"lovers of beauty," 95
PERU
adopts Code Napoleon, 180
PETITION, RIGHT OF
First Amendment, 16
imbedded in common law, 349
PHILIPPINES
penetrated by Islam, 237
PHILOSOPHY
See also Aristotle; Natural Law; Plato;
   Positivism, Legal
Confucius, 318
"end justifies means," 482
Gandhi, 66
influence of Greek, 154
legacy of Greek, 103, 108
Marxist, 4
Nehru, 68
Socrates, 106-108
Sophists, 104
Stoic, 118
PHOENICIA
law of, 33
Mediterranean influence, 33
PHYSICIANS AND SURGEONS
See also Medical Science
fees fixed in Babylonia, 31
Greece, 100
malpractice liability, 367
PHYSICS
Babylonia, 29
Egypt, 20
Greece, 95
Islam, 243
PILGRIM FATHERS
at Plymouth Rock, 4
Mayflower Compact, 232
PLATO
See also Greece
community of wives, 110
each to his own talent, 109
education stressed, 110
how war comes, 111
no individual freedom, 113
political wisdom necessary, 111, 112
Republic, 108
rulers must obey law, 109
"the just man", 112
wisdom related to truth, 112
women's position, 110
   Plessy v. Ferguson, 469-471

PLUTARCH, 94
POLAND, 228, 291
POLICE POWER, 113, 452
POLITICAL PARTIES, 159, 283
POLITICAL SOCIETY, 10
See also Government; State
POLITICS
as Law in Russia, 303-305
POLLOCK, SIR FREDERICK, 182, 186,
   189
POLYBIUS, 96
POLYGAMY, 238
See also Marriage
PONTIUS PILATE, 136
See also Christ, Jesus
PORTER, LORD, 411
PORTUGAL, 52, 178, 180
POSITIVISM, LEGAL
See also Philosophy
effect in Europe, 324
in Germany, 296
POTHIER, 180
POUND, ROSCOE
debt to Greece, 103
law and order, 7
on criminal law, 390
on freedom, 413
on natural law, 155
on Pashukanis, 302
on Soviets, 304
POWER
See also Pressure groups
government, 12
Plutarch's comment, 158
sovereign, limitation, 398
PRAETORS
See also Roman Law
edict, 150
judex assignment, 149
judicial function, 148
law "in breast of judges" 206
natural law influence, 181
praetor peregrinus, 152, 187
procedure, 149
works in general, 174
PRAVDA, 302
PRECEDENTS, 423, 465-467
PRE-NATAL INJURIES, 422
PRESBYTERIANISM, 230
PRESSURE GROUPS, 15
PRICE REGULATION, 31, 168
PRINTING, 170
PRIVACY, RIGHT OF
definition, 417
fingerprints, 421
limited by public interest, 418, 419
nature, 416, 417
origin, 416
PRIVATE LAW MAKING.
family, 123, 124
organized groups, 15
PRIVY COUNCIL, ENGLISH
appeals from India, 58, 62
PROCEDURE
See also Trial by Jury
administrative, 450
bail, 398
China, 315, 316
confrontation by witnesses, 397
declaratory judgment, 387, 429

discovery before trial, 428, 429
due process requirements, 397, 399, 457
English reforms, 427, 428
federal, 352
Federal Employers' Liability Act, 444
Field Code, 428
fines, 398
grand jury, 397
Greece, 100
habeas corpus, 402
Hebrew Law, 206
information or accusation, 397
injunctions, 408
motion for directed verdict, 355, 356
oath ex officio, 226
pre-trial hearing, 429
process for witnesses, 397
punishment for crime, 398
restitution, 387
review of administrative action, 453-456
Roman Law of Twelve Tables, 145
secret, Soviet Russia, 305
speedy and public trial, 397
star chamber, 230
stare decisis, 465
trial by jury, 397, 401
warrant, 397
witnesses, 397
writ of prohibition, 349
PROPERTY
See also Contracts; Corporations; Wills
absentee ownership, 339
Babylonia, 31
business, liability for injuries, 368, 369
Canon Law, 234
common law, 388
community law, 351, 352
customary law, India, 57
Decalogue on, 331
"dram-shop" liability, 439
economic changes, 333-340
enlarging concept, 416
Fifth Amendment protection, 332, 397
Free Homestead Act, 334
landlord's liability, 370-372
Laws of Manu, 43
marital interests, 351, 352
married women, 434
origin of concept, 330
ownership common to all, 340
ownership in U. S., 330
police power limitations, 113
restrictions on usage, 332
right to hold, 328
Roman law, 124, 125, 126
Roman Law of Twelve Tables, 145
tangible and intangible, 389
tenement house regulation, 392
PRUSSIA
See also Germany
rise, 266
PUBLIC SCHOOLS
See also Education
Roman Catholic Church and, 234
PUBLIC SCHOOL SEGREGATION
CASE, 469
"PUBLIC WELFARE" OFFENSES, 391
PURITANS, 230, 231
QUEBEC, 180
QUO WARRANTO, 349

RADIO
libel or slander by, 359
Radovich v. National Football League, 467
RAPE
common law crime, 391
REASON
See also Conscience
divine faculty of, 155
key to truth, 108
man's highest faculty, 113
natural law, 184
power of, 296
recognized by Greeks, 104
Roman religion, 121
Stoic, universal, 118
RED CHINA
See also China
aggression in Korea, 480
class justice, 319, 320
confiscation, 320
constitution, 319
governmental purpose, 322
judiciary, 321, 322
no checks on power, 321
People's Congress, 321
Procurator General, 322, 323
"rights" and "duties", 320
war atrocities, 480
REFORMATION
See also Roman Catholic Church
impact of, 228
RELIGION
See also Babylonia; Buddhism; Christianity; Egypt; Hinduism; Islam; Judaism;
Religious Organizations
ancestor worship, 316
animal and human sacrifice, 29
animal worship, 24
basis of Spartan constitution, 86
common origin with law, 21, 22
concepts of ancient, 24
concern of, 23
early coercive order, 9
freedom of, 233
freedom under Islam, 246
Greek, 83, 84
integrated with law, 265
Islamic as law, 244
legislative force, 87
"no law establishing", 233
relation to conscience, 23
Rome, 120
Roman Republic, 142
source of despotism, 25
RELIGIOUS ORGANIZATIONS
See also Church
as pressure groups, 15
RESTATEMENT OF THE LAW
contracts, 382
REVOLUTIONARY WAR, 132
RIGHTS
See also Bill of Rights; Individual Liberty
clarified by Aristotle, 116
in rem and *in personam*, 375
limited by police power, 452
travel, 399
RIO TREATY, 481
ROAD, RULE OF THE, 186
ROBBERY, 391
ROBINSON, EDWARD VAN DYKE, 97,

115
ROMAN CATHOLIC CHURCH
See also Canon Law; Christians; Christ-
    ianity; Church; Ecclesiastical Courts
Albigensian Crusade, 227
"Babylonian Captivity," 227, 228
clergy, power of, 220
Council of Constance, 227, 228
Council of Nicaea, 169, 170
Courts, 235
Crusades, 226
decretals, 233
England, 226, 229
excommunication, 225, 227
exercises civil powers, 223
foundation, 220
"Great Schism", 227, 228
inquisition, 226
interdiction, 225, 226
oath ex officio, 226, 230
Peace of Augsburg, 229
privilege of clergy, 222
public schools, 234
relation to feudalism, 224
relation to United States, 234
simony, 225
temporal influence, 225
wealth, 222, 223
ROMAN EMPIRE
See also Rome; Roman Republic; Roman
    Law
ancient gods, 163
art, 163
as world government, 489
Augustus assumes power, 161
book burning, 168
Caligula's inaccessible laws, 458
Christian persecution, 165
Christianity state religion, 84, 169
consuls, 161
decurions, 168
divisions, 170
emasculation of tribunes, 161
fall of West, 171
imperial constitutions, 166
literature, 163
majestas, law of, 164
occupation of England, 412
praetorian guard, 161
senate, 161, 175
"sold" by praetorian guard, 167
wine and circuses, 162
ROMAN LAW
See also Cicero; Justinian; Las Siete
    Partidas; Praetors; Natural Law; Ro-
    man Republic; Roman Empire; Theo-
    dosian Code; Twelve Tables, Law of
advent of lawyers, 154
Babylonian content, 33
Breviary of Alaric, 177
compared with Greek, 134
compared with common, 151
contracts, 128, 153
contributions, 173
custom, 143
early symbolism, 128
edict of Theodoric, 177
elements in common law, 350, 351
emancipation ceremony, 129
equity, 403

fictions, use of, 125
France, 179
Fuero Real, 178
Imperial Consistory, 174
Imperial Constitutions, 166, 174
improvisation, genius for, 125
influence of Greek philosophy, 154
inheritance, 126
in provinces, 133, 134
jurisconsults, 154
jus civile, 150
jus gentium, 152
jus honorarium, 150, 173
natural law influence, 181
praetors, 148
praetors peregrinus, 151, 187
property, 124-126
relation to Canon Law, 233
scope of influence, 189
tonic to common law, 344
trusts, 128
wills, 126, 127, 128
ROMAN REPUBLIC
See also Caesar; Cicero; Roman Law;
    Rome
Anthony and Cleopatra, 158
beginnings of conquest, 131
Catilinian conspiracy, 157
censors, 140
citizenship, 137-139
College of Pontiffs, 142
comitia centuriata, 139
consuls, 139
Decimvirs, 144
demise of, 156
dictator, 140
government, 139
jurisconsults, 154
Licinian Laws, 146
military booty, 136
military service, 137
municipalities, 133
no political parties, 159
no representative government, 136
outlying provinces, 134
plebeian "sit-down", 141
prosecution of Verres, 157
reasons for fall, 158
religion, 142
senate, 140
suffrage, 147
treatment of conquered peoples, 133
treaties, 133
tribunes, 139
Valerio-Horatian Laws, 145
ROME
See also Caesar; Cicero; Praetors; Roman
    Empire; Roman Republic; Roman Law;
    Twelve Tables, Law of
beginnings, 120
classes of people, 122
comitia centuriata, 130
comitia curiata, 127
concilium plebis, 130
constitution, no formal, 130
contribution of order, 174
family, 123
military service, 129
no individual liberty, 325
paterfamilias, power, 124